New Perspectives on

Microsoft® Office FrontPage® 2003

Introductory

Jessica Evans

THOMSON
COURSE TECHNOLOGY

Australia • Canada • Mexico • Singapore • Spain • United Kingdom • United States

THOMSON
COURSE TECHNOLOGY

New Perspectives on Microsoft® Office FrontPage® 2003—Introductory
is published by Course Technology.

Managing Editor:
Rachel Goldberg

Senior Product Manager:
Kathy Finnegan

Senior Technology Product Manager:
Amanda Young Shelton

Product Managers:
Karen Stevens, Brianna Germain

Editorial Assistant:
Abigail Z. Reider

Senior Marketing Manager:
Rachel Stephens

Associate Marketing Manager:
Caitlin Wight

Developmental Editor:
Judy Adamski

QA Manuscript Reviewers:
John Freitas, Marc Spoto, Alex White

Production Editor:
Summer Hughes

Composition:
GEX Publishing Services

Text Designer:
Steve Deschene

Cover Designer:
Nancy Goulet

Printed in the United States of America

1 2 3 4 5 6 7 8 9 BM 08 07 06 05 04

For more information, contact Course Technology, 25 Thomson Place, Boston, Massachusetts, 02210.

Or find us on the World Wide Web at: www.course.com

ISBN 0-619-21377-9

Preface

Real, Thought-Provoking, Engaging, Dynamic, Interactive—these are just a few of the words that are used to describe the New Perspectives Series' approach to learning and building computer skills.

Without our critical-thinking and problem-solving methodology, computer skills could be learned but not retained. By teaching with a case-based approach, the New Perspectives Series challenges students to apply what they've learned to real-life situations.

Our ever-growing community of users understands why they're learning what they're learning. Now you can too!

See what instructors and students are saying about the best-selling New Perspectives Series:

> "I have used books from the New Perspectives series for about ten years now. I haven't been able to find anything else that approaches their quality when it comes to covering intermediate and advanced software application topics."
> — Karleen Nordquist, College of St. Benedict & St. John's University

...and about New Perspectives on Microsoft Office FrontPage 2003:

> "I appreciate that the 'design' aspect is included in Tutorial 1. Often books either do not cover design principles at all or add them as an afterthought. I think that from the very beginning these issues need to be addressed."
> — Kim Blosser, Blue Ridge Community College

> "Overall, the text is excellent! Tutorial 4 is one of my favorite tutorials as this is where you can use shared borders, themes, photo galleries, and word art to make a project much easier to do and change it from an ordinary Web site to an extra-ordinary one."
> — Fred Parce, Texas State Technical College Harlingen

www.course.com/NewPerspectives

Why *New Perspectives* will work for you

Context
Each tutorial begins with a problem presented in a "real-world" case that is meaningful to students. The case sets the scene to help students understand what they will do in the tutorial.

Hands-on Approach
Each tutorial is divided into manageable sessions that combine reading and hands-on, step-by-step work. Screenshots—now 20% larger for enhanced readability—help guide students through the steps. **Trouble?** tips anticipate common mistakes or problems to help students stay on track and continue with the tutorial.

Review

Review
In New Perspectives, retention is a key component to learning. At the end of each session, a series of Quick Check questions helps students test their understanding of the concepts before moving on. And now each tutorial contains an end-of-tutorial summary and a list of key terms for further reinforcement.

Apply

Assessment
Engaging and challenging Review Assignments and Case Problems have always been a hallmark feature of the New Perspectives Series. Now we've added new features to make them more accessible! Colorful icons and brief descriptions accompany the exercises, making it easy to understand, at a glance, both the goal and level of challenge a particular assignment holds.

Reference Window

Task Reference

Reference
While contextual learning is excellent for retention, there are times when students will want a high-level understanding of how to accomplish a task. Within each tutorial, Reference Windows appear before a set of steps to provide a succinct summary and preview of how to perform a task. In addition, a complete Task Reference at the back of the book provides quick access to information on how to carry out common tasks. Finally, each book includes a combination Glossary/Index to promote easy reference of material.

Reinforce

Lab Assignments
Certain tutorials in this book contain Lab Assignments, which provide additional reinforcement of important skills in a simulated environment. These labs have been hailed by students and teachers alike for years as the most comprehensive and accurate on the market. Great for pre-work or remediation, the labs help students learn concepts and skills in a structured environment.

Student Online Companion
This book has an accompanying online companion Web site designed to enhance learning. This Web site includes:

- Lab Assignments for selected tutorials
- Student Data Files and PowerPoint presentations
- Links to Web sites for additional information

Certification
If you've used the New Perspectives FrontPage book in the past, you may have noticed the Microsoft Office Specialist logo on the cover. With this release, Microsoft has decided not to offer a certification exam for FrontPage 2003. Rest assured that this title contains the same comprehensive level of instruction you expect from New Perspectives.

www.course.com/NewPerspectives

New Perspectives offers an entire system of instruction

The New Perspectives Series is more than just a handful of books. It's a complete system of offerings:

New Perspectives catalog

Our online catalog is never out of date! Go to the catalog link on our Web site to check out our available titles, request a desk copy, download a book preview, or locate online files.

Brief
Introductory
Comprehensive
Advanced

Coverage to meet your needs!

Whether you're looking for just a small amount of coverage or enough to fill a semester-long class, we can provide you with a textbook that meets your needs.

- Brief books typically cover the essential skills in just 2 to 4 tutorials.
- Introductory books build and expand on those skills and contain an average of 5 to 8 tutorials.
- Comprehensive books are great for a full-semester class, and contain 9 to 12+ tutorials.
- Power Users or Advanced books are perfect for a highly accelerated introductory class or a second course in a given topic.

So if the book you're holding does not provide the right amount of coverage for you, there's probably another offering available. Go to our Web site or contact your Course Technology sales representative to find out what else we offer.

Instructor Resources

We offer more than just a book. We have all the tools you need to enhance your lectures, check students' work, and generate exams in a new, easier-to-use and completely revised package. This book's Instructor's Manual, ExamView testbank, PowerPoint presentations, data files, solution files, figure files, and a sample syllabus are all available on a single CD-ROM or for downloading at www.course.com.

How will your students master Microsoft Office?

SAM (Skills Assessment Manager) 2003 helps you energize your class exams and training assignments by allowing students to learn and test important computer skills in an active, hands-on environment. With SAM 2003, you create powerful interactive exams on critical Microsoft Office 2003 applications, including Word, Excel, Access, and PowerPoint. The exams simulate the application environment, allowing your students to demonstrate their knowledge and to think through the skills by performing real-world tasks. Designed to be used with the New Perspectives Series, SAM 2003 includes built-in page references so students can create study guides that match the New Perspectives textbooks you use in class. Powerful administrative options allow you to schedule exams and assignments, secure your tests, and run reports with almost limitless flexibility. Find out more about SAM 2003 by going to www.course.com or speaking with your Course Technology sales representative.

Distance Learning

Enhance your course with any of our online learning platforms. Go to www.course.com or speak with your Course Technology sales representative to find the platform or the content that's right for you.

www.course.com/NewPerspectives

About This Book

This book offers a case-based, problem-solving approach to learning Microsoft FrontPage 2003. Students will learn how to create and publish Web pages using links, graphics, tables, and frames.

- Updated for the new software! Includes features new to FrontPage 2003 such as custom link bars, custom themes, multiple browser preview, and Split view, which displays both the design and code views simultaneously.
- This edition features a new running tutorial case and two new case problems.
- Increased emphasis on design issues, including Web-safe colors, expanded coverage of fonts, and how to use various picture file formats.
- Includes 120-day trial of the full version FrontPage 2003 software!

New to this edition!

- Larger screenshots!
- Sequential page numbering!
- New end-of-tutorial material provides additional conceptual review in the form in the form of key terms and a tutorial summary.
- New labels and descriptions for the end-of-tutorial exercises makes it easy for you to select the right exercises for your students.

Acknowledgments

I would like to thank several people who very carefully reviewed the published previous edition of this book and the manuscript as I developed it for this book for their excellent comments and suggestions: Joanne Walters, J Sargeant Reynolds Community College; Jay Human, Lexington CC; Fred Parce, Texas State Technical College Harlingen; and Kim Blosser, Blue Ridge Community College. Your many comments and suggestions were a great resource for me as I worked to improve this book's content and cases.

I have always been blessed to be a part of the best publishing team in the business. I would like to thank Rachel Goldberg, Managing Editor, who has been a terrific resource and a good friend over the years in addition to being a great leader of the New Perspectives Team; and Karen Stevens, Product Manager, who has provided support and much-needed encouragement during this book's development. I would also like to thank my Developmental Editor, Judy Adamski, for her constant support and wisdom and her willingness to go the extra mile to help me meet this book's fast-paced schedule. I have also been fortunate to have a great set of quality assurance testers on all of my projects, and this one is no different. Thank you to John Freitas, Marc Spoto, and Alex White for helping to improve this book and for carefully checking all of my solution files. Finally, I am grateful to Summer Hughes, Production Editor, for all of her efforts to ensure that this book was published quickly and accurately.

I would also like to acknowledge the contributions of my friends and neighbors, Brett and Shelly Greer and Scott and Carla Swenson, for allowing me to adapt and expand their successful Web sites and use them as new case problems in this book. The new cases in this edition are fun, interesting, and a true reflection of how real businesses use Web sites in today's economy.

And last but not least…I am fortunate to be surrounded by many people who support me in my personal and professional endeavors. To my husband, Richard and our daughter, Hannah, thank you for support, encouragement, love, and confidence and pride in what I do.

— Jessica Evans

www.course.com/NewPerspectives

New Perspectives on

Microsoft® Office FrontPage® 2003

Read This Before You Begin: Tutorials 1 & 2

To the Student

Data Disks

To complete the Tutorials, Review Assignments, and Case Problems in this book, you will need the starting student Data Files. Your instructor will either provide you with these Data Files or ask you to obtain them yourself.

The FrontPage Tutorials 1 and 2 require the folders shown in the next column to complete the Tutorials, Review Assignments, and Case Problems. You will need to copy these folders from a file server, a standalone computer, or the Web to the drive and folder where you will be storing your Data Files. Your instructor will tell you which computer, drive letter, and folders contain the files you need. You can also download the files by going to www.course.com; see the inside front cover for more information on downloading the files to your working folder, or ask your instructor or technical support person for assistance.

You will need to store your Data Files on a Zip disk, hard drive, or network drive that you can access. You will also need a location in which to create and save Web sites; the default location used in this book is C:\My Webs\[YourName], where "[YourName]" is your first and last names. You cannot complete this book using floppy disks.

▼**FrontPage**
- Tutorial.01
- Tutorial.02

Course Labs

Tutorial 1 features two interactive Course Labs to help you understand Internet and hypermedia concepts. There are Lab Assignments at the end of Tutorial 1 that relate to these labs. Contact your instructor or technical support person for assistance in accessing these labs.

To the Instructor

The Data Files and Course Labs are available on the Instructor Resources CD for this title. Follow the instructions in the Help file on the CD-ROM to install the programs to your network or standalone computer. See the "To the Student" section above for information on how to set up the Data Files that accompany this text. To complete the tutorials in this book, students must have a Web browser, access to a Web server with the FrontPage 2002 Server Extensions or Windows SharePoint Services installed on it, and an Internet connection. You are granted a license to copy the Data Files and Course Labs to any computer or computer network used by students who have purchased this book.

System Requirements

If you are going to work through this book using your own computer, you need:

- **Computer System** Microsoft Windows 2000 Professional or higher, Microsoft FrontPage 2003, and Microsoft Office 2003 must be installed on your computer. (The screens shown in this book use Microsoft Windows XP Professional. If your computer has Microsoft Windows 2000 Professional, your screens will look slightly different.) This book assumes a typical installation of FrontPage 2003 and Office 2003.

  The recommended browser for viewing Web pages is Internet Explorer 6.0 or higher.

- **Data Files** You will not be able to complete the tutorials or exercises in this book using your own computer until you have a set of Data Files.

- **Course Labs** See your instructor or technical support person to obtain the Course Lab software for use on your own computer.

Objectives

Session 1.1
- Study the five-part process for developing a Web site
- Use FrontPage to create a Web site and a Web page
- Set default technologies and a default page size for a Web site
- Enter and spell check text in a Web page
- Insert a file and paste text into a Web page
- Save a Web page and close a Web site

Session 1.2
- Open a Web site
- Create a heading
- Align text
- Use fonts, font colors, and special characters in a Web page
- Preview and print a Web page

Session 1.3
- Learn about Hypertext Markup Language
- Use FrontPage and a browser to view an HTML document
- Create meta tags in a Web page
- Use the FrontPage Help system

Lab

Student Data Files

To complete this tutorial, you will need the following Data Files. Additional Data Files needed to complete the end-of-tutorial exercises are listed with the Review Assignments and Case Problems.

▼**Tutorial.01**

▽ Tutorial folder

link.doc
list.doc

Creating a Web Site

Creating the Web Site for the Sunshine Landscape & Garden Center

Case

Sunshine Landscape & Garden Center

Brett Kizer graduated from college with a master's degree in business administration. At first, he tried the traditional MBA career path and worked for a financial institution. He soon determined, however, that he was not going to be happy working in an office. When an opportunity arose for him to purchase an established garden center in the Texas Hill Country, he quickly came up with the resources to do so, and he and his wife, Shelly, became the owners of the Sunshine Landscape & Garden Center. Because Brett and Shelly knew very little about plants and landscaping when they bought the business, Brett took several courses at a local college to become more knowledgeable about his new role. In addition, he took the required course of study to become a licensed irrigator and acquired an existing business that installed commercial and residential irrigation systems. With the addition of irrigation to the nursery's existing services, Sunshine soon had several new commercial and residential clients and hired several employees to support the nursery's increase in services and sales.

A short time later, Brett purchased several computers with Microsoft Windows XP and Microsoft Office 2003 installed on them. He then computerized the nursery's accounting, inventory, and ordering systems. The transition from the previous owner's paper-based system to a computerized system helped Brett and Shelly better manage the nursery by eliminating inventory that did not sell well and increasing orders in those areas of the business that generated the most profits.

As part of his business plan, Brett wants to create a Web site for the center so he can provide information to the community about the services offered by the business. Because Sunshine's employees spend a good deal of time troubleshooting common gardening problems and counseling local residents about appropriate plants for the area, Brett also wants to make the Web site a resource for information about what types of plants to install, when to plant them, how to maintain them, and other information that local residents frequently request from the nursery's expert employees. Brett hopes that the Web site will make it easy for Sunshine's customers to rely on the nursery for information and all their gardening needs.

In the several months since Brett hired you, you have been working in various positions at the nursery and have acquired a good sense of the overall operation of the business. In your capacity as a landscape designer, you have counseled residential and commercial customers about their landscaping needs, recommended plants to install, and helped customers troubleshoot various problems with new and existing landscaping. Brett thinks that you are an ideal candidate to manage the development of the new Web site because, in addition to your experience at the nursery, you have taken several college-level courses on Web site design and development. After considering several alternatives, you and Brett decide to use FrontPage to create, manage, and maintain the site. You will create the Web site and, at the same time, teach Brett how to use FrontPage so he will be able to utilize it in the future to contribute to and help maintain the site.

Session 1.1

The Internet: World Wide Web

Web Servers

The **Internet** is a large, worldwide collection of computer networks that are connected to one another. In a **network**, two or more computers are connected together for the purposes of sharing resources and communicating. Within a network, one computer is designated as the server, which functions as the network's central computer. The **network server**, or **host**, is a powerful computer that stores and distributes information and resources across the network to individual computers. The Internet is not a single, massive computer, but rather a collection of connected networks through which users exchange information. The Internet allows you to communicate and share data with people in the next office, across the street, or around the world.

The Internet's resources are organized in a **client/server architecture**. The server runs software that coordinates and communicates with the other computers connected to it. These other computers are called **clients**; a personal computer that is connected to the Internet is one example of a client. The server to which the client is connected stores information and processes the client's requests for that information. When a client requests information from a server, that request is transferred in the form of a file. The server then finds the information and returns it to the client, also in the form of a file. This file travels over the Internet from one server to another until it eventually reaches the client that requested it. Sometimes the file travels through many different servers before finally reaching this client.

To access the Internet, you need an account with an Internet service provider. An **Internet service provider (ISP)** is a business that provides a connection to the Internet for individuals, businesses, and organizations for a fee. An ISP might be a small, local business or a large, national provider such as EarthLink or America Online. Many colleges, universities, and large businesses have their own direct connections to the Internet and, in effect, act as their own ISP.

To function as a Web server, a server connected to the Internet must run special software that enables it to receive and execute clients' requests for Web pages. When you install Windows 2000 Professional or higher, you can also install Microsoft Internet Information Services, or IIS, which lets your computer function as a Web server. In this book, you will use IIS or a compatible server to process Web pages.

What Is FrontPage?

Microsoft FrontPage is a program that simplifies the development, maintenance, and publication of a Web site. A **Web site** consists of the Web pages, files, and folders that a business or organization presents via the Internet. You can use FrontPage to create, view, edit, and publish your Web site; insert and edit text, pictures, and photo galleries in your Web pages; import and export files; add, test, and repair hyperlinks to and within your pages; and generate a variety of reports about your Web site's function and usage. FrontPage also includes features that simplify Web site creation, such as templates for creating Web pages and built-in functions for processing Web pages on a server.

To create professional-looking Web pages, you don't need to be an experienced HTML programmer. **Hypertext Markup Language (HTML)** is the language that creates the **HTML documents** that a Web browser, such as Microsoft Internet Explorer or Netscape Navigator, interprets to display Web pages. You can create Web pages by learning HTML and using it to produce the necessary tags to create the content of a Web page and define its format. You can create an HTML document using an HTML authoring program or a text editor such as Notepad. Notepad does not insert any HTML tags into its document file. Instead, you must write and edit the tags yourself, and, therefore, you need to know each tag's name and its attributes. Writing HTML documents can prove tedious when you are creating a complex Web page. By contrast, FrontPage creates HTML tags automatically so you can create an HTML document without learning HTML. Regardless of the method you use to create a Web page, you can work with FrontPage to open and revise the Web page. The Student Online Companion page for Tutorial 1 has links to other programs that you can use to develop a Web site and resources for learning and understanding HTML.

In addition to creating the HTML document for you, FrontPage includes many features that make it easy to create Web pages and publish Web sites. When you publish a Web site, you transfer copies of the Web site's files and folders to a Web server or other location. If the location to which you have published your Web site is connected to the Internet, publishing the Web site makes it available to people using the Internet.

Web pages are usually classified into two categories: dynamic and static. A **static Web page** is one that displays information that does not change, such as text that describes a business, its address, and a map of the route to that business. A **dynamic Web page** is one that contains data that changes on a schedule, such as stock market and weather data, pricing changes made to a database, and forms that let you search a Web site for a specific keyword. When a Web page contains dynamic content, it must contain instructions to tell the Web server how to process it. A programmer can write small programs, called scripts, to provide these processing instructions. Instead of requiring its users to develop scripts to process dynamic content, you can publish a Web site to a Web server that uses a set of programs and script files called the **FrontPage Server Extensions** or **SharePoint Services**. The FrontPage Server Extensions and SharePoint Services are programs that run on a Web server and provide the processing instructions for dynamic Web pages. You will learn more about the FrontPage Server Extensions and SharePoint Services in Tutorial 6.

You can create and publish a FrontPage Web site on your computer, on a local area network, or on a Web server connected to the Internet. A **local area network (LAN)** is a group of computers that are located near one another and connected so as to share data, files, software, and hardware. By starting with a **disk-based Web site**, which lets you store and retrieve Web pages on a computer's disk drive, you will be able to test the Web site before making it accessible to Internet visitors. To access a disk-based Web site, you use a drive letter and the page's pathname with backslashes—for example, C:\My Webs\garden\index.htm. Some Web sites are created as disk-based Web sites on the developer's computer or on a LAN to control access to the site and to test its functionality. Because you must publish a Web site to a Web server running the FrontPage Server Extensions or SharePoint Services, the testing of more advanced features of a Web site, such as the ability to process forms or conduct searches, requires a server. A **server-based Web site** uses Web server software that is installed on either a client or a server. You open a server-based Web site by typing the prefix "http:"

and the file's pathname with forward slashes—for example, http://localhost/garden/index.htm. The computers in the offices of the Sunshine Landscape & Garden Center are configured in a LAN. You tell Brett that he can create a disk-based Web site and then publish it to his computer's server to test its functionality, appearance, and content. When he is satisfied that the Web site is complete and functioning correctly, he can publish it to the Web server at the ISP he has chosen to host it, making it accessible to Internet visitors. At that point, Brett would need to continue testing the site on the ISP's server to make sure that everything works as expected.

Before getting started on creating the actual Web site, you tell Brett that the most important first step is to plan the Web site's development. Using the five-part process that you'll teach Brett will ensure a successful site.

Developing a Web Site

The task of developing a Web site might be undertaken by an individual or by a team of people working together to meet certain established goals. A Web site often results from the efforts of a development team consisting of a copywriter, an editor, a graphic designer, a programmer, a systems administrator, and a marketing representative, with a Web design director, sometimes called a **webmaster**, as the team's coordinator. Figure 1-1 shows some of the general responsibilities of each team member. Individuals who own a small business or who have information to put on the Internet sometimes create and develop their own Web sites without the input from a team.

Figure 1-1 **Web development team**

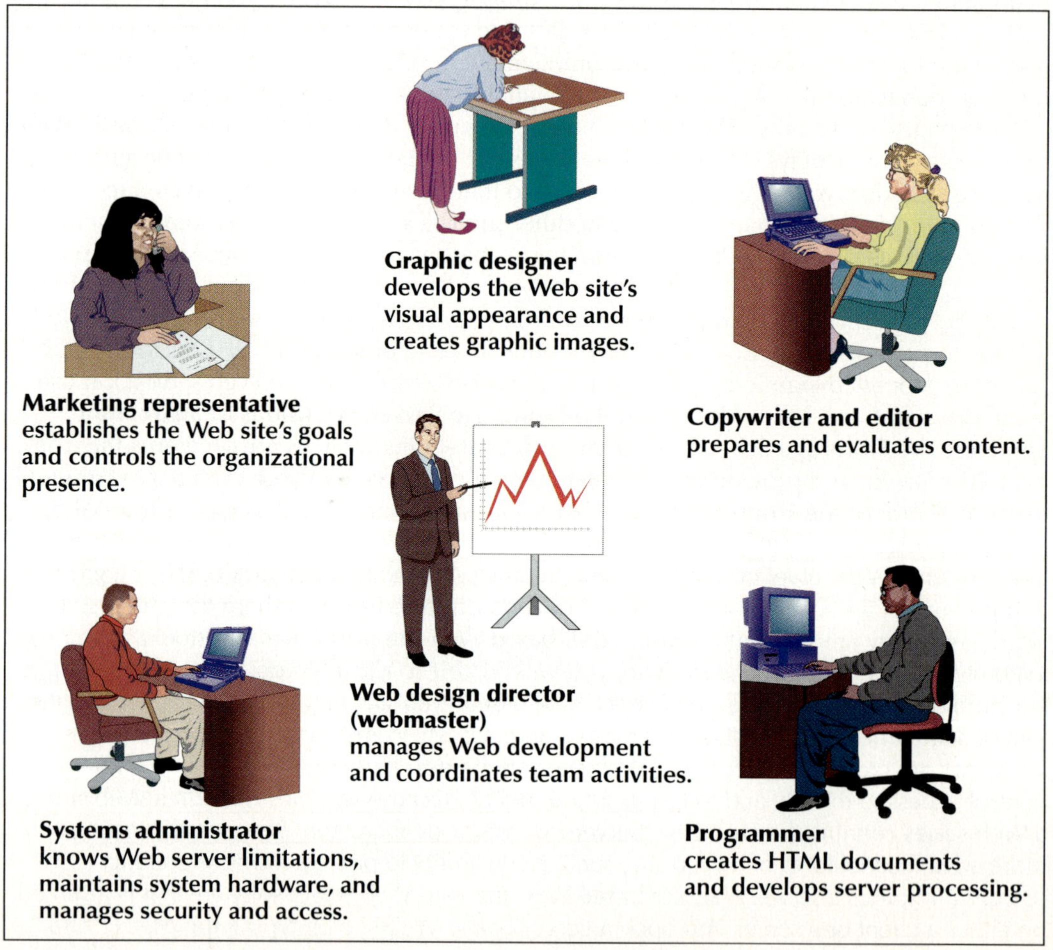

Regardless of who is responsible for developing a Web site, FrontPage makes it easy to perform the various activities required to create and maintain it because FrontPage generates the HTML documents as well as the scripts and other programs required to create your Web site. In addition, FrontPage includes a collection of clip-art images and other graphics that you can use to enhance your site's appearance. The Internet itself is also a great resource for beginning Web site developers, as many sites provide free graphics and scripts that you can use to enhance your own site. The Student Online Companion page for Tutorial 1 includes links to resources that provide graphics and other design information that you might find helpful when developing your own Web site.

Developing a Web site is a multitask process that includes the following activities:

- Defining the goal and purpose of the Web site
- Determining and preparing the Web site's contents
- Designing the Web site
- Building the Web site
- Testing the Web site

Your first objective is to meet with Brett to define the site's overall goal and purpose to ensure that the Web site you develop will meet the needs of its visitors.

Defining the Goal and Purpose of the Web Site

As the first step in creating a Web site, you must clearly define the site's goal and purpose. What do you want to achieve with your site? What will a Web site help you accomplish that other marketing media cannot? Who is your target audience? After meeting with Brett and several other key employees at the nursery, you determine that the Sunshine Landscape & Garden Center wants to develop a Web site that promotes the services provided by the nursery and offers information about products and plants sold at the nursery.

After agreeing on the Web site's goal and purpose, you meet with the people responsible for different services offered by the nursery, such as irrigation, landscape design, and rock work, to obtain the preliminary information necessary to begin developing the site. Specific factors to consider when planning a Web site include the following:

- **Primary intent:** What is the purpose of the Web site? Will you use the Web site to promote the business, accept online orders, or provide information?
- **Short- and long-term goals:** What specific goals should the Web site meet? For example, do you want to market your company's products to boost sales or to increase the company's visibility?
- **Intended audience:** Who do you want or expect to visit your Web site? What research have you completed to describe your site's target audience? What information does your audience need? Have you completed any research about the browsers your audience will use to access the Web site?

Most Web sites include multiple Web pages that are linked together in a hierarchy. The site's top-level page, called the **home page**, includes hyperlinks to the pages that appear at the next level. **Hyperlinks**, or **links**, are keywords, phrases, or pictures in a Web page that, when clicked using a mouse, connect to related information located in the same Web page, in the same Web site, or in another Web site. A hyperlink might open another Web page or play a video clip or a sound file. The process of using a hyperlink to connect to another location on the Internet is called linking. When you click a hyperlink with your mouse, you retrieve the hyperlink's file from the Web server on which it resides. Your Web browser then opens or plays this file on your computer.

Computer History Hypermedia

Figure 1-2 shows your notes after talking with several key employees at the nursery. Your Web site plan contains all the information you need to begin working on the Web site for the Sunshine Landscape & Garden Center.

Figure 1-2 Web site plan for Sunshine Landscape & Garden Center

Web Site Plan

Objectives

Develop a Web site that provides the following information:

- Descriptions of services available at the Sunshine Landscape & Garden Center, including landscape design, rock work, and irrigation, and photographs of completed projects
- Photographs and information about plants and other gardening supplies available for purchase at the nursery
- Seasonal suggestions about plants to install in the area and how to maintain them
- Answers to common gardening questions
- Seasonal suggestions about common gardening tasks to perform during the current month

Requirements

The following information is required to complete the Web site:

- Descriptions of landscape design, rock work, and irrigation services
- Information about plants, their care, and how to install them
- Monthly gardening feature
- Photographs of completed landscaping projects, plants and gardening supplies available for purchase, and different rocks and landscaping materials available
- Information about irrigation services
- The company's logo

Results

The Web site will contain the following main pages:

- Home page
- Garden Center page
- Landscape & Rock Work page
- Bulk Goods page
- Irrigation page

Determining and Preparing the Web Site's Contents

After completing your Web site plan, you are ready to begin developing the Web site's contents. You should gather relevant documents, workbooks, presentations, and other data that you might use or adapt for use in the Web site. As part of this step, you might need to revisit people who were involved in planning the Web site to see if they have material that you can use in your Web pages.

Content is the most fundamental aspect of Web design because the success of any Web site ultimately depends on the quality of its information.

Designing the Web Site

Your next step in developing a Web site is to design the site. In the commercial and competitive realm of the Web, good design is crucial. The overall layout and quality of the pictures and graphics in a Web page should enhance the page's contents and make it interesting for its users to view. Web site design is very different from the page designs you find in newspapers, magazines, and other print media. For example, it's fine in a print publication to include long blocks of text with few pictures or graphics. In a Web page, however, you need to use headings and graphics to make your content easy to view and read on a computer screen. In addition, you have to develop your site for users who view it with different Web browsers, operating systems, monitors, and screen resolutions. You also need to develop your site with individual users in mind. A site geared toward college-aged visitors should look very different than a site developed for seniors. Your selection of graphics, fonts, and other design elements can make the site look very appealing to your target audience or it can turn them away.

During the design stage, you should ask and answer questions related to your company's organizational image. What message is your company trying to convey? What distinguishes your organization from its competitors? Should the Web site be classic, stylish, or contemporary? You should also determine other factors that can influence the site's appearance. Depending on your target audience and Web site goals, these factors might include selecting a specific type style to use in your pages or developing custom graphics.

Armed with the answers to these questions, you can sketch a design of the site, including its individual pages. In this way, you can plan the relationships among Web pages before creating them and connecting them using hyperlinks. Figure 1-3 shows your plan for linking the pages in the Web site for the Sunshine Landscape & Garden Center. The plan specifies which Web pages you must create and the likely hyperlinks that will connect the Web pages.

Preliminary sketch of the Web site **Figure 1-3**

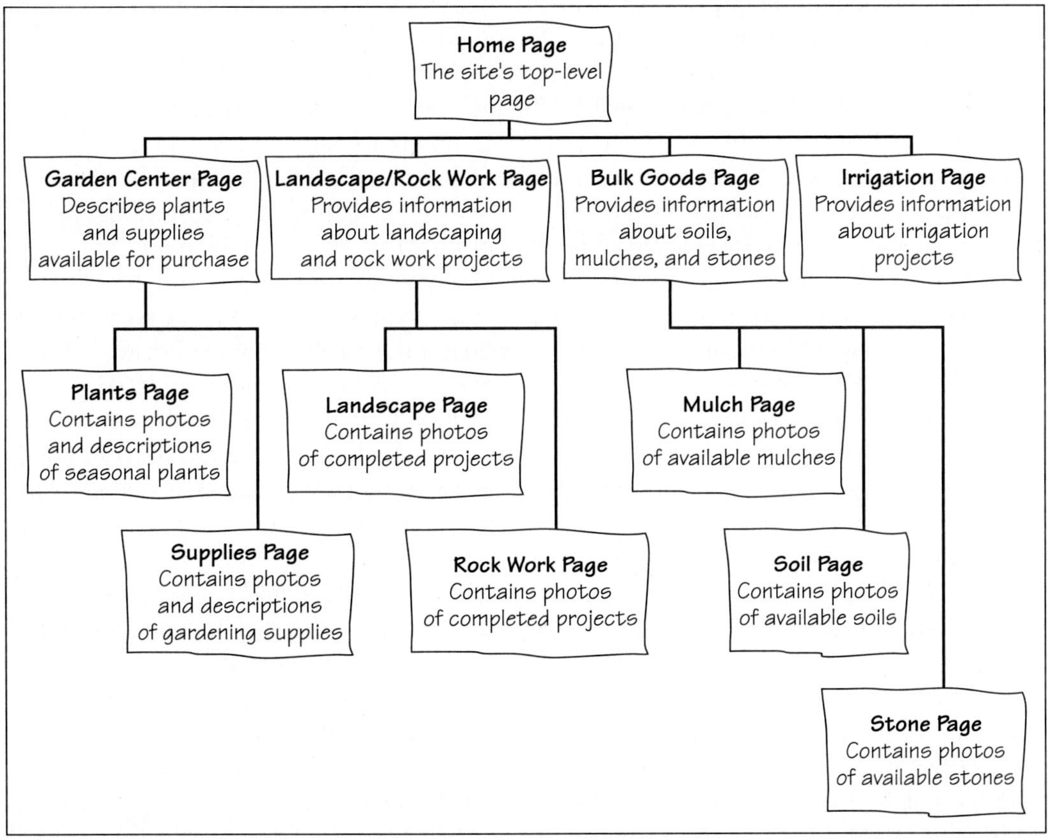

With your Web design plan in place, you can begin developing the Web pages. You will create all of the pages for the Web site as you work through the tutorials in this book.

Building the Web Site

As you transform your Web site's plan into a Web site, it is important to recognize that Internet Explorer and other popular Web browsers, such as Netscape Navigator, might display your pages in slightly different ways. When creating a Web site, you should always test your pages in different browsers to ensure that your pages will be displayed correctly. Fortunately, FrontPage includes an option that you can set before developing any Web pages to ensure compatibility with certain browsers and Internet technologies. For example, if your research indicates that your Web site will be viewed using both Internet Explorer and Netscape Navigator, you might choose to develop it with the settings enabled for creating pages that are supported by both browsers. When you set this option, FrontPage dims commands that are not supported by both browsers. If you do not have information about which browsers will access your site, you can ask your ISP or visit Internet Web sites that conduct browser research to learn more about popular Web browsers used by Internet visitors. The Student Online Companion page for Tutorial 1 includes links to companies that conduct research about the popularity of different Web browsers.

Another important consideration during this phase is that the best Web sites are visually appealing, convey information correctly and succinctly, and download quickly. Keep the following guidelines in mind while you are building a Web site:

- Know and adhere to the stated goals for the site as you decide how to present its information.
- Consider your audience's reaction to every piece of information and every picture to be included.
- Include components that download quickly. People often leave a site if downloading its pages takes too long. Large pictures can download slowly; if you must include them, provide an option to download them as separate Web pages.
- Make the site visually appealing. Strike a balance between a site design that is too simple and one that is chaotic. Make the text large enough for easy viewing, and use color and font variations to draw attention to items. However, don't use so many different fonts, colors, or features on a page that the excessive formatting becomes distracting.
- Organize your content into groups of related information. For example, if you are designing a Web site for a bookstore, arrange the material according to subject areas.
- Include appropriate navigation options, including hyperlinks that make it easy to return to the home page. Users should be able to move around easily within your site.
- Contact your ISP to inquire about any special naming conventions for your Web site and its pages. For example, some Web servers will only process pages with filenames that use all lowercase letters. Some ISPs also place restrictions on the use of spaces and special characters (such as $ and #) in filenames because some Web servers do not support files containing spaces and special characters in their filenames. Another common restriction is limiting filenames to eight characters. There might be other restrictions on the name of the home page, how to name the Web site's folder, and the features you can include in your Web site. The best way to plan for these types of conventions and restrictions is to know in advance about the filename conventions and restrictions that the ISP you choose to host your site will enforce. You tell Brett that a good rule of thumb is to use only lowercase letters in filenames and no spaces or special characters, and to limit the size of your filenames to eight characters. You will use these conventions when developing the Sunshine Landscape & Garden Center Web site.

Testing the Web Site

The final step in developing a Web site is to test it. This step includes verifying that all hyperlinks work correctly and that all multimedia files are available. You should thoroughly test a Web site before and after publishing it to a Web server. In these tutorials, you will test Web pages using FrontPage and a browser. It is also important to test your Web site using different browsers, and different versions of those browsers, to ensure that all pages function and appear correctly.

Starting FrontPage

Through the five-part Web development process, you and Brett identified a clear vision of the Web site to be developed for the Sunshine Landscape & Garden Center, and you are ready to begin creating the Web site. First, however, you need to start FrontPage and explore some important features of the FrontPage program window.

To start FrontPage:

1. Make sure that you know the location of the Data Files that you will use as you complete the tutorials in this book, and the location where you will create your Web sites.

   Trouble? You must have the FrontPage Data Files to complete the tutorials in this book. The "Read This Before You Begin" section of this book includes information about where to get the Data Files and how to use them.

   Trouble? The steps in this book are written for students who will create their Web sites in the following folder on their computer's hard drive: C:\My Webs\[StudentName], where "[StudentName]" is your first and last name. However, you can create your Web sites in any folder or on any network or server that supports FrontPage Web sites. If you are unsure of the location where you will create your Web sites for this book, ask your instructor or technical support person for assistance.

2. Click the **Start** button on the taskbar, point to **All Programs**, point to **Microsoft Office**, and then click **Microsoft Office FrontPage 2003** to start FrontPage. A blank Web page opens in the FrontPage program window. See Figure 1-4.

Figure 1-4 **Microsoft FrontPage program window**

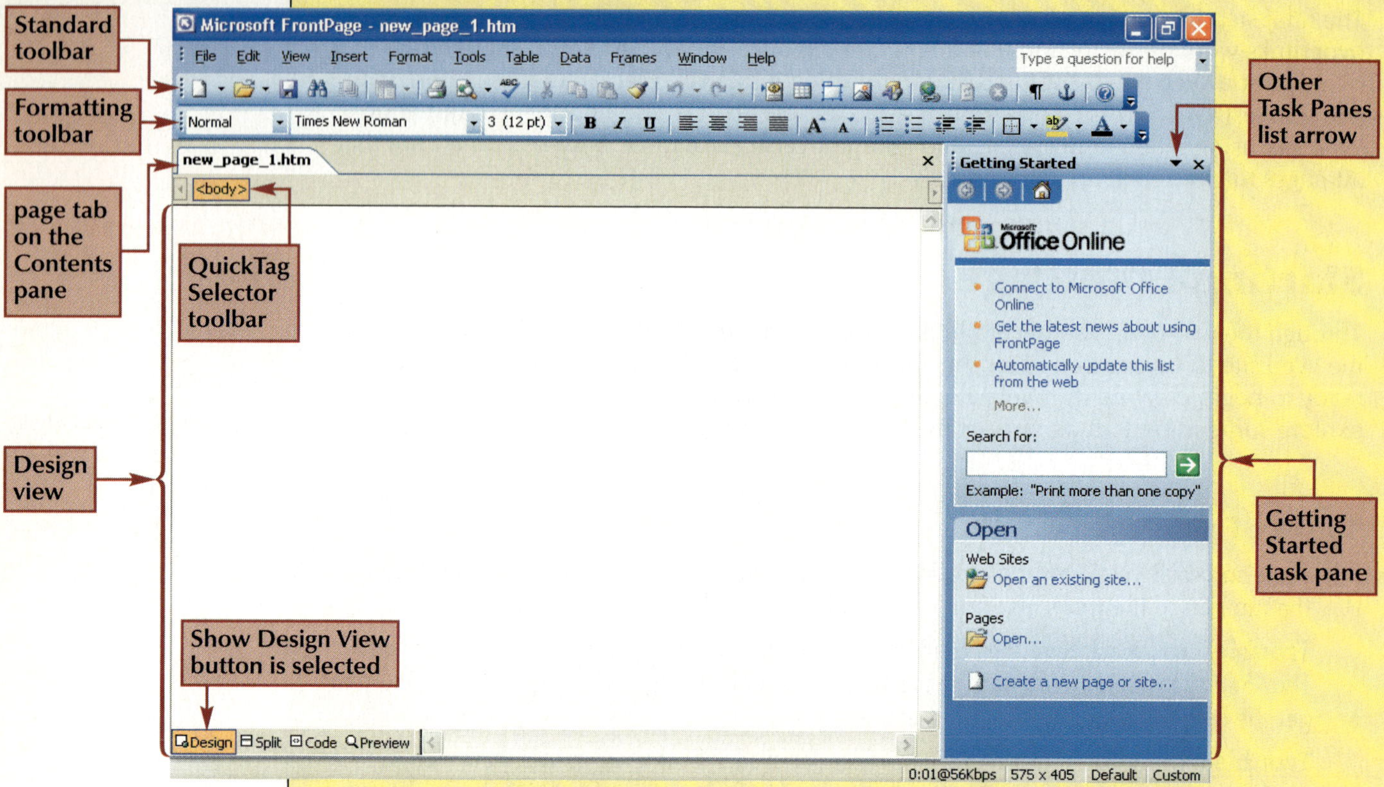

Trouble? If a User Name dialog box opens and asks you to enter your full name and initials, provide this information in the appropriate text boxes, and then click the OK button.

Trouble? If a dialog box opens and asks whether you would like to make FrontPage your default Web page editor, click the No button.

Trouble? If your Microsoft FrontPage 2003 title bar contains a path to a Web site (such as C:\My Webs\site), click File on the menu bar, and then click Close Site to close it. If you want to set FrontPage so that it doesn't automatically open the Web site that was open the last time FrontPage was used, click Tools on the menu bar, click Options, click the General tab, and then click the Open last Web automatically when FrontPage starts check box to clear it. Click the OK button to close the Options dialog box.

Trouble? If the Show Design View button shown in Figure 1-4 is not selected, you are in a different Page view. Click the Show Design View button to change to Design view.

Figure 1-4 shows the default FrontPage program window. Before creating the garden Web site, you want to tell Brett about some important FrontPage features.

When you first start FrontPage, a new Web page opens in the Design view window within the Contents pane. By default, this page is named new_page_1.htm. This filename appears as a tab at the top of the Contents pane. As you open and create other Web pages, their filenames will appear on new tabs. You can switch between Web pages by clicking these tabs.

The area below the tabs, called the **QuickTag Selector toolbar**, shows the HTML for the content in the Web page that contains the insertion point. Because you are viewing a Web page with no content, only the <body> tag appears on the QuickTag Selector toolbar. If you click an HTML tag on the QuickTag Selector toolbar, the text affected by that tag is selected in the Web page and you can use the QuickTag Selector toolbar to make changes to the selected text. This feature makes it easy for you to examine the HTML tags that format the selected text and to make changes to text affected by the tags.

When you first start FrontPage, the Getting Started task pane opens on the right side of your screen. You can use the options in the Getting Started task pane to search for Help on a specific topic, or to create or open a Web site or create or open a Web page. Clicking the Other Task Panes list arrow displays a list of other task panes, as shown in Figure 1-5. Notice that there are task panes for a variety of common tasks you might perform when working in a Web site, such as creating tables or inserting clip-art images. As you work in FrontPage, the task pane sometimes might close automatically so you can see more of the Web page on which you are working; you can close the task pane yourself by clicking the Close button on its title bar. In addition, as you work in FrontPage, different task panes might open automatically to provide shortcuts for working on the current task. The shortcuts available in the different task panes are also available through the menu commands and toolbar buttons.

Figure 1-5 **Task pane options**

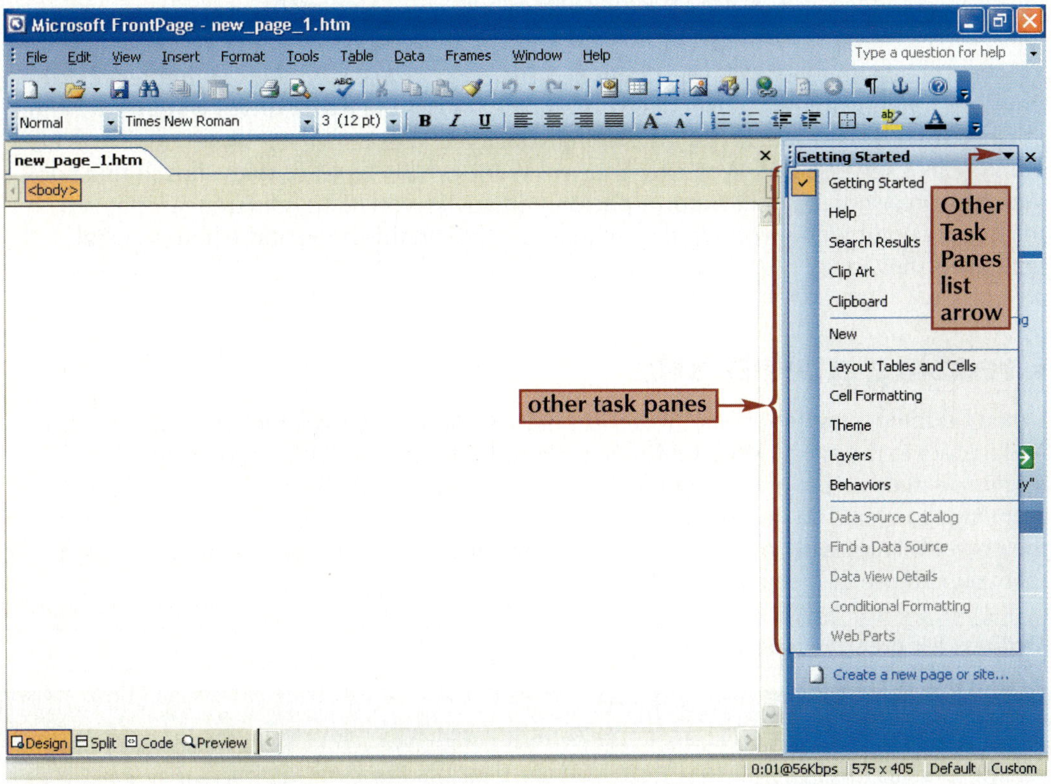

Finally, just as in other Office programs, you can customize the toolbars and menu bars in FrontPage so that the Standard and Formatting toolbars appear on one or two rows, and so that menus show your frequently used commands first. To change these settings, click Tools on the menu bar, click Customize, and then click the Options tab. If you want your screens to match the ones shown in this book, change your settings to match those shown in Figure 1-6.

Figure 1-6 **Customize dialog box**

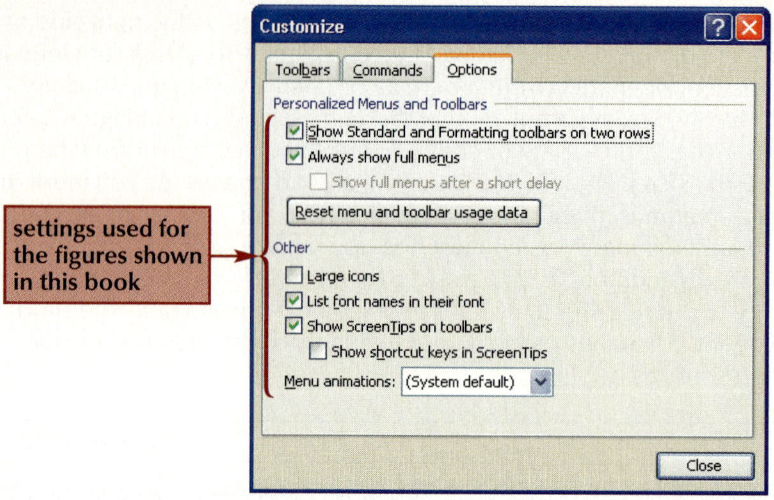

If you are storing the Web sites that you create in this book on your computer's hard drive, on a removable drive (such as a Zip drive), or on a network drive, you are working in a disk-based Web site. If you are storing your Web sites on a Web server, then you are working in a server-based Web site. You will work in both types of Web sites in this book. Your instructor or technical support person will advise you of any differences that you might encounter while working through the tutorials in this book and where to create your Web sites.

Creating a Web Site

When building a new Web site, you must first create a folder in which to store the files and folders in the site. A **Web folder** is a Windows folder, similar to a folder that you might use in other programs, but it is configured to store a Web site. You always use FrontPage to create the folder for your Web site. The Web site that you create depends on the content that it will contain. Figure 1-7 describes the various templates and wizards that you can use to create a new Web site.

Figure 1-7 **Options for creating a new FrontPage Web site**

Template or Wizard	Description
One Page Web Site	Creates a Web site that contains one blank page named index.htm or Default.htm, which becomes the site's home page
Corporate Presence Wizard	Creates a Web site with pages that a corporation might use
Customer Support Web Site	Creates a Web site that contains pages useful for companies providing customer support, particularly software companies
Database Interface Wizard	Creates a Web site that you can connect to a database in which you can add, view, update, and delete records
Discussion Web Site Wizard	Creates a Web site that contains a table of contents, full-text searching capability, and threads organized around a specific discussion topic
Empty Web Site	Creates a Web site that contains no pages
Import Web Site Wizard	Creates a Web site that contains pages imported from another location, such as another Web site or a hard drive

Figure 1-7

Options for creating a new FrontPage Web site (continued)

Template or Wizard	Description
Personal Web Site	Creates a Web site that an individual might use to publish pages about his or her interests and favorite Web sites
Project Web Site	Creates a Web site that contains a list of members, a schedule, status information, and a discussion archive related to a specific project
SharePoint Team Site	Creates a Web site with tools that group members can use to collaborate on a project, including a calendar, a library for storing shared documents, a tasks list, and a contacts list

Because you need to create a Web site that includes a home page for the Sunshine Landscape & Garden Center, you will use the One Page Web Site template. After creating the Web site, you will add pages and other content to it.

To create the garden Web site:

1. Click the **Other Task Panes** list arrow, and then click **New** to display the New task pane. This task pane contains options for creating new Web pages and Web sites. See Figure 1-8.

Figure 1-8

New task pane

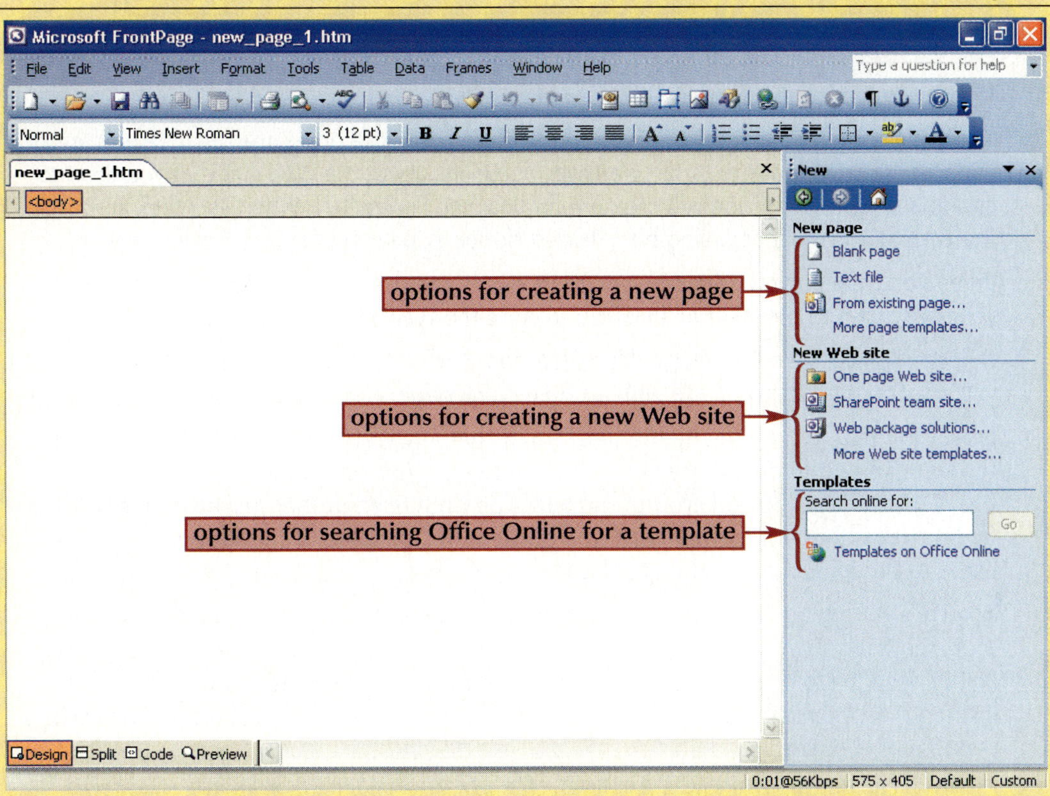

2. In the New Web site section of the New task pane, click **More Web site templates**. The Web Site Templates dialog box opens. See Figure 1-9.

Figure 1-9 **Web Site Templates dialog box**

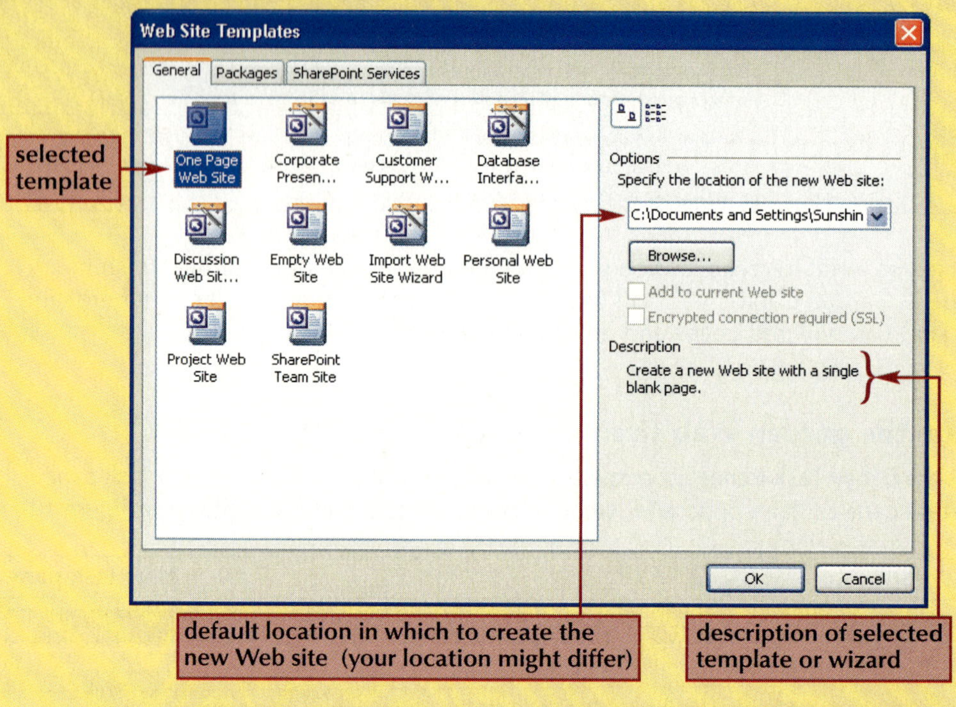

The options in this dialog box let you create a new Web site using one of six templates, or you can use one of four wizards to answer questions about the Web site that you want to create and then FrontPage will create it for you (see Figure 1-7). When you click an icon in the Web Site Templates dialog box, its description appears in the Description section.

When you create a new Web site, you must select a template or wizard on which to base your new site and the location in which to store the Web site's files and folders.

3. If necessary, click the **One Page Web Site** icon. Notice that the Description box shows that you will create a new Web site with a single blank page.
4. Select the text in the Specify the location of the new Web site text box, type the path to the drive and folder where you will create your Web site, and then type the name of the Web site that you will create, **garden**. The path used in the figures in this book is C:\My Webs\[Student Name]\garden; "garden" is the name of the Web site and the name of the folder that will store the Web site's files.

   Trouble? If you are storing your Web sites on a different drive or in a different folder, your instructor might provide you with a location different from that given in Step 4. You do not need to store your Data Files and your Web sites in the same location. Ask your instructor or technical support person for help if you are unsure of the location in which to create your Web sites.
5. Click the **OK** button to create a new Web site using the One Page Web Site template. FrontPage creates the garden Web site in the location you specified and closes the New task pane. When you create a new Web site, FrontPage creates some folders and hidden files that it uses to run the Web site. Because you used the One Page Web Site template to create the garden Web site, FrontPage also created a home page named index.htm. (If you created your Web site on a server, FrontPage names the home page Default.htm.) The garden Web site appears in Figure 1-10.

Web site in Folders view

Figure 1-10

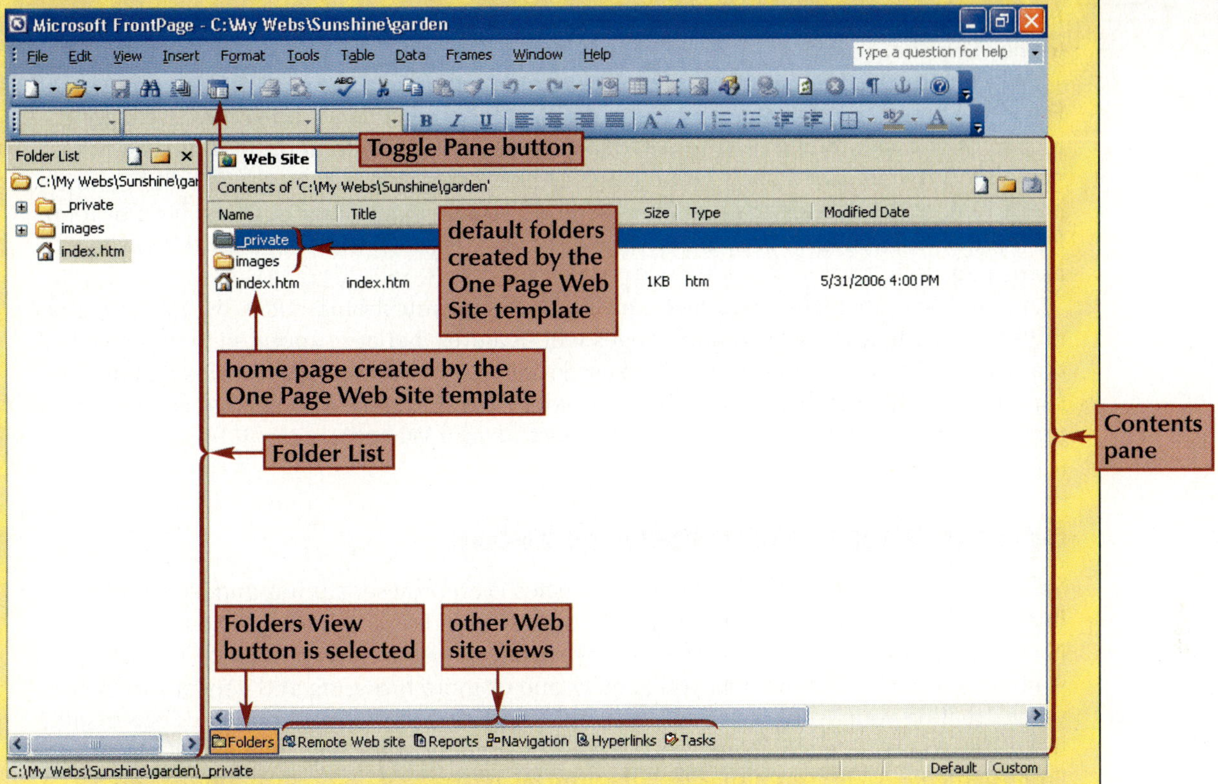

Trouble? If a dialog box opens and indicates that FrontPage must convert this folder to a FrontPage Web site, click the Yes button to continue.

Trouble? If your Folder List is hidden, click the Toggle Pane button on the Standard toolbar to display it.

Notice that the FrontPage program window has a different appearance when it displays a Web site instead of just the Web page shown in Figure 1-4. A Web site is a collection of folders and files for an entire site, and not just a single Web page. Because a Web site is more complicated than a single Web page, FrontPage displays additional features to make it easy for you to view the entire contents of a Web site. Notice the Folder List that opens on the left side of your screen. The Folder List shows the root folder (also called the root Web) for the current Web site, which in this case is the garden folder. The garden folder includes two subfolders, _private and images, and the home page file, index.htm, that FrontPage created. The three buttons on the Folder List let you create a new Web page , create a new folder , and close the Folder List ×. You can click the Toggle Pane button on the Standard toolbar to open and close the Folder List. Displaying the Folder List is a matter of personal preference; you might want to keep it visible as you work in FrontPage so you can see all of the files and folders in your Web site. For this book, however, you will close the Folder List when you don't need it so you can see more of the Web page as you do your work.

The Contents pane shows the same information as the Folder List but provides details about the title, size, file type, last modification date, the name of the author who last modified the file, and optional comments about each file in the Web site (you might need to scroll the Contents pane to see all of these columns). Notice that the path to the current Web site appears on the Microsoft FrontPage 2003 title bar; your path might differ. Finally, the buttons at the bottom of the Contents pane let you change the Web site view and examine other details about the site's files, hyperlinks, and features. You will learn more about Web site views after you have added additional content and hyperlinks to the Web site.

When you used the One Page Web Site template to create the garden Web site, FrontPage created and saved the garden Web site's home page as **index.htm**. It's a good idea to check with the ISP you selected to host your Web site to find out if it has any filename requirements for a site's home page. Other acceptable names are default.htm and home.htm, and some servers require different filename extensions, such as .html or .php, for a site's home page. A Web browser will recognize any of these files as a Web site's home page.

You tell Brett that when you first create a Web site, you should check the Web site's settings to verify that you are creating pages with features that are supported by the browsers that you expect to access the site. Because FrontPage lets you create features that are not supported by all Web browsers, it also includes options that let you disable certain features so you can easily refrain from using them in your Web site.

Specifying a Browser Version

You checked an Internet Web site that publishes Web browser studies and learned that Internet Explorer is the most popular Web browser used on the Internet. Netscape Navigator is also a popular browser, as are browsers used by different ISPs, such as America Online. FrontPage lets you specify one or more browsers and versions to target when creating your Web pages, so you can be sure that these target browsers can display the pages you will create. When you change the default authoring settings for a Web site, FrontPage will use those settings for all future Web sites that you create, unless you change them. Therefore, it is a good idea to check these settings for all new Web sites that you create to ensure their accuracy.

To change the authoring settings of the garden Web site:

1. Point to the **Authoring Settings** pane on the status bar. Figure 1-11 shows the word "Default" on this panel; your current setting might differ. When you point to the pane, a ScreenTip appears and displays information about the current authoring settings.

Figure 1-11

Using the Authoring Settings feature

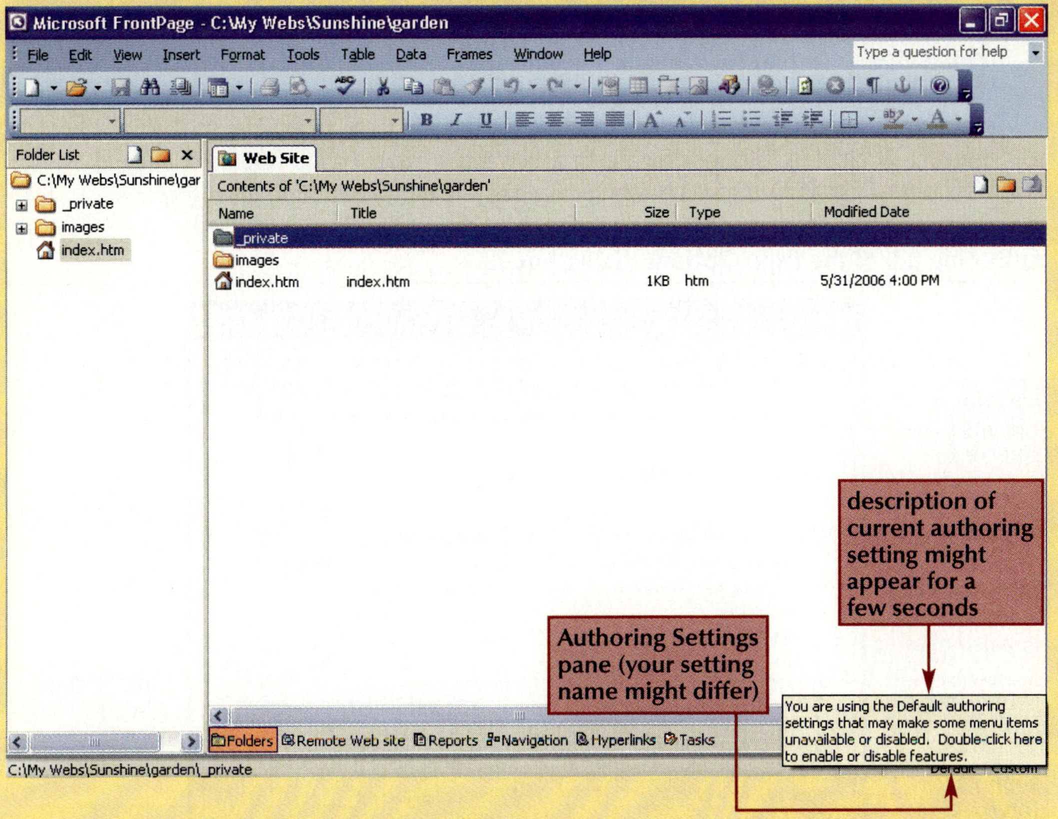

2. Double-click the **Authoring Settings** pane on the status bar. The Page Options dialog box opens with the Authoring tab selected. Read the message at the top of the Authoring tab, which indicates that changing these settings might disable some menu and dialog box options so as to ensure that Web sites you create will contain only those features supported by the browsers and options that you select. In the future, if you attempt to create a feature in a Web site and that feature's menu command is disabled, you can check the Web site's settings to see whether that feature has been disabled.
3. Click the **FrontPage and SharePoint technologies** list arrow, and then click **Custom**. You tell Brett that you will not use Generator and ProgID tags or downlevel image files in the garden Web site, so he can disable these features. You will use Author-time Web Components to create navigation bars and shared borders, so you will enable these options.
4. If necessary, click the **Generator and ProgID tags** check box and the **Downlevel image file** check box to deselect them; then make sure that every other check box in the FrontPage and SharePoint technologies section contains a check mark.
5. Click the **Browsers** list arrow, and then click **Microsoft Internet Explorer only**. FrontPage will allow you to use only those features supported by Internet Explorer. People who access the Web site using another Web browser will still be able to view its content, but the browser might not be able to display some features you have created. You'll identify these features for Brett as he creates the Web site.

6. Click the **Browser versions** list arrow, and then click **5.0/6.0 browsers and later**. When you specify a browser setting, FrontPage automatically selects and deselects Internet technologies that the selected browser(s) and version(s) support. As shown in Figure 1-12, FrontPage changes the settings in the dialog box to enable features supported by versions 5.0, 6.0, and later of the specified browser, Internet Explorer. If you need to change the default settings, you can click the check box for the technology that you want to enable or disable, at which time one or all of the settings for the browser and browser version would change to "Custom," indicating that you have customized the default authoring settings.

Figure 1-12 **Authoring tab of the Page Options dialog box**

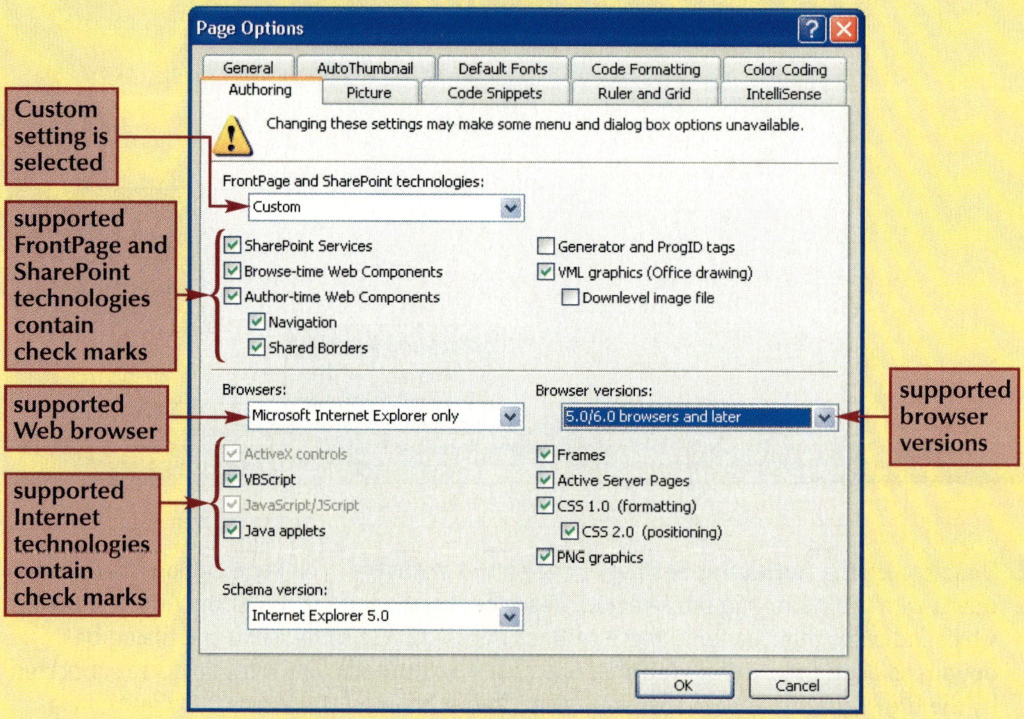

7. Click the **OK** button to close the dialog box. Notice that the Authoring Settings pane shows the "Custom" authoring setting and that the Browser Settings pane next to the Authoring Settings pane shows "IE 5.0/6.0+," which indicates custom authoring settings and support for Internet Explorer versions 5.0, 6.0, and higher.

Specifying a Page Size

If you have experience using the Internet on different computers with different monitors, you might already have discovered that Web pages don't have the same standard dimensions as sheets of paper. When you view a Web page on a computer, you might see the full page or need to use a scroll bar to view all of its contents. Figure 1-13 shows how a Web page might look to users with monitors set to different resolutions. The Web page on the left is being viewed in a browser that displays 640 × 480 pixels. The same Web page on the right is being viewed in a browser that displays 1024 × 768 pixels. A **pixel** is a single point of an image. For most monitors, you can use Windows to control the number of pixels that appear on the screen at the same time. For a monitor set to 640 × 480 resolution, you will see approximately 307,000 pixels on the screen at the same time—640 pixels on each of 480 lines. As you increase the resolution, you will see more pixels and more lines of the Web page. For this reason, monitors with high resolutions display more content.

Figure 1-13 **Comparing the same Web page displayed at different resolutions**

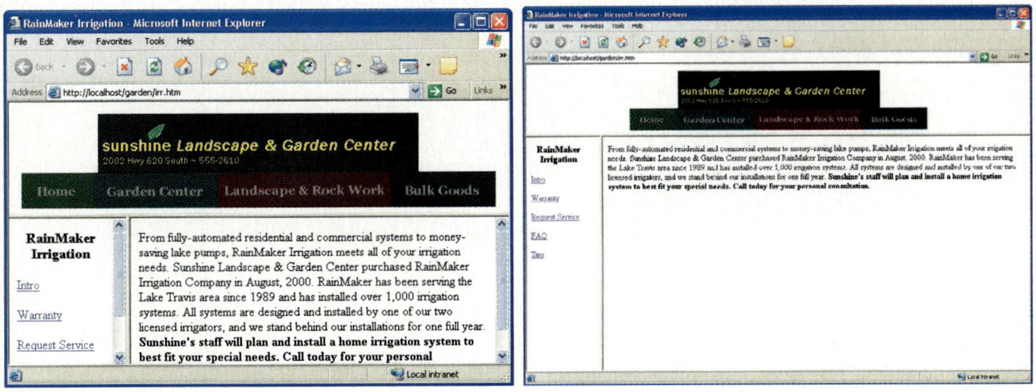

640 × 480 resolution **1024 × 768 resolution**

Because people who view your Web pages will use different monitors with different resolutions, part of your testing process should include viewing your Web site using different computers and monitors. In addition, you can use FrontPage to set your default page size. For most Web sites, this page size (or resolution) is 800 × 600. FrontPage includes a feature that lets you set your default page size and change it to see how your site looks when viewed at different resolutions. Brett wants to set the page resolution now so the pages will already be optimized for people viewing the pages at 800 × 600 resolution. You will set the page size by opening the home page, but all other pages that you create in the Web site will use the same page size.

To open the home page and set the default page size:

1. Double-click **index.htm** in the Folder List. The home page, which contains no content yet, opens in Design view. Notice the Page Size pane on the status bar.
2. Click the **Page Size** pane to open a menu of preset sizes. The current page size appears at the top; your value might differ from what appears in Figure 1-14. This menu includes settings for the most commonly used browser settings. You can click a new setting or click Modify Page Sizes to open the Modify Page Sizes dialog box, where you can add, modify, and reset the commonly used settings.

Figure 1-14 Home page in Design view

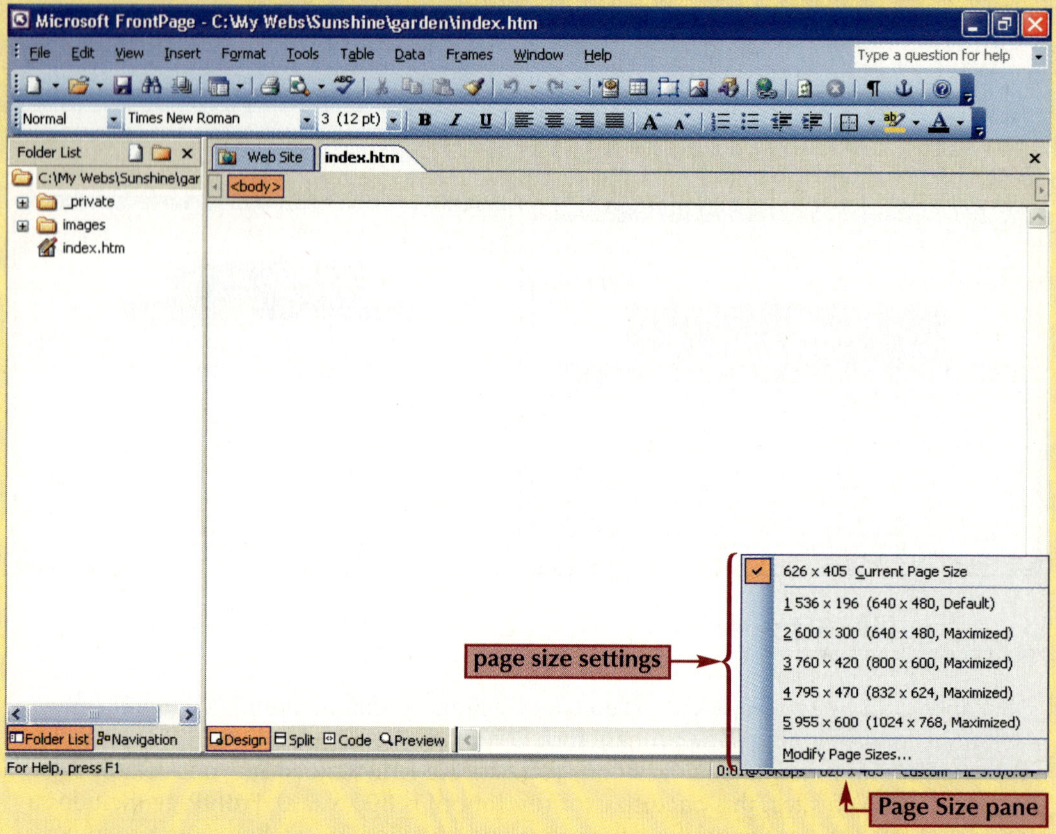

3. Click **760 × 420** in the menu. The Page Size pane on the status bar shows that the default page size is locked at 760 × 420 pixels, which is the size allowed for a monitor with 800 × 600 resolution.

Entering Text in a Web Page

After creating a Web site, you can create its individual Web pages. FrontPage automatically created and saved the index.htm home page when you used the One Page Web Site template to create the garden Web site. The home page doesn't contain any content yet, so your first task is to add content to it. Brett wants to add the company's name and address to the site's home page. So you will be able to view more of the home page as you work, you will close the Folder List.

To close the Folder List and enter text in a Web page:

1. Click the **Close** button × on the Folder List. Notice that the name of the home page—index.htm—appears both as a page tab at the top of the Contents pane and on the Microsoft FrontPage 2003 title bar. Because you have not yet added any content to the home page, it is blank.
2. Type **Sunshine Landscape & Garden Center**, and then press the **Enter** key. FrontPage creates a new paragraph in the Web page. Notice that the default setting for a paragraph in a Web page is to add some white space between lines.

3. On the new line, type **2002 Hwy 620 South**, press the **Enter** key, and then type **555-2610**. You have added the nursery's name, address, and phone number to the Web page.

Brett wants to include information that changes regularly on the home page to make that page more interesting to site visitors. He asks you to speak with Clara McShane, the company's chief landscaper, to see if she has some content you can insert for now.

Inserting a File into a Web Page

You can enter new content for a Web page by typing all the necessary text in Design view. If the content already exists in another text-based file format or in a Word, Excel, or PowerPoint file, you can insert it directly into the page instead of retyping it. When you include content from another file in a Web page, FrontPage automatically converts the new content to HTML. Being able to insert the contents of a file into a Web page allows members of a Web site development team to divide the tasks required to complete a Web page and to exchange information.

Inserting a File into a Web Page

Reference Window

- Place the insertion point where the new content should appear.
- Click Insert on the menu bar, click File, and then use the Look in list arrow to browse to the location that contains the desired file.
- Click the Files of type list arrow, and then click All Files (*.*) to display a list of all available files or click the file type for which you are searching.
- Double-click the desired file to insert its contents.

As you catch up with Clara between jobs, she tells you that she used Microsoft Word to prepare a feature that includes a checklist of information about the tasks that local gardeners should perform during the current month. She prepared the checklist for February. When the site is published, she will give you the correct checklist for the current month. You can insert her text from the Word file to save yourself some typing.

To insert a Word file into a Web page:

1. Press the **Enter** key to position the insertion point below the phone number, click **Insert** on the menu bar, and then click **File**. The Select File dialog box opens.
2. If necessary, click the **Look in** list arrow, change to the drive or folder that contains your Data Files, double-click the **Tutorial.01** folder to display its contents, and then double-click the **Tutorial** folder to open it.

   By default, FrontPage displays only HTML files. You need to display Word files, however, to find Clara's document. Word files have a .doc file extension.
3. Click the **Files of type** list arrow to display a list of available file types, and then click **Word 97-2003 (*.doc)** to display a list of Word files.
4. Double-click **list.doc** to select this file, to convert its content to HTML, and to insert it into the home page. Figure 1-15 shows the home page with the new text inserted from the Word file.

   Trouble? If Windows is configured to hide filename extensions, double-click the list file (without the filename extension).

Trouble? If a Microsoft FrontPage dialog box opens and informs you that it can't import the specified format because it is not currently installed, insert your Microsoft FrontPage 2003 CD into the correct drive, and then click the Yes button. If you do not have this CD, ask your instructor or technical support person for help, or simply type the text shown in Figure 1-15.

Figure 1-15 **Home page with new content**

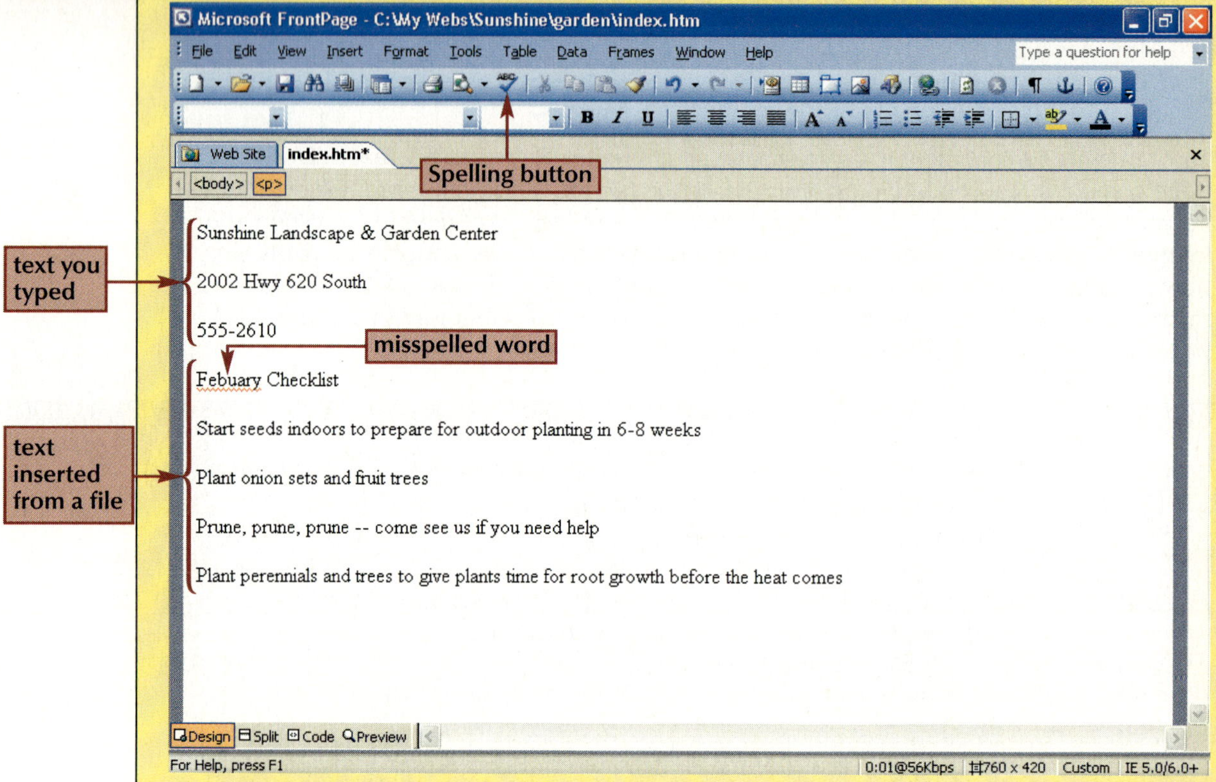

After creating the content of a Web page, you tell Brett that it's a good idea to check the document for spelling errors.

Spell Checking a Web Page

Brett asks you about the wavy red line below the word "Febuary" in the content he inserted from Clara's file. You tell him that this line indicates a word that the dictionary doesn't recognize. To correct a single misspelled word, you can right-click it and then select the correctly spelled word from the menu that opens. To check the spelling in the entire Web page, you tell Brett that he can use the spell check feature.

Spell Checking a Web Page

Reference Window

- Click the Spelling button on the Standard toolbar to open the Spelling dialog box.
- As potentially misspelled words are highlighted in the Spelling dialog box, either click the correct suggestion and then click the Change button, click the Ignore button to accept the original spelling, or type the correct word in the Change To text box and then click the Change button.
- To ignore all instances of a word or to change the spelling of all instances of a misspelled word, click the Ignore All button or the Change All button, respectively.
- When the spell check feature is complete, click the OK button to close the message box.

To check the spelling in a Web page:

1. Click the **Spelling** button on the Standard toolbar. The word "Febuary" is selected in the Web page and the Spelling dialog box opens with the word "Febuary" displayed in the Not in Dictionary box. See Figure 1-16.

Figure 1-16 Spelling dialog box

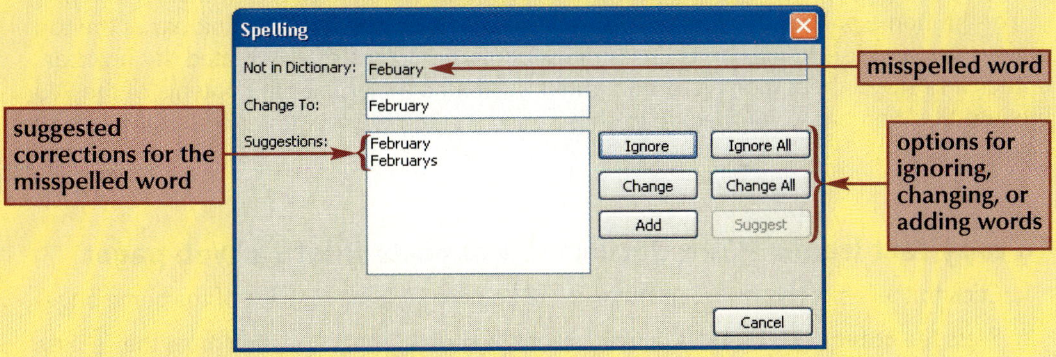

Trouble? If a different word appears in the Not in Dictionary box, you may have typed another word incorrectly. Use the information in the following paragraph to ignore or change the word as appropriate.

Trouble? If you do not encounter any misspelled words in your Web page, then the word "Febuary" is in your dictionary. Click the OK button to close the Spelling dialog box, and then edit the word to change it to "February."

You can click one of the suggested corrections in the Suggestions list box to change the spelling of the selected word, and then click the Change button. Alternatively, you can type a new spelling in the Change To text box, and then click the Change button. If the selected word is spelled correctly, click the Ignore button. You can also click the Change All or Ignore All button to avoid checking the spelling of the same word again. If you want to add a word to FrontPage's dictionary, click the Add button; normally, you should add only those words to the dictionary that you will type often, such as your name.

2. Click **February** in the Suggestions list box, and then click the **Change** button.
3. If necessary, correct any other misspellings that appear in the Spelling dialog box. When you are finished, click the **OK** button in the message box that opens to tell you that the spell check is complete.

After completing the spell check, you remind Brett that he cannot rely on the spell check feature to catch all of the errors in a document, and that he needs to read everything to make sure that it is grammatically correct before finalizing it.

Adding a Link Bar

Based on Brett's plan for the entire Web site, you know that you need to create the hyperlinks on the home page that will let visitors open other pages in the Web site. Even though you haven't created these pages yet, you can add the text for the hyperlinks as placeholders until you are ready to create the actual pages and the links to them. The feature in a Web page that contains hyperlinks that open other pages in the Web site is called a **link bar**. One way to create a link bar is to type the text you want to use and then format that text as hyperlinks to open other Web pages. Another type of link bar is a link bar component, which is a group of hyperlinks that FrontPage creates and manages for you. Because you have not created any other pages in the Web site yet, you will just type the text to use as the links that appear on the home page.

When you create a link bar using text that you type, you can separate the entries in the link bar using one of several options. One popular way to separate entries is to use characters, such as a vertical bar (|) or square brackets ([ ]), as the separators. A single vertical bar is typically placed between entries, whereas square brackets surround each entry.

For the home page of the garden Web site, you decide to place the link bar at the top of the page and use square brackets as the separators. Brett already created the link bar entries and saved them in a Word document. Instead of inserting the contents of the Word file into the Web page, you decide to show him how to copy the text and paste it into the Web page.

To copy text from a Word document and paste it into a Web page:

1. Click to the left of the word **Sunshine** at the beginning of the first line of the home page.
2. Press the **Enter** key to insert a line before the first paragraph, and then press the ↑ key. The insertion point moves to the beginning of the new line, where you will insert the text for the link bar.
3. Click the **Start** button on the taskbar, point to **All Programs**, point to **Microsoft Office**, and then click **Microsoft Office Word 2003** to start Word.
4. Click the **Open** button on the Standard toolbar, click the **Look in** list arrow and browse to the drive and folder where your Data Files are stored, double-click the **Tutorial.01** folder to open it, double-click the **Tutorial** folder to open it, and then double-click the **link.doc** file to open it. This document contains text that you will copy and then paste into the home page.
5. Click **Edit** on the menu bar, and then click **Select All**. The text in the document is selected.
6. Click the **Copy** button on the Standard toolbar to copy the selected text to the Windows Clipboard.
7. Click the **Close** button on the Microsoft Word title bar to close Word. If necessary, click the **Microsoft FrontPage** program button on the taskbar to return to FrontPage.

   The insertion point appears on the first line of the home page. You will paste the text into this location.
8. Click the **Paste** button on the Standard toolbar. The text that you copied from the Word document appears in the Web page. See Figure 1-17.

Copied text added to Web page

Figure 1-17

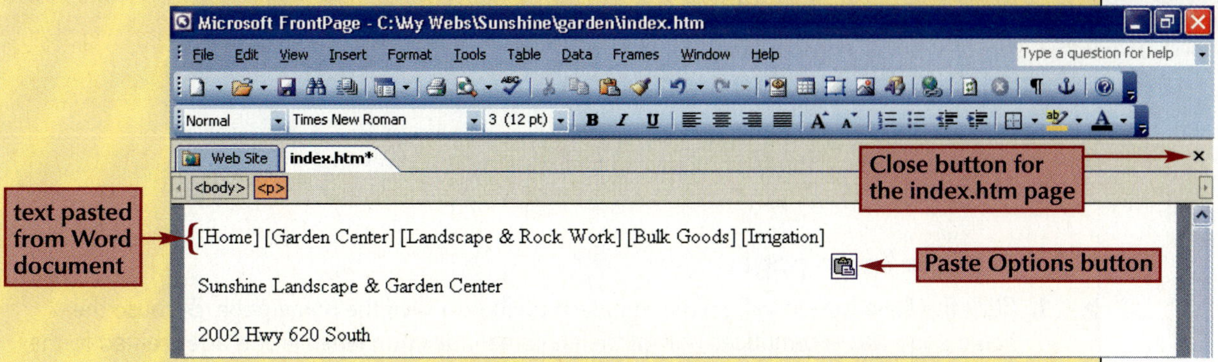

Notice the Paste Options button that appears below the pasted text. The Paste Options button is a **smart tag**, which provides choices for establishing the layout and content of pasted text in a Web page. When you paste text into a Web page, FrontPage provides up to three options related to the format of the pasted text. The first option, Use Destination Styles, removes any styles in the original document in which the text appeared and uses defined styles in the Web page in their place. The second option, Keep Source Formatting, ensures that any formatting applied to the original text is retained in the Web page. For example, if the pasted text uses specific fonts or colors, choosing this option would ensure that these characteristics carry over to the Web page. The third option, Keep Text Only, pastes just the text, without retaining any formatting. Depending on the format of the pasted text, some of these options might not appear in the list. Working with plain text gives you greater flexibility as you work in FrontPage, so you tell Brett to choose this option.

9. Click the **Paste Options** button that appears below the pasted text, and then click the **Keep Text Only** option button. Now you have plain text, without any formatting. The Paste Options button will disappear when you perform another task in the document. If you don't select an option after pasting text in a Web page, the default selection is to keep the source formatting. If you know that you want to keep the source formatting, you can ignore the Paste Options button and it will disappear when you perform another task.

Brett asks you about the asterisk that appears on the index.htm page tab. You tell him that the asterisk is a reminder that the page contains unsaved changes. Brett is finished with his work on the home page for now, so you will show him how to save it.

Saving a Web Page

Saving your work on a regular basis is important. You use the Save command on the File menu or the Save button on the Standard toolbar to save a Web page. Keep in mind that using the Save command or Save button does not create a separate version of your old Web page; instead, it replaces the old version with the new version. To retain the original file and create a new file, you must save the Web page with a different filename by using the Save As command on the File menu.

Reference Window

Saving a Web Page

- Click the Save button on the Standard toolbar.

or

- Click File on the menu bar, and then click Save.

Brett needs to save the home page before closing the Web site.

To save the home page:

1. Click the **Save** button on the Standard toolbar to save the home page. Because the home page was automatically given the filename index.htm when FrontPage created it, the page is saved immediately without requesting a filename. Notice that the asterisk following the index.htm text on the page tab disappears.

Brett's work on the home page is finished, so you will show him how to close the page, the garden Web site, and FrontPage.

Closing a Web Page, a Web Site, and FrontPage

You can close a single Web page, a Web site, or FrontPage by choosing the appropriate Close command. When you close FrontPage, it automatically closes any open page. If you did not save your changes to a Web page, FrontPage will prompt you to do so before closing the page. Next, you will show Brett how to close the home page, the garden Web site, and FrontPage.

To close a Web page, a Web site, and FrontPage:

1. Click the **Close** button for the index.htm page to close it. You have not made any changes since the last time you saved the page, so the home page closes. Because there are no other pages open in Page view, the Web site is displayed in Folders view.

   Trouble? If you changed the Web page since you last saved it, a FrontPage message box opens and asks whether you want to save the file. Click the Yes button to save your changes and to close the home page.

2. Click **File** on the menu bar, and then click **Close Site**. The garden Web site closes, but FrontPage remains open.

   Trouble? If you do not see the Close Site command on the File menu, click the double arrow that appears at the bottom of the File menu. The rest of the menu will open and display the Close Site command.

3. Click the **Close** button on the Microsoft FrontPage 2003 title bar to close FrontPage.

Brett is pleased with his progress in creating the home page. In the next session, you will teach him how to format the home page to make it more visually interesting.

Session 1.1 Quick Check

Review

1. What is the difference between a static Web page and a dynamic Web page?
2. List the five major tasks involved in developing a Web site.
3. What is a hyperlink?
4. What filename does FrontPage give the home page in a disk-based Web site?
5. Why should you determine and set a default page size before working on the pages in a Web site?
6. What are three ways to enter text into a Web page?
7. What is a smart tag?
8. To close a FrontPage Web site, click File on the menu bar, and then click ______________.

Session 1.2

Opening a Web Site

Unlike other programs with which you might be familiar, FrontPage has two "open" options: You can open a single Web page or an entire Web site. In most cases, you will open a Web site so that you have access to all of the Web pages and files that make up the entire site. When you open a Web site, you select the folder that contains the Web site. Because of these two options, the Open button on the Standard toolbar has two options and icons. The first option, Open , lets you open a specific file. The second option, Open Site , lets you open a Web site. The button changes appearance based on its previous use. If you don't see the option you need, clicking the list arrow on the button lets you select either open option.

Opening a Web Site

Reference Window

- Click the list arrow for the Open button on the Standard toolbar.
- Click Open Site in the list.
- Click the folder that contains your Web site.
- Click the Open button.

If you have just started FrontPage, you can use the Getting Started task pane to open an existing Web site. Because you closed FrontPage at the end of the previous session, you will need to open the garden Web site to continue your work. You will open the garden Web site using the Getting Started task pane.

To start FrontPage, open the garden Web site, and open the home page:

1. Start FrontPage. A blank Web page opens in the FrontPage program window, and the Getting Started task pane opens on the right side of the screen.

   Trouble? If the Getting Started task pane does not open automatically, click View on the menu bar, and then click Task Pane.

2. In the Web Sites section of the Open section of the Getting Started task pane, click the **More** link or the **Open an existing site** link. The Open Site dialog box opens.

   Trouble? If the Open File dialog box opens, you clicked the More link or the Open link in the Pages section. Click the Cancel button and then repeat Step 2.

3. If necessary, use the **Look in** list arrow to browse to the location where you are storing your Web sites, and then click the **garden** folder. (The location used in the figures in this book is C:\My Webs\[YourName].) When you use FrontPage to create a Web site, FrontPage adds a blue dot to the folder to indicate that it stores a Web site.
4. Click the **Open** button. The Open Site dialog box closes, the Getting Started task pane closes, and the garden Web site opens in Folders view. See Figure 1-18.

Figure 1-18 **Web site in Folders view**

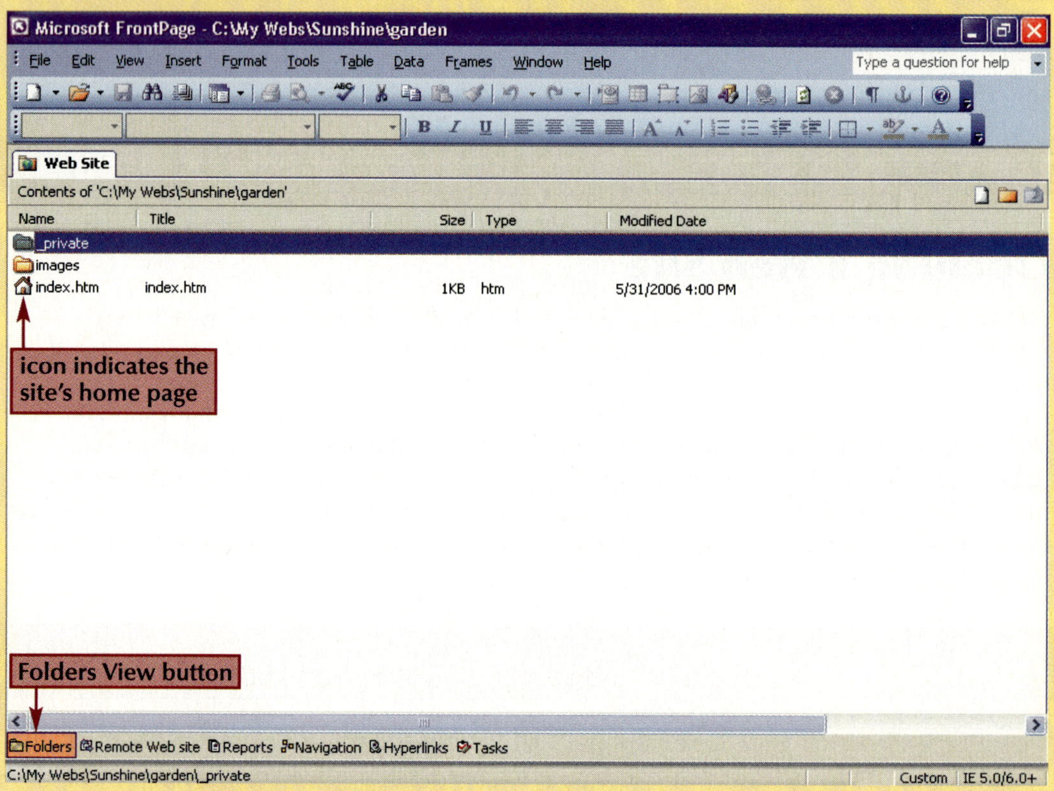

In Figure 1-18, the icon indicates that this page is the Web site's home page. If you open the garden Web site in a browser and do not request a specific file, index.htm will open automatically. The other files in the Web site will use different page icons to indicate that they are HTML and other types of documents.

Trouble? If the Folder List opens, click its Close button to close it.

Trouble? If a different view of the Web site opens, click the Folders View button Folders at the bottom of the Contents pane to change to Folders view.

5. Double-click **index.htm** to open the home page in Design view.

Now that the home page is open in Design view, you can start formatting the text in the page.

Formatting a Web Page

Formatting is the process of changing the appearance of text in a Web page; it does not alter the Web page's content, but it does make changes to the HTML document that creates the page. You usually work in Design view to apply formatting. You can access the FrontPage formatting options in three ways:

- Use the Format menu commands, which provide access to all formatting commands, ranging from revising paragraph organization to creating numbered lists.
- Right-click the text or an object in a Web page to open the shortcut menu, which provides quick access to many formatting commands, such as those for fonts, numbered lists, or special effects. You can use the shortcut menu commands to apply formatting to specific characters, words, text, or pictures.
- Click the buttons on the Formatting toolbar. Figure 1-19 describes the Formatting toolbar buttons and their uses in more detail.

Formatting toolbar buttons — **Figure 1-19**

Button Name	Button	Function
Style list box	Normal	Lets you apply different styles, such as headings, to paragraphs in your document; contains styles compatible with HTML
Font list box	Times New Roman	Lets you apply a font to a selection; contains fonts that are available on your system
Font Size list box	3 (12 pt)	Lets you apply different font sizes to a selection; contains sizes compatible with HTML, where 1 is the smallest, 7 is the largest, and 3 is the default
Bold	B	Changes selected text to bold
Italic	I	Changes selected text to italic
Underline	U	Underlines the selected text
Align Left		Aligns the selected paragraph or object to the left
Center		Centers the selected paragraph or object
Align Right		Aligns the selected paragraph or object to the right
Justify		Justifies the selected paragraph
Increase Font Size	A	Increases the font size of the selected text to the next higher HTML level
Decrease Font Size	A	Decreases the font size of the selected text to the next lower HTML level
Numbering		Changes a list of selected items to a numbered list
Bullets		Changes a list of selected items to a bulleted list
Decrease Indent		Moves the indentation of a selected paragraph or object left by one tab stop (0.5 inch)
Increase Indent		Moves the indentation of a selected paragraph or object right by one tab stop (0.5 inch)
Borders		Adds a border to the selected text; use the list arrow to select a border option other than the one displayed on the button
Highlight	ab	Highlights the selected text; click the list arrow to choose a highlight color other than the one displayed on the button or to choose None to remove highlighting from the selected text
Font Color	A	Changes the color of the selected text; click the list arrow to choose a text color other than the one displayed on the button

The first thing that Brett wants to do is to make the words "February Checklist" more prominent. To make this change, you will show him how to format this text as a heading.

Creating a Heading

Headings in a Web page affect paragraphs. In a Web page, a paragraph might be a single line containing one word, a single line containing multiple words, or several lines. The heading options available for a Web page are limited to those defined by HTML tags. HTML provides six levels of headings, identified as h1, h2, h3, h4, h5, and h6. The h1 tag creates the largest font; the h6 tag creates the smallest font. Figure 1-20 shows the default formatting options for the six levels of headings that you can create in a Web page.

Figure 1-20 **HTML headings**

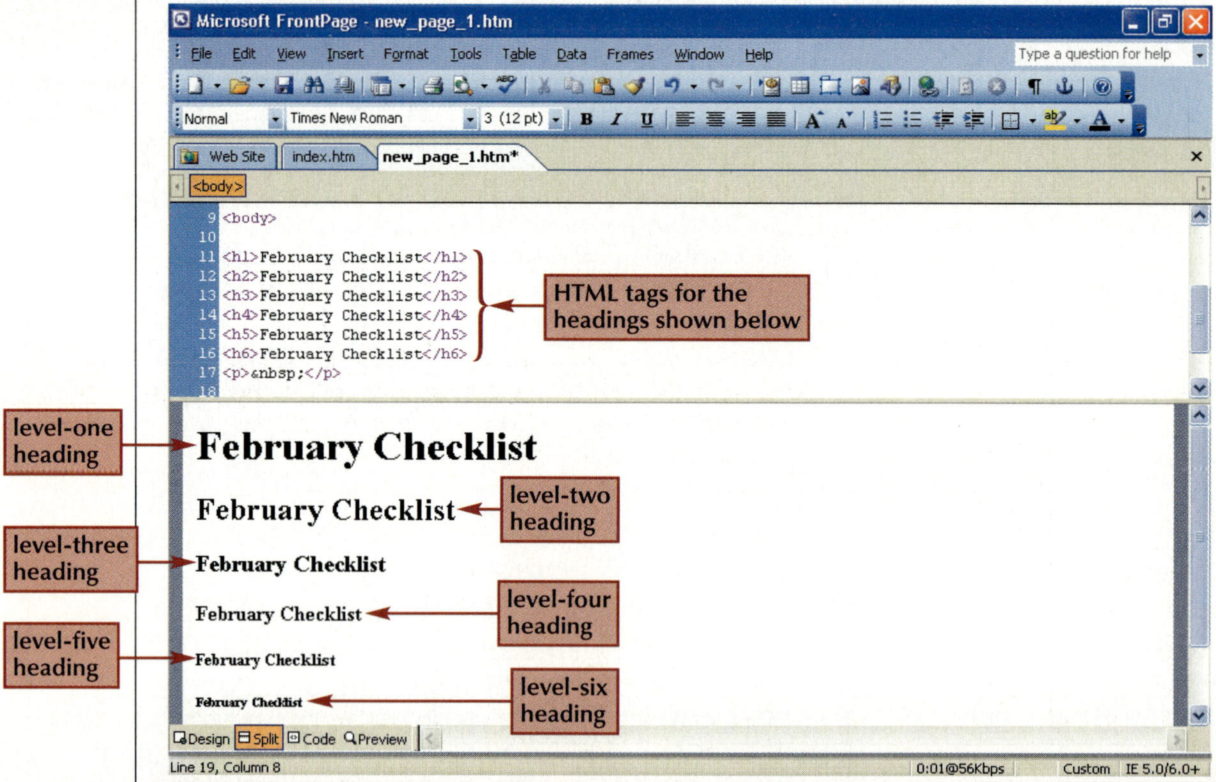

Reference Window **Creating a Heading in a Web Page**

- Click anywhere in the paragraph that you want to format as a heading.
- Click the Style list arrow on the Formatting toolbar to display a list of available paragraph format styles, and then click the desired heading style.

Because the words "February Checklist" already exist in the Web page, you only need to select the paragraph that contains them and change their style from the default style, Normal, to a heading. Selecting a paragraph is different from selecting a word or all of the text in a paragraph. To select a paragraph, you only need to click in it to position the insertion point in the paragraph; you do not need to use the pointer to select all of the text in the paragraph. To make the heading prominent, you will format it using the Heading 1 style.

To change text to a heading:

1. Click anywhere in the line that contains the text "February Checklist." Notice that the QuickTag Selector toolbar shows that the HTML <p> tag, which creates a paragraph in a Web page, formats this text.
2. Point to the **<p>** tag on the QuickTag Selector toolbar, as shown in Figure 1-21.

Figure 1-21 **Using the QuickTag Selector toolbar**

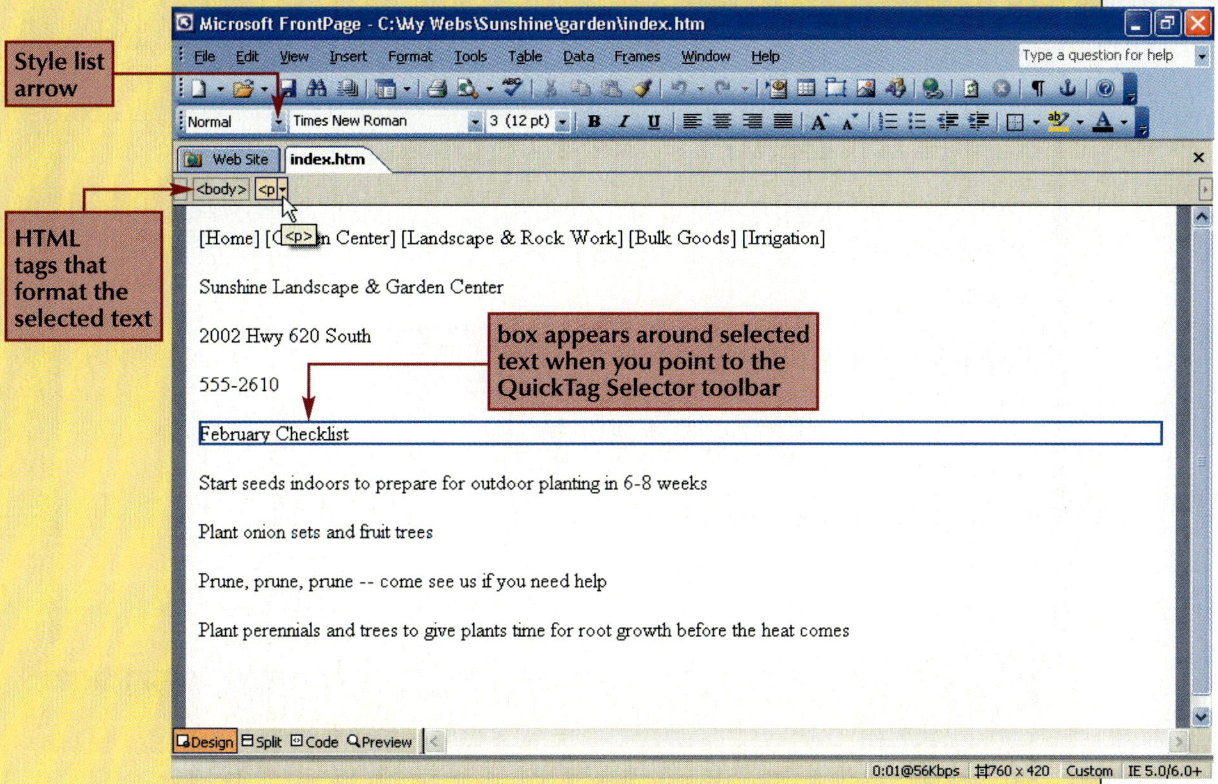

Notice that the paragraph you selected appears with a box around it. If you click the list arrow on the <p> tag, you can select from the options available for formatting paragraphs and the change you make will appear in the selected paragraph. You can use this method to make changes in a WYSIWYG (what you see is what you get) environment while at the same time seeing the HTML tags that create and format your text. For now, you will teach Brett how to use the Formatting toolbar to make his changes.

3. Click the **Style** list arrow on the Formatting toolbar to display the list of available paragraph styles. These styles correspond to the HTML tags that you can use to define the various paragraphs in a Web page.
4. Click **Heading 1** to apply this style to the heading. Because headings format entire paragraphs, all of the text in the current paragraph changes to the Heading 1 style, which is 24 points and bold.

   Brett wants to format the link bar using a heading. You tell him he can change this text to the Heading 2 style to emphasize it.
5. Click anywhere in the link bar at the top of the page (beginning with "[Home]") to select it.
6. Click the **Style** list arrow on the Formatting toolbar, and then click **Heading 2**. The paragraph changes to the Heading 2 style, which is 18 points and bold.

   Brett thinks that the text in the link bar is too large and wants to reduce its size.

7. Click the **Style** list arrow on the Formatting toolbar, and then click **Heading 3**. The paragraph changes to the Heading 3 style, which is 14 points and bold. The home page now contains two headings. See Figure 1-22.

Figure 1-22 **Home page with headings**

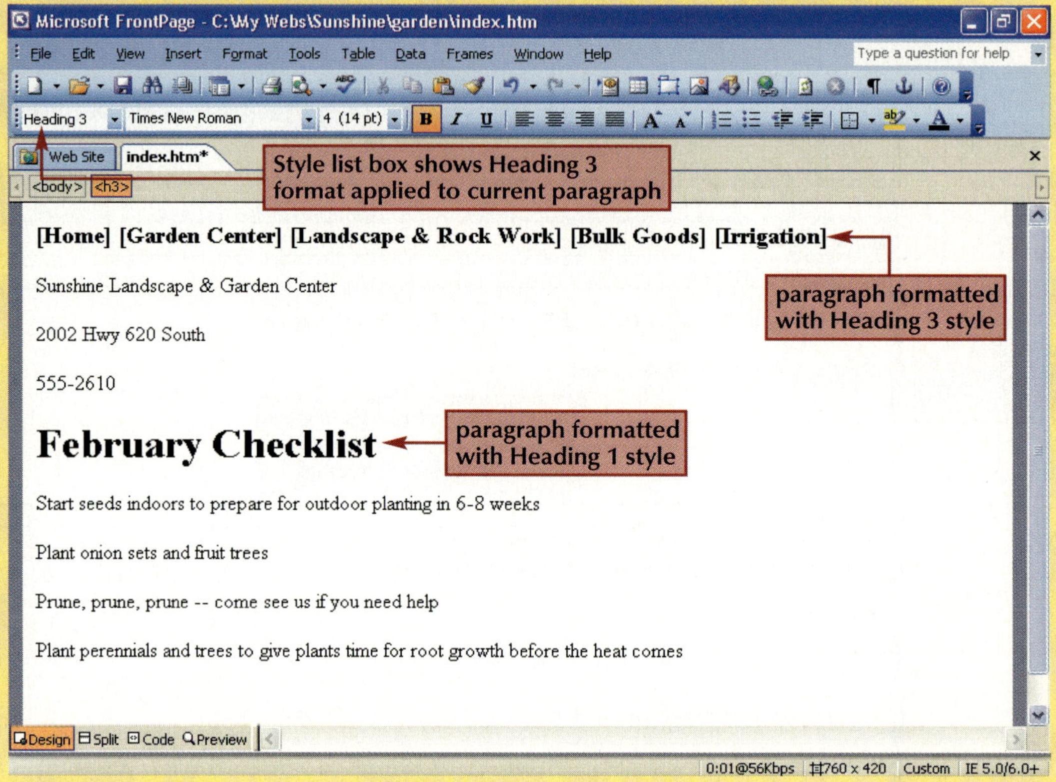

Aligning Text

Like a word-processing program, you can use FrontPage to justify, left-align, center, or right-align paragraphs in a Web page. When you type text in a Web page, the default alignment is set to left. You can use the alignment buttons on the Formatting toolbar to change text alignment.

Reference Window

Aligning a Paragraph in a Web Page

- Click in the paragraph you want to align.
- Click one of the alignment buttons on the Formatting toolbar to apply the desired alignment.

or

- Right-click the paragraph to open the shortcut menu, click Paragraph, click the Alignment list arrow, click the desired alignment, and then click the OK button.

Brett wants to center the paragraph that contains the link bar and the heading that contains the words “February Checklist.”

To center a paragraph in a Web page:

1. With the insertion point positioned in the paragraph that contains the link bar at the top of the page, click the **Center** button on the Formatting toolbar to center the paragraph.
2. Click anywhere in the paragraph that contains the words "February Checklist."
3. Click to center the paragraph. See Figure 1-23.

Home page with aligned paragraphs **Figure 1-23**

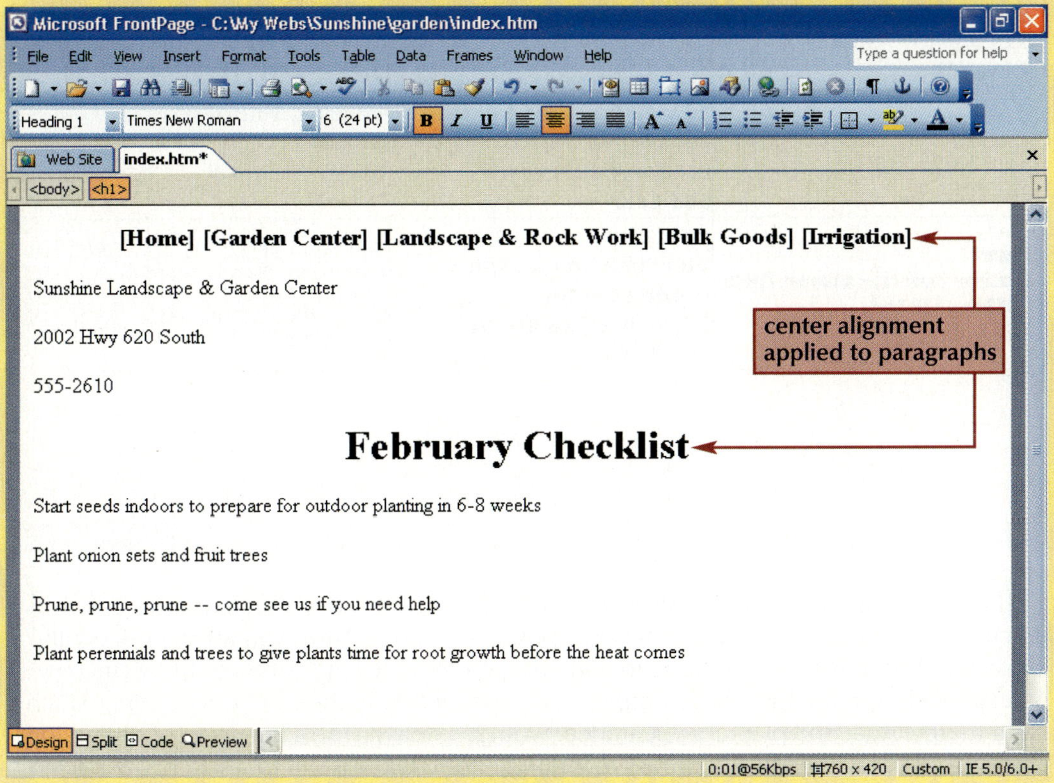

Using Fonts

A **font** is a design for a set of letters, numbers, and symbols distinguished by their typeface, point size, and style. When you select fonts to use in your Web pages, you need to keep several things in mind. First, a font is a group of characters that is installed on your computer. When you install a program, such as FrontPage, on your computer, the program might install fonts with it. Or, you can install fonts on your computer by downloading them from Web sites or from standalone programs that install fonts. Thus, the fonts you have on your computer are ones that you have installed, which might not match the fonts another user has on his or her computer. Because the user's browser can display only fonts that are installed on the user's computer, you have to be careful about which fonts you use in your Web pages. If you format text using a font that a site visitor doesn't have on his or her computer, the user's browser will substitute another font in its place. Sometimes, the browser might select a font that's close to the one you used in your Web page; other times, the font might be quite different in appearance or, even worse, it might be a collection of symbols (like the Wingdings font). The safest fonts to use in a Web page are Times New Roman and Arial, because most computers have these fonts. Other fonts that are commonly installed on computers are Verdana, Georgia, Comic Sans, Trebuchet MS, Impact, Arial Black, and Courier New. Figure 1-24 shows some sample text using each of these fonts.

Figure 1-24 Commonly installed fonts

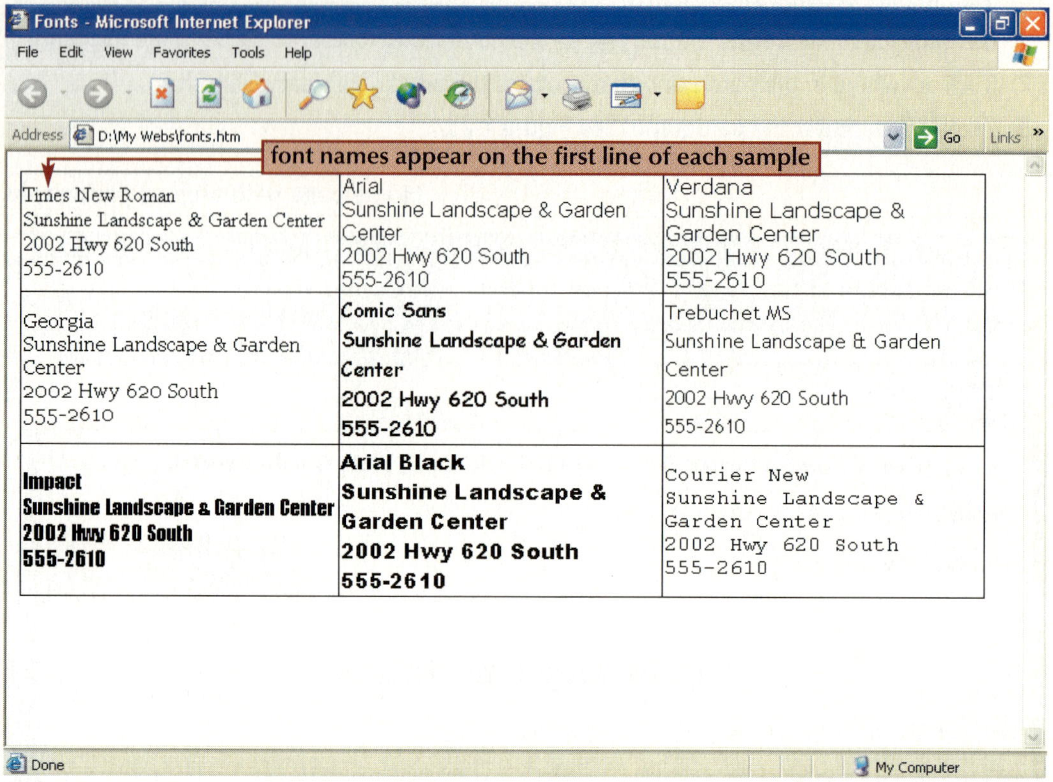

The second thing to keep in mind when selecting a font is that different fonts convey different messages. In most business correspondence, Times New Roman is a frequently chosen font because it is easy to read and has a professional appearance. Receiving an official letter from the CEO of a company that was written in the Comic Sans font, which has a more casual and playful appearance, wouldn't convey the same level of professionalism as a letter written in the Times New Roman font. Likewise, if that letter was written in the Arial Black font, it might be hard to read. In addition to using fonts that your site visitors are likely to have on their computers, you should choose fonts based on the mood you want to create in your pages. If your site is formal, choose Times New Roman. If your site is developed for parents and children, use a more playful font like Comic Sans. If you want an easy-to-read, informal font, use Arial.

For almost any font you use, you can create characters in different sizes and styles. The sizes of fonts are limited to those supported by HTML. Fonts with size 1 are the smallest (8 points), and fonts with size 7 are the largest (36 points). You can also create different styles of text in your Web pages. The default font is called regular; other styles are italic, bold, and bold italic. Some fonts, like Arial Black, already have a bold appearance.

Brett wants to include a copyright notice at the bottom of the home page so it is clear that the Web page belongs to the Sunshine Landscape & Garden Center. You will apply a different font and italics to the text to distinguish it from other text in the page.

To enter and format text:

1. Press **Ctrl + End** to move to the bottom of the home page.
2. Type **Copyright 2006 Sunshine Landscape & Garden Center**.

3. Press **Shift + Enter** to advance to a new line without starting a new paragraph and without inserting a blank line between paragraphs. When you press the Enter key, you create a new paragraph, which has white space above and below it. Pressing Shift + Enter creates a new line in the current paragraph (using the HTML <br> tag), which does not create any additional white space.

   Notice that a dotted line appears near the text you typed. This line tells you that visitors viewing the page with a browser set to 800 × 600 pixels will need to scroll down the page to see the text. In other words, the dotted line represents the number of lines and pixels that visitors will see in one window, based on the page size setting you selected. If your Web page includes content outside the dotted line, visitors can use the scroll bars for their browser to view it.

4. Type **All rights reserved.**

   Now that you've entered the copyright information, you will format it in a different font.

5. Use the pointer to select the two lines that you just typed.

6. Click the **Font** list arrow on the Formatting toolbar. The fonts that are installed on your computer appear in a scrollable list. Notice that the font name appears in the font's face so it is easy to preview the font's appearance. Because you want to ensure that all browsers will render the font correctly, you ask Brett to format the text using the Arial font.

7. Click **Arial** in the list. The Font list box closes and the text changes to the Arial font.

8. With the two lines of text still selected, click the **Italic** button on the Formatting toolbar, and then click anywhere in the selected text to deselect it. The completed copyright information now appears as Arial, italic font, as shown in Figure 1-25.

Figure 1-25 New font and italics applied to copyright text

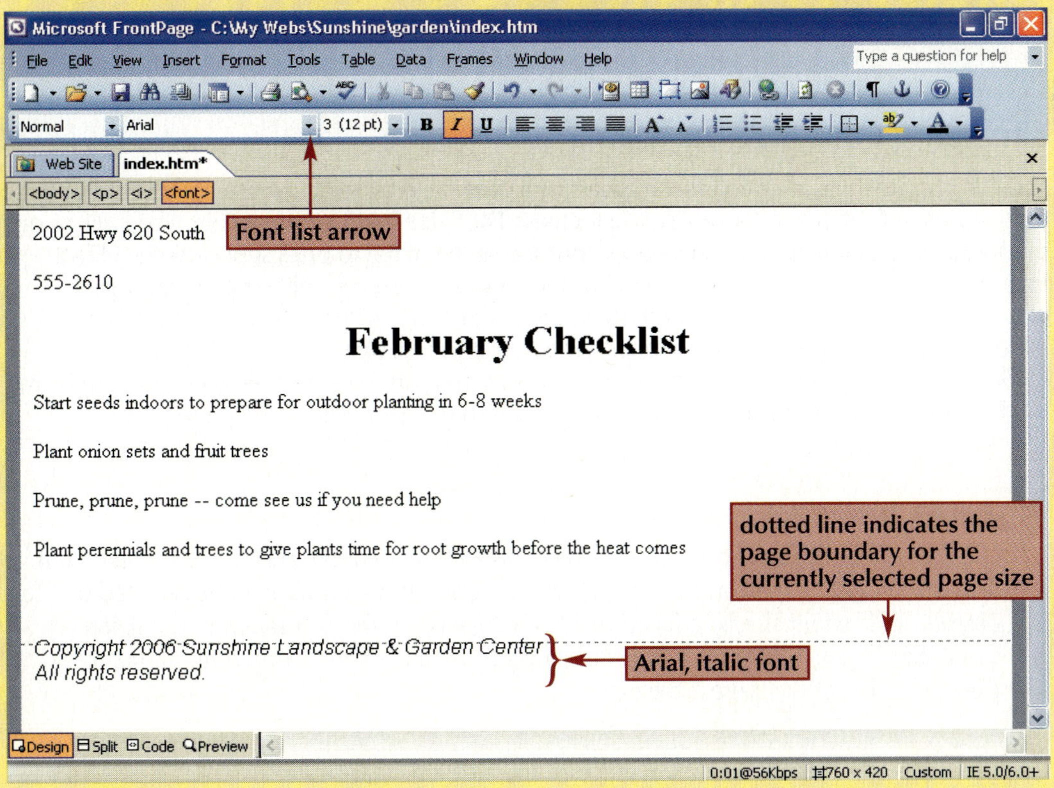

Inserting Special Characters

You can insert special characters, such as the copyright symbol (©), in the text of a Web page just as you can in other types of documents. In FrontPage, you insert special characters using the Symbol dialog box. Brett wants to add a copyright symbol after the word "Copyright."

To insert a special character:

1. Click to the left of the number **2** in the year 2006. You will place the copyright symbol here.
2. Click **Insert** on the menu bar, and then click **Symbol** to open the Symbol dialog box. The copyright symbol, ©, might appear in the list of recently used symbols or you might need to scroll the complete list of symbols to locate it.
3. Find the © symbol and click it. If you do not see the © symbol in the Recently used symbols list, scroll down to the seventh row of symbols, and then click the © symbol (ninth character from the left).
4. With the © symbol selected, click the **Insert** button, and then click the **Close** button. The Symbol dialog box closes and the copyright symbol appears to the left of 2006.
5. Press the **spacebar** to insert a space between the © symbol and 2006.

   When you insert a symbol into a Web page, it's a good idea to change the symbol's font to the same font used in the text in which it appears because the symbol might be inserted from a different font or character set. The text in which the copyright symbol appears is formatted with the Arial font, so you'll change the copyright symbol's font to Arial.
6. Select the first line (which begins with the word "Copyright"), click the **Font** list arrow on the Formatting toolbar, and then click **Arial**. The copyright symbol is formatted using the Arial font.

Changing Font Size

You can change the size of text that appears in a Web page by selecting the desired text and then using the Font Size list arrow or the Increase Font Size and Decrease Font Size buttons on the Formatting toolbar. Just like headings, font sizes are limited to ones supported by HTML. Font size 1 is the smallest, and font size 7 is the largest. However, unlike headings, font changes affect only selected text, and not entire paragraphs. When designing a Web page, you often will need to experiment with font sizes to find the best one for your purposes.

Brett wants to de-emphasize the copyright information, so you need to show him how to change the size of this text so that it is smaller than other text in the page.

To change font size:

1. Use the pointer to select both lines of the copyright information, click the **Decrease Font Size** button on the Formatting toolbar, and then click anywhere in the selected text to deselect it. The font size is reduced to 10 points, which is the equivalent of HTML font size 2. See Figure 1-26. Notice that the Font Size list box on the Formatting toolbar now displays "2 (10 pt)" to reflect the new size.

Reduced font size for the copyright information

Figure 1-26

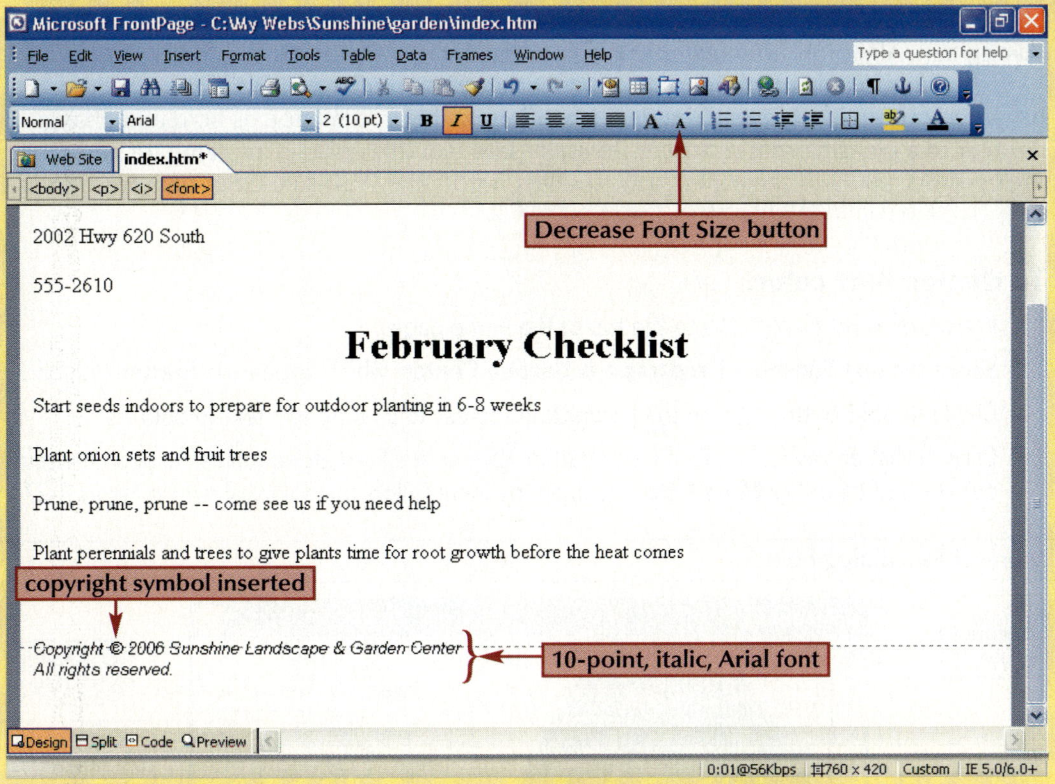

2. Click the **Save** button on the Standard toolbar to save the home page.

Changing Font Color

Although FrontPage lets you select any standard color or create your own custom color, some colors are considered to be "Web safe." If you create a custom color in a Web page using a monitor with high resolution and 16.7 million colors (32-bit color), you might be surprised when viewing the page on a lower-resolution monitor that is set for 256 colors—the colors might look dithered (speckled), washed out (faded), or completely different. Computers with different operating systems (Macintosh, Windows 95/98/Me/2000/NT/XP, and so on) use different color palettes. A color that you create on a Macintosh computer might look different—or even terrible—when viewed on a computer running Windows Me. Although the color palettes of different operating systems are different, they do have 216 colors in common. These colors are called **Web-safe colors** because a browser, regardless of the operating system on which it is running, will display these colors consistently. The Student Online Companion page for Tutorial 1 includes links to sites that identify these colors. FrontPage identifies the 216 Web-safe colors in the More Colors dialog box. If you want to make sure that the color you select will appear consistently for all of your Web site's visitors, select a color from this dialog box.

In HTML, there are 16 colors that are specified using their names. These colors are aqua, black, blue, fuschia, gray, green, lime, maroon, navy, olive, purple, red, silver, teal, white, and yellow. If you want to use shades of these colors or other colors, you must specify the amount of red, green, and blue (abbreviated **RGB**) in the mix that creates the desired color. In HTML, colors are written as a pound sign (#) followed by two characters each to represent the amount of red, green, and blue in the color. For example, the RGB value #008000 specifies the color green. The digits in the RGB value are expressed in

hexadecimal, which is a numbering system that uses 16 characters (0 through f) to represent values in a base-16 numbering system. For example, the RGB value of #008000 combines 00 amounts of red, 80 amounts of green, and 00 amounts of blue to produce the color green. All colors are created through combinations of red, green, and blue.

Brett wants to call attention to the center's name so it will stand out better on the home page. To accomplish this goal, he decides to format this information as bold and change its color to a pleasing shade of blue. To make sure that this color is the same for all of the site's visitors, you will show him how to select it from the Web-safe color palette.

To change font color:

1. Press **Ctrl + Home** to scroll to the top of the home page.
2. Select the text **Sunshine Landscape & Garden Center**, which appears below the link bar.
3. Click the **Bold** button on the Formatting toolbar to change this text to bold.
4. Click the **list arrow** for the Font Color button on the Formatting toolbar to open the color palette, and then click **More Colors** to open the More Colors dialog box shown in Figure 1-27.

Figure 1-27 More Colors dialog box

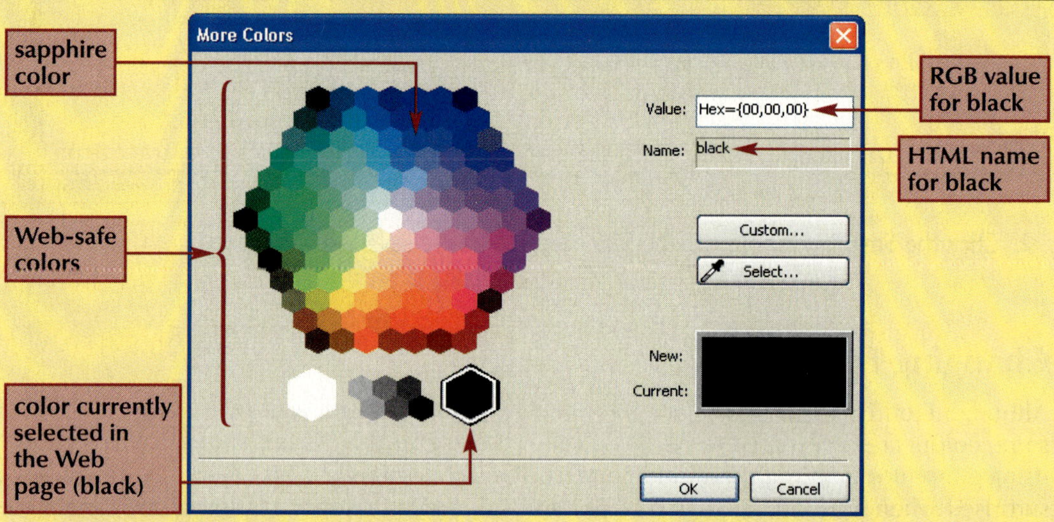

The color palette shown in the More Colors dialog box includes only the Web-safe colors. Any color you select from this palette will appear consistently in any browser that displays it. As you select colors in the palette, the value for the selected color appears in the Value text box. For colors that you can specify by name, such as black or navy, the HTML color name will also appear in the Name text box. For example, the color black is selected. In the More Colors dialog box, its value is Hex={00,00,00} and its HTML name is "black."

If you need to create a different color, clicking the Custom button in the More Colors dialog box opens the Color dialog box, where you can specify colors using RGB values or by clicking the desired color in a color spectrum. Because it is considered good Web design to use the Web-safe colors, you will choose one from the color palette in the More Colors dialog box.

5. Click the **sapphire** color (third row, fourth color tile from the right) to select it. The value in the Value text box should be Hex={00,66,FF}.
6. Click the **OK** button to close the More Colors dialog box and apply the sapphire color to the selected text.
7. Click anywhere in the Web page to deselect the text.

Using the Format Painter

Brett wants to change the center's address and phone number to match formatting he applied to the name. You tell him that he could select the address and phone number, change their text style to bold, and then change their color to sapphire. An easier way to achieve this goal, however, is to use the Format Painter. The **Format Painter** lets you copy the format from existing formatted text and paste it to new text.

To use the Format Painter:

1. Click anywhere in the text **Sunshine Landscape & Garden Center** to select it.

   If you click the Format Painter button once, you can copy the format of the selected text and apply it once to any other text. If you double-click the Format Painter button, you can continue to apply the format to additional locations until you click the button again to turn it off. Brett needs to copy the format and apply it twice, so he will double-click the Format Painter button.
2. Double-click the **Format Painter** button on the Standard toolbar to set the button to apply the format more than once.
3. Use the pointer, which changes to a shape, to select the address. The text is selected and changes to bold, sapphire text.
4. Repeat Step 3 to change the phone number on the next line to bold, sapphire text.
5. Click to turn off the Format Painter, and then click the selected text to deselect it.
6. Save the home page.

Before finishing your work for the day, you want to show Brett how to view the Web page in a browser and how to print it.

Previewing a Web Page

Working in Design view lets you see a Web page as you create it, but this view also includes dotted lines and other formatting to indicate the page size and other features. If you want to see how the page will appear in a Web browser, you can examine it in one of two ways. The first way is to click the Show Preview View button at the bottom of the Contents pane to change to Preview view. Using the Show Preview View button lets you look at the Web page without actually opening it in a browser. In most cases, the appearance of your Web page in Preview view will be the same as or very similar to the way it looks in Design view. The second way is to open the page in a browser. When you click the list arrow for the Preview button on the Standard toolbar, you can choose a Web browser from a list of installed browsers on your computer to open the page. Once you select a browser from the list, you can click the Preview button on the Standard toolbar to preview pages using the Web browser you selected because it becomes your default Web browser.

You tell Brett that browsers can display fonts and other Web page elements differently, so it's a good idea to check your Web pages in one or more Web browsers periodically as you work on them to verify that your pages are rendered correctly in different situations. As you add other features (such as hyperlinks) to your Web pages, you should confirm that they work correctly by testing them in the browser.

Reference Window

Previewing a Web Page

- Click the Show Preview View button at the bottom of the Contents pane.
- Click the Show Design View button at the bottom of the Contents pane to return to Design view.

or

- Click the list arrow for the Preview button on the Standard toolbar, and then select the desired browser from the list that opens.
- Close the browser to return to FrontPage.

So that Brett can use both methods to preview the home page, you'll have him open it in Preview view, and then use the Preview button to open it in a Web browser.

To preview the Web page:

1. Click the **Show Preview View** button at the bottom of the Contents pane. The home page opens in Preview view.
2. Click the **list arrow** for the Preview button on the Standard toolbar. A list of installed Web browsers and page size settings opens, as shown in Figure 1-28. Your list of browsers and page size settings might differ, depending on the Web browsers installed on your computer. Clicking a browser in the list starts that browser and opens the current Web page. If you select a screen size, FrontPage will start the Web browser with the indicated screen size. If more than one browser is installed on your computer and you want to preview the Web page using multiple browsers, clicking the Preview in Multiple Browsers option starts all browsers on your computer and opens the home page in each one. You can also select a screen size using one of the Preview in Multiple Browsers options that includes a screen size (such as 640 × 480).

Figure 1-28 Options for previewing the Web page using a browser

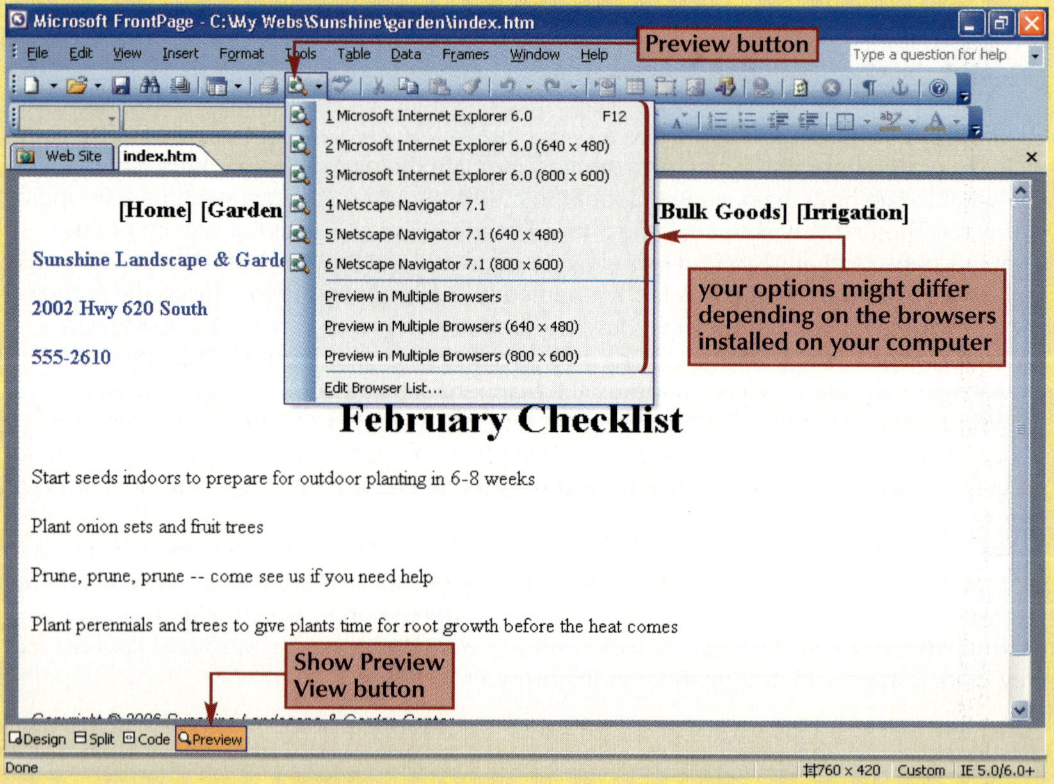

At this time, Brett wants to view the page using Internet Explorer, so he'll select that option.

3. Click the **Microsoft Internet Explorer 6.0** option in the list. FrontPage starts a maximized program window of Internet Explorer and opens the home page, as shown in Figure 1-29.

Home page in a maximized Internet Explorer window **Figure 1-29**

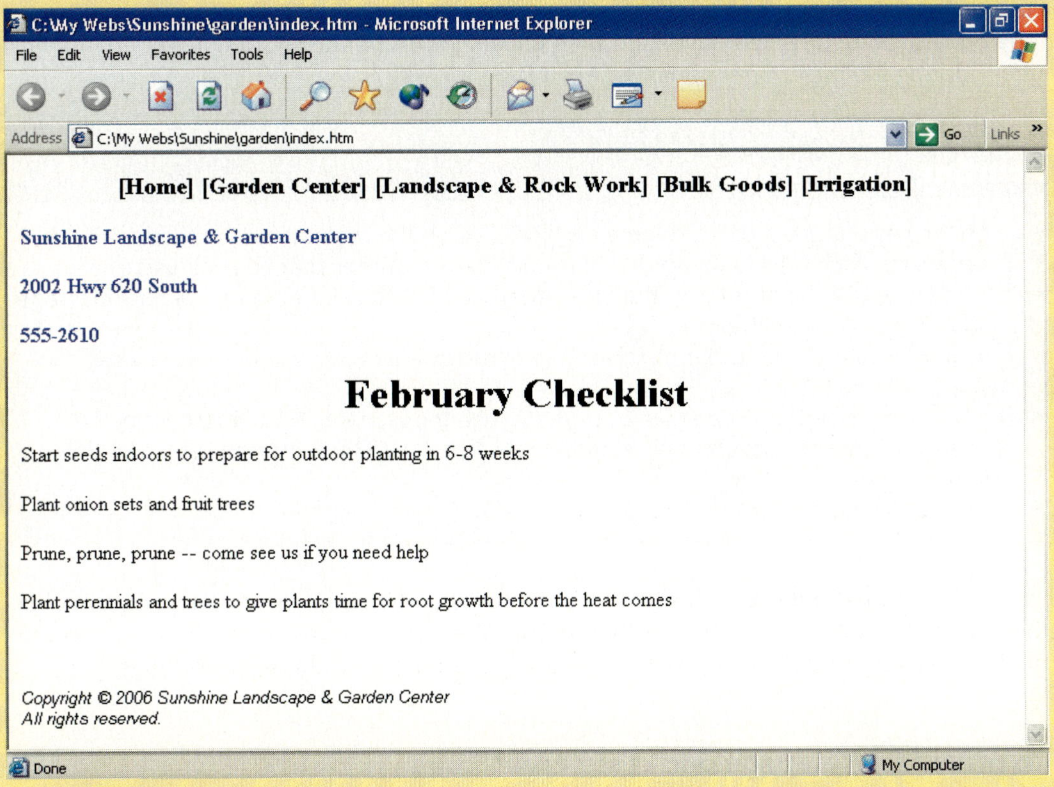

Trouble? If you do not have the Microsoft Internet Explorer 6.0 option, select another browser in the list.

4. Click the **Close** button on the browser title bar to close it. You want Brett to see how the page looks with 640 × 480 resolution, so you ask him to preview the page in Internet Explorer again, but this time at the lower resolution.

5. Click the **list arrow** for the Preview button on the Standard toolbar, and then click **Microsoft Internet Explorer 6.0 (640 × 480)**. Internet Explorer opens again, but this time the window size is set to 640 × 480 resolution. Notice that less of the page is visible in this window. As you work on future Web pages together, you tell Brett that he will need to keep in mind that some users will view the Web pages at this resolution.

6. Click the **Close** button on the browser title bar to close it.

Closing the Web browser as you are working in FrontPage is a personal choice. You might want to leave the browser open and then use the Refresh button or the Reload button on the browser's toolbar to refresh the page. Refreshing the page loads the most recently saved version of the page in the browser window. If you leave the browser open, you can check the page's appearance in the browser window without having to click the Preview button on the Standard toolbar in FrontPage.

Printing a Web Page

Brett wants to print a copy of the home page so he can share it with other staff members and obtain their feedback. You can print a Web page in Design view using the Print/File menu when you need to change the printer to use or the number of copies to print. If you do not need to change or verify your printer's settings, clicking the Print button on the Standard toolbar prints the page. If the Web page appears in Preview view, you can print it by right-clicking the Web page, and then clicking Print on the shortcut menu that opens. After printing the page, Brett can close FrontPage.

Reference Window

Printing a Web Page

- With the page displayed in Design view, click File on the menu bar, and then click Print.
- If necessary, click the Name list arrow and select the printer that you will use.
- If necessary, use the options in the Print range section to print all pages, a specific page range, or a page selection.
- If necessary, use the Number of copies list arrow to select the number of copies of the page(s) to print.
- If necessary, click the Properties button and use the options in the dialog box that opens to change the settings for your printer. Click the OK button to return to the Print dialog box.
- Click the OK button.

After using the Print dialog box to select a printer and change its settings, you can click the Print button on the Standard toolbar to print Web pages in the future. You need to use the Print dialog box only when you need to select a printer or change its settings.

To print the Web page and close FrontPage:

1. Click the **Show Design View** button Design at the bottom of the Contents pane to return to Design view.
2. Click **File** on the menu bar, and then click **Print**. The Print dialog box opens.
3. If necessary, click the **Name** list arrow and select the printer that you will use to print your Web page, make sure that the **All** option button is selected in the Print range section, and then click the **OK** button. FrontPage prints the home page using the printer you selected.
4. Click **File** on the menu bar, and then click **Close Site**. The home page and the garden Web site close.
5. Click the **Close** button on the Microsoft FrontPage 2003 title bar to close FrontPage.

In the next session, you will review with Brett some basic HTML tags and their use. Although you and Brett will use FrontPage to create and edit Web pages, it is important for FrontPage users to have a basic understanding of the HTML that creates those pages. If you want to learn more about HTML, the Student Online Companion page for Tutorial 1 includes several resources about working with HTML.

Session 1.2 Quick Check

Review

1. Describe the three methods that you can use to access the formatting commands in Design view.
2. Which HTML heading style creates a heading with the largest font size?
3. Which HTML font size creates the largest font?
4. A set of letters, numbers, and symbols that are distinguished by their typeface, point size, and style is called a(n) ______________.
5. What is a Web-safe color?
6. How would you use the Format Painter to apply the formatting of selected text to one other location in a Web page?
7. What are the two methods you can use to preview a Web page?

Session 1.3

Understanding Hypertext Markup Language

As you learned in Session 1.1, Web pages are written in Hypertext Markup Language (HTML). HTML documents use a standard group of characters, called a **character set**, that all computers recognize. In addition, each HTML document contains special tags that a Web browser interprets to display data in the desired format on a client computer. The browser interprets the tags in an HTML document to display the Web page. The tags in an HTML document specify the appearance of text in terms of its font (such as Arial or Times New Roman), its style (such as a heading or bold), or its position (such as a fixed or floating position). An HTML document also specifies the playing of media files, the placement of pictures, and the appearance of the page's background, if these elements are used. A Web browser interprets the HTML tags in a Web page to determine how to display and use these elements on the page.

The name of an HTML tag is enclosed in angle brackets (< >). Most tags are **two-sided tags**; that is, they are used in pairs that consist of an opening tag and a closing tag. The **opening tag** tells the browser to turn on a particular feature and apply it to the document content that follows this tag. The browser continues applying the feature until it encounters the **closing tag**, which tells the browser to stop applying the feature. The forward slash character (/) identifies a closing tag in the tag name. For example, the tags <body> and </body> specify the beginning and end of the body of an HTML document, respectively, and the tags <b> and </b> indicate the beginning and end of bold text, respectively.

Some tags are **one-sided tags** and require only an opening tag. With this type of tag, the browser stops applying the formatting indicated by the one-sided tag when it finishes reading the tag. The HTML <br> tag, which specifies a line break in a Web page, is an example of a one-sided tag.

Figure 1-30 lists some common HTML tags. The ellipsis (...) in the tag indicates the content that is entered by the developer, either between two-sided tags or within a one-sided tag.

Figure 1-30 **Selected HTML tag descriptions**

HTML Tag	Description	Use
<!-- ... -->	Creates a comment, which is not displayed in the Web page	Identifies the HTML document's content, creator, and other documentation
<a> ... </a>	Defines a hyperlink or an anchor	Indicates an internal or external hyperlink and the file or location that will open
<b> ... </b>	Changes text to bold	
<bgsound src=...>	Specifies a background sound	Indicates the filename containing the sound
<body> ... </body>	Encloses the body of the HTML document	
 	Creates a line break	
<dd> ... </dd>	Specifies a definition within a glossary list	Provides a heading line for a defined term
<dl> ... </dl>	Specifies a definition or glossary list	
<dt> ... </dt>	Specifies a defined term within a glossary list	Provides the font size and indentation information for a defined term
<em> ... </em>	Emphasizes text, usually with italic	
<h1> ... </h1> <h2> ... </h2> <h3> ... </h3> <h4> ... </h4> <h5> ... </h5> <h6> ... </h6>	Specifies a heading and its level	Indicates the format of a heading (h1 has the largest size; h6 has the smallest size)
<head> ... </head>	Encloses the head section of the HTML document	Contains meta tags and the page's title, which appears in the browser's title bar
<hr>	Inserts a horizontal line across the page	Provides a visual break for sections of a page
<html> ... </html>	Encloses the entire HTML document	Identifies the file as one that contains HTML tags
<i> ... </i>	Changes text to italic	
<img> ... </img>	Specifies the appearance of a picture in a page	Inserts a picture file into the HTML document
<li> ... </li>	Specifies an individual element in a bulleted or numbered list	
<ol> ... </ol>	Specifies an ordered list of elements	Creates numbered elements in a list
<p> ... </p>	Divides text into paragraphs separated by blank lines	
<strong> ... </strong>	Strongly emphasizes text, usually with bold	
<table> ... </table>	Creates a table	Organizes data in a row-and-column table arrangement
<td> ... </td>	Defines the data contained in a table's cells	
<th> ... </th>	Creates a row of headings in a table	
<title> ... </title>	Defines the text that appears in the Web browser's title bar	Creates the Web page's title
<tr> ... </tr>	Indicates a row in a table	
<ul> ... </ul>	Specifies an unordered list of elements	Creates bulleted elements in a list

Just as important as the tags themselves is the order of their placement. Tags often appear within each other; this is called a **nested tag**. The browser first processes the tag on the outside, called the **outside tag**; it then processes the tag on the inside, called the **inside tag**. When nesting tags, you must close the inside tag before closing the outside tag. When you create a nested list—for example, a bulleted list within a numbered list—FrontPage handles the opening and closing of each pair of tags automatically. You need to be concerned with nesting the tags only if you decide to make changes directly to your HTML document, which is not the recommended approach when using FrontPage. However, it is helpful to understand how a browser applies different formats to a single code segment.

Many HTML tags require one or more **attributes**, or **properties**, that specify additional information about the tag. When you changed the color of the center's address in the home page, you used an attribute to identify the color for the selected text. Attributes appear within the brackets that enclose the tag.

Even though HTML uses a standard character set to ensure that documents can be easily transferred and viewed by many different types of computers, not all Web browsers will interpret these tags and display the requested Web page in exactly the same way. For example, text that is formatted as bold might be displayed as bold text by one browser and as blue text by another browser. Even with this limitation, the use of HTML in storing, transferring, and viewing HTML documents among the many different computers that are connected to the Internet is the key element in providing a standard method for displaying information.

Viewing the HTML Document That Creates a Web Page

By viewing the HTML document for a Web page, you can see how a particular feature has been implemented using HTML tags. In this book, you will create and edit Web pages using FrontPage. You will also study the HTML document that FrontPage creates to gain a better understanding of how HTML works. Some Web page developers find it easier to make changes directly to the HTML document, even when they are working in FrontPage. You can examine a Web page's HTML document by using FrontPage or a Web browser.

Viewing an HTML Document Using FrontPage

The work you have done in FrontPage so far has been in Design or Preview view. There are two other Page views that let you see the HTML document you have created. You can use Split view to see the HTML document and your Web page at the same time, or you can use Code view to examine only the HTML document that creates your Web page. A nice feature of Split view is that it lets you work in the HTML document and view your changes in the Web page at the same time. Because you think it's important for Brett to understand the HTML that creates the home page, you ask him to examine the HTML document and then to make changes to it to see the results in the Web page.

To examine a Web page in Code view:

1. Start FrontPage, open the **garden** Web site from the location where you are storing your Web sites, and then open the **index.htm** page in Design view. If necessary, close the Folder List.
2. Click the **Show Code View** button [Code] at the bottom of the Contents pane to display the HTML document that creates the Web page, as shown in Figure 1-31. Notice that the text you entered in the Web page and the HTML tag names are black, HTML properties are red, and the values for HTML properties are blue. For example, the tag that formats the text "555-2610" as sapphire text is <font color="#0066FF">. The HTML tag is *font*, the HTML property is *color*, and the HTML value for sapphire is "*#0066FF.*"

Figure 1-31 **HTML document for the home page**

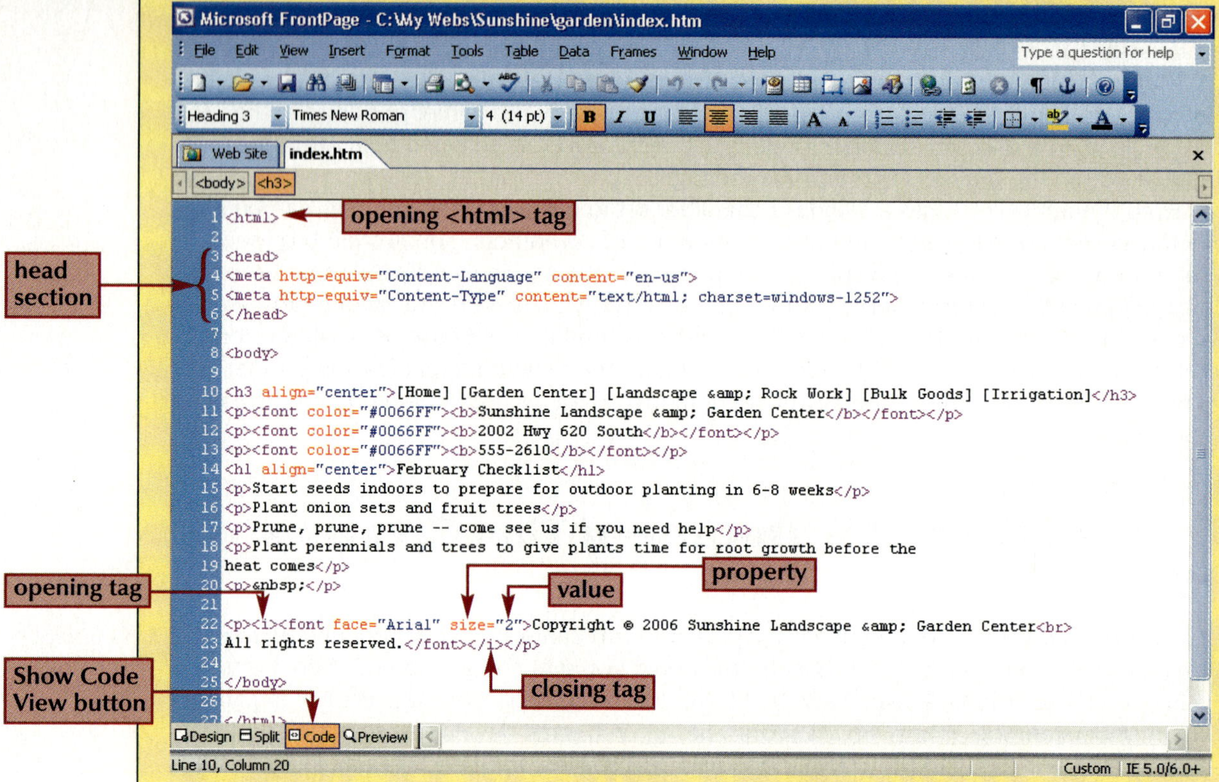

Trouble? You can customize FrontPage to display HTML tags in different ways. The colors in your HTML document might differ. In addition, you might see HTML tags and property names in all uppercase letters. Both of these differences cause no problems.

3. Inspect the HTML document and try to identify which tags provide the formatting instructions that create the home page. As you work through the tutorials in this book, you will learn about the various HTML tags that specify the appearance of the Web pages for the Sunshine Landscape & Garden Center.
4. Click the **Show Design View** button [Design] to return to Design view.

Split view shows the HTML document and the Web page at the same time. When you make changes to the HTML document in Code view, pressing the F5 key updates the Web page in Design view to reflect the changes. Using Split view is an excellent way to see the results of changes to your HTML document, so you ask Brett to make a change using Split view.

To work in Split view:

1. Click the **Show Split View** button [Split]. The size of the Design view window is reduced and the Code view window is added above it, as shown in Figure 1-32. Each window has its own scroll bar so you can examine the complete HTML document and Web page. Code view includes line numbers to make it easy to document and examine the HTML document.

Split view of the home page

Figure 1-32

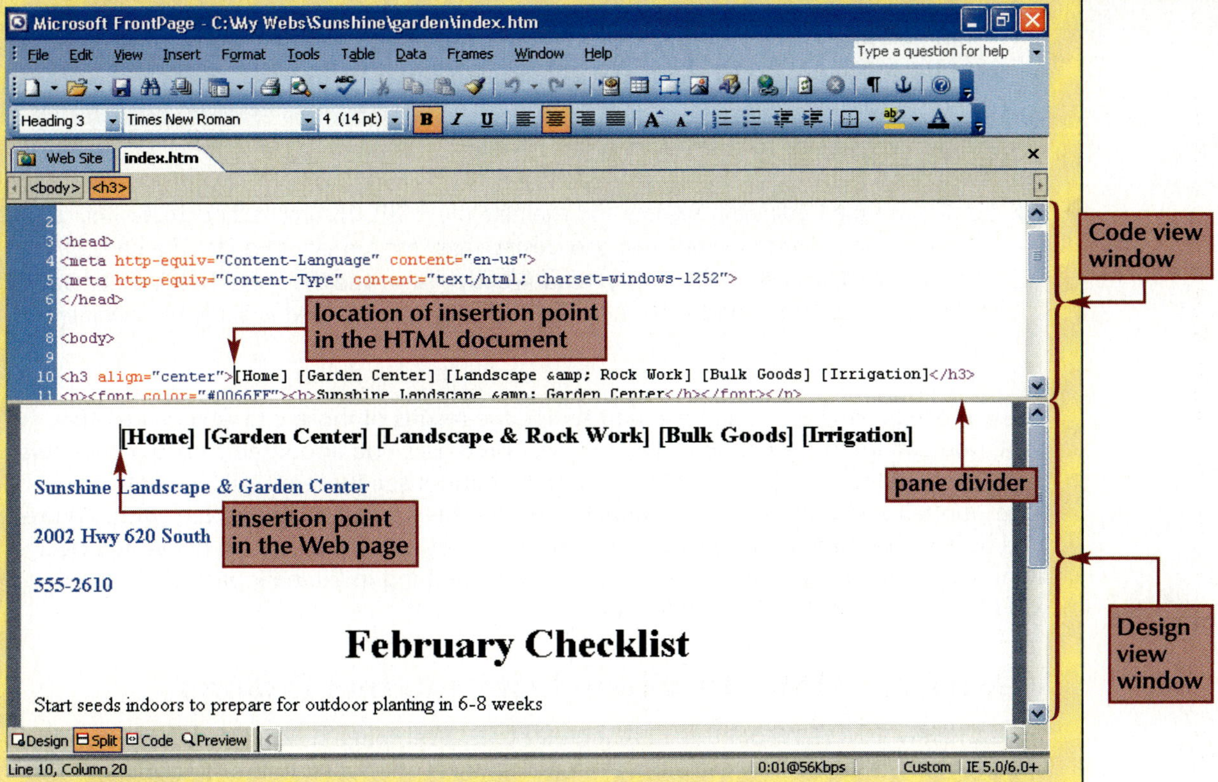

Trouble? The sizes of your Code and Design view windows might differ from what is shown in Figure 1-32. You can increase and decrease the size of the windows by positioning the ‡ pointer on the pane divider and dragging it up or down to resize the windows.

2. In the Code view window, use the pointer to select the text **Sunshine Landscape & Garden Center**, which appears on line 11. Notice that the ampersand character (&) is written as & in the HTML document. As you select the text in the HTML document, the same text is selected in the Design view window.

   Trouble? The line numbers in your HTML document might differ depending on the way FrontPage is configured to create tags in new documents. If your line numbers are different, just make sure that you are working in the correct line of your HTML document.

3. Click the **list arrow** for the Font Color button on the Formatting toolbar, click the **Red** color in the menu that opens, and then click the selected text in the Design view window to deselect it. The text in the Design view window is now red, and the HTML document now shows the font color for this text as "#FF0000" for red.

4. In the Design view window, select the text **Sunshine Landscape & Garden Center**, click the **list arrow** for the Font Color button, and then click the **Sapphire** color in the Document Colors section of the menu that opens (the ScreenTip is Hex={00,66,FF}). Click the text in the Design view window to deselect it, and then notice that the text returns to its previous color and the HTML document shows the color property for the sapphire color again.

5. On line 10 of the HTML document, change the opening tag that creates the level-three heading from <h3 to **<h4**. When you make this change, the paragraph it affects is selected in the Design view window. To update the Design view window, you need to press the F5 key.

6. Press the **F5** key and watch the selected text in the Design view window, which changes to the Heading 4 style. To complete this change, you need to update the closing HTML tag as well.

7. Change the closing </h3> tag at the end of line 10 in the Code view window to **</h4>**, and then save the page.

   FrontPage includes features that make it easy to type HTML tags directly in Code view. For example, when you type an opening HTML tag, such as <h1> to create a level-one heading, FrontPage will automatically insert the required </h1> closing tag for you. However, when you change existing tags, as you did in Step 7, you need to update the opening and closing tags yourself.

8. Scroll down the Code view window and examine the HTML document that creates the rest of the home page. Notice the opening and closing tags that format the page. The body of the Web page appears within the <body> and </body> tags, and the entire HTML document is enclosed in the <html> and </html> tags. These tags are required in all HTML documents.

By making changes in one view and seeing the results of those changes in the other view, you can learn a great deal about HTML. Brett asks you about the   characters that appear in the HTML document because he cannot see these characters in the Web page. You tell him that this set of characters represents a nonbreaking space, which is created by the character set when you press the Enter key in a Web page to create the equivalent of an "empty paragraph." When you type something in the new paragraph, the text you type replaces the   characters.

Viewing an HTML Document Using Internet Explorer

You can view the HTML document that creates any Web page using a Web browser. This option is convenient when you want to inspect the HTML document for a Web page that was created by someone else and that you opened from a Web site. Next, you will view the HTML document for the home page using Internet Explorer.

To view an HTML document using Internet Explorer:

1. Click the **Preview** button on the Standard toolbar. The home page opens in the default browser for your computer.

   Trouble? If you need to change your default browser, close the browser window that opened, click the list arrow for the Preview button on the Standard toolbar, and then select the browser you would like to use.

2. Click **View** on the menu bar, click **Source**, and then maximize the Notepad window, if necessary. Notepad displays the HTML document used to create the home page. When you view the HTML document in Notepad, it's a good idea to turn on the Word Wrap feature so that the lines in the HTML document won't scroll to the right and out of view.

   Trouble? If you are using Netscape Navigator as your browser, click View on the menu bar, and then click Page Source to view the HTML document for the home page.

3. Click **Format** on the Notepad menu bar, and then click **Word Wrap**. The HTML document matches the one you viewed in Code view, except Notepad does not use colors to identify content, tags, properties, and values.

   Trouble? If the Word Wrap command has a check mark in front of it, then the Word Wrap feature is already on. If you accidentally turned off the Word Wrap feature, repeat Step 3 to turn it back on.

   Trouble? If you are using Netscape Navigator as your browser, click View on the menu bar, and then click Wrap Long Lines.

4. Click the **Close** button ☒ to close the Notepad window (or the window that opened and displayed the HTML document for the home page).
5. Click ☒ on the browser's title bar to close it.

Brett asks you about the content of line 4. You tell him that FrontPage automatically inserts tags that identify the file as an HTML document. One important tag that Brett needs to understand is the meta tag, which is important when marketing a Web site.

Using Meta Tags

A Web site can be an effective marketing tool for a company—but only if people are aware that the site exists. Most people find information on the Internet using a **search engine**, which is a Web site that automatically gathers and maintains information about sites on the Internet. Sometimes the process of getting a Web site listed with a search engine is accomplished automatically when a search engine reads the tags in your HTML document and adds your site to its index. An **index** is a database that stores information about specific Web sites. Each search engine uses a different method to index the Web, so your search results using different search engines might vary.

Most search engines gather information about Web sites by either accepting requests from Web site developers to add their sites to the search engine's index or by collecting data based on meta tags entered into the HTML document by the Web page's developer. A **meta tag** is an HTML tag that includes information about a Web page, such as the character set it uses, the name of its developer, how often the page is refreshed, and the keywords and description of the page's contents. (A developer can also use a meta tag to prevent a site from being indexed.) For example, if a user enters the search term "landscaping" in a Web search engine, Brett wants the search engine to find the home page for the Sunshine Landscape & Garden Center. To accomplish this objective, you will add a keywords meta tag with the phrase "landscaping" to the home page. To control how the search engine describes the Web site for the nursery, you'll add a description meta tag to provide the description you want the search engine to display.

In addition to their use with search engines, meta tags provide instructions for Web servers and Web browsers when transferring and interpreting data. FrontPage automatically creates a meta tag in all FrontPage-created documents with properties and values that indicate the page's default character set and content. All meta tags must appear at the beginning of the HTML document in the head section. The **head section** of an HTML document is enclosed by the <head> and </head> tags. Except for the Web page title, which also appears in the head section and is displayed by the browser in its title bar, information stored in the head section does not affect the appearance of the Web page.

Inserting a Meta Tag into a Web Page

Reference Window

- Right-click anywhere in the Web page to open the shortcut menu, click Page Properties, and then click the Custom tab.
- Click the Add button in the User variables section.
- Type the meta tag name in the Name text box, and then press the Tab key.
- Type the desired text for the meta tag in the Value text box.
- Click the OK button.
- Click the Add button, and then repeat the process to add additional meta tags as necessary.
- Click the OK button.

To promote the Web site for the Sunshine Landscape & Garden Center, Brett wants to include indexing information in the home page to increase the chances of the home page being added to the indexes of various Web search engines. You will add two meta tags—description and keywords—to the home page.

To insert meta tags in the home page:

1. Right-click anywhere in the Design view window to open the shortcut menu, click **Page Properties** to open the Page Properties dialog box, and then click the **Custom** tab.
2. In the User variables section, click the **Add** button to open the User Meta Variable dialog box.

   Trouble? If you click the Add button in the System variables section, the System Meta Variable (HTTP-EQUIV) dialog box opens instead of the User Meta Variable dialog box. Click the Cancel button, and then repeat Step 2. (Creating system variables is beyond the scope of this tutorial.)
3. Type **description** in the Name text box, and then press the **Tab** key to move the insertion point to the Value text box. You will use the description meta tag to summarize the Web site's contents.
4. With the insertion point in the Value text box, type **The Texas Hill Country's premiere full-service landscaping center, specializing in rock work, irrigation systems, and landscape design.** As you type, the text automatically scrolls across the text box. See Figure 1-33.

Figure 1-33 Adding meta tags to the home page

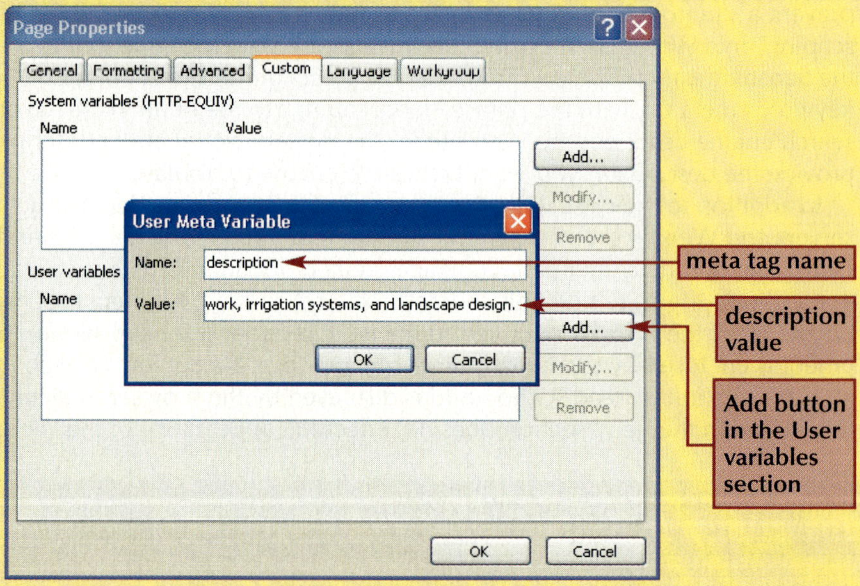

5. Click the **OK** button to return to the Page Properties dialog box. Notice that the text you just typed in the Name and Value text boxes now appears in the Name and Value columns in the User variables section.
6. Click the **Add** button in the User variables section again, type **keywords** in the Name text box, and then press the **Tab** key to advance to the Value text box. Web search engines use the keywords meta tag to catalog your Web site.

7. Type **Sunshine, Texas Hill Country, garden, gardening, flower, plant, herb, landscaping, landscape design, rock work, irrigation** in the Value text box as the desired keywords.

8. Click the **OK** button in the User Meta Variable dialog box to return to the Page Properties dialog box, and then click the **OK** button to close the Page Properties dialog box. Figure 1-34 shows the meta tags you added to the HTML document. Notice that the appearance of the Web page in the Design view window does not change.

Meta tags added to the home page **Figure 1-34**

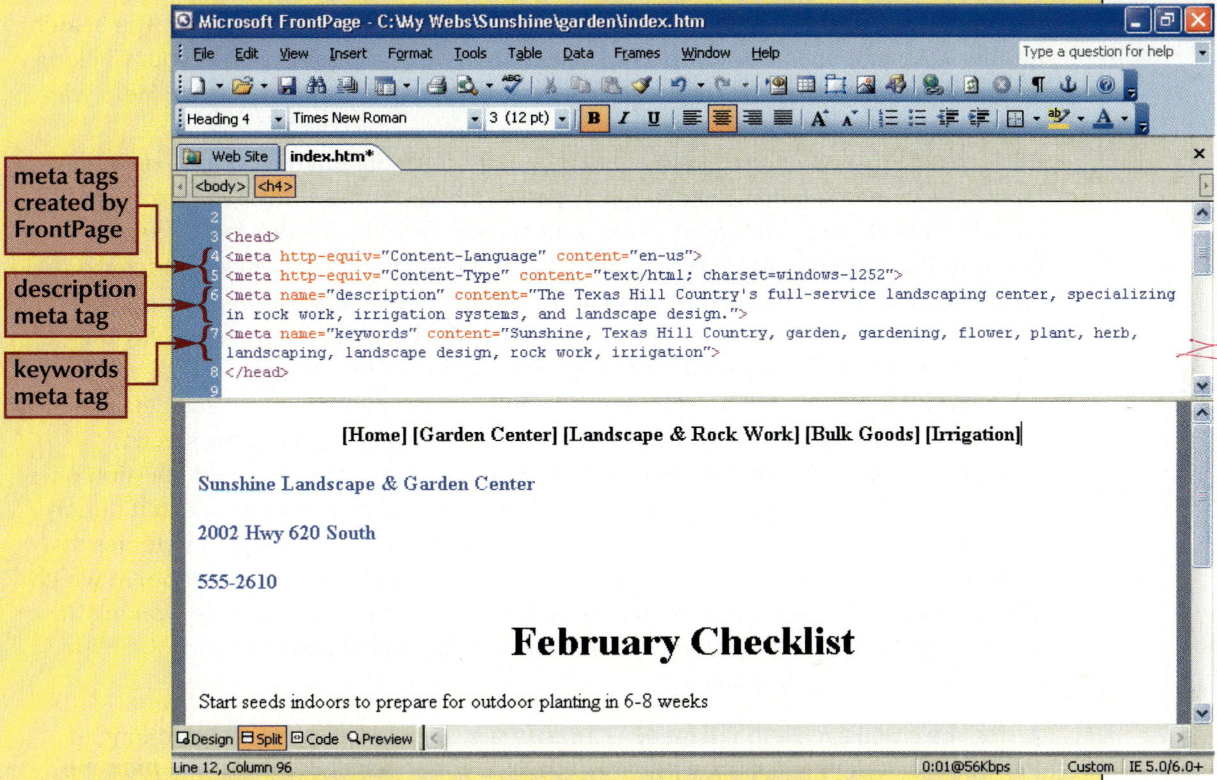

Trouble? If necessary, scroll up the Code view window so you can see the meta tags you added.

Trouble? If the meta tags scroll off the screen instead of wrapping to the next line as shown in Figure 1-34, click Tools on the menu bar, click Page Options, and then, in the Code View Options section of the General tab, click the Word wrap check box to select it. Click the OK button to close the Page Options dialog box.

9. Click the **Save** button on the Standard toolbar to save the home page.

10. Click the **Show Design View** button Design.

As you finish working on the home page, you tell Brett that the process of adding meta tags does not ensure that a search engine will list the nursery's Web site in its results. As you continue working on the Web site, you will need to conduct some additional research to learn how to submit the nursery's site to one or more search engines to make sure that it appears in the search engine's index. The Student Online Companion page for Tutorial 1 includes resources to sites that provide information about using meta tags and getting your site indexed by the many search engines available on the Internet.

As your last task for the day, you decide to show Brett how to get Help in FrontPage, in case he is working on a task and needs additional instructions.

Getting Help in FrontPage

The FrontPage Help system provides instructions and answers common questions for FrontPage users as they do their work. In addition to the Help files that are installed with FrontPage, you can access several online resources that provide additional Help files. The primary benefit of using the online resources is that Microsoft updates these resources frequently. There are several different ways to use the Help system, so you can choose the one that you like best. The different ways of accessing Help are as follows:

- Type a question or keywords in the Type a question for help text box, which appears on the menu bar. After you type your question or keywords, press the Enter key. The Search Results task pane opens and displays a selection of topics that might help you. Clicking a topic in the Search Results task pane opens the Microsoft Office FrontPage Help window and displays the specified Help topic.
- Click the Microsoft Office FrontPage Help button on the Standard toolbar to open the FrontPage Help task pane. You can type your search keywords in the Search for text box and click the Start search button to run your search, or you can click the Table of Contents link to search for information by category. In either case, clicking a topic opens the Microsoft Office FrontPage Help window and displays your requested topic.
- Click Help on the menu bar, and then click Show the Office Assistant to display the Office Assistant, a customizable character that provides a text box into which you can ask a question. (You might need to install the Office Assistant to use it.) The default Office Assistant is a paper clip that opens in the lower-right corner of the screen. Clicking the Office Assistant opens a window in which you can type your question or keywords in the What would you like to do? text box and then click the Search button to run your search. The Search Results task pane opens and displays links to topics that might help you. Some users like to have the Office Assistant always turned on, in which case it periodically provides Help for the task on which they are currently working. If you want to turn off or hide the Office Assistant, right-click it and then click the Hide command on the shortcut menu.

Using the FrontPage Help task pane is an easy way to get Help as you are working in FrontPage. In addition to having a printed copy of the Web page, Brett wants to print the HTML document. To learn how to print the HTML document, you will show him how to use the Help system.

To use the FrontPage Help task pane to get Help:

1. Click the **Microsoft Office FrontPage Help** button on the Standard toolbar. The FrontPage Help task pane opens and the insertion point is blinking in the Search for text box.
2. Type **How do I print an HTML document?** in the Search for text box, and then click the **Start searching** button. Figure 1-35 shows the Search Results task pane, which indicates that Help found 20 topics that might answer your question.

Search Results task pane

Figure 1-35

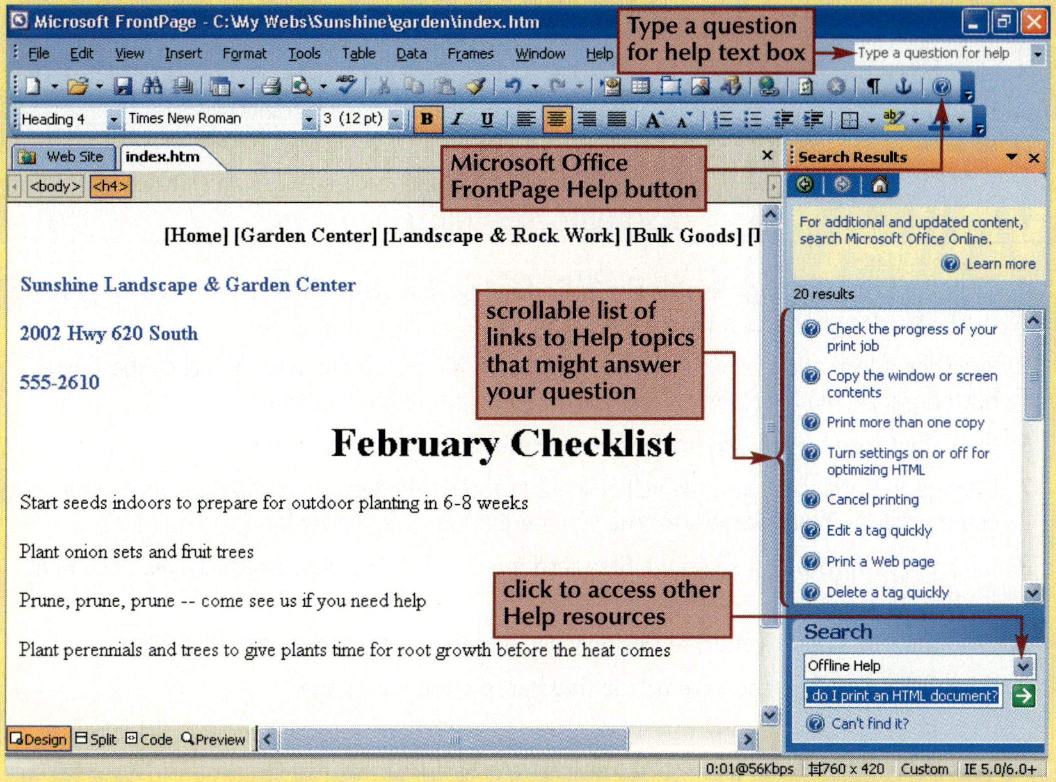

Figure 1-35 shows topics from Offline Help, which is the resource that FrontPage uses that does not require an active Internet connection. If you are connected to the Internet, your Search Results task pane might look different because it might display Help topics from Microsoft Office Online. If you don't find the help you need from the Offline Help files, you can connect to the Internet, click the list arrow in the Search panel, click Microsoft Office Online, and then click the Start searching button to connect to Microsoft Office Online Help. The offline and online Help resources include many of the same topics; however, the online topics are updated frequently by Microsoft and might provide additional help.

Trouble? If you are connected to the Internet, your Search Results task pane might look different. To display the Offline Help topics, click the list arrow in the Search panel, click Offline Help, and then click the Start searching button.

3. Scroll down the search results as necessary, and then click **Print a Web page**. The Microsoft Office FrontPage Help window opens. If necessary, click the **Maximize** button on the Microsoft Office FrontPage Help window title bar to maximize it. Figure 1-36 shows the Microsoft Office FrontPage Help window, which lists three topics that might answer your question. Notice the Show All link in the upper-right corner of the window. Clicking this link displays all of the information available for the topics listed. After you click the Show All link, it changes to the Hide All link, which returns the topics to the format shown in Figure 1-36.

Figure 1-36 Microsoft Office FrontPage Help window

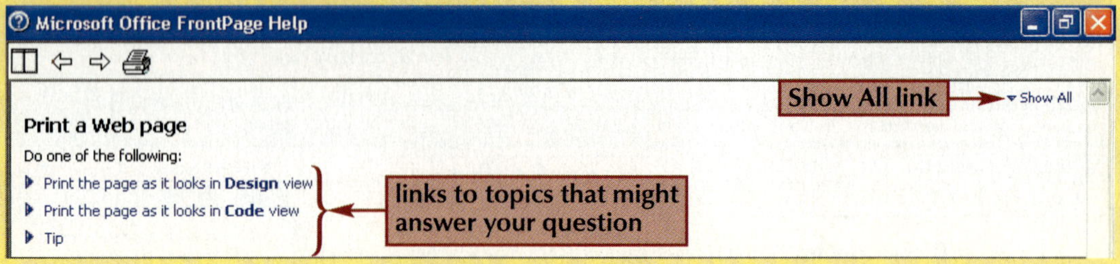

4. Click the **Print the page as it looks in Code view** link. Help displays the steps for printing the HTML document for a Web page.
5. Read the information provided for printing an HTML document, and then click the **Close** button on the Microsoft Office FrontPage Help title bar to close it.
6. Click the **Close** button on the Search Results task pane to close it.
7. Change to Code view, and then click line 2 of the HTML document and type your name as a comment (**<!-- Your Name -->**). The comment appears in a gray font.
8. Click the **Print** button on the Standard toolbar. FrontPage prints the HTML document for the home page.
9. Save the home page, return to Design view, and then close the garden Web site.
10. Click on the Microsoft FrontPage title bar to close FrontPage.

After creating the home page and formatting its contents, Brett is excited about continuing his work on the Web site. In Tutorial 2, you will show him how to create additional pages in the Web site and how to add hyperlinks and graphics to the pages.

Review

Session 1.3 Quick Check

1. True or False: Most HTML tags are one-sided.
2. How are the <html> and </html> tags used in an HTML document?
3. Write the HTML tag to italicize the words "home page" in a Web page.
4. How do you view the HTML document that creates a Web page in FrontPage? In Internet Explorer?
5. What is a nested tag?
6. How do you update a Web page when you make changes to the HTML document while working in Split view?
7. What is a meta tag?
8. What are three ways to get Help while working in FrontPage?

Review

Tutorial Summary

In this tutorial, you learned the five-part process for developing a Web site. You used FrontPage to create a Web site with a single Web page, entered and formatted text in a Web page, and learned about HTML. You also used the FrontPage Help system to answer a question as you completed your work in a Web site.

Because FrontPage includes an easy-to-use interface and templates for creating Web sites and Web pages, you will find that it is an easy tool to use to create your own Web sites.

Key Terms

attribute
character set
client
client/server architecture
closing tag
disk-based Web site
dynamic Web page
font
Format Painter
FrontPage Server Extensions
head section
hexadecimal
home page
host
HTML document
hyperlink
Hypertext Markup Language (HTML)
index
index.htm
inside tag
Internet
Internet service provider (ISP)
link
link bar
local area network (LAN)
meta tag
Microsoft FrontPage
nested tag
network
network server
one-sided tag
opening tag
outside tag
pixel
property
QuickTag Selector toolbar
RGB
search engine
server-based Web site
SharePoint Services
smart tag
static Web page
two-sided tag
Web folder
Web-safe color
Web site
webmaster

Practice

Practice the skills you learned in the tutorial using the same case scenario.

Review Assignments

There are no Data Files needed for the Review Assignments.

At a recent meeting, Brett passed around the printout he made of the new home page for the Sunshine Landscape & Garden Center. Everyone was very pleased with the content of the page. However, Brett did receive a few suggestions for changing the way text is formatted, all of which he would like to implement. You'll help him make these changes.

If necessary, start FrontPage, and then do the following:

1. Open the **garden** Web site that you created in this tutorial from the location where you are storing your Web sites. Open the home page (**index.htm**) in Design view, and if necessary, close the Folder List.
2. Select the nursery's name, address, and phone number, which appear on lines 2 through 4 of the home page, and change their alignment to center.

3. Select the link bar at the top of the home page, and then change its color to green. (*Hint:* Use the ScreenTips to find the Green tile in the Standard Colors section on the Font Color menu.)
4. Select the last two lines at the bottom of the home page (the copyright information), and then change the font to Verdana. (*Note:* If you do not have this font, select another font.)
5. Save the home page, and then preview it in Preview view. Scroll the page as necessary to see the changes you made in Design view.
6. Display the home page in Split view, and then use the Code view window to change the font color of the text in the link bar to navy. (*Hint:* Find the RGB value in the opening <font> tag that specifies the current color, and then change the value to the HTML value "navy.") Press the F5 key to update the text in the Design view window, and then save the home page.
7. Preview the home page in a Web browser, and then close the browser.
8. Use FrontPage to print the Web page and the HTML document that creates it.
9. Close the **garden** Web site, and then close FrontPage.

Apply

Apply the skills you learned in the tutorial to create a Web site for a retail business.

Case Problem 1

Data Files needed for this Case Problem: buffalo.doc, link.doc

Buffalo Trading Post Buffalo Trading Post (BTP) is a regional retail clothing business that specializes in buying, selling, and trading used clothing. The company buys its merchandise from people who take items to one of its trading post stores. Employees then sort items based on style, size, fabric, and garment condition. BTP specializes in clothing items made of natural fabric, but it also carries a limited inventory of polyester, acetate, Lycra, and other manufactured fibers in order to follow current styles and trends. BTP accepts only clothing in good condition for resale and attracts a loyal following of fashion enthusiasts and bargain hunters.

The president of the company, Nicole Beirne, hired you to lead the Web site development team. Nicole wants you to prepare a plan for BTP's Web site and create its home page. As you finished your first meeting with the Web site development team, you agreed that, in addition to the home page, the site should include five more pages with the following titles: (1) Who, (2) How, (3) What, (4) Where, and (5) Contact. Nicole asks you to begin your work by developing a Web site plan, the Web site, and the home page.

If necessary, start FrontPage, make sure you have your Data Files, and then do the following:

Explore

1. Use the information provided in the case problem description to prepare a Web site plan for the BTP Web site.

Explore

2. Prepare a preliminary sketch of the Web site that shows the desired Web pages and the expected hyperlinks from the home page.

3. Use the One Page Web Site template to create the **buffalo** Web site in the location where you are storing your Web sites.
4. Open the home page in Design view, and then make sure that the Web site's authoring settings are set to enable SharePoint Services, Browse-time Web Components, Author-time Web Components (including Navigation and Shared Borders), and VML graphics, and to support Internet Explorer versions 5.0/6.0 and later.
5. Make sure that the default page size is 800 × 600 maximized.
6. Insert into the home page the **buffalo.doc** file from the Tutorial.01\Case1 folder included with your Data Files.
7. Check the spelling in the home page and correct any misspelled words.
8. Change to Split view. In the Web page, click to the left of the sentence that begins "We also carry" and then press the Enter key, observing the change in the HTML document.
9. Return to Design view, create a new paragraph at the top of the home page, and then type "Welcome to the Buffalo Trading Post!" in the new paragraph. Center this paragraph, and then change it to the Heading 1 style.
10. Create a new paragraph above the heading you created in Step 9. Start Word, and then copy the text from the **link.doc** file in the Tutorial.01\Case1 folder included with your Data Files. Close Word, and then paste the text you copied on the new paragraph at the top of the home page. Choose the Keep Text Only option, and then change the paragraph that contains the pasted text to the Normal style.
11. Change the color of the text in the link bar to navy and its style to bold.
12. In a new paragraph at the bottom of the page, type the following text: "BTP™ is a registered trademark of Buffalo Trading Post". (*Hint:* Use the symbol set to insert the trademark character.) Change this text to 10-point, Arial font.
13. Format the text "Buffalo Trading Post" in the first sentence of the page as bold and change its color to navy. Then use the Format Painter to change other text occurrences of "Buffalo Trading Post" in the same and next paragraphs in the home page to match.

Explore

14. Create meta description and keywords tags in the home page using values that you provide.
15. Save the home page, examine it in Preview view, and then preview it in a Web browser. Use the browser to print the home page, and then close the browser.
16. Use FrontPage to print the HTML document for the home page. On the printout, circle the meta tags that you created.
17. Close the **buffalo** Web site, and then close FrontPage.

Apply

Apply the skills you learned in the tutorial to create a Web site for a restaurant.

Case Problem 2

Data Files needed for this Case Problem: grill.doc, linkbar.doc

Garden Grill Garden Grill is a growing national chain of casual, full-service restaurants. Its moderately priced menu features delicious dishes taken from various locations around the world. Garden Grill uses sophisticated consumer marketing research techniques to monitor customer satisfaction and evolving customer expectations. It strives to be a market leader in its segment by utilizing technology as a competitive advantage. Since 1976, management has used in-store computers to assist in the operation of the restaurants. The corporate office provides support seven days a week, 24 hours a day. Management believes that its information systems have positioned the chain to handle both its current needs and its future growth.

The corporate office has prepared a long-range information systems plan, which it reviews annually with all levels of management. Management's plan for the coming year includes the development of a Web site. Meghan Elliott just completed her management training at the corporate offices of Garden Grill and was assigned to work with Callan Murphy, who manages the information systems department. Last week, Callan's job responsibilities were increased to include managing the company's Web site development team. Callan wants Meghan to help him prepare the Web site design plan and create a home page for Garden Grill.

Callan and Meghan just met with the rest of the Web site development team. All agreed that, in addition to the home page, the company's Web site should include six additional pages with the following titles: (1) Company Profile, (2) Menu, (3) Franchise Info, (4) Employment, (5) Feedback, and (6) Search. Callan has asked you to assist Meghan with the design and development activities.

If necessary, start FrontPage, make sure you have your Data Files, and then do the following:

Explore

1. Use the information provided in the case problem description to prepare a Web site plan for the Garden Grill Web site.

Explore

2. Prepare a preliminary sketch of the Web site that shows the desired Web pages and the expected hyperlinks from the home page.
3. Use the One Page Web Site template to create the **grill** Web site in the location where you are storing your Web sites.
4. Open the home page in Design view, and then make sure that the Web site's authoring settings are set to enable SharePoint Services, Browse-time Web Components, Author-time Web Components (including Navigation and Shared Borders), and VML graphics, and to support Internet Explorer versions 5.0/6.0 and later.
5. Make sure that the default page size is 800 × 600 maximized.

6. Insert into the home page the **grill.doc** file from the Tutorial.01\Case2 folder included with your Data Files.
7. Check the spelling in the home page and correct any misspelled words.
8. Change to Split view. In the Web page, click to the left of the sentence that begins "Garden Grill is a premier" and then press the Enter key, observing the change in the HTML document.
9. Return to Design view, create a new paragraph at the top of the home page, and then type "Welcome to Garden Grill" in the new paragraph. Center this paragraph, change its style to Heading 3, change its font color to red, and change its font to Comic Sans MS. (*Hint:* Red is a standard color. Use the ScreenTips to locate it on the Font Color menu. The Comic Sans MS font might appear on your computer as "Comic Sans.")
10. Create a new paragraph above the heading you created in Step 9. Start Word, and then copy the text from the **linkbar.doc** file in the Tutorial.01\Case2 folder included with your Data Files. Close Word, and then paste the text you copied on the new paragraph at the top of the home page. Choose the Keep Text Only option, and then change the paragraph that contains the pasted text to the Normal style.

Explore

11. Change the font color of the text in the link bar to purple and its style to bold, and make sure its font is Times New Roman. (*Hint:* Purple is a standard color. Use the ScreenTips to locate it on the Font Color menu.)

Explore

12. In a new paragraph at the bottom of the page, insert a copyright symbol and then type a space, the current year, and the company name. Press Shift + Enter to create a new line, and then add the text "Last updated" and a date field that indicates when the page was last edited. (*Hint:* To add the date field, click Insert on the menu bar, and then click Date and Time.) Format the date with the day of the week and the full date with the month spelled out. Do not include the time.
13. Change the style of the text you created in Step 12 to italic, 10-point, Arial font.

Explore

14. Create meta description and keywords tags in the home page using values that you provide.
15. Save the home page, examine it in Preview view, and then preview it in a browser. Use the browser to print the home page, and then close the browser.
16. Use FrontPage to print the HTML document for the home page. On the printout, circle the meta tags that you created.
17. Close the **grill** Web site, and then close FrontPage.

Challenge

Apply the skills you learned in the tutorial to create a Web site for a service-oriented business.

Case Problem 3

Data Files needed for this Case Problem: link.doc, swenson.doc

Swenson Auctioneers Scott Swenson became a professional auctioneer in 1983 when he left his job at a real estate brokerage to become an approved auctioneer for the U.S. Bankruptcy Court. As an auctioneer before the Bankruptcy Court, he realized that he was very comfortable in the position of auctioneer and really enjoyed working with people in different types of businesses. After several years, he left his job and started his own firm, Swenson Auctioneers. At first, the firm handled auctions of personal estates only, but it soon expanded to handle auctions for commercial and industrial institutions, government entities, financial institutions, national retailers, law firms, manufacturers, and small businesses. As the business expanded and Scott began handling multiple auctions each month, he hired an assistant auctioneer, a marketing representative, an appraiser, an auction clerk, and a collectibles specialist. To handle the daily business of the office, Scott also hired a receptionist and a personal assistant. After 10 years, Swenson Auctioneers has grown from a small, local "mom and pop" organization to one of the leading auctioneering firms in the Midwest.

Scott wants to create a Web site for the business as part of his commitment to customer service. He thinks that the Web site can offer current and potential clients information about the types of auctions that Swenson Auctioneers handles, and provide a way for the new clients to get information about upcoming auctions that might interest them. As part of his overall vision for the Web site, Scott wants to showcase the business's past auctions and provide information about its key employees. After discussing the Web site at a recent staff meeting, Scott decides that in addition to the home page, he wants to create pages with the following titles: (1) Upcoming Auctions, (2) Auction & Appraisal Services, (3) Our Team, and (4) Mailing List. Scott has hired you to teach him how to develop and maintain his FrontPage Web site. You'll start by creating a Web site plan, the Web site, and the home page.

If necessary, start FrontPage, make sure you have your Data Files, and then do the following:

Explore

1. Use the information provided in the case problem description to prepare a Web site plan for the Swenson Auctioneers Web site.

Explore

2. Prepare a preliminary sketch of the Web site that shows the desired Web pages and the expected hyperlinks from the home page.
3. Use the One Page Web Site template to create the **swenson** Web site in the location where you are storing your Web sites.
4. Open the home page in Design view, and then make sure that the Web site's authoring settings are set to enable SharePoint Services, Browse-time Web Components, Author-time Web Components (including Navigation and Shared Borders), and VML graphics, and to support Internet Explorer versions 5.0/6.0 and later.
5. Make sure that the default page size is 800 × 600 maximized.

6. Insert into the home page the **swenson.doc** file from the Tutorial.01\Case3 folder included with your Data Files.
7. Check the spelling in the home page and correct any misspelled words.

Explore

8. Change to Split view. In the HTML document, select the text "Swenson Auctioneers" in the first sentence of the first paragraph, and then use the More Colors dialog box to change this text to the red color with the value Hex={FF,00,00}. Click anywhere in the Web page to deselect the text.
9. In the HTML document, select the text "Swenson Auctioneers" again, and then use the Bold button on the Formatting toolbar to change the text to bold, noticing the nested tag created in the HTML document. Click anywhere in the Web page to deselect the text.
10. Return to Design view, and then use the Format Painter to apply the formatting you applied in Steps 8 and 9 to the text "Swenson Auctioneers" in the second paragraph.
11. Create a new paragraph at the top of the home page. In this new paragraph, type "Swenson Auctioneers provides nationwide auction and appraisal services for a variety of industries."
12. Change the paragraph you inserted in Step 11 to the Heading 4 style.
13. Create a new paragraph above the paragraph you created in Step 11. Start Word, and then copy the text from the **link.doc** file in the Tutorial.01\Case3 folder included with your Data Files. Close Word, and then paste the text you copied into the new paragraph at the top of the home page. Choose the Keep Text Only option, and then change the paragraph that contains the pasted text to the Normal style.

Explore

14. Click anywhere in the link bar at the top of the page, change the alignment to center, and then apply a solid border around the paragraph. (*Hint:* Click the list arrow for the Borders button on the Formatting toolbar, and then use the ScreenTips to find and click the Outside Borders option in the menu that opens.)

Explore

15. In a new paragraph at the bottom of the page, insert a copyright symbol and then type a space, the current year, and the company name on the first line. Press Shift + Enter to create a new line, and then add the text "Last updated" and a date field that indicates when the page was last edited. (*Hint:* To add the date field, click Insert on the menu bar, and then click Date and Time.) Format the date with the day of the week and the full date with the month spelled out. Do not include the time.
16. Change the style of the text you created in Step 15 to bold, italic, 10-point, Arial font.

Explore

17. Create meta description and keywords tags in the home page using values that you provide.
18. Save the home page, examine it in Preview view, and then preview it in a browser. Use the browser to print the home page, and then close the browser.
19. Use FrontPage to print the HTML document for the home page. On the printout, circle the meta tags that you created.
20. Close the **swenson** Web site, and then close FrontPage.

Research

Examine Internet Web sites that provide residential mortgage loans, and then create a Web site for an online mortgage broker.

Case Problem 4

Data File needed for this Case Problem: loan.doc

Mortgage Services, Inc. While working her way through college, Natalie Fuselier worked part-time as a teller at a small regional bank in her hometown of Baton Rouge. After she graduated from Louisiana State University with a degree in finance, she accepted a position at the bank as a loan officer. Loan officers typically specialize in commercial, consumer, or mortgage loans. Natalie was assigned to manage commercial loans, where she worked with companies seeking loans to pay for new equipment and business expansions. As part of her duties, Natalie was responsible for contacting businesses in the area and persuading them to use the bank for their loan needs. As she found new clients, Natalie would help them apply for the loan, and then she would manage the process of verifying the information provided by the business to make a decision about the business's ability to repay the loan. If the business could provide sufficient collateral to insure the loan, Natalie would approve it and then service the account over the term of the loan.

For five straight years, Natalie was the bank's top loan officer, closing millions of dollars in loans per year. Part of her success was due to her ability to develop effective working relationships with others and her enthusiasm for ensuring a smooth process for businesses. Natalie enjoyed her position but realized that working with commercial loans was cyclical and tied to the nation's economy. In an economic downturn, the number of business loans decreases. Natalie feared that her job might be tied to the needs of her clients, so she decided to leave her position to start her own company. Natalie decided to work with consumers this time. She counted on the existing relationships she had built with realtors in the area and started asking them to recommend her to provide residential home loans to their clients. As business increased, Natalie determined that a Web site would automate much of the loan application process and has hired you to help her design and create a Web site. To help her make some decisions about the kind of site to produce, she wants to examine some existing Internet Web sites that are set up to access applications from individuals.

If necessary, start FrontPage, make sure you have your Data Files, and then do the following:

Explore

1. Start your Web browser, and then open the home page for the search engine of your choice or the Google home page (**www.google.com**). Type the search expression "online mortgage application" in the search engine's text box, and then initiate the search. Examine the list of sites returned by the search engine and explore a few sites that provide applications for residential mortgages. As you explore the sites, notice features that make it easy to apply for a loan and the type of information the sites provide. (*Note:* Do not complete any on-screen forms at any of the sites that you visit.)

Explore

2. Use the information provided in the case problem description and the Web sites you explored in Step 1 to prepare a Web site plan for Natalie's Web site.
3. Prepare a preliminary sketch of the Web site that shows the desired Web pages and the expected hyperlinks from the home page. In addition to the home page, the Web site should include a minimum of the following pages: Loan Types, Application, Post Application Help, Resources, and Contact Us.

4. Use the One Page Web Site template to create the **loan** Web site in the location where you are storing your Web sites.
5. Open the home page in Design view, and then make sure that the Web site's authoring settings are set to enable SharePoint Services, Browse-time Web Components, Author-time Web Components (including Navigation and Shared Borders), and VML graphics, and to support Internet Explorer versions 5.0/6.0 and later.
6. Make sure that the default page size is 800 × 600 maximized.
7. Insert into the home page the **loan.doc** file from the Tutorial.01\Case4 folder included with your Data Files.
8. Check the spelling in the home page and correct any misspelled words.

Explore

9. Change to Split view and click the blank line between the opening <body> tag and the opening <p> tag in the HTML document. Add a level-one heading to the Web page using the text "Mortgage Services, Inc." (*Hint:* When you type the opening tag, FrontPage will insert the closing tag for you automatically.) Press the F5 key to update the Web page.

Explore

10. In the HTML document, select the text in the level-one heading that you added in Step 9, and then change its color to a blue color with the value Hex={00,00,CC} and change its alignment to center. Return to Design view.
11. Create a new paragraph above the heading. Create a centered link bar using the information you prepared in Steps 2 and 3. Format the link bar using the Normal style and a font, font style, and font color of your choice.

Explore

12. Switch to your Web browser, and then use a search engine of your choice to learn more about the different properties of the HTML meta tag. (*Hint:* Use the search expression "HTML meta tag" and follow some of the links to Web sites that provide HTML tutorials and resources.) After examining the resources you find, use the User Meta Variable dialog box to add three meta tags to the home page: description, keywords, and robots. Select appropriate values for the description and keywords properties, and set the robots value to "all."
13. Save the home page, examine it in Preview view, and then preview it in a browser. Use the browser to print the home page, and then close the browser.
14. Use FrontPage to print the HTML document for the home page. On the printout, circle the meta tags that you created.
15. Close the **loan** Web site, and then close FrontPage.

Reinforce

Lab Assignments

The New Perspectives Labs are designed to help you master some of the key concepts and skills presented in this text. The steps for completing this Lab are located on the Course Technology Web site. Log on to the Internet and use your Web browser to go to the Student Online Companion for New Perspectives Office 2003 at **www.course.com/np/office2003**. Click the Lab Assignments link, and then navigate to the assignments for this tutorial.

Computer History Hypermedia The Computer History Hypermedia Lab is an example of multimedia hypertext, or hypermedia, that contains text, pictures, and recordings that trace the origins of computers. This Lab provides you with two benefits: First, you learn how to use hypermedia links, and second, you learn about some of the events that took place as the computer age dawned.

The Internet: World Wide Web One of the most popular services on the Internet is the World Wide Web. This Lab is a Web simulator that teaches you how to use Web browser software to find information. You can use this Lab whether or not your school provides you with Internet access.

Review

Quick Check Answers

Session 1.1

1. A static Web page is one that displays information that does not change; a dynamic Web page contains data that changes on a schedule, such as stock market information.
2. defining the goal and purpose of the Web site, determining and preparing the Web site's contents, designing the Web site, building the Web site, and testing the Web site
3. a keyword, phrase, or picture in a Web page that, when clicked using a mouse, connects to related information located in the same Web page, in the same Web site, or in another Web site
4. index.htm
5. Determining a default page size lets you customize the appearance of your Web pages for the majority of your visitors. Viewing the Web site's pages at different resolutions is an important part of testing to ensure that all visitors will see your pages as you intend them to be viewed.
6. Type the text, insert the text from a file, and paste the text from an existing document.
7. A smart tag appears when you paste text in a Web page and provides options for working with that text, such as keeping the text's original formatting or only pasting the text.
8. Close Site

Session 1.2

1. Use the Format menu commands, right-click the text and use the shortcut menu commands, or use the Formatting toolbar buttons.
2. h1 (Heading 1)
3. 7
4. font
5. One of 216 colors common to all computer operating systems. A browser will display these colors consistently regardless of the computer on which the browser is installed.
6. Select the text whose format you want to copy, click the Format Painter button on the Standard toolbar once, and then select the text to which you want to copy the format with the Format Painter pointer.
7. Click the Show Preview View button at the bottom of the Contents pane, or click the Preview button list arrow on the Standard toolbar and select the browser(s) to use to open the page.

Session 1.3

1. False
2. The <html> tag identifies the beginning of the HTML document, and the </html> tag identifies the end of the HTML document.
3. <i>home page</i>
4. In FrontPage, click the Show Code View button at the bottom of the Contents pane; in Internet Explorer, click View on the menu bar, and then click Source.
5. an HTML tag that appears within another HTML tag
6. Press the F5 key.
7. an HTML tag that includes information about a Web page, such as the character set it uses, the name of its developer, how often it is refreshed, and the keywords and description of the page's contents
8. Type a question or keywords in the Type a question for help text box; click the Microsoft Office FrontPage Help button on the Standard toolbar; and click Help on the menu bar, and then click Show the Office Assistant.

Objectives

Session 2.1
- Change the background color of a Web page
- Insert a background picture into a Web page
- Save a Web site's embedded files
- Create a marquee
- Insert a picture into a Web page
- Learn about different picture file formats

Session 2.2
- Import a Web page into a Web site
- Create hyperlinks to other Web pages and to an e-mail address
- Create an image map
- Use a picture as a hyperlink

Session 2.3
- Create a thumbnail picture
- Change the characteristics of a picture
- Create an interactive button, a page transition, and animated text

Working with Graphics and Hyperlinks

Creating Graphics and Hyperlinks for the Sunshine Landscape & Garden Center Web Site

Case

Sunshine Landscape & Garden Center

The Web site for the Sunshine Landscape & Garden Center currently includes only the home page that you created in Tutorial 1. You formatted the page using different fonts and colors and added the text to use as entries in the link bar that will connect the home page to other pages that you will develop in the Web site.

Because nurseries are very colorful places, Sunshine's owner, Brett Kizer, wants to make sure that the pages in the Web site are colorful and attractive, like the nursery itself. Toward that goal, Brett hired a graphic designer to create a company logo and other graphics to include in the Web site. Brett also began taking digital pictures of the plants arriving at the nursery for use in the Garden Center page. The graphic designer also created a map with directions to the nursery for Brett to use in a Map page.

In this tutorial, you will continue enhancing the home page by adding a background color, a company logo, and some animated text. Then you will create hyperlinks to connect the home page to the Garden Center and Map pages. Finally, you will use features that create dynamic elements in Web pages, including page transitions and interactive buttons.

Student Data Files

To complete this tutorial, you will need your ending files from Tutorial 1 and the following Data Files. Additional Data Files needed to complete the end-of-tutorial exercises are listed with the Review Assignments and Case Problems.

▼**Tutorial.02**

▽ Tutorial folder

back.jpg	gc_pic.gif	map_page.htm
center.htm	map.jpg	sun_logo.gif

Session 2.1

Changing the Background Color of a Web Page

The background color of a Web page can enhance its appearance and readability. If you don't specify a background color, the default background color is white. You can select any available color as the background of a Web page, but you should follow good design principles and select Web-safe colors that provide sufficient and complementary contrast with the rest of the Web page's contents. You might need to try several colors before you find one that provides the desired appearance for your Web page.

You can select a background color for a Web page using the Page Properties dialog box.

Reference Window

Setting the Background Color of a Web Page

- Click Format on the menu bar, and then click Background to open the Page Properties dialog box with the Formatting tab selected.
- In the Colors section, click the Background list arrow, and then click the desired color. If you want to use a color that is not listed, click More Colors, click a color in the color palette, and then click the OK button.
- Click the OK button to apply the new background color and close the Page Properties dialog box.

Although Brett likes the current white background of the home page, he asks you to select another color to see whether it might be more attractive.

To set the background color of the home page:

1. Start **FrontPage**, open the **garden** Web site from the location where your Web sites are stored, and then open the home page in Design view. If necessary, close the Folder List.
2. Click **Format** on the menu bar, and then click **Background** to open the Page Properties dialog box with the Formatting tab selected, as shown in Figure 2-1. In the Colors section, the background color is currently set to Automatic, which produces the default background color, white.

Figure 2-1

Background settings for the home page

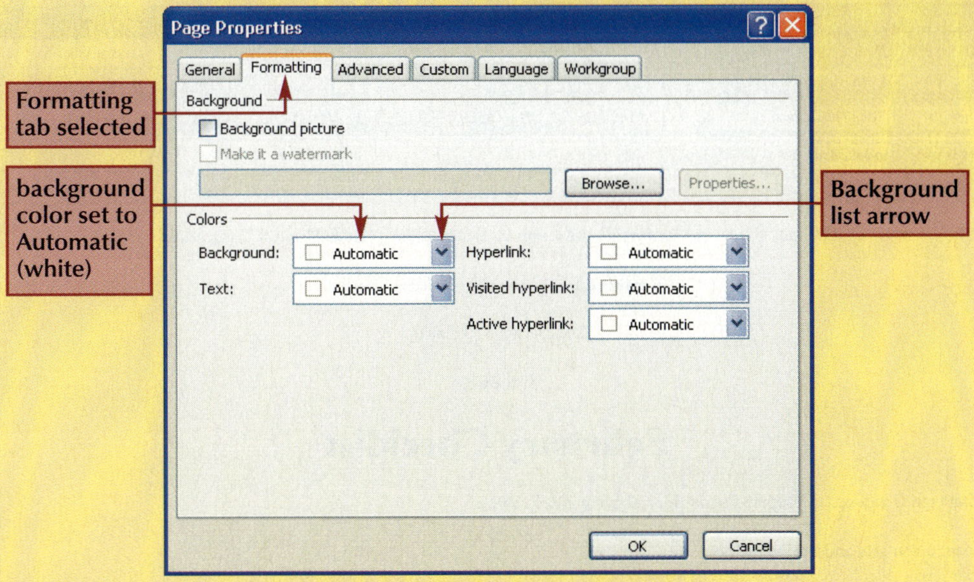

3. In the Colors section, click the **Background** list arrow. The menu includes 16 standard colors and a section named "Document Colors," which includes the colors used in the current Web page. Because you used the sapphire and navy colors in Tutorial 1 to change the font colors in the home page, these are the only two colors listed in the Document Colors section. Clicking More Colors opens the More Colors dialog box, which contains the 216 Web-safe colors.
4. Point to the **Yellow** color in the Standard Colors section. After a few seconds, a ScreenTip identifies the color as "Yellow." See Figure 2-2.

Figure 2-2

Changing the background color of the home page

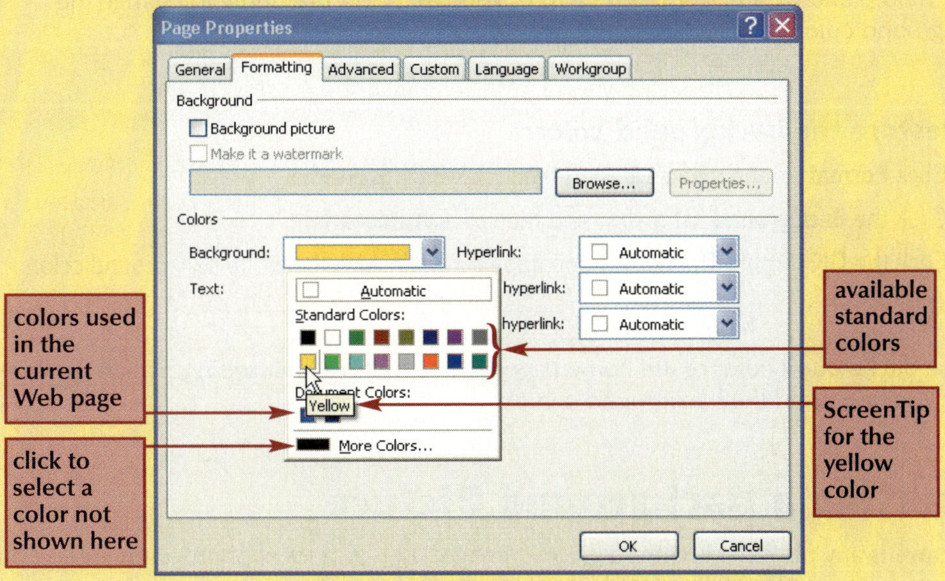

5. Click the **Yellow** color to select it, and then click the **OK** button to close the Page Properties dialog box. The background color of the home page changes to yellow. See Figure 2-3.

Figure 2-3 Home page with yellow background color

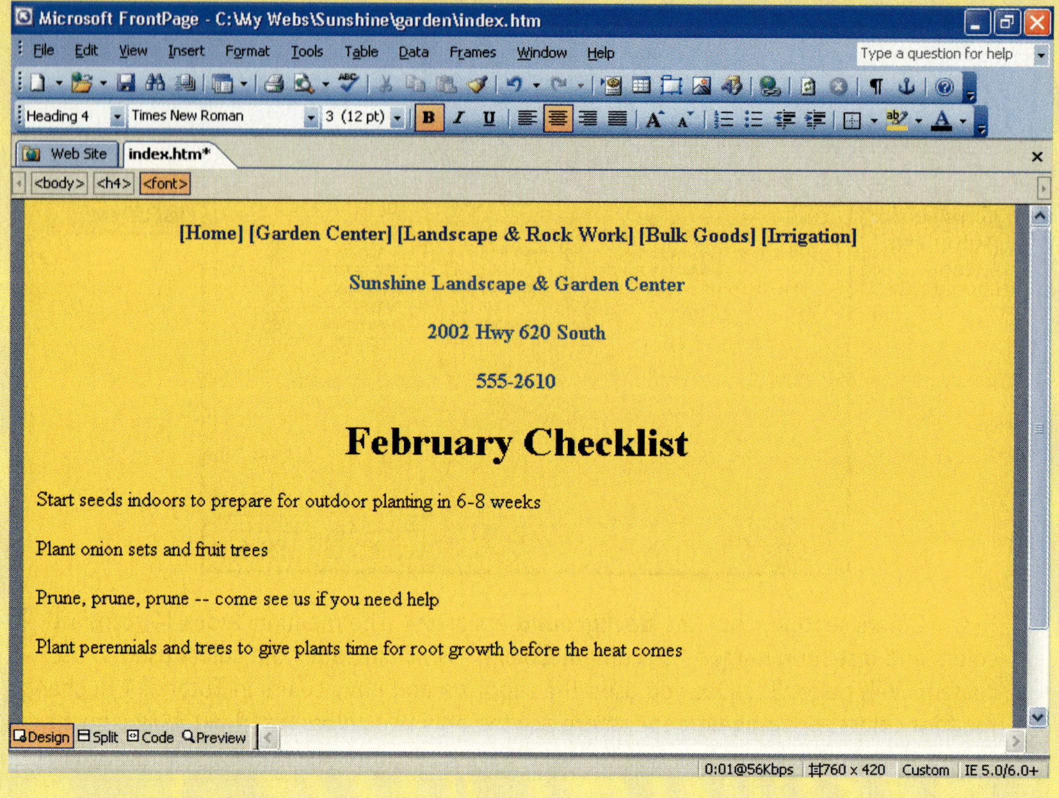

The yellow background provides a good contrast with the text in the home page, but Brett thinks that it is too bright. Instead of trying a different background color, Brett wonders how the page would look with a background picture that his graphic designer created. Before adding a background picture, you will show Brett how to change the background color back to Automatic (white).

To restore the background color:

1. Click **Format** on the menu bar, and then click **Background**.
2. Click the **Background** list arrow, and then click **Automatic**.
3. Click the **OK** button. The home page appears again with the white background color.

The background color of the home page returns to its default setting, which is white. Now you can insert the background picture.

Inserting a Background Picture

A **picture** is any file that contains a graphic image, such as a logo, photograph, or computer-generated image. Almost every Web site that you visit contains pictures to enhance the site's appearance and provide visual representations of people and products. Because the Internet is a highly visible medium, many of its users have high expectations when viewing a Web site for the first time. They expect to find pictures of products and interesting graphics to enhance their use of the site. Pictures are an expected and vital part of communication; a Web site's users often perceive a Web site without pictures as having little or no value. As you work in a Web site, you will find many ways to use pictures to enhance the appearance and functionality of your pages. Even simple graphics can meet this goal. For example, the logo that Brett wants to include in the home page identifies the company's corporate logo, connecting the Web site in the virtual world to the nursery's physical location in the real world. The logo also includes the business's name, address, and phone number.

To include a picture in a Web page, it must be stored as a file. This file might be a digital picture that you purchase from a company that sells them, a digital picture that you take with a digital camera, a scanned copy of a picture that exists on paper, or a clip-art image that you find at a Web site or in the Microsoft Office Clip Art gallery. Pictures can be saved in a variety of file formats, but there are certain formats that are commonly used on the Web because they produce high-quality images with low file sizes and low download times. In most cases, the content of the graphic dictates the file type you choose for it. Three of the most popular formats for picture files are:

- **JPG** (or **JPEG**), pronounced "jay-peg," stands for **Joint Photographic Experts Group**, which is the name of the group that wrote this file standard. JPEG uses lossy compression technology to compress the file. **Lossy compression** technology eliminates redundant and unnecessary data in an image to reduce its file size, which reduces the amount of time it takes to download the file from the Web server on which it is stored and display it in the Web page. In most cases, the discarded data is invisible to the human eye. Because it supports 16 million colors, JPEG is used primarily for photographs and complex graphics.
- **GIF**, pronounced "giff" (with a hard "g"), stands for **Graphics Interchange Format**. GIF uses a **lossless compression** technology that reduces the file size of an image without any loss of data. The algorithm that compresses GIF files is owned by Unisys, which requires a licensing fee when the algorithm is used to compress GIF files. However, the licensing fee does not apply to people using GIF files in their Web pages; it only applies to companies that create programs that output GIF files. This format supports color and different screen resolutions. Because GIF files are limited to 256 colors, they are suitable for scanned images, line drawings, and simple graphics, but not photographs. In addition, GIF files can be combined to create animated images in a Web page.
- **PNG**, pronounced "ping," stands for **Portable Network Graphic**. The PNG format was created as a license-free alternative to GIF. PNG also uses lossless compression technology, but its compression algorithm produces files that are smaller than GIF files. PNG files support up to 16 million colors, but unlike GIF files, you cannot combine PNG files to create animation.

Most Web browsers will display pictures that are created using the GIF and JPEG formats. Some browsers cannot display PNG files, so this format is less popular on the Internet. The Student Online Companion page for Tutorial 2 includes resources that you can use to learn more about different graphics resources available on the Web and the picture file formats used on the Web.

A **background picture**, which appears behind the Web page content, can be almost any picture file, but some pictures work better than others. When you surf the Internet, you might find businesses that use background pictures to enhance the appearance of their Web pages. These background pictures might be a single copy or multiple small copies of a company logo, a picture or clip-art image that represents the business, or an interesting graphic, such as a three-dimensional shape or a series of lines. You can use any picture as a background in a Web page, but the primary goal of any background is to enhance the content of the Web page and ensure its readability.

Reference Window

Inserting a Background Picture into a Web Page

- Click Format on the menu bar, and then click Background.
- In the Background section, click the Background picture check box to select it, and then click the Browse button to open the Select Background Picture dialog box.
- Browse for and select the desired background picture file.
- Click the Open button to return to the Page Properties dialog box, and then click the OK button to insert the background picture.

Brett received a file from the graphic designer that he wants to use as the background for the home page. You'll show him how to make this change next.

To insert the background picture:

1. Click **Format** on the menu bar, and then click **Background** to open the Page Properties dialog box with the Formatting tab selected.
2. In the Background section, click the **Background picture** check box to select it, and then click the **Browse** button. The Select Background Picture dialog box opens. You will insert the background picture from your Data Files.
3. Click the **Look in** list arrow, select the drive or folder that contains your Data Files, open the **Tutorial.02** folder, and then open the **Tutorial** folder.
4. Select **back.jpg** in the list box, and then click the **Open** button. The Page Properties dialog box reappears, and the text box in the Background section shows the path to the file you selected as a background picture. See Figure 2-4.

Figure 2-4 Background picture selected for the home page

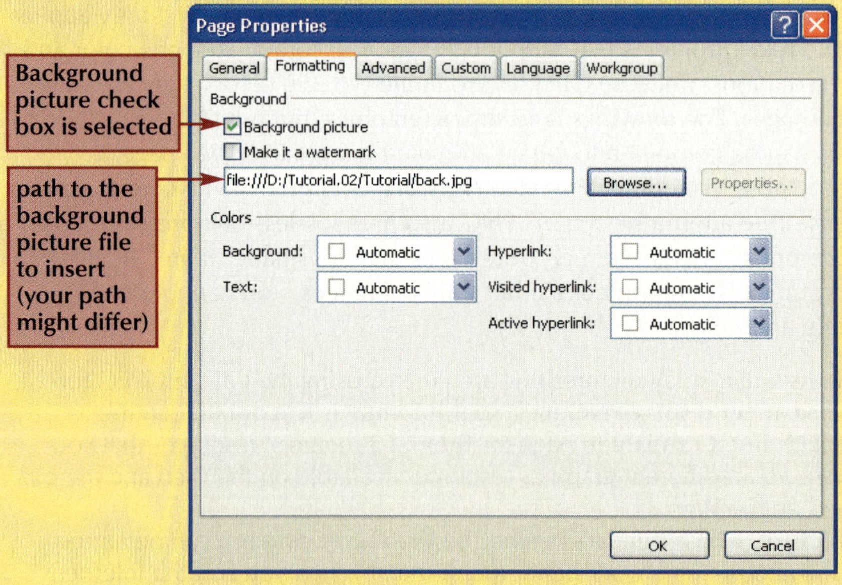

Trouble? The path to the back.jpg file on your computer might differ. Just make sure that you see "back.jpg" in the path. If you do not see "back.jpg," click the Browse button and repeat Steps 3 and 4 to select it.

5. Click the **OK** button to close the Page Properties dialog box. The background picture now appears in the home page for the Sunshine Landscape & Garden Center. Notice that the text from the page appears on top of the background picture.

Saving an Embedded File in a Web Site

When you insert a picture into a Word or other Office document, the picture is saved *with* the document. In FrontPage, however, inserting a file only adds an HTML tag in the HTML document that creates the Web page to indicate *where* the file that contains the picture is stored. Until you save the page, the reference for the background picture points to the location from which you inserted it. This location might be a removable drive, hard drive, or server. Because an HTML tag can only insert a picture from a file location into your Web page, a picture is called an **embedded file**. This embedded file does not become part of your Web site until you save it in the Web site's images folder, which most developers use to store all picture and multimedia files that are used in the Web site. Saving the embedded background picture file in your Web site ensures that all of your Web site's files are saved within the Web site itself and that they will be accessible to all users.

Saving a Web Page That Contains an Embedded File

Reference Window

- Click the Save button on the Standard toolbar. The Save Embedded Files dialog box opens.
- If necessary, click the Change Folder button, select the images folder for the current Web site, and then click the OK button.
- Click the OK button to save the Web page and the embedded file.

Before saving the file, you want to show Brett the HTML tag that inserts the background picture into the Web page. To accomplish this goal, you ask him to change to Split view.

To change to Split view and save the home page and the embedded picture file:

1. Click the **Show Split View** button Split at the bottom of the Contents pane to change to Split view, and then examine the HTML document to find the HTML tag that inserts the background picture. This tag appears below the closing </head> tag and begins <body background=. The file location, which appears in quotation marks, is the location of the back.jpg file on your computer; Figure 2-5 shows the HTML document for Brett's computer.

Figure 2-5 Split view of the home page after inserting the background picture

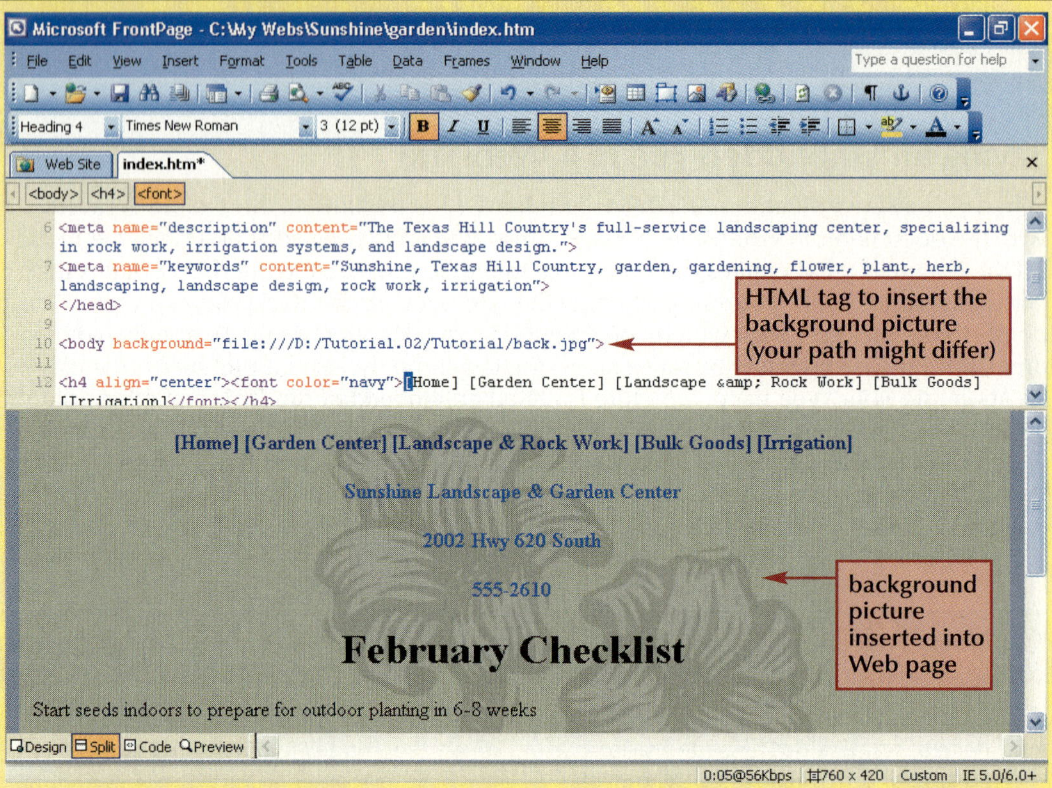

2. Click the **Save** button on the Standard toolbar. The Save Embedded Files dialog box opens, as shown in Figure 2-6. Notice that the Save Embedded Files dialog box shows the name of the embedded file (back.jpg), the action to perform (Save), and a preview of the picture. You can use this dialog box to rename the picture, to change the folder in which to save it, or to change the action either to save or avoid saving the file in the Web site. In addition, clicking the Picture File Type button lets you change the picture's properties. For example, you might change the file from one format to another or change the quality of the image. (You will learn about changing a file's type and properties later in this tutorial.)

Figure 2-6 Save Embedded Files dialog box

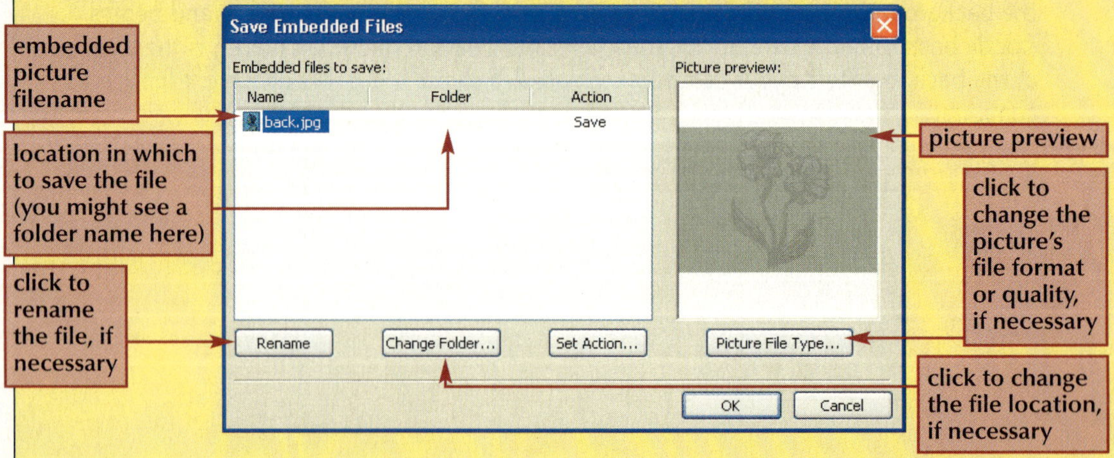

You will save the background picture file, back.jpg, in the garden Web site's images folder.

Trouble? As you use FrontPage to save Web pages with embedded files, FrontPage might select the images folder for you automatically based on your previous actions. If the images folder is already listed in the Folder column, skip to Step 5.

3. Click the **Change Folder** button. The Change Folder dialog box opens and displays the folders in the garden Web site.
4. Click the **images** folder to select it, and then click the **OK** button. The Save Embedded Files dialog box shows the folder in which to save the back.jpg file as "images/."
5. Click the **OK** button to save the back.jpg file in the garden Web site's images folder and to save the changes you made to the home page. The back.jpg file is still with your Data Files, but now it is also saved in the garden Web site. These files are independent and are not linked to each other in any way. Notice that the <body> tag in the Code view window now shows that the file is saved in the images folder of the current Web site (the garden Web folder).
6. Return to Design view, click the **Web Site** tab at the top of the Contents pane, and then double-click the **images** folder to open it. The back.jpg file is stored in the images folder.
7. Click the **index.htm** tab at the top of the Contents pane to return to the home page in Design view.

Brett likes the appearance of the home page with the background picture. He asks you about using other techniques to enhance the appearance of the home page and call attention to important specials or promotions at the nursery. You suggest using a marquee to display important text in the home page.

Using a Marquee

A **marquee** is a text box that displays a scrolling text message in a Web page. You can create a marquee by using existing text or by entering new text. Most businesses use marquees to call attention to important announcements, promotions, and other messages. You should use marquees sparingly, however, because they can easily overpower a Web page and distract users. Most browsers can animate the text in a marquee; if a browser does not support the <marquee> tag, then it will display the text in the marquee without the animation. Internet Explorer can display and animate marquee text. However, certain versions of Netscape Navigator cannot animate the text or display the text box; a person using Navigator to view a Web page that contains a marquee might see static text, or the text might scroll across the screen in a smaller text box.

Reference Window

Creating a Marquee in a Web Page

- Select the text in the Web page that you want to include in the marquee.
- Click the Web Component button on the Standard toolbar to open the Insert Web Component dialog box.
- If necessary, click Dynamic Effects in the Component type list, and then click Marquee in the Choose an effect list.
- Click the Finish button. The Marquee Properties dialog box opens.
- If necessary, edit the text that will appear in the marquee in the Text text box.
- In the Behavior section, click the option button to implement the desired behavior for the marquee's text.
- Specify any other desired characteristics of the marquee, such as the direction, speed, or size of the text and the background color of the text box, or accept the default settings for these characteristics.
- If necessary, click the Style button, click the Format button in the Modify Style dialog box, and then click an option in the list that opens to change the settings for the marquee's font, paragraph, border, bullets, and position. Click the OK button to close any open dialog boxes and return to the Marquee Properties dialog box.
- Click the OK button.

Brett wants to call attention to the nursery's new shipments of plants for the spring growing season, and he wants to put this notice in a marquee. Placing this text in a marquee will animate it when the user views the home page in a browser. You tell Brett that the text in a marquee should fit on one line, and that shorter phrases or sentences work better than longer ones.

To create and test the marquee:

1. Scroll down the home page as necessary, click the blank paragraph above the copyright information, and then type **Vegetables and perennials arrive next month!** You will use this text in the marquee.

   When you create a marquee, you need to make sure that you select only text, and not the paragraph mark at the end of the paragraph. If you select the paragraph mark, the paragraph below the marquee will move up to the same line as the marquee. To help Brett select the text correctly, you ask him to turn on the display of the nonprinting characters in the home page.

2. Click the **Show All** button ¶ on the Standard toolbar. Paragraph marks appear at the end of each paragraph. See Figure 2-7.

Nonprinting characters in a Web page | **Figure 2-7**

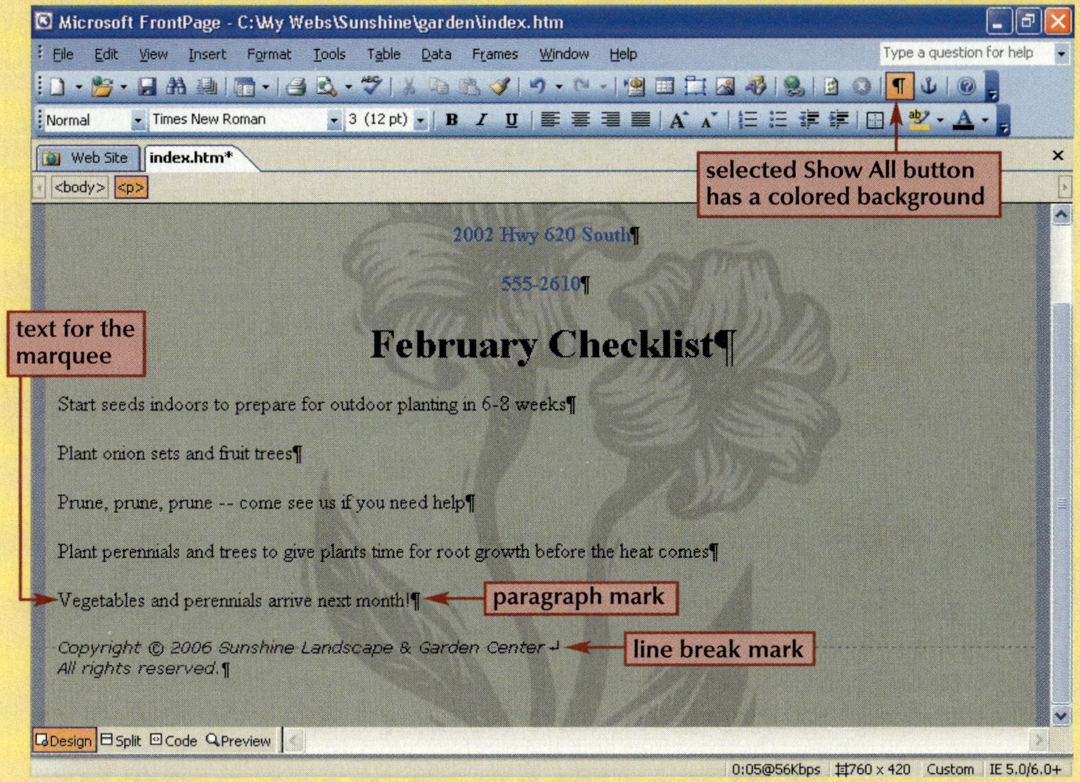

Trouble? If the Show All button has a colored background, then this feature is already enabled and you do not need to click the Show All button. (Clicking the Show All button again turns this feature off.)

3. Select the text that you typed in Step 1, but not the paragraph mark at the end of the line.
4. Click the **Web Component** button on the Standard toolbar. The Insert Web Component dialog box opens.

   Trouble? If your Web site is set to support Netscape Navigator browsers, the Marquee option in the Choose an effect list will be dimmed and a message will appear in the dialog box indicating that you need to change the authoring settings for the Web site because Navigator cannot display marquees. To complete these steps, click the Cancel button in the Insert Web Component dialog box, click Tools on the menu bar, click Page Options, select the Authoring tab, click the Browsers list arrow and click Microsoft Internet Explorer only, click the Browser versions list arrow and click 5.0/6.0 browsers and later, and then click the OK button. Repeat Steps 3 and 4.
5. Make sure that **Dynamic Effects** is selected in the Component type list and **Marquee** is selected in the Choose an effect list. A description of the Marquee Web component appears in the dialog box.
6. Click the **Finish** button. The Marquee Properties dialog box opens, as shown in Figure 2-8. Notice that the text you selected in the home page appears in the Text text box. This is the text that will appear in the marquee. You can change this text if you need to do so by editing the text in the Text text box.

Figure 2-8 Marquee Properties dialog box

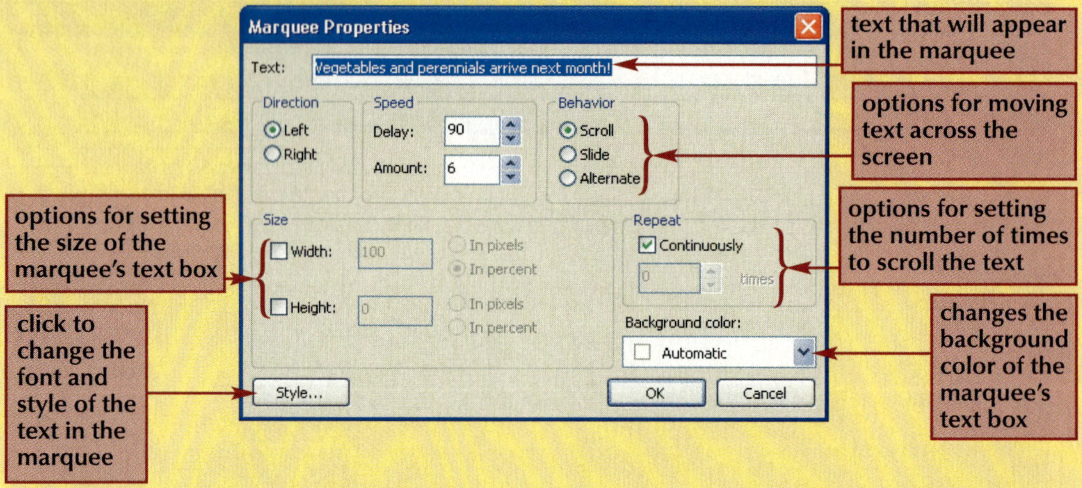

7. Click the **Alternate** option button (if necessary) in the Behavior section. Selecting this setting causes the marquee's text to move back and forth across the screen. The Scroll setting causes the text to move across the screen in only one direction, and the Slide setting causes the text to scroll across the screen and then stop.
8. In the Size section, click the **Width** check box to select it, select the value in the Width text box and type **90**, and then (if necessary) click the **In percent** option button to select that screen measurement. These settings limit the width of the marquee to 90% of the screen's width. Notice that you can set similar limits on the marquee's height or use pixels as the unit of measurement.

   Trouble? If you accidentally close the Marquee Properties dialog box, double-click the marquee text in the Web page to reopen it.

   Brett wants to use a different background color for the marquee's text box so that it will stand out in the page.
9. Click the **Background color** list arrow to open the list of available colors.
10. Click the **White** color in the Standard Colors section.

    Notice that you can change other marquee options as well. For example, selecting the Continuously check box in the Repeat section causes the marquee's text to remain animated indefinitely while the page is open. If you clear this check box, you can specify the number of times that the marquee's text will move across the screen. You can also set the text's direction of movement so that it scrolls from the left or right side of the page. You can specify delay and speed parameters in the Speed section. In the Delay text box, you can specify the amount of time, in milliseconds, that the text should wait before it begins to move. In the Amount text box, you can specify the speed at which the text should move in the marquee. The default settings for these options are acceptable, so you will close the dialog box.
11. Click the **OK** button. The Marquee Properties dialog box closes and a marquee with a white background encloses the text you typed in Step 1. No movement is shown, however. To test this feature, you must save the page and change to Preview view.
12. Click the **Save** button on the Standard toolbar, and then click the **Show Preview View** button (Preview) at the bottom of the Contents pane to preview the page. If necessary, scroll down the page to see the marquee. The text moves back and forth in the white marquee.
13. Return to Design view.

The logo picture that Brett received from the graphic designer includes the nursery's name, address, and phone number. Brett wants to replace the text at the top of the home page with the new logo. Because the logo is a picture, you'll show Brett how to insert a picture into a Web page.

Inserting a Picture into a Web Page

Inserting a picture into a Web page uses the same techniques as inserting a background picture into a Web page. Just as for background pictures, a picture in a Web page might be any file format, with JPEG, GIF, and PNG being the most popular formats used on the Internet. When inserting pictures in a Web page, try to insert files with the smallest file sizes to meet your objectives. You might have a beautiful picture to include in your site, but if it takes two or three minutes for people to download it, they will quickly become frustrated when viewing your site.

Inserting a Picture into a Web Page

Reference Window

- Click the location in the page where you want to insert the picture.
- Click the Insert Picture From File button on the Standard toolbar.
- In the Picture dialog box, browse to and then select the desired file.
- Click the Insert button to insert the picture.

Brett wants to replace the text in the home page that identifies the nursery's name, address, and phone number with the logo created by the graphic designer. To make this change, he'll need to select the text and then replace it with the file that contains the logo.

To add a picture to a Web page:

1. Scroll up the home page as necessary, and then use the pointer to select the text on lines 2, 3, and 4 of the Web page, containing the nursery's name, address, and phone number, as shown in Figure 2-9. Because this text was centered, the picture that you insert in this location will also be centered.

Figure 2-9 **Text to replace with a picture**

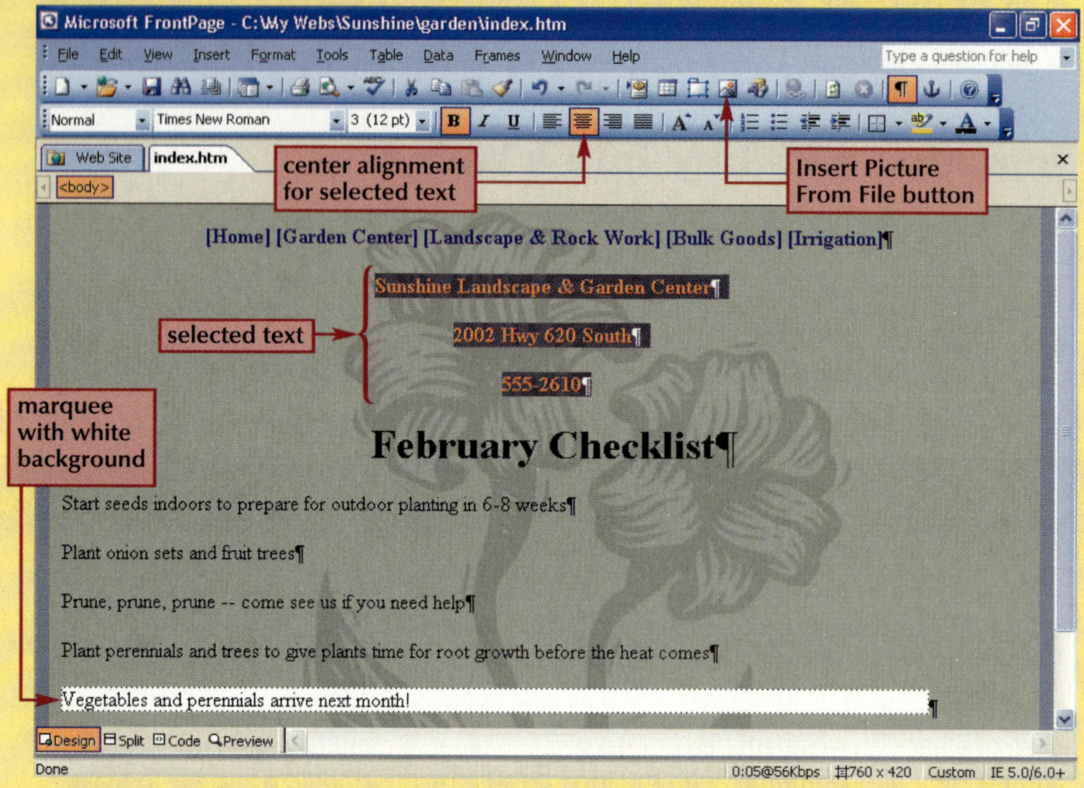

2. Click the **Insert Picture From File** button on the Standard toolbar. The Picture dialog box opens.
3. If necessary, click the **Look in** list arrow, change to the drive or folder that contains your Data Files, and open the **Tutorial.02\Tutorial** folder to display its contents.
4. Click **sun_logo.gif** to select it, click the **Insert** button to insert the picture into the Web page, and then, if necessary, press the **Enter** key to make the picture appear on its own line.

   Trouble? If your picture is not centered, click the picture to select it, and then click the Center button on the Standard toolbar.
5. Click the picture to select it. See Figure 2-10.

Figure 2-10 **Picture inserted into the home page**

Notice the **sizing handles**—eight small squares around the picture—that you can use to resize the selected picture. When you are working with a picture, you can display the Pictures toolbar to gain access to common commands used for pictures. You'll display the Pictures toolbar next.

To display the Pictures toolbar:

1. Click **View** on the menu bar, and then point to **Toolbars**. The Toolbars submenu includes all of the FrontPage toolbars. A toolbar that is displayed has a check mark to the left of its name. Clicking a toolbar name either displays or hides it.

   Trouble? If the Pictures command on the Toolbars submenu has a check mark to the left of its name, this toolbar is already displayed. Skip to Step 3.

2. Click **Pictures** on the Toolbars submenu. The Pictures toolbar opens. It might appear as either a floating or docked toolbar, depending on how it was last used. Figure 2-11 shows the default setting, which is a floating toolbar. You can move a toolbar by dragging its title bar to a new location. Working with toolbars is a matter of personal preference, but to make sure that you can see all of the Web page in Design view, you'll dock toolbars at the top of the window.

Figure 2-11 Pictures toolbar

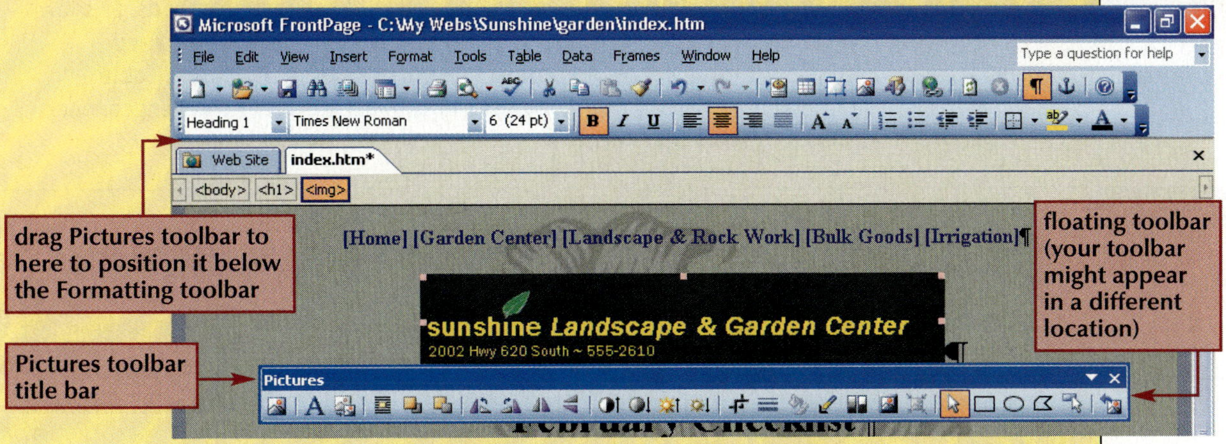

3. If your Pictures toolbar is not docked below the Formatting toolbar, click the title bar of the Pictures toolbar, and then drag it to below the Formatting toolbar. When the toolbar appears below the Formatting toolbar, release the mouse button. Now the Pictures toolbar is docked below the Formatting toolbar. When you display a toolbar in the FrontPage window, the size of the Web page decreases slightly to make room for the new toolbar. Because you see less of your Web page, it is a good practice to hide toolbars that you don't need as you complete your work.

When you start adding graphics to a Web page, it is a good idea to keep an eye on the Estimated Time to Download pane on the status bar. The speed at which you view Web pages in a browser on your computer is dependent upon the way you connect to the Internet. If you use a dial-up connection, pages will load more slowly for you than for a user with a high-speed Internet connection, such as a cable modem or Digital Subscriber Line (DSL), both of which download data very quickly. The Estimated Time to Download pane uses a download speed that you select to estimate the amount of time required to download the page and its embedded files from the Web server on which they are stored. Remember that when you use a Web browser to view a Web page, the browser uses your Internet connection to download the HTML document that creates the Web page and the embedded files that are displayed in the page. HTML documents are usually small text files, but pictures can vary in size from a few to several hundred or thousand kilobytes. Because file sizes can vary based on content, it's important to check the file sizes of pictures you include in a Web site and to use the appropriate file format to compress the files as much as possible to make them download more quickly. Some Internet Web sites and ISPs provide research data about the types of connections people make to access different servers, and some cities have a much higher percentage of high-speed connections than others. A good rule of thumb is to assume that some of your site's visitors will use dial-up connections. You'll check the options for setting the download speed next, and then make sure it is set to 56 Kbps (kilobits per second), which is a "fast" dial-up connection.

To view the Estimated Time to Download options:

1. Point to the **Estimated Time to Download** pane on the status bar so the ScreenTip "Estimated Time to Download" appears.
2. Click the **Estimated Time to Download** pane to open a list of connection speeds, as shown in Figure 2-12. The first two options, 28.8 and 56, are connection speeds for dial-up modems. DSL transfers data at a rate of approximately 256 Kbps to 512 Kbps. Cable modems transfer data at a rate of 1,000 Kbps, and T1 connections are the fastest connections, with transfers of up to 1,500 Kbps.

Figure 2-12 **Estimated Time to Download options**

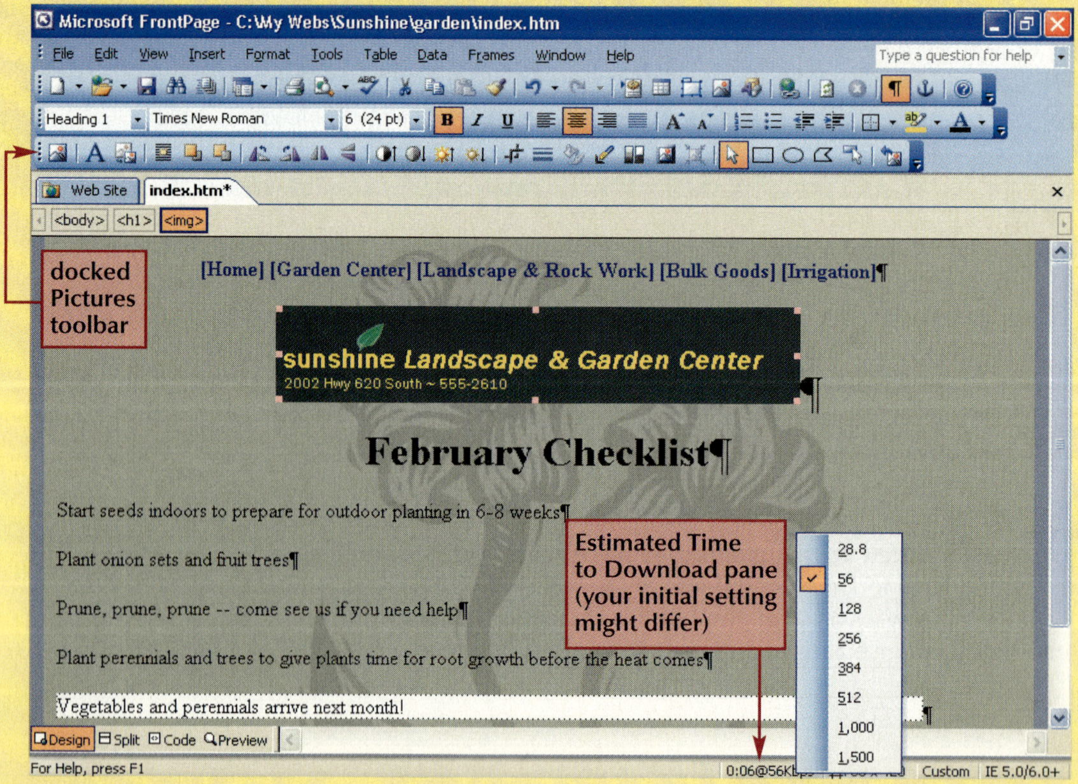

3. Click **1,000** in the Estimated Time to Download menu. The list closes and the Estimated Time to Download pane shows that the page requires 0:01, or one second, to be downloaded at 1,000 Kbps (a cable modem).
4. Click the **Estimated Time to Download** pane again, and then click **56**. The page requires 0:06, or six seconds, to be downloaded using a dial-up connection. This download time tells you that even with the simple graphics you have included, the page will take six seconds to be downloaded over a dial-up connection.

As you are working on your Web pages, it is important to consider the audience you are trying to reach and how it will access the site. For example, your preliminary planning should give you a good idea of the kind of information to include and which browsers visitors will use to access the site. When you begin using graphics in your pages, you should consider the needs of your Web site visitors who are using text-only browsers (which cannot display graphics) and visually impaired visitors using special software to read the content of Web pages. One way to enhance your Web site for this audience is to include alternative text with pictures.

Alternative text is a short phrase that identifies or describes a picture in a Web page using the HTML alt property. For example, the alternative text for the picture you just added could be "logo" or "Sunshine Landscape & Garden Center logo," which would identify the picture's function as decorative. For pictures that are used as hyperlinks, you might identify the picture's function as "Bulk Goods page hyperlink," so a user can infer its purpose in the page. This optional setting is important for two reasons. First, it identifies the picture's contents while it is being downloaded from the server. People viewing the pages with fast connections won't see the alternative text unless they point to the picture, but people viewing the page with slow connections will see the text in the place where the picture will eventually appear. Alternatively, people using browsers that cannot display pictures will see the alternative text *instead* of the picture. The second reason for adding alternative text is to identify the picture for visually impaired and other people using software that reads a Web page. Even though visually impaired users won't see the pictures in your Web pages, alternative text can tell them that the picture is included and describe its function.

When adding alternative text to a picture, be sure to include a short description and not just the picture's filename or the word "picture." Some developers use alternative text such as "decorative photo" to describe pictures that simply complement the Web page's appearance and alternative text such as "picture of Hewlett-Packard 1100A printer" for descriptions that are more important to conveying a message. This subtle difference is one to consider as you add alternative text to your pictures because it will increase the utility of your Web pages for all users.

Adding Alternative Text to a Picture

Reference Window

- Right-click the picture to open the shortcut menu, and then click Picture Properties.
- Click the General tab.
- Click the check box to the left of the Text text box to select it.
- Type the alternative text in the Text text box in the Alternative representations section, and then click the OK button.

Because he replaced the center's name, address, and phone number with the logo, Brett realizes that he deleted this important information for users who cannot view pictures. He wants to add alternative text to the picture to include this information in the Web page.

To add alternative text to a picture:

1. Right-click the picture to open the shortcut menu, and then click **Picture Properties** to open the Picture Properties dialog box.
2. Click the **General** tab.
3. Click the **check box** to the left of the Text text box to select it.
4. Click the **Text** text box in the Alternative representations section, type **Sunshine Landscape & Garden Center, 2002 Hwy 620 South, 555-2610**, and then click the **OK** button. The Picture Properties dialog box closes and the alternative text is added to the HTML document.

   You can see the alternative text that you added by viewing the HTML document or by pointing to the picture in a browser.
5. Click the **Show Code View** button Code at the bottom of the Contents pane. The alt property includes the alternative text that you added to the picture. See Figure 2-13.

Figure 2-13 **HTML document for the home page**

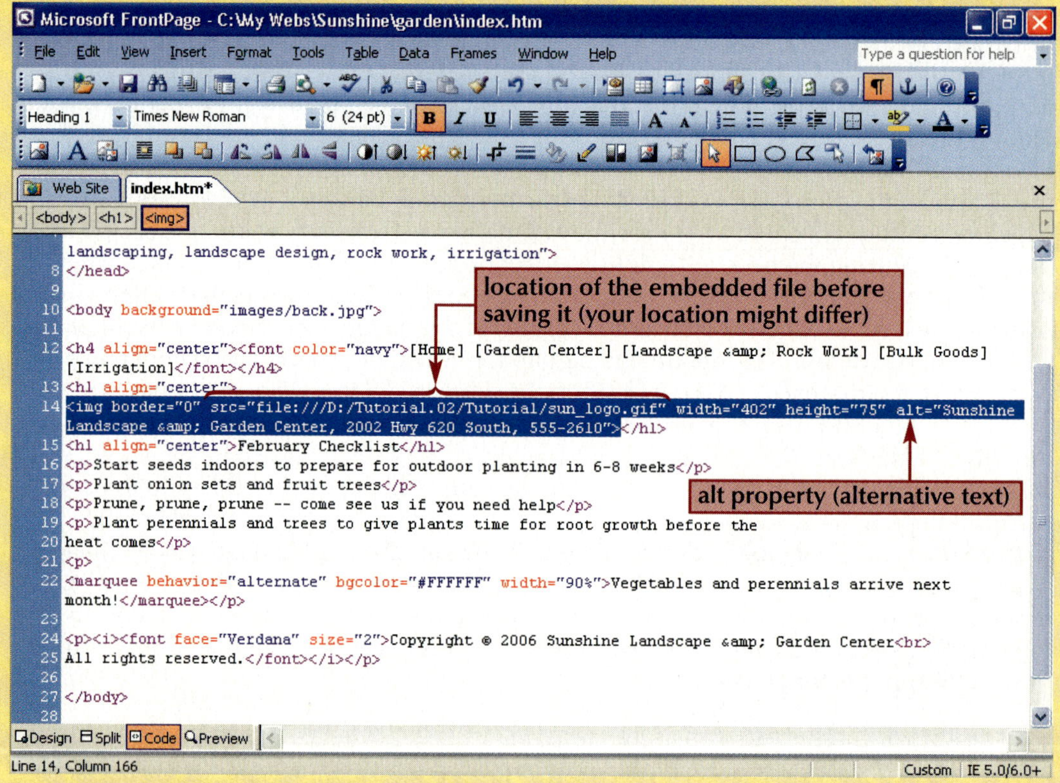

6. Click the **Show Preview View** button Preview at the bottom of the Contents pane to change to Preview view, and then point to the picture so the ScreenTip displays the alternative text that you added to the picture. After a few seconds, the alternative text will disappear.
7. Click the **Show Design View** button Design at the bottom of the Contents pane to return to Design view.

Brett added another picture to the Web site, so you remind him that he needs to save its file in the garden Web site's images folder.

To save the home page and the picture:

1. Click the **Save** button on the Standard toolbar. The Save Embedded Files dialog box opens and displays the name of the new embedded file (sun_logo.gif), the folder in which to save it (images/), and the action to perform (Save). Notice that the Picture preview box shows a preview of the picture.

   Trouble? If the images folder is not selected automatically, click the Change Folder button, select the images folder in the garden Web site, and then click the OK button and continue with Step 2.

2. Click the **OK** button to save the embedded file in the garden Web site and your changes to the home page. After a few seconds, the file is saved and the Web site is updated.

Working with Pictures in Different Formats

When you are working in a photo-editing program, such as Adobe Illustrator or PhotoShop, you can edit a picture's characteristics; for example, you might change the background color or add special effects to the picture's edges. FrontPage includes tools that let you change some of a picture's characteristics to enhance its appearance in a Web page. For example, you can rotate and flip a picture to change its orientation, increase and decrease the picture's contrast and brightness, crop a picture to remove an unwanted area, change the picture to black and white or gray, or add a beveled edge. For pictures saved as GIF files, you can also change a color in the picture to transparent, which lets the background color of the Web page show through the picture.

Because the different picture formats support different features, you will find as you work on a Web site that there are effects that don't work as well or at all with some pictures. For example, if you insert a JPEG picture into a Web page and want to change its background to transparent, FrontPage will first require you to convert it to a GIF picture because JPEG pictures do not support transparency. When you convert a picture from JPEG to GIF, you are converting an image with up to 16 million colors to one limited to 256 colors. The converted GIF file might look fine in your Web page, but when you try to change the background to transparent, the image might look like the one shown in Figure 2-14.

Figure 2-14 JPEG file converted to a GIF file with a transparent background

Instead of a solid background color, the conversion created different shades of the background color. The shades aren't visible to you until you convert the picture. If this problem occurs as you work in your Web pages, you will need to use a photo-editing program to change the background color to solid and change the file format to GIF. Although FrontPage has tools to convert pictures from one format to another, the pictures you use in your Web sites might make the FrontPage tools unusable. For this reason, it's important to have a graphic designer to make changes to pictures for you or for you to learn how to use a photo-editing program and make the changes yourself.

Reference Window

Converting a Picture to Another Format

- Right-click the picture to open the shortcut menu, click Picture Properties to open the Picture Properties dialog box, and then click the General tab.
- Click the Picture File Type button to open the Picture File Type dialog box.
- Click the option button to select the format to which you want to convert the picture.
- For GIF and JPEG files, use the Settings options to change the picture's settings as necessary.
- Click the OK button.

Next, you will show Brett the options for converting a picture to another format.

To examine the options for changing a picture's file type:

1. Right-click the picture to open the shortcut menu, and then click **Picture Properties**.
2. Click the **General** tab to select it.
3. Click the **Picture File Type** button. The Picture File Type dialog box opens and displays four formats for pictures, as shown in Figure 2-15. You can tell that the picture is saved as a GIF file because the GIF option button is selected. Notice that the Settings options at the bottom of the dialog box show settings that only GIF files support. Clicking the Interlaced check box causes a GIF picture to be displayed with increasing detail as it is being downloaded from the server. You also can make the background of a picture transparent, so that the background of the Web page shows through the picture, by checking the Transparent check box (when this option is enabled). Also notice that there are two options for PNG files. PNG-8 has better color support than GIF, and PNG-24 uses a lossless compression technique, resulting in a larger file size. The note for both of these formats indicates that some browsers do not support them.

Figure 2-15 Picture File Type dialog box

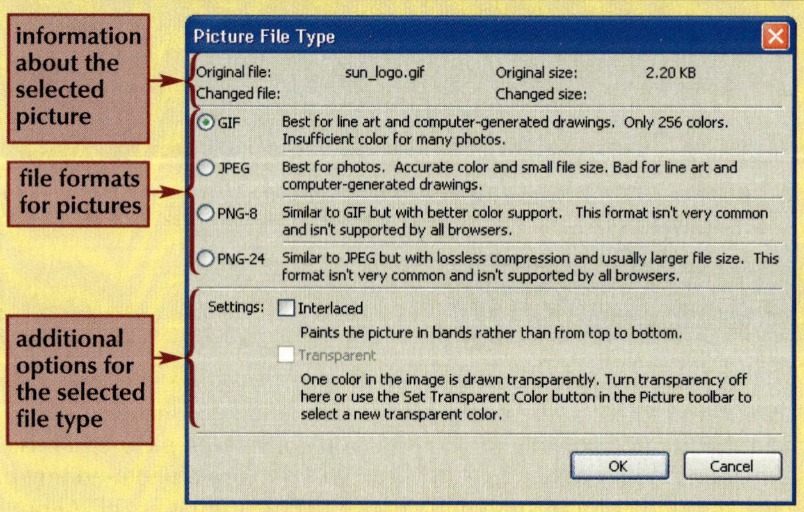

4. Click the **JPEG** option button to select it. Notice that the information at the top of the dialog box changes to show the original filename and size and the changed filename and size. As expected, a JPEG file requires more space than a GIF file because this format includes more colors and detail. Also notice that the Settings options change to show the available settings for a JPEG file. Because the JPEG format does not support transparency or interlacing, these options are not available. For a JPEG picture, you can set the desired quality as a number from 1 to 100, with 100 being the best. In addition, you can set the number of progressive passes as a number from 0 to 100, with 100 being the most passes; the browser will then make this number of passes to display the picture before it is completely downloaded from the server.
5. Click the **PNG-8** option button to select it. The file size increases slightly. Because there are no additional settings for PNG files, the Settings options disappear.
6. Click the **Cancel** button to close the dialog box without making any changes, and then click the **Cancel** button to close the Picture Properties dialog box.

When you save a picture for the first time as an embedded file in a Web site, you can click the Picture File Type button in the Save Embedded Files dialog box to change the picture's format. However, after you save the file the first time, you need to use the Picture Properties dialog box to change the file's format. For more information about editing pictures and setting their characteristics, consult FrontPage Help.

Brett wants to see how the logo will look with a transparent background.

Changing a Color in a Picture to Transparent

One way to enhance the appearance of a picture in a Web page is to change one of the picture's colors to transparent. A transparent color will not be visible in the picture, thereby allowing the page's background to show through the picture.

Changing a Color in a Picture to Transparent

Reference Window

- Click the picture to select it.
- Click the Set Transparent Color button on the Pictures toolbar.
- Click the color in the picture that you want to make transparent.

Brett wants to change the green background of the picture to transparent to see how it looks.

To change a color in a picture to transparent:

1. If necessary, click the picture to select it so sizing handles appear around the picture.
2. Click the **Set Transparent Color** button on the Pictures toolbar.
3. Point to the green color in the picture. The pointer changes to a shape. See Figure 2-16.

Figure 2-16 **Changing a color to transparent**

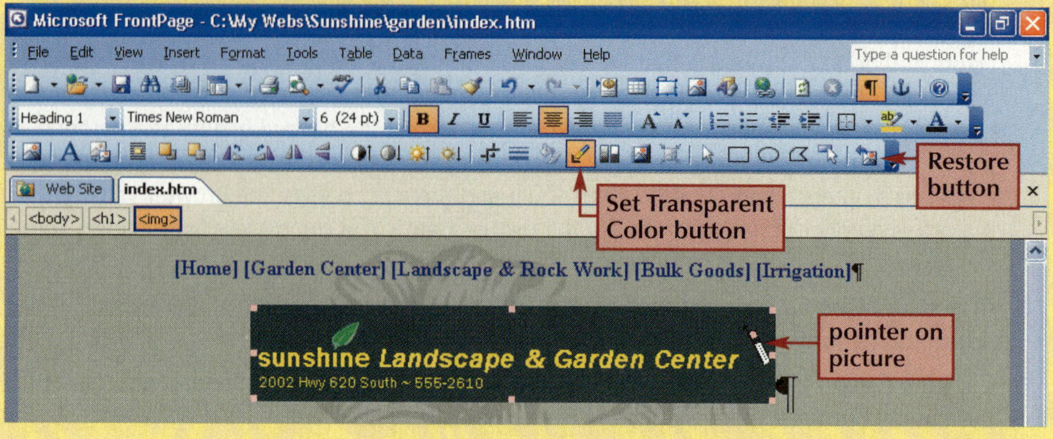

4. Make sure that the small arrow of the pointer points to the green color that you want to make transparent, and then click the green color. The green background of the picture becomes transparent, allowing the background of the Web page to show through.

   Trouble? If you change the wrong color in the picture to transparent, click the Undo button on the Standard toolbar, and then repeat Steps 1 through 4.

   Without the background color, Brett decides that the logo isn't as attractive and wants to cancel this change. You tell him that he could click the Undo button on the Standard toolbar, but instead you will show Brett how to restore a picture to its original settings.

5. Click the **Restore** button on the Pictures toolbar. The picture returns to its original state with the green background. Clicking the Restore button erases any changes you have made to a picture since the last time you saved it.

6. Click the **Save** button on the Standard toolbar. Even though you restored the picture, the Save Embedded Files dialog box opens with the "Overwrite" command in the Action column. This command will save the picture by overwriting the one that is saved in the images folder. If you do not want to overwrite the picture, clicking the Set Action button lets you select the option to cancel this action. You'll accept the default setting and overwrite the existing file.

7. Click the **OK** button to overwrite the picture file and save the home page.

Inserting a Horizontal Line

The last graphic that you want to show Brett is the **horizontal line**, which is frequently used for emphasis or to divide a Web page into sections. There are two ways to create horizontal lines in a Web page. The first way is to use the HTML <hr> tag (which stands for "horizontal rule"). This tag draws a line in a Web page. After inserting a horizontal line, you can change its characteristics by adjusting its length, width, and color. The second way is to insert a picture of a horizontal line, such as the one shown in Figure 2-17. When you use a picture to create a divider in a Web page, the line can be more visually interesting than the horizontal line drawn by the HTML <hr> tag. Keep in mind that using a picture does add to the overall download time for the Web page, so you need to use picture dividers carefully. You can search for picture dividers to use in your Web pages by displaying the Clip Art task pane and searching using the keyword "dividers."

Figure 2-17

Picture used as a horizontal line

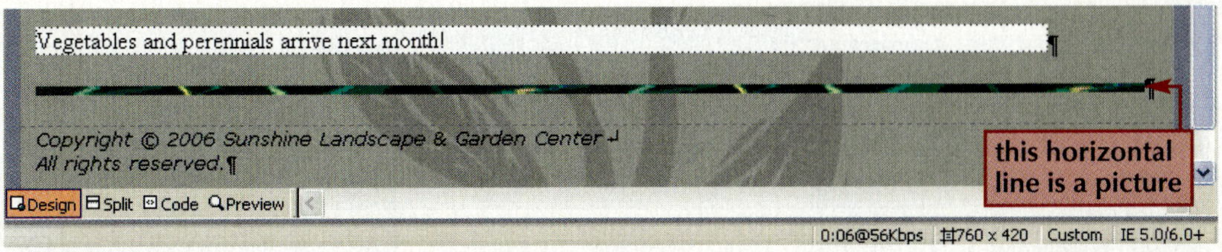

Inserting a Horizontal Line and Changing Its Properties

Reference Window

- Click at the beginning of the line directly below the location in which to insert the horizontal line.
- Click Insert on the menu bar, and then click Horizontal Line to insert a horizontal line.
- If necessary, double-click the horizontal line in the Web page, and then use the Horizontal Line Properties dialog box to change its characteristics.

To provide a visual break between the content of the home page and the copyright information at the bottom of the page, Brett wants to insert a horizontal line.

To insert a horizontal line in the home page:

1. Scroll down the home page as necessary, and then click to the left of the word **Copyright** at the bottom of the home page. The insertion point is now positioned below the location in which to insert the horizontal line.
2. Click **Insert** on the menu bar, and then click **Horizontal Line**. A horizontal line is inserted above the first line of the copyright information.

Next, Brett wants to make the line more prominent by making it shorter and wider and by changing its color.

To change horizontal line settings:

1. Double-click the **horizontal line** to select it and open the Horizontal Line Properties dialog box. See Figure 2-18.

Figure 2-18 **Horizontal Line Properties dialog box**

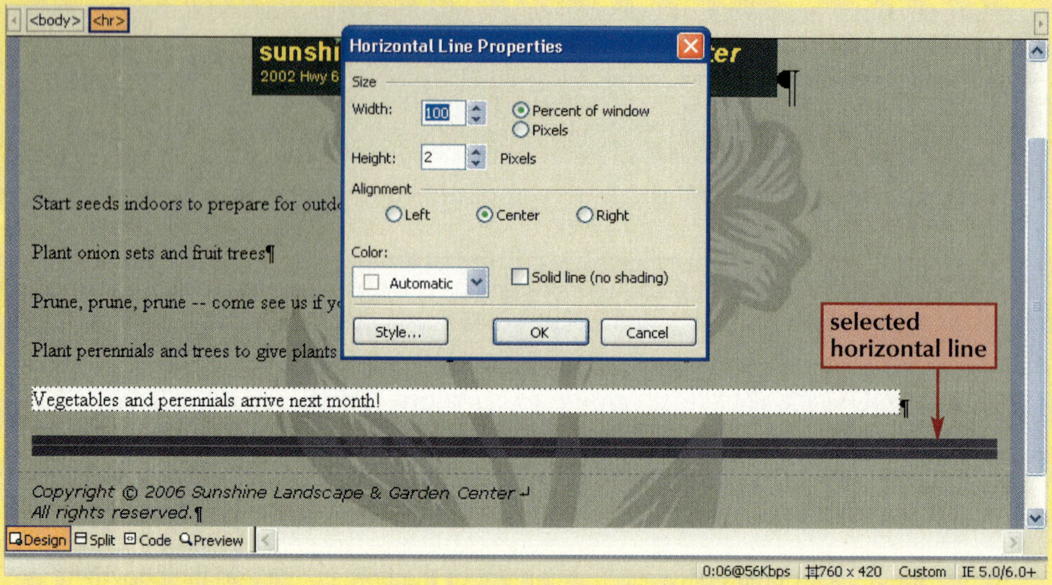

2. In the Size section, replace the selected text in the Width text box by typing **90**. The line's width will now be 90% of the screen's width.
3. Click the **Height** up arrow until the value changes to **5**. The height of the line is set to five pixels.
4. Click the **Color** list arrow, and then click the **Navy** color in the Document Colors section. The horizontal line will be the same navy color as the text in the link bar.
5. Click the **OK** button, and then click below the horizontal line to deselect it. The horizontal line appears as a centered, thicker, shorter, navy line. See Figure 2-19.

Figure 2-19 **Horizontal line with new properties**

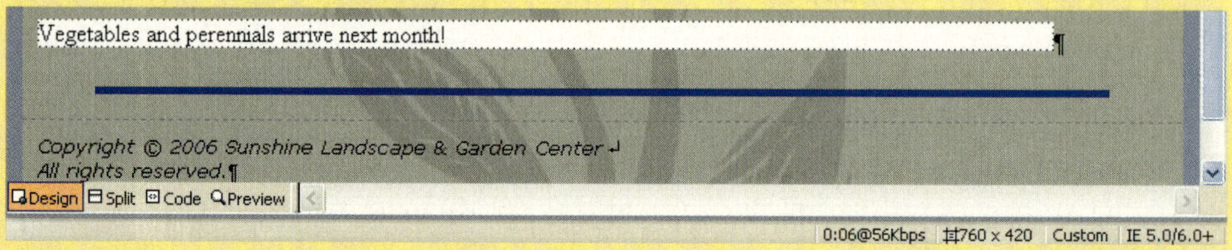

6. Click the **Save** button on the Standard toolbar to save the home page. Because a horizontal line is created with the HTML <hr> tag, you do not need to save it as an embedded picture file in the Web site.
7. Close the garden Web site, and then exit FrontPage.

In the next session, you will show Brett how to import a Web page into a Web site, create hyperlinks to Web pages and an e-mail address, and use pictures as hyperlinks.

Session 2.1 Quick Check

Review

1. If you do not specify a background color for a Web page, which color appears in the background when a browser opens the page?
2. What are the three popular file formats for pictures on the Internet? What are the primary characteristics and uses of each file type?
3. True or False: All Web browsers can display marquees in a Web page.
4. Explain why it is important to use the Estimated Time to Download pane when creating Web pages.
5. What are two important uses of alternative text?
6. True or False: You can change a color in a GIF picture to transparent.
7. True or False: You can specify a horizontal line's size as a percentage of the screen's width.

Session 2.2

Importing a Web Page into a Web Site

In Tutorial 1, you learned how to copy text from a Word document and insert it into a Web page, and how to insert a Word file into a Web page. When you perform these tasks, FrontPage converts the content to HTML and adds it to the Web page. Sometimes the content you need to add to your Web site already exists as an HTML document. This content may have been created using FrontPage or another program that creates HTML files. When you want to use a Web page that exists outside of your Web site, you can import it into the Web site. When you import a Web page into a Web site, you add a copy of the file that contains the Web page to your Web site. Importing a Web page saves you time and eliminates the need to retype material.

Clara McShane, the nursery's chief landscape designer, used Notepad to create a draft of the Garden Center page for the Web site. This page will contain links to pictures of current inventory at the nursery. Instead of retyping Clara's material, you will show Brett how to import Clara's document into the garden Web site.

Importing an Existing Web Page into a Web Site

Reference Window

- If necessary, open the Web site into which to import the Web page, and then display the Folder List.
- Click the folder in the Web site into which you want to import the file.
- Click File on the menu bar, click Import, and then click the Add File button in the Import dialog box. The Add File to Import List dialog box opens.
- Use the Look in list box to browse to the desired file, click the file to select it, and then click the Open button.
- Click the OK button in the Import dialog box to import the page.

After importing a Web page into a Web site, you tell Brett that he can use it just like any other Web page created by FrontPage.

To open the garden Web site and import an existing Web page into it:

1. Make sure you have your Data Files, start **FrontPage**, open the **garden** Web site from the location where your Web sites are stored and, if necessary, display the Pictures toolbar and dock it below the Formatting toolbar.

2. If necessary, click the **Toggle Pane** button on the Standard toolbar to display the Folder List.

   When you import a Web page into a Web site, you must select the folder into which you want to save the file. The Garden Center page will be stored in the Web site's root folder, so you will select the root folder before importing the page.

3. If necessary, click the Web site's root folder to select it.
4. Click **File** on the menu bar, and then click **Import** to open the Import dialog box.
5. Click the **Add File** button to open the Add File to Import List dialog box.
6. If necessary, click the **Look in** list arrow and change to the drive or folder that contains your Data Files, and then open the **Tutorial.02\Tutorial** folder.
7. Click **center.htm** to select this file, and then click the **Open** button. The Add File to Import List dialog box closes and the center.htm file appears in the Import dialog box. Clicking the Add Folder button lets you import a folder and all of its files into the Web site. Clicking the From Site button starts the Import Web Site Wizard, which you can use to import Web pages from a disk, network, or URL.

   Trouble? If you selected the wrong file to import, make sure that the file you selected by mistake is highlighted, click the Remove button in the Import dialog box, and then repeat Steps 5 through 7 to select the correct file.

8. Click the **OK** button. The Garden Center page, center.htm, is now in the garden Web site. See Figure 2-20.

Figure 2-20 **Garden Center page imported into the garden Web site**

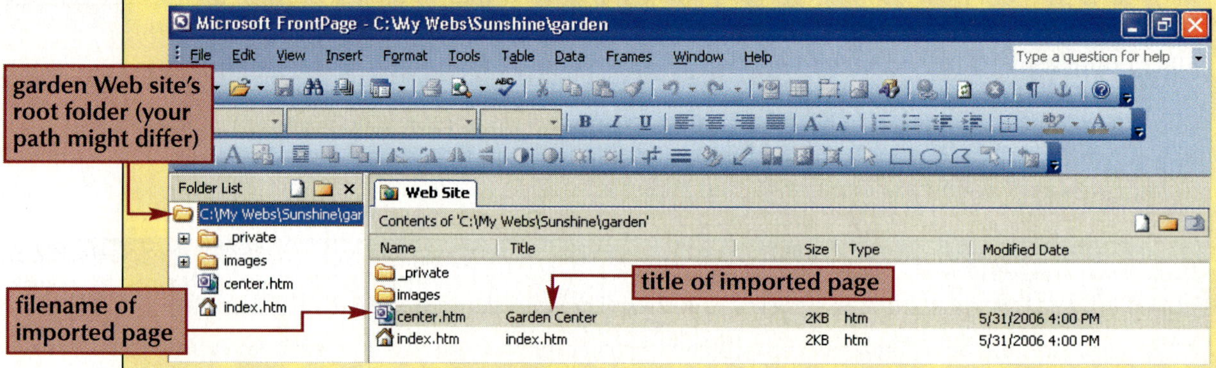

When Clara created the Garden Center page, she gave it a descriptive title, "Garden Center," using the HTML <title> </title> tags. The page's title appears in Folders view in the Title column. Brett notices that FrontPage used the title "index.htm" when it created the home page and the garden Web site. Because the title appears in the browser's title bar, "index.htm" is not a good choice. You tell Brett that he can change the title easily in Folders view.

To change a page's title in Folders view:

1. Click **index.htm** to select the file. FrontPage highlights the entire line of information about this file.
2. Click **index.htm** in the Title column to select the page title. The title is selected and FrontPage changes to editing mode by adding an insertion point.

3. With the title selected, type **Sunshine Landscape & Garden Center home page**, and then press the **Enter** key. FrontPage changes the title and selects the entire line again. If the text you entered exceeds the column width, an ellipsis (…) appears in the title. You can increase the width of the Title column to see the complete title.
4. If necessary, point to the right side of the Title column so the pointer changes to a ↔ shape, as shown in Figure 2-21.

Figure 2-21 **Increasing a column's width in Folders view**

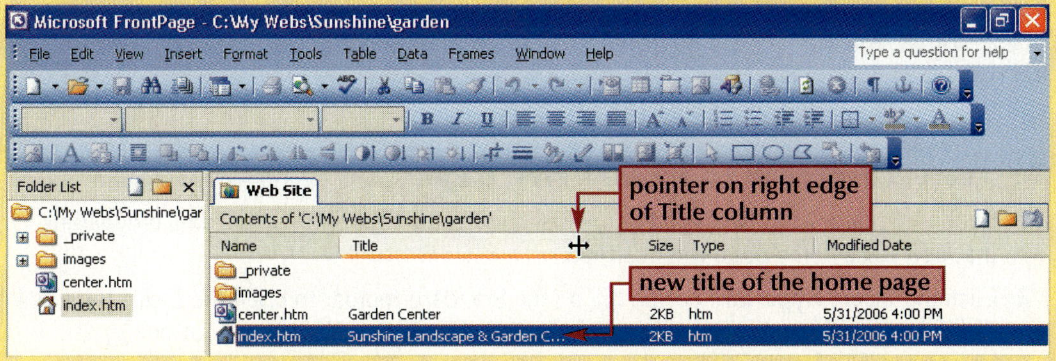

5. Double-click ↔ on the right side of the Title column. FrontPage resizes the Title column and displays the complete title. Because the width of the Title column increased, some other columns scrolled to the right of the screen. To see these columns, you would click the right arrow on the horizontal scroll bar.

Now that Brett has imported the Garden Center page into the garden Web site, he can open it just like any other Web page.

To open the imported Web page:

1. Double-click **center.htm** to open the partially completed Web page in Design view, and then close the Folder List. Notice that the Garden Center page appears with the default white background.

The first thing that Brett wants to do is link the home page and the Garden Center page to each other.

Linking to Other Web Pages

In Tutorial 1, you told Brett that a hyperlink is text or a picture in a Web page that, when clicked using a mouse, connects to related information located in the same Web page, the same Web site, or another Web site. The most common use of a hyperlink is to connect to different pages in the same Web site. When connecting Web pages with a hyperlink, the page that opens when the hyperlink is clicked is called the hyperlink's **target** or **target page**.

Reference Window

Creating a Hyperlink to an Existing Web Page in the Same Web Site

- Select the text or picture to use as the hyperlink.
- Click the Insert Hyperlink button on the Standard toolbar. If necessary, click the Existing File or Web Page button on the Link to bar.
- Browse to and then select the target of the hyperlink.
- Click the OK button.

Brett wants to create one hyperlink from the Garden Center page to the home page and another hyperlink from the home page to the Garden Center page to connect these pages to each other. You will show him how to use the link bar text that he created in Tutorial 1 to create the hyperlinks.

To create a hyperlink to another Web page:

1. Double-click the word **Home** in the link bar to select it. This text will become a hyperlink that opens the home page when clicked.
2. Click the **Insert Hyperlink** button on the Standard toolbar to open the Insert Hyperlink dialog box, and then, if necessary, click the **Existing File or Web Page** button on the Link to bar. See Figure 2-22.

Figure 2-22 **Insert Hyperlink dialog box**

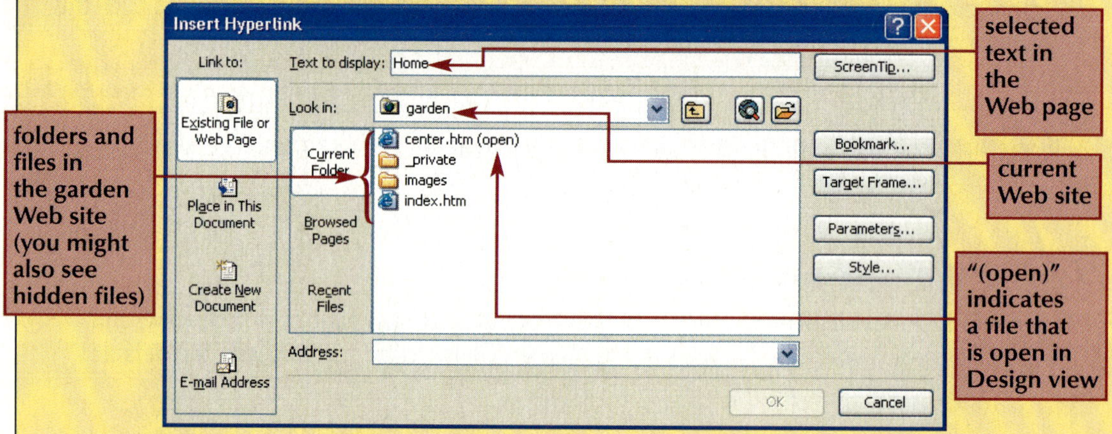

Trouble? If you see additional files and folders in the Insert Hyperlink dialog box, FrontPage might be configured to display hidden files and folders. This difference causes no problems.

The list box includes all of the folders and files in the garden Web site. The "center.htm (open)" entry indicates that this page is currently open in Design view.

Also notice that you can link to existing files in the current folder (in this case, the garden Web site), to browsed pages (pages you have opened in a Web browser), to recent files (files that you have recently opened in FrontPage), and to an e-mail address.

3. Click **index.htm** to select it as the target of the hyperlink. Notice that the Address list box now displays the filename for the selected page, index.htm.
4. Click the **OK** button to close the Insert Hyperlink dialog box and return to the center.htm page.
5. Click **Home** in the link bar to deselect the hyperlink. "Home" is now formatted as underlined text, which is the default format for a hyperlink.

6. Point to the **Home** hyperlink. The target of the hyperlink, "index.htm," appears on the status bar. The ScreenTip tells you that pressing and holding the Ctrl key and then clicking the hyperlink will open the hyperlink's target in Design view.
7. Save the center.htm page.

Brett created the hyperlink from the Garden Center page to the home page; now you will show him how to create the hyperlink from the home page to the Garden Center page. Although he could use the same method to create the return hyperlink, you decide to show Brett another method.

Creating a Hyperlink Using Drag and Drop

Drag and drop is another method you can use to create a hyperlink between pages in a Web site. By default, the title of the linked page (the target page) becomes the text for the hyperlink in the Web page that contains the hyperlink (the **source page**). Therefore, you might want to consider a title for a Web page that you can use later as the text for its hyperlink.

To use drag and drop to create a hyperlink, open the source page in Design view and then open the Folder List. Select the filename of the target page in the Folder List and drag the pointer to the location where you want to insert the hyperlink. When you release the mouse button, FrontPage creates a hyperlink using the target page's title. You can change the hyperlink's name by editing it after placing the hyperlink in the Web page.

Creating a Hyperlink Using Drag and Drop

Reference Window

- If necessary, open the source page in Design view.
- If necessary, click the Toggle Pane button on the Standard toolbar to display the Folder List.
- Drag the filename of the target page from the Folder List to the location in the source page where you want to create the hyperlink.
- Release the mouse button to create the hyperlink.

You ask Brett to create the hyperlink from the home page to the Garden Center page using drag and drop.

To create a hyperlink using drag and drop:

1. In the Garden Center page, point to the **Home** hyperlink in the link bar, press and hold the **Ctrl** key, click the **Home** hyperlink, and then release the **Ctrl** key. The home page opens in Design view.
2. Click the **Toggle Pane** button on the Standard toolbar. The Folder List opens and displays the files and folders in the garden Web site.
3. Click **center.htm** (the target page) in the Folder List to select it, and then hold down the left mouse button as you drag the pointer from the Folder List to the home page. The pointer changes to a ⃠ shape while you are moving the file out of the Folder List; it changes to a shape when it is in Design view. Do *not* release the mouse button yet.
4. While still holding down the mouse button, move the pointer to the left of the **G** in "Garden Center" in the link bar in the home page. See Figure 2-23.

Figure 2-23 **Creating the hyperlink to the Garden Center page**

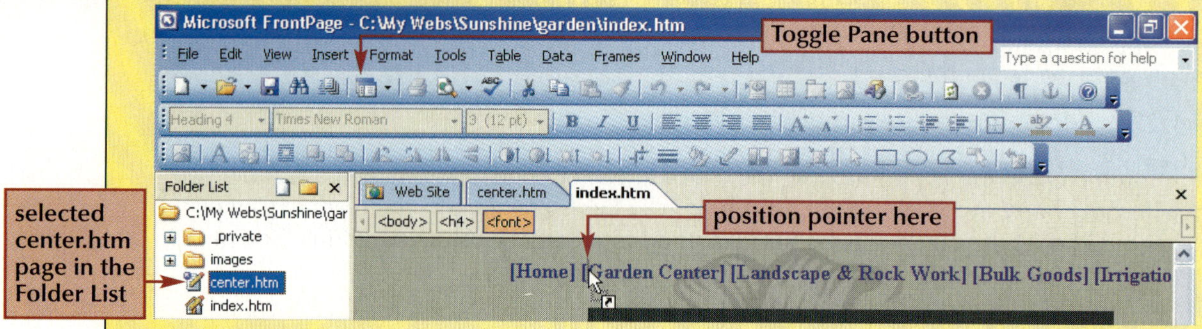

5. Release the mouse button to create the hyperlink. A Garden Center hyperlink is inserted into the link bar in the home page, using the page title from the center.htm page. See Figure 2-24. The text in the link bar now appears as "Garden CenterGarden Center" because the page title was inserted in front of the text already present in the link bar.

Figure 2-24 **Hyperlink added to the link bar**

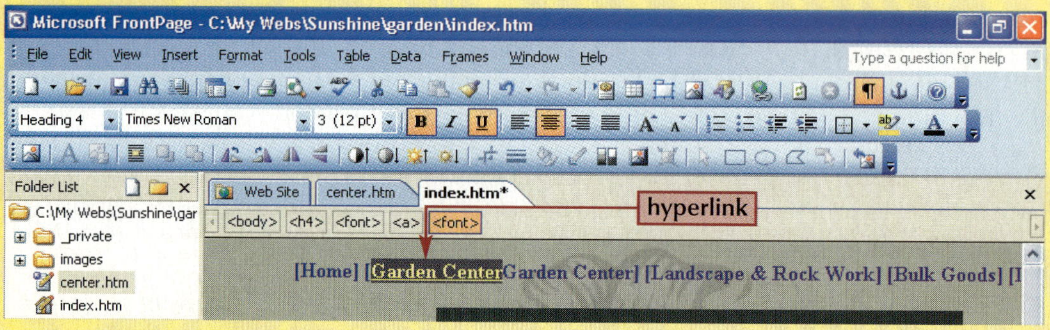

Next, remove the extra "Garden Center" text to create the desired entry in the link bar.

6. Select the **Garden Center** text that is *not* underlined in the link bar, and then press the **Delete** key to remove it. The Garden Center hyperlink (the underlined text) remains in the link bar.
7. Click to close the Folder List.
8. Save the home page.

Now Brett can test the hyperlinks between the home page and the Garden Center page in a browser.

To test hyperlinks between Web pages in a browser:

1. Click the **Preview** button on the Standard toolbar to open the home page in your browser. Notice that the Garden Center entry in the link bar is underlined, indicating that it is a hyperlink.
2. Point to the **Garden Center** hyperlink. The target of the hyperlink, the center.htm page, appears on the status bar to confirm that this hyperlink connects to a different Web page.
3. Click the **Garden Center** hyperlink in the link bar. The Garden Center Web page opens.

4. Click the **Home** hyperlink in the link bar of the Garden Center Web page to reopen the home page.
5. Close your browser and return to FrontPage.

Brett is excited about linking pages in the Web site. Next, you want to show Brett how to create a hyperlink to an e-mail address.

Creating a Hyperlink to an E-mail Address

A **mailto** is a hyperlink that contains an e-mail address. When a user clicks a mailto link in a Web page, the user's default e-mail program automatically opens and addresses a message to the address contained in the mailto. The user then can type the message and send it as usual.

When you type an e-mail address followed by a space in a Web page in Design view, FrontPage automatically creates a mailto and changes the appearance of the e-mail address to a hyperlink.

Creating a Mailto

Reference Window

- Click the location where you want to place the mailto, type the e-mail address, and then press the spacebar.

or

- Select the text to format as a mailto, and then click the Insert Hyperlink button on the Standard toolbar.
- In the Insert Hyperlink dialog box, click the E-mail Address button on the Link to bar.
- Type the target e-mail address in the E-mail address text box.
- If desired, type an optional subject in the Subject text box.
- Click the OK button.

Brett wants to format the nursery's name, which appears in the copyright information in the home page, as a mailto so visitors can click it to send an e-mail message to him. Because this text already exists, you'll need to show him how to format it as a hyperlink.

To create a mailto from existing text:

1. If necessary, scroll to the bottom of the home page, and then select the text **Sunshine Landscape & Garden Center**.
2. Click the **Insert Hyperlink** button on the Standard toolbar. The Insert Hyperlink dialog box opens.
3. Click the **E-mail Address** button on the Link to bar to select it. The options for working with mailtos appear in the dialog box.
4. Click the **E-mail address** text box, and then type your full e-mail address. (If you do not have an e-mail address, make one up.) As you begin typing, FrontPage adds "mailto:" to the beginning of your e-mail address.

   When you create a mailto using the Insert Hyperlink dialog box, you can also specify a subject that will appear automatically in all messages sent using the mailto link. To help Brett identify messages sent from the Web site from other messages sent to him, he can add the subject "Web Site" to the mailto link. When Brett receives the messages, he will be able to determine those messages sent from the Web site by the message subject.

5. Press the **Tab** key to move to the Subject text box, and then type **Web Site**. The mailto is complete.
6. Click the **OK** button to close the Insert Hyperlink dialog box. The text is underlined, indicating that you created a hyperlink.
7. Click the mailto link to deselect it, and then point to the mailto link you just created. The target of the hyperlink, which in this case is an e-mail address, appears on the status bar. Notice that the mailto contains your e-mail address, followed by a question mark and the subject you specified, "Web Site." See Figure 2-25.

Figure 2-25 Mailto link created in the home page

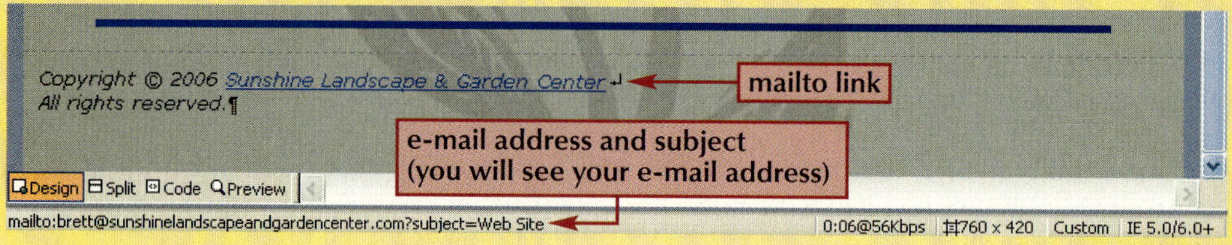

8. Save the home page.

Brett's e-mail address is now included in the home page. Next, Brett can test this feature in a browser.

To test a mailto:

1. Click the **Preview** button on the Standard toolbar to open the home page in the browser, and then press **Ctrl + End** to scroll to the bottom of the page.
2. Click the **Sunshine Landscape & Garden Center** link to start your default e-mail program and to open a new message. Figure 2-26 shows the New Message window for Microsoft Outlook Express (the default e-mail program for Internet Explorer). If your computer uses an e-mail program other than Outlook Express, your e-mail window will look different. Notice that Brett's e-mail address was entered automatically in the To field, and that the subject you specified, "Web Site," appears in the Subject field.

Figure 2-26 Microsoft Outlook Express New Message window

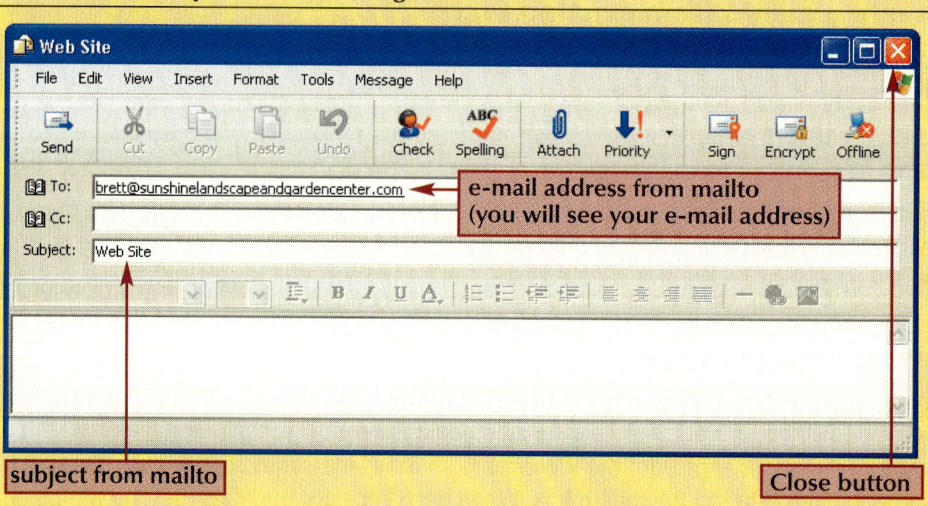

Trouble? If an Outlook Express dialog box opens and asks whether you want to specify a default e-mail program, click the No button.

Trouble? If an Internet Connection Wizard dialog box opens, click the Cancel button, and then click the Yes button to close the dialog box.

Trouble? If a Microsoft Outlook dialog box opens and indicates that no e-mail client is specified for your computer, click the OK button to continue.

Because Outlook Express started when you clicked the mailto link in the Web page, your test is complete. A Web site visitor who wants to send a message would type the message text and click the Send button to mail it. Because you are just testing the mailto to see whether it links to your e-mail program, rather than actually sending a message, you can close the New Message window.

3. Click the **Close** button ☒ on the New Message window title bar to return to the home page.
4. Click ☒ on the browser title bar to close it.

Now visitors can click the mailto link to send a message.

Using Pictures as Hyperlinks

You remind Brett that a picture can do more than enhance the appearance of a Web page. A picture can also contain a hyperlink that opens another Web page. There are two ways to use a picture as a hyperlink. The first method is to create an **image map**, which is a picture that contains one or more hotspots. A **hotspot** is an area of a picture that, when clicked, opens the hyperlink target. A hotspot can have a rectangular, circular, or polygonal shape. The second method is to format the entire picture as a hyperlink. Clicking any part of the picture opens the target of the hyperlink. You'll show Brett how to create an image map first.

Creating an Image Map

To demonstrate how to create an image map, you'll show Brett how to format the word "sunshine" in the logo in the Garden Center page as a hotspot that opens the home page.

Creating an Image Map

Reference Window

- Click the picture in which to create the hotspot to select it.
- Click the button for the desired hotspot shape on the Pictures toolbar.
- Click and hold down the mouse button while you drag the pointer to specify the desired size of the hotspot on the picture, and then release the mouse button. The Insert Hyperlink dialog box opens.
- Click the button on the Link to bar to specifiy the target of the hyperlink (an existing file or Web page, a place in the document, a new document, or an e-mail address), and then specify the target of the hyperlink on the page that opens.
- Click the OK button.

Because the content is rectangular in shape, Brett needs to create the hotspot as a rectangle.

To create a rectangular hotspot:

1. Click the **center.htm** tab at the top of the Contents pane, and then click the picture (the Sunshine logo) in the Garden Center page to select it.
2. Click the **Rectangular Hotspot** button on the Pictures toolbar, and then position the pointer in the upper-left corner of the picture. The pointer changes to a shape when it is pointing to the picture. See Figure 2-27.

Figure 2-27 **Creating a hotspot**

3. Hold down the left mouse button and drag the pointer down and to the right until you have enclosed the word "sunshine" and the leaf graphic in the hotspot box. As you drag the pointer, the box that appears on the picture indicates the size and location of the hotspot.
4. Release the mouse button. The Insert Hyperlink dialog box opens. If necessary, click the **Existing File or Web Page** button on the Link to bar.
5. Double-click **index.htm (open)** in the list to select the home page as the target of the hotspot. The Insert Hyperlink dialog box closes and the rectangle on the picture indicates the location of the hotspot you just created.

   Trouble? If your hotspot appears in the wrong location, press the Delete key to remove it, select the picture, and then repeat Steps 2 through 5, or use the sizing handles on the hotspot to resize it.
6. Save the Garden Center page.

Brett successfully created the hotspot that opens the home page. Now users of the garden Web site can click either the word "sunshine" in the logo or the word "Home" in the link bar to open the home page.

Highlighting Hotspots in a Picture

When you create a hotspot, you usually can see its shape while it is selected. Depending on the picture, however, it might be difficult to see the hotspot or hotspots it contains. By highlighting a picture's hotspots, you can see their location more clearly and confirm their placement.

Highlighting Hotspots in a Picture

Reference Window

- Click the picture that contains the hotspot(s) to select it.
- Click the Highlight Hotspots button on the Pictures toolbar.
- Click the Highlight Hotspots button again to turn off the highlights.

Next, you will check the location of the hotspot and verify its placement.

To highlight the hotspot:

1. Make sure that the picture is still selected, and then click the **Highlight Hotspots** button on the Pictures toolbar. The hotspot in the picture appears as a dark square in a white picture. See Figure 2-28.

Figure 2-28 Highlighting hotspots in a picture

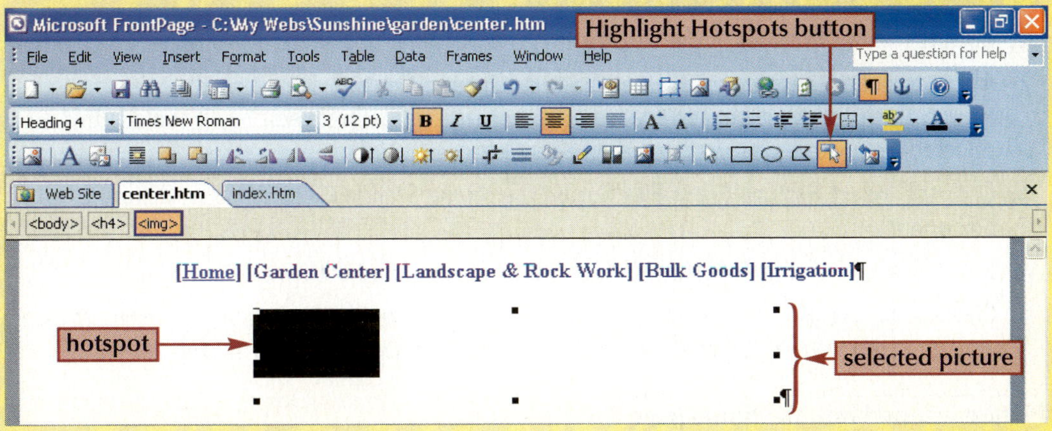

Trouble? If the hotspot is selected when you click the Highlight Hotspots button, it will appear as a solid black image, as shown in Figure 2-28. If the hotspot is not selected, it will appear as a white object with a black outline.

2. Click the **Highlight Hotspots** button to turn off the hotspot highlights, and then press **Ctrl + Home** to deselect the picture and scroll to the top of the page.
3. Point to the word "sunshine" in the picture, which is the hotspot. Notice that the filename for this hyperlink—index.htm—appears on the status bar, confirming that it is a hyperlink.

Next, Brett will test the hotspot in the browser to verify that it works correctly.

To test a hotspot in the browser:

1. Click the **Preview** button on the Standard toolbar to open the Garden Center page in a browser.
2. Point to the word "sunshine" in the picture. The pointer changes to a shape, and the filename for the hyperlink appears on the status bar; both of these changes indicate that the word "sunshine" is a hyperlink.
3. Click the word "sunshine" in the picture to open the home page.

4. Click **Garden Center** in the link bar in the home page to return to the Garden Center page.
5. Close your browser.

The hotspot in the picture provides users with another way to return to the site's home page.

Inserting a Picture Hyperlink into a Web Page

Next, you'll show Brett how to use an entire picture as a hyperlink. The graphic designer created small pictures for each page in the Web site. You'll insert these pictures in place of the text that you created in the link bar. Brett hopes that the graphics will be more visually interesting than the text.

To insert a picture into a Web page:

1. Click the **index.htm** tab at the top of the Contents pane to switch to this page.
2. At the top of the home page, select the text **[Garden Center]**, including the brackets around the words, but not the spaces on either side of the brackets. You'll replace this selected text with a picture that has the same text.
3. Click the **Insert Picture From File** button on the Standard toolbar. The Picture dialog box opens.
4. If necessary, open the **Tutorial.02\Tutorial** folder included with your Data Files.
5. Click the **gc_pic.gif** file to select it, and then click the **Insert** button. As shown in Figure 2-29, a picture with the text "Garden Center" replaces the text you selected in Step 2.

Figure 2-29 **Picture inserted into the home page**

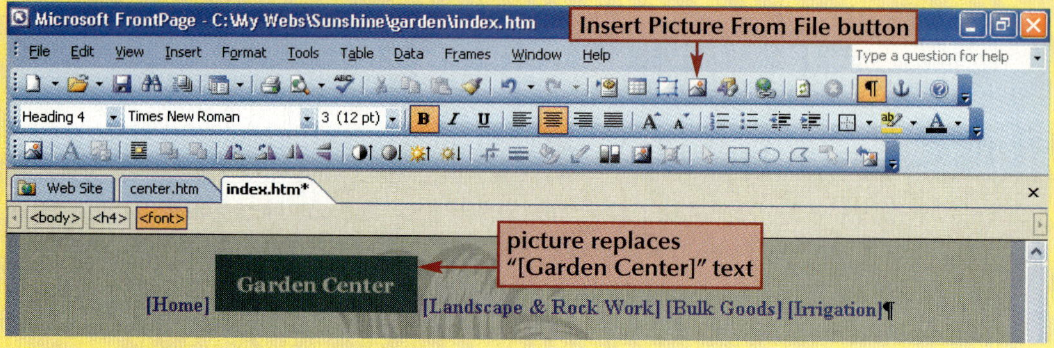

Now that Brett has inserted the picture, you can show him how to format it as a hyperlink. The target of the hyperlink will be the center.htm page in the Web site; clicking anywhere on the picture will open the Garden Center page. Formatting a picture as a hyperlink is different from creating an image map, which only uses the specified part of the picture (the hotspot) as the hyperlink.

To format the picture as a hyperlink:

1. Click the Garden Center picture to select it.
2. Click the **Insert Hyperlink** button on the Standard toolbar. The Insert Hyperlink dialog box opens.
3. If necessary, click the **Existing File or Web Page** button on the Link to bar. The files and folders in the garden Web site appear in the dialog box. The target of the hyperlink is the center.htm page, so you'll select this page.
4. Click **center.htm (open)** in the list box, and then click the **OK** button. The picture is formatted as a hyperlink that opens the Garden Center page.
5. Save the home page and save the gc_pic.gif file in the Web site's images folder.

To test the hyperlink, you ask Brett to open the home page in a browser.

To test the picture hyperlink:

1. Click the **Preview** button on the Standard toolbar. The home page opens in a browser.
2. Click the Garden Center picture at the top of the page. The Garden Center page opens.
3. Click the word "sunshine" in the picture on the Garden Center page. The home page opens.
4. Close your browser.

Brett likes the picture in the link bar better than the plain text. When you complete the Review Assignments at the end of this tutorial, you will replace the remaining text entries in the link bars on the home and Garden Center pages with pictures and format them as hyperlinks.

Examining HTML for a Picture Hyperlink and an Image Map

Brett is curious about the differences in the HTML document between using an entire picture as a hyperlink and using a part of a picture as a hyperlink. To explain the differences, you decide to show him the HTML documents for the home page and the Garden Center page.

To view the HTML documents and examine the picture hyperlinks:

1. With the home page displayed in Design view, click the Garden Center picture to select it, and then click the **Show Code View** button Code at the bottom of the Contents pane. The HTML document that creates the home page opens. Figure 2-30 shows the HTML <a> </a> tags that create the hyperlink from the gc_pic.gif file to the center.htm page. Notice that the <img> tag is nested in the anchor tags.

Figure 2-30 HTML document for the home page

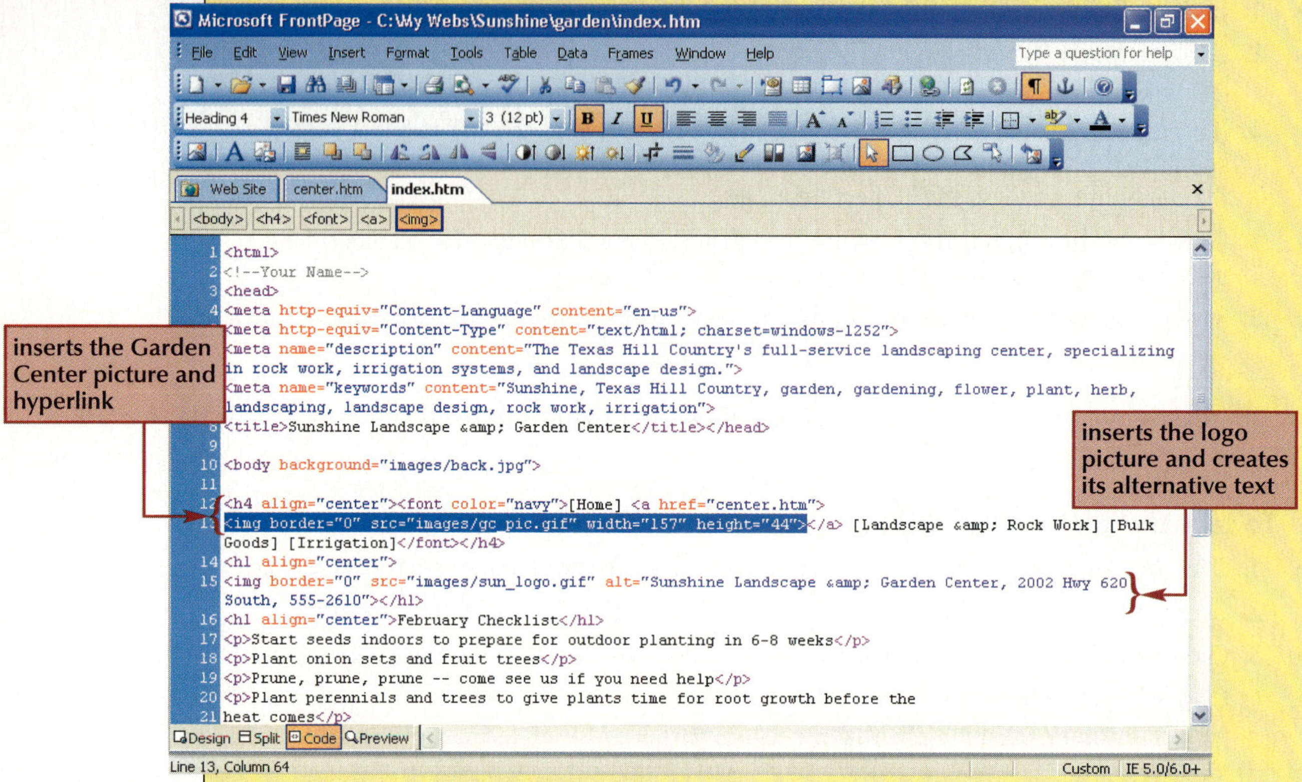

The second <img> tag in this document creates the logo at the top of the page. Notice the alt attribute, which contains the alternative text you added to this picture.

2. Click the **center.htm** tab at the top of the Contents pane, and then change to Code view for this page. Figure 2-31 shows the HTML <map> </map> tags that create the rectangular hotspot in the logo. Notice that the shape property defines the area as "rect" (for rectangle) and that the coords property defines the pixel locations for the four corners of the rectangular hotspot (your coordinates might be slightly different). The href property identifies the target of the hyperlink, index.htm, which is the home page.

Figure 2-31 HTML document for the Garden Center page

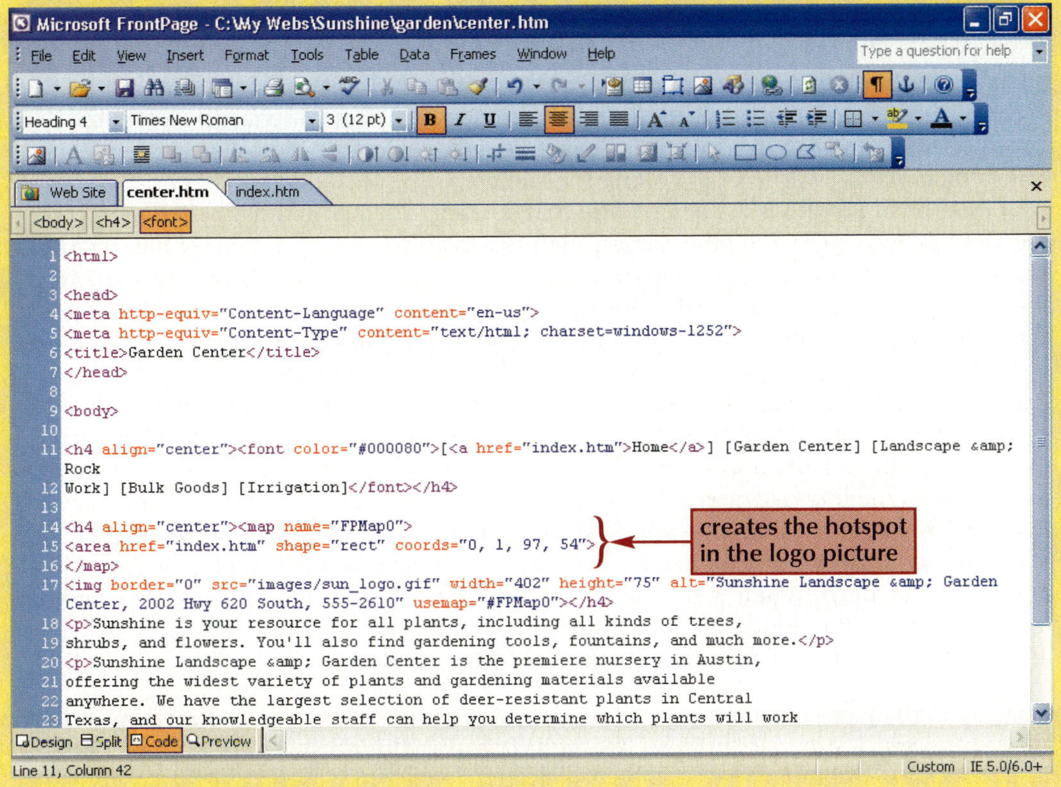

3. Return to Design view for the center.htm and index.htm pages.
4. Close the garden Web site, and then exit FrontPage.

In the next session, you'll show Brett how to create a small version of a picture that contains a hyperlink to the original picture. You'll also teach Brett how to change a picture's characteristics, create an animated button that contains a hyperlink, use a page transition, and create animated text in a Web page.

Session 2.2 Quick Check

Review

1. True or False: You can import a folder and its contents into a Web site.
2. What are three common targets of a hyperlink?
3. What is a source page? What is a target page?
4. What is a mailto, and what happens when you click one in a Web page?
5. What are the three shapes of hotspots that you can create using FrontPage?
6. What is the difference between an image map and a picture that is formatted as a hyperlink?

Session 2.3

Creating a Thumbnail Picture

So far in this book, you have included pictures in your Web pages to increase visual interest and create hyperlinks to other pages. You can use FrontPage to change a picture's appearance in other ways, as well. For example, you can create a smaller version of a picture, a picture with washed-out colors, or a picture with special edges.

A **thumbnail picture** is a small picture that contains a hyperlink to a larger version of the same picture, or to any other target, such as a Web page. Using a thumbnail picture is appropriate when some users might not need the larger version. Users who want to view the larger picture can click the thumbnail picture, which contains a hyperlink that opens the larger picture. Thumbnail pictures are commonly used in Web pages that contain catalog items, such as a clothing or shoe store. Using thumbnail pictures reduces the download time of the Web page for all users, especially for users with dial-up connections.

The hyperlink in a thumbnail picture might connect to a picture file or to a Web page that contains the picture and some text. When the thumbnail's target is a picture file (such as a GIF file), the browser opens the picture file; the user must then click the browser's Back button to return to the previous Web page. If the hyperlink opens a Web page that contains the larger picture, the page can include hyperlinks to other Web pages, just like any other Web page. When you create a thumbnail of a larger picture, FrontPage automatically creates the thumbnail picture, inserts it in place of the larger picture, and then creates a hyperlink from the thumbnail picture to the larger picture.

Reference Window

Creating a Thumbnail Picture

- If necessary, insert the full-size picture into the Web page in the desired location.
- Select the picture.
- Click the Auto Thumbnail button on the Pictures toolbar.

Brett received a picture of a map to the nursery's location from the graphic designer and has asked you to show him how to insert it into the home page. To save space in the home page and to decrease its download time, you suggest that he instead use a thumbnail of the map with a hyperlink to the full-size map.

To open the home page and create the thumbnail picture:

1. Make sure you have your Data Files, start **FrontPage**, open the **garden** Web site from the location where your Web sites are stored, open the **index.htm** page in Design view, and, if necessary, display the Pictures toolbar and dock it below the Formatting toolbar.
2. Click at the end of the marquee, press the **Enter** key to create a new paragraph, and then click the **Center** button on the Formatting toolbar to center the paragraph.
3. Click the **Insert Picture From File** button on the Standard toolbar, open the **Tutorial.02\Tutorial** folder included with your Data Files, and then double-click **map.jpg**. The picture of a map to the nursery is inserted into the home page. The picture is large, and adding it to the home page increased the download time of the home page from seven to 14 seconds (at 56 Kbps).
4. Click the map picture to select it.
5. Click the **Auto Thumbnail** button on the Pictures toolbar to create the thumbnail picture. See Figure 2-32.

Thumbnail picture added to the home page **Figure 2-32**

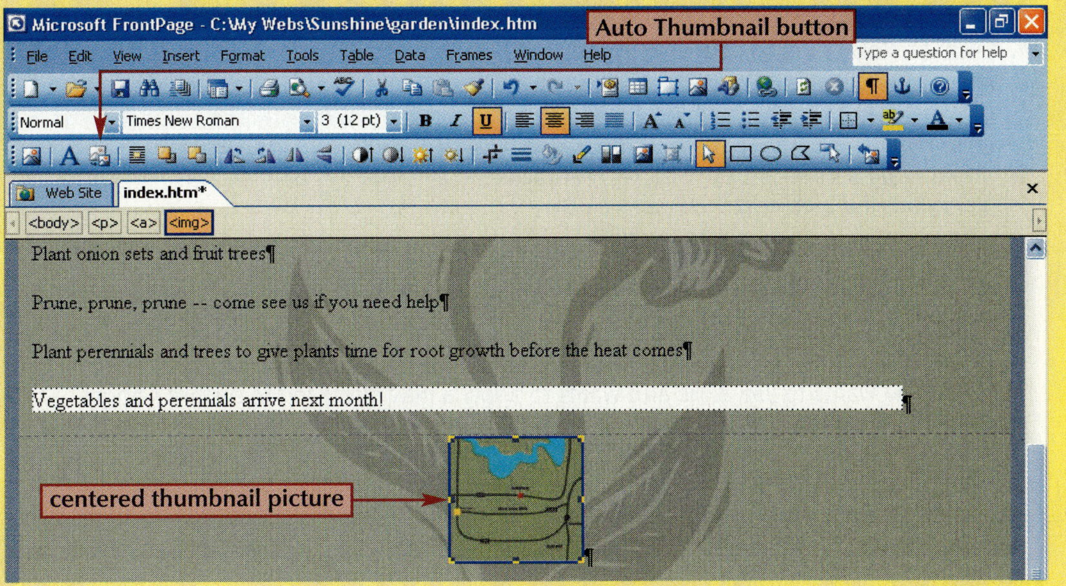

The thumbnail picture replaces the full-size picture in the home page. FrontPage created a hyperlink from the thumbnail to the map.jpg file in the Tutorial.02\Tutorial folder included with your Data Files, which is the location of the original, full-size picture from which the thumbnail was created. When you save the home page, you will need to save both pictures in the garden Web site. Before you save the pictures, however, Brett wants you to show him how to change the characteristics of the thumbnail picture.

Changing Picture Characteristics

You can use FrontPage to change many picture characteristics. For example, you can convert a picture to black and white, rotate it, change its contrast or brightness level, add a beveled edge to the picture, or wash out a picture. When you **wash out** a picture, you reduce its brightness and contrast to create a faded appearance. You can also change a picture's position; for example, you can position it in front of or behind text and other page elements.

In viewing the thumbnail picture, Brett wonders if site visitors will know to click the picture to display a larger version of the map. You tell Brett that he can add text on top of the picture to indicate its function. Because the map image is dark, it would be appropriate to wash out the colors to make the text more readable.

To change picture characteristics:

1. With the thumbnail picture still selected, click the **Color** button on the Pictures toolbar. A menu opens, providing four options: Automatic, Grayscale, Black & White, and Wash Out. Only the Grayscale and Wash Out effects are enabled for a color picture. If you select the Grayscale option, FrontPage will convert the picture to use shades of gray instead of colors. When it is enabled, the Black & White option lets you change a picture's colors to black and white, with no shading. This option is available for pictures without any shading.

2. Click **Grayscale**. The picture changes to light and dark shades of gray instead of colors.
3. Click the button, and then click **Grayscale** to restore the colors to the thumbnail picture.
4. Click the **Rotate Left 90°** button on the Pictures toolbar. The picture flips on its left side.
5. Click the **Rotate Right 90°** button to rotate the picture 90 degrees to the right, which returns the picture to its original orientation.
6. Click the button, and then click **Wash Out**. Notice that the colors in the picture become faded, but the picture still contains colors.
7. Click the **Restore** button on the Pictures toolbar to remove the wash-out effect and restore the picture to its original state. Clicking the Restore button removes all previously applied, unsaved picture effects.

   Brett believes that the wash-out effect provides the best appearance for the thumbnail picture, so he wants to use it. He also wants to apply a new effect to the picture's edges.
8. Click the **Undo** button on the Standard toolbar to return to the thumbnail picture with the wash-out effect.
9. Click the **Bevel** button on the Pictures toolbar. Notice that the edges of the picture change to include a raised effect. The picture now has a wash-out effect and a beveled edge.
10. Click the **Save** button on the Standard toolbar to open the Save Embedded Files dialog box. You need to save the original picture file, map.jpg, and the thumbnail picture, which FrontPage automatically named map_small.jpg, in the images folder of the garden Web site. FrontPage names a thumbnail by appending "_small" to the filename of the full-size picture.
11. Make sure that the files will be saved in the garden Web site's images folder, and then click the **OK** button. The picture files are saved in the garden Web site.

Next, you'll show Brett how to add text on top of a picture so users can easily identify its function.

Adding Text on Top of a Picture

When you insert a picture that you plan to use as a hyperlink into a Web page, a good design practice is to add descriptive text on top of the picture to identify its function. You place text on a picture by selecting the picture and then using the Text button on the Pictures toolbar to add the text. To add text on a picture, the picture must be saved as a GIF file. FrontPage will convert the picture to a GIF file, if necessary, when you try to add text on it.

Reference Window

Adding Text on a Picture

- Click the picture to select it.
- Click the Text button on the Pictures toolbar to open a text box on top of the selected picture. If necessary, click the OK button to convert the picture to a GIF file.
- Type the desired text. If necessary, press the Enter key to start a new line, and format the text as desired.
- Click anywhere in the Web page to close the text box.

Brett wants to add text on the picture to indicate that it opens a map to the nursery. You ask him to use the Formatting toolbar to format the text so it is easy to read.

To add text on a picture:

1. If necessary, click the thumbnail picture to select it. Sizing handles appear around the edge of the picture.
2. Click the **Text** button on the Pictures toolbar. Because the thumbnail is a JPEG file, a FrontPage message box opens and tells you that you'll need to convert the picture to a GIF file.
3. Click the **OK** button in the message box to convert the picture to a GIF file. A text box with eight sizing handles and an insertion point opens on top of the picture.
4. Type **Map to**, press the **Enter** key to start a new line, and then type **Sunshine**. This text will appear on top of the picture. By default, text is centered, but it looks left-aligned when you are in editing mode.
5. Click outside the picture to deselect the picture and the text box, and then click the text on the picture to select the picture and the text box. Sizing handles appear around the picture and the text box. The text isn't vertically centered on the image. You can resize a text box using a sizing handle or by dragging it to a new location. You'll move the text box up.
6. Click anywhere in the text box and hold down the left mouse button, drag the text box up so it looks like the one shown in Figure 2-33, and then release the mouse button.

Figure 2-33 Text added on thumbnail picture

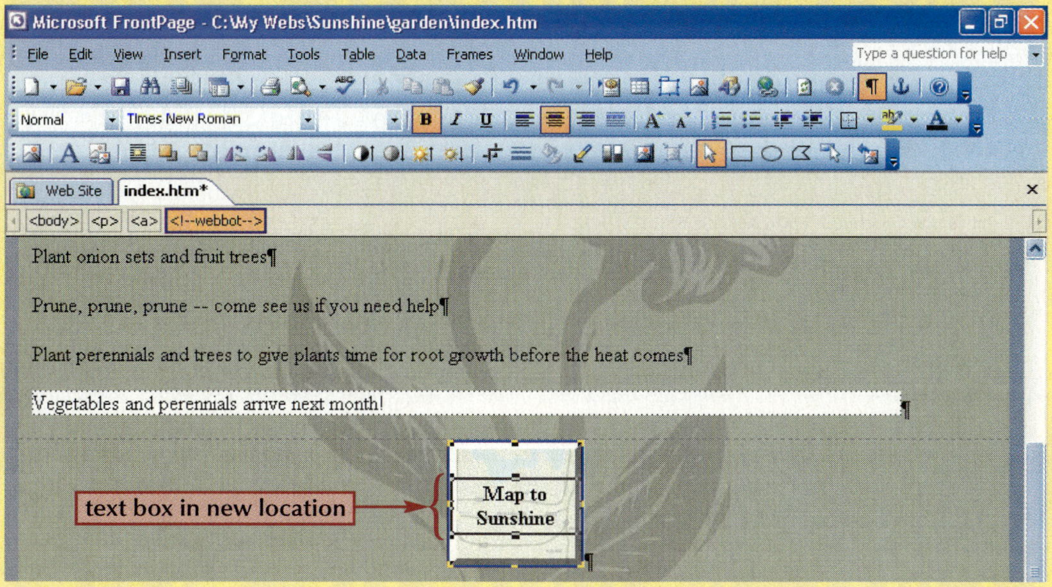

Trouble? If you click in the text box and release the left mouse button, you will change to editing mode, which displays an insertion point. If this problem occurs, repeat Steps 5 and 6.

When you add text on a picture, the text is not treated as regular text in the HTML document; the text box is coded as an image map. However, you can format the text just like any other text in a Web page. Brett wants to change the font color and style of the text to make it more prominent. After he makes this change, you'll show Brett the HTML document so he understands the difference between text in a Web page, alternative text for a picture, and an image map that contains text.

To change the font color and style of the text:

1. Click the text **Map to Sunshine**. The insertion point appears in the text and the text box changes to editing mode.
2. Use the mouse to select the text **Map to Sunshine**.
3. Click the **list arrow** for the Font Color button on the Formatting toolbar to open the color palette, and then click the **Navy** color in the Document Colors section. The text that you added on top of the thumbnail picture changes from black to navy, but you won't see this change until you deselect the text.
4. Click the **Italic** button on the Formatting toolbar to change the text to italic.
5. Click outside the picture to deselect it and the text box. The completed thumbnail picture appears in Figure 2-34.

Figure 2-34 **Completed thumbnail picture**

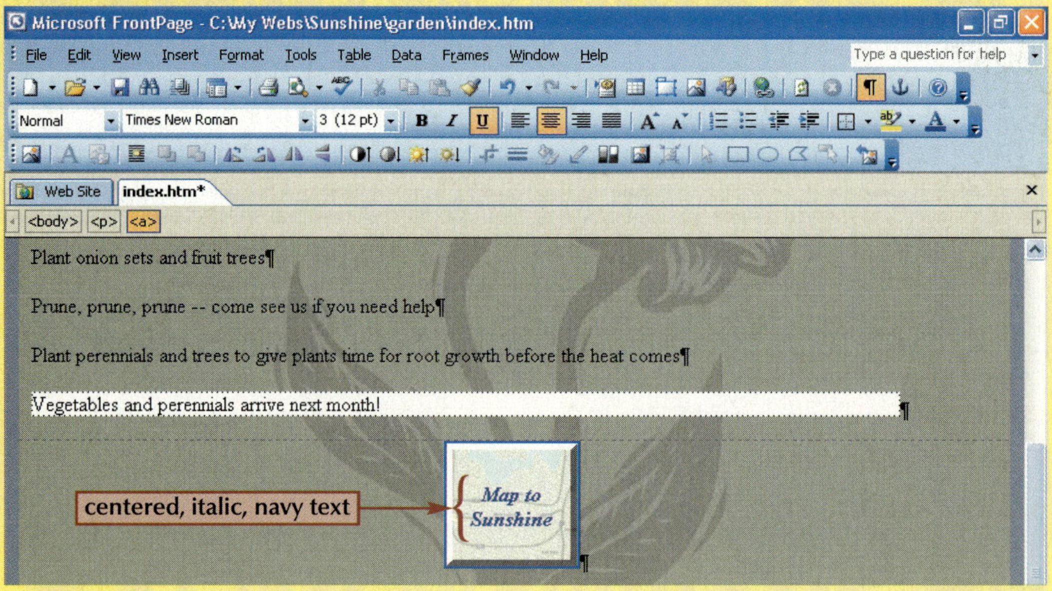

6. Save the home page. Because you converted the thumbnail to a GIF file, you need to save the map_small.gif file in the garden Web site. Make sure that the images folder is selected in the Save Embedded Files dialog box, and then click the **OK** button.

Now Brett has created a thumbnail picture, changed several of its characteristics, and added text on it. You ask him to test the thumbnail picture to make sure the hyperlink works correctly and opens the full-size map picture.

To test the thumbnail picture:

1. Click the **Preview** button on the Standard toolbar to open the home page in a browser, and then scroll to the bottom of the page (if necessary) so you can see the thumbnail picture.
2. Point to the thumbnail picture. The pointer changes to a shape. The path on the status bar indicates that this picture contains a hyperlink to the map.jpg file.

3. Click the thumbnail picture. The map.jpg file opens in your browser. The URL in the Address bar indicates that this page is a JPEG file and not an HTML document. Because you opened a picture file and not a Web page with hyperlinks, you will need to use your browser's Back button to return to the home page.
4. Click your browser's **Back** button to return to the home page, and then close your browser.

To return to the previous Web page, you had to click your browser's Back button. Some Web users might not know to do this, so you tell Brett that he will need to provide a hyperlink to return to the home page. To do so, he needs to include the full-size map picture in a Web page. You already created a Web page that contains the map picture, so Brett only needs to import that page into the garden Web site and then create the appropriate hyperlink.

To import the Web page into the garden Web site:

1. Click the **Web Site** tab on the top of the Contents pane, click the **Toggle Pane** button on the Standard toolbar to display the Folder List, and then make sure the garden Web site's root folder is selected.
2. Click **File** on the menu bar, and then click **Import** to open the Import dialog box.
3. Click the **Add File** button to open the Add File to Import List dialog box, open the **Tutorial.02\Tutorial** folder included with your Data Files, and then double-click **map_page.htm**. The map_page.htm file is listed in the Import dialog box.
4. Click the **OK** button to import the Web page into the garden Web site.

With the Web page imported into the garden Web site, you are ready to show Brett how to add the link back to the home page. First, he'll need to change the link from the thumbnail picture in the home page to the imported Map to Sunshine Landscape & Garden Center page (map_page.htm). Then he'll need to create the link from the Map page to the home page.

To change the hyperlink for the thumbnail picture:

1. Click the **index.htm** tab to switch to the home page in Design view, and then close the Folder List.
2. Right-click the thumbnail picture (not the "Map to Sunshine" text) to select it and open the shortcut menu, click **Hyperlink Properties**, and then, if necessary, click the **Existing File or Web page** button on the Link to bar. The Address text box displays the current hyperlink to the map.jpg file in the Web site's images folder.

   Trouble? If the Insert Hyperlink dialog box opens and the Address text box is empty, then you right-clicked the picture's text box. Click the Cancel button, and then repeat Step 2.
3. Click **map_page.htm** in the list box to set this page as the target of the hyperlink, and then click the **OK** button to close the Edit Hyperlink dialog box.
4. Save the home page.

After changing the target of the hyperlink, Brett needs to test the page to verify that the hyperlink from the thumbnail picture opens the correct Web page.

To test the hyperlink from the thumbnail picture:

1. Click the **Preview** button on the Standard toolbar.
2. If necessary, scroll down the home page until you see the thumbnail picture, and then click the Map to Sunshine picture to open the Map page. The URL in the Address bar specifies the map_page.htm Web page, and not the map.jpg file. The page doesn't include a hyperlink back to the home page yet, so you will need to add one.
3. Close your browser.
4. Right-click the thumbnail picture (not the "Map to Sunshine" text) to open the shortcut menu, and then click **Follow Hyperlink**. The map_page.htm file opens in Design view.

Brett successfully created the link from the home page to the Map page. Now he needs to complete the link in the other direction—from the Map page to the home page. You tell Brett that a fun way to do this is to use an interactive button.

Creating an Interactive Button

You have already shown Brett how to create hyperlinks from text and pictures. Another way to create a hyperlink is to use an interactive button. An **interactive button** is a button that displays special effects to change its appearance depending on how the user interacts with it. When the user clicks the button, it opens the target location. You can set special effects from a list of available effects, or you can use the custom option to create a picture that changes on mouse over. **Mouse over**, or **mouse fly over**, is the act of moving the pointer over an interactive button or picture. When you point to an interactive button, the appearance of the button changes to match the mouse-over effect specified for that button.

Brett wants you to create an interactive button in the Map page that changes on mouse over and contains a hyperlink that opens the home page.

Reference Window

Creating an Interactive Button in a Web Page

- Click the location in the Web page to insert the interactive button.
- Click Insert on the menu bar, and then click Interactive Button. The Interactive Buttons dialog box opens.
- On the Button tab, select the type of button you want to create. Select the default text in the Text text box, and then type the text that you want to appear on the button. Finally, click the Browse button to select the target of the hyperlink.
- If desired, click the Text tab to change the default font, font style, font size, font color, and alignment of the button.
- If desired, click the Image tab to change the button's size, characteristics, background color, or transparency.
- Click the OK button.

Brett wants the interactive button to display the text "Return to Home Page," to contain a hyperlink that opens the home page, and to use coordinated colors for the interactive button's effects.

To create an interactive button:

1. Click the blank paragraph between the logo picture and the map picture.
2. Click **Insert** on the menu bar, and then click **Interactive Button**. The Interactive Buttons dialog box opens.

   The Text text box displays the default text, "Button Text," which you will change to "Return to Home Page." Then you will preview several buttons to view their colors and effects by selecting a button in the Buttons list box and pointing to the sample button that appears in the Preview box.
3. Select the text **Button Text** in the Text text box, and then type **Return to Home Page**. This text will appear on the button to indicate its function. As you type, notice that the sample button in the Preview box is updated, as shown in Figure 2-35.

Interactive Buttons dialog box **Figure 2-35**

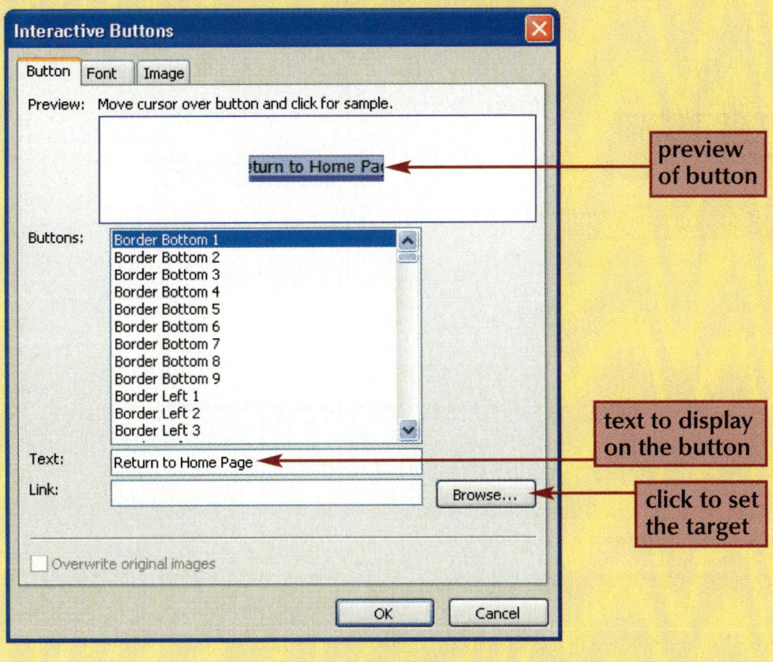

The text you entered exceeds the current button's size, so you will need to change the button's size. You change the button's size using the Image tab. However, because changing the button type returns the button to its default dimensions, you should change the button size as your last task so you don't have to resize it twice.

4. Click a few of the button types in the Buttons list box and preview their samples. Notice that the buttons have different default shapes and color combinations.

   Brett likes the Embossed Capsule 1 button because its color coordinates well with the map picture in the page.
5. Scroll the Buttons list as necessary, and then click **Embossed Capsule 1**. (The button types are listed alphabetically.)

   Next, you'll select the button's target.
6. Click the **Browse** button. The Edit Hyperlink dialog box opens. If necessary, click the **Existing File or Web page** button on the Link to bar.
7. Click **index.htm (open)** in the list, and then click the **OK** button.

Next, Brett needs to change the default size of the button so all of the text that appears on it is visible. You ask him to make this change using the Image tab.

To change the interactive button's size:

1. Click the **Image** tab. If you know the exact size in pixels for the button you want to create, you can enter those values in the Width and Height text boxes. In most cases, however, you'll need to increase or decrease the button size by viewing the changes as you make them.
2. Click the **Width** up arrow several times and watch the sample button in the Preview box. As you click the Width up arrow, the width of the button increases. Keep clicking the **Width** up arrow until you can see all of the button text. (You will need to change the width to approximately 140 pixels to accommodate the text.) See Figure 2-36.

Figure 2-36 **Revised button size**

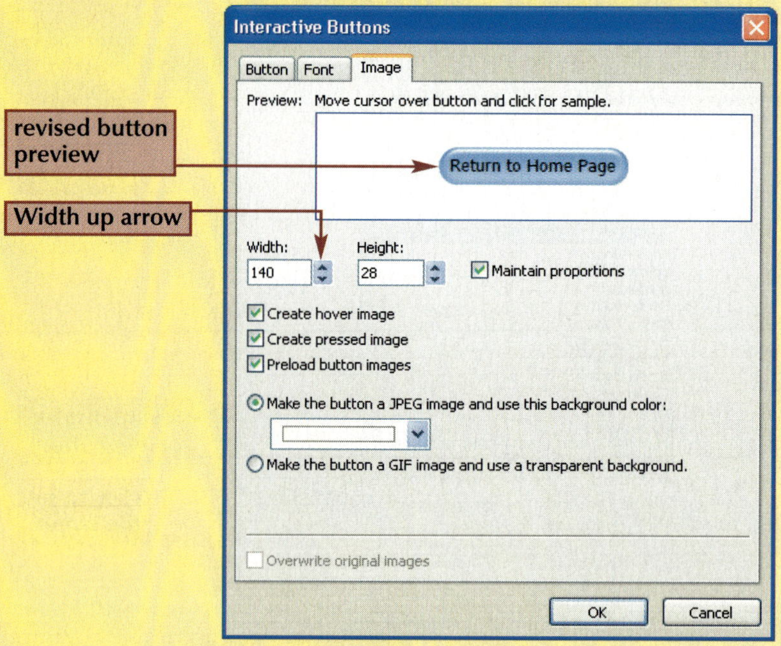

Now all of the text is visible on the button. The last change that you'll ask Brett to make is to change the button's text color. You tell him that he can set three different colors for a button's text: inactive (original), hover, or clicked (pressed).

To change the button's effects:

1. Click the **Font** tab to display those options. The message at the top of the Font tab indicates that you can move the pointer over and click the button in the Preview box to view its behavior in the Web page.
2. Click the **Original Font Color** list arrow, and then click the **Navy** color. When the button is inactive, the button's text will be navy.
3. Click the **Hovered Font Color** list arrow, and then click the **Maroon** color. When you point to the button, the text color will change to maroon.

4. Click the **Pressed Font Color** list arrow, and then click the **Fuchsia** color. When you click the button, the text color will change to fuchsia. The completed Font tab appears in Figure 2-37.

Revised button effects **Figure 2-37**

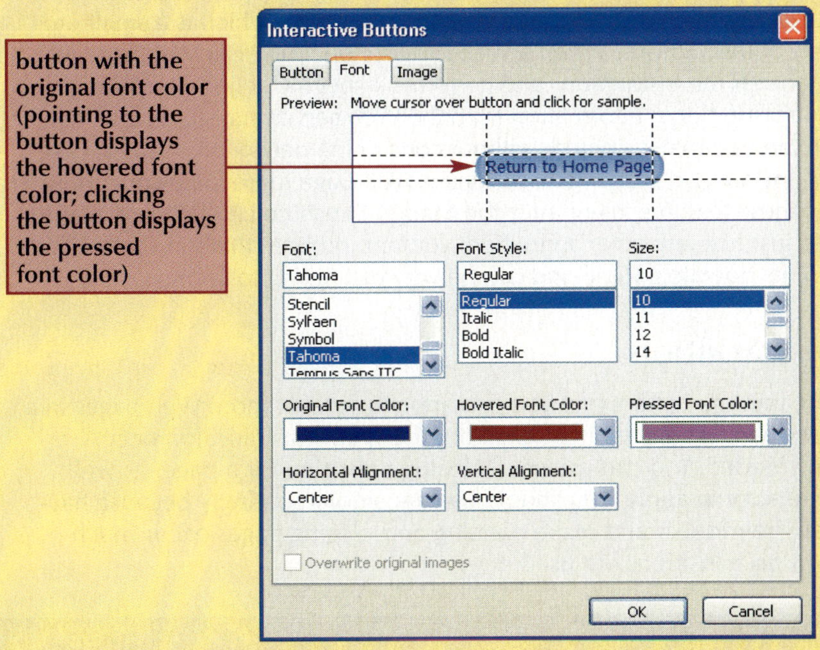

5. Point to and then click the sample button in the Preview box to view your changes. If you need to make any changes to the button, you could do so. You could also use this tab to change the font, font style, and font size of the button text.

The interactive button is complete, so Brett can close the dialog box and test the changes in a browser.

To test the interactive button:

1. Click the **OK** button to close the Interactive Buttons dialog box and to insert the button into the Map page.
2. Save the Map page, and save the button files created by FrontPage for the interactive button in the Web site's images folder. Three picture files are created to represent each state of the interactive button: original, hovered, and pressed.
3. Preview the Map page in a browser, and then point to and click the interactive button, noting the effects for each situation. When you click the interactive button, the home page opens.
4. Click the thumbnail picture to return to the Map page, and then close your browser. Your test is successful.

The interactive button provides an attractive, animated way of creating a hyperlink to another Web page. The interactive button effect helps draw the user's attention to the button for selecting the hyperlink. As with other Web page features, you should apply these effects carefully to avoid overwhelming or distracting users.

Using Dynamic HTML

Dynamic HTML (**DHTML**) gives you the ability to control the display of text and objects, such as pictures, in a Web page. When a DHTML command is applied to text or a picture, Internet Explorer (and other Web browsers that support DHTML) will animate the text or picture (or apply other effects that you specify) by executing a **script**, which is a small program that contains a set of instructions. When a Web browser encounters a Web page that contains a script, it interprets the instructions and performs a specific action. Because DHTML does not require additional information from the Web server that stores the Web page, it is very efficient and animates content without consuming network resources. Page transitions and animations are two methods of making a Web page more interesting. Brett wants to apply each of these features to enhance the Map to Sunshine Landscape & Garden Center page. However, just like any other animation, you remind Brett that too many effects in a Web page increase its download time and can be very distracting to users.

Creating a Page Transition

A **page transition** is an animated effect that you can apply to one or more Web pages in a Web site. When a user opens a page with a transition, the specified transition occurs while the page is being loaded. You can specify a closing transition for a page, as well. Although transitions are easy to apply, you should use transitions sparingly because having too many can overwhelm users and make opening and closing pages occur much more slowly than when no transitions are used.

Reference Window

Applying a Page Transition

- With the desired page open in Design view, click Format on the menu bar, and then click Page Transition to open the Page Transitions dialog box.
- If necessary, click the Event list arrow, and then select the desired event.
- Enter a value (in seconds) in the Duration (seconds) text box.
- Click the desired transition effect.
- Click the OK button.

Brett wants to add a transition effect to the Map page.

To add a page transition:

1. Click **Format** on the menu bar, and then click **Page Transition** to open the Page Transitions dialog box shown in Figure 2-38.

Figure 2-38 Page Transitions dialog box

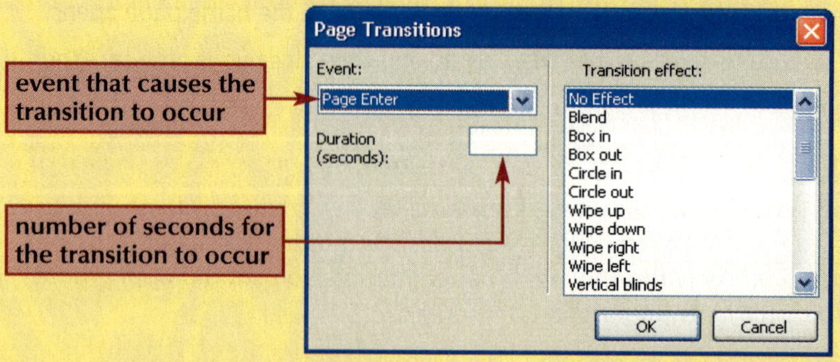

The default event is Page Enter, which means that the transition will occur when the page is opened or refreshed in the browser. Three other options are available: Page Exit, which applies the transition when the user leaves the page; Site Enter, which applies the transition when the user opens any page in the Web site; and Site Exit, which applies the transition when the user leaves the Web site.

Trouble? If the Event list box is not set to Page Enter, click the Event list arrow, and then click Page Enter.

2. Click the **Duration (seconds)** text box, and then type **5** as the number of seconds that the transition should occur.
3. In the Transition effect list box, click **Wipe right** to select that effect.

   Trouble? If you do not have the Wipe right transition, select another transition effect.
4. Click the **OK** button to complete the page transition specifications. FrontPage creates a script to execute the action you selected. When a browser that can interpret the script opens the Map page, it will create the page transition.
5. Save the Map page.

In addition to page transitions, you tell Brett that he can also control the manner in which text and individual objects, such as pictures, are displayed in a Web page.

Creating Animated Text in a Web Page

Animation is an effect that causes an element to "fly" into view from a corner or side of the page or in some other eye-catching way, such as a spiraling motion. You can apply animation to either text or a picture. Animation is also created using a script that FrontPage creates.

Creating Animated Text or an Animated Picture in a Web Page

Reference Window

- Select the text or picture that you want to animate.
- Click View on the menu bar, point to Toolbars, and then click DHTML Effects to display the DHTML Effects toolbar.
- Click the On list arrow, and then select an event on which you want the effect to occur.
- Click the Apply list arrow, and then select an effect to apply.
- If it is active, click the Effect list arrow and select a direction from which to apply the effect.

Brett wants to see how the home page would look with animated text. To demonstrate this effect, you'll animate the "February Checklist" heading.

To add text animation:

1. Click the **index.htm** tab at the top of the Contents pane.
2. Scroll the page as necessary and select the text **February Checklist**. To access the commands for animating text, you'll need to display the DHTML Effects toolbar.

3. Click **View** on the menu bar, point to **Toolbars**, and then click **DHTML Effects**. The DHTML Effects toolbar opens, as either a docked or floating toolbar. If necessary, drag this toolbar and dock it below the Pictures toolbar. Then make sure that the Highlight Dynamic HTML Effects button on the DHTML Effects toolbar has an orange background to indicate that this feature is enabled, so that DHTML elements will be highlighted in Design view, making them easier to locate.

   Next, specify the effects for the selected text.

4. Click the **On** list arrow on the DHTML Effects toolbar, and then click **Page load**. This setting will apply the effect when the page is opened or refreshed in the browser.

   You can specify three other effects for pictures: Click, which causes the animation to occur when the user clicks the element; Double click, which causes the animation to occur when the user double-clicks the element; and Mouse over, which causes the animation to occur on mouse over.

5. Click the **Apply** list arrow on the DHTML Effects toolbar, and then click **Fly in**. This setting will cause the selected text to fly into the page from a direction that you specify. When you select certain effects, you must also indicate the direction from which to apply the effect. You will know that you need to select a direction if the Effect list arrow becomes active.

6. Click the **Effect** list arrow on the DHTML Effects toolbar, which displays the text "< Choose Settings >" when it is active, and then click **Along corner**. See Figure 2-39. This setting indicates that the specified effect will occur from the corner of the window. Notice that the DHTML element in the Web page has a light-blue background; this background will not be visible in the browser.

Figure 2-39 **Animated text added to the home page**

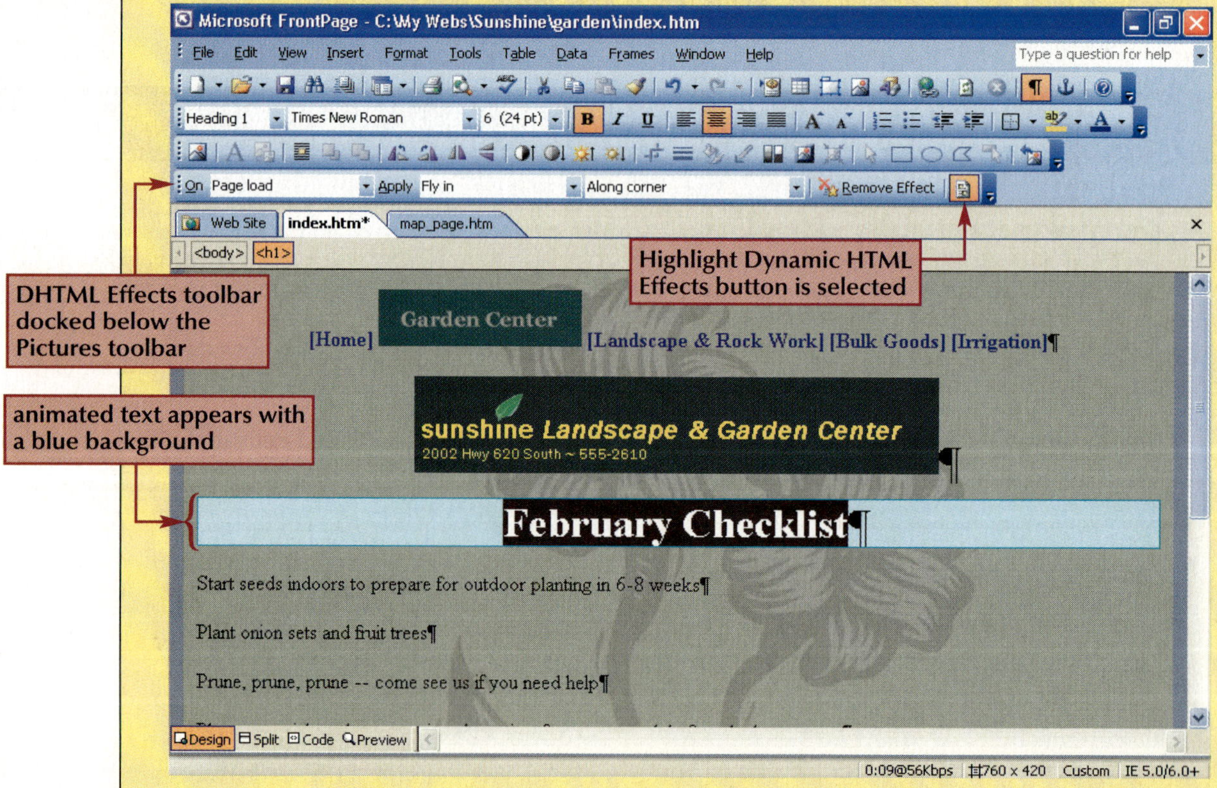

You are finished setting the text animation.

7. Save the home page.

If a browser cannot process these effects, it will ignore them and open the page anyway. To verify that these effects work correctly, you must use a browser to test the page transition and text animation.

To test the text animation and page transition:

1. Click the **Preview** button on the Standard toolbar to open the home page in the browser. The animation occurs for the "February Checklist" text.

   Trouble? If you do not see the text animation in the page, refresh the Web page.
2. Click the thumbnail picture to open the Map to Sunshine Landscape & Garden Center page. As the browser loads the page, the page transition occurs.
3. Click the interactive button. The "February Checklist" text is animated again.
4. Close your browser.

So Brett will better understand the different effects that he created in this tutorial, you'll show him the HTML document for the home page and the Map page.

Examining the HTML for Pages with Special Effects

When you created the interactive button for the Map page, FrontPage created a Java applet and inserted it into the HTML document. The page transition and text animation were implemented with Java scripts. An **applet** uses a series of parameters that specify an object's behavior. You can see this program by examining the page that contains it in Code view. Before exiting FrontPage, you ask Brett to hide the DHTML Effects and Pictures toolbars.

To view the HTML documents for the pages containing special effects:

1. Click **View** on the menu bar, point to **Toolbars**, and then click **DHTML Effects**. The DHTML Effects toolbar closes.
2. Click **View** on the menu bar, point to **Toolbars**, and then click **Pictures** to close the Pictures toolbar.
3. With the home page displayed in Design view, click the **Show Code View** button Code to change to Code view. The HTML document for the home page appears in Figure 2-40.

Figure 2-40 HTML document for the home page

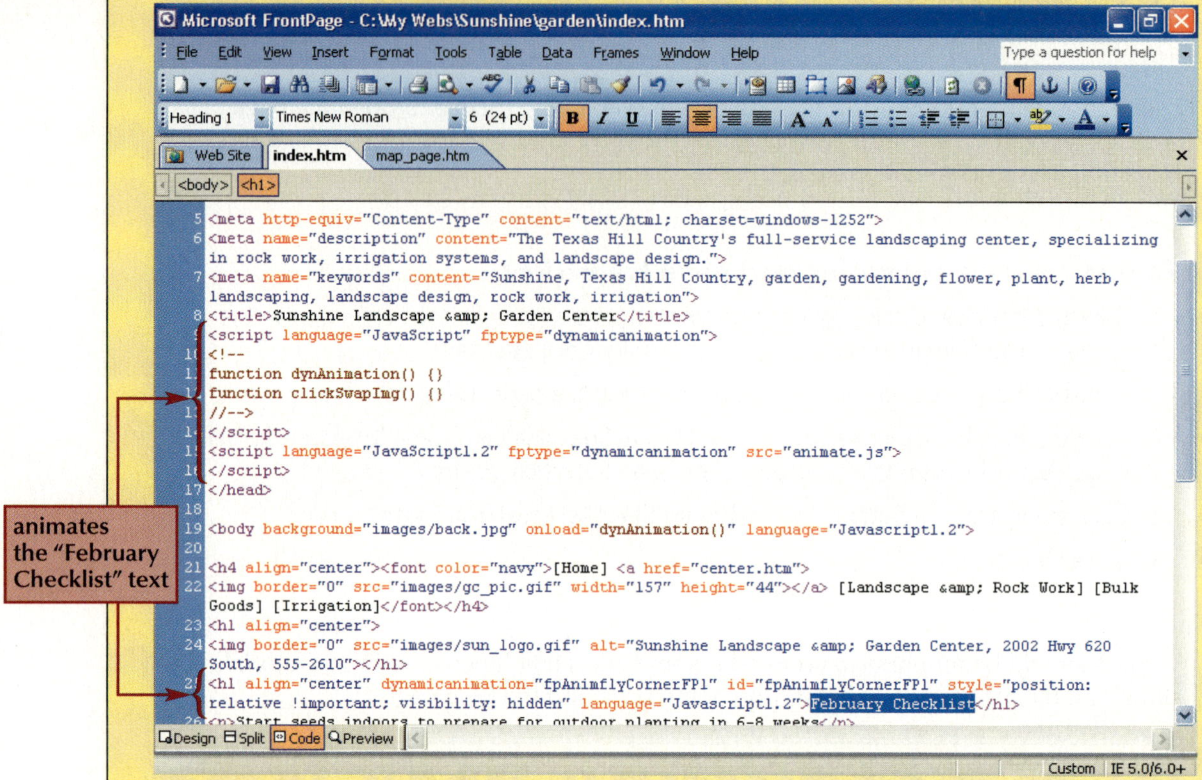

4. Return to Design view for the home page, and then click the **map_page.htm** tab and change to Code view.

5. Press **Ctrl + Home** to scroll to the top of the page. The first half of the HTML document for the Map page appears in Figure 2-41.

HTML document for the Map page

Figure 2-41

creates the page transition (scroll down to see the rest of the code)

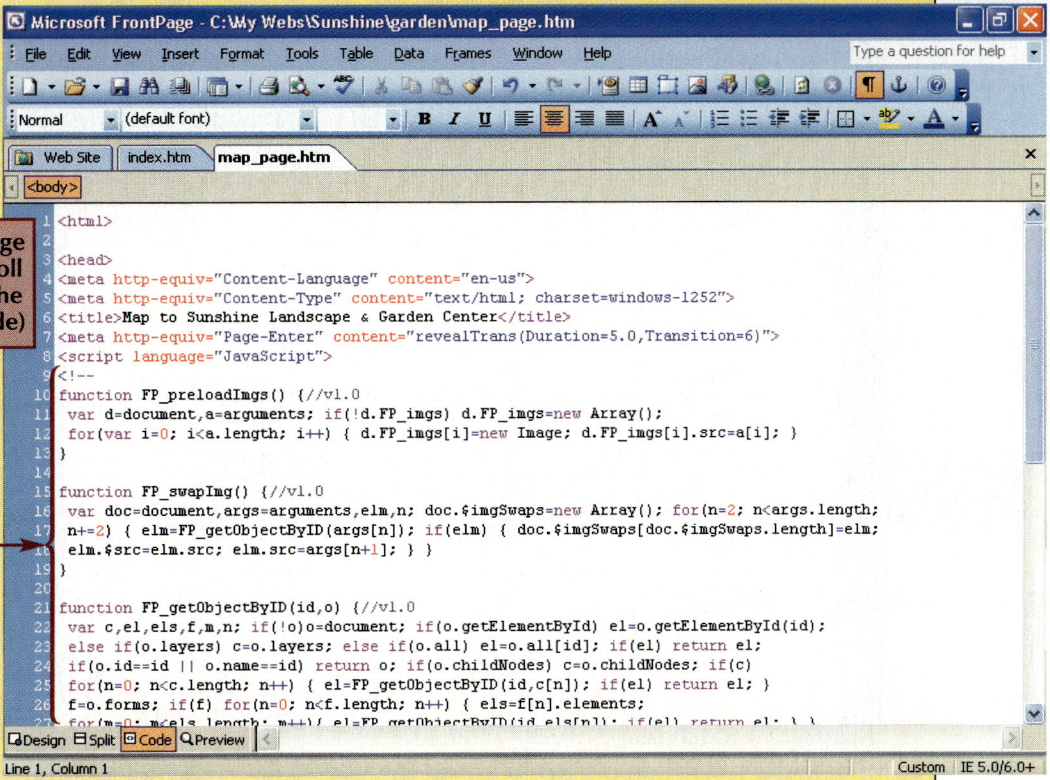

6. Press **Ctrl + End** to scroll to the bottom of the Map page, and then examine the rest of the HTML document shown in Figure 2-42.

Figure 2-42 **HTML document for the rest of the Map page**

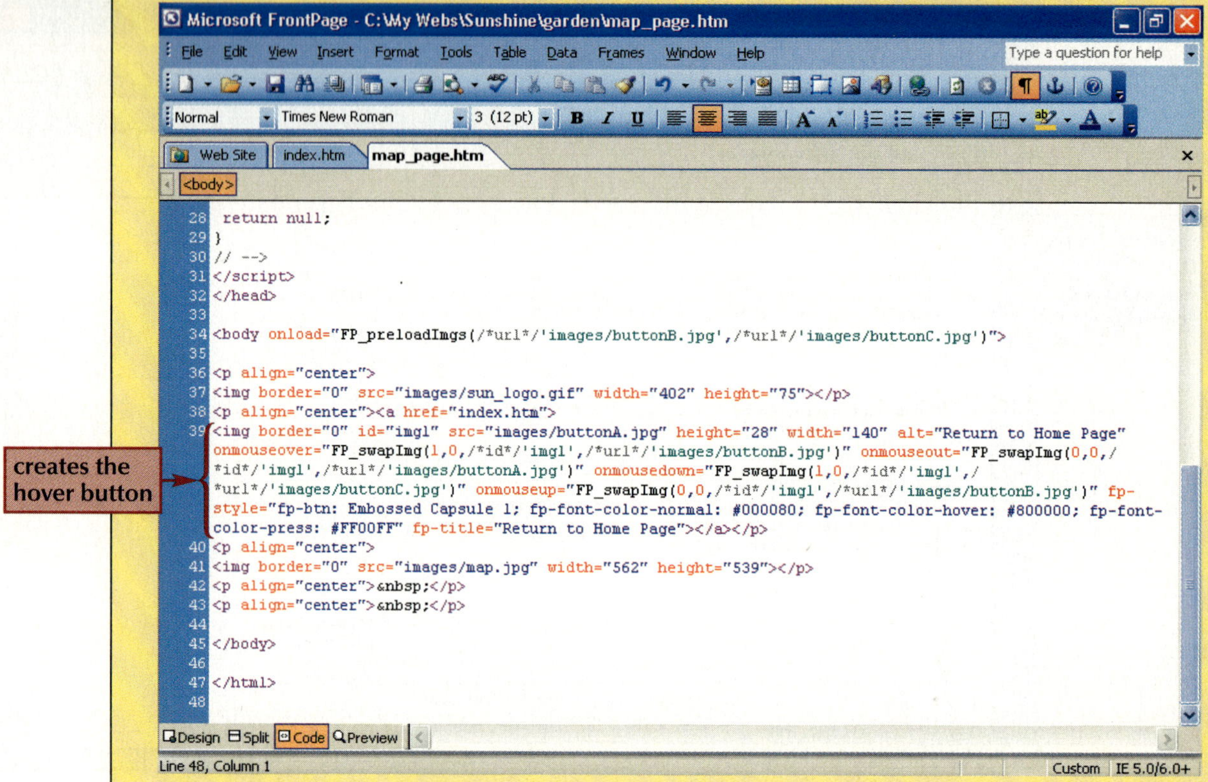

7. Return to Design view for the Map page. You are finished with your work, so you can close FrontPage.
8. Close the garden Web site, and then exit FrontPage.

The Web site for the Sunshine Landscape & Garden Center now contains three pages that are linked together. In the next tutorial, you will help Brett to learn more about hyperlinks and to examine the different views of a Web site.

Review

Session 2.3 Quick Check

1. When you create a thumbnail picture in a Web page, FrontPage automatically creates a(n) ______________ to the original picture that was used to create the thumbnail.
2. List three effects that you can apply to a picture using the Pictures toolbar.
3. Describe the process for adding text on top of a picture in a Web page.
4. Moving the pointer over an interactive button is called ______________.
5. True or False: An HTML tag creates an interactive button in a Web page.
6. True or False: A page transition reduces the speed at which a Web page opens and closes.
7. True or False: Animation is an effect that causes an element to "fly" into view from a designated area of the page.

Review

Tutorial Summary

In this tutorial, you learned how to add graphics to a Web site, create page transitions, and create animated text. You also learned about the different file formats of pictures and the advantages and disadvantages of each type. Finally, you learned how to create hyperlinks using text, e-mail addresses, and pictures.

As you use FrontPage to create your own Web sites, be sure to include graphics to increase the visual interest and functionality of your pages, but keep in mind that different users will see and use your site's pictures in many ways. If you use the proper file format for individual pictures, you can be sure that your pictures download as quickly as possible from the server. If you need to include pictures with large file sizes in your Web pages, try using thumbnails to leave the choice to the user as to whether to display the full picture. Finally, if you cannot reduce the file size of your picture by changing its format and it requires a significant amount of time to download, try using a corner sizing handle to reduce the size of the picture, and then click the Resample button to reduce the file size of the image. You might lose some of the image's quality by reducing the picture's size, but you can ensure that all of your site's visitors will be able to download the picture and use it.

Key Terms

alternative text
animation
applet
background picture
dynamic HTML (DHTML)
embedded file
Graphics Interchange Format (GIF)
horizontal line
hotspot
image map
interactive button
Joint Photographic Experts Group (JPEG or JPG)
lossless compression
lossy compression
mailto
marquee
mouse fly over
mouse over
page transition
picture
Portable Network Graphic (PNG)
script
sizing handle
source page
target
target page
thumbnail picture
wash out

Practice

Practice the skills you learned in the tutorial using the same case scenario.

Review Assignments

Data Files needed for the Review Assignments: bulk_pic.gif, home_pic.gif, irr_pic.gif, land_pic.gif

Brett is pleased with the progress he has made on the garden Web site. He asks you to finish changing the text in the link bar on the home page to pictures, which you will format as hyperlinks. You'll also add alternative text to these pictures.

If necessary, start FrontPage, make sure you have your Data Files, and then do the following:

1. Open the **garden** Web site from the location where your Web sites are stored, and then open the home page in Design view.
2. Select the text "[Home]" in the link bar at the top of the page, and then replace it with the **home_pic.gif** file in the Tutorial.02\Review folder included with your Data Files.

3. Repeat Step 2 to replace the text "[Landscape & Rock Work]" with the **land_pic.gif** file, the text "[Bulk Goods]" in the link bar with the **bulk_pic.gif** file, and the text "[Irrigation]" with the **irr_pic.gif** file. If necessary, delete any spaces that remain between the pictures you inserted so the pictures look like one large picture instead of five smaller pictures. Save your changes to the home page and save the pictures in the Web site's images folder.
4. Format the Landscape & Rock Work, Bulk Goods, and Irrigation pictures as hyperlinks that open new pages with the filenames **land.htm**, **bulk.htm**, and **irr.htm**, respectively, that you create in the Web site at the same time. (*Hint:* Click the Create New Document button on the Link to bar in the Insert Hyperlink dialog box for the first hyperlink, and then type the filename that you need to create in the Name of new document text box. Click the option to edit the new document later, and then click the OK button.)
5. In Folders view, change the titles of the **land.htm**, **bulk.htm**, and **irr.htm** pages that you created in Step 4 to "Landscape & Rock Work," "Bulk Goods," and "Irrigation," respectively.
6. Format the Home picture in the home page as a hyperlink that opens the home page.
7. For each picture in the link bar, create alternative text to identify the picture's function, such as "Home page hyperlink." When you are finished, save the home page.
8. Copy the picture link bar at the top of the home page by selecting it and clicking the Copy button on the Standard toolbar, and then use Ctrl + Click to open the Garden Center page. Select the text link bar at the top of the Garden Center page, and then replace it with the picture link bar you copied from the home page. (*Hint:* Do not use the Paste Options button to change the pasted pictures.) Save the Garden Center page.
9. On the home page, animate the thumbnail picture with the Page load event and the Wave animation.
10. Remove the effect that you applied to the "February Checklist" heading. (*Hint:* Click the heading to select it, and then click the Remove Effect button on the DHTML Effects toolbar.) Save the home page.
11. Preview the home page in a browser and test the hyperlinks you created in the home page and in the Garden Center page. (The new pages you added to the Web site will be blank; you will add their content in another tutorial.) When you are finished, close your browser.
12. Use FrontPage to print the HTML documents for the home page and the Garden Center page.
13. If necessary, hide the Pictures and DHTML Effects toolbars.
14. Close the **garden** Web site, and then exit FrontPage.

Apply

Apply the skills you learned in the tutorial to create new pages with pictures and hyperlinks in a Web site.

Case Problem 1

Data Files needed for this Case Problem: buffalo.gif, how.htm, how_logo.jpg, w_mark.gif, who.htm, who_logo.gif

Buffalo Trading Post Business at Buffalo Trading Post remains strong. Nicole Beirne and her sales staff receive approximately 50 phone calls each day from potential customers. To serve these customers better, Nicole wants to add a "How" page to the Web site that describes the company's procedures for trading and selling clothes. Nicole and the sales staff agree that one page should contain sections entitled "Frequently Asked Questions" and "How It Works" to describe the process of buying and selling clothing. They also want a "Choose To Re-Use" section that will describe Buffalo's overall commitment to reselling reusable materials. Nicole created this page and wants you to add it to the Web site. She also created a "Who" page that describes the history and philosophy of the business. After importing these pages, you will add logos and other graphics, hyperlinks, and features to enhance the overall appearance of the Web site.

If necessary, start FrontPage, make sure you have your Data Files, and then do the following:

1. Open the **buffalo** Web site from the location where your Web sites are stored, and then, if necessary, display the Folder List. (If you did not create this Web site in Tutorial 1, ask your instructor for assistance.)
2. If necessary, select the root folder of the **buffalo** Web site, and then import the **how.htm** page from the Tutorial.02\Case1 folder included with your Data Files into the Web site. After importing the page, open it in Design view, close the Folder List, and quickly examine the page contents.
3. In the centered paragraph above the link bar, insert the **how_logo.jpg** picture from the Tutorial.02\Case1 folder. Add the alternative text "How page logo" to the picture to describe its fu126nction.

Explore

4. Save the How page, use the Picture File Type dialog box to convert the JPEG picture that you added in Step 3 to a GIF picture, and then save it in the Web site's images folder.
5. Insert the **w_mark.gif** file from the Tutorial.02\Case1 folder as the background picture for the How page. Select the option to make the background picture a watermark.

Explore

6. Type your e-mail address at the bottom of the Web page in a new paragraph below the "For additional information please contact us:" text. (If you don't have an e-mail address, create one or use one provided by your instructor.) Set the message subject to "How Page." (*Hint:* After typing the mailto and pressing the spacebar, right-click the mailto link to open the shortcut menu, and then click Hyperlink Properties to open the Edit Hyperlink dialog box.)
7. Save the How page, and save the background picture file in the Web site's images folder.
8. Create a hyperlink in the link bar from the How page to the home page, and then create a hyperlink in the link bar from the home page to the How page. Click File on the menu bar, and then click Save All to save both pages.
9. Create a rectangular hotspot that encloses the "Buffalo Trading Post" text in the logo picture at the top of the How page. Set the target of the hotspot to the home page.

Explore

10. Use the What entry in the link bar of the How page to create a hyperlink to the **what.htm** page. (*Hint:* Click the Create New Document button on the Link to bar in the Insert Hyperlink dialog box, and then type the filename in the Name of new document text box. Click the option to edit the new document later, and then click the OK button.)
11. In Folders view, change the title of the **what.htm** page to "What." Then change the title of the home page to "Buffalo Trading Post."
12. Import the Who page (**who.htm**) from the Tutorial.02\Case1 folder into the **buffalo** Web site's root folder. Insert the **who_logo.gif** picture from the Tutorial.02\Case1 folder on the centered line at the top of the page. Add the alternative text "Who page logo" to the picture to describe its function. Save the picture in the Web site's images folder.
13. Create the hyperlinks between the Home, Who, How, and What pages so that each page has an active hyperlink to the other three pages. (Do not create any links in the What page, which is blank.) Save each page after creating its hyperlinks. Use a browser to test these hyperlinks, and then close your browser.
14. Change the background color of the home page to a Web-safe, light-yellow color of your choice. In a new, centered paragraph below the link bar in the home page, insert the **buffalo.gif** picture from the Tutorial.02\Case1 folder, and then change its background to transparent and add the alternative text "Buffalo Trading Post logo" to describe its function. Save the home page and save the embedded file in the Web site's images folder.
15. Change the "Welcome to the Buffalo Trading Post" heading on the home page to use an animation of your choice, and then save the home page.

Explore

16. In the How page, change the e-mail address you typed at the bottom of the page to an interactive button. (*Hint:* Select the text in the mailto link and then open the Interactive Buttons dialog box. Change the button text to your e-mail address, and then click the Browse button. On the E-mail Address tab, select your e-mail address in the Recently used e-mail addresses list (make sure that you choose the e-mail address that has the subject "How Page;" the space character will appear as "%20"), and then click the OK button). Change the button's properties to select a button type of your choice, increase the button size as necessary so it displays your complete e-mail address, and change the original, hovered, and pressed font colors to complementary colors of your choice. When you are finished, save the How page and save the embedded files in the Web site's images folder.
17. Use your browser to test the hyperlinks you created, including the interactive button. When you are finished, close your browser and the window that opens when you clicked the interactive button.
18. Use FrontPage to print the HTML documents for the home page, the How page, and the Who page.
19. If necessary, hide the Pictures and DHTML Effects toolbars.
20. Close the **buffalo** Web site, and then exit FrontPage.

Challenge

Expand the skills you learned in the tutorial by creating multiple hotspots in a single picture, copying and pasting an image map, and changing a text hyperlink to an interactive button.

Case Problem 2

Data Files needed for this Case Problem: about.htm, garden.gif, jobs.htm, link_bar.gif

Garden Grill Hiring and retaining the best possible staff is key to the continued growth of Garden Grill. Recently, Callan Murphy and Meghan Elliott met with the corporate Human Resources director to discuss the content of the planned Job Opportunities Web page. They want the page to emphasize that Garden Grill is a fun place to work and that employees are well rewarded. All agreed that the Job Opportunities page should include information about both management and staff associate positions. Meghan began developing the Job Opportunities page based on the detailed requirements from the meeting. Callan wants you to help Meghan complete the development and testing of this Web page. In addition to this work, you will import the About Us page into the site and work on enhancing the site's appearance and functionality with graphics and hyperlinks.

If necessary, start FrontPage, make sure you have your Data Files, and then do the following:

1. Open the **grill** Web site from the location where your Web sites are stored. (If you did not create this Web site in Tutorial 1, ask your instructor for assistance.)
2. In Folders view, change the title of the home page to "Garden Grill."
3. Display the Folder List, make sure the Web site's root folder is selected, and then import the **jobs.htm** page from the Tutorial.02\Case2 folder included with your Data Files into the Web site. Open the page in Design view and examine its contents.
4. In the centered paragraph at the top of the page, insert the **link_bar.gif** picture from the Tutorial.02\Case2 folder. In a new, centered paragraph below the picture you just inserted, insert the **garden.gif** file from the Tutorial.02\Case2 folder. Save the page and save the embedded files in the Web site's images folder.

Explore

5. Create two hotspots in the appropriate locations in the link bar of the Job Opportunities page so that one opens the home page and the other opens the **jobs.htm** page. Then create hotspots using the text entries in the picture link bar to open new pages that you create in the Web site as follows: Menu opens **menu.htm**; About Us opens **about.htm**; Franchise opens **fran.htm**; Feedback opens **feedback.htm**; and Search opens **search.htm**. (*Hint:* Click the Create New Document button on the Link to bar in the Insert Hyperlink dialog box, and then type the filename in the Name of new document text box. Click the option to edit the new document later, and then click the OK button.)

Explore

6. Highlight the hotspots you created and make sure that none of the hotspots overlap each other. To change the size of a hotspot, turn off the display of hotspots, click a hotspot to select it, and then use a sizing handle to change its size. Turn off the hotspot highlights, and then save the **jobs.htm** page.
7. Use Folders view to change the titles of the **menu.htm**, **about.htm**, **fran.htm**, **feedback.htm**, and **search.htm** pages to "Menu," "About Us," "Franchise Info," "Feedback," and "Search," respectively.

Explore

8. Include your e-mail address in a new paragraph at the bottom of the **jobs.htm** page below the "For additional information please contact us:" text. (If you don't have an e-mail address, create one or use one provided by your instructor.) Set the message subject to "Job Opportunities Page." (*Hint:* After typing the mailto and pressing the spacebar, right-click the mailto link to open the shortcut menu, and then click Hyperlink Properties to open the Edit Hyperlink dialog box.)

Explore

9. Save the **jobs.htm** page, and then copy the link bar picture and hotspots you created. (*Hint:* To copy the picture and the hotspots you created, click to the left of the picture, press and hold the Shift key, and then click to the right of the picture and release the Shift key. The Copy button on the Standard toolbar becomes active if you do this task correctly.) Use Ctrl + Click to open the home page, select the text link bar in the home page, and then paste the picture you copied in its place. (*Hint:* Do not use the Paste Options button to change the pasted pictures.) After pasting the picture, center it, and then point to each text entry in the link bar to make sure that you copied all of the hotspots. If you did not, copy and paste the picture again. Save the home page.
10. If necessary, display the Folder List, make sure the Web site's root folder is selected, and import the About Us page (**about.htm**) from the Tutorial.02\Case2 folder into the Web site, replacing the page that you created in Step 5. Review the page contents.
11. Replace the "Welcome to Garden Grill" heading in the home page with the **garden.gif** file from the Tutorial.02\Case2 folder. Add the alternative text "Garden Grill logo" to the picture to describe its function, and then save the home page and overwrite the embedded file in the Web site's images folder.
12. Insert a horizontal line above the copyright information on the home page. Change the line's properties so it is 95% of the window's width, five pixels high, and purple.

Explore

13. In a new paragraph above the horizontal line you inserted, insert a centered, scrolling marquee that is 95% of the window's width with the text "See the store manager for information about our new catering services!" Change the marquee's text to Arial, bold, 10-point, white font. (*Hint:* Click the Style button in the Marquee Properties dialog box, click the Format button, and then click Font to change the marquee text font color and style.) In the Marquee Properties dialog box, use the Background color list arrow to change the background color of the marquee to purple. Save the home page.

Explore

14. In the Job Opportunities page, change the e-mail address you typed at the bottom of the page to an interactive button. (*Hint:* Select the text in the mailto link and then open the Interactive Buttons dialog box. Change the button text to your e-mail address, and then click the Browse button. On the E-mail Address tab, select your e-mail address in the Recently used e-mail addresses list (make sure that you choose the e-mail address that has the subject "Job Opportunities Page;" the space character will appear as "%20"), and then click the OK button). Change the button's properties to select a button type of your choice, increase the button size as necessary so it displays your complete e-mail address, and change the original, hovered, and pressed font colors to complementary colors of your choice. When you are finished, save the page and save the embedded files in the Web site's images folder.

15. Use your browser to test the hyperlinks you created, including the interactive button. When you are finished, close your browser and the window that opened when you clicked the interactive button.
16. Use FrontPage to print the HTML documents for the home page, the About Us page, and the Job Opportunities page.
17. If necessary, hide the Pictures toolbar.
18. Close the **grill** Web site, and then exit FrontPage.

Apply

Apply the skills you learned in the tutorial to enhance a Web site with a picture, hyperlinks, and a background picture.

Case Problem 3

Data Files needed for this Case Problem: back.gif, mail.htm, services.htm, sw_logo.gif, team.htm, upcoming.htm

Swenson Auctioneers Scott Swenson likes the home page that you created for the new Swenson Auctioneers Web site. In accordance with his Web site plan, Scott and his staff created the content of the four main pages in the Web site: Upcoming Auctions, Auction & Appraisal Services, Our Team, and Mailing List. Today, Scott asks you to add these pages to the Web site. Also, he wants you to add hyperlinks to these pages to connect them to each other. His graphic designer completed the Swenson Auctioneers logo, and Scott wants to include this logo in each page in the Web site. Finally, Scott asks you to make changes to create subtle, professional backgrounds and graphics in the pages to enhance their appearance and functionality.

If necessary, start FrontPage, make sure you have your Data Files, and then do the following:

1. Open the **swenson** Web site from the location where your Web sites are stored. (If you did not create this Web site in Tutorial 1, ask your instructor for assistance.)
2. Use Folders view to change the title of the home page to "Swenson Auctioneers."
3. **Explore** If necessary, display the Folder List, make sure the Web site's root folder is selected, and then import the **mail.htm**, **services.htm**, **team.htm**, and **upcoming.htm** pages from the Tutorial.02\Case3 folder included with your Data Files into the Web site. (*Hint:* In the Add File to Import List dialog box, select the first file to import, press and hold the Ctrl key, click the other files to import to select them, and then release the Ctrl key and click the Open button.)
4. Open the home page in Design view, and then change the text in the link bar to hyperlinks that open the correct pages in the Web site.
5. To the left of the "Upcoming Auctions" link in the link bar, insert the **sw_logo.gif** picture from the Tutorial.02\Case3 folder. Insert two spaces between the picture and the word "Upcoming." Add the alternative text "Swenson Auctioneers logo" to the picture to describe its function.
6. Change the alignment of the paragraph that contains the picture and the link bar to left.
7. **Explore** Remove the border from the link bar. (*Hint:* Click the link bar to select it, click the list arrow for the Borders button on the Formatting toolbar, and then click the No Border button.)

8. Format the picture you inserted in Step 5 as a hyperlink that opens the site's home page.
9. Save the home page, and save the picture in the Web site's images folder.
10. Copy the link bar in the home page (including the picture), and paste it at the top of the **mail.htm**, **services.htm**, **team.htm**, and **upcoming.htm** pages. Make sure the link bar text is formatted using the Normal style. Save each page as you complete it.
11. Add the **back.gif** file from the Tutorial.02\Case3 folder as a background picture in all five pages of the Web site. Save the picture in the Web site's images folder, and save each page as you complete it.
12. Add a horizontal line that is 100% of the window width, four pixels high, and red to the home page. Position the horizontal line above the copyright information, and then save the home page.
13. Add a page transition of your choice to the **team.htm** page, and then save the **team.htm** page.

Explore

14. At the end of the last sentence on the **services.htm** page, insert your e-mail address as a mailto by typing your address and pressing the spacebar. Then change the e-mail address you typed to an interactive button. (*Hint:* Select the text in the mailto link and then open the Interactive Buttons dialog box. Change the button text to your e-mail address, and then click the Browse button. On the E-mail Address tab, type your e-mail address in the E-mail address text box and "Web Site" in the Subject text box.) Change the button's properties to select a button type of your choice, increase the button size as necessary so it displays your complete e-mail address, and change the original, hovered, and pressed font colors to complementary colors of your choice. When you are finished, save the page and save the embedded files in the Web site's images folder.
15. Use your browser to test the hyperlinks you created, including the interactive button. When you are finished, close your browser and the window that opened when you clicked the interactive button.
16. Use FrontPage to print the HTML documents for the home page and the **team.htm** page.
17. If necessary, hide the Pictures toolbar.
18. Close the **swenson** Web site, and then exit FrontPage.

Apply

Apply the skills you learned in the tutorial to enhance the loan Web site with graphics and hyperlinks.

Case Problem 4

Data Files needed for this Case Problem: back.gif, collage.gif, loantype.htm, help.htm, repair.htm, resource.htm

Mortgage Services, Inc. After examining multiple Web sites that have the same functionality as the one that she has hired you to create, Natalie Fuselier now has a better sense of the overall content and appearance that she wants to see in the new Web site for her company, Mortgage Services, Inc. Natalie began working on the content of several pages in the Web site and has given you the HTML documents to import into the Web site. She wants you to work on linking the pages together and enhancing the site with graphics and some animation. Because Natalie deals with many clients who need credit repair services, she has decided to include a Web page for this service in the Web site. Because these applicants will have different needs than her applicants who do not need credit repair services, she asks you to format the Credit Repair Services page with a different appearance to differentiate between the different kinds of loans.

If necessary, start FrontPage, make sure you have your Data Files, and then do the following:

1. Open the **loan** Web site from the location where your Web sites are stored. (If you did not create this Web site in Tutorial 1, ask your instructor for assistance.)
2. Use Folders view to change the title of the home page to "Mortgage Services, Inc."
3. **Explore** If necessary, display the Folder List, make sure the **loan** Web site's root folder is selected, and then import the **help.htm**, **loantype.htm**,**repair.htm**, and **resource.htm** pages from the Tutorial.02\Case4 folder included with your Data Files into the Web site. (*Hint:* In the Add File to Import List dialog box, select the first file to import, press and hold the Ctrl key, click the other files to import to select them, and then release the Ctrl key and click the Open button.)
4. **Explore** Open the home page in Design view, and then change the text in the link bar to hyperlinks that open the correct pages in the Web site. For the Application and Contact Us entries, create new pages in the Web site with the filenames **apply.htm** and **contact.htm**. (*Hint:* Click the Create New Document button on the Link to bar in the Insert Hyperlink dialog box, and then type the filename that you need to create in the Name of new document text box. Click the option to edit the new document later, and then click the OK button.) If your link bar contains other entries, delete them.
5. In Folders view, change the titles of the **apply.htm** and **contact.htm** pages to "Application" and "Contact Us," respectively.
6. Create a hyperlink from the text "credit repair services" in the last sentence on the home page to the **repair.htm** page. Save the home page.
7. **Explore** In a new, centered paragraph below the heading in the home page, insert the **collage.gif** file from the Tutorial.02\Case4 folder. Note the number of seconds required to download the home page at 56 Kbps. Then select the picture, use a corner-sizing handle to reduce the size of the picture by approximately one-half, and then click the Resample button on the Pictures toolbar to resize the picture. Note the number of seconds required to download the page after resizing the picture.
8. Add the alternative text "Decorative photograph" to the picture you added in Step 7 to describe the picture's function. Save the home page and save the embedded file in the Web site's images folder.
9. Add the **back.gif** file from the Tutorial.02\Case4 folder to the background of the home page, the **resource.htm** page, the **loantype.htm** page, and the **help.htm** page. Save each page as you complete it and save the embedded file in the Web site's images folder.
10. Change the background color of the **repair.htm** page to the light-yellow color with hex FF,FF,CC, and then save the page.

11. Format the heading "Mortgage Services, Inc." in the home page as a hyperlink that opens the home page. Then copy the link bar and the heading and paste them at the top of the **resource.htm**, **loantype.htm**, and **help.htm** pages.
12. In the **repair.htm** page, create a centered interactive button below the heading at the top of the page with the text "Return to Mortgage Services, Inc. home page." Choose a button type, colors, and other features for the button. Set the target of the interactive button to the site's home page. Save the **repair.htm** page and save the embedded files in the Web site's images folder.
13. Add a page transition of your choice to the **repair.htm** page, and then save the page.
14. Click File on the menu bar, and then click Save All to save all of the changes you have made. Use your browser to test the hyperlinks you created, including the interactive button. When you are finished, close your browser.
15. Use FrontPage to print the HTML documents for the home page and the **repair.htm** page.
16. If necessary, hide the Pictures toolbar.
17. Close the **loan** Web site, and then exit FrontPage.

Review

Quick Check Answers

Session 2.1

1. white
2. JPEG, GIF, and PNG. A JPEG file has up to 16 million colors and is suitable for photographs. A GIF file has up to 256 colors and is suitable for scanned images, line drawings, and simple graphics. GIF files can be combined to create animated images. PNG files are similar to GIF files but can have up to 16 million colors. PNG files are smaller than GIF files but cannot be combined to create animated images. Some browsers cannot display PNG files.
3. False
4. The Estimated Time to Download pane estimates the time needed to download the page using the specified connection speed. Because some users might have dial-up connections, it is important to monitor the download time as you add graphics to a Web page to ensure that pages will load quickly for all users.
5. (1) Alternative text identifies a picture's contents while the picture is being downloaded from the server. Users who cannot see the picture will see the alternative text instead of the picture, which identifies the missing content. (2) Alternative text is used to describe a picture's contents for visually impaired users who are using software that reads a Web page.
6. True
7. True

Session 2.2

1. True
2. a Web page in the same site, a Web page in another site, or related information in the same Web page
3. A source page contains a hyperlink; a target page is the page that opens when the hyperlink in the source page is clicked.
4. A mailto is a hyperlink that contains an e-mail address. When you click a mailto link, your default e-mail program starts and opens a new message addressed to the e-mail address specified by the mailto.
5. rectangular, circular, or polygonal
6. An image map is a picture that contains one or more hotspots. Clicking a hotspot opens the target of the hyperlink. When you format a picture as a hyperlink, clicking any area of the picture opens the target.

Session 2.3

1. hyperlink
2. any three of: convert to black and white, rotate, change contrast or brightness level, add a beveled edge, and wash out colors
3. Click the picture to select it, click the Text button on the Pictures toolbar, click the OK button, if necessary, to convert the picture to a GIF file, type the desired text, and then click anywhere in the Web page to deselect the text.
4. mouse over (or mouse fly over)
5. False
6. True
7. True

New Perspectives on

Microsoft® Office FrontPage® 2003

Read This Before You Begin: Tutorials 3–6

To the Student

Data Disks

To complete the Tutorials, Review Assignments, and Case Problems in this book, you will need the starting student Data Files. Your instructor will either provide you with these Data Files or ask you to obtain them yourself.

FrontPage Tutorials 3–6 require the folders shown in the next column to complete the Tutorials, Review Assignments, and Case Problems. You will need to copy these folders from a file server, a standalone computer, or the Web to the drive and folder where you will be storing your Data Files. Your instructor will tell you which computer, drive letter, and folders contain the files you need. You can also download the files by going to www.course.com; see the inside front cover for more information on downloading the files to your working folder, or ask your instructor or technical support person for assistance.

You will need to store your Data Files on a Zip disk, hard drive, or network drive that you can access. You will also need a location in which to create and save Web sites; the default location used in this book is C:\My Webs\[YourName], where "[YourName]" is your first and last names. You cannot complete this book using floppy disks.

▼FrontPage

Tutorial.03
Tutorial.04
Tutorial.05
Tutorial.06

The Data Files you work with in each tutorial build on the work you did in the previous tutorial. Thus when you begin Tutorial 3, you will use the Data Files that resulted after you completed the steps in Tutorial 2 and the Tutorial 2 Review Assignments.

Course Labs

Tutorial 3 features an interactive Course Lab to help you understand HTML concepts. There are Lab Assignments at the end of Tutorial 3 that relate to this lab. Contact your instructor or technical support person for assistance in accessing this lab.

To the Instructor

The Data Files and Course Labs are available on the Instructor Resources CD for this title. Follow the instructions in the Help file on the CD-ROM to install the programs to your network or standalone computer. See the "To the Student" section above for information on how to set up the Data Files that accompany this text. To complete the tutorials in this book, students must have a Web browser, access to a Web server with the FrontPage 2002 Server Extensions or Windows SharePoint Services installed on it, and an Internet connection. You are granted a license to copy the Data Files and Course Labs to any computer or computer network used by students who have purchased this book.

System Requirements

If you are going to work through this book using your own computer, you need:

- **Computer System** Microsoft Windows 2000 Professional or higher, Microsoft FrontPage 2003, and Microsoft Office 2003 must be installed on your computer. (The screens shown in this book use Microsoft Windows XP Professional. If your computer has Microsoft Windows 2000 Professional, your screens will look slightly different.) This book assumes a typical installation of FrontPage 2003 and Office 2003. To publish your Web sites in Tutorial 6, you also must have Internet Information Services version 5.0 or higher, Microsoft Windows 2003 Server, or access to a compatible Web server and a network connection, and the Microsoft FrontPage 2002 Server Extensions or Windows SharePoint Services installed on the Web server. You can install Internet Information Services from your Windows 2000 Professional or Windows XP Professional CD and you can download the FrontPage 2002 Server Extensions from www.msdn.com. The recommended browser for viewing Web pages is Internet Explorer 6.0 or higher.
- **Data Files** You will not be able to complete the tutorials or exercises in this book using your own computer until you have a set of Data Files.
- **Course Labs** See your instructor or technical support person to obtain the Course Lab software for use on your own computer.

Objectives

Session 3.1

- Create bulleted, numbered, and definition lists
- Create nested lists
- Create anchors in a Web page
- Create hyperlinks to anchors

Session 3.2

- Work with advanced features of Page view
- Work with advanced features of Folders view
- Examine a Web site in Reports view
- Use Hyperlinks view to examine the hyperlinks in a Web page
- Add, sort, change, and delete tasks in Tasks view

Lab

Web Pages & HTML

Student Data Files

To complete this tutorial, you will need your ending files from Tutorial 2 and the following Data Files. Additional Data Files needed to complete the end-of-tutorial exercises are listed with the Review Assignments and Case Problems.

▼Tutorial.03

▽ Tutorial folder

contact.gif	land.htm	rock_sam.gif
contact.htm	land_sam.jpg	sun.gif
land.gif	rock_pic.gif	

Using Lists, Anchors, and Web Site Views

Creating the Contact Sunshine Web Page

Case

Sunshine Landscape & Garden Center

In a weekly staff meeting, Brett Kizer, owner of the Sunshine Landscape & Garden Center, comments that he is pleased with the appearance and content of the Web site you are developing. The site's basic structure is now in place. The home page contains a link bar with links to the other pages in the site: Garden Center, Landscape & Rock Work, Bulk Goods, and Irrigation. In addition, the thumbnail picture that you inserted into the home page opens a page with a map that customers can use to find the center. At this point, you have added some content to the Garden Center page, but the other pages (Landscape & Rock Work, Bulk Goods, and Irrigation) are blank. As you continue developing the Web site, you will add content to these pages.

Because many grocery and discount stores in the area sell landscaping materials and plants, Brett wants to add a page to the Web site that will showcase the combined experience of the center's staff so that prospective customers will know they can trust the advice the staff gives and feel confident they are buying the best products and plants for use in their landscapes. Brett already collected biographical material from the center's senior employees and has prepared a draft of the page. Because this page contains a lot of content, Brett asks you to show him how to format information in bulleted lists and add hyperlinks that scroll to different locations in the document. You tell Brett that this type of hyperlink is easy to create, and you turn your attention to working on the new Contact Sunshine page.

Session 3.1

Web Pages & HTML

Creating Lists

Just like in word-processing documents, you can use different types of lists to organize content in a Web page. The basic list types are bulleted, numbered, and definition. A bullet character, such as a dot, precedes each item in a **bulleted list**. You can customize a bulleted list to use almost any graphic to enhance its appearance. A **numbered list** displays items preceded by numbers, letters, or Roman numerals. A **definition list** is used to format defined terms and their definitions. A **defined term** is the term being explained; the paragraph below the defined term contains a definition to describe the term.

When you use the tools in Design view to create these types of lists, FrontPage generates the HTML tags that create the lists. Figure 3-1 shows the basic list types and the HTML tags that create them. A bulleted list is also called an **unordered list** because items in the list are not sequentially organized. The <ul></ul> tags, which stand for "unordered list," create a bulleted list in a Web page. Notice that each item in the list is enclosed in <li></li> tags, which stand for "line item." A numbered list is also called an **ordered list** because items in the list are sequentially organized. The <ol></ol> tags, which stand for "ordered list," create a numbered list in a Web page. Items in an ordered list also are enclosed by the <li></li> tags. A definition list is different from unordered and ordered lists because it contains different tags to format the defined terms and definition items in the list. The <dt></dt> tags, which stand for "defined term," enclose the terms in the list. The <dd></dd> tags, which stand for "defined definition," enclose the definitions for each defined term in the list. The <dl></dl> tags, which stand for "definition list," enclose all of the <dt></dt> and <dd></dd> items in the list. Although FrontPage generates these tags for you automatically, it's often helpful to understand their presentation in an HTML document for those times when you need to make minor adjustments to the tags that you cannot perform using the tools in Design view.

Figure 3-1 **Basic list types**

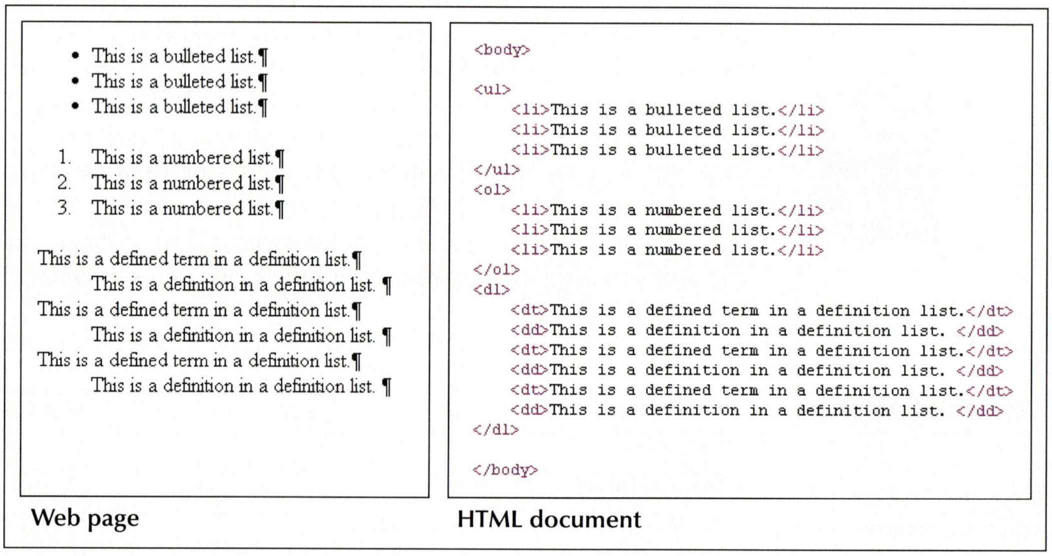

The items in a list can themselves be lists. A **nested list** is one that is contained within another list. A list that contains one or more nested lists is also called a **multi-level list** or **outline list**. Multi-level lists can use the same or different list types for each level. To create a standard outline, for example, you would nest numbered lists; each level would use the same numbered list type but a different number, letter, or Roman numeral format. In contrast, you would use different list types for each level when nesting a numbered list within a bulleted list or vice versa.

Brett finished the biographies that he wants to include in the Contact Sunshine page and has sent the page to you via e-mail. Now he wants you to import his page into the garden Web site. Then you will examine the page together and decide what types of lists would be appropriate to organize the content of the page.

To import the Contact Sunshine page into the Web site and open it in Design view:

1. Start **FrontPage** and then open the **garden** Web site from the location where your Web sites are stored.
2. If necessary, display the Folder List and make sure the root folder of the garden Web site is selected in the Folder List.
3. Click **File** on the menu bar, and then click **Import**. The Import dialog box opens.
4. Click the **Add File** button, open the **Tutorial.03\Tutorial** folder included with your Data Files, click the **contact.htm** file to select it, and then click the **Open** button. The contact.htm file appears in the Import dialog box.
5. Click the **OK** button to import the page into the Web site.
6. Close the Folder List and then open the **contact.htm** page in Design view. The Contact Sunshine page appears in Figure 3-2.

Figure 3-2 Contact Sunshine page

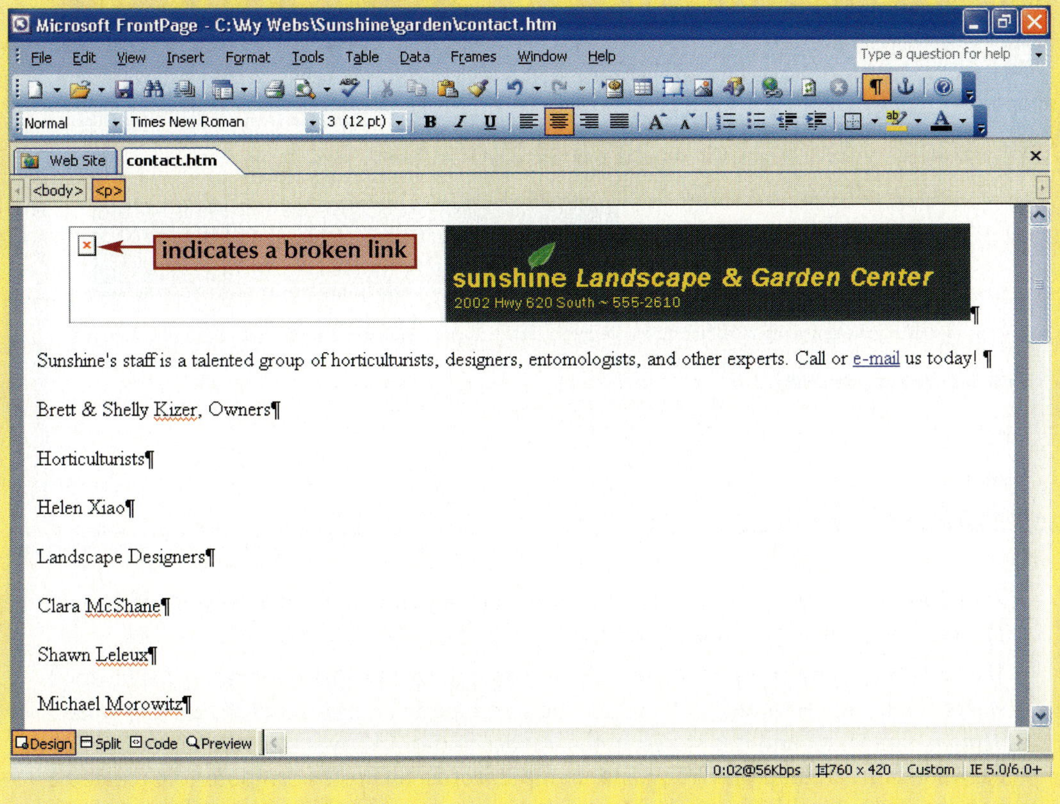

The first thing that Brett notices about the page he gave you is that the logo for the Sunshine Landscape & Garden Center appears in the upper-right corner of the page.

However, an empty box with a icon appears to the left of the logo. Brett explains that he inserted a "Contact Sunshine" logo picture in that location when he created the page on his computer. He wonders why this picture doesn't appear on your computer. You tell Brett that the Sunshine logo appears in the page because it is already stored in the Web site's images folder. However, the picture on the left, which appears as a **broken link**, is not stored in the Web site. To show Brett this problem, you decide to switch to Split view, so Brett can see the HTML document and the Web page simultaneously.

To switch to Split view and examine the broken link:

1. Click the **broken link** at the top of the page. Sizing handles appear around the missing picture.
2. Click the **Show Split View** button Split at the bottom of the Contents pane. The HTML document for the Contact Sunshine page appears in the Code view window and the Web page appears in the Design view window. Because you selected the broken link in Design view, the HTML tag for the broken link is selected in the Code view window, as shown in Figure 3-3.

Figure 3-3 **Split view of the Contact Sunshine page**

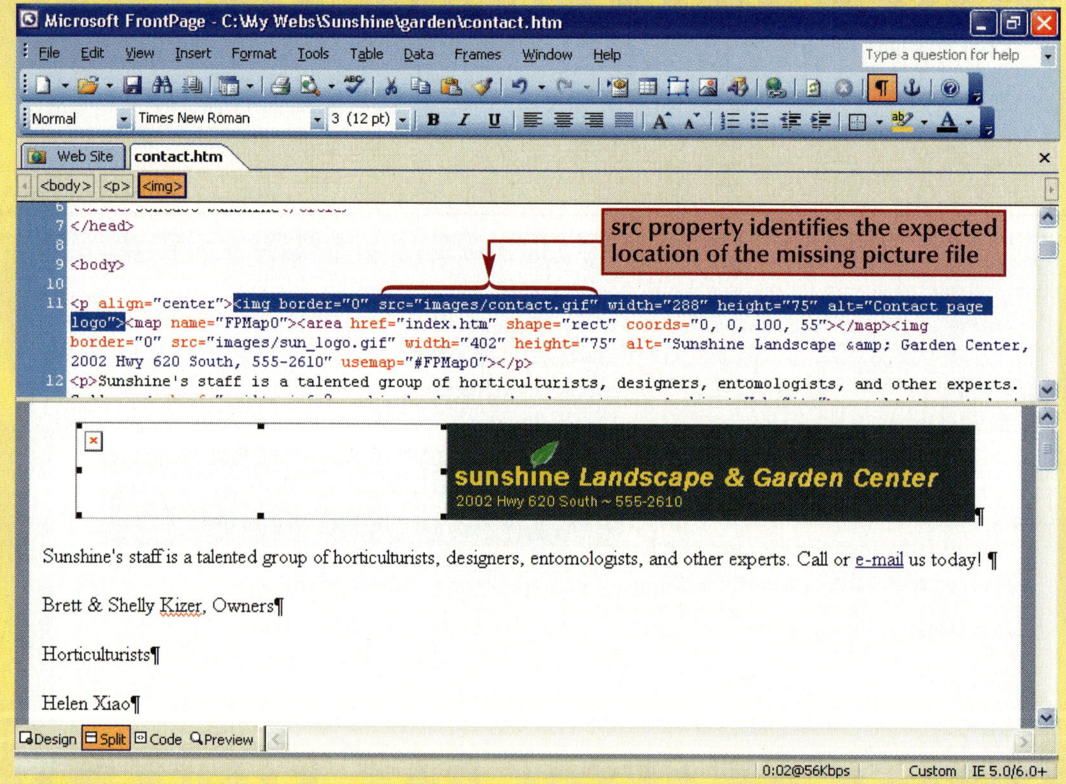

Trouble? If necessary, scroll down the HTML document in the Code view window so you can see the HTML tag for the broken link.

The <img> tag inserts a picture into a Web page; the src property identifies the location where the picture is stored. In this case, the src property indicates that the picture's filename is contact.gif and it is stored in the images folder. This was the original location of the file when Brett created this Web page. In other words, on Brett's computer, he created a page named contact.htm, inserted two pictures (contact.gif and sun_logo.gif), and saved the picture files in the Web site's images folder. You imported the contact.htm Web page into the garden Web site on your computer, but you did not import the contact.gif file. Because FrontPage cannot locate the picture file, it appears as a broken link. When you see icons in a Web page, the picture files used in the Web page are not stored in the location indicated by the src property. When this situation occurs, you can insert the picture file into the location referenced by the src property, change the path to the picture file so it points to the correct location, or delete the picture from the page. Brett can supply the missing picture file to you so that you can import it into the Web site's images folder, which will correct the problem.

3. Return to Design view for the Contact Sunshine page, and then display the Folder List.
4. Click the **images** folder in the Folder List to select it. You will import the missing contact.gif file into the images folder.
5. Click **File** on the menu bar, and then click **Import**.
6. Click the **Add File** button, open the **Tutorial.03\Tutorial** folder included with your Data Files (if necessary), click the **contact.gif** file to select it, click the **Open** button, and then click the **OK** button. The contact.gif file is added to the Web site's images folder, and the picture now appears in the contact.htm Web page. You corrected the broken link problem.
7. Close the Folder List, and then use the vertical scroll bar in Design view to examine the contents of the Contact Sunshine page. When you are finished viewing the page's contents, press **Ctrl + Home** to scroll to the top of the page.

After reviewing the page's contents, you decide that the information at the top of the page would benefit from being formatted differently. You suggest that the general title of each position, such as "Horticulturists" and "Landscape Designers," be formatted as a bulleted list. You also recommend formatting the names appearing below each title as a numbered list. Further down the page, each person's name and title appear on a line above a paragraph that describes his or her biography. This material would work very well in a definition list. Figure 3-4 shows the plan for the various lists you will create in the Contact Sunshine page.

Plan for the Contact Sunshine page | **Figure 3-4**

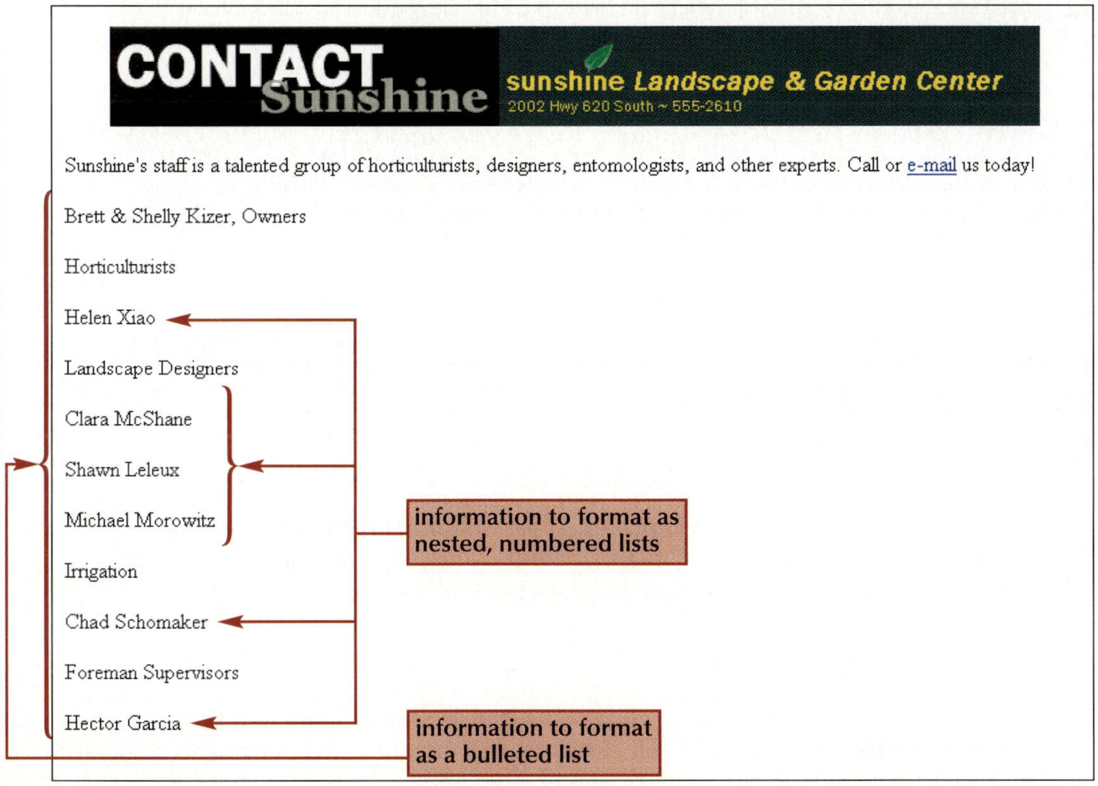

Figure 3-4 **Plan for the Contact Sunshine page (continued)**

Brett & Shelly Kizer, Owners

Sunshine Landscape & Garden Center has been a family owned and operated business since 1976 when the Carpenters first opened their shop. In August 1998, Brett and his wife, Shelly, became part of the Sunshine family, purchasing the business from the Carpenters. Over the years Brett and Shelly have expanded the products and services available at Sunshine and they continue to offer the highest level of quality and expertise that has made Sunshine the best garden center in the area. In August 2000, when Sunshine purchased Rainmaker Irrigation Company, Brett took courses and became a licensed irrigator.

Helen Xiao, Horticulturalist

Helen wasn't born in Texas but she got here as fast as she could! Raised and educated in Columbus, Ohio, Helen holds two horticulture degrees from Ohio State University, one of our nation's best horticulture programs. She has worked in the nursery industry for 28 years and has lived in Texas since 1971. Helen is an expert in native Texas plants; she holds the TNLA certification Texas Master Certified Nursery Professional from Texas A&M. Helen also has 14 years of experience with landscape design and installation having worked for commercial and residential landscape firms across central Texas.

Clara McShane, Chief Landscape Designer

defined term

definition

Clara came to Sunshine in March 2001 as sort of a "relief pitcher" to help out during the busy spring season and she hasn't left yet! Clara's passion has always been gardening, and after graduating from UT she studied plants and practiced landscape design for over 10 years. Her expertise ranges from designing the perfect entryway for a home to coordinating large-scale installations. Clara's creative abilities are also on display in our monthly newsletter as she serves as Sunshine's publicist.

Shawn Leleux, Landscape Designer

information to format as a definition list

Shawn joined Sunshine in March 2000 only two years after graduating from Texas A&M University, but he has wisdom beyond his years. He earned his degree in Entomology and is Sunshine's resident expert on insects and how to treat them. Shawn comes to Sunshine from Marble Falls, Texas, where he grew up enjoying outdoor activities, including hunting, fishing, camping, and hiking. His love for nature is one of the reasons he designs and builds such beautiful and successful landscapes.

Michael Morowitz, Landscape Designer

A landscape painter and portrait artist from McLean, Virginia, Mike was certified as a Master Gardener in 1996. He is a member of the education committee at Zilker Botanical Garden here in Austin. For several years, Mike owned a successful design business in Austin and worked with Sunshine on many projects. He officially joined Sunshine in October 2002. "I love my work because I get to dream up beautiful things and watch them become reality."

Chad Schomaker, Irrigation

Chad has been the Supervisor of RainMaker Irrigation since May 2002. He's originally from Salem, Oregon, where he worked his way through school as an Agricultural Irrigator. After moving to Texarkana in 1981, he continued to work in irrigation. He then made his way to Houston and then to Austin, where he has specialized in residential and commercial underground irrigation systems for three years. Chad has been installing landscape lighting for 13 years. In 1999, Chad earned his backflow certification and is able to conduct tests required by local municipalities.

Hector Garcia, Foreman

Hector has been with Sunshine since 1982 and he has done it all. He has worked on the maintenance crew, the landscape crew, and is now the head of the rock crew and foreman of all Sunshine crews. Hector is a real professional and a true hardscape genius. He can build patios, fountains, benches, fireplaces, walls, walkways, and columns with precision. Because of his ability to build exactly what a customer wants, even when they can't fully describe it, some customers think he can read minds!

Finally, looking ahead, you tell Brett that after you format the lists in the page, you can create hyperlinks from a person's name at the top of the page to the place in the page that describes that person. Your first task is to create the bulleted list using the titles.

Creating a Bulleted List

A bulleted list, or an unordered list, contains items that are not sequentially organized. Each item in the list begins with a bullet character; the default bullet character displayed by most Web browsers is a dot. You can create a bulleted list either by clicking the Bullets button on the Formatting toolbar before typing the items in the list, or by selecting existing text and then clicking the Bullets button.

Creating a Bulleted List

Reference Window

- Select the paragraph that will contain the first item in the bulleted list.
- Click the Bullets button on the Formatting toolbar.
- Type each item in the list, pressing the Enter key after each item.
- If necessary, press the Enter key twice to end the bulleted list.

Bulleted lists are indented by one tab stop when you first create them. You can change this indention if desired by using the Decrease Indent button or the Increase Indent button on the Formatting toolbar. To create the bulleted list, you will select all of the items at the top of the page, and then use a toolbar button. To create the nested, numbered lists, you will need to select the items individually and format them as numbered lists.

To create a bulleted list:

1. Click to the left of the word **Brett** at the top of the Contact Sunshine page, scroll down as necessary, press and hold the **Shift** key as you click to the right of the word **Garcia**, and then release the **Shift** key. You selected 11 lines in the Web page.
2. Click the **Bullets** button on the Formatting toolbar to format these lines as a bulleted list, and then scroll up the page as necessary and click the first item in the list to deselect the entire bulleted list. See Figure 3-5.

Figure 3-5 **Information formatted as a bulleted list**

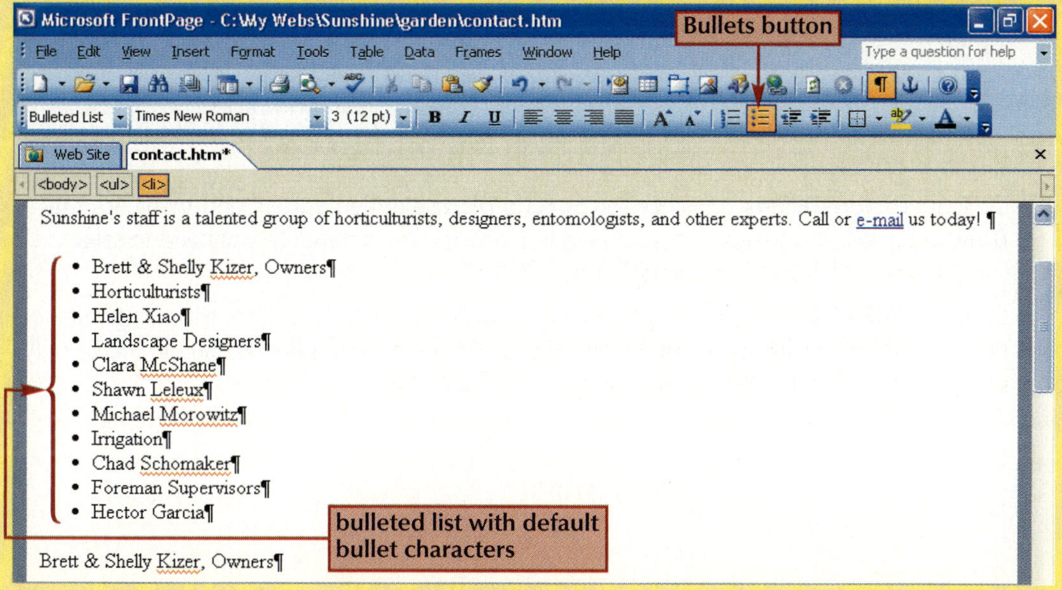

Notice that the items in the bulleted list appear with the default bullet and that the entire list is indented by one tab stop (one-half inch). Brett asks about changing the default bullet character to a small sun that the graphic designer created for him. You can use almost any graphic as a bullet character, as long as it is sized in proportion to the text. In other words, a graphic such as the contact.gif picture wouldn't work as a bullet character, but a small graphic of an arrow would work well. When you change the default bullet character to a picture, you must store the picture in the Web site; otherwise, visitors will see a broken link icon instead of the bullets.

To change the default bullet character in the bulleted list:

1. Select all 11 lines in the bulleted list.
2. Click **Format** on the menu bar, and then click **Bullets and Numbering**. The Plain Bullets tab of the List Properties dialog box opens, as shown in Figure 3-6. The current bullet character, the dot, is selected. Notice that you can change the dot to a small, open circle or to a small, solid square by clicking these samples on the Plain Bullets tab. To change the bullet to a picture, you need to select the Picture Bullets tab.

Figure 3-6 **List Properties dialog box**

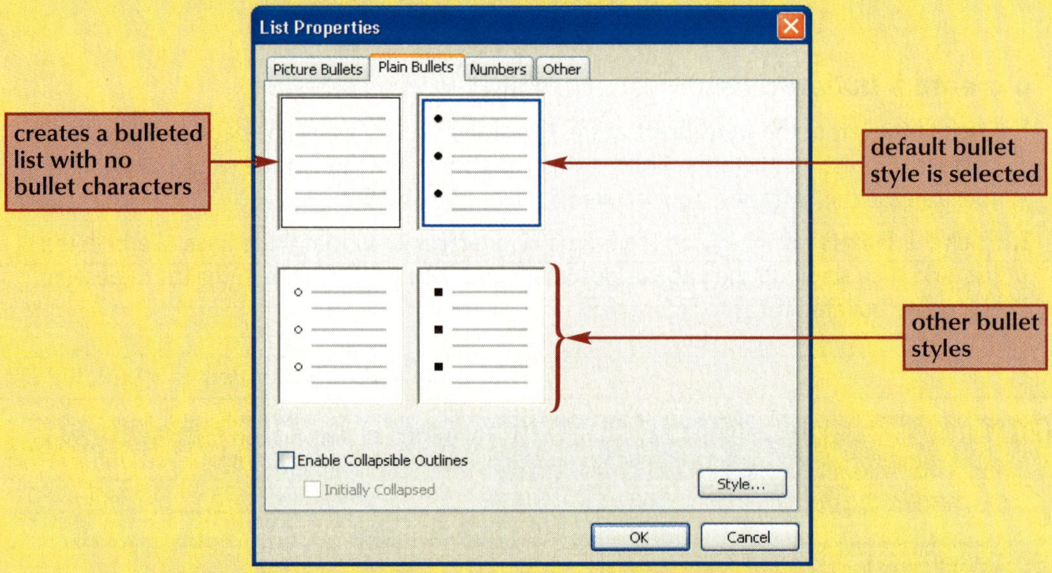

3. Click the **Picture Bullets** tab, click the **Specify picture** option button, and then click the **Browse** button. The Select Picture dialog box opens. The picture file you need to select, sun.gif, is stored in the Tutorial.03\Tutorial folder.
4. Open the **Tutorial.03\Tutorial** folder included with your Data Files, click the **sun.gif** file to select it, and then click the **Open** button. The path to the sun.gif file appears in the Specify picture text box on the Picture Bullets tab. See Figure 3-7.

Figure 3-7 Completed Picture Bullets tab

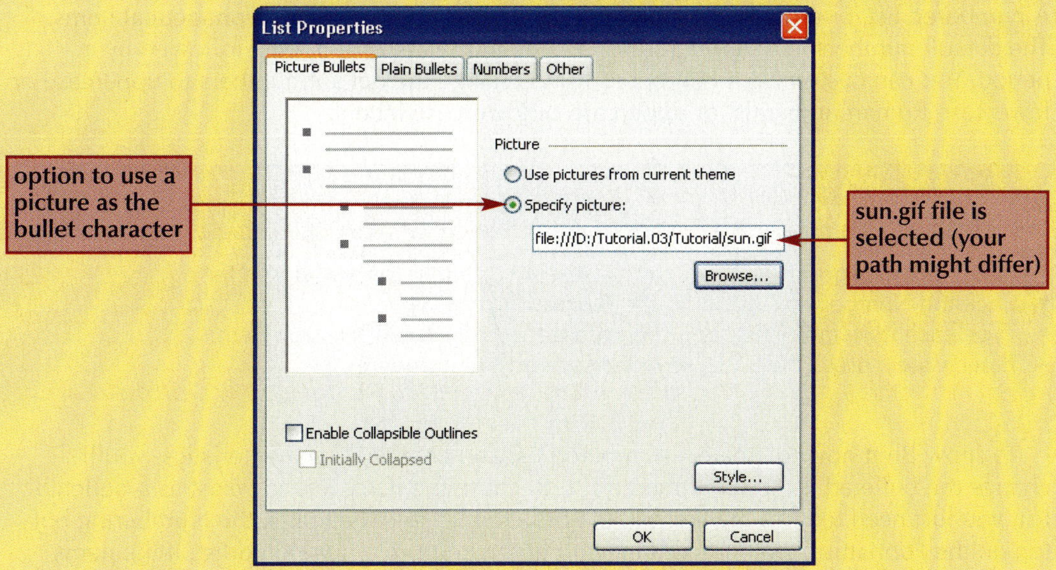

5. Click the **OK** button, and then click the first bulleted item in the list to deselect the list. The bullets are pictures, as shown in Figure 3-8.

Figure 3-8 Bulleted list with picture bullets

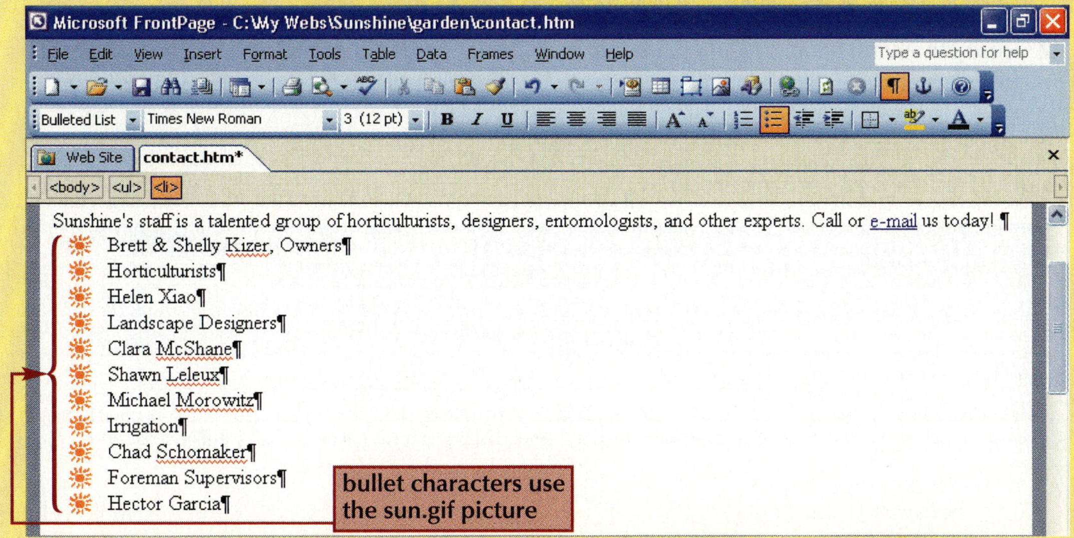

Because you inserted a picture into the Web page, you need to save the picture file in the Web site's images folder.

6. Click the **Save** button on the Standard toolbar, and then save the sun.gif picture in the Web site's images folder.

According to your plan, you need to change the bullets next to people's names to numbered lists. Before making this change, you want to show Brett how to create a numbered list.

Creating a Numbered List

A numbered list, or ordered list, contains sequentially numbered or alphabetical items. The default numbers in a numbered list are the numerals 1, 2, 3, etc., followed by a period. You can customize a numbered list to change the default numbers to uppercase or lowercase Roman numerals, or uppercase or lowercase letters.

Reference Window

Creating a Numbered List

- Select the paragraph that will contain the first item in the numbered list.
- Click the Numbering button on the Formatting toolbar.
- Type each item in the list, and then press the Enter key after each item.
- If necessary, press the Enter key twice to end the numbered list.

To show Brett how to create a numbered list and change its characteristics, you'll change the bulleted list to a numbered list. Because the items already exist as a bulleted list, you just need to click any item in the bulleted list and then click the Numbering button on the Formatting toolbar to change all of the items to a numbered list. If the items were not already formatted as a list, you would need to select all of the items to format in a numbered list before clicking the Numbering button.

To create a numbered list and examine its default settings:

1. Click any item in the bulleted list at the top of the page.
2. Click the **Numbering** button on the Formatting toolbar. Because the items were already formatted as a bulleted list, all of the items in the bulleted list change to a numbered list, as shown in Figure 3-9.

Figure 3-9 **Items formatted as a numbered list**

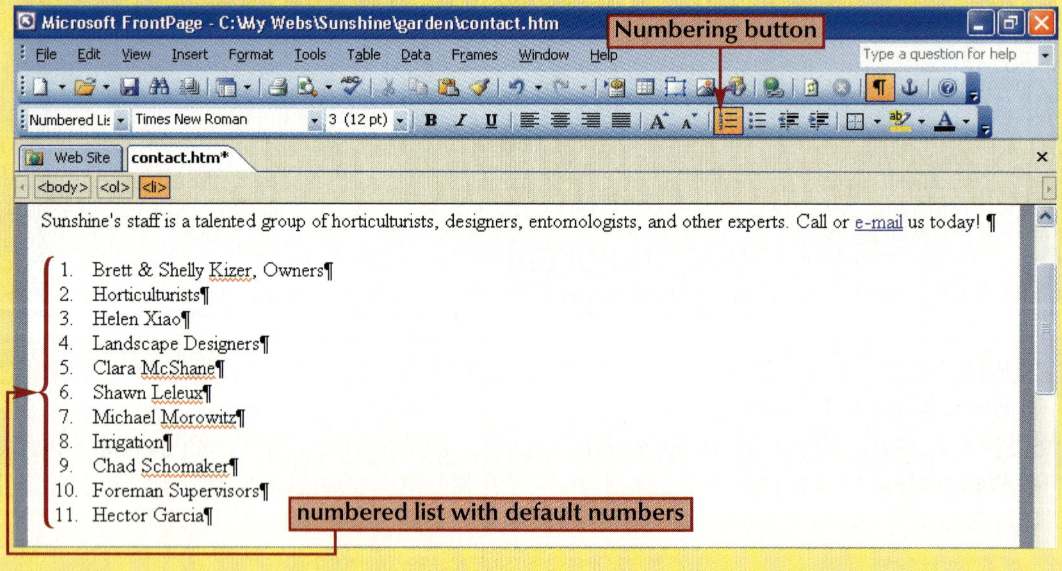

3. Click **Format** on the menu bar, click **Bullets and Numbering**, and then click the **Numbers** tab. See Figure 3-10.

Figure 3-10 Numbers tab in the List Properties dialog box

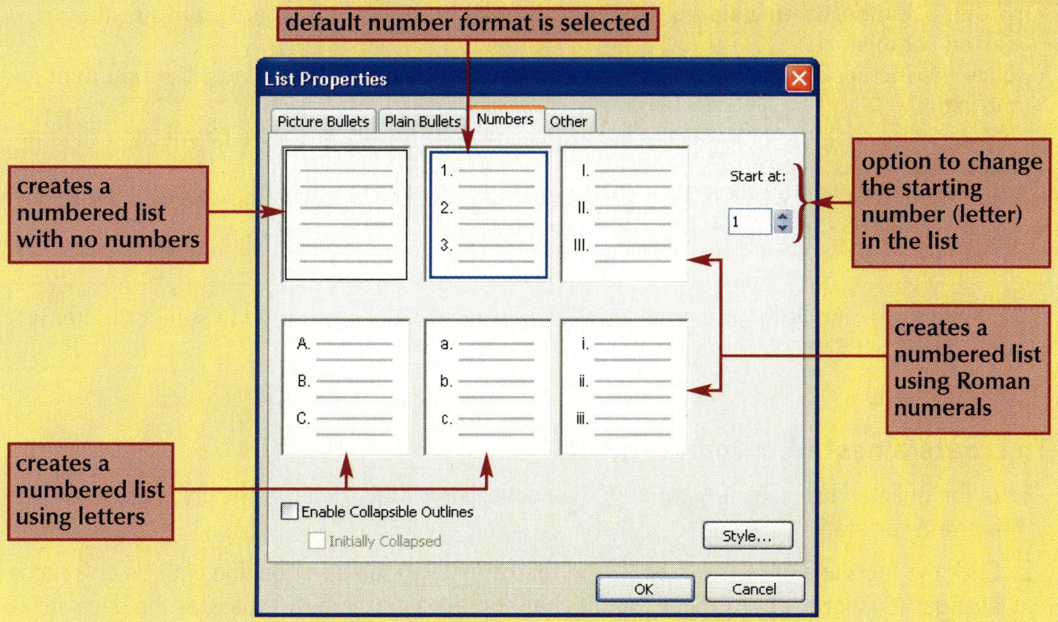

The default number in a numbered list is a numeral, which is the currently selected item. You can format the numbered list using uppercase or lowercase Roman numerals or uppercase or lowercase letters. Notice the Start at list box, which shows that the current starting number is 1. When you need to start a numbered list with a specific number, Roman numeral, or letter, you can change the Start at value to the beginning value you need.

Because you don't want to change the items to a numbered list, you will close the List Properties dialog box without making any changes, and then you will undo the change you made.

To return the items to a bulleted list:

1. Click the **Cancel** button in the List Properties dialog box to close it.
2. Click the **Undo** button on the Standard toolbar. The numbered list returns to a bulleted list with picture bullets.

Now you can change the people's names to nested, numbered lists.

Creating a Nested, Numbered List

A nested list contains one or more items that appear within another list. You can create a nested, numbered list or a nested, bulleted list within an existing numbered or bulleted list.

Reference Window

Creating a Nested List

- Within a numbered or bulleted list, insert or select the list item where you want the nested list to start.
- Click the Increase Indent button on the Formatting toolbar twice to nest the first item in the list.
- If necessary, click the Numbering button or the Bullets button on the Formatting toolbar to change the list type.
- Type each item in the list, pressing the Enter key after each item. Do not press the Enter key after typing the final item in the nested list.

To format specific items in an existing list as a nested list, you need to select the items for the nested list first.

To create a nested, numbered list:

1. In the bulleted list, click anywhere in the name **Helen Xiao**. Helen is the only horticulturist currently on staff.
2. Click the **Increase Indent** button on the Formatting toolbar. The line with Helen's name changes to a normal paragraph. Notice that additional space now separates the line with Helen's name in it from the bullet that appears above her name. In addition, Helen's name no longer contains a bullet.
3. Click the button again. The line with Helen's name changes to a nested, bulleted list. If you wanted to create the nested list using the same bullet as the original list, no further action would be necessary. However, if you want to change the nested list's type from bulleted to numbered, you must click the Numbering button on the Formatting toolbar.
4. Click the **Numbering** button on the Formatting toolbar. The number 1 appears to the left of Helen's name. You created a nested, numbered list.

   Trouble? If the nested list still uses the sun.gif picture as its bullet character, you clicked the Increase Indent button only once. Click the Numbering button on the Standard toolbar again to change the list type.
5. Click anywhere in the name **Clara McShane**, and then repeat Steps 2 through 4 to format this item as a nested, numbered list.
6. Change the following names to nested, numbered lists: **Shawn Leleux**, **Michael Morowitz**, **Chad Schomaker**, and **Hector Garcia**. When you are finished, your list should look like the one shown in Figure 3-11. Notice that the list with more than one item is formatted automatically to use sequential numbers, and that the second, third, and fourth numbered lists all begin with the number 1.

Figure 3-11 Nested, numbered lists created

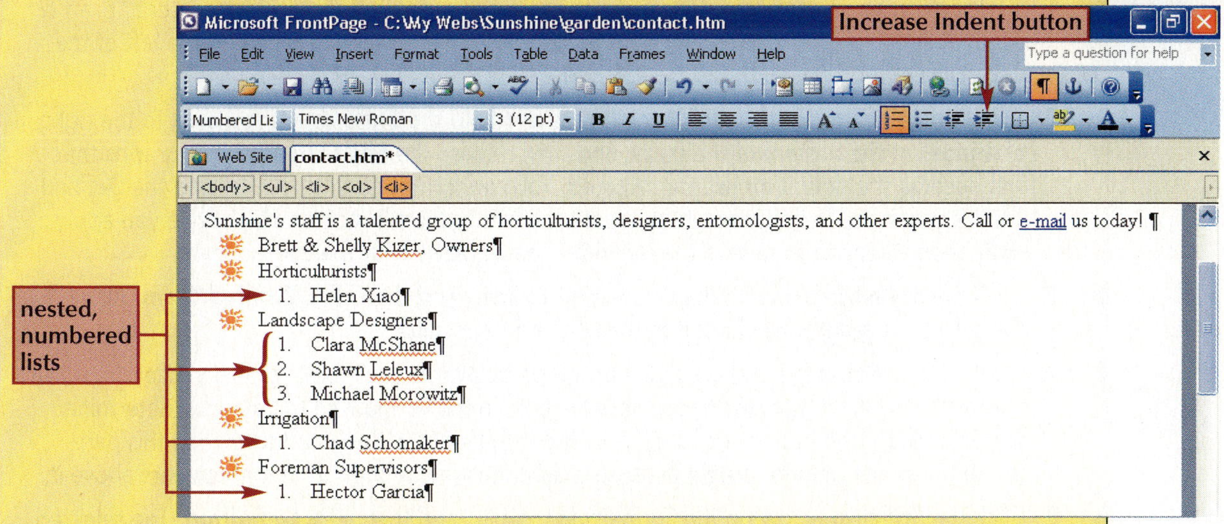

7. Click the **Save** button on the Standard toolbar to save your changes, and then click the **Preview** button on the Standard toolbar to view the page in your browser. Depending on the browser you use, you might see blank lines above and below the nested lists that did not appear in Design view. You could change the HTML document to change the tags for the nested lists to eliminate the extra space, but you decide not to do so at this time. However, this situation does show the importance of testing your pages in a browser to note any changes that occur when a browser interprets the HTML document. Some differences you discover in a browser are acceptable, like this one, but others are not.
8. Close your browser.

Now you can create the definition list.

Creating a Definition List

A definition list contains defined terms and their definitions. The default organization of a definition list is for the defined term to appear on a left-aligned line by itself, and the definition for that defined term to appear in an indented paragraph below the defined term.

Creating a Definition List

Reference Window

- Select the paragraph that will contain the first item in the definition list, and then type the term you want to define.

or

- Click an item in an existing list that you want to use for the defined term.
- Click the Style list arrow on the Formatting toolbar, and then click Defined Term.
- Press the Enter key, and then type the definition for the term.
- If necessary, press the Enter key twice to end the definition list.

Brett already provided the content for the defined terms and their definitions, so you only need to change the format of this content in the Web page. You'll accomplish this task by using the Style list arrow on the Formatting toolbar.

To change existing paragraphs to a definition list:

1. If necessary, scroll down the Web page so you see the paragraph with the content "Brett & Shelly Kizer, Owners" (the one without a bullet character), and then click to the left of the word **Brett**.
2. Scroll to the bottom of the Web page, press and hold the **Shift** key as you click to the right of **minds!** at the bottom of the page, and then release the **Shift** key. The paragraphs that will become the definition list are selected. You can format all of the text using the Defined Term style or the Definition style to create the list; it doesn't matter which style you apply first. Then you need to format the individual paragraphs with the correct style.
3. Click the **Style** list arrow on the Formatting toolbar, and then click **Defined Term**. All of the selected paragraphs change to the Defined Term style.
4. Scroll up the Web page and click the paragraph below the text "Brett & Shelly Kizer, Owners" to select it. Looking at the Style list box on the Formatting toolbar, you determine that this paragraph has the Defined Term style applied to it. You need to change this paragraph to use the Definition style because it describes the defined term that appears above it.
5. Click the **Style** list arrow on the Formatting toolbar, and then click **Definition**. The selected paragraph changes to the Definition style. The default format for a paragraph with the Definition style is indented one tab stop. See Figure 3-12.

Figure 3-12 **Definition list created**

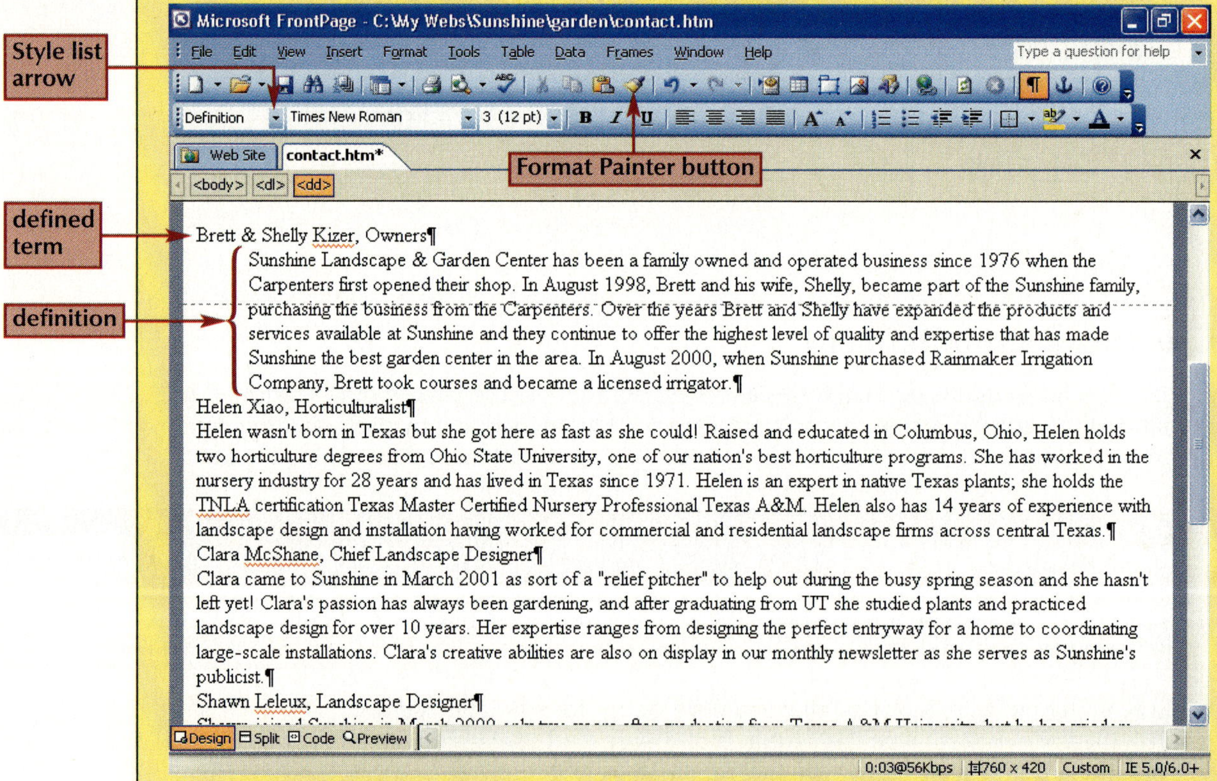

You can format the remaining paragraphs that appear below a person's name and title with the Definition style using the Format Painter button.

6. With the insertion point positioned in the paragraph with the Definition style applied to it, double-click the **Format Painter** button on the Formatting toolbar, and then scroll down the Web page as necessary and click the paragraphs that appear below a person's name and title to change them to the Definition style.

Trouble? If you change a person's name and title to the Definition style by mistake, click the Undo button on the Standard toolbar, and then use the Style list arrow on the Formatting toolbar to change the paragraph to the Defined Term style.

7. After formatting the last paragraph in the page, click the **Format Painter** button on the Formatting toolbar to turn off the Format Painter. Scroll to the top of the page, checking to make sure that you have formatted the page correctly.
8. Save the page.

The Contact Sunshine page now uses lists to organize its contents. Next, you will format the names at the top of the Web page as hyperlinks that jump to the section in the Web page that describe them.

Creating Anchors and Hyperlinks to Anchors

In Tutorial 2, you created hyperlinks to link the pages in the garden Web site to each other. A hyperlink consists of two parts—the text or object that is linked and a target location. For example, the home_pic.gif picture in the center.htm page is the object that is linked to the index.htm page in the Web site. Clicking the picture opens the home page. In this example, the target is another page in the Web site. You can also create hyperlinks to locations in the *same* Web page. To create links to locations in the same Web page, you need a way to identify the location of the target. In HTML, you identify a location in a Web page by creating an anchor. An **anchor** is specially marked text or an object that identifies a named location in a Web page. (In FrontPage, anchors are called **bookmarks**.) When you create a hyperlink to an anchor, the anchor becomes the target of the hyperlink. For example, if you create an anchor named "top" at the beginning of a Web page, you could also create a hyperlink from the text "Back to Top" at the bottom of the Web page that links to the "top" anchor. In this case, a user can click the "Back to Top" text, and the browser will jump to the target, which is the "top" anchor, and as a result, the user is able to scroll immediately to the top of the page. The "top" anchor isn't visible in the Web page itself; it is just a way of identifying a location in the document. You can create an anchor using text, a picture, or a location in a Web page that is not based on text or a picture.

Brett wants to format the list at the top of the Contact Sunshine page so that users can scroll to each person's biography by clicking the person's name in the list. You can place bookmarks (anchors) anywhere in a Web page to make it easier for users to navigate the page, and you can create multiple hyperlinks in a Web page to the same anchor.

When viewed in Design view, text in a bookmark appears as dashed, underlined text. A bookmark that is not based on text appears as a icon when viewed in Design view. When you view a page with bookmarks using a browser, there is no underlining or other identification of the bookmark.

Each bookmark within a Web page must have a unique name. You can use the name that FrontPage suggests for the bookmark—which is taken from the text that you selected when you created it—or you can assign a new name. For Web sites stored on some servers, the names of bookmarks—just like filenames for Web pages—cannot contain any spaces or mixed-case filenames, and cannot exceed eight characters. For this reason, it is a good idea to use bookmark names that will work on any Web server, even if you know that the Web server on which you will eventually publish your Web site supports filenames containing spaces, mixed-case filenames, and filenames exceeding eight characters. The bookmark's name serves only to identify its location in the Web page, so using bookmark names that will work on any server does not affect the content of the Web page.

Creating a Text-Based Bookmark

The Contact Sunshine page contains content that you organized using bulleted, numbered, and definition lists. Now you need to create the bookmarks in the Web page, so when a user clicks a name at the top of the page, the browser will scroll to the bookmark you created for that link. For the names, you will create text-based bookmarks using the defined terms in the definition list.

Reference Window

Creating a Text-Based Bookmark in a Web Page

- Select the text for the bookmark.
- Click Insert on the menu bar, and then click Bookmark.
- Type a bookmark name in the Bookmark name text box, or accept the suggested name.
- Click the OK button to create the bookmark.

You'll create the first bookmark for Brett and Shelly's biography.

To create a text-based bookmark:

1. Double-click the word **Brett** in the first defined term in the Web page (not the word "Brett" in the bulleted list). The word "Brett" will become the location of the bookmark you will create. You could have also selected the entire line, "Brett & Shelly Kizer, Owners," or any combination of words on this line when creating the bookmark. The browser would still scroll to this location in the Web page.
2. Click **Insert** on the menu bar, and then click **Bookmark** to open the Bookmark dialog box. See Figure 3-13.

Figure 3-13 Bookmark dialog box

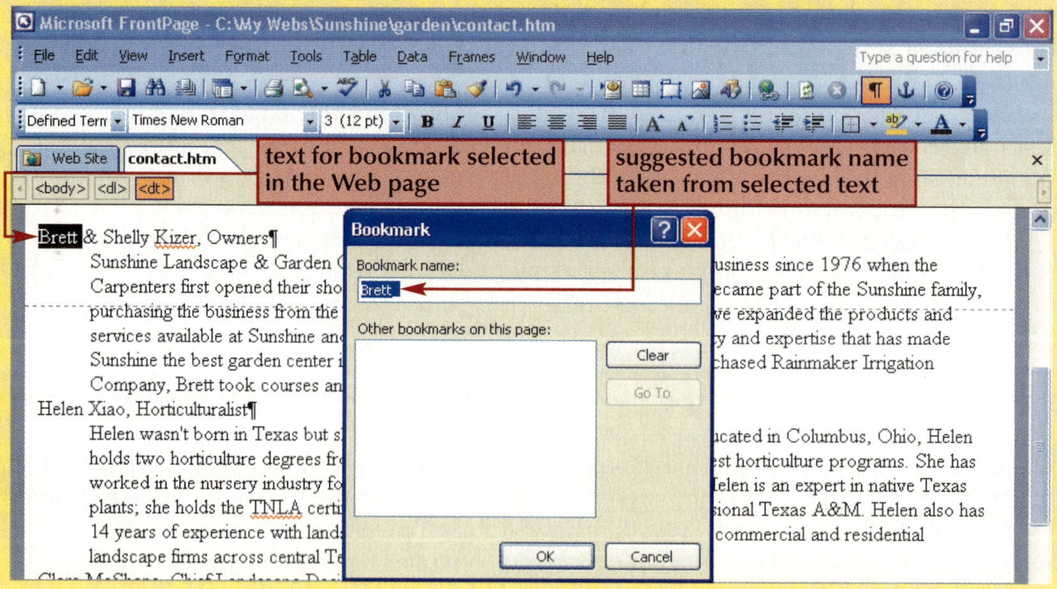

FrontPage used the text you selected to create the bookmark name. When you double-clicked the word "Brett" to select it, you selected the word "Brett" and the space that follows it. Because a bookmark cannot contain a space, FrontPage changed the space character to an underscore character. You could accept the suggested bookmark name of

"Brett_" but decide to delete the underscore character. In addition, to ensure that this bookmark is valid on any Web server, you will change it to all lowercase letters.

3. With Brett_ selected in the Bookmark name text box, type **brett** (with all lowercase letters), and then click the **OK** button. The selected word "Brett" in the Web page has a dashed underline, indicating the location of the bookmark you just created.
4. Scroll down the Web page as necessary, double-click the word **Helen** in the next defined term to select it, click **Insert** on the menu bar, and then click **Bookmark**. The Bookmark dialog box opens again, as shown in Figure 3-14. This time, notice that the brett bookmark you created appears in the Other bookmarks on this page list. As you create bookmarks in a Web page, they will appear in this dialog box. By giving the bookmarks simple names, it makes it easier for you to remember and identify where you created them in the Web page. This association will be helpful when you create hyperlinks to the bookmarks.

Bookmark created in the Web page | **Figure 3-14**

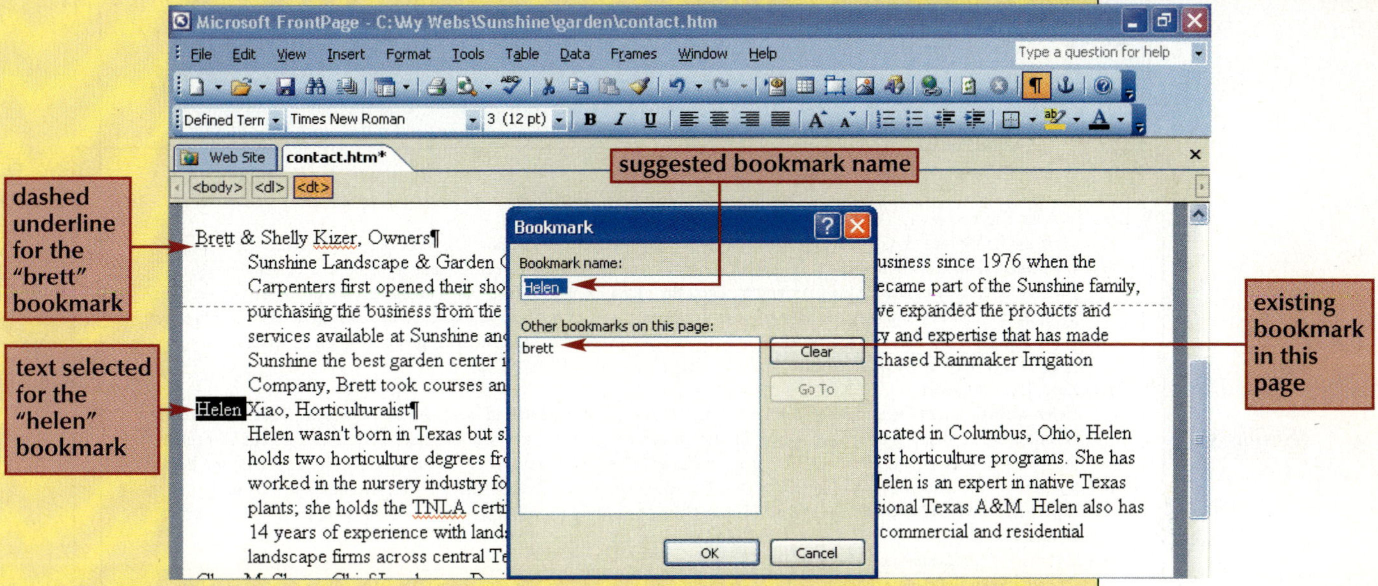

5. Type **helen** (with all lowercase letters) in the Bookmark name text box, and then click the **OK** button to create the bookmark.
6. Repeat Steps 1 through 3 to create bookmarks using the words **Clara**, **Shawn**, **Michael**, **Chad**, and **Hector** in the remaining defined terms in the Web page. For each bookmark, change the default bookmark name to the same name but with all lowercase letters and no underscore character.
7. When you have finished creating the bookmarks, scroll to the top of the page.

Your next task is to create hyperlinks from the names at the top of the page to the associated bookmark in the definition list.

Creating a Hyperlink to a Bookmark

After you format the names at the top of the page as hyperlinks, clicking a link will scroll the Web page to the bookmark. Figure 3-15 illustrates how these bookmarks will work.

Figure 3-15 **Hyperlinks and bookmarks for the Contact Sunshine page**

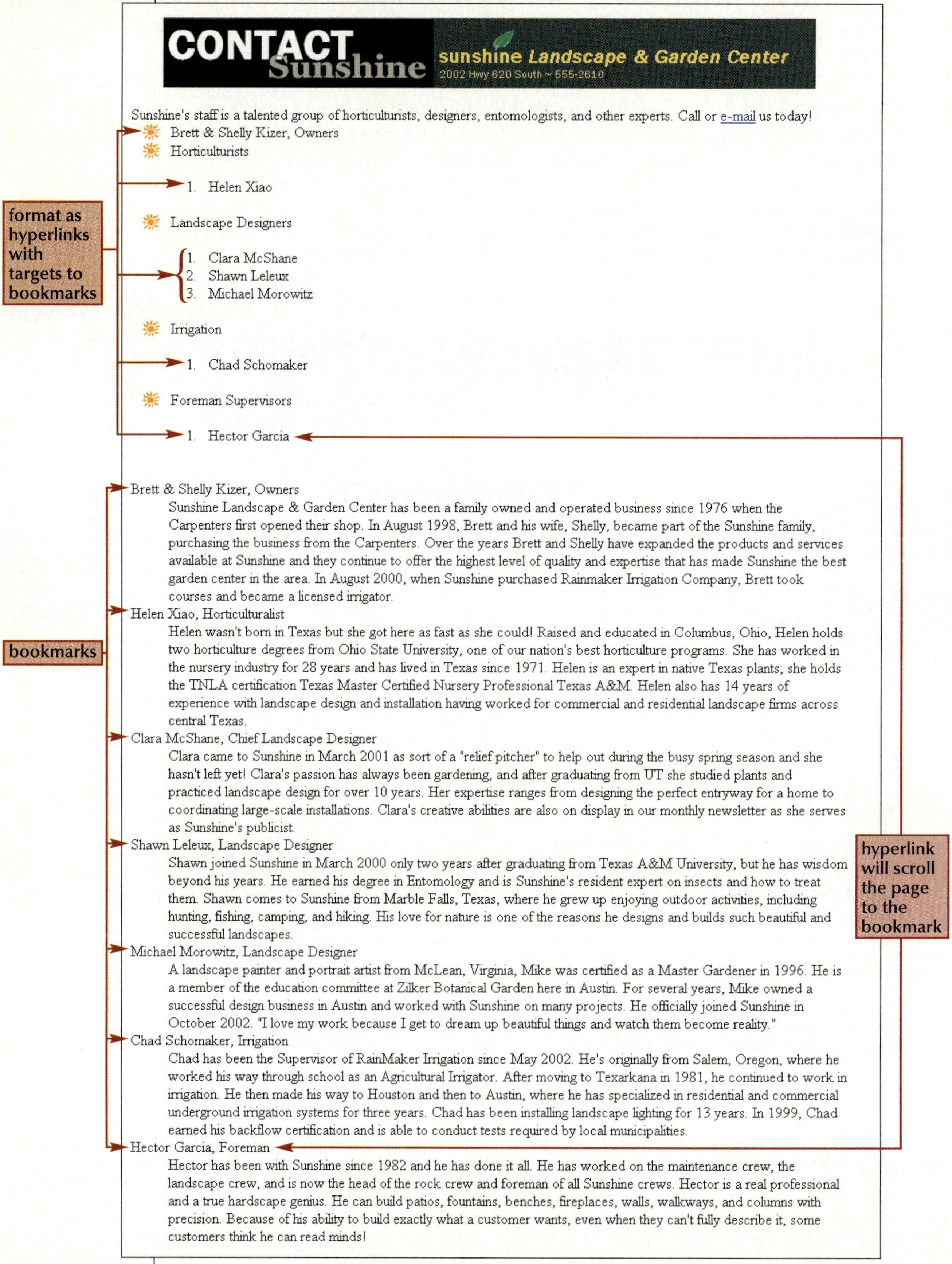

CONTACT Sunshine
sunshine Landscape & Garden Center
2002 Hwy 620 South ~ 555-2610

Sunshine's staff is a talented group of horticulturists, designers, entomologists, and other experts. Call or e-mail us today!

- Brett & Shelly Kizer, Owners
- Horticulturists
  1. Helen Xiao
- Landscape Designers
  1. Clara McShane
  2. Shawn Leleux
  3. Michael Morowitz
- Irrigation
  1. Chad Schomaker
- Foreman Supervisors
  1. Hector Garcia

Brett & Shelly Kizer, Owners

Sunshine Landscape & Garden Center has been a family owned and operated business since 1976 when the Carpenters first opened their shop. In August 1998, Brett and his wife, Shelly, became part of the Sunshine family, purchasing the business from the Carpenters. Over the years Brett and Shelly have expanded the products and services available at Sunshine and they continue to offer the highest level of quality and expertise that has made Sunshine the best garden center in the area. In August 2000, when Sunshine purchased Rainmaker Irrigation Company, Brett took courses and became a licensed irrigator.

Helen Xiao, Horticulturalist

Helen wasn't born in Texas but she got here as fast as she could! Raised and educated in Columbus, Ohio, Helen holds two horticulture degrees from Ohio State University, one of our nation's best horticulture programs. She has worked in the nursery industry for 28 years and has lived in Texas since 1971. Helen is an expert in native Texas plants; she holds the TNLA certification Texas Master Certified Nursery Professional Texas A&M. Helen also has 14 years of experience with landscape design and installation having worked for commercial and residential landscape firms across central Texas.

Clara McShane, Chief Landscape Designer

Clara came to Sunshine in March 2001 as sort of a "relief pitcher" to help out during the busy spring season and she hasn't left yet! Clara's passion has always been gardening, and after graduating from UT she studied plants and practiced landscape design for over 10 years. Her expertise ranges from designing the perfect entryway for a home to coordinating large-scale installations. Clara's creative abilities are also on display in our monthly newsletter as she serves as Sunshine's publicist.

Shawn Leleux, Landscape Designer

Shawn joined Sunshine in March 2000 only two years after graduating from Texas A&M University, but he has wisdom beyond his years. He earned his degree in Entomology and is Sunshine's resident expert on insects and how to treat them. Shawn comes to Sunshine from Marble Falls, Texas, where he grew up enjoying outdoor activities, including hunting, fishing, camping, and hiking. His love for nature is one of the reasons he designs and builds such beautiful and successful landscapes.

Michael Morowitz, Landscape Designer

A landscape painter and portrait artist from McLean, Virginia, Mike was certified as a Master Gardener in 1996. He is a member of the education committee at Zilker Botanical Garden here in Austin. For several years, Mike owned a successful design business in Austin and worked with Sunshine on many projects. He officially joined Sunshine in October 2002. "I love my work because I get to dream up beautiful things and watch them become reality."

Chad Schomaker, Irrigation

Chad has been the Supervisor of RainMaker Irrigation since May 2002. He's originally from Salem, Oregon, where he worked his way through school as an Agricultural Irrigator. After moving to Texarkana in 1981, he continued to work in irrigation. He then made his way to Houston and then to Austin, where he has specialized in residential and commercial underground irrigation systems for three years. Chad has been installing landscape lighting for 13 years. In 1999, Chad earned his backflow certification and is able to conduct tests required by local municipalities.

Hector Garcia, Foreman

Hector has been with Sunshine since 1982 and he has done it all. He has worked on the maintenance crew, the landscape crew, and is now the head of the rock crew and foreman of all Sunshine crews. Hector is a real professional and a true hardscape genius. He can build patios, fountains, benches, fireplaces, walls, walkways, and columns with precision. Because of his ability to build exactly what a customer wants, even when they can't fully describe it, some customers think he can read minds!

Creating a Hyperlink to a Bookmark

Reference Window

- Select the text for the hyperlink.
- Click the Insert Hyperlink button on the Standard toolbar.
- Click the Place in This Document button on the Link to bar to display the list of bookmarks created in the Web page.
- Click the desired bookmark to select it, and then click the OK button.

When you created the bookmarks, you could use one word or the entire line as the bookmark location in the document. When you create the hyperlinks, however, you must select the exact text that you want to format as a hyperlink. Now you are ready to create the hyperlinks to the bookmarks you created.

To create the hyperlinks to the bookmarks:

1. In the bulleted list at the top of the page, select the text **Brett & Shelly Kizer, Owners**. This is the text that you will format as a hyperlink.
2. Click the **Insert Hyperlink** button on the Standard toolbar to open the Insert Hyperlink dialog box. Because you are creating a hyperlink to a location in the current document, you must display the options for working with bookmarks.
3. Click the **Place in This Document** button on the Link to bar to display a list of bookmarks in the Contact Sunshine page. See Figure 3-16.

Figure 3-16 **Selecting a bookmark as the hyperlink target**

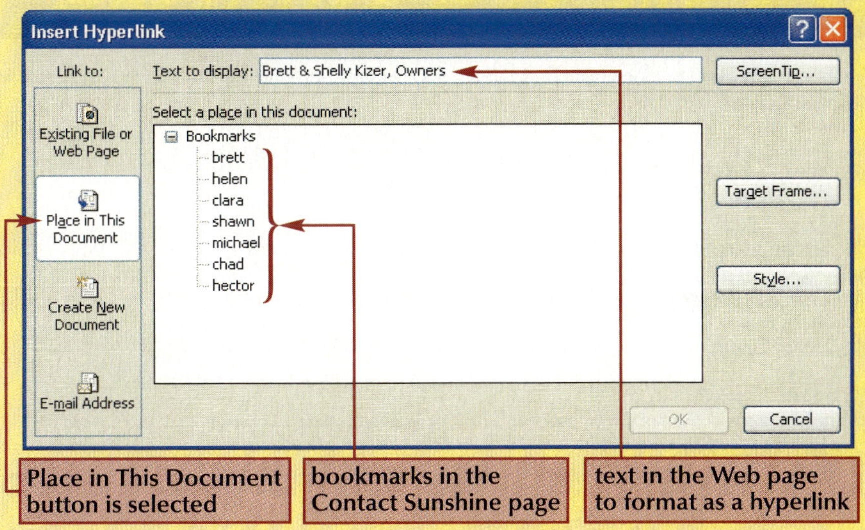

Trouble? If you do not see the bookmarks in the page, click the plus box to the left of the word "Bookmarks" in the list box.

4. Click **brett** to select it, and then click the **OK** button. The Insert Hyperlink dialog box closes, and the first item in the bulleted list is formatted as a hyperlink.
5. Click the text **Brett & Shelly Kizer, Owners** to deselect it. This text now appears with a solid underline, indicating that it is a hyperlink.
6. Point to the hyperlink you created. When you point to the hyperlink, the status bar displays the text #brett, which identifies the bookmark's location in the Web page. The pound sign (#) indicates that the target of the hyperlink is a bookmark.
7. Select the text **Helen Xiao** in the nested, numbered list, and then repeat Steps 2 through 5 using the **helen** bookmark.
8. Repeat Steps 2 through 5 to create hyperlinks using the text **Clara McShane**, **Shawn Leleux**, **Michael Morowitz**, **Chad Schomaker**, and **Hector Garcia** in the nested, numbered lists to their associated bookmarks. When you are finished, deselect any selected text. See Figure 3-17.

Figure 3-17 **Hyperlinks created using bookmarks as their targets**

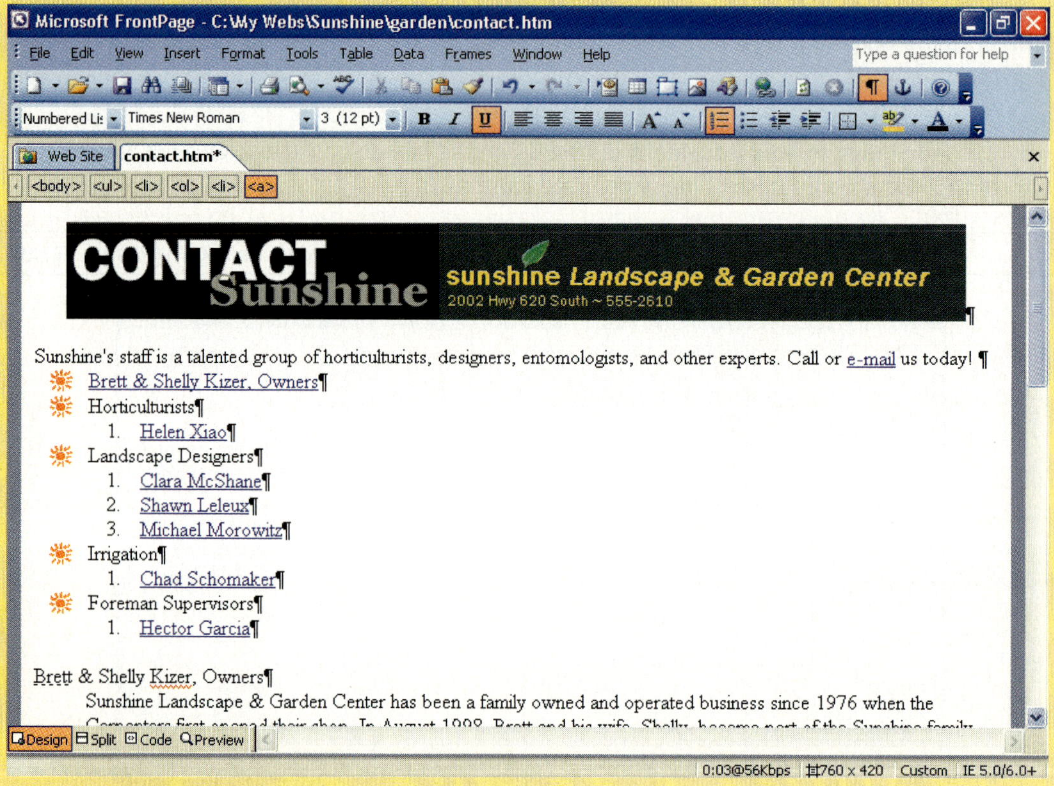

You could have named the bookmarks differently, but Brett now sees that using text from the bookmark's location has made it very easy to associate the hyperlink text with the correct bookmark in the Web page.

9. Click the **Save** button on the Standard toolbar to save your changes.

Before continuing, you need to verify that the hyperlinks to the bookmarks work correctly. You will test the hyperlinks in a browser.

To test an internal hyperlink using a browser:

1. Click the **Preview** button on the Standard toolbar.
2. Point to the **Helen Xiao** hyperlink at the top of the page. The pointer changes to a shape.
3. Click the **Helen Xiao** hyperlink. The Web page scrolls so that the helen bookmark's location is at the top of the window. Notice that the word "Helen," which is the text for the helen bookmark, does not have a dashed underline.
4. Scroll to the top of the page, and then click the **Hector Garcia** hyperlink. Hector's biography appears at the bottom of the Web page, so you see the bottom of the Web page instead of seeing the hector bookmark at the top of the window.
5. Close your browser.

All of the bookmarks that you have created so far used text in the Web page to identify their locations. You can also use a picture to create a bookmark that works exactly like one that uses text. You create a bookmark to a picture by selecting the picture, opening the Bookmark dialog box, and giving the picture a name. Next you'll learn how to create a third type of bookmark, one that is not based on text or a picture.

Creating Nontext-Based Bookmarks

As you were testing the Contact Sunshine page, you had to scroll up the page to return to the hyperlinks. Most users expect and appreciate a "Top of Page" link that scrolls to the top of the page. As the anchor for such a link, you could create a "top" bookmark in the Contact Sunshine page using the contact.gif picture at the top of the page. However, you decide to show Brett something new—you'll create a bookmark that is based on a specific location in the page. In this case, a icon will appear in Design view to identify the bookmark's location. When you view the Web page in a browser, the icon is not visible.

You'll create a bookmark at the top of the page, and then you'll create a "Top of Page" hyperlink after each definition in the Web page that will scroll back to the top of the page.

To create a nontext-based bookmark:

1. Click the **contact.gif** picture at the top of the page, and then press the **left arrow** key ← to move the insertion point to the left of the picture. The picture should *not* be selected.
2. Click **Insert** on the menu bar, and then click **Bookmark** to open the Bookmark dialog box. Because you did not select any text, FrontPage does not suggest a name for the bookmark. When you create bookmark names, it is a good idea to select ones that describe the location in which the bookmark appears, so it is easy to recognize a bookmark in the page. When you click the "Top of Page" hyperlink in this page, the page will scroll to the bookmark. For this reason, "top" is a good bookmark name.
3. Type **top** in the Bookmark name text box as the name for this new bookmark, click the **OK** button, and then press the **End** key to deselect the bookmark icon, which has a dashed underline. See Figure 3-18.

Figure 3-18 **Creating a bookmark that is not based on text**

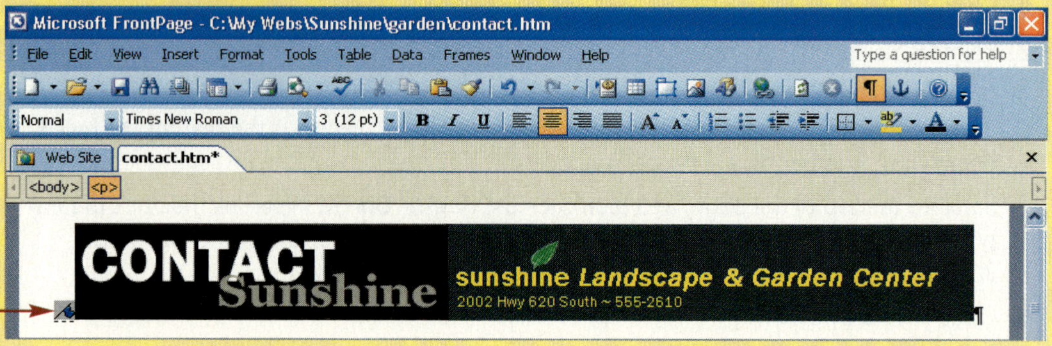

"top" bookmark

Next, you will create a "Top of Page" hyperlink below the first definition in the definition list. After creating this hyperlink, you can copy and paste it below other definitions in the list so the user can scroll back to the top of the page after reading any person's biography in the page.

Creating Multiple Hyperlinks to a Bookmark

A bookmark can have many hyperlinks to it from different locations within a Web page. Regardless of which biography the user reads, he needs an easy way to return to the top of the page. You can create a single bookmark in the Web page and then create as many hyperlinks as necessary to that bookmark. When multiple hyperlinks reference a single bookmark, the bookmark has multiple hyperlinks, or multiple references, to it.

With the bookmark already created at the top of the page, you can create a hyperlink to it.

To create multiple hyperlinks to a bookmark:

1. Scroll down the Web page, and then click to the right of **irrigator.** at the end of the first definition in the definition list (the definition paragraph for Brett & Shelly).
2. Press the **Enter** key to create a new paragraph, click the **Style** list arrow on the Formatting toolbar, and then click **Normal**. The new paragraph changes to the Normal style.
3. Type **Top of Page** as the text for the new hyperlink.
4. Select the text **Top of Page**, click the **Insert Hyperlink** button on the Standard toolbar to open the Insert Hyperlink dialog box, and then, if necessary, click the **Place in This Document** button on the Link to bar to display the list of available bookmarks.
5. Click the **top** bookmark, and then click the **OK** button. The Insert Hyperlink dialog box closes and the text "Top of Page" is formatted as a hyperlink.
6. With the Top of Page hyperlink still selected, click the **Copy** button on the Standard toolbar to copy the hyperlink to the Clipboard.
7. Scroll down the Web page, click to the right of **Texas.** at the end of the definition for Helen, press the **Enter** key to create a new paragraph, change the new paragraph to the **Normal** style, and then click the **Paste** button on the Standard toolbar. The hyperlink to the top bookmark now appears below the definition for Helen, as shown in Figure 3-19. Because you want to copy the text and its formatting, which is the default option, you can ignore the Paste Options button that might appear when you paste the text.

Hyperlinks created to bookmark target **Figure 3-19**

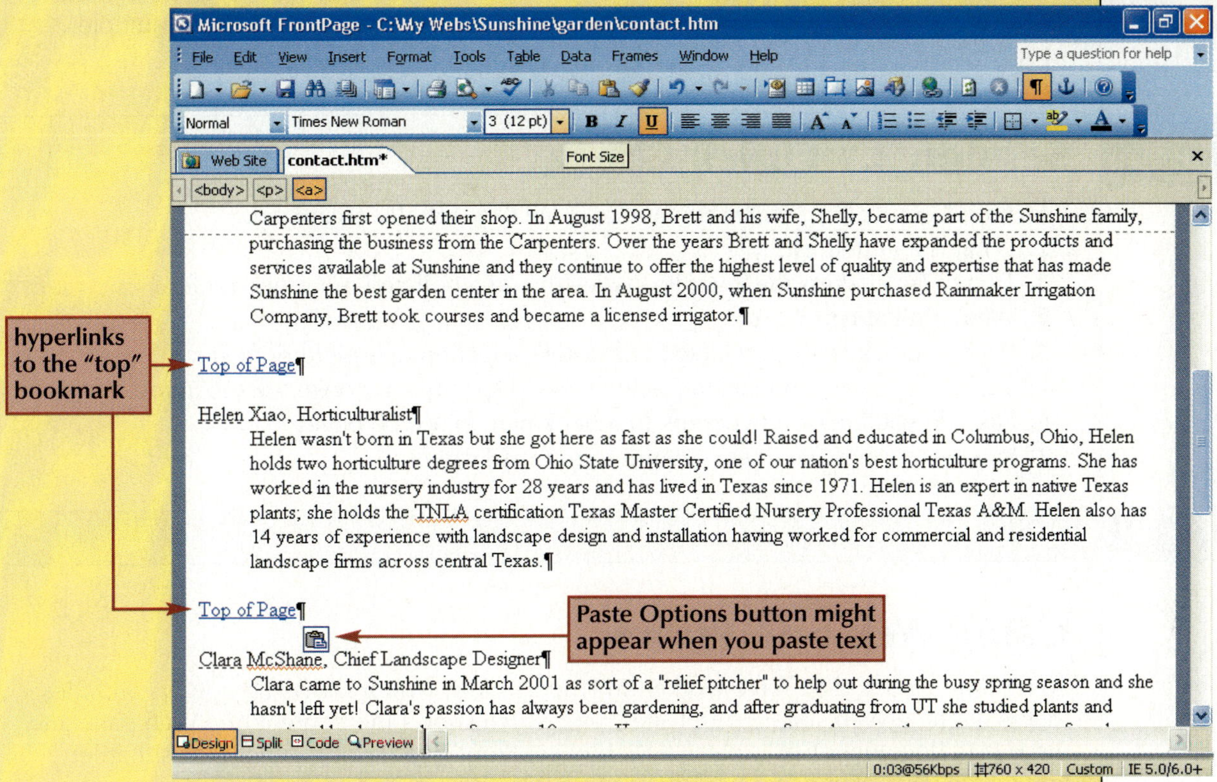

8. Repeat Step 7 to create Top of Page hyperlinks below the definition paragraphs for Clara, Shawn, Michael, Chad, and Hector.
9. Save the Contact Sunshine page.

Now you will use a browser to test all the hyperlinks you have created.

To test the hyperlinks in a browser:

1. Click the **Preview** button on the Standard toolbar. The Contact Sunshine page opens in a browser.
2. Test each hyperlink that you created in this session to make sure that it works correctly. Depending on your monitor and its resolution, clicking the last several hyperlinks in the bulleted list might result in the browser scrolling to the bottom of the page instead of displaying the defined term at the top of the window.

   Trouble? If you have problems with a hyperlink, return to Design view and make any necessary changes. When you are finished, save the page and preview it again in a browser.
3. Close your browser.
4. Close the **garden** Web site, and then exit FrontPage.

The hyperlinks to bookmarks you created in the Contact Sunshine page work as expected. Brett is pleased with the final version of this page and feels confident that his customers will be able to use the page to learn more about the center's expert employees.

In the next session, you will show Brett how to use different Web site views to learn about the Web site's organization, reports, and hyperlinks. You will also show Brett how to use Tasks view to organize the tasks required to complete a Web site when it has multiple contributors.

Review

Session 3.1 Quick Check

1. A(n) ______________ list is one that is not sequentially organized.
2. What is a nested list?
3. True or False: Press the Enter key twice to end a bulleted or numbered list.
4. What is an anchor?
5. If a bookmark is not associated with a text selection or a picture, then a(n) ______________ appears in Design view to specify the bookmark's location.
6. How do you create a hyperlink to a bookmark in a Web page?
7. In a hyperlink, what does a pound sign (#) indicate?

Session 3.2

Using Web Site Views

So far in this book, you have worked in Folders view, which shows the folders and files that make up a Web site, and in Page view, which shows the content of a Web page and the HTML document that creates a Web page. FrontPage has five other views that let you create your Web pages and manage your Web sites. The seven Web site views are described in Figure 3-20. In this session, you will learn about Hyperlinks view, Reports view, and Tasks view. You will also learn more about the views in which you have been working, Page view and Folders view. In Tutorial 4, you will learn about Navigation view when you create the Web site's navigation structure to identify how pages in the Web site are related to each other. Finally, you will learn about Remote Web Site view in Tutorial 6 when you publish the garden Web site to a server.

Figure 3-20 **FrontPage Web site views**

View	Description
Page	Use to create, edit, format, and view the content of a Web page
Folders	Use to view, create, delete, copy, rename, and move folders and files in the current Web site
Remote Web Site	Use to publish a Web site to another location and to synchronize copies of the Web site stored in different locations
Reports	Use to analyze, summarize, and produce various types of reports about a Web site
Navigation	Use to create or display a Web site's navigation structure, which identifies the relationships among pages
Hyperlinks	Use to examine the hyperlinks in a Web site
Tasks	Use to maintain a list of the tasks required to complete a Web site

Page View

Most of the work you have completed thus far in the garden Web site has been in **Page view**, which is the Web site view you use to create, edit, format, and view the content of the site's Web pages. Page view has four different ways of displaying a Web page. You can work in Design view, which shows the formatted content of the Web page. Code view shows the HTML document that creates the Web page. Split view shows the HTML document and the formatted Web page at the same time, so you can see both the code that creates the content of the Web page and the appearance of the Web page simultaneously. Finally, Preview view shows the Web page as it will appear when viewed using a browser.

Because Brett has been working in Page view for some time now, you decide that he is ready to learn more about some of the settings that are important for using FrontPage to its full potential, but that might overwhelm a new FrontPage user. You decide to show him a few tricks to help him become more proficient at using FrontPage. The first thing you'll show him is how to use the Clipboard task pane.

To display the Clipboard task pane:

1. Start **FrontPage**, open the **garden** Web site from the location where your Web sites are stored, and then open the home page in Design view.
2. Click **View** on the menu bar, and then click **Task Pane**.
3. Click the **Other Task Panes** list arrow, and then click **Clipboard**.

The **Windows Clipboard** is a temporary storage area in Windows that stores items that you cut and copy from FrontPage and from other programs. The content of the Clipboard is accessible using the Clipboard task pane. If you just started Windows and FrontPage, then your Clipboard task pane is empty. If you have been working in FrontPage or another program and have copied or cut text or other objects, then you might see these objects on the Clipboard task pane. The items on the Clipboard are deleted when you click the Clear All button on the Clipboard task pane or when you turn off your computer.

While working on the Contact Sunshine page in the previous session, you used the Copy button on the Standard toolbar to copy a hyperlink, and then you used the Paste button on the Standard toolbar to paste that hyperlink in other locations in the same Web page. As you cut and copy text and graphics, they are stored on the Clipboard task pane (and on the Windows Clipboard), even if the Clipboard task pane isn't visible. Because the Clipboard task pane can store up to 24 items, it can save you a lot of time. For example, you tell Brett that the link bar and Sunshine logo need to be inserted into other Web pages. You will show him how to use the Clipboard task pane to make these changes.

To use the Clipboard task pane:

1. Position the pointer to the left of the link bar in the home page so it changes to a shape, and then click the left margin. The link bar is selected.
2. Click the **Copy** button on the Standard toolbar. A picture appears on the Clipboard task pane, making it easy to recall the item later. The link bar you copied is really five separate pictures, but only the Home picture is visible in the Clipboard task pane. The Home picture just reminds you what you copied; the full content of the item you copied or cut does not always appear on the Clipboard task pane.

3. Click the logo picture on the next line, and then click [Copy button]. The logo is copied and a reduced image of it appears on the Clipboard task pane. The Clipboard task pane lists the most recently cut or copied item at the top of the list, so the logo picture appears first in the list.
4. Click the **Web Site** tab, if necessary change to Folders view, and then open the **bulk.htm** page in Design view.
5. Click the Home picture on the Clipboard task pane. The link bar and its hotspots are pasted into the bulk.htm page. Because you pasted pictures, you can ignore the Paste Options button that might appear on your screen.
6. Click the logo picture on the Clipboard task pane. The logo is pasted into the Web page, as shown in Figure 3-21.

Figure 3-21 **Using the Clipboard task pane**

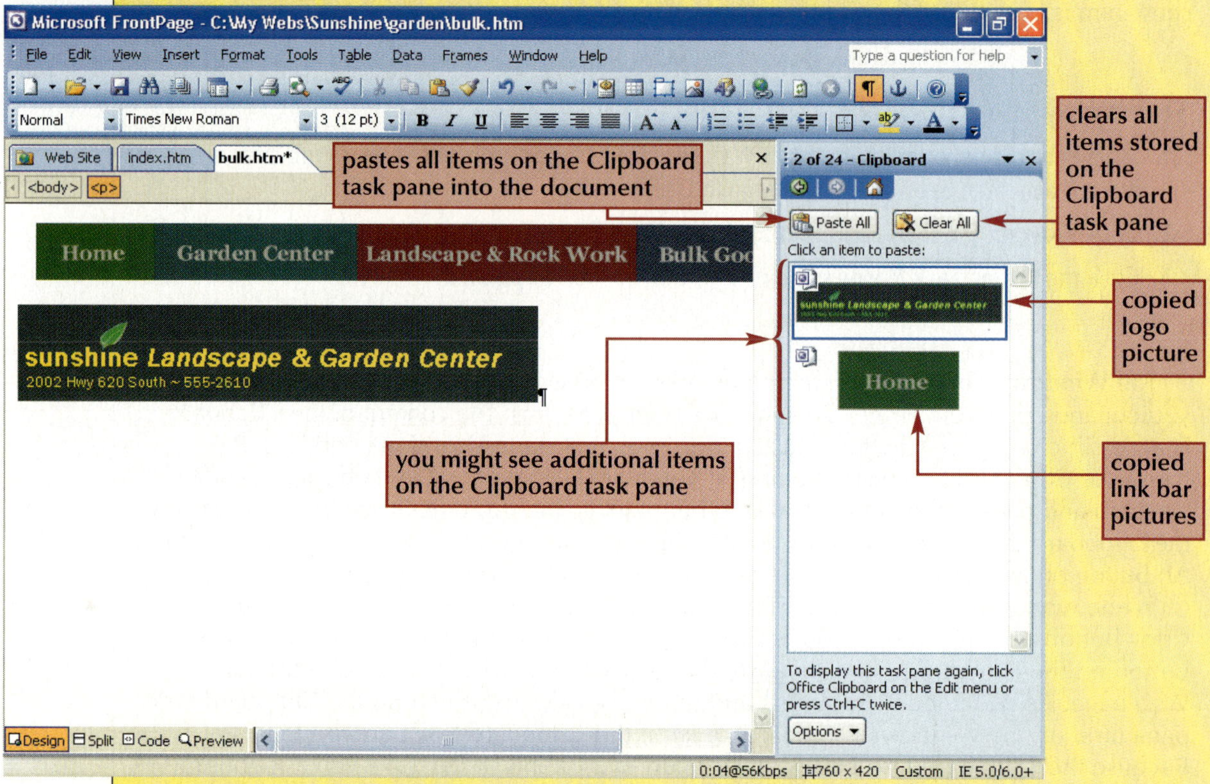

You need to center the paragraph that contains the logo picture.

7. Click the **Center** button [Center button] on the Formatting toolbar.

   Trouble? If you see any blank paragraphs in the page, select and delete them.

   Trouble? If the link bar isn't centered on the page, click any picture in the link bar, and then click the Center button on the Formatting toolbar.

8. Save the bulk.htm page, and then click the **Close** button [Close button] on the Clipboard task pane to close it.

The items you cut or copy from FrontPage and other programs will remain on the Clipboard task pane until you turn off your computer or delete them. If you want to paste all items on the Clipboard task pane at the same time, click the Paste All button. To clear the contents in the Clipboard task pane, click the Clear All button.

Another thing that you want to demonstrate to Brett is how to document your work in a Web page. Many developers use HTML **comments** to identify the pages on which they have worked, the date the page was last revised, and notes about the page's content or format. These comments appear in the HTML document, but not in the Web page. In FrontPage, there are two ways to add a comment to a Web page. The first way is to type the HTML comment tags (<!-- and -->) directly into the HTML document shown in Code view. The text you want to insert as a comment appears between the tags, such as <!--This document was last revised by Brett Kizer.--> This content will not appear in the Web page because the browser ignores content in comment tags.

When you insert a comment into the HTML document, you can see it only in Code view. If you want to see the comment in Design view, you can use the Comment command on the Insert menu to insert the comment. The text you type appears within the HTML comment tags in Code view, but it is also visible in Design view. However, when you view the page in a browser, the browser ignores the comment.

Inserting a Comment into a Web Page

Reference Window

- Click the location where you want to insert the comment.
- Click Insert on the menu bar, and then click Comment.
- In the Comment text box, type the content of your comment, and then click the OK button.

You'll show Brett how to insert a comment into the bulk.htm page so it will show up in Design view.

To insert a comment into a Web page so it appears in Design view:

1. Press the **Enter** key to create a new paragraph below the logo picture, and then click the **Align Left** button on the Formatting toolbar to left-align the paragraph.
2. Click **Insert** on the menu bar, and then click **Comment**. The Comment dialog box opens and the insertion point appears in the Comment text box.
3. Type **Clara will take the photographs to include in this page.** and then click the **OK** button. The comment appears as purple text in the Web page, as shown in Figure 3-22.

Figure 3-22 Comment added in Design view

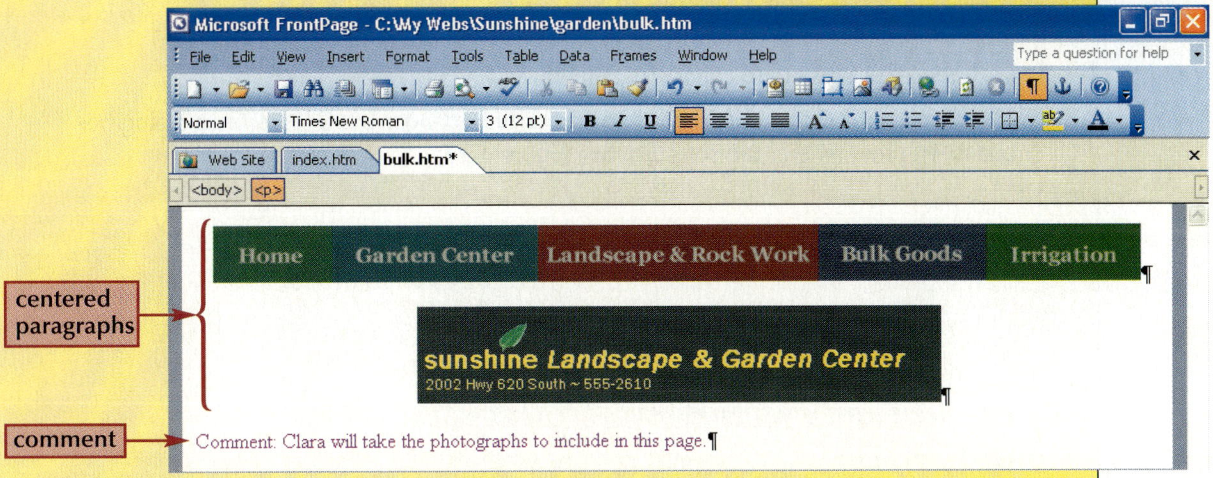

To see the HTML comment tags, you need to change to Code view.

4. Select the comment you inserted in Step 3, and then change to Code view. The comment is selected in the HTML document. Notice the HTML comment tags that enclose the comment. The bot and PREVIEW properties that FrontPage added to your comment make it visible in Design view, but a browser will ignore everything in the <!-- and --> tags.
5. Click the **Show Preview View** button Preview at the bottom of the Contents pane. The comment does not appear in Preview view.
6. Return to Design view, and then save and close the bulk.htm page.

Brett appreciates the tips you have given him for working in Page view. He asks if there are any helpful things that he needs to know about Folders view.

Folders View

You use **Folders view** to display and navigate the folders in a Web site. Clicking a folder in Folders view shows the folder's contents, along with valuable information about each file in the folder, such as its size, type, title, the name of the person who last modified it, and the date and time it was last modified. Using Folders view is very similar to using Windows Explorer to examine files. When you double-click the filename of a Web page in Folders view, that page opens in Design view.

When you first create a Web site, you must indicate the location in which to store the Web site and give it a name. By default, FrontPage creates the images folder in a Web site, in which you can store all of your site's multimedia files, and the _private folder, in which you can store files that you do not want to make accessible to Web site visitors after you publish your site. When a folder name begins with an underscore character, it is called a hidden folder. The _private folder is always visible in Folders view; depending on how FrontPage is configured, you might see other hidden folders that FrontPage creates as you work in your Web site.

You can examine and change a Web site's settings using the Site Settings dialog box. You decide to show Brett the Site Settings dialog box so he knows how to change some of the Web site's general settings, including how to change the Web site's name, check the settings of the Web site's server and the version of the FrontPage Server Extensions or SharePoint Services that are in use, delete temporary files, and display a Web site's hidden folders.

To examine a Web site's general settings:

1. Click the **Web Site** tab to change to Folders view.
2. Click **Tools** on the menu bar, and then click **Site Settings**. The Site Settings dialog box opens with the General tab selected. See Figure 3-23.

Figure 3-23 General tab of the Site Settings dialog box

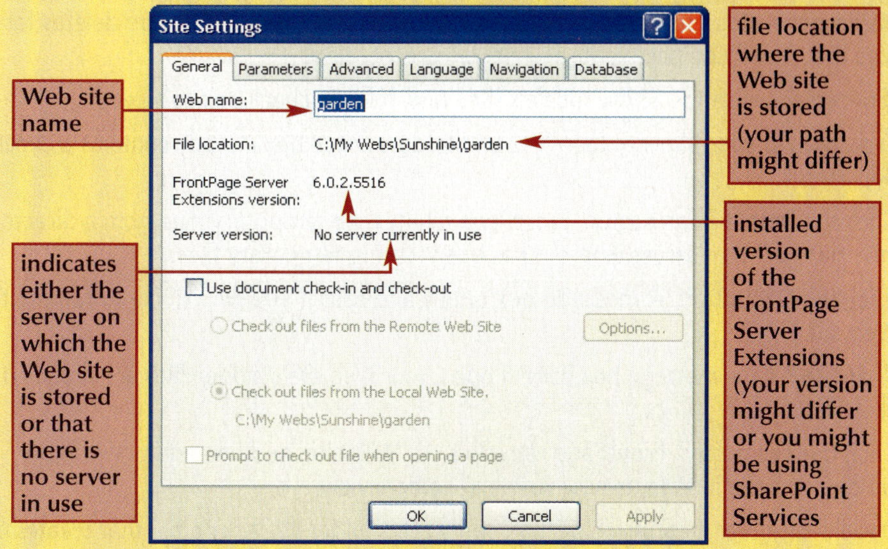

The Web site name, garden, appears in the Web name text box. If Brett needs to change the name of the Web site, he could type a new one in the Web name text box. FrontPage would change the name of the Web site's root folder and update the hyperlinks and pages in the Web site to use the new folder name.

You tell Brett that he will learn more about publishing a Web site in Tutorial 6, but you want to point out the information provided on the General tab about the FrontPage Server Extensions or SharePoint Services version and server version used in the current site. When you are working in a disk-based Web site, there is no server version indicated on the General tab. When you publish the Web site, the General tab will tell you the version of FrontPage Server Extensions or SharePoint Services in use and the server on which the current Web site is stored.

3. Click the **Advanced** tab. See Figure 3-24.

Figure 3-24 Advanced tab of the Site Settings dialog box

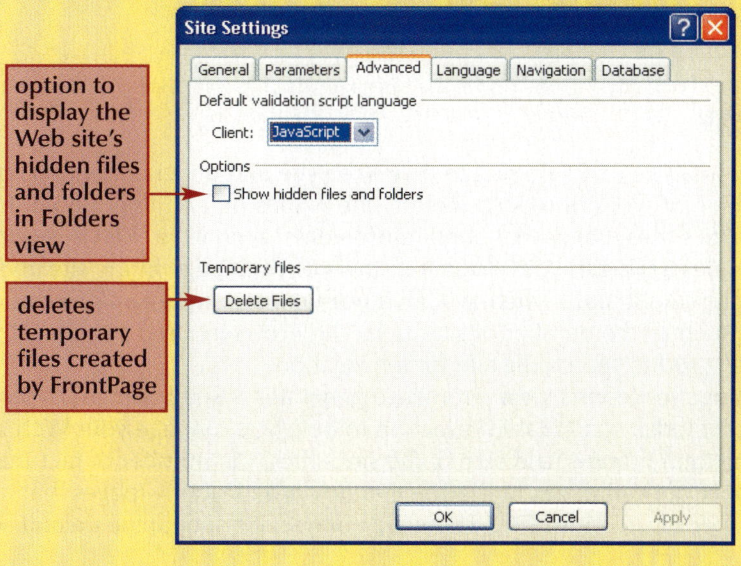

The Advanced tab lets you set the default validation script language (a feature that is beyond the scope of this tutorial). Selecting the Show hidden files and folders check box displays the Web site's hidden files and folders. The Delete Files button deletes temporary files that FrontPage has created while you are working.

4. If necessary, click the **Show hidden files and folders** check box to select it.

   Trouble? If your Show hidden files and folders check box already contains a check mark, skip Step 4.

5. Click the **Delete Files** button. FrontPage deletes the temporary files from a directory on your hard drive or server where it has been storing temporary files.

6. Click the **OK** button. A message box opens and asks if you would like to refresh the Web site.

   Trouble? If the message box doesn't open, your Web site's hidden files are already displayed. Skip Step 7.

7. Click the **Yes** button. FrontPage refreshes the Web site, and one additional folder, _overlay, which had been hidden, is now visible in Folders view.

8. Double-click the **_overlay** folder to open it. This folder stores one file that creates the text on the thumbnail picture in the home page. (You might see additional files, depending on how FrontPage is configured.)

9. Click the **Up One Level** button at the top of the Contents pane. The contents of the root folder are displayed again. Notice that there are two other buttons on the Contents pane in Folders view. The New Page button creates a new page in the current folder, and the New Folder button creates a subfolder in the current folder. You can use folders to organize the pages in your Web site to make them easier for you to locate and use.

   Trouble? If you do not see the files in the root folder, click the Refresh button on the Standard toolbar.

10. Click **Tools** on the menu bar, click **Site Settings**, click the **Advanced** tab, click the **Show hidden files and folders** check box to clear it, click the **OK** button, and then click the **Yes** button. FrontPage refreshes the Web site and hides the Web site's hidden files and folders.

Brett appreciates knowing more about changing the Web site's general settings. Next you'll show him how to use Reports view.

Reports View

Reports view lets you analyze and summarize your Web site and generate reports about your Web site. The different types of reports identify the names of, and important information about, all of the site's files; pages that contain problems, such as broken hyperlinks; workflow information describing the development status of each page in the site and the person assigned to complete it; and, when available from the server, usage information about your Web site, such as the number of site users, the browsers used to access the site, and the keywords used to search the site for information.

When you first change to Reports view, FrontPage generates a Site Summary report. The **Site Summary report** includes statistical information to help you manage your Web site, such as data about the total number and size of the site's files, the number of pictures in the site, and the number of Web pages in the site that download slowly (pages that take longer than a set number of seconds using a specific connection speed; the default setting is 30 seconds).

To change to Reports view:

1. Click the **Reports View** button [Reports] at the bottom of the Contents pane. Figure 3-25 shows a Site Summary report for the garden Web site. (The statistics in your report might look different, but you should see the same list of reports.)

Site Summary report in Reports view | **Figure 3-25**

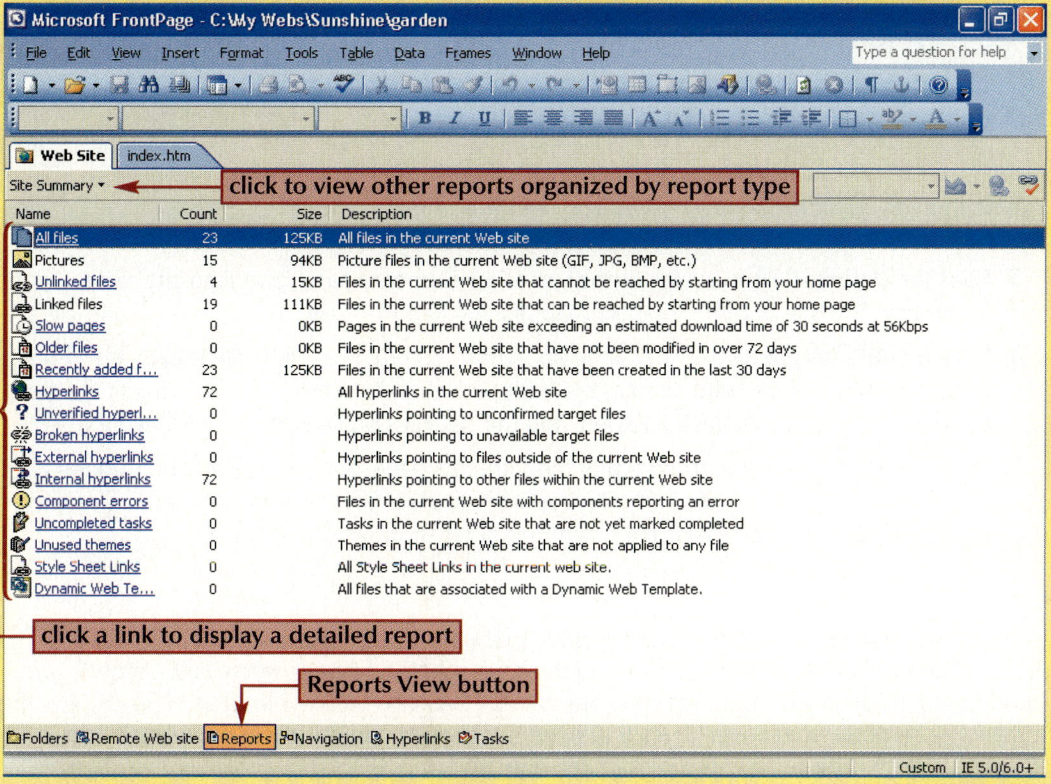

Each hyperlink in the first column of Reports view opens another report with detailed information. For example, clicking the Unlinked files link opens a list of files in the Web site that are not linked to any other files in the Web site.

2. Click the **Unlinked files** link in the Site Summary report. Figure 3-26 shows that there are four files in the Web site that aren't linked to any other file. (Depending on how FrontPage is configured, you might see additional unlinked files.) The contact.gif file is a graphic and does not need to be linked to any other page, and you saved the map_small.jpg file as map_small.gif when you converted it to a GIF file and applied effects to it. The sun.gif file is the picture bullet that you used in the contact.htm page. All of these unlinked files are acceptable. However, seeing that the contact.htm file is not linked to any other page is a problem because site visitors will have no way to access this file. As you work in Reports view, you will find that there are some problems that you need to correct, and others that you can ignore.

Figure 3-26 Unlinked Files report

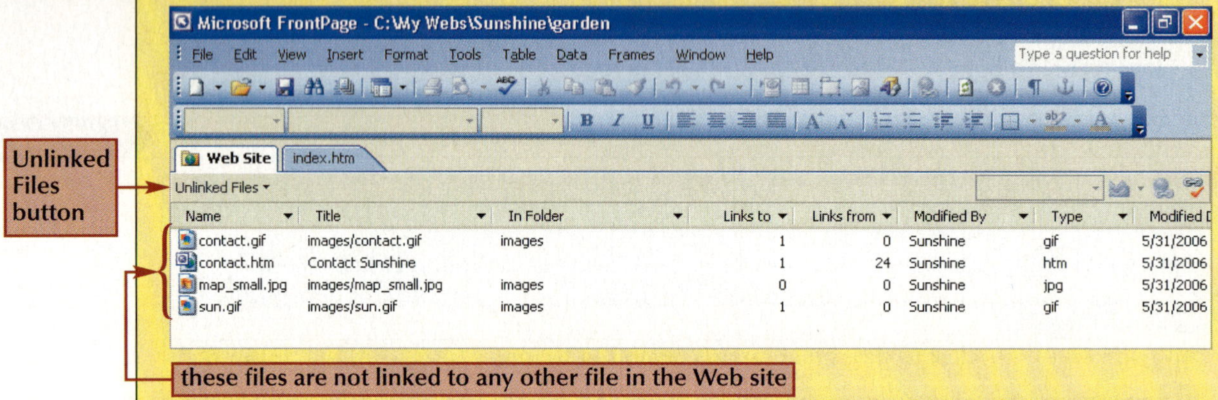

3. Click the **Unlinked Files** button at the top of the Contents pane, and then click **Site Summary**. The Site Summary report reappears in Reports view.
4. Click the **All files** link in the Site Summary report. The All Files report lists each file in the garden Web site along with its title, the folder in which it is stored, its file size, its file type, the date and time it was last modified, and the person's name who last modified it.
5. Click the **All Files** button at the top of the Contents pane, and then click **Site Summary**. The All files entry in the Site Summary report indicates that the Web site has 23 files that use 125 KB of file space. (Your file size might differ slightly.)

Brett also notices the other reports, many of which display zero as their counts. The descriptions indicate that some of the reports have specific settings, such as the Slow pages report, which lists pages that require more than 30 seconds to download at 56 Kbps, and the Older Files report, which lists pages that have not been modified in the previous 72 days. You tell Brett that these reports are customizable and decide to show him how to change their default settings.

To change time intervals for reports:

1. Click **Tools** on the menu bar, and then click **Options**. The Options dialog box opens.
2. Click the **Reports View** tab. As shown in Figure 3-27, you can change the settings for the reports that list recent files, older files, and slow pages. In addition, when your Web site is stored on a server, you can change the way usage data is displayed by specifying the number of months to show in the report.

Reports View tab in the Options dialog box

Figure 3-27

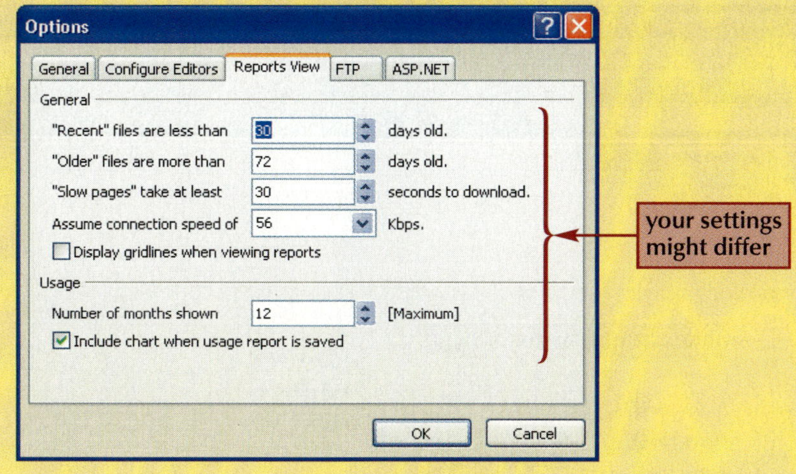

3. If necessary, change your settings to match the ones shown in Figure 3-27, and then click the **OK** button to close the Options dialog box.

You tell Brett that after the garden Web site is published on a Web server, he can learn about his site's visitors by examining the Usage reports, which are accessible by clicking the Site Summary button at the top of the Contents pane, pointing to Usage, and then clicking the desired report. (The Web server on which the site is stored must be configured to support these reports. Some ISPs provide usage data reporting other ways.) These reports include usage statistics about the number of page hits, the operating systems and browsers used to access the site, and information about the domain names of site visitors. Brett can use these reports to monitor usage of the site and to determine the popularity of different pages in the Web site.

Hyperlinks View

Hyperlinks view shows the hyperlinks that connect the pages in a Web site, along with hyperlinks to locations outside the Web site and other types of links, such as mailtos. As you develop a Web site, you can get an overview of it by using Hyperlinks view to examine the hyperlinks that connect the site's pages. You should check Hyperlinks view periodically to verify that your links are set up correctly. Because it is easier to check your site's hyperlinks after you've added only a few hyperlinks to its pages, you might prefer to check smaller parts of the Web site as you go, instead of waiting until the entire Web site has been completed. A completed Web site might contain hundreds of hyperlinks, so checking them as you create them makes it easier to confirm that they are set up as desired.

You want to show Brett how to use Hyperlinks view to examine the Web site's pages for missing hyperlinks and to see the overall structure of the Web site.

To view the Web site in Hyperlinks view:

1. Click the **Hyperlinks View** button [Hyperlinks] at the bottom of the Contents pane, display the Folder List, and then click **index.htm** in the Folder List. Hyperlinks view of the home page for the garden Web site appears, as shown in Figure 3-28.

Figure 3-28 Hyperlinks view of the home page

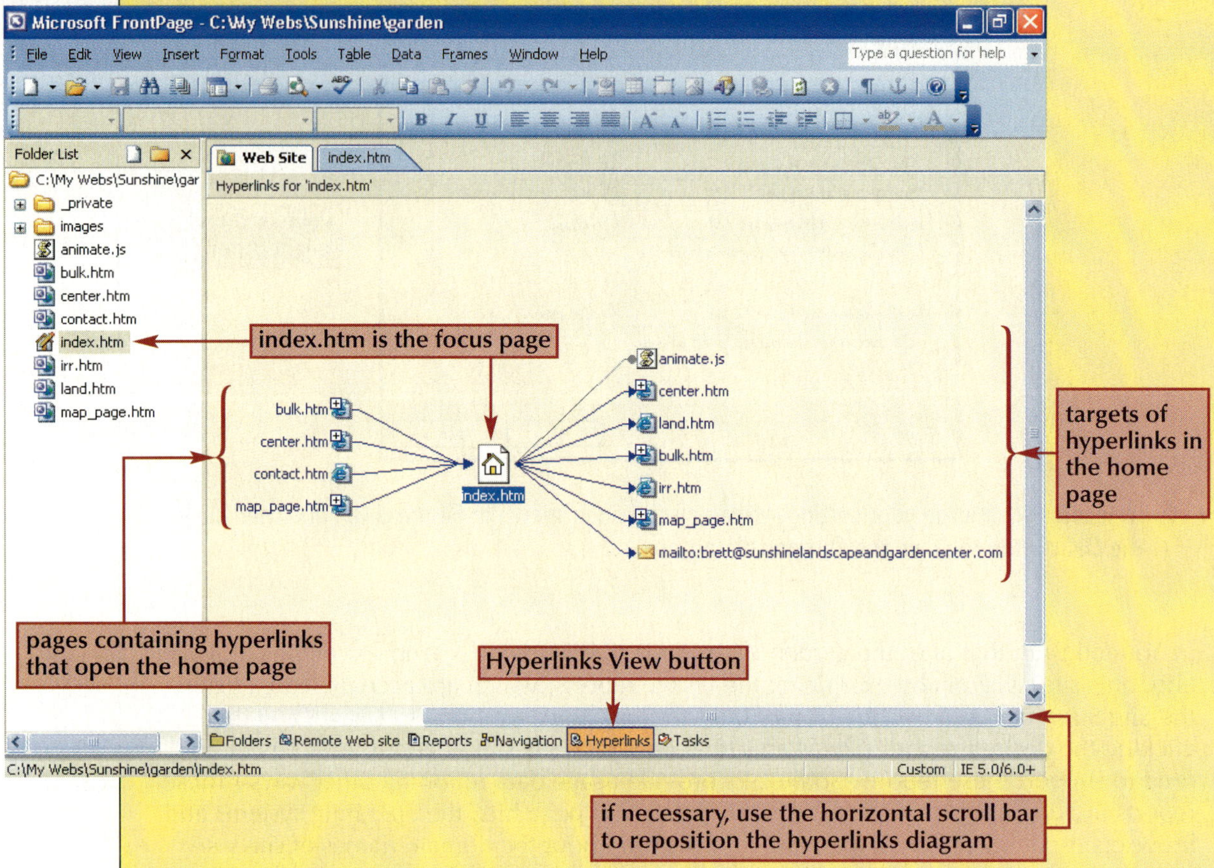

Trouble? If necessary, use the horizontal scroll bar to scroll the Contents pane to the right until the hyperlinks are centered in the window as shown in Figure 3-28.

Trouble? You can customize Hyperlinks view to display page titles instead of page filenames. Figure 3-28 shows filenames; your Hyperlinks view might display page titles. To display the page filenames, right-click an empty area in the Contents pane to open the shortcut menu, and then click Show Page Titles to turn this feature off.

The page you selected, index.htm, appears in the center of the diagram in Hyperlinks view. The selected page is called the focus page; in this case, the home page is the focus page. The links to the left of the focus page contain hyperlinks that open the focus page. In other words, the bulk.htm, center.htm, contact.htm, and map_page.htm pages contain at least one hyperlink that opens the home page. The links to the right of the focus page are targets of hyperlinks in the focus page. For example, the home page contains hyperlinks that open the center.htm, land.htm, bulk.htm, irr.htm, and map_page.htm pages. The home page also contains a link to the animate.js file, which is a JavaScript file that creates the animation for the thumbnail picture in the home page, and the mailto, which includes your e-mail address.

2. Right-click an empty area in the Contents pane to open the shortcut menu, and then click **Hyperlinks to Pictures**. Hyperlinks view of the home page now includes hyperlinks to pictures in the home page. See Figure 3-29.

Figure 3-29

Hyperlinks view of the home page with picture hyperlinks displayed

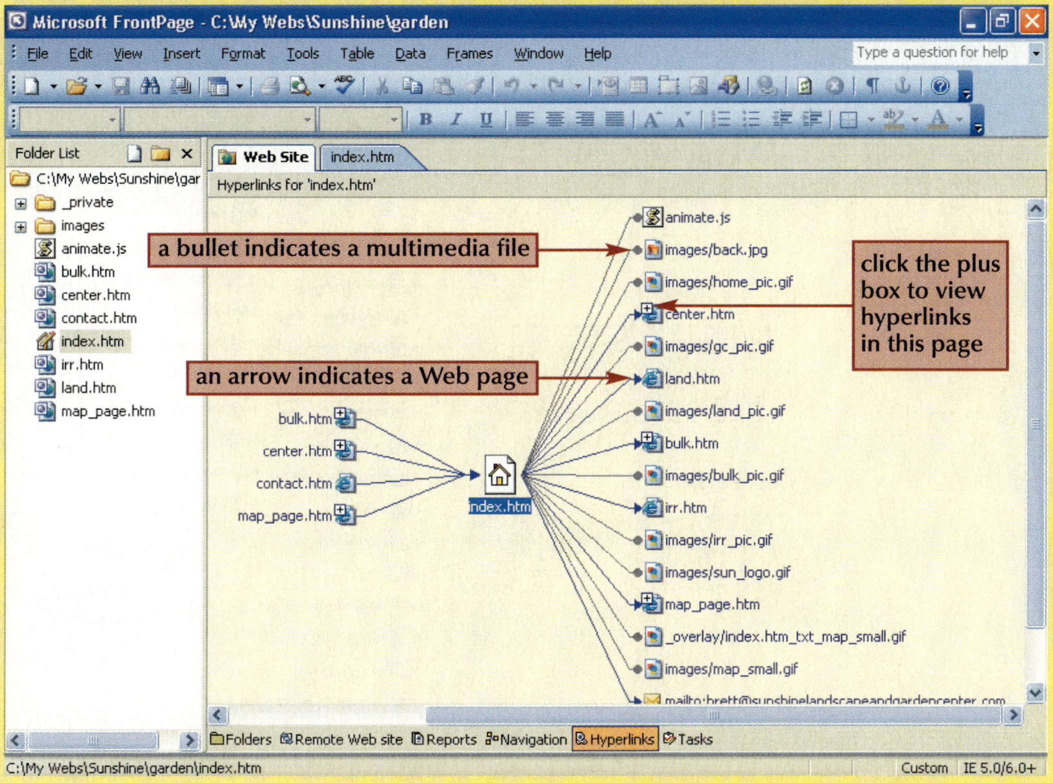

Trouble? If you see a check mark to the left of the Hyperlinks to Pictures command on the shortcut menu, this feature is already turned on and you do not need to click it.

A hyperlink that ends with an arrow indicates a hyperlink to a Web page in the Web site; a hyperlink that ends with a bullet indicates a hyperlink to a picture or other multimedia file or a script file. The animate.js file creates the animation that you applied to the thumbnail picture in the home page. The other files with bullets are pictures that appear in the home page. The envelope icon indicates a hyperlink to the mailto you created in the home page (you will see your e-mail address in the mailto).

Notice also the plus box on the upper-left corner of the center.htm icon to the right of the focus page. You can follow the hyperlinks from one document to another by expanding (showing) or contracting (hiding) the hyperlinks. Clicking the plus box expands the hyperlinks in the page; clicking the minus box collapses the hyperlinks in the page. Expanding the hyperlinks enables you to see how the pages in a Web site are connected.

To expand the hyperlinks for the center.htm page:

1. Click the **plus box** on the center.htm icon to the right of the focus page to expand this hyperlink and display the hyperlinks it contains. Figure 3-30 shows the hyperlinks in the center.htm page.

Figure 3-30 Hyperlinks in the center.htm page

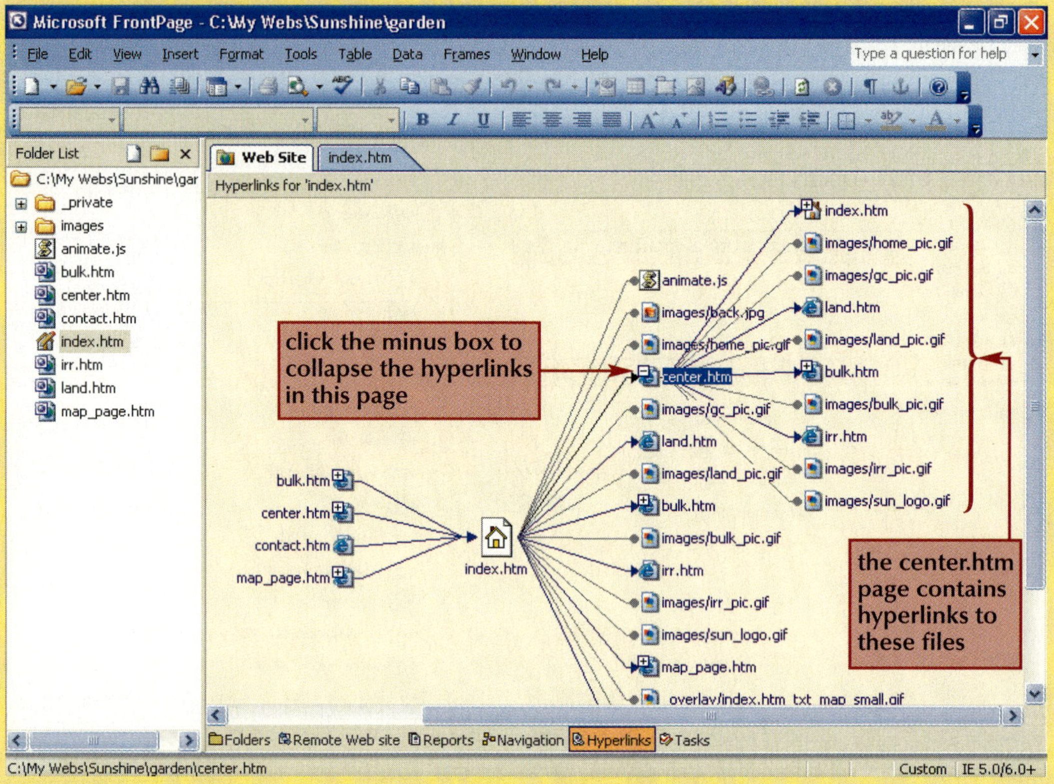

Trouble? If necessary, use the vertical and horizontal scroll bars on the Contents pane to view the expanded hyperlinks from the center.htm page.

2. Click the **minus box** on the center.htm icon to the right of the focus page to collapse this hyperlink.

You can change the focus page in Hyperlinks view by clicking a new page in the Folder List.

To change the focus page in Hyperlinks view:

1. Click the **center.htm** page in the Folder List. The Contents pane shows the center.htm page as the focus page of Hyperlinks view. There are two pages that contain hyperlinks that open the center.htm page, and the center.htm page contains hyperlinks that open four pages (index.htm, land.htm, bulk.htm, and irr.htm). In addition, the center.htm page contains six picture files, all indicated with bullets in Hyperlinks view.
2. Click the **land.htm** page in the Folder List. There are three pages in the Web site that contain hyperlinks that open this page, but the land.htm page does not contain any pictures or links that open other pages. This lack of hyperlinks in the page indicates a problem in the Web site.
3. Double-click **land.htm** in the Folder List. The land.htm page opens in Design view and is empty. You note this problem so you can correct it later.
4. Close the land.htm page.

Displaying Repeated Hyperlinks

Some pages contain hyperlinks with the same target. When a single target of a hyperlink appears in more than one location in a Web page, it is called a **repeated hyperlink**. You can display repeated hyperlinks in Hyperlinks view. First, you'll turn off the hyperlinks to pictures so you can see the repeated links better.

To display repeated hyperlinks:

1. Click the **Web Site** tab to return to Hyperlinks view, right-click an empty area of the Contents pane to open the shortcut menu, and then click **Hyperlinks to Pictures**.
2. Click **index.htm** in the Folder List to select this page as the center focus of Hyperlinks view. If necessary, use the scroll bars to center the hyperlinks diagram in the Contents pane.
3. Right-click an empty area of the Contents pane to open the shortcut menu, and then click **Repeated Hyperlinks** to display the repeated hyperlinks for this page. Because each page listed to the right of the home page appears only once, you determine that there are no repeated hyperlinks in this page.
4. Click the **center.htm** page in the Folder List. The center.htm page becomes the focus of Hyperlinks view. As shown in Figure 3-31, there are two links to the index.htm page, indicating a repeated hyperlink.

Figure 3-31 Repeated hyperlinks in the center.htm page

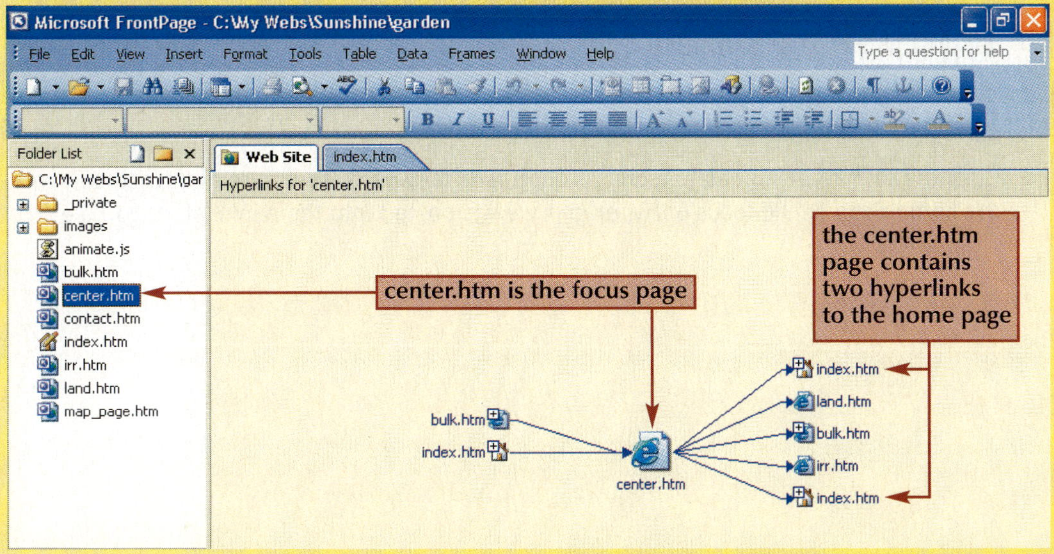

5. Double-click **center.htm** in the Folder List to open the page in Design view. There are two hyperlinks to the home page. The first one is in the link bar (the "Home" picture). The second link is the image map you created in the logo picture (using the word "sunshine").
6. Close the center.htm page.

Printing Hyperlinks View

When you are working in Hyperlinks view, the Print button is disabled. Sometimes it is helpful to have a printout of the hyperlinks for a specific page, especially if you work with a team to develop a Web site. To print Hyperlinks view, you must copy it to the Windows Clipboard, paste it into a document that you can print, and then print that document. You can paste the picture into a new document created by WordPad or Microsoft Word, but an easier way is to paste the picture into a new Web page. After pasting the picture, you can resize it to reduce its size or print it as usual. Because the pasted picture is wider than it is long, you will need to print it in landscape orientation. After printing the Web page, you can close the page without saving changes. You want to show Brett how to print Hyperlinks view before finishing your work in this view.

To copy and paste the screen in Hyperlinks view:

1. Click the **Web Site** tab to return to Hyperlinks view, click the **index.htm** page in the Folder List, and then, if necessary, use the scroll bars to center the hyperlinks diagram in the Contents pane.
2. Press the **Print Screen** key. A picture of your screen (called a screenshot) is copied to the Windows Clipboard. You will paste the picture into a new Web page.
3. Click the **Create a new normal page** button on the Standard toolbar. A new page opens in Design view, and the Layout Tables and Cells task pane opens.

   Trouble? If the Layout Tables and Cells task pane does not open, click View on the menu bar, and then click Task Pane. Don't worry about which task pane opens; you'll change it in the next step.
4. Click the **Other Task Panes** list arrow, and then click **Clipboard**. The picture of your screen appears on the Clipboard task pane.
5. Click the picture of your screen on the Clipboard task pane. A picture of your screen with the home page as the focus of Hyperlinks view is pasted into the new Web page. See Figure 3-32.

New Web page created **Figure 3-32**

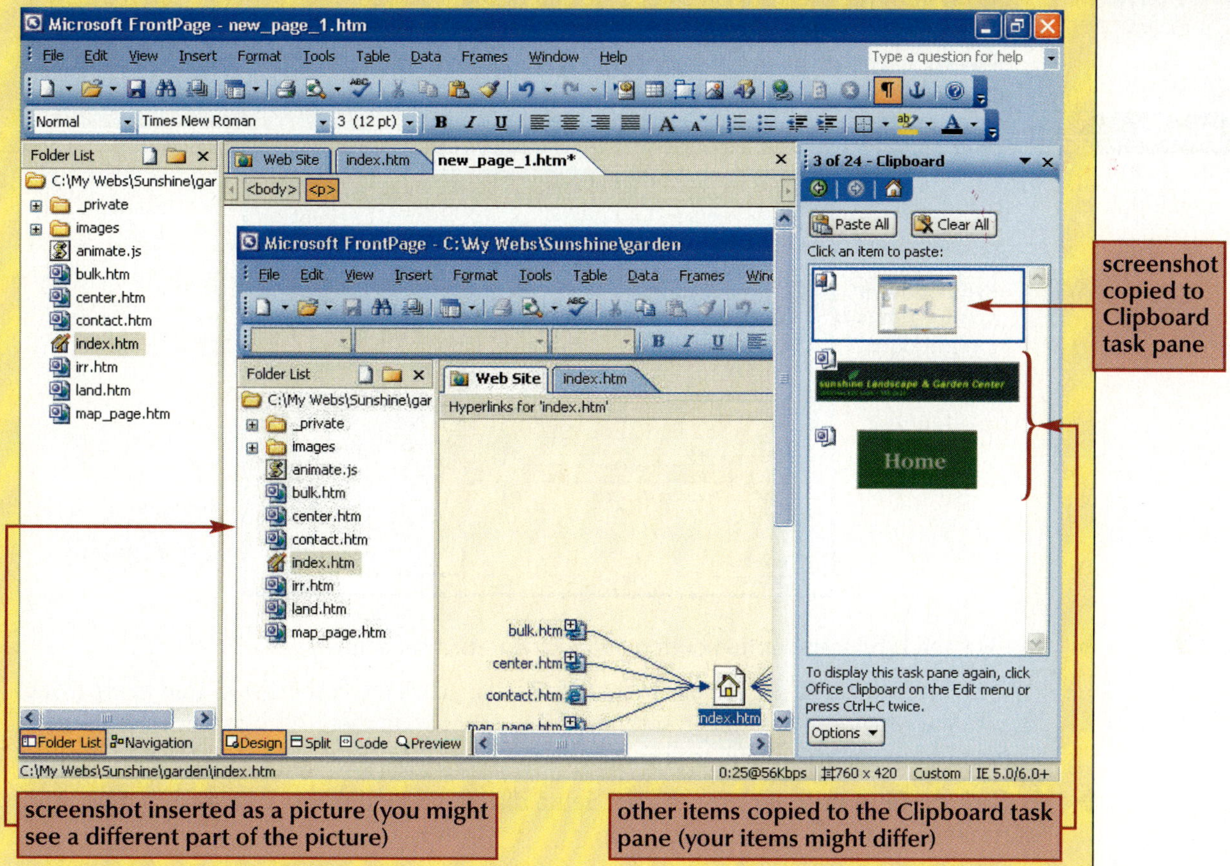

To make sure your screenshot prints on one page, you'll reduce the picture's size.

To reduce the picture's size and print it:

1. Close the Clipboard task pane.
2. Click the picture to select it. Sizing handles appear around the picture.
3. Point to the sizing handle in the upper-left corner of the picture so the pointer changes to a ↖↘ shape, and then drag the sizing handle toward the center of the picture. Release the mouse button when the pointer is about two inches from the upper-left corner of the picture. The picture looks blurry because you resized it. To correct this problem, you'll resample the picture.
4. Find the **Picture Actions** button, which should appear in the lower-right corner of your screen.
5. Click the button, and then click the **Resample Picture To Match Size** option button. The picture is resampled and the image is clear.
6. Click **File** on the menu bar, and then click **Page Setup**. The Print Page Setup dialog box opens.

7. Click the **Options** button. The Print Setup dialog box opens and displays options unique to the printer you have installed and connected to your computer, so your Print Setup dialog box might look different from the one show in Figure 3-33. As you print Web pages using different printers, you might see different options and settings in the Print Setup dialog box.

Figure 3-33 **Print Setup dialog box**

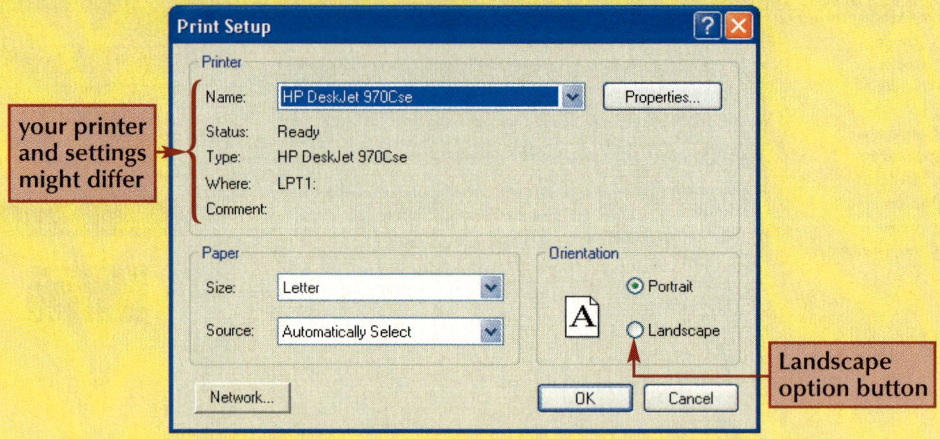

8. Click the **Landscape** option button in the Orientation section.

   Trouble? If you do not see an Orientation section, click the Properties button to see if you can locate the print orientation settings. If you cannot find these settings, click the OK button to close the dialog box, then continue with Step 10.

9. Click the **OK** button to close the Print Setup dialog box, and then click the **OK** button to close the Print Page Setup dialog box.
10. Click **File** on the menu bar, and then click **Print Preview**. Make sure that the picture will print on one page. If not, click the Close button above the page (not the Close button for the new_page_1.htm page), repeat Steps 2 through 5 to reduce the size of the picture, and then preview the page again. When the picture fits on one page, click the Close button above the page.
11. Click the **Print** button to print the page, and then if necessary click the **OK** button in the dialog box that opens.
12. Close the new page and click the **No** button to skip saving the page.
13. Close the index.htm page.

You're finished working in Hyperlinks view, so you will turn off the display of repeated hyperlinks and close the Folder List.

To turn off the display of repeated hyperlinks and close the Folder List:

1. Right-click an empty area of the Contents pane to open the shortcut menu, and then click **Repeated Hyperlinks**.
2. Click the **Close** button × on the Folder List to close it.

The final Web site view that you want to demonstrate for Brett is Tasks view.

Tasks View

To manage a Web site developed by one or many people, you can use **Tasks view** to organize tasks as you work on the site. Each task can include the person assigned to complete it, the task's name and description, and an assigned priority. When a task is finished, you can mark it as completed and then archive or delete it from the Web site. When many people are collaborating to develop a new Web site, they can use Tasks view to manage the Web site's overall development.

Adding a Task to Tasks View

You can add new tasks in Tasks view or by clicking the list arrow for the Create a new normal page button on the Standard toolbar, and then clicking Task. You can add general tasks to the Web site from any view. If you want to associate a task with a specific Web page, change to Folders view and select the page you want to associate with the task or open the page in Design view, and then create the task. In Tasks view, the task will be associated with the page you selected.

Adding a Task to Tasks View

Reference Window

- In any Web site view, click the list arrow for the Create a new normal page button on the Standard toolbar, and then click Task. To associate a Web page with the task, select the Web page in Folders view or open the Web page in Design view before creating the new task.
- In the New Task dialog box, type a task name, assign the task to the appropriate person or group, type a description, and then click an option button as necessary to assign the task a priority.
- Click the OK button.

During your exploration of Hyperlinks view, you noted that the land.htm page did not contain any content. To show Brett how to create a task in the Web site, you will add a task to complete this page and assign the work to yourself. Because the land.htm page already exists in the Web site, you will associate the new task with this page.

To add a task to the Web site:

1. Click the **Folders View** button [Folders] at the bottom of the Contents pane to change to Folders view, and then click the **land.htm** page to select it.
2. Click the **list arrow** for the Create a new normal page button on the Standard toolbar, and then click **Task**. The New Task dialog box opens, as shown in Figure 3-34. Notice that the land.htm page is associated with this task. The default assignment of tasks is to the user who is currently logged on. You might see your name or the logon you use for your computer in the Assigned to list box. The Created by date shows today's date and time. The default priority for all tasks is medium. The user determines the priority for a task; you might give all tasks medium priority or choose to have a system for ranking tasks as high, medium, or low priority.

Figure 3-34 New Task dialog box

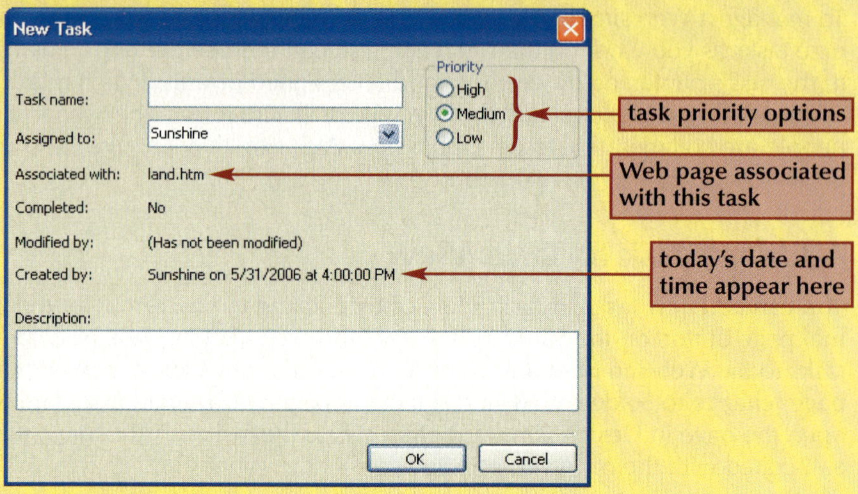

3. In the Task name text box, type **Add content to Landscape & Rock Work page**, and then press the **Tab** key.
4. If your name is selected in the Assigned to list box, press the **Tab** key to move the insertion point to the Description text box. If your name is not selected in the Assigned to list box, type your first and last names, and then press the **Tab** key.
5. Type **Talk to Clara about the content for this page.** The task has a name and description and you assigned the task to yourself.
6. Click the **High** option button in the Priority section. The task is complete.
7. Click the **OK** button. The New Task dialog box closes and the task is added to the Web site.

   Brett reminds you that the irr.htm page is also blank and that the bulk.htm page only has a link bar and the Sunshine logo. You decide to add these tasks to the Web site.
8. Select the **irr.htm** page in Folders view, and then repeat Steps 2 through 7 to add a task to the Web site with **Add content to Irrigation page** as the task name and **Talk to Chad about the content for this page.** as the description. Assign the task to yourself and give it a high priority.
9. Select the bulk.htm page in Folders view, and then repeat Steps 2 through 7 to add a task to the Web site with **Finish bulk.htm page** as the task name and **Get the file for this page from Michael.** as the description. Assign the task to yourself give it a high priority.

To see the tasks you created, you need to change to Tasks view. You can use Tasks view to sort tasks by different values and change them as necessary to update their status.

Sorting, Changing, and Deleting Tasks

If you are working on a large Web site with a team, the site might contain hundreds of tasks, so keeping it organized is important. You can sort tasks in many ways to organize their presentation. For example, you might want to sort tasks by priority, by the people assigned to complete them, or alphabetically by task name. You want to show Brett how to sort and change tasks now, while the list is still small, so he can practice this skill. In the future, Brett might rely on Tasks view to organize the work required to create and maintain the Web site.

To sort Tasks view and change a task:

1. Click the **Tasks View** button [Tasks] at the bottom of the Contents pane to change to Tasks view. The three tasks you added appear in the list, as shown in Figure 3-35.

Figure 3-35 **Tasks added to the Web site**

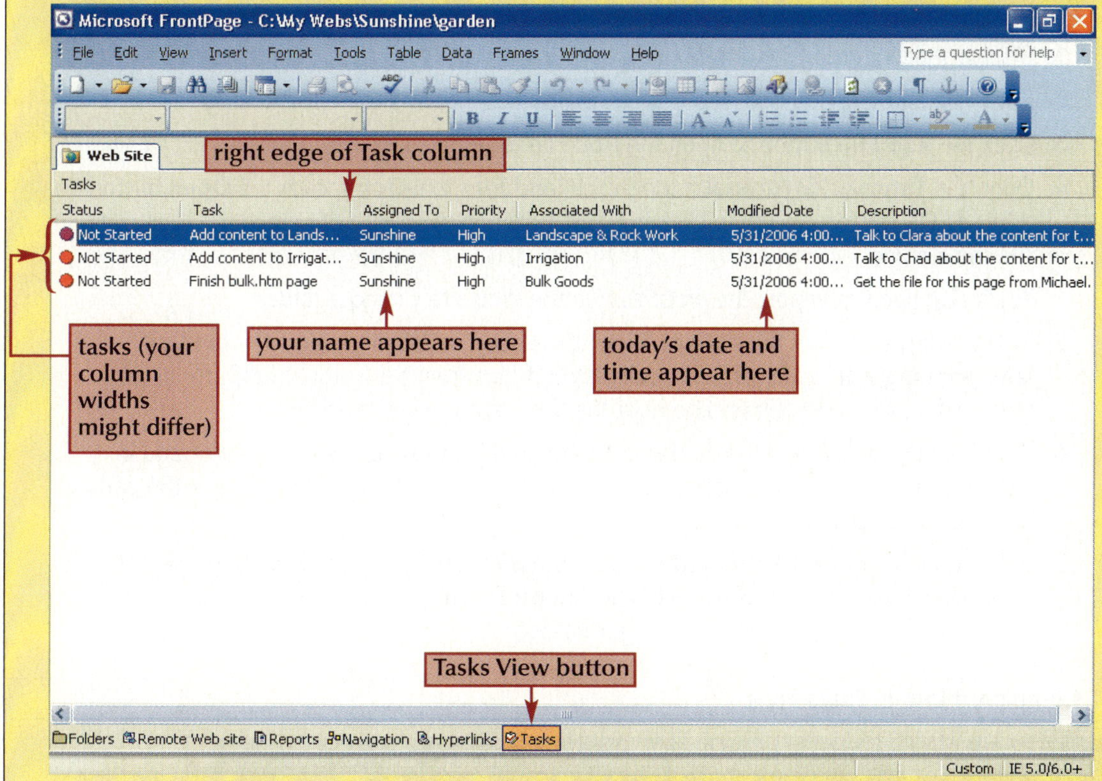

You can resize the columns in Tasks view using the pointer. You will show Brett how to resize the columns so he can read the task names better.

2. Point to the right edge of the Task column so the pointer changes to a ↔ shape, and then double-click the column. The Task column's width increases so that the longest entry is completely visible in the column. The columns to the right of the Task column scroll further to the right. You can use the horizontal scroll bar to see columns that have scrolled off the screen.
3. Click the **Task** column heading to sort the tasks alphabetically by task name.
4. Click the **Task** column heading again to sort the tasks in descending alphabetical order.

   You can double-click any task to see its details.

5. Double-click the **Finish bulk.htm page** task to open the Task Details dialog box. In this dialog box, you can change the priority of a task, its description, or the person assigned to complete it.
6. Type **Finish Bulk Goods page** in the Task name text box to provide a more descriptive name for the task.

   You could click the Start Task button to open the page associated with this task (bulk.htm) in Design view so you can begin working on the page. For now, you will simply close the Task Details dialog box.

7. Click the **OK** button. The task is updated.

Clara just sent Brett the files for the land.htm page, so he tells you that you can complete this task. You'll import the new land.htm and its picture files into the Web site, and then you can mark the task as complete. The process of completing a task can entail anything from importing a new page to updating a hyperlink in an existing page.

To complete a task:

1. Display the Folder List, and then make sure the garden Web site's root folder is selected.
2. Click **File** on the menu bar, and then click **Import** to open the Import dialog box.
3. Click the **Add File** button to open the Add File to Import List dialog box.
4. Open the **Tutorial.03\Tutorial** folder, click **land.htm** to select it, click the **Open** button, click the **OK** button, and then click the **Yes** button to overwrite the file in the Web site with the same name.

   You'll also need to import the pictures into the Web site's images folder.
5. In the Folder List, click the **images** folder to select it, and then import the **land.gif**, **land_sam.jpg**, **rock_pic.gif**, and **rock_sam.gif** files from the Tutorial.03\Tutorial folder into the images folder. (Press and hold the Ctrl key to select multiple files.)
6. Double-click **land.htm** in the Folder List to open the Landscape & Rock Work page in Design view. Use the scroll bars to examine the page contents, and then close the page and the Folder List.
7. In Tasks view, right-click the **Add content to Landscape & Rock Work page** task to open the shortcut menu, and then click **Mark Complete**. The task's status changes from Not Started to Completed, as shown in Figure 3-36.

Figure 3-36 Completed task in Tasks view

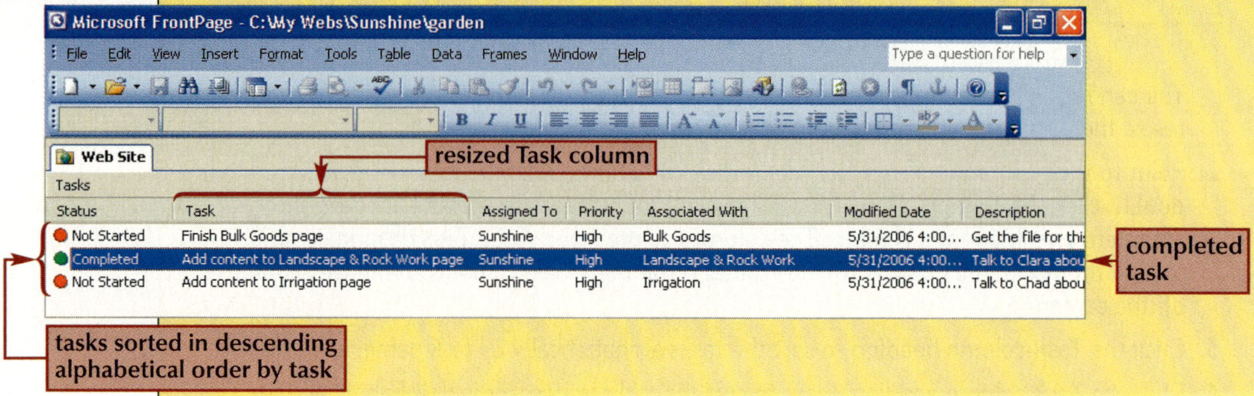

After finishing a task, you can mark it as completed. The task will remain in Tasks view after you change its status. However, if you close the Web site and then reopen it in Tasks view, you'll need to turn on the task history to see completed tasks. Because it might seem like completed tasks have disappeared, you want to show Brett how to turn on the task history. You will simulate closing the Web site by refreshing it. You also want to show Brett how to delete a task, so you will delete the completed task from the site.

To turn on task history and delete a task:

1. Click the **Refresh** button on the Standard toolbar. Notice that the Add content to Landscape & Rock Work page task, which was marked as completed, no longer appears in Tasks view. To display completed tasks, you must show the task history.
2. Right-click an empty area in Tasks view to open the shortcut menu, and then click **Show History**. Tasks view now shows unfinished and completed tasks.

   Trouble? If the Show History command has a check mark to the left of its name on the shortcut menu, then the task history is already enabled. Click outside the shortcut menu to close it, and then continue with Step 3.
3. Right-click the **Add content to Landscape & Rock Work page** task to open the shortcut menu, and then click **Delete Task**. The Confirm Delete dialog box opens and asks you to confirm the deletion.
4. Click the **Yes** button. The task is deleted from Tasks view.
5. Right-click an empty area in Tasks view to open the shortcut menu, and then click **Show History** to turn this feature off.
6. Change to Folders view, close the **garden** Web site, and then exit FrontPage.

Brett is pleased with the Contact Sunshine page and appreciates the tour of the different views of a Web site. In the next tutorial, you will show Brett how to use Navigation view and how to create shared borders and themes in a Web site.

Session 3.2 Quick Check

Review

1. How many items can you store in the Clipboard task pane at the same time?
2. How would you change the name of the folder that stores a Web site?
3. What does an underscore character indicate when it is the first character in a folder in a Web site?
4. When you change to Reports view, what does FrontPage automatically generate?
5. What is a repeated hyperlink?
6. True or False: Click the Print button on the Standard toolbar to print Hyperlinks view.
7. How do you add a task to a Web site and associate the task with a specific Web page?
8. True or False: Marking a task as completed deletes the task from the Web site.

Tutorial Summary

Review

In this tutorial, you learned how to create bulleted, numbered, definition, and nested lists. You learned about creating anchors (bookmarks) in a Web page to increase the ease of use for that page's user. Finally, you learned about the different Web site views available in FrontPage. In Page view, you learned how to use the Clipboard task pane and how to enter comments in a Web page. In Folders view, you learned how to display a Web site's hidden files and folders and how to delete temporary files created by FrontPage. You examined a Site Summary report in Reports view and examined a few of the Web site's detailed reports. In Hyperlinks view, you learned how to examine the hyperlinks leading to and coming from a single Web page. Finally, you used Tasks view to create, change, and delete tasks.

As you work on your own Web sites in the future, you will make your Web pages easier to use if you create anchors and hyperlinks to anchors in pages that contain a lot of information. As you saw in this tutorial, creating anchors and hyperlinks to those anchors makes it easier for your site's visitors to find the content they need.

As you develop a Web site, you will do most of your work in Page view and Folders view. Some developers use Tasks view to coordinate the tasks required to complete a Web site, but others do not. Regardless of your preference, Tasks view can be an effective way of managing the many details involved in creating a Web site. You can use Hyperlinks view to see the hyperlinks in your Web pages, and you will use this view in the future when you test the Web site to identify broken links. Finally, after publishing a Web site, you can use Reports view to study the ways different users access your site. This information is both interesting and informative and should be a part of the overall maintenance of a Web site.

Key Terms

anchor	Folders view	Page view
bookmark	Hyperlinks view	repeated hyperlink
broken link	multi-level list	Reports view
bulleted list	nested list	Site Summary report
comment	numbered list	Tasks view
defined term	ordered list	unordered list
definition list	outline list	Windows Clipboard

Practice

Practice the skills you learned in the tutorial using the same case scenario.

Review Assignments

Data Files needed for the Review Assignments: bulk2.htm, bulk.gif, bulk.htm, bulk_sam.jpg, irr.htm, mlch_art.gif, mulch.jpg, soil.jpg, soil_art.gif, stne_art.gif, stone.jpg

Brett is happy with the way the garden Web site is shaping up. He is pleased that you were able to include the content for the Landscape & Rock Work page, but he is concerned about other missing content in the site's pages. He asks you to review the entire Web site and add tasks to the Web site for the remaining work, and then to complete as much of the work as possible using files that have been developed to date by the Sunshine staff.

If necessary, start FrontPage, make sure you have your Data Files, and then do the following:

1. Open the **garden** Web site from the location where your Web sites are stored, and then preview the home page in a browser. Use the browser to examine all of the pages in the Web site. As you note problems in the pages that you open, use the Windows taskbar to switch between the browser and FrontPage to add appropriate tasks in Tasks view. (You already added two of these tasks to the Web site in Session 3.2.) Assign tasks you find to yourself and give them a medium priority. If necessary, associate the task with a specific Web page.
2. When you have finished examining the Web site using your browser, close your browser and switch to Hyperlinks view. For each Web page in the site (**bulk.htm**, **center.htm**, **contact.htm**, **index.htm**, **irr.htm**, **land.htm**, and **map_page.htm**), examine the hyperlinks leading to and from the page. With the exception of the **map_page.htm** page, each page should contain links that open the other pages in the Web site. The **contact.htm** page should be accessible using a hyperlink in the home page. If you need to make any changes to these planned links, note the changes as tasks in the Web site.

3. Compare your notes to Figure 3-37, and then, if necessary, update Tasks view in your Web site to match. When you have finished, sort the tasks alphabetically by task name.

Figure 3-37

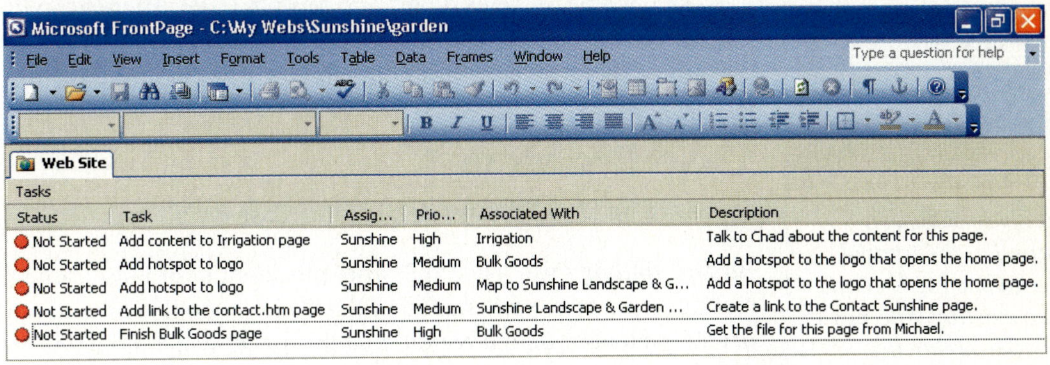

4. Display the Folder List, and then import the following pages from the Tutorial.03\Review folder included with your Data Files into the root folder of the **garden** Web site: **bulk2.htm**, **bulk.htm**, and **irr.htm**. When prompted to overwrite the **bulk.htm** and **irr.htm** files, click the Yes button.
5. Import the following files from the Tutorial.03\Review folder into the images folder of the garden Web site: **bulk.gif**, **bulk_sam.jpg**, **mlch_art.gif**, **mulch.jpg**, **soil.jpg**, **soil_art.gif**, **stne_art.gif**, and **stone.jpg**.
6. Open the home page in Design view. Select the word "us" in the third line on the page and change it to "our expert staff." Then format the "our expert staff" text as a hyperlink that opens the **contact.htm** page. Save the home page.
7. Copy the link bar in the home page and paste it at the top of the **contact.htm** page. Make sure to insert the link bar so the top bookmark remains at the top of the page. (*Hint:* Press the right arrow key to move the insertion point between the bookmark icon and the **contact.gif** file, and then insert the link bar. If necessary, delete any blank lines above the link bar.) Save the **contact.htm** page.
8. In the **bulk2.htm** page, select the broken link to the **mulch_art.gif** file, and then open the Picture Properties dialog box and display the General tab. Change the picture from **mulch_art.gif** to **mlch_art.gif**, and then save the **bulk2.htm** page.
9. Copy the logo picture in the **bulk2.htm** page, open the **map_page.htm** page, and then replace the logo picture in the **map_page.htm** page with the one you copied. Make sure that the hotspot that opens the home page appears in the pasted logo picture, and then save the **map_page.htm** page.
10. Open the **bulk.htm** page in Design view, and then verify that the logo picture in the revised **bulk.htm** page that you imported into the Web site contains a hotspot that opens the home page.
11. Open the home page in a browser, and then use the links in the Web site to open all of its pages. (*Note:* You will continue adding pages to the Web site as you complete this book. There are still some missing pages that are linked to the **land.htm** and **bulk2.htm** pages.)
12. Close your browser.
13. In Tasks view, mark the tasks you created for linking the home page and the **contact.htm** page, adding the content to the Irrigation page, and adding the hotspot to the logo picture in the **bulk.htm** and **map_page.htm** pages as complete. Print Tasks view. (*Hint:* There is no Print command in Tasks view, so you will need to print a screenshot.)

14. Change to Hyperlinks view, and set the **contact.htm** page as the focus page. If necessary, center the hyperlinks diagram in the Contents pane, and then print Hyperlinks view.
15. Close the Folder List and then change to Reports view. Change the Slow Pages report so it lists pages that take longer than 10 seconds to download at 56 Kbps, and then open the Slow Pages report and print it. (*Hint:* There is no Print command in Reports view, so you will need to print a screenshot.)
16. Close the **garden** Web site, and then close FrontPage.

Apply

Apply the skills you learned in the tutorial to organize the content of an existing Web page and to examine the Web site in Hyperlinks, Reports, and Tasks view.

Case Problem 1

There are no Data Files needed for this Case Problem.

Buffalo Trading Post Nicole Beirne, president of Buffalo Trading Post, wants you to format the How page you created in the Web site so it is easy to navigate. In reviewing the page's contents, you tell Nicole that this page, which contains answers to commonly asked questions, would be an ideal candidate for a bulleted list and a definition list. To make the page easier to scroll, you also suggest adding anchors to the page and hyperlinks to them.

Nicole also wants you to examine the Web site and create a list of its remaining tasks. Nicole knows that the content of the What page is missing and the Where page has not been added to the Web site. She will assign the creation of these pages to an associate and ask her to send the files to you later. For now, you will note these problems to ensure their future completion.

Because you have completed some of the initial design work, you tell Nicole that you will also examine the Web site in Hyperlinks view and Reports view to look for any problems that you can fix now.

If necessary, start FrontPage, and then do the following:

1. Open the **buffalo** Web site from the location where your Web sites are stored. (If you did not create this Web site in Tutorial 1 and change it in Tutorial 2, ask your instructor for assistance.)
2. Open the **who.htm** page in Design view, and then change the numbered list at the bottom of the page to a bulleted list. After creating the bulleted list, change the default bullet character from a dot to a solid square, and then save the **who.htm** page.
3. Open the **how.htm** page in Design view, and then format the first three paragraphs below the link bar as a bulleted list with solid square bullet characters.
4. Create a bookmark for each heading in the page ("How It Works," "Frequently Asked Questions," and "Choose to Re-Use") using a lowercase name of your choice that does not contain spaces or exceed eight characters. Then create a hyperlink from each item in the bulleted list to its corresponding bookmark.
5. Format the paragraphs beginning with the bold "How It Works" text and ending with the paragraph ending "per person per day." as a definition list. Format the paragraphs with the headings "How It Works," "Frequently Asked Questions," and "Choose to Re-Use" as defined terms.
6. Create a bookmark named "top" to the left of the picture at the top of the page. Below the first definition paragraph in the definition list, create a "Back to top of page" hyperlink using the top bookmark as its target. Format the paragraph containing this link with the Normal style.

7. Copy the "Back to top of page" hyperlink you created in Step 6 and paste it on a new line below each of the other definition paragraphs. (For the "Frequently Asked Questions" definition, paste the link after the last answer.) Format each paragraph containing this link with the Normal style. When you are finished, save the **how.htm** page.
8. Add a task to the Web site to get the content of the **what.htm** page from its developer and associate the task with the existing page with the same name. Assign the task to yourself, add an appropriate description and task name, and give it a medium priority.

Explore

9. Add another task to the Web site to get the **where.htm** Web page from its developer and import it into the Web site. Assign the task to yourself, add an appropriate description and task name, and give it a medium priority. (*Hint:* Create the task in Tasks view to create the task without associating it with a page.)
10. Display the **how.htm** page in Hyperlinks view. If necessary, center the hyperlinks diagram in the Contents pane. Display the hyperlinks to pictures in the page, and then print Hyperlinks view.
11. Use Hyperlinks view to examine the hyperlinks in the Web site for the **index.htm**, **what.htm**, and **who.htm** pages, and then turn off the display of hyperlinks to pictures.

Explore

12. Change to Reports view and then open the Broken Hyperlinks report. Use the information in this report to identify the filename of the broken hyperlink and the page in which it is located. Open the **who.htm** page in Design view, and then change the broken link to the watermark background picture from **bwmark.gif** to the **w_mark.gif** file in the Web site's images folder. When you have corrected the broken link, save the **who.htm** page, and then run another Site Summary report in Reports view.
13. Open the home page in a browser and test the hyperlinks between pages and the hyperlinks to bookmarks you created. (*Note:* You will add content to the **what.htm** page in another tutorial.) Print the **how.htm** page, and then close your browser.
14. In a new paragraph below the horizontal line at the bottom of the **who.htm** page, add a comment that you can see in Design view with the following content: "This page last updated by [Your Name]." Save and print the **who.htm** page.
15. Close the **buffalo** Web site, and then close FrontPage.

Apply

Apply the skills you learned in the tutorial to organize the content of an existing Web page and to examine the Web site in Hyperlinks, Reports, and Tasks view.

Case Problem 2

Data File needed for this Case Problem: bullet.gif

Garden Grill Meghan Elliott provided you with the content of the new Job Opportunities page, and you added this content to the jobs.htm page. As the list of new positions grows, Meghan wants to make sure that it is easy for people to scroll to the job description in which they are interested. Meghan asks you to format the Job Opportunities page to make it easier to navigate. She also wants you to examine the existing hyperlinks in the Web site to locate any pages that are not linked to other pages in the site. Meghan will use your research to coordinate her work with Callan Murphy, who will either develop missing pages or assign the work to the appropriate staff.

If necessary, start FrontPage, make sure you have your Data Files, and then do the following:

1. Open the **grill** Web site from the location where your Web sites are stored. (If you did not create this Web site in Tutorial 1 and change it in Tutorial 2, ask your instructor for assistance.)
2. Open the **jobs.htm** page in Design view and then review its contents.

3. Format the second and third paragraphs in the page (with the text "Managers" and "Staff Associates") as a bulleted list. Change the bullet character to the **bullet.gif** picture, which is stored in the Tutorial.03\Case2 folder included with your Data Files. Save the **jobs.htm** page and save the picture in the Web site's images folder.
4. Change the five paragraphs below the paragraph that begins "Garden Grill's managers are outstanding..." to a bulleted list with the **bullet.gif** picture. (*Hint:* Insert the **bullet.gif** picture from the Web site's images folder.)
5. Change the six paragraphs below the paragraph that begins "Garden Grill is one of the most..." to a bulleted list with the **bullet.gif** picture.
6. Create a bookmark for each heading in the page (the bold "Managers" and "Staff Associates" text) using a lowercase name of your choice that does not contain spaces or exceed eight characters. Then create a hyperlink from each item in the first bulleted list in the page to its corresponding bookmark.
7. Create a bookmark named "top" to the left of the picture link bar at the top of the page.
8. Format the two paragraphs beginning with the bold "Managers" heading and ending with the paragraph that ends "the following qualifications:" as a definition list. The paragraph with the bold "Managers" heading is a defined term and the paragraph below it is the definition.

Explore

9. Indent the bulleted list below the definition paragraph you created in Step 8 one additional tab stop. (*Hint:* Select the bulleted list and then use a toolbar button.)
10. Format the two paragraphs beginning with the bold "Staff Associates" heading and ending with the paragraph that ends "at a Garden Grill location near you:" as a definition list. The paragraph with the bold "Staff Associates" heading is a defined term and the paragraph below it is the definition. Indent the bulleted list below the definition paragraph by one additional tab stop.

Explore

11. Create a new paragraph below the third bulleted list, and then decrease the paragraph's indentation to zero. (*Hint:* Click at the end of the "Bartenders" item in the list, press the Enter key twice to end the bulleted list and create a new paragraph, and then use a toolbar button to change the new paragraph so it is not indented.)
12. In the new paragraph you created in Step 11, create a "Top of Page" hyperlink using the top bookmark as its target.
13. Create a "Top of Page" hyperlink to the top bookmark below the bulleted list that appears below the "Managers" heading. Save the **jobs.htm** page.

Explore

14. Display each page in the Web site as the focus page in Hyperlinks view. If a page does not contain any hyperlinks that open other pages in the Web site, add a task associated with the focus page to finish the page. Assign the task to yourself, add an appropriate description and task name, and give it a medium priority. (*Hint:* You should add four tasks to the Web site. You can add the tasks in Hyperlinks view as you examine the pages.)

Explore

15. Change to Reports view. Set the time for the Slow Pages report to 20 seconds and the connection speed to 28.8 Kbps, and then print the Site Summary report. (*Hint:* There is no Print command in Reports view, so you will need to print a screenshot.)
16. Open the home page with a browser and test the hyperlinks between pages and the hyperlinks to bookmarks you created. (*Note:* You will add content to the **menu.htm**, **fran.htm**, **feedback.htm**, and **search.htm** pages in another tutorial.) Use your browser to print the **jobs.htm** page, and then close your browser.
17. In a new paragraph at the bottom of the **jobs.htm** page, add a comment that you can see in Design view with the following content: "This page last updated by [Your Name]." Save the **jobs.htm** page, and then print the HTML document for the **jobs.htm** page.
18. Close the **grill** Web site, and then close FrontPage.

Apply

Apply the skills you learned in the tutorial to organize the content of an existing Web page and to examine the Web site in Hyperlinks view and Reports view.

Case Problem 3

There are no Data Files needed for this Case Problem.

Swenson Auctioneers Scott Swenson, president of Swenson Auctioneers, has reviewed your progress on the Web site. He likes the background picture that you added to each Web page and the overall presentation of material. One change that he asks you to make is to organize the content of the Our Team page so it is easy to scroll to a specific person's information. You will also examine the pages in the Web site to make sure they are linked together as desired and examine the Site Summary report for the entire site.

If necessary, start FrontPage, and then do the following:

1. Open the **swenson** Web site from the location where your Web sites are stored. (If you did not create this Web site in Tutorial 1 and change it in Tutorial 2, ask your instructor for assistance.)
2. Open the **team.htm** page in Design view and examine its contents. As you conduct your examination, decide the best way to format the organization in this page so it will be easy for its users to scroll the page's contents.
3. Display the Clipboard task pane. If any items appear in the list, click the Clear All button.
4. If necessary, display the nonprinting characters in the page so you can see paragraph marks and line breaks. Use the pointer to select each person's name, but not the line break character at the end of the line on which the name appears. Do not select the person's title. After selecting each person's name, copy it to the Clipboard.
5. Scroll to the top of the page, and then create a new paragraph below the "Swenson Auctioneers takes pride…" paragraph. Click a toolbar button to start a bulleted list.
6. **Explore** Use the Clipboard task pane to paste each name you copied in the Web page into the bulleted list in the order the names appear in the Web page. (Scott's name should be first, then Tucker's, etc.) Each name should appear as an item in the bulleted list.
7. **Explore** Create a bookmark for each person's biography using a lowercase name of your choice that does not contain spaces or exceed eight characters. Then create a hyperlink from the person's name in the bulleted list to the person's biography.
8. **Explore** After the last paragraph in each person's biography, create a new paragraph containing a link that scrolls to the Swenson logo at the top of the page. After you have finished, save the **team.htm** page.
9. Add a task to the Web site to create the form in the **mail.htm** page. Associate the task with the **mail.htm** page, assign the task to yourself, add an appropriate description and task name, and give the task a high priority.
10. Display each page in the Web site as the focus page in Hyperlinks view with the hyperlinks to pictures and page titles displayed. As you view each page, examine the hyperlinks leading to and coming from the focus page so you understand how the pages are linked. Display the **team.htm** page as the focus page, and then print Hyperlinks view. Turn off the display of page titles.
11. **Explore** Change to Reports view. Set the time for the Slow Pages report to 10 seconds and the connection speed to 28.8 Kbps, and then print the Slow Pages report. (*Hint:* There is no Print command in Reports view, so you will need to print a screenshot.)
12. Open the home page with a browser, and then test the hyperlinks between pages and the hyperlinks to bookmarks you created. Use your browser to print the **team.htm** page, and then close your browser.

13. In a new paragraph at the bottom of the **team.htm** page, add a comment that you can see in Design view with the following content: "This page last updated by [Your Name]." Save the **team.htm** page, and then print the HTML document for the **team.htm** page.
14. Close the **swenson** Web site, and then close FrontPage.

Create

Explore a Web site's structure and settings by examining it in Hyperlinks view, and organize page content using lists.

Case Problem 4

Data File needed for this Case Problem: arrow.gif

Mortgage Services, Inc. Natalie Fuselier, owner of Mortgage Services, Inc., is pleased with the pages and appearance of the Web site you are creating for her. She wants to review the structure of the Web site and make improvements to some of its pages.

If necessary, start FrontPage, make sure you have your Data Files, and then do the following:

1. Open the **loan** Web site from the location where your Web sites are stored. (If you did not create this Web site in Tutorial 1 and change it in Tutorial 2, ask your instructor for assistance.)
2. Change to Hyperlinks view and then display the Folder List. Display each page in the Web site as the focus page and examine its hyperlinks. Each page in the Web site should open all of the other pages in the Web site, with the exception of the **repair.htm** page, which should be accessible from the home page and contain a hyperlink to the home page. If you find any pages that do not meet these specifications, add a task to the Web site for finishing the page. Associate the page with the task, assign the task to yourself, add an appropriate description and task name, and give it a medium priority.

Explore

3. Open the **loantype.htm** page in Design view and close the Folder List. Review the page contents and formulate a plan to organize it so a user can click a loan type at the top of the page to scroll to the description of that loan type.
4. Create a bulleted list using the loan types at the top of the page. Use the **arrow.gif** file in the Tutorial.03\Case4 folder included with your Data Files as the bullet character. Save the page and save the picture file in the Web site's images folder.

Explore

5. Create bookmarks and hyperlinks in the page according to the plan you developed in Step 3. Use lowercase bookmark names of your choice that do not contain spaces or exceed eight characters.

Explore

6. Use existing text in the page to create hyperlinks that scroll to the "Loan Types" heading near the top of the page.
7. Change each level-three heading in the Web page to the Defined Term style, and then change the paragraph below the defined term to the Definition style. (The "Back to top" text should retain the Normal style.) The text in the paragraphs formatted using the Defined Term style should be bold. When you have finished, save the **loantype.htm** page.
8. Open the **help.htm** page in Design view, and then format its contents using Figure 3-38 as a guide. (*Hint:* Use the **arrow.gif** file to format the bulleted list. The bullets in the nested lists are the default bullet character.) When you have finished, save the **help.htm** page.

Figure 3-38

[Loan Types] [Application] [Post Application Help] [Resources] [Contact Us]

Mortgage Services, Inc.

Post Application Help

▶ What Happens After I Apply Online?

1. You receive an e-mail message confirming receipt of your application.
2. We review your loan application and credit history.
3. We contact you and tell you how much you can borrow.
4. You send us the required documents we need to verify your loan application. This page describes the original documents necessary to start processing your loan. During processing, additional information may be required. Do not send these forms until you receive an e-mail message from us requesting you to mail them.

▶ Please provide these documents for the Borrower and Co-Borrower:

- **Bank Statements:** Last three months of consecutive statements on every account showing liquid funds/cash to close (include all pages of statements)
- **IRA, 401K, Stocks, Bonds, etc.:** Most recent statements showing balances for the last three months or two quarters (include all pages of statements)
- **W-2 Statements:** Past two years
- **Pay Stubs:** Consecutive pay stubs covering one complete month's salary (if paid by personal check, supply canceled checks from each company)
- **(Homeowner's) Insurance Agent:** Name, company, and phone number of agent

▶ If you are self-employed, please provide the following information:

- **Personal Federal Income Tax Returns:** Past two years, signed, all schedules
- **Business Federal Income Tax Returns:** Past two years, signed, all schedules
- **Business Financial Statements:** Within three months of today's date, signed
- **Business Profit/Loss Statements:** Within three months of today's date, signed

▶ If you own income-producing property, please provide the following information:

- **Leases:** Current copies for each leased property
- **Income/Expense/Payment:** Information for each leased property

▶ If you are divorced, please provide the following information:

- **Final Judgment:** Divorce and child support agreements, fully executed

We will review the documents and will approve or not approve your loan based on the information you provided and according to the conditions of the lender.

Once approved, you are ready to buy or refinance your home!

When you find a house you like, your offer will have a much better chance of being accepted because the seller knows that you have already been approved for a loan from one of over 400 recognized national or local lenders. Along with your real estate agent, we will help guide you through the rest of the home buying process until closing.

Please keep in mind that lenders do not provide the final approval for a loan until after the close of the sale. Funds are disbursed when all conditions of the mortgage approval and real estate sale have been met. Conditions include the following, among other things: verification of borrower's employment and funds for down payment, acceptable appraised value of the house, survey of property, title commitment, signatures on all closing documents, and other standard requirements involved in any real estate transaction.

9. Open the home page in a browser, and then examine all of the site's pages and check the bookmarks you created in the Loan Types page. (You will add content to the **apply.htm** and **contact.htm** pages in another tutorial.) When you have finished examining all of the pages, use your browser to print the Post Application Help and Loan Types pages, and then close your browser.
10. Close the **loan** Web site, and then close FrontPage.

Reinforce

Lab Assignments

The New Perspectives Labs are designed to help you master some of the key concepts and skills presented in this text. The steps for completing this Lab are located on the Course Technology Web site. Log on to the Internet and use your Web browser to go to the Student Online Companion for New Perspectives Office 2003 at **www.course.com/np/office2003**. Click the Lab Assignments link, and then navigate to the assignments for this tutorial.

Review

Quick Check Answers

Session 3.1

1. bulleted (unordered)
2. a list within another list
3. True
4. An anchor is specially marked text or an object that identifies a named location in a Web page.
5. icon
6. Create the bookmark in the page by selecting the text, picture, or location for it, clicking Insert on the menu bar, and then clicking Bookmark. Accept the default bookmark name or provide a new name, and then click the OK button. Select the text or picture in the page that will contain the hyperlink to the bookmark, click the Insert Hyperlink button on the Standard toolbar, click the Place in This Document button on the Link to bar, select the bookmark, and then click the OK button.
7. The hyperlink's target is a bookmark.

Session 3.2

1. 24
2. Click Tools on the menu bar, click Site Settings, click the General tab, type a new name in the Web name text box, and then click the OK button.
3. The folder is hidden.
4. a Site Summary report
5. more than one hyperlink in a Web page that opens the same target
6. False
7. In Folders view, select the page with which to associate the task or open the page in Design view, click the list arrow for the Create a new normal page button on the Standard toolbar, click Task, supply the required information in the New Task dialog box, and then click the OK button.
8. False

Objectives

Session 4.1
- Add pages to a Web site's navigation structure
- Create shared borders in a Web site
- Edit a shared border
- Delete, rename, and create new pages in Navigation view
- Add a link bar component and page banner to a page
- Create a custom link bar

Session 4.2
- Apply a theme to a Web site
- Customize an existing theme
- Delete a theme
- Create a new theme

Session 4.3
- Add a photo gallery to a page
- Learn about using drawings and AutoShapes
- Create a WordArt object in a page

Using Shared Borders and Themes

Updating the Content and Appearance of the Garden Web Site

Case

Sunshine Landscape & Garden Center

Brett Kizer, owner of the Sunshine Landscape & Garden Center, has been examining the garden Web site with a careful eye for detail. He wants to make sure that the Web site is colorful, professional, and reflects the atmosphere at the nursery. As he examined the site's current pages with several of the nursery's key employees, he noticed that the pages do not share a common presentation of material. Brett likes certain elements included in each page, but no one page stands out as a potential design sample. For example, he likes the background picture included with the home page, but does not like the white background in other pages. He likes the link bar and the Sunshine logo that appear in most pages, but thinks they take up too much space in the browser window. As a result, Brett decided to make some changes to the Web site, with the goal of freeing up space at the top of pages and using consistent formatting in all pages. You told Brett that these goals are very attainable and spent some time changing the pages to prepare them for the updates he requested. For the pages in the Web site, you deleted the link bar and Sunshine logo at the top of the pages, and then you deleted extra pictures and other content that were inconsistently formatted and presented. You will import these revised pages into the garden Web site and overwrite the pages with the same names.

Student Data Files

To complete this tutorial, you will need your ending files from Tutorial 3 and the following Data Files. Additional Data Files needed to complete the end-of-tutorial exercises are listed with the Review Assignments and Case Problems.

▼Tutorial.04

▽ Tutorial

bulk.htm
bulk2.htm
center.htm
contact.htm
deer.htm
garden2.htm
garden3.htm
garden4.htm
garden57.jpg
garden82.jpg
garden98.jpg
index.htm
irr.htm
land.htm
land2.htm
leon.jpg
map_page.htm
mulch.htm
rock.htm
soil.htm
stone.htm
bulk_pic (folder)
gc_pics (folder)
land_pic (folder)
rock_pic (folder)

As you were talking with Brett, Clara McShane, the nursery's senior landscape designer, told you that she has finished some additional pages that should be linked to the Garden Center, Landscape & Rock Work, and Bulk Goods pages. She gave you these files and their embedded pictures on a disk and asked you to add them to the Web site. You told Brett that with the addition of these pages, it's more important now to use the tools in FrontPage to format the site's hyperlinks and page formatting. These tools—shared borders, link bars, and themes—are dependent upon the Web site's navigation structure, which you create in Navigation view. By maintaining these features with FrontPage, you can ensure that all pages in the Web site have a consistent look and feel, and that future updates to the Web site are reflected automatically in the site's link bars.

Session 4.1

Understanding Shared Borders and Link Bars

Up to this point, you have been creating hyperlinks to other pages in the Web site using a link bar with pictures formatted as hyperlinks and with text formatted as hyperlinks. You also added the Sunshine logo to most pages. You have completed this work manually by inserting text and pictures into each Web page in the site. Although this system has worked well, it will soon be impractical to continue inserting link bars and logos in all future pages. This effort requires time, and the possibility for error increases. For example, if you add a new page to the Web site, you would need to add a link to it in the site's existing pages to make it accessible from the home page and other pages in the Web site.

If your Web site contains many pages, you can use Navigation view to identify the way pages are related to each other in a hierarchical manner. For example, a site's home page is usually the top page in a Web site and contains links that open pages at the next level. When you create a Web site, FrontPage adds the site's home page to the navigation structure in Navigation view, but you must add the remaining pages to the navigation structure to identify their relationships. You can think of a Web site's navigation structure as an organizational chart, with the home page as an organization's president. The next level of pages would include the top-level managers, the assistants would appear at the next level, and so forth. In this context, the home page is the called a **parent page**, and the pages below the home page are **child pages** of the home page. In some cases, you will add every page in a Web site to the navigation structure; in other cases, you might exclude pages based on their content.

After you identify how pages in a Web site are related to each other, you can enable features in the Web site that use the navigation structure to enable navigation-related features. A **link bar component** is a link bar that FrontPage maintains and updates automatically, thus saving time and ensuring that the links to other pages are always consistent and accurate. In many cases, you will create a link bar component in one or more shared borders. A **shared border** is an area at the top, bottom, right, or left side of a page that contains content that appears in every page that uses it. You can set up the Web site to use one or more of these borders in a page. For example, you might use a top shared border for the company's name and a link bar component, and a bottom shared border for copyright and other information about the company. A shared border presents the same information in all Web pages that use it, so it ensures consistency in the site's pages. Because FrontPage maintains the links in a link bar component, you don't have to worry about updating the link bars in all pages in the site as you add new pages to it and delete pages from it. For a new page, you would just need to create the new page in the Web site (or import its file into the Web site), position the page in the navigation structure to identify its relationship to other pages, and activate the shared borders that you want to use in the new page. After saving your changes, FrontPage automatically makes appropriate changes to the link bar component.

After creating the navigation structure and activating the shared border(s), you add the content of a shared border to your Web site in any page that uses the border. In Design view, a dashed line indicates the boundary of a shared border in a Web page; these boundary lines are not displayed in the browser. When you edit the content of a shared border in a single Web page, your changes apply to *all* pages in the Web site that use the shared border. For example, adding a company name and logo to a top shared border in one page will cause all other pages in the Web site that use the top shared border to display the same name and logo in the same location.

Brett likes the idea of maintaining the Web site's hyperlinks with link bar components. You tell Brett that enabling the Web site's shared borders will make it easy to accommodate his request for the link bars, but first he must import the revised pages into the Web site and position them in the navigation structure in Navigation view to identify the relationships among pages in the site.

Adding Pages to the Site's Navigation Structure

After you import or create Web pages in a Web site, you must add them to the navigation structure in Navigation view to identify how they are related to each other. When you first change to Navigation view, only the site's home page will appear in the navigation structure. You can drag and drop files from the Folder List and position them in the navigation structure according to your Web site plan.

To import the revised pages into the Web site and add pages to the navigation structure:

1. Start **FrontPage** and then open the **garden** Web site from the location where your Web sites are stored.
2. Display the Folder List and make sure that the garden Web site's root folder is selected, click **File** on the menu bar, click **Import**, click the **Add File** button, open the **Tutorial.04\Tutorial** folder included with your Data Files, press and hold the **Ctrl** key, click the files **bulk.htm**, **bulk2.htm**, **center.htm**, **contact.htm**, **index.htm**, **irr.htm**, **land.htm**, and **map_page.htm**, release the **Ctrl** key, and then click the **Open** button. Eight files are listed in the Import dialog box.
3. Click the **OK** button, and then click the **Yes to All** button to overwrite the files in the Web site with the same names.
4. Change to Navigation view by clicking the **Navigation View** button Navigation at the bottom of the Contents pane. When you first change to Navigation view, only the site's home page appears in the navigation structure. To add pages to Navigation view, you drag a file from the Folder List to the navigation structure, and then release the mouse button when the page is in the correct position. You'll add the center.htm page first.
5. Click **center.htm** in the Folder List, and then drag it to the navigation structure. Position the center.htm page below the home page, as shown in Figure 4-1.

Figure 4-1 **Adding a page to the navigation structure**

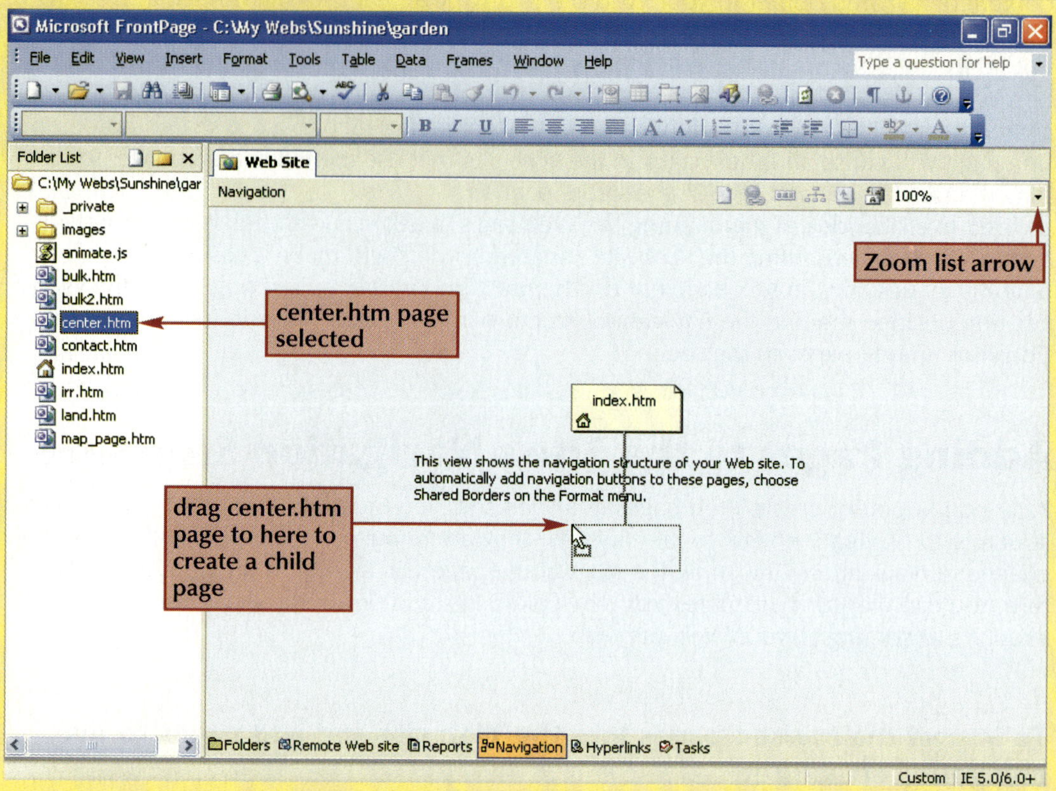

Trouble? Your home page might display part of the page title "Sunshine Landscape & Garden Center home page" instead of the filename. This difference causes no problems, because you will change this page title later.

6. When you have positioned the page as shown in Figure 4-1, release the mouse button to add it to the navigation structure. The page's title, Garden Center, appears in the page icon you added. If you need to know the filename of a page in the navigation structure, you can click it and the page's filename will appear on the status bar.

Trouble? If your page icons are larger or smaller than those shown in Figure 4-1, click the Zoom list arrow on the Contents pane, and then click 100%.

7. Repeat Steps 5 and 6 to add the **land.htm** and **irr.htm** pages as child pages of the home page and to the right of the Garden Center page, and then click anywhere in a blank area of the Contents pane to deselect the pages. See Figure 4-2.

Three child pages added to the navigation structure — **Figure 4-2**

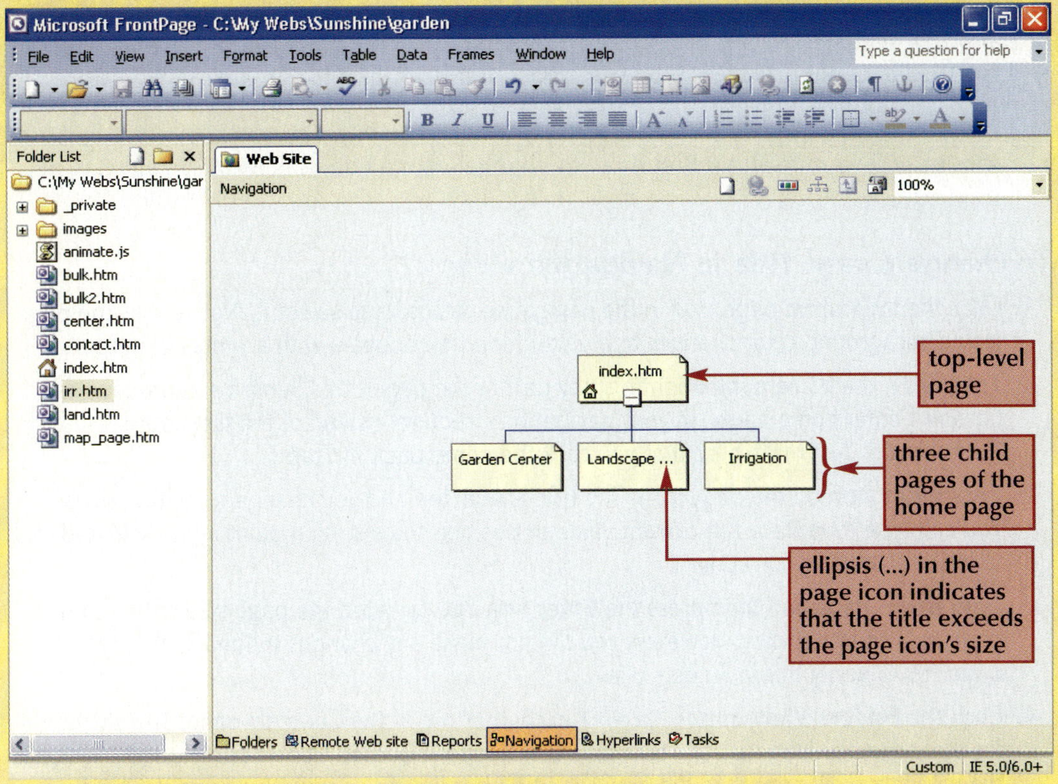

Trouble? If you drop a page in the wrong position, click the page that you need to fix and drag it into the correct position. If you drag the wrong page into the navigation structure, right-click the page icon to open the shortcut menu, click Delete, click the Remove page from the navigation structure option button, and then click the OK button.

As you add pages to the navigation structure, you'll notice that the titles for some pages exceed the size of the page icon, as is the case for the land.htm page, whose title is "Landscape & Rock Work." When the page title exceeds the size of the page icon, an ellipsis (…) appears in the page title. To see the entire title, you click it once to select it, and then again to change to editing mode.

Brett wonders why the page title for the home page is "index.htm," instead of "Sunshine Landscape & Garden Center home page," which is the page title in Folders view. You tell Brett that the page titles in Folders view and Navigation view are separate. The page title that you see in Folders view is the HTML title of the Web page, which appears in the <title> and </title> tags. The page title in Navigation view is not always the same as the HTML title; it is the page name that will appear in the site's link bars. In some cases, the HTML page title might be long to convey the page's contents; in those instances, you might not want to use the long title to identify the page in the site's link bars because it would require a lot of space.

Reference Window

Renaming a Page's Title in Navigation View

- Right-click the page icon in the navigation structure to open the shortcut menu, and then click Rename.
- Type the new page title, and then press the Enter key.

For now, you want to show Brett how to change a page title in Navigation view.

To change a page title in Navigation view:

1. Click the **index.htm** page icon in the navigation structure to select it. Notice that the page icon's background color changes to blue and the title appears with a white background.

   Trouble? The home page might display part of the page title "Sunshine Landscape & Garden Center home page" in your navigation structure instead of the filename "index.htm." Just make sure that you click the home page in Step 1.

2. Click **index.htm** on the page icon. The title is selected and you change to editing mode. You can type to replace the current value or position the insertion point in the selected text to make an editing correction.
3. Type **Home Page** and then press the **Enter** key. You updated the page title of the home page in Navigation view. However, you did not make any changes to the HTML title of the page. You'll verify this in Folders view.
4. Click the **Folders View** button Folders at the bottom of the Contents pane. The page title for the index.htm page is still "Sunshine Landscape & Garden Center home page," which is the value that will appear in the browser's title bar when you view this page in a browser.

   Trouble? If the title of the home page changed to "Home Page" in Folders view, click the title to select it and change to editing mode, type Sunshine Landscape & Garden Center home page, and then press the Enter key.

5. Return to Navigation view.

Now you can finish adding pages to the navigation structure.

To continue adding pages to the navigation structure:

1. Click the **bulk.htm** page in the Folder List to select it, and then position it to the left of the Irrigation page in the navigation structure.
2. Position the **contact.htm** page to the left of the Bulk Goods page.
3. Position the **map_page.htm** page to the right of the Irrigation page.
4. Position the **bulk2.htm** page below the Bulk Goods page, as shown in Figure 4-3. The bulk2.htm page is now a child page of the bulk.htm page and you have finished adding pages to the navigation structure.

Figure 4-3

Completed navigation structure

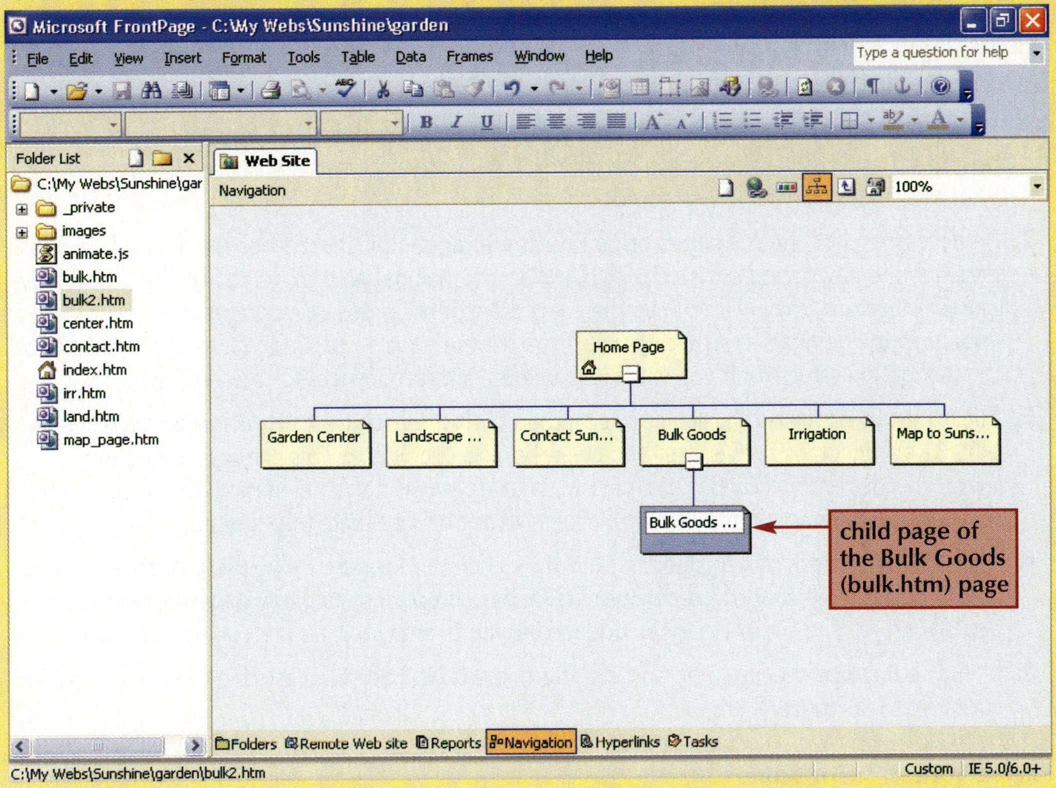

Now that you have created the navigation structure, you can create the shared borders and the link bar components.

Creating Shared Borders in a Web Site

After you position pages in the navigation structure, you can create one or more shared borders in those pages. You can create shared borders at the top, bottom, left, and right sides of the page. FrontPage automatically adds the page title to the top shared border, and provides the option to use the navigation structure to create link bar components in the top, left, and right shared borders.

Creating Shared Borders for a Web Site

Reference Window

- If necessary, position pages in the navigation structure.
- Click Format on the menu bar, and then click Shared Borders.
- Select the option button for applying the shared border to all or selected pages, select the shared border(s) to add, select the option to include navigation buttons if desired, and then click the OK button.

Your next task is to create the shared borders for the Web site. Brett wants the pages in the Web site to have three shared borders: a top shared border containing the page's title and a link bar with links to pages at the same level, the home page, and the parent page; a left shared border containing a link bar with links to child pages; and a bottom shared border with the company's copyright information. All pages appearing in the navigation structure will use the same shared borders. You can create the shared borders with any page selected in the navigation structure.

To create the shared borders:

1. Click **Format** on the menu bar, and then click **Shared Borders**. The Shared Borders dialog box opens and displays a sample page. You have not yet added any shared borders to the Web site, so no options are selected.
2. If necessary, click the **All pages** option button to apply the shared borders you select to all pages in the navigation structure; if your Web site has pages that do not appear in the navigation structure, they will not use the shared borders. In this case, pages that do not appear in the navigation structure will display a message to remind you to add the page to the navigation structure if you want it to use the shared borders for the Web site.
3. Click the **Top** check box to select it, and then click the **Include navigation buttons** check box, which becomes active after you click the Top check box. This change adds a top shared border with a link bar component to every page in the navigation structure. Notice that the sample page in the Shared Borders dialog box reflects this change.
4. Click the **Left** check box to select it, and then click the **Include navigation buttons** check box to add the left shared border with a link bar component to every page in the navigation structure. The sample page is updated again to show top and left shared borders.
5. Click the **Bottom** check box to add a bottom shared border to every page in the navigation structure. See Figure 4-4.

Figure 4-4 **Shared Borders dialog box**

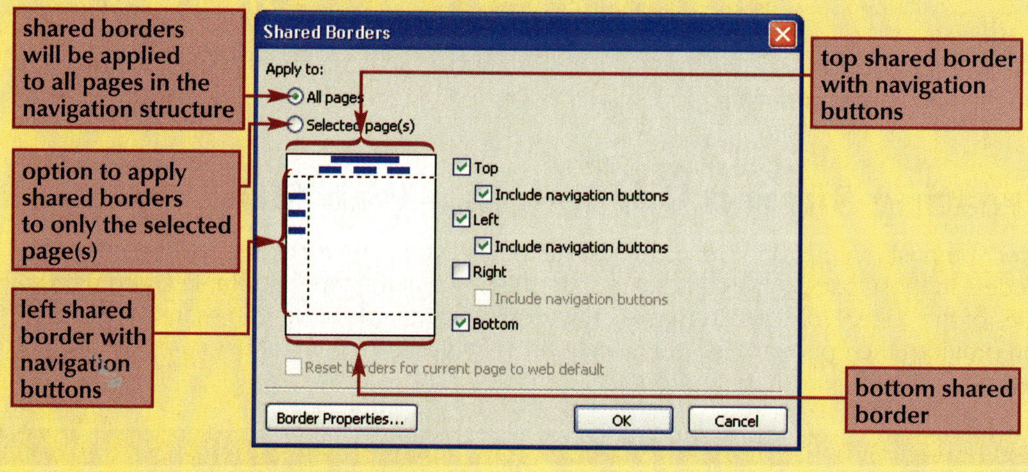

6. Click the **Border Properties** button. The Border Properties dialog box opens. See Figure 4-5.

Figure 4-5 **Border Properties dialog box**

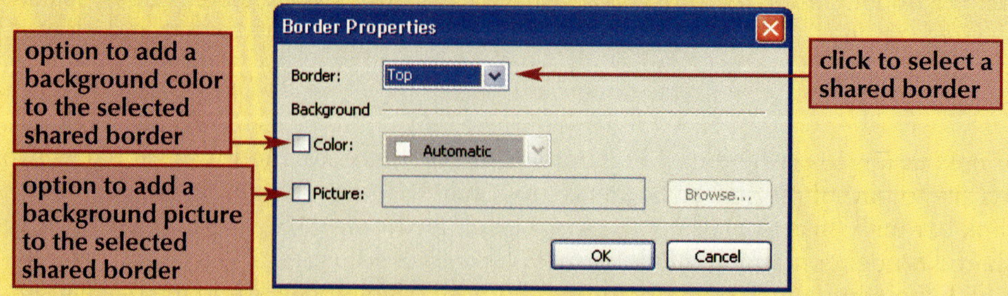

You can use the options in the Border Properties dialog box to add a background color or background picture to the different shared borders. For example, by selecting the Color check box, you can use the list box to select a background for a shared border. By selecting the Picture check box and then selecting a file, you can display a background picture in a shared border. Brett doesn't want to include these options, so he can close the Border Properties dialog box and then finish creating the shared borders.

7. Click the **Cancel** button to close the Border Properties dialog box, and then click the **OK** button to close the Shared Borders dialog box and to create the top, bottom, and left shared borders in pages you added to the navigation structure. The status bar will display some messages indicating that the Web site's shared borders are being created. This process might take a few seconds, depending on where your Web site is stored.
8. Close the Folder List.

Although FrontPage created the shared borders, you can't see them in your Web site in Navigation view. When you open any page that appears in Navigation view in Design view, however, you will see the shared borders. Next, you will open the Bulk Goods page in Design view.

To open the Bulk Goods page in Design view:

1. Double-click the **Bulk Goods** page icon (the child page of the home page, bulk.htm) to open that page in Design view. See Figure 4-6.

Shared borders in the Bulk Goods page **Figure 4-6**

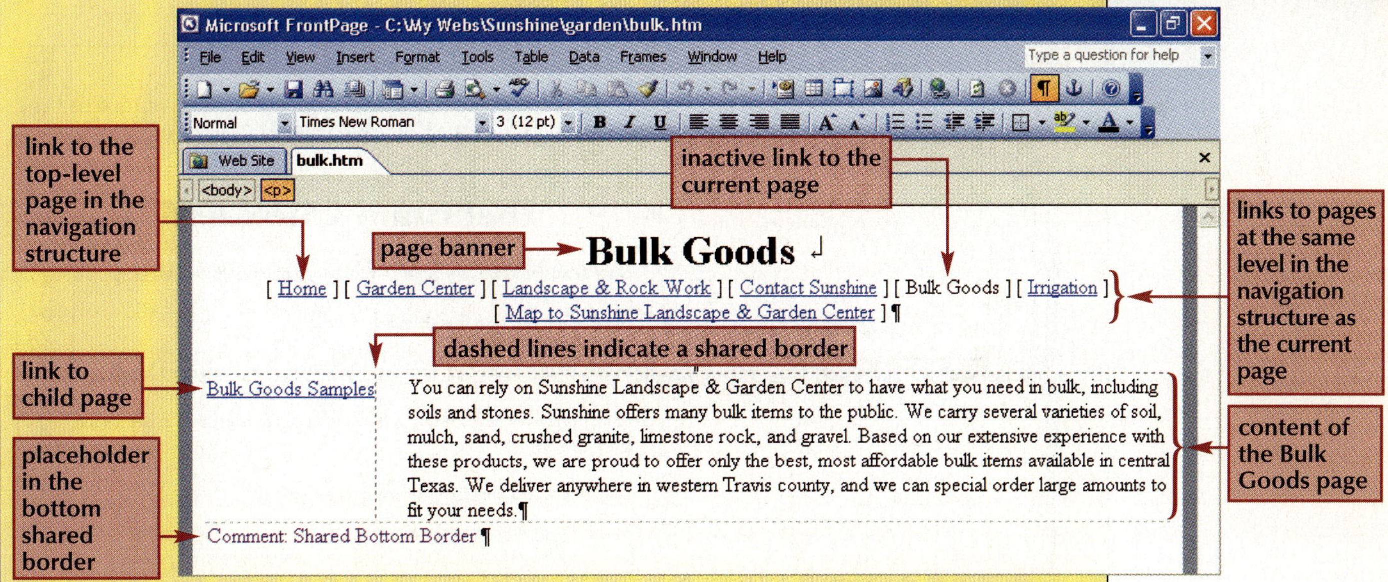

Trouble? If the Bulk Goods page does not open in Design view, repeat Step 1 and double-click the icon, not the page title.

The top shared border includes the page's title (Bulk Goods) and a link bar component that includes links to the home page and to pages at the same level in the navigation structure as the Bulk Goods page. The page title is called a **page banner**. A page banner can be text, as shown in Figure 4-6, or a picture. Its text is taken from the page's title in Navigation view. The hyperlinks below the page banner and in the left shared border appear in link bar components. The option for including the home page was automatically selected for the top shared border. When this option is selected, FrontPage inserts the link named "Home" in the link bar and creates a link to the site's top-level page.

The Bulk Goods page is currently the only child page in the Web site with its own child page, and the link to that page (Bulk Goods Samples) appears automatically in the left shared border. If a page contains no links in a border for which navigation buttons have been specified, a message in that border will indicate that you can edit the link bar's properties to display hyperlinks. The bottom shared border does not yet contain any content; the "Comment: Shared Bottom Border" text is an HTML comment that will not be displayed when the page is viewed using a browser. To add content to the bottom shared border, you would select the comment and type the new content to replace it.

The home page does not contain any links in the top shared border, as you will see next.

To examine the shared borders for the home page:

1. Click the **Web Site** tab to return to Navigation view.
2. Double-click the **Home Page** page icon to open this page in Design view. See Figure 4-7.

Figure 4-7 **Shared borders in the home page**

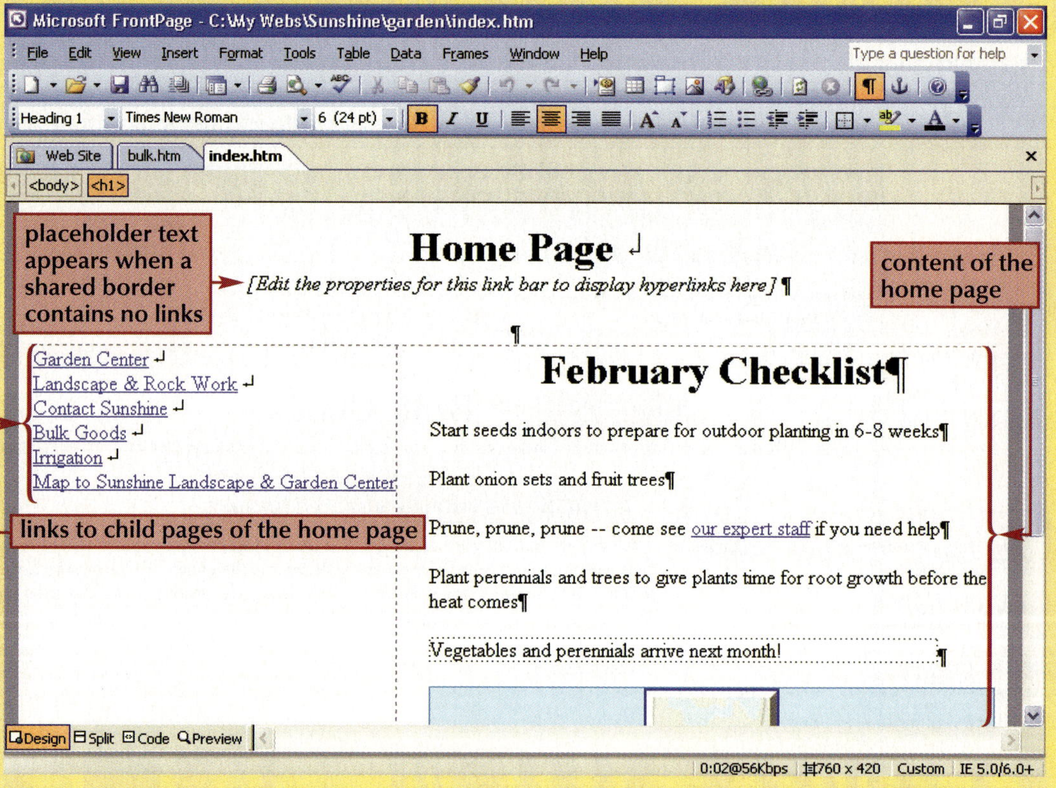

The top shared border displays the page's title and a message. The top shared border does not contain a link bar because the home page is the top-level page in the Web site and no "higher" or same-level pages exist in the navigation structure. The left shared border contains links to the child pages of the home page. The bottom shared border contains a comment.

You decide to show Brett the Web site in a browser so he can better understand how the shared borders work and see how FrontPage creates the link bars.

To test the shared borders and link bars in a browser:

1. Click the **Preview** button on the Standard toolbar. The home page opens in a browser. The top shared border displays the page's title and the left shared border displays the links to child pages of the home page. Notice that the page title in the top shared border is "Home Page," which is this page's title in Navigation view. The browser's title bar displays the HTML title for the document, which is the same title you see in Folders view and that appears in the HTML document's <title> and </title> tags. See Figure 4-8.

Figure 4-8 Home page in a browser

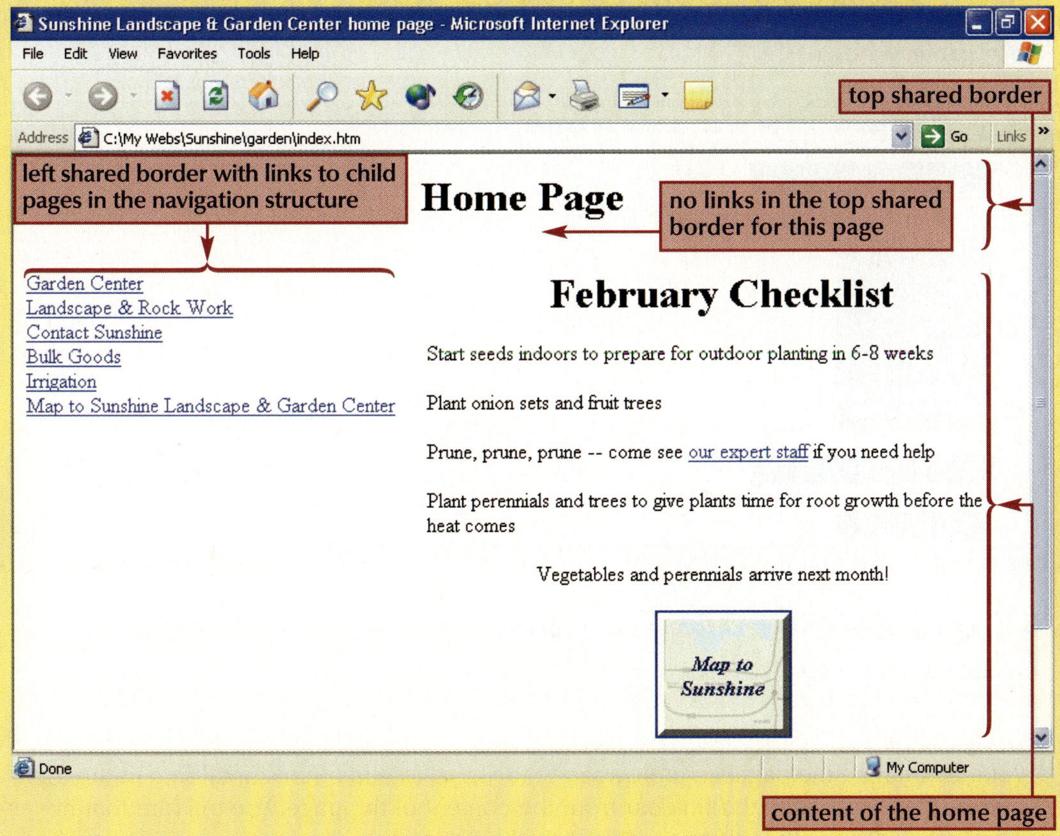

2. Click the **Garden Center** link in the left shared border to open that page. The top shared border for this page includes the page's title, plus links to the home page and to pages in the navigation structure at the same level as the Garden Center page. The left shared border is empty because the Garden Center page does not have any child pages in the navigation structure.
3. Click the **Bulk Goods** link to open that page. The top shared border includes the page's title and links to the home page and to same-level pages in the navigation structure. Because the Bulk Goods page has a child page in the navigation structure, a hyperlink to the child page, Bulk Goods Samples, appears in the left shared border.

4. Click the **Bulk Goods Samples** link to open that page. Because this page has no child pages in the navigation structure, the left shared border is empty. The top shared border includes links entitled "Home" and "Up." Clicking the Home link opens the home page. Clicking the Up link opens the parent page, which in this case is the Bulk Goods page, which is the parent of the Bulk Goods Samples page in the navigation structure. See Figure 4-9.

Figure 4-9 **Bulk Goods Samples page in a browser**

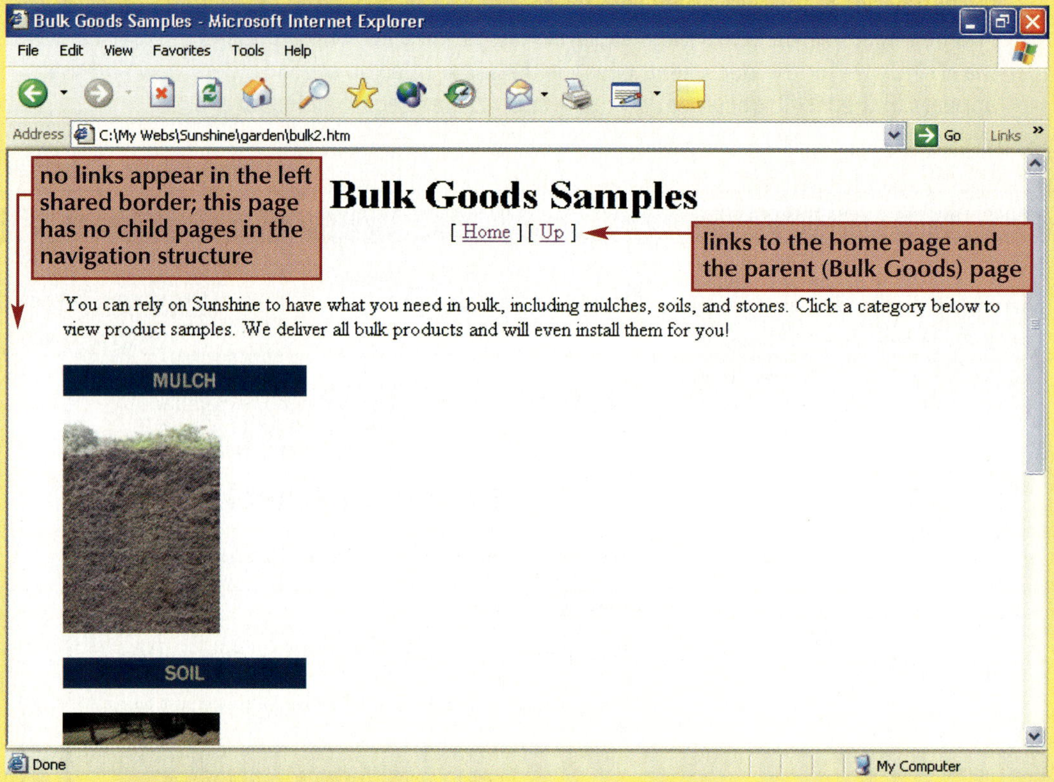

5. Click the **Up** link. The Bulk Goods page opens.
6. Close your browser.

After examining the pages in a browser, Brett wants to add a horizontal line in the top shared border to separate the link bar from the content of the page. You tell him that he can make this change by editing the top shared border.

Editing a Shared Border

After creating a shared border, you can modify it by opening any page in Design view that uses the shared border and then making the desired changes. Remember that all of the Web pages included in the navigation structure use the *same* shared borders, so any changes that you make to a shared border are automatically applied to all pages that use it. You can change the content of the shared border using the same techniques that you would use to revise any page in Design view.

Brett wants to add a horizontal line below the link bar component in the top shared border to separate the border from the page content. He also wants to add a copyright notice to the bottom shared border. You will show him how to make these changes in

Design view for the home page. He could also make these changes using any page in the Web site because all of the pages currently use the same shared borders.

To edit the top and bottom shared borders:

1. In the home page, move the pointer over the text that begins "Edit the properties" in the link bar component in the top shared border of the home page until the pointer changes to a shape, and then click the link bar placeholder text to select it.
2. Press the **down** arrow key ↓ on the keyboard to position the insertion point on the next line, and then press the **Delete** key to remove this line.
3. Click **Insert** on the menu bar, and then click **Horizontal Line**. A horizontal line appears in the shared border below the link bar placeholder text.

   Brett wants to use the copyright information at the bottom of the home page as the content for the bottom shared border. He can cut and paste this text to move it to the bottom shared border.
4. Scroll down the home page as necessary, use the pointer to select the last two lines in the home page (beginning "Copyright" and "All," and including the paragraph mark at the end of the second line), and then click the **Cut** button on the Standard toolbar.
5. Click the comment placeholder text in the bottom shared border to select it, press the **Enter** key, and then click the **Paste** button on the Standard toolbar. As shown in Figure 4-10, the copyright information now appears in the bottom shared border. A blank paragraph appears above and below the pasted text.

Pasting the content of the bottom shared border — **Figure 4-10**

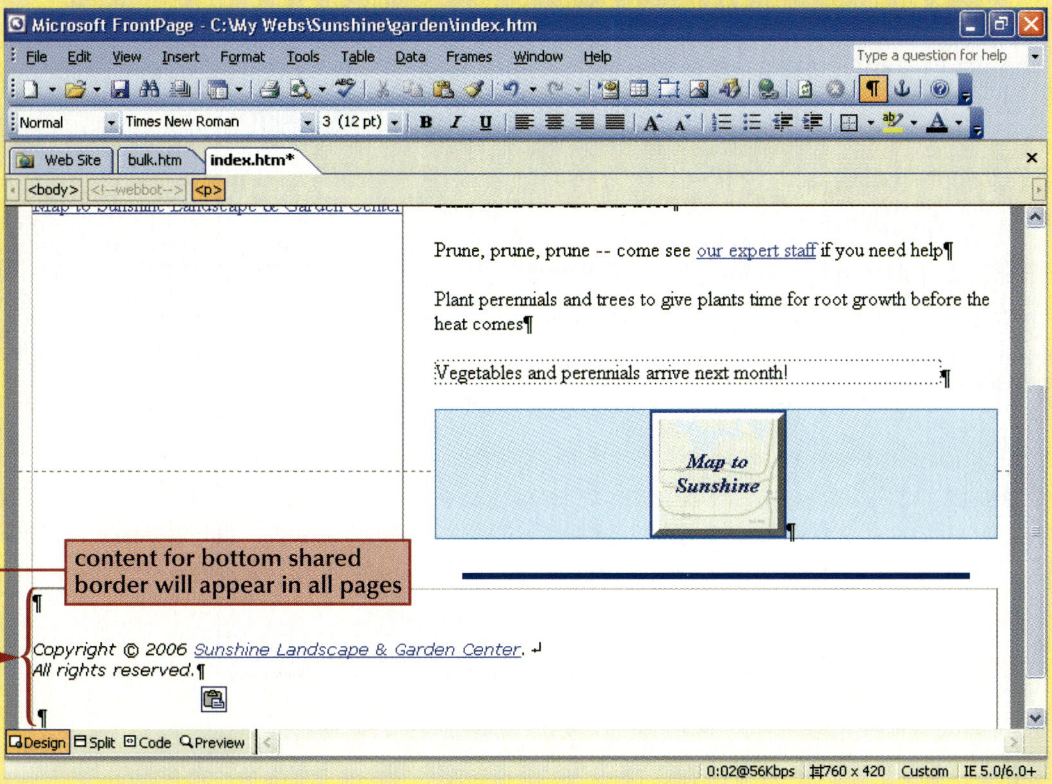

Trouble? If you don't have a blank paragraph in the bottom shared border above the "Copyright" line, click at the beginning of that line, and then press the Enter key.

6. Save the home page. FrontPage saves the home page and the changes you made to the top and bottom shared borders.
7. Click the **bulk.htm** page tab to open the Bulk Goods page in Design view. Notice that the horizontal line appears in the top shared border for this page and the copyright information appears in the bottom shared border.

You tell Brett that he can make other types of changes to the shared borders, as well. For example, he might want to add a company logo to the top shared border or the date and time the page was last updated to the bottom shared border. To make changes to a link bar component, however, he needs to know how to use the Link Bar Properties dialog box. You want to show Brett this dialog box in case he needs to change the default settings of a link bar.

Revising a Link Bar Component

After you create a link bar component, you might need to revise it to change the hyperlinks or to change the style of the links.

To open the Link Bar Properties dialog box:

1. Double-click the link bar component in the top shared border to open the Link Bar Properties dialog box for the link bar component in the top shared border. See Figure 4-11. Notice that most of the choices are option buttons, so only one selection is permitted.

Figure 4-11 Link Bar Properties dialog box for the link bar component in the top shared border

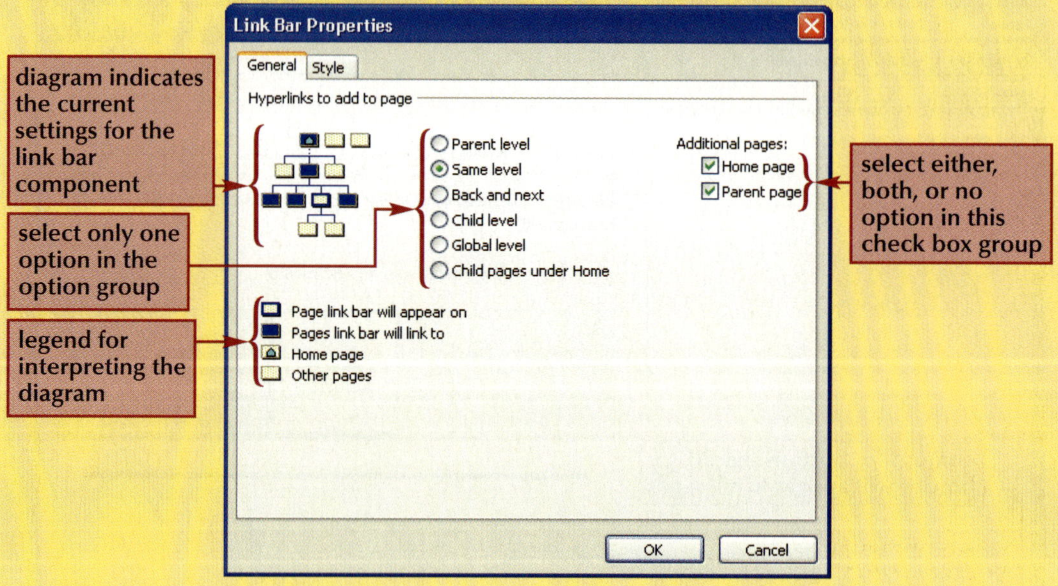

Figure 4-12 describes the settings on the General tab in the Link Bar Properties dialog box and provides examples of how these settings would apply to the Bulk Goods page. When you change an option in this dialog box, the sample diagram changes to reflect the new links. Make sure that you study these settings and understand how they work before continuing.

Figure 4-12 **Link bar property descriptions and examples**

Option	Description	Example for the Bulk Goods page in the garden Web site
General tab: Select one option button and one or both check boxes.		
Parent level option button	All pages will include a link to the parent-level page.	Home link only (the parent page)
Same level option button	All pages will include links to pages at the same level as the current page.	Links to the Garden Center, Landscape & Rock Work, Contact Sunshine, Irrigation, and Map to Sunshine Landscape & Garden Center pages
Back and next option button	All pages will include links to the pages immediately to the left and right of the current page, based on page positions in the navigation structure.	Back and Next links, which open the Contact Sunshine and Irrigation pages, respectively
Child level option button	All pages will include a link to child pages of the current page, when applicable.	Link to the Bulk Goods Samples page only
Global level option button	All pages will include a link to the top-level page in the Web site.	Home link only (the top-level page in the navigation structure)
Child pages under Home option button	All pages will include links to child pages of the home page.	Links to the Garden Center, Landscape & Rock Work, Contact Sunshine, Irrigation, and Map to Sunshine Landscape & Garden Center pages
Home page check box	All pages will include a link to the home page, regardless of what other options are selected.	Home link, plus any other links included by the option button selected in the Hyperlinks to add to page section
Parent page check box	All pages will include a link to the parent-level page of the current page, regardless of which other options are selected.	Home link (which is the parent page of the Bulk Goods page), plus any other links included by the option button selected in the Hyperlinks to add to page section

To change the link bar properties:

1. Click the **Back and next** option button to select it. The Home page and Parent page check boxes are still selected. Notice that the diagram in the dialog box shows these changes to the hyperlinks included in the link bar.
2. Click the **Same level** option button to select it and to return to the original configuration.
3. Click the **Style** tab. See Figure 4-13.

Figure 4-13 **Style tab for the link bar component in the top shared border**

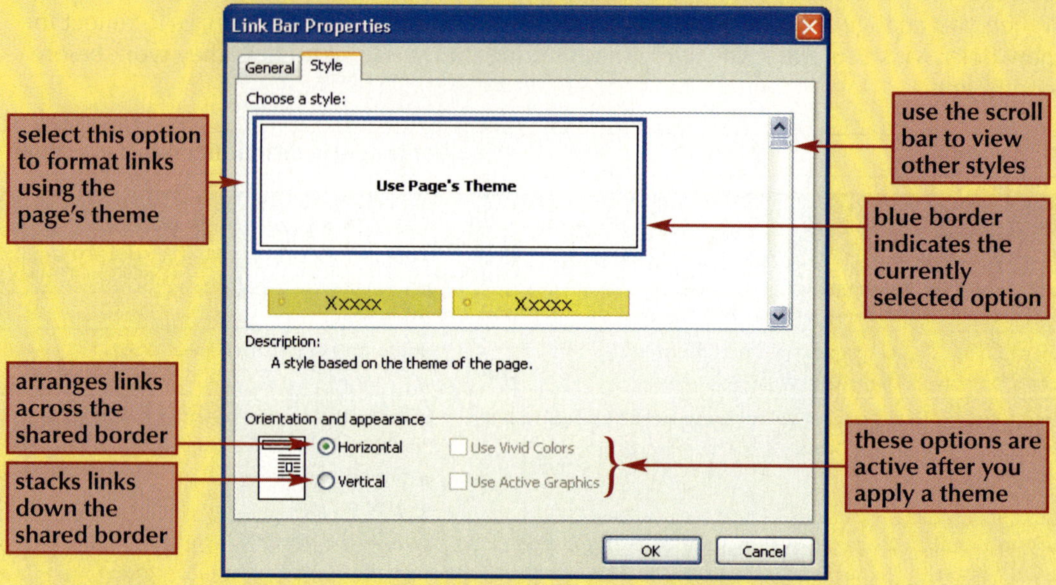

The options on the Style tab control the appearance of the links that you selected on the General tab. By scrolling the Choose a style list box, you can select a theme or text style as the basis for formatting your links. In the Orientation and appearance section, clicking the Horizontal option button arranges the hyperlinks in the link bar across the shared border; clicking the Vertical option button vertically stacks the hyperlinks in the link bar in the shared border. When you select a theme to format the hyperlinks, the Use Vivid Colors and Use Active Graphics check boxes become active so you can choose to apply these options, as well.

For now, Brett wants to keep the buttons arranged horizontally across the top shared border and to select the default style, which is to use the page's theme. You'll show him how to apply a theme to the garden Web site in the next session.

4. Make sure that the **Use Page's Theme** option and the **Horizontal** option button are selected, and then click the **OK** button. The link bar component in the top shared border does not change because you did not change any of its settings.

   You can also examine the selections in the left shared border.

5. Double-click the link bar component in the left shared border to open the Link Bar Properties dialog box for the link bar component in the left shared border. The top shared border will include a link to the home page, so you don't need to repeat that link in the left shared border.
6. Make sure that the **Child level** option button is selected and that the **Home page** and **Parent page** check boxes do not contain check marks, and then click the **Style** tab.
7. Scroll up the Choose a style list and click the **Use Page's Theme** option, make sure that the **Vertical** option button is selected, and then click the **OK** button. The Link Bar Properties dialog box for the left shared border closes. The link in the left shared border looks the same, even though you changed its style. The link's appearance will change when you apply a theme to the Web site in the next session.
8. Save the page.

These changes to the shared borders will appear in every page in the Web site that uses them. You won't see some of the changes you made, however, until you apply a theme in Session 4.2.

Making Changes in Navigation View

As you work on a Web site, you will frequently return to Navigation view to update the site. For example, as you add pages to the Web site, you'll need to add them to the navigation structure. You also can delete pages from the navigation structure or set a page so its link will not appear in a link bar. You can drag the page icons in the navigation structure to rearrange their order in the link bars.

Deleting a Page from the Navigation Structure

When examining the Web pages in a browser, Brett noticed that the link to the map_page.htm page has a very long title. As he considers the function of this page, he realizes that it does not need to be accessible from every Web page in the site; the thumbnail picture and hyperlink in the home page are sufficient. You tell Brett that he is correct to discover that some Web pages aren't part of the main structure of the Web site and don't need to appear in the navigation structure. Because the map_page.htm page is the target of a hyperlink that appears in the home page, you can choose not to make it accessible from other pages in the site. If you decide later that you want visitors to be able to open the map_page.htm page from any page in the Web site, you could add it back to the navigation structure.

You can use Navigation view to delete a page from the navigation structure only or from the navigation structure *and* the Web site. If you delete the page from the navigation structure only, then the page is deleted from any link bar components that include it, but it remains in the Web site. Deleting the page from the Web site permanently removes the page from the navigation structure, the site's link bars, and the Web site.

Deleting a Page in Navigation View

Reference Window

- Right-click the page icon in the navigation structure that you want to delete to select the page and open the shortcut menu.
- Click Delete to open the Delete Page dialog box.
- Click the Remove this page from the navigation structure option button to delete the page from only the navigation structure, or click the Delete this page from the Web option button to delete the page from the navigation structure and the Web site.
- Click the OK button.

If you need to make a page in the navigation structure temporarily unavailable through the site's link bar components, you can right-click the page icon in the navigation structure to open the shortcut menu, and then click Included in Link Bars. If you choose this option, the page icon's background color changes from yellow to gray, as shown in Figure 4-14, and the page's link is removed from the site's link bar components. To add the page back to the site's link bar components, right-click it again, and then click Include in Link Bars on the shortcut menu.

Figure 4-14 **Omitting a page from a site's link bar components**

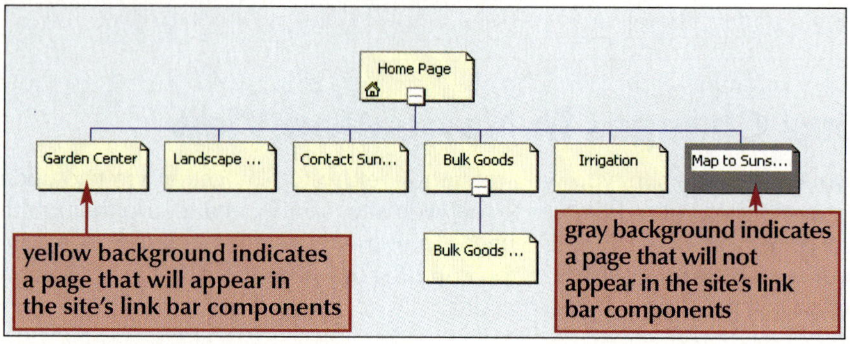

Brett wants to delete the Map to Sunshine Landscape & Garden Center page from the navigation structure, but not from the Web site.

To delete a page from the navigation structure:

1. Return to Navigation view.
2. Right-click the **Map to Sunshine Landscape & Garden Center** page icon to open the shortcut menu, and then click **Delete** to open the Delete Page dialog box.
3. Click the **Remove page from the navigation structure** option button to select it (if necessary), and then click the **OK** button. The page is deleted from the navigation structure, but its file (map_page.htm) is still in the Web site.

You can also add Web pages to the navigation structure, which creates the page in the Web site and positions the page in the navigation structure at the same time.

Creating a New Page in Navigation View

Helen Xiao, Sunshine's senior horticulturist, told Brett this morning that customers frequently request a list of products that deter deer from eating landscaping materials and a list of deer-resistant plants to install. Helen asks if this would be a good page to include in the Web site, so staff members could point customers to the Web site for a complete list of anti-deer products and deer-resistant plants. Brett agrees with Helen's suggestion and asks you to show him how to create a new page in the Web site. Helen said that she would create the content for this new page and send it to Brett in a couple of days.

When you use Navigation view to create a new Web page, you add it to the navigation structure and to the Web site at the same time. Because the planned content of this new page deals with plants, Brett will add the new page as a child page of the center.htm page.

Reference Window

Creating a New Page in Navigation View

- Right-click the page icon that will be the parent for the new page to select it and to open the shortcut menu.
- Point to New on the shortcut menu, and then click Page.
- Right-click the page icon for the new page to open the shortcut menu, click Rename, enter the page's title, and then press the Enter key. FrontPage will create the Web page using the title you entered. To change the default filename, change to Folders view, click the filename of the new page to select it, type a new filename, and then press the Enter key.

FrontPage uses the title you entered (or the default title's filename, new_page_1.htm, if you don't enter a title) as the filename for a new Web page that you create in Navigation view. If you change the default title to one that contains spaces, FrontPage will save the filename with underscore characters in place of the spaces. You'll show Brett how to add the new page to the Web site, and then you will show him how to change its page title and filename.

To add a new page to the Web site and change its title and filename:

1. Right-click the **Garden Center** page in the navigation structure to select it and to open the shortcut menu, point to **New**, and then click **Page**. A new page with the default title of "New Page 1" and the temporary filename of new_page_1.htm is added to the navigation structure and to the Web site.

   Trouble? If your default page title includes another number, don't worry. Just make sure that a new page was created.

   Next, rename the new page.

2. Right-click the **New Page 1** page icon to open the shortcut menu, and then click **Rename**.
3. Type **Anti-Deer Products** as the page's title, and then press the **Enter** key.
4. Double-click the **Anti-Deer Products** page icon. The page opens in Design view. Notice the shared borders at the top, bottom, and left side of the page. See Figure 4-15. These are the same shared borders that you set for all pages in the Web site.

Figure 4-15 Design view of the Anti-Deer Products page

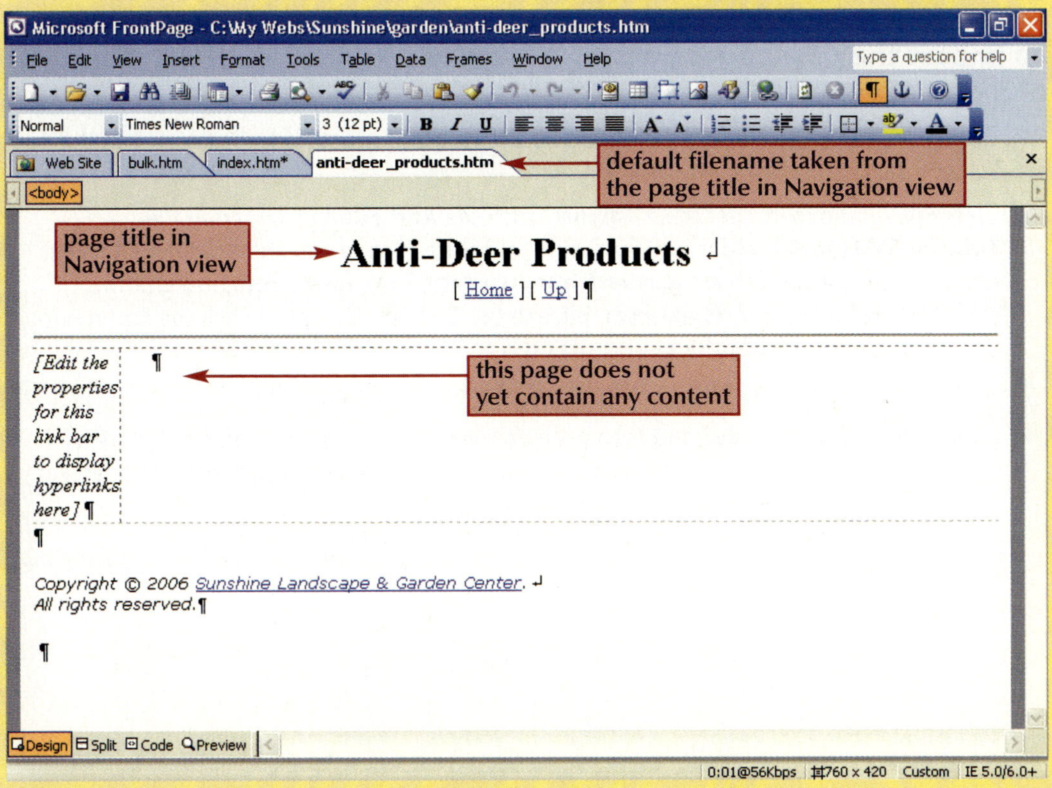

Trouble? FrontPage might assign the filename new_page_1.htm to the Anti-Deer Products page. This is not a problem; you will change the filename next.

5. Click the **Web Site** tab at the top of the Contents pane, and then change to Folders view.
6. In Folders view, right-click the filename **anti-deer_products.htm** to select it and to open the shortcut menu, click **Rename**, type **deer.htm**, and then press the **Enter** key. FrontPage updates the filename in the Web site.

   Trouble? If you see new_page_1.htm in Folders view, right-click that filename instead of anti-deer_products.htm in Step 6.

Brett reminds you that Clara finished some of the pages that are linked to the existing land.htm, center.htm, and bulk2.htm pages in the Web site. Keeping with Brett's overall vision of the Web site, Clara used photographs in the new pages to provide pictures of landscaping and rock work jobs Sunshine has completed and pictures of the different available soils, mulches, and stones. Brett will import these pages into the Web site, and then you will help him position them in the navigation structure to identify their relationships to their parent pages. You will also help him include links to these pages in the site's link bar components.

Adding New Pages to the Navigation Structure

Clara sent Brett the new Web pages and the embedded pictures they contain. Because Clara needed a way to organize the pictures, she saved them in folders. You tell Brett he can import the pages into the Web site, and then position them in Navigation view to enable the shared borders. Then he can import the folders that contain the pictures into the Web site.

To import the new pages into the Web site and position them in Navigation view:

1. Display the Folder List, and then make sure the Web site's root folder is selected in the Folder List.
2. Click **File** on the menu bar, click **Import**, click the **Add File** button, open the **Tutorial.04\Tutorial** folder included with your Data Files, press and hold the **Ctrl** key, click the files **garden2.htm**, **garden3.htm**, **garden4.htm**, **land2.htm**, **mulch.htm**, **rock.htm**, **soil.htm**, and **stone.htm**, release the **Ctrl** key, and then click the **Open** button. Eight files appear in the Import dialog box.
3. Click the **OK** button. The files are imported into the garden Web site.
4. Change to Navigation view, and then position the pages in the navigation structure as shown in Figure 4-16. Use the horizontal scroll bar as needed to display different parts of the navigation structure as you position the pages.

Figure 4-16 **Imported pages positioned in the navigation structure**

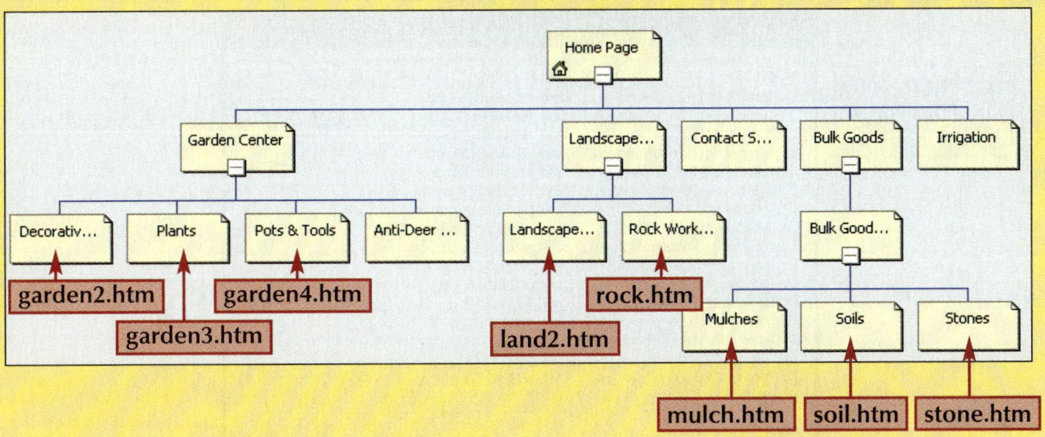

5. Double-click the **Decorative Items** page icon to open the garden2.htm page in Design view. This page and the other new pages you imported into the Web site will not use the Web site's shared borders until you activate this feature.
6. Click **Format** on the menu bar, click **Shared Borders**, click the **All pages** option button to select it, make sure the **Top**, **Left**, and **Bottom** check boxes contain check marks and that the **Include navigation buttons** check boxes contain check marks, and then click the **OK** button. Now the new pages you imported into the Web site use the Web site's existing shared borders.

Brett notices that the Decorative Items page contains broken links to the pictures that Clara inserted into the page. To correct these broken links, he must add the pictures to the Web site. Clara stored the pictures in four folders. To make it easier to identify the pictures used with the new pages, you'll show him how to import the folders into the Web site.

To import folders into the Web site:

1. In the Folder List, click the Web site's root folder to select it.
2. Click **File** on the menu bar, click **Import**, and then click the **Add Folder** button. The File Open dialog box opens.
3. Open the **Tutorial.04\Tutorial** folder included with your Data Files. Four folders appear in the list. You can't select multiple folders for importing, so you'll need to select the folders individually.
4. Click the **bulk_pic** folder to select it, and then click the **Open** button. The File Open dialog box closes and the Import dialog box reappears. Each file in the bulk_pic folder appears in the list. You can continue adding the additional folders and import everything at the same time.
5. Click the **Add Folder** button, click the **Up One Level** button in the File Open dialog box, click the **gc_pics** folder to select it, and then click the **Open** button.
6. Repeat Step 5 to select the **land_pic** and **rock_pic** folders. The Import dialog box lists all of the files you have selected. See Figure 4-17.

Figure 4-17 **Folders and files selected for importing**

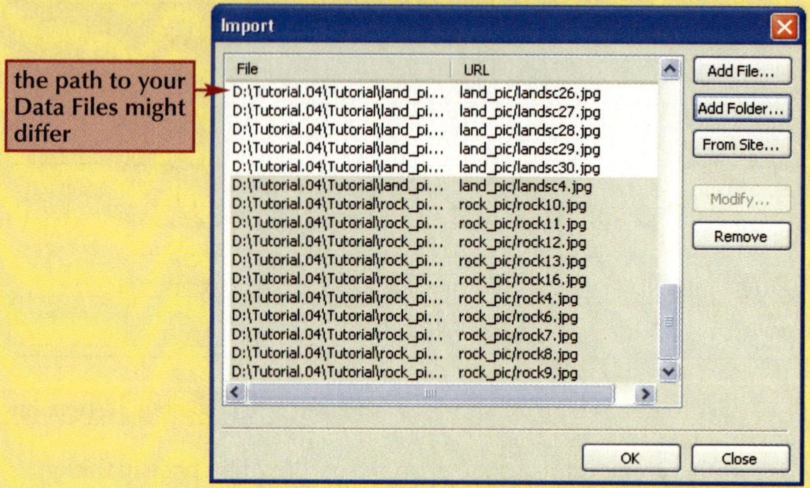

7. When you have selected all four folders, click the **OK** button in the Import dialog box. The folders and their contents are imported into the Web site and the pictures appear in the garden2.htm page.

Brett asks if he can move the folders and their contents from the Web site's root folder to the Web site's images folder without creating broken hyperlinks to the pictures. You tell Brett that using FrontPage to move files and folders automatically updates the links to the files. You'll show him how to move the folders into the Web site's images folder next.

To move the folders into the Web site's images folder:

1. Click the **Web Site** tab at the top of the Contents pane, and then change to Folders view.
2. If necessary, scroll the Folder List so you can see the Web site's root folder at the top of the list, and then scroll Folders view so you can see the bulk_pic, gc_pics, land_pic, and rock_pic folders.
3. In Folders view, click the **bulk_pic** folder to select it, press and hold the **Ctrl** key, click the **gc_pics**, **land_pic**, and **rock_pic** folders to select them, and then release the **Ctrl** key. All four folders are selected in Folders view.
4. Point to the **bulk_pic** folder, click and hold the left mouse button, and then drag the pointer to the **images** folder in the Folder List. While you are dragging the mouse, the pointer with a ⃠ shape appears. When you point to the images folder, the pointer changes to a shape, indicating a valid operation.
5. While pointing to the **images** folder in the Folder List, release the left mouse button. FrontPage moves the selected folders into the images folder and updates the hyperlinks to these pictures.
6. Click the **garden2.htm** tab to display the page in Design view. The pictures appear in the page because FrontPage updated the path to the files.

   Trouble? Don't worry if the pictures or text appears to be cut off. They will appear correctly in a browser.
7. Close the Folder List.

You tell Brett that moving files and folders stored in a Web site using Windows Explorer or another file management program would not update the hyperlinks. Because Brett used FrontPage to move the folders and their contents, FrontPage updated all of the paths to the embedded pictures in the Web pages.

Disabling Shared Borders in a Page

Brett asks if there is a way to turn off the shared borders for one or more pages in the Web site without removing the page from the site's link bar components. You tell him that this is possible and that it's common for the content of a shared border to be inappropriate for one or more pages. You can disable one or all of the shared borders in a page using the Shared Borders dialog box.

Disabling Shared Borders for a Single Web Page

Reference Window

- Open the page in Design view.
- Click Format on the menu bar, and then click Shared Borders to open that dialog box.
- Click the Current page option button to select it.
- Click the Top, Left, Right, and Bottom check boxes, as necessary, to turn off the appropriate shared borders.
- Click the OK button.

Brett noticed that the home page does not include any links in the top shared border because it is the top-level page in the Web site and the top shared border includes only links to the top-level and same-level pages. Because the top shared border of the home page does not contain any links, Brett asks you to turn it off. He also wants to change the appearance of the home page to remove the links that appear on the left side of the page, so that the marquee and text will appear centered in the browser window. You'll turn off the left shared border to make this change.

To turn off shared borders for a single Web page:

1. Click the **index.htm** tab to display the home page, click **Format** on the menu bar, and then click **Shared Borders** to open the Shared Borders dialog box.
2. Click the **Current page** option button to select it, and then click the **Top** and **Left** check boxes to clear them. The sample diagram changes to display a page with a bottom shared border, but not top and left shared borders.
3. Click the **OK** button to close the Shared Borders dialog box and to turn off the top and left shared borders in the home page. The other Web pages in the navigation structure still use the top, left, and bottom shared borders.
4. Save the home page.

Without the shared borders, Brett notices that the home page no longer has a page title or link bar. You will show him how to add this content back to the home page by manually inserting a page banner and a link bar component.

Adding a Link Bar Component to a Page

You can add a link bar component to any Web page, not just to a shared border. Brett wants to include a link bar component in the home page with links to its child pages in the Web site. When you include a link bar component in a Web page, you can use a different arrangement of hyperlinks than what is available in the shared borders. FrontPage will use the information in the navigation structure to create the link bar in the home page, just as it does for the link bar in the site's shared borders.

To add a link bar component to the home page:

1. Press **Ctrl + Home** to scroll to the top of the home page, press the **Enter** key, and then press the **up** arrow key ↑ to move the insertion point to the new paragraph you created. Before inserting the link bar component, you'll change the style of the new paragraph to Normal.
2. Click the **Style** list arrow on the Formatting toolbar, and then click **Normal**.
3. Click **Insert** on the menu bar, and then click **Navigation**. The Insert Web Component dialog box opens, with the Link Bars component type selected. You can choose from three styles of link bars: a bar with custom links to pages in the current Web site or to pages in other Web sites, a bar with Back and Next links to pages in the current site, or a bar based on the arrangement of pages in the navigation structure. You'll choose the third option so the hyperlinks match the appearance and content of other link bars in the Web site.
4. In the Choose a bar type list box, click **Bar based on navigation structure**, and then click the **Next** button. The second dialog box opens, in which you choose a style for the link bar.
5. Make sure that the **Use Page's Theme** option is selected, and then click the **Next** button. The third dialog box opens, in which you select an option for the arrangement of the hyperlinks. You'll use the horizontal option, which is the default.
6. Make sure that the page with horizontal links is selected (the page on the left), and then click the **Finish** button. The Link Bar Properties dialog box shows that the default setting is for the link bar to contain links to child-level pages.
7. Click the **OK** button. The link bar component is inserted at the top of the page. See Figure 4-18.

Link bar component added to the home page — Figure 4-18

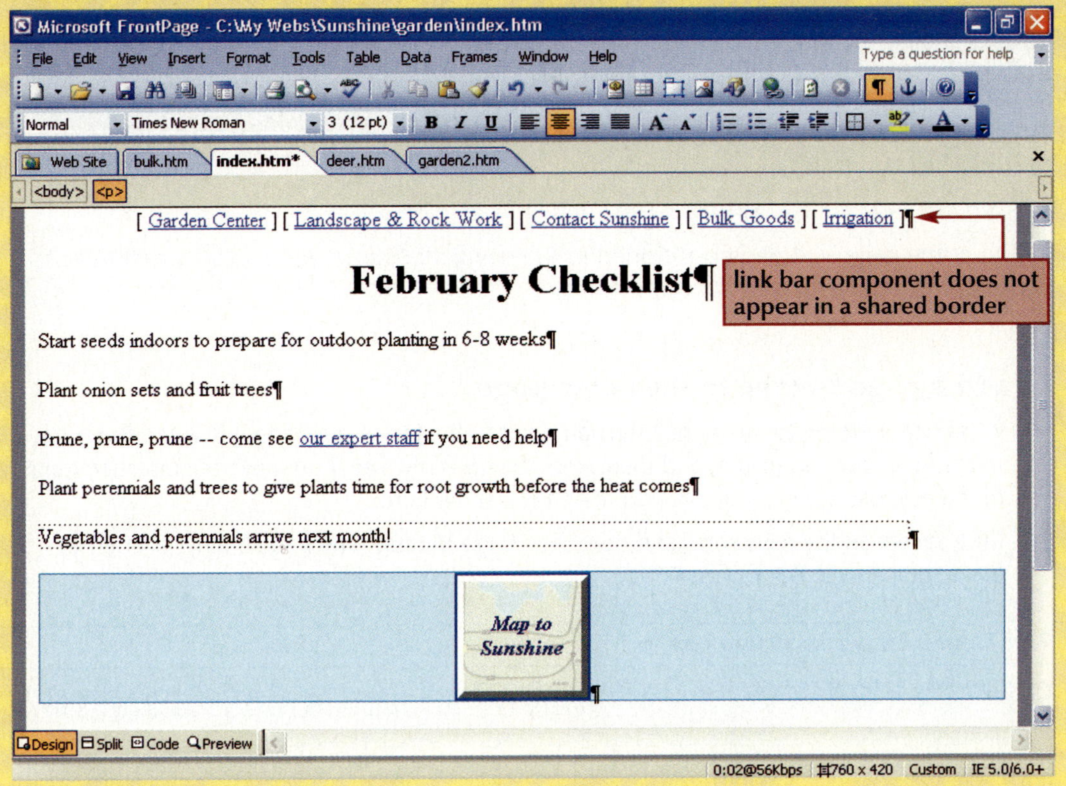

Other pages in the Web site have a horizontal line below the link bar, so you'll add one to the home page to match this style.

8. With the insertion point positioned to the right of the link bar component, click **Insert** on the menu bar, and then click **Horizontal Line**. A horizontal line is inserted below the link bar.
9. Save the home page.

You added a link bar component to the home page that is separate from the link bar component that appears in the top shared border of other Web pages in the site. When Brett adds new pages to the Web site, FrontPage will update this link bar automatically to include hyperlinks to the new pages after you add those pages to the navigation structure.

When he turned off the top shared border for this page, Brett removed the title from the top of the page. Brett wants the home page to include a title, but not a shared border. You explain that you can add a page banner to identify a page's content.

Adding a Page Banner to a Page

A page banner is a text or picture object that usually appears at the top of each page in a Web site. You can add a page banner to any page, but the page must appear in the navigation structure to use this feature.

Reference Window

Creating a Page Banner

- If necessary, position the page in the site's navigation structure.
- Click the location in the Web page where you want the banner to appear.
- Click Insert on the menu bar, and then click Page Banner.
- Select the Picture or Text option button to indicate the type of banner to create.
- Edit the text in the Page banner text text box as necessary.
- Click the OK button.

The home page is already positioned in the navigation structure, so you won't need to perform this step.

To add a page banner to the home page:

1. Press **Ctrl + Home** to move the insertion point to the top of the page, press the **Enter** key to create a new paragraph, and then press the **up** arrow key ↑ to move the insertion point to the new paragraph. You will add the page banner here.
2. Click **Insert** on the menu bar, and then click **Page Banner**. The Page Banner Properties dialog box opens. See Figure 4-19.

Figure 4-19 **Page Banner Properties dialog box**

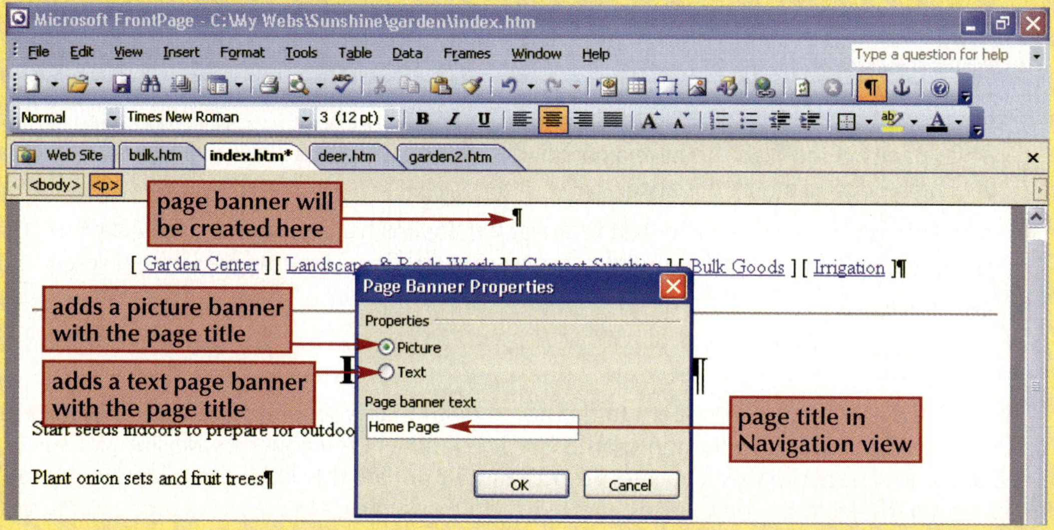

Brett notices that you can change the page title in this dialog box. He asks you to change the title of this page to "Sunshine Landscape & Garden Center." You will change the page title in the Page Banner Properties dialog box.

3. Make sure that the **Picture** option button is selected, select the text in the Page banner text text box, type **Sunshine Landscape & Garden Center**, and then click the **OK** button to insert the page banner into the page. FrontPage automatically updates the page title in Navigation view.
4. Save the home page. The page banner, Sunshine Landscape & Garden Center, appears at the top of the Web page. Brett asks why the page banner is displayed as regular text instead of as a picture. You explain that you could use the Formatting toolbar to change the appearance of the text in the page banner, but an easier way is to apply a theme that automatically formats the entire page—including the page banner—using predefined pictures and fonts. You'll show Brett how to apply a theme in the next session.

5. Preview the home page in a browser, and then follow some of the links in the Web site's pages to examine the new pages you added to the Web site and the link bars created by FrontPage. As you examine the pages, notice that the link bar components display links based on the configuration of pages in the navigation structure. For example, the bulk.htm page contains links in the top shared border to the home page and to Web pages at the same level in the navigation structure. The left shared border contains a link to its child page, bulk2.htm. When you click the Bulk Goods Samples link, the bulk2.htm page opens. Because this page contains child pages in the navigation structure, links to these child pages appear in the left shared border. To return to the parent page (bulk.htm), click the Up link in the top shared border. The link to the site's home page is named "Home," even though you changed the title of the home page in Navigation view. The default setting for the link bar component is to use a "Home" link, even if you change the title of the home page.
6. When you have finished examining the pages in the Web site and understand how the link bar components work, close your browser.

Brett is satisfied with the current content and appearance of the Web site. However, he asks if there is a way to include a link to the page that contains a map to the nursery in the link bar of the home page. He deleted this page from the navigation structure because he doesn't want it to appear as a link in the site's shared borders. You tell Brett that this request can be met by creating a custom link bar.

Creating a Custom Link Bar

When you inserted the link bar component into the home page, the Insert Web Component dialog box included three options for the bar type: Bar with custom links, Bar with back and next links, and Bar based on navigation structure. You created the link bar component in the home page using the third option so the links would match the pages in the Web site's navigation structure. Sometimes you might need to include a link to one or more pages in a Web site, but you don't want to include these links in all pages in the navigation structure. This situation is the one Brett has described: He wants to include a link to the Map page in the link bar component in the home page, but he does not want this link to appear in any other pages positioned in the navigation structure. To add the Map link to the link bar component in the home page, you tell Brett that he needs to create a custom link bar to replace the link bar based on the navigation structure that currently appears in the home page.

There are two ways to create a custom link bar. The first way is to position the insertion point where you want to insert the custom link bar, and then to insert a link bar based on custom links using the Insert Web Component dialog box. When you choose this method, you add the custom link bar to the Web site and Web page at the same time, and use the Link Bar Properties dialog box to select the links to include in the custom link bar. When you choose this method, the links use filenames unless you change them by editing the text to display in the link.

If you know you want to use page titles as your link names, you can create the custom link bar in Navigation view. You can still change the link names by renaming the page icons that appear in the custom link bar navigation structure. This method takes a little less time because you can drag and drop pages into the custom link bar's navigation structure instead of selecting pages individually.

Reference Window

Creating a Custom Link Bar in Navigation View

- Change to Navigation view, and, if necessary, display the Folder List.
- Make sure that no page icon is selected in the navigation structure, and then click the New Custom Link Bar button on the Contents pane.
- Right-click the New Link Bar page icon to select it and to open the shortcut menu, type a name for the custom link bar, and then press the Enter key.
- Drag the filename of the first page you want to include in the custom link bar from the Folder List and position it in the custom link bar navigation structure. Repeat this step to include the appropriate pages in the custom link bar.
- Open the page in which to display the custom link bar, position the insertion point where you want to insert it, click Insert on the menu bar, and then click Navigation. Select the Bar with custom links option in the Choose a bar type list, click the Next button, choose the desired bar style, click the Next button, choose the desired orientation, and then click the Finish button.
- In the Link Bar Properties dialog box, click the Choose existing list arrow and select the custom link bar to use in the page. (If your Web site has only one custom link bar, then the one you created will be selected automatically.)
- Use the Add link, Remove link, and Modify link buttons to add new links and delete or modify existing links. To move a link's position in the link bar, select it and then click the Move up or Move down buttons to position it in the desired location.
- Click the OK button.

You'll show Brett how to create a custom link bar in Navigation view. The custom link bar will include the same links as the one currently in the home page plus a new link to the Map page.

To create a custom link bar:

1. Switch to Navigation view, and then, if necessary, display the Folder List.
2. Click any blank area in the Contents pane to deselect any selected page icons, and then click the **New Custom Link Bar** button on the Contents pane. A New Link Bar page icon is added to the Contents pane. See Figure 4-20.

Figure 4-20
Custom link bar created

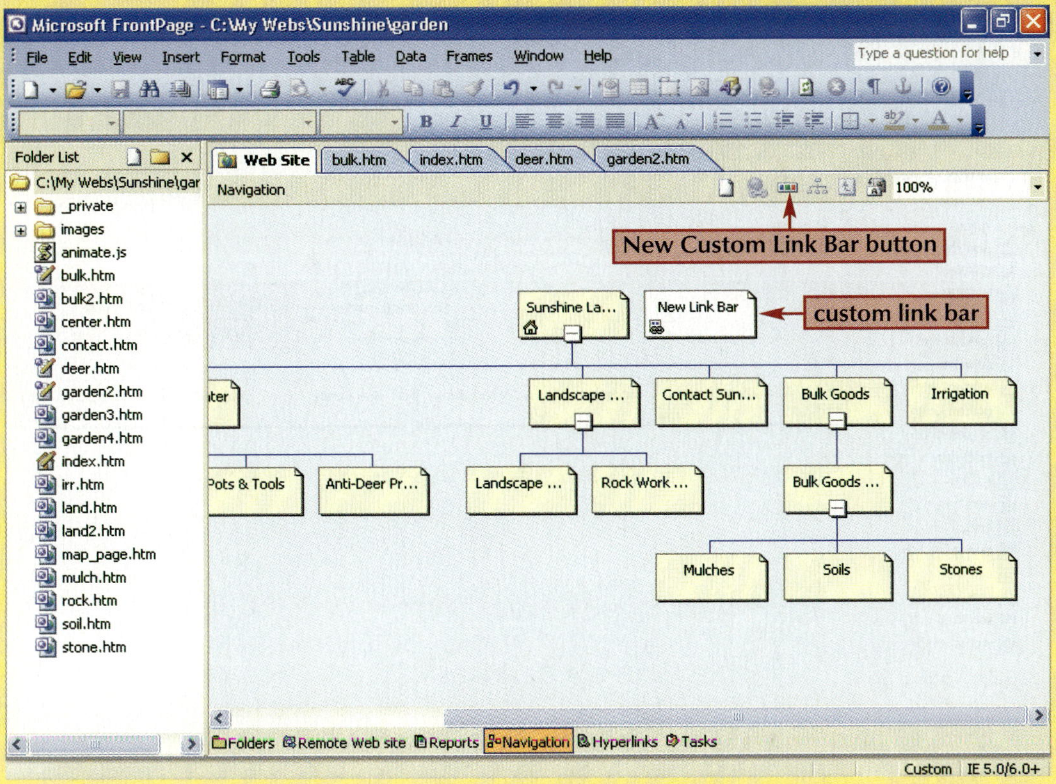

Trouble? If you cannot see the New Link Bar page icon, use the horizontal scroll bar to scroll the Contents pane to the left.

Trouble? If your New Link Bar page icon appears within the navigation structure for the Web site, then a page icon was selected when you created the custom link bar. Right-click the New Link Bar page icon to select it and open the shortcut menu, click Delete, and then repeat Step 2.

To add links, you drag files from the Folder List and position them below the New Link Bar page icon.

3. Drag the **center.htm** file from the Folder List and position it as a child page of the New Link Bar page icon. Release the mouse button to add the Garden Center page to the custom link bar.

4. Repeat Step 3 to add the **land.htm**, **contact.htm**, **bulk.htm**, **irr.htm**, and **map_page.htm** pages to the right of the Garden Center page icon in the navigation structure for the custom link bar. Figure 4-21 shows the navigation structure for the custom link bar.

Figure 4-21 Navigation structure for the custom link bar

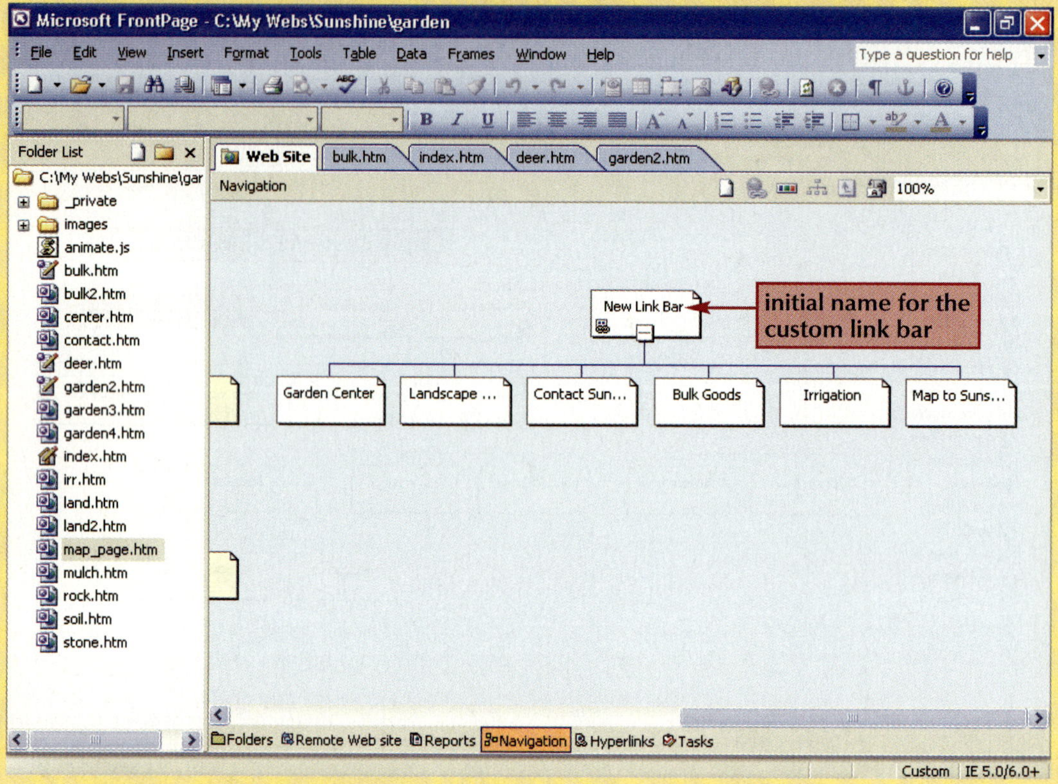

Trouble? If you cannot see the navigation structure for the custom link bar, scroll the Contents pane to the left.

When you create a custom link bar, FrontPage assigns it the name "New Link Bar." You can name the custom link bar using this suggested name or you can give it a name that describes the links it contains or the page in which you plan to use it. You suggest changing the name of the link bar to "Home Page" so Brett remembers the page in which this custom link bar will appear. Even though you created the link bar for a specific page, you can use it in other pages in the Web site. You can also create additional custom link bars to use in other pages of the Web site.

After renaming the custom link bar, you'll insert it into the home page.

To rename the custom link bar and insert it into the home page:

1. Right-click the **New Link Bar** page icon to select it and to open the shortcut menu, and then click **Rename**.
2. Type **Home Page** to identify the new link bar, and then press the **Enter** key. The name of the custom link bar changes to "Home Page."
3. Click the **index.htm** tab to change to the home page in Design view.

4. Click the **link bar component** to select it, and then press the **Delete** key. You deleted the existing link bar component, which was based on the Web site's navigation structure. You will replace it with the custom link bar component you just created.
5. Click **Insert** on the menu bar, and then click **Navigation**. The Insert Web Component dialog box opens, with the Link Bars component type selected and the Bar with custom links bar type selected.
6. Click the **Next** button, make sure the **Use Page's theme** option is selected, click the **Next** button, make sure the horizontal option is selected, and then click the **Finish** button. The Link Bar Properties dialog box opens. Because the Home Page custom link bar is the only custom link bar in the Web site, it is selected in the Choose existing list box. The links that appear in the custom link bar appear in the Links list box. See Figure 4-22.

Figure 4-22 **Link Bar Properties dialog box for the custom link bar**

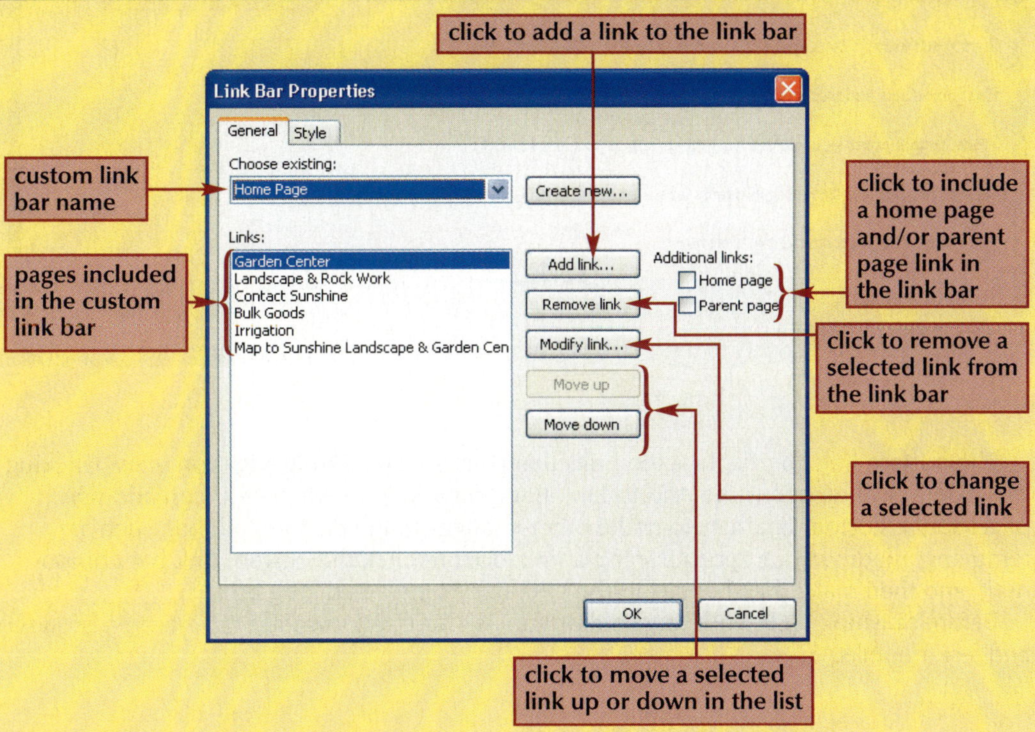

At this point, you could make changes to the custom link bar, but these settings are correct, so you can just insert it into the home page.

7. Click the **OK** button, close the Folder List, and then save the home page. Figure 4-23 shows the custom link bar in the home page.

Figure 4-23 **Custom link bar added to the home page**

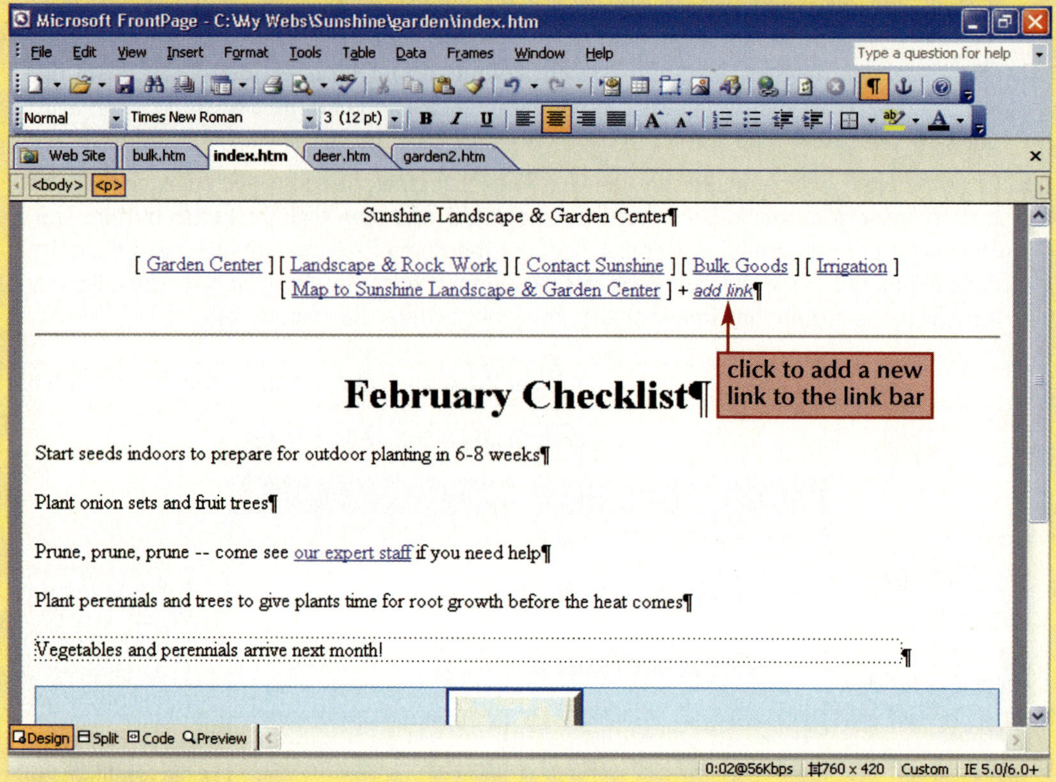

The custom link bar displays the links that Brett specified in Navigation view. Clicking the "add link" link opens the Add to Link Bar dialog box, in which you can add new pages to the custom link bar. To make other changes to the custom link bar, such as removing, modifying, or repositioning a link, double-click the custom link bar component, and then make the changes in the Link Bar Properties dialog box.

Before finishing your work for the day, you ask Brett to view the Web site in a browser and test the links.

To test the links:

1. Click the **Preview** button on the Standard toolbar. The home page opens in your browser.
2. Use the links that you created to navigate the pages in the Web site. When you are finished, close your browser.
3. Close the garden Web site and FrontPage.

Now Brett can be sure that people can find the map to the nursery. In the next session, you will show him how to apply a theme to the Web site to change the overall appearance of pages in the site.

Session 4.1 Quick Check

Review

1. What is the main reason for positioning pages in the navigation structure in Navigation view?
2. Where can you create shared borders in a Web page? Which shared borders can contain optional link bar components?
3. True or False: Renaming a Web page in Navigation view updates the HTML title of the page.
4. True or False: You can add shared borders to a Web page that does not appear in the Web site's navigation structure.
5. True or False: Editing a shared border in a Web page updates the shared border for all Web pages that use that shared border.
6. When you delete a page from the navigation structure, which two options are available?
7. How do you turn off a shared border for a page?
8. True or False: You can insert a link bar component into a Web page even if that page does not use a Web site's shared borders.

Session 4.2

Applying a Theme to a Web Site

By creating shared borders, link bar components, and page banners in the garden Web site, you have made the pages easy to identify and navigate. Brett wants you to focus now on the appearance of the Web site's pages to make them visually interesting and professional, reflecting the atmosphere of the nursery itself. Brett's first suggestion is to add a background picture and change the format of text that appears in each page in the Web site to create this visual interest. However, you tell Brett that an easier way of applying the same formatting to all pages in a Web site is to apply a theme to its pages.

A **theme** is a collection of design elements—bullets, backgrounds, table borders, fonts, and pictures—that you can apply to an entire Web site or to only one or more specific Web pages. A Web site with a theme applied to it has a consistent appearance because the formatting applied by the theme is the same in every page. Everything in the page—from its bullets to its background picture—is professionally designed to fit together. When you insert new bullets, horizontal lines, page banners, link bars, and other features into a page that uses a theme, these features are formatted automatically by the theme. Also, if you add a new page to a Web site that has a theme applied to it, the new page will use the same theme automatically. FrontPage includes many themes with styles ranging from conservative to flashy; you can visit the Microsoft Web site to download and install additional themes. When you apply a theme, you can change it to use vivid colors, active graphics, or a background picture. You can even modify a theme to customize it for your needs.

Reference Window

Applying a Theme to a Web Site

- In Design view, Folders view, or Navigation view, click Format on the menu bar, and then click Theme.
- Scroll the themes in the Theme task pane to find one of interest. If a page is open in Design view, clicking the theme temporarily applies the theme to the page.
- If desired, select the options for Vivid colors, Active graphics, and a Background picture in the Theme task pane.
- When you locate an appropriate theme, click the list arrow that appears when you point to the desired theme. To apply the theme to the entire Web site, click Apply as default theme in the menu. To apply the theme to the currently selected page(s) in Folders, Navigation, or Design view, click Apply to selected page(s) in the menu.
- Click the Yes button to apply the theme.

You can use the Theme task pane to preview the themes installed on your computer. Brett wants to find one that has easy-to-read text and complementary colors that he can apply to the entire Web site. Because Brett wants to preview the theme before applying it to the entire Web site, you'll ask him to open the home page in Design view. You tell Brett, however, that he can preview the theme with any page in Design view.

To apply a theme to a Web site:

1. Start **FrontPage**, open the **garden** Web site from the location where your Web sites are stored, and then open the home page **(index.htm)** in Design view.
2. Click **Format** on the menu bar, and then click **Theme**. The Theme task pane opens, as shown in Figure 4-24.

Figure 4-24 **Theme task pane**

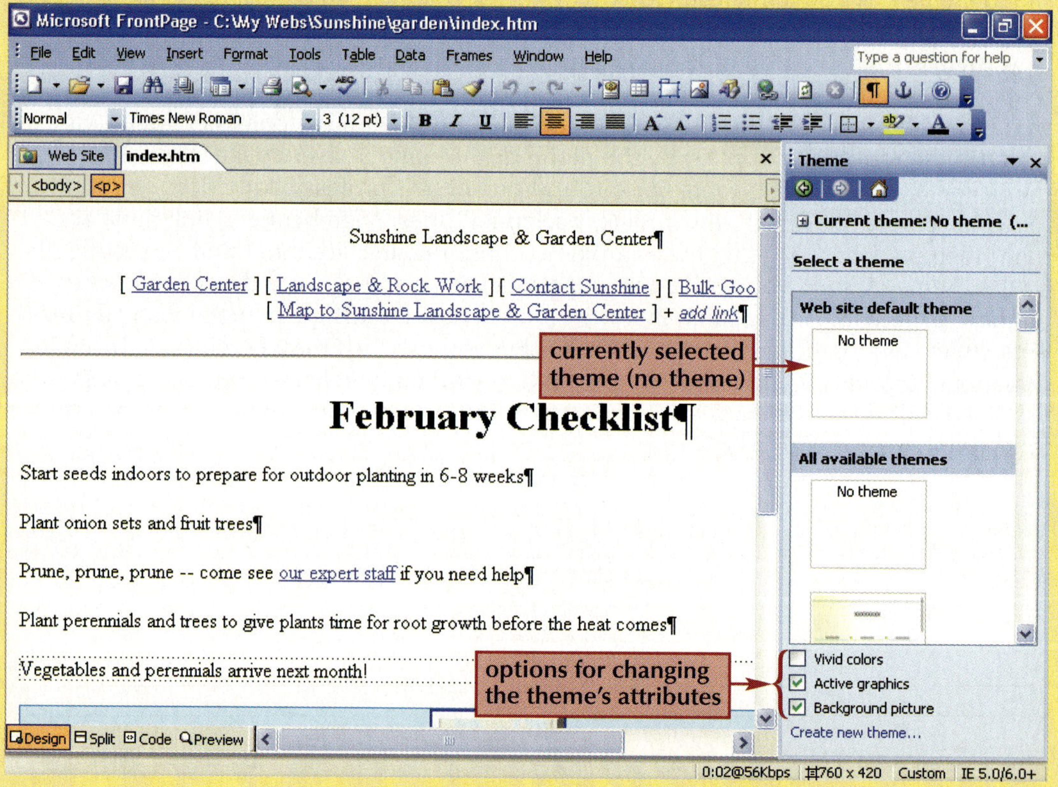

The first entry in the Select a theme section shows the Web site's current default theme, which is "No theme" because you have not applied a theme yet. After you apply a theme to the Web site, the theme you select will appear in this location. You might see a Recently used themes section below the Web site default theme section, which displays previews of themes that you (or other users) have recently applied to other Web sites or pages. This list changes as you use FrontPage. If you scroll the Select a theme list, the All available themes section shows the themes installed on your computer; this list will vary depending on whether you have installed other themes from the FrontPage 2003 CD or from the Microsoft Web site. As you scroll the list, you'll see the previews and names of the themes available on your computer.

3. Scroll down the Select a theme list so you see the "All available themes" heading. The first option, No theme, deletes a previously applied theme. The remaining entries are the available themes on your computer, displayed in alphabetical order by theme name.

4. Click the first theme (but not the No theme theme) in your list of available themes. (The default first theme is "Afternoon.") As shown in Figure 4-25, the home page is formatted using the elements of the Afternoon theme (or the theme that you clicked in the Theme task pane). Notice that the theme uses different fonts and a background picture. The link bar component now uses buttons for the hyperlinks, instead of plain text. The page banner is formatted according to the theme, which simply changes the font of the text.

Figure 4-25 **Afternoon theme temporarily applied to the home page**

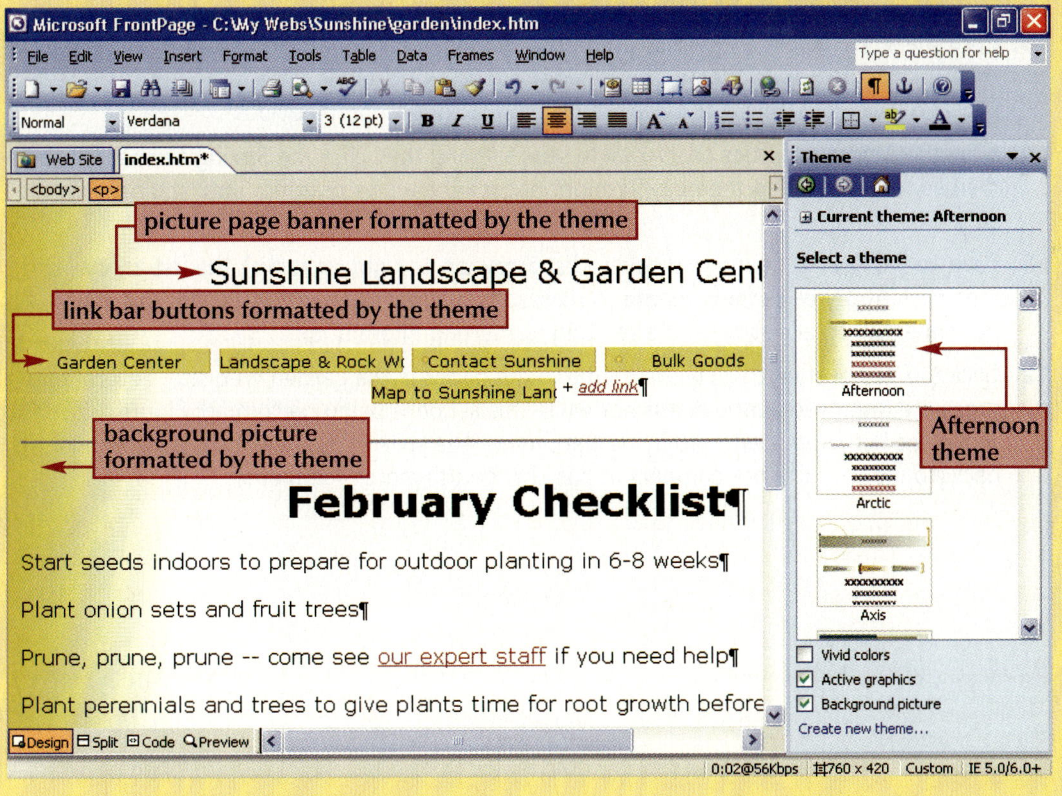

5. Scroll down the themes in the Select a theme list and click some of the themes in the list. Notice that the theme's name might indicate its contents. For example, the Checkers theme displays a checkerboard in the page.

   Trouble? Depending on your installation of FrontPage and other Microsoft Office programs, you might see a different list of themes than those identified in the text. If you don't have a specified theme, select another theme.

6. Scroll down the list of available themes until you see Spring, and then click **Spring** to preview this theme for the home page. Brett likes this theme.

   You can change a theme to use vivid colors, active graphics, and a background picture. As you select these features, you can update the preview of the theme to see their effect.

7. If necessary, clear the **Vivid colors**, **Active graphics**, and **Background picture** check boxes, and then click the **Spring** theme again. The home page now uses a white background instead of a background picture. The options for active graphics and vivid colors are disabled. When you enable active graphics for a theme, certain theme elements, such as the buttons in the link bar, will change their appearance on mouse over. For most themes, the vivid color set is a collection of brighter, more intense colors. You may have previewed some sample themes in Step 5 that use dark background colors. In some cases, you might like the theme but not the background picture. You can disable the background picture by clearing its check box.
8. Click the **Background picture** check box, and then click the **Spring** theme. The home page now uses a background picture.
9. Click the **Vivid colors** check box to select it, and then click the **Spring** theme. For some themes, like the Spring theme, there might not be a noticeable difference between the regular and vivid color sets. For other themes, the change is more obvious.
10. Click the **Active graphics** check box to select it, and then click the **Spring** theme. For some themes, like the Spring theme, you might not see the active graphics until you preview the page in a browser.
11. Point to the **Spring** theme to display a list arrow on its right side, click the **list arrow**, and then click **Apply as default theme**. A message box opens and indicates that this action will permanently replace some of the existing formatting information.
12. Click the **Yes** button to apply the theme to the pages in the garden Web site. Several messages are displayed on the status bar while this action is being performed; Figure 4-26 shows the home page after applying the theme. The style of the headings, page banner, background, and link bar component has changed to match the theme.

Spring theme applied to the home page

Figure 4-26

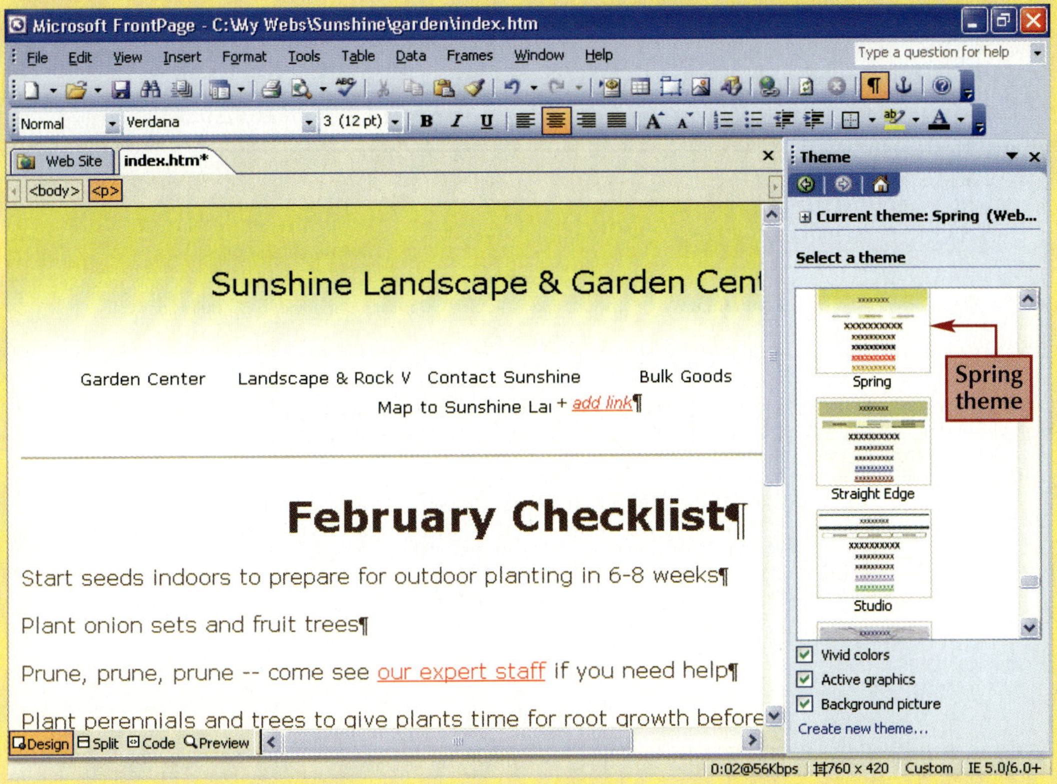

Trouble? It might take several minutes to apply the theme if your Web site is saved on a server or a removable disk. If you are storing your Web site on a hard drive, themes are applied and saved quickly.

Next, you ask Brett to open the home page in a browser and test the link bar component.

To view the page in a browser and test the link bar:

1. Close the Theme task pane, and then preview the home page in a browser. Click the **Yes** button when prompted to save your changes.
2. Point to the **Garden Center** button in the link bar. The button's appearance changes to add a background color. This animation occurs because you chose the active graphics option when you applied the theme.
3. Click the **Garden Center** button in the link bar to open that page. See Figure 4-27. The link bars in the top and left shared borders, the page banner, and the horizontal line are formatted by the theme. You selected these settings when you created the link bar in the top and left shared borders and the page banner. The Garden Center button in the top shared border has a background color; for this theme, the background color on a button indicates that it is the currently displayed page. If you point to the Garden Center button, you'll notice that it is not a hyperlink; FrontPage disables hyperlinks to the current page in a link bar component. The other buttons in the link bar are active hyperlinks. As Brett examines the Garden Center page, he notices that the link to the Landscape & Rock Work page is incomplete; part of the "W" and the rest of the word "Work" are missing.

Figure 4-27 **Garden Center page with Spring theme applied**

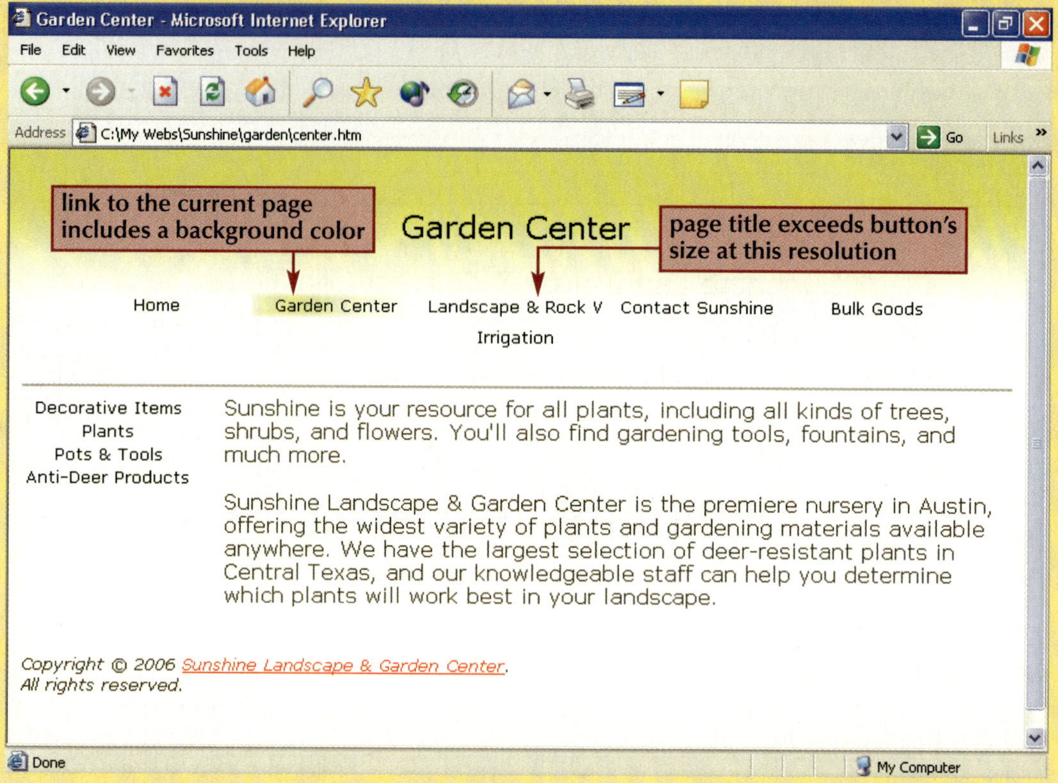

Trouble? If your monitor displays more than 800 × 600 pixels, your link bar might appear on a single line. This difference is not a problem.

4. Use the link bars to examine the pages in the Web site and note how the theme formats the pages. When you are finished, close your browser.

Brett likes the Spring theme but wants to make a couple of changes and asks you how to make them. You tell him that it's easy to customize an existing theme.

Customizing an Existing Theme

After selecting a theme, you might want to make some changes to it. For the Spring theme, you have already noticed that the font the theme applies to the buttons in the link bar components is too large to display the full page titles. You could change the names of pages in Navigation view to decrease their size and make them fit. Another solution is to customize the theme to use a smaller font size for the buttons. You can also customize a theme by changing the colors, graphics, and fonts it uses.

Customizing an Existing Theme

Reference Window

- Click Format on the menu bar, and then click Theme to open the Theme task pane.
- Point to the theme that you want to customize, and then click the list arrow that appears.
- Click Customize in the menu that opens. The Customize Theme dialog box opens.
- Click the Colors button to customize the colors used in the theme, click the Graphics button to customize pictures and other graphic elements used in the theme, or click the Text button to customize the fonts and font styles of text elements used in the theme.
- When you have finished customizing the desired theme elements, click the Save button, type a name for the custom theme, click the OK button, and then click the Yes button.

When you customize a theme, all pages that use the theme will display the changes. In addition, the theme is saved on your hard drive so you can use it to format future Web sites.

To customize the Spring theme:

1. Click **Format** on the menu bar, and then click **Theme**. The Theme task pane opens.
2. Scroll to the top of the Select a theme list. Notice that the Theme task pane now identifies the default theme for the Web site as Spring.
3. Point to the **Spring** theme in the Web site default theme section of the Theme task pane, click the **list arrow** that appears, and then click **Customize** in the menu that opens. The Customize Theme dialog box opens, as shown in Figure 4-28. The "What would you like to modify?" section of the dialog box includes buttons that let you change the theme's colors, graphics, and text.

Figure 4-28 Customize Theme dialog box

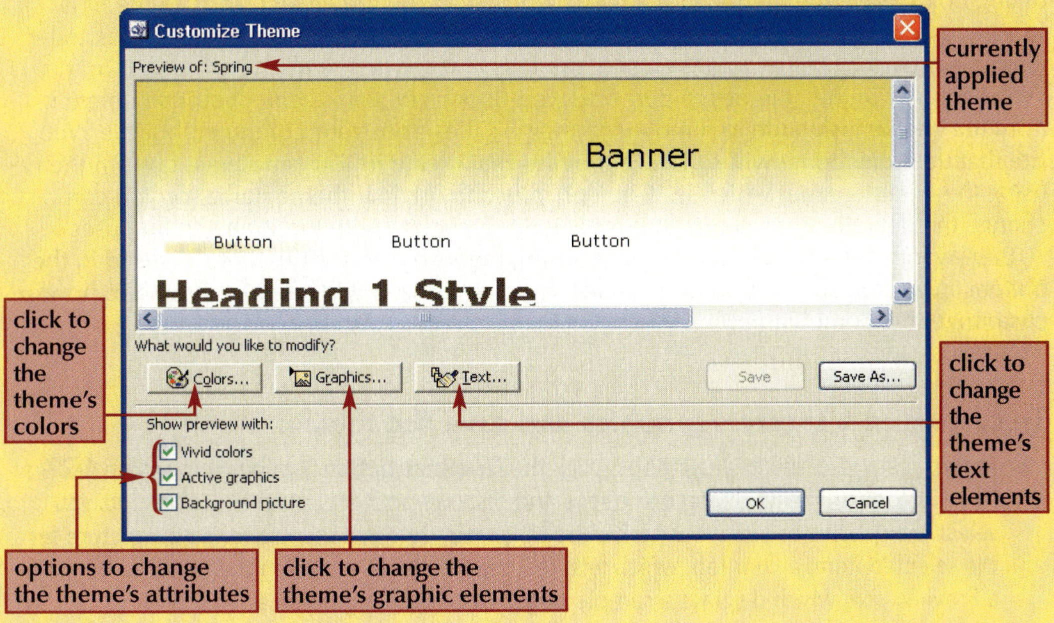

As you work with themes and customize them, you'll become more familiar with which button to click to change the theme's various features. The Colors button opens a dialog box in which you can change the color scheme used in the pages. The **color scheme** is the coordinated collection of colors used in the page's fonts, headings, background, and other elements. You can also change the intensity of the color scheme to make colors lighter or darker. Finally, you can apply custom colors to specific elements, such as the background color, the Heading 1 text, and horizontal lines.

Clicking the Graphics button lets you change the pictures used in specific graphics, such as a background picture, a page banner, or the different buttons used in the link bar components. For graphics that include fonts, such as a page banner or a button in a link bar component, you can also change the style, size, horizontal alignment, vertical alignment, and font of the button. There are several types of buttons used in a theme. The horizontal navigation buttons appear horizontally across the page in a link bar component, usually in the top shared border. The vertical navigation buttons appear vertically down a page in a link bar component, usually in the left or right shared border. The quick back, quick home, quick next, and quick up buttons include the words "Back," "Home," and "Up" in a link bar; these buttons appear when you have set a link bar to display links to the back and next pages, to the home page, and to the parent page. The bullet list buttons are the bullet characters in a bulleted list. When you set a page banner to display a picture, the picture is created using the banner picture for the theme. Finally, the global navigation buttons are buttons used in the theme but not in any of the preceding categories. If you specify the use of active graphics in a theme, you will see three pictures used for some graphic elements to represent samples of the button, the selected button (after it is clicked), and the hovered button (the button on mouse over).

The Text button lets you change the font and text styles of paragraphs formatted using the Normal, Heading 1, Heading 2, Heading 3, Heading 4, Heading 5, and Heading 6 styles. Paragraphs formatted with the Normal style are collectively called body text; paragraphs formatted with any of the heading styles are collectively called headings.

When you create a custom theme, you use the Save button in the Customize Theme dialog box to save the theme with a new name. After you create a custom theme, it is stored on your computer so you can use it to format other Web sites or Web pages. After applying a custom theme to a Web site, the files that create the theme are stored in the Web site itself in the _themes folder. After you apply a custom theme, you can delete it from the Theme task pane to remove the theme's files from your computer, but the Web site that uses the theme will still have the files that create it. You can save a custom theme using the default name, which is "Copy of" plus the original theme name, or you can change the default name to one that is easier to associate with the Web site that uses it.

Brett wants to customize the existing Spring theme to reduce the font size used in the buttons in the top shared border. To make this change, you will need to show him how customize the theme's graphics.

To customize a theme's graphics and save the theme:

1. In the Customize Theme dialog box, click the **Graphics** button. As shown in Figure 4-29, a new Customize Theme dialog box opens and displays an Item list arrow, which lets you select the graphic to customize; a Picture tab, which lets you browse for a new picture for the selected item; a Font tab, which lets you change the font used in the selected item; and a Preview box, which displays a sample page with the changes you apply.

Figure 4-29 Changing the theme's graphic elements

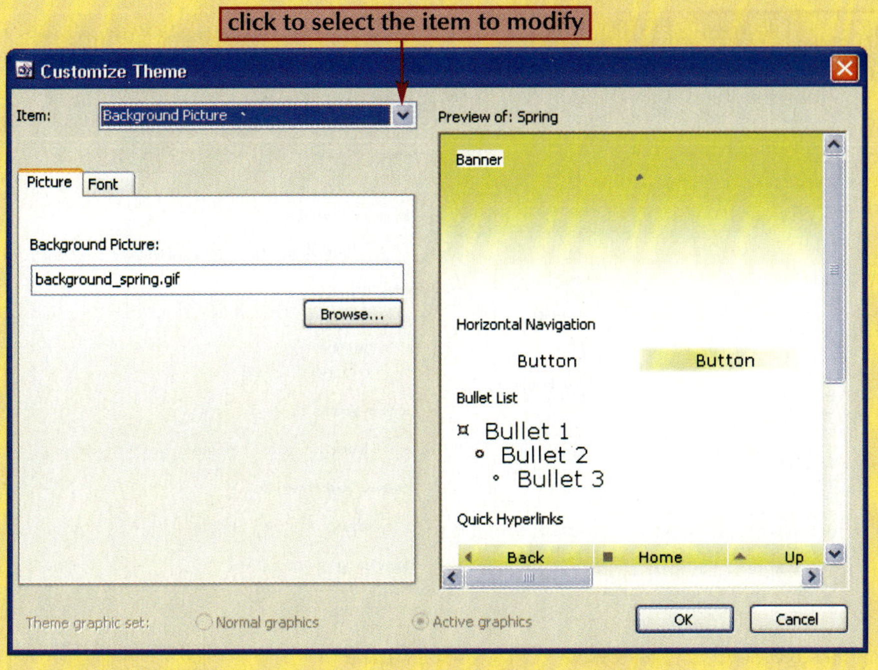

2. Click the **Item** list arrow, and then click **Horizontal Navigation**. Because you enabled active graphics for this theme, there are three pictures for creating the horizontal navigation buttons: one for the button, one for the selected (clicked) button, and one for the hovered button. You can change any of these pictures using the Browse button. If you change the theme to use normal graphics, the hovered picture will be disabled, and depending on the theme you applied, the buttons might change.
3. Click the **Font** tab. The Font tab shows the font, font style, font size, horizontal alignment, and vertical alignment for text that appears on the horizontal navigation buttons. You need to make the text smaller, so you will change the font size.
4. Click the **Size** list arrow, and then click **1 (8 pt)**. Notice that the preview changes to show horizontal buttons with 8-point text. See Figure 4-30.

Figure 4-30 **Changing the font used on the horizontal navigation buttons**

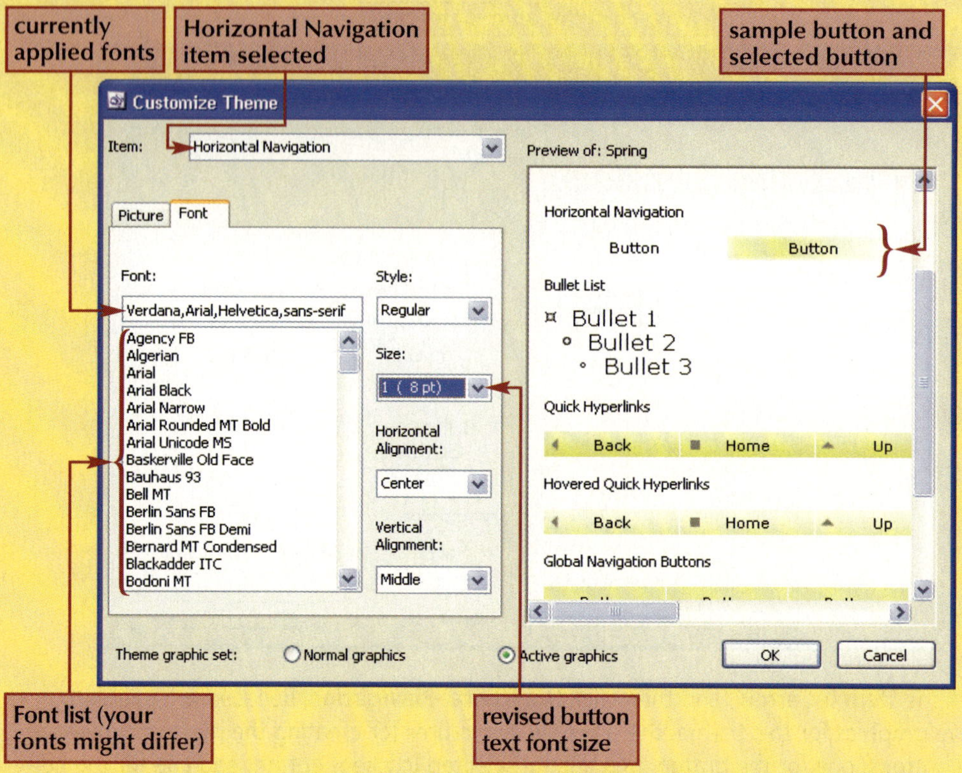

To make the buttons in the top and left shared borders match, you'll make this same change to the vertical navigation buttons.

5. Click the **Item** list arrow, and then click **Vertical Navigation**. The current settings for the vertical navigation buttons appear on the Font tab and the preview scrolls automatically to display the sample vertical navigation buttons.
6. Click the **Size** list arrow, and then click **1 (8 pt)**. The preview shows the revised font for the vertical navigation buttons.
7. Click the **OK** button. For now, you do not need to make any other changes to the custom theme. You'll save the theme using the Web site name so it's easy to identify it later.
8. Click the **Save** button. The Save Theme dialog box opens and displays the default theme title, Copy of Spring.

   Trouble? If another user already created a Copy of Spring theme, your initial theme name will differ. This difference causes no problems.
9. Type **Garden Web Site** in the Save Theme dialog box, and then click the **OK** button.

   Trouble? If another user already created the Garden Web Site theme, add your initials to the theme or a number to save it with a unique name.
10. Click the **OK** button to close the Customize Theme dialog box, and then click the **Yes** button to apply your changes as the new default theme for the Web site. After a few moments, the Garden Web Site theme is applied to every page in the Web site.
11. Save the home page, and then preview it in a browser and examine the revised theme.

Brett notices that the reduced font size only partially corrected the problem with the link for the Landscape & Rock Work page. In addition, he notices that the link for the Map to Sunshine Landscape & Garden Center page also has some dropped text. You tell him that you could apply another theme to the Web site, or customize the theme's buttons to find ones that have more space. Because you've already tried reducing the font size, you decide to fix this problem by renaming the affected pages in Navigation view. Because there are two link bars (the link bar created from the navigation structure and the custom link bar for the home page) in the garden Web site, you will need to change the page title for the land.htm page twice.

To change page titles in Navigation view:

1. Close your browser.
2. Change to Navigation view and close the Theme task pane.
3. Right-click the **land.htm** page icon in the navigation structure to select it and open the shortcut menu, click **Rename**, type **Landscape/Rock Work**, and then press the **Enter** key.

   Trouble? If you are unsure of which page icon is the land.htm page, click the page icons and look at the path on the status bar until you see the land.htm page.
4. Scroll the navigation structure so you can see the navigation structure for the custom link bar, right-click the **land.htm** page icon to select it and to open the shortcut menu, click **Rename**, type **Landscape/Rock Work**, and then press the **Enter** key.

   Next, you'll rename the page title for the map_page.htm page. This page icon appears only in the navigation structure for the custom link bar.
5. Right-click the **Map to Sunshine Landscape & Garden Center** page icon in the custom link bar navigation structure to select it and to open the shortcut menu, click **Rename**, type **Map to Sunshine**, and then press the **Enter** key.
6. Click the home page icon in the navigation structure (not in the custom link bar), and then click the **Preview** button on the Standard toolbar. The home page opens in a browser. If necessary, refresh the page in the browser to display the revised titles for the Landscape/Rock Work and Map to Sunshine buttons. Now the page titles fit on the buttons. See Figure 4-31.

Figure 4-31 **Home page with revised theme**

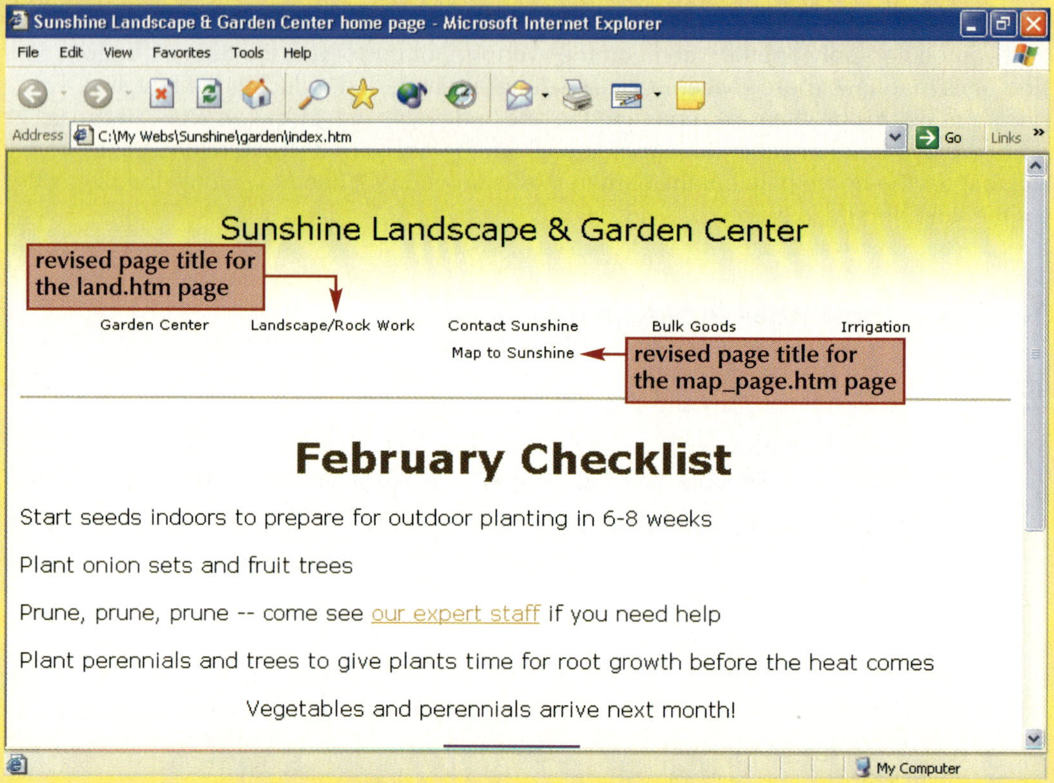

7. Click the **Garden Center** link in the top shared border.

Brett likes the changes to the link bars. Now he asks you to show him how to customize the theme again to left-align the links in the left shared border.

To change text alignment in a custom theme:

1. Close your browser.
2. Click **Format** on the menu bar, and then click **Theme** to open the Theme task pane.
3. Point to the **Garden Web Site** theme in the Web site default theme section of the Theme task pane, click the **list arrow** that appears, and then click **Customize**. The Customize Theme dialog box opens.
4. Click the **Graphics** button.
5. Click the **Item** list arrow, and then click **Vertical Navigation**.
6. Click the **Font** tab.
7. Click the **Horizontal Alignment** list arrow, and then click **Left**. The sample buttons in the theme preview change to use a left alignment.
8. Click the **OK** button, click the **Save** button to save your changes to the custom theme, click the **OK** button to close the Customize Theme dialog box, and then click the **Yes** button to apply the theme to the entire Web site.

9. Click the **Garden Center** page icon in the navigation structure, and then preview it in a browser. The links in the left shared border are left-aligned. See Figure 4-32.

Figure 4-32 **Garden Center page with revised theme**

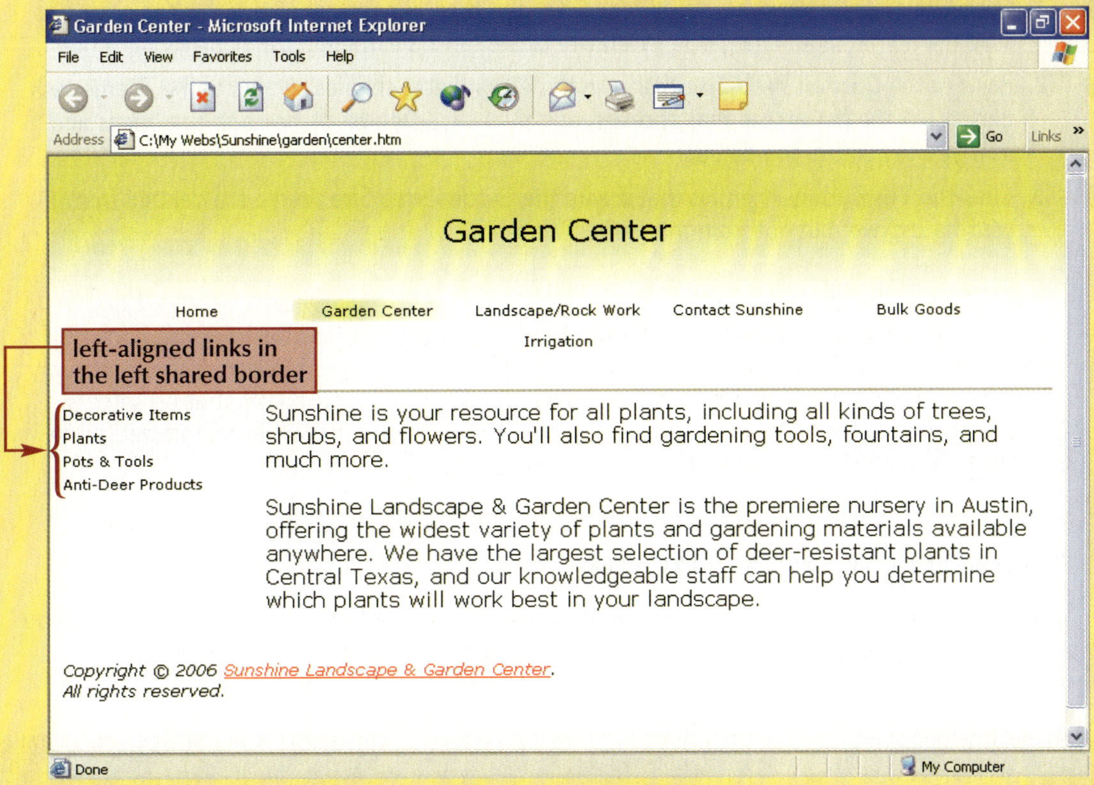

10. Close your browser.

Brett likes the revised theme. Because Brett is concerned about file management on his computer, he asks you how to remove the custom theme from his computer.

Deleting a Custom Theme From Your Hard Drive

After you create a theme, you can delete it from your hard drive to save disk space. After you apply a custom theme to a Web site, you can delete it from your hard drive after closing the Web site; the files for the theme will continue to be stored in the Web site that uses the custom theme.

Deleting a Custom Theme From Your Hard Drive

Reference Window

- If necessary, close all open Web sites in FrontPage.
- Click Format on the menu bar, and then click Theme to open the Theme task pane.
- Locate and click the custom theme in the All available themes section that you want to delete.
- Click Delete in the menu that opens.
- Click the Yes button in the message box that opens.

Brett wants to delete the theme from his computer.

To delete a custom theme from your hard drive:

1. Click **File** on the menu bar, click **Close Site**, and then, if necessary, click the **Yes** button to save the home page. The garden Web site closes, and the Theme task pane remains open.
2. Point to the **Garden Web Site** theme in the All available themes section of the Theme task pane, click the **list arrow** that appears, and then click **Delete**. A message box opens and asks you to confirm the deletion.
3. Click the **Yes** button. The files that create the Garden Web Site theme are deleted from your hard drive, but not from the garden Web site.

Brett really likes the customized theme that he created, but he also likes the background picture that he used in the first version of the home page. He asks if there is a way to create a new theme that uses a background picture, fonts, and colors that he selects. You tell him that FrontPage does include an option to create a new theme and decide to show it to him next.

Creating a New Theme

When you create a new theme, you can customize any or all of a theme's elements. If you choose not to customize a theme element, such as a heading or the way a followed hyperlink appears, then FrontPage applies the default formatting to it.

Reference Window

Creating a New Theme

- In the Theme task pane, click the Create new theme link.
- Use the Colors, Graphics, and Text buttons to apply the desired formatting to different elements of the theme.
- Click the Save button and provide a name for the new theme, and then click the OK button.
- Click the OK button to close the Customize Theme dialog box.

Brett wants you to show him how to create a new theme using the back.jpg file as the background picture. He also wants to select a color scheme and specific fonts.

To create a new theme:

1. Click **File** on the menu bar, point to **Recent Sites**, and then click the **garden** Web site.
2. At the bottom of the Theme task pane, click the **Create new theme** link. The Customize Theme dialog box opens. This is the same dialog box that you use to customize an existing theme. Notice that the preview name is "New Theme" and that the default formatting is applied to the elements shown in the preview. See Figure 4-33.

Figure 4-33 Customize Theme dialog box

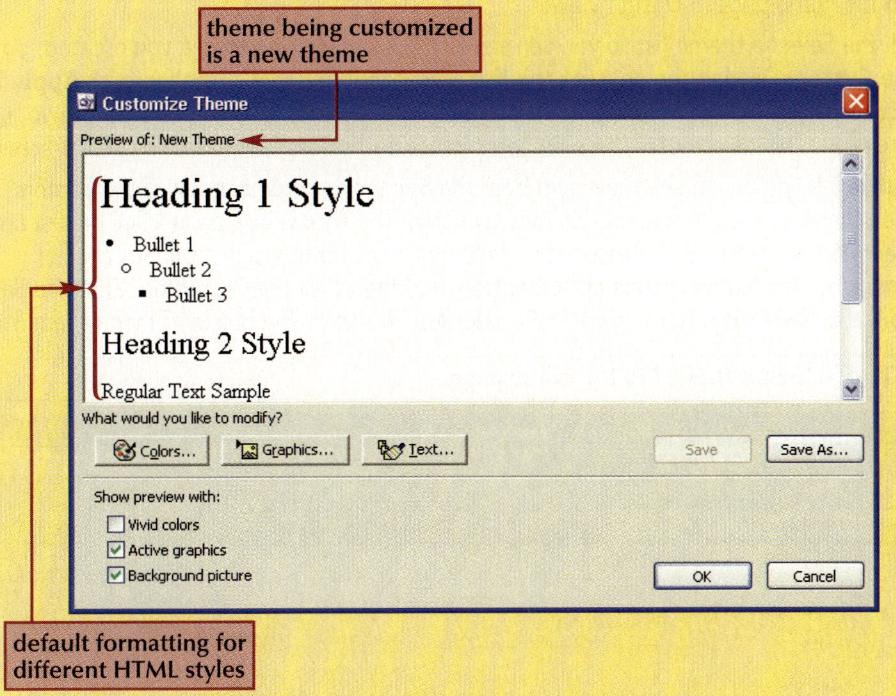

The first thing Brett wants to do is select a color scheme.

3. Click the **Colors** button. The Color Schemes tab displays the names and sample colors of the color schemes available on your computer. When you click a color scheme, a preview of it using text samples representing different styles of text appears in the Preview box.
4. Make sure that the **Normal colors** option button is selected in the Theme color set section, scroll down the color schemes list, click **Spiral**, and then scroll down the Preview box to view the samples of the colors used in this color scheme.
5. Click the **OK** button, and then click the **Graphics** button. "Background Picture" is the selected item in the Item list box.
6. Click the **Browse** button on the Picture tab, open the **images** folder of the garden Web site (if necessary), and then double-click **back.jpg**. The theme now uses the back.jpg picture, and a preview of this background picture appears in the Preview box.
7. Click the **OK** button, click the **Save** button, type **Custom Garden** in the Save Theme dialog box, click the **OK** button to close the Save Theme dialog box, and then click the **OK** button to close the Customize Theme dialog box.

The Custom Garden theme Brett created is now available for use just like any other theme, and it appears in the All available themes section of the Theme task pane. Brett wants to preview the theme he created before applying it to the entire Web site.

To preview the new theme:

1. Open the home page in Design view.
2. Scroll the Select a theme list so you can see the Custom Garden theme you created, point to the **Custom Garden** theme, click the **list arrow** that appears, and then click **Apply to selected page(s)**. The Custom Garden theme is applied to the home page, as shown in Figure 4-34. This theme uses the back.jpg picture and colors from the Spiral color scheme.

   Trouble? If you do not see the colors from the Spiral color theme, point to the Custom Garden theme in the All available themes section of the Theme task pane, click the list arrow that appears, and then click Customize. Click the Colors button, select the Spiral color scheme, click the Normal colors option button, and then click the OK button. Click the Save button, click the OK button to close the Customize Theme dialog box, and then repeat Step 2.

Figure 4-34 Custom Garden theme applied to the home page

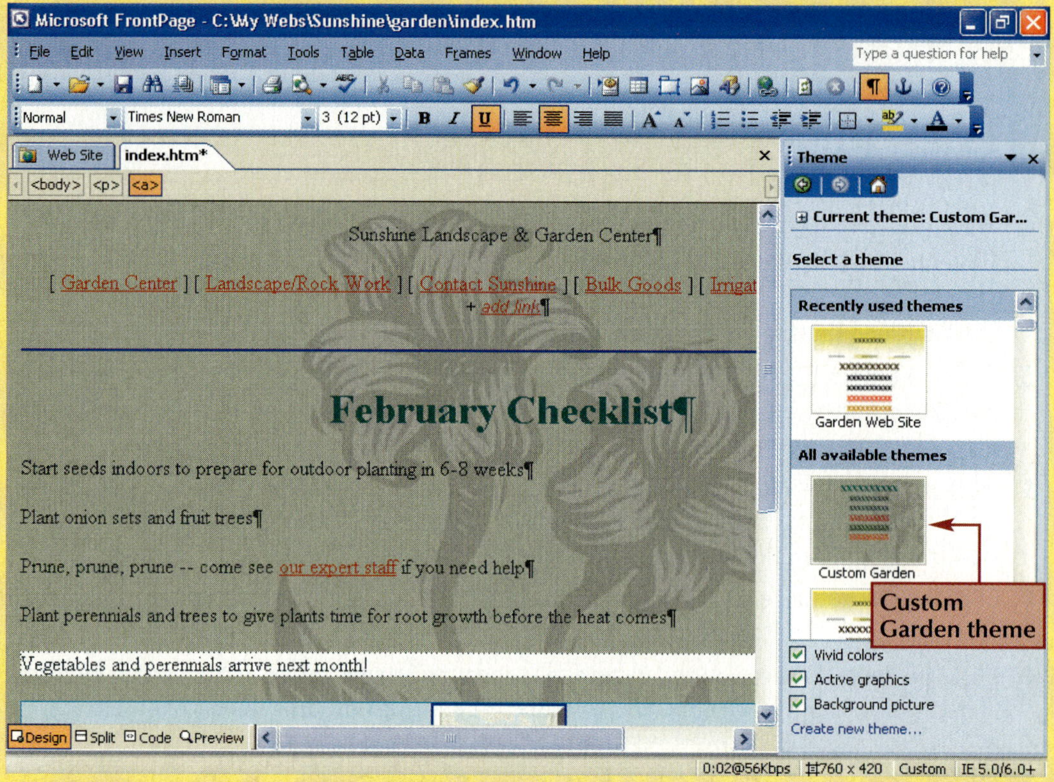

Brett realizes that creating a new theme requires a lot more effort than just applying a background picture and selecting a color scheme. He sees that he will need to create buttons to use in the link bar component and a picture to use in the page banner. Brett wants to check with his graphic designer to inquire about creating custom graphics to use in this new theme. You also suggest browsing one of the many free clip-art sites on the Internet to see if Brett can find graphics that he can use. Because Brett isn't prepared to finish this work today, he wants to restore the Garden Web Site theme. Instead of just reapplying the Garden Web Site theme to the home page, you want to show Brett how to remove a theme from a page first so he knows how to do this.

Removing a Theme From a Page

To remove a theme from a page, you just apply the "No theme" theme to it, which removes the link to the files that create the theme. You can also remove a theme from an entire Web site.

Removing a Theme From a Page or Web Site

Reference Window

- To remove a theme from a Web page, open the page in Design view, open the Theme task pane, point to the No theme theme in the All available themes section, click the list arrow that appears, and then click Apply to selected page(s).
- To remove a theme from a Web site, open the Theme task pane, point to the No theme theme in the All available themes section, click the list arrow that appears, click Apply as default theme, and then click the Yes button.

First, you'll show Brett how to remove the Custom Garden theme from the home page.

To remove a theme from a Web page:

1. If necessary, scroll the Select a theme list so you can see the No theme theme in the All available themes section.
2. Point to the **No theme** theme, click the **list arrow** that appears, and then click **Apply to selected page(s)**. The Custom Garden theme is removed from the home page.

   Now you can reapply the Garden Web Site theme.
3. Scroll up the Select a theme list until you see the Garden Web Site theme, point to the **Garden Web Site** theme, click the **list arrow** that appears, and then click **Apply to selected page(s)**. The home page is formatted using the Garden Web Site theme.
4. Save the home page.
5. Close the Theme task pane, the garden Web site, and FrontPage.

Brett likes the changes that he made to the Web site. The customized theme is not only attractive, but it also helps to unify the Web site's pages with a consistent, professional appearance. In the next session, you'll show Brett another way to present pictures and art in a Web page.

Session 4.2 Quick Check

Review

1. What is a theme?
2. True or False: You can temporarily apply a theme to a page by opening the page in Design view, and then clicking the theme to apply.
3. In a theme, what changes when you select the Vivid colors option?
4. True or False: When you customize a theme, the files for the customized theme are saved in the Web site and on your computer's hard drive.
5. What are three categories of elements that you can customize in a theme?
6. True or False: You can apply a custom theme to only a single Web site.

Session 4.3

Creating a Photo Gallery in a Page

In Tutorial 2, you learned how to insert pictures into a Web page and change their characteristics, and how to create thumbnail pictures with hyperlinks that open larger pictures and Web pages. You can insert pictures into any Web page and position them using the alignment and formatting tools in FrontPage. In some cases, however, you might want to present a group of thumbnail pictures that, when clicked, display a larger version of the same picture. A **photo gallery** lets you add pictures with captions and descriptions to your Web pages. The advantage of using a photo gallery is that you can create and format the captions, descriptions, and thumbnail pictures automatically. After creating a photo gallery, you can change its properties by revising the captions and descriptions or by adding and deleting pictures. A photo gallery is an excellent way to organize photos and descriptions of their contents.

Reference Window

Creating a Photo Gallery in a Page

- Click the desired location in which to add the photo gallery.
- Click Insert on the menu bar, point to Picture, and then click New Photo Gallery.
- Click the Add button, click Pictures from Files, and then browse to and double-click a picture file to include in the photo gallery.
- Click in the Caption text box, and then type the photo's caption.
- Press the Tab key, and then type the photo's description.
- If necessary, click the Override and use custom font formatting option button to enable the options to format the caption and description using the Formatting toolbar options in the dialog box.
- Add more photos and their captions and descriptions to the photo gallery as necessary.
- Click the Layout tab, and then select a layout for the photo gallery.
- When you are finished adding photos, click the OK button.

Helen Xiao, Sunshine's senior horticulturist, contacted Brett this morning to tell him that she has been working on the content of the Anti-Deer Products page. So far, she has some content describing the anti-deer products available for purchase at the nursery. Because many people believe that deer-resistant plants are less colorful than plants that are not deer-resistant, she suggests including pictures of beautiful, flowering, deer-resistant plants that are in season at the nursery, but she's not sure how to incorporate this content. She has some descriptions and photos that she can send to you. You tell Helen and Brett that this content is an excellent candidate for a photo gallery. You'll begin by importing Helen's files into the Web site, and then you'll create the photo gallery.

To import the files into the Web site:

1. Start **FrontPage**, and then open the **garden** Web site from the location where your Web sites are stored. You'll import Helen's files into the root folder, and then you'll move the pictures into the Web site's images folder.
2. Display the Folder List (if necessary), make sure the garden Web site's root folder is selected, click **File** on the menu bar, click **Import**, click the **Add File** button, open the **Tutorial.04\Tutorial** folder included with your Data Files, press and hold the **Ctrl** key, click **deer.htm** and **leon.jpg**, release the **Ctrl** key, and then click the **Open** button. Two files are selected to import into the Web site.

3. Click the **OK** button. When the Confirm Save dialog box opens, click the **Yes** button to overwrite the existing deer.htm page in the Web site.
4. In the Contents pane, select the file **leon.jpg**, and then drag it to the **images** folder in the Folder List. When the pointer changes to a shape, release the mouse button.
5. Close the Folder List, and then open the **deer.htm** page in Design view and examine its contents. The first thing you should notice is that the page does not use the Web site's theme. You can apply the theme using the Theme task pane.
6. Click **Format** on the menu bar, click **Theme**, point to the **Garden Web Site** theme in the Web site default theme section, click the **list arrow** that appears, and then click **Apply to selected page(s)**. The page is formatted using the Garden Web Site theme.

   To add the shared borders to this page, you need to open the Shared Borders dialog box.
7. Click **Format** on the menu bar, click **Shared Borders**, make sure that the **Current page** option button is selected, and then click the **OK** button. Because you already positioned this page in the navigation structure, the shared borders contain links to other pages in the Web site.
8. Close the Theme task pane.

With Helen's page and pictures imported into the Web site, you can create the photo gallery. You'll create the photo gallery at the bottom of the page. As the nursery gets new stock, you can add new pictures to the photo gallery.

To create the photo gallery:

1. Press **Ctrl + End** to scroll to the bottom of the deer.htm page, and then press the **Enter** key to start a new paragraph.
2. Click **Insert** on the menu bar, point to **Picture**, and then click **New Photo Gallery**. The Photo Gallery Properties dialog box opens. The pictures that you will add to the photo gallery are saved with your Data Files.
3. Click the **Add** button, and then click **Pictures from Files**. The File Open dialog box opens. Open the **Tutorial.04\Tutorial** folder included with your Data Files, and then double-click **garden57.jpg**. The picture's filename and a preview appear in the dialog box. See Figure 4-35.

Figure 4-35 Photo Gallery Properties dialog box

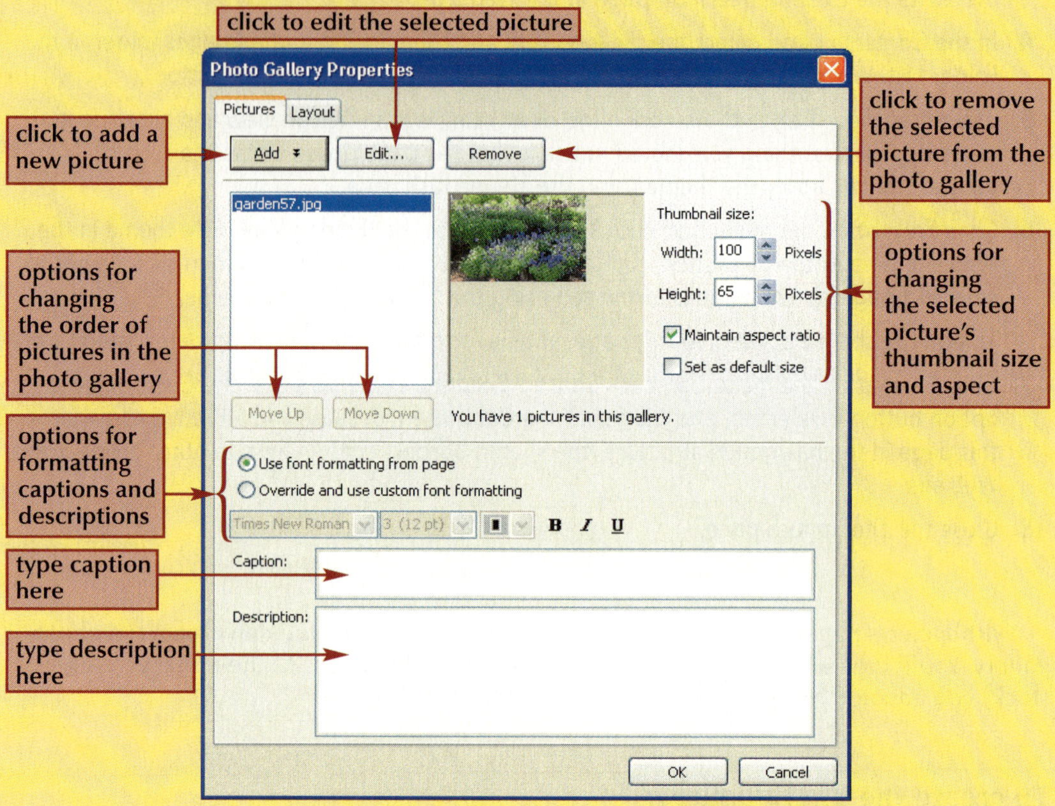

The next step is to add the caption and description for this photo. Notice the two option buttons in the middle of the dialog box. If you want the caption and description to use the same formatting as other text in the page, click the Use font formatting from page option button. If you want to format the caption and description using the formatting options in the dialog box, click the Override and use custom font formatting option button.

Because the deer.htm page uses a theme, you will not use custom formatting, which will ensure that the photo gallery has the same font style as other text in the page.

4. Click the **Caption** text box, and then type **Mexican Bush Sage**.
5. Press the **Tab** key to move to the Description text box, and then type **Sages are very drought-tolerant and deer-resistant plants. They need good drainage and full sun, and come in a variety of colors.**
6. Repeat Steps 3 through 5 to add the **garden82.jpg** picture to the photo gallery with the caption **Salvia Greggii** and the description **This plant comes in many colors and blooms from spring to the first freeze. Very drought-tolerant and the deer don't like it!**
7. Repeat Steps 3 through 5 to add the **garden98.jpg** picture to the photo gallery with the caption **Black-eyed Susan** and the description **This self-seeding perennial thrives in most soil types, loves full sun, and blooms all summer.**
8. Click the **OK** button. FrontPage creates the photo gallery in the deer.htm page. (Scroll down the page as necessary to see the photo gallery.) See Figure 4-36.

Photo gallery added to the deer.htm page — **Figure 4-36**

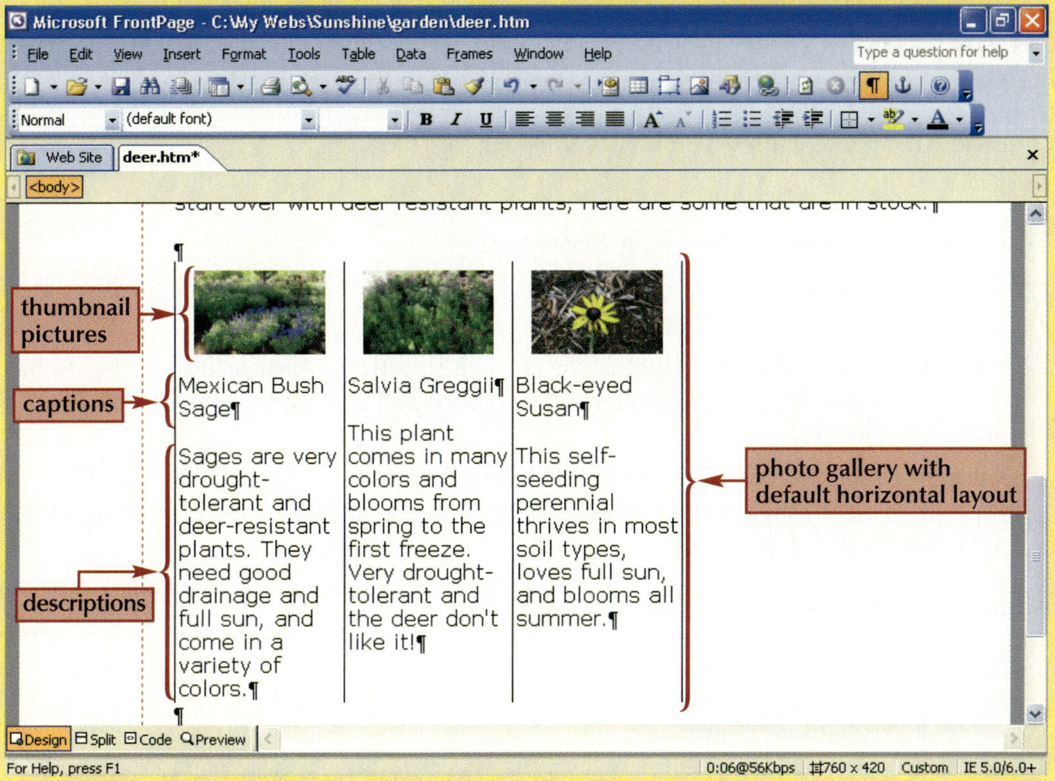

When you create a photo gallery, the default style is the horizontal layout, which arranges thumbnails of the pictures you selected into rows, with their captions and descriptions positioned below the pictures. Clicking a thumbnail picture opens the full-size version of the picture. There are three other layouts that you can use for a photo gallery. Brett wants to see the other layouts, so you need to open the Photo Gallery Properties dialog box again.

To change the photo gallery's layout:

1. Double-click the photo gallery to open the Photo Gallery Properties dialog box, and then click the **Layout** tab. The Layout tab contains options for arranging the pictures in the photo gallery. The default, Horizontal Layout, displays each picture, its caption, and its description in a row format. You can change the number of pictures to display in each row by changing the value in the Number of pictures per row box. The default value is to display five pictures in each row.
2. Click the **Montage Layout** option. This layout arranges pictures as a collage. When you point to a picture in the collage, its caption appears. This layout does not support descriptions.
3. Click the **Slide Show** option. This layout arranges the pictures in a scrollable format, with the selected image being displayed in its full size with a description below it.
4. Click the **Vertical Layout** option. This layout displays pictures in columns with their captions and descriptions.

   Brett likes the Slide Show layout, so you will select that one.

5. Click the **Slide Show** option, click the **OK** button, and then click the **down** arrow key ↓ to deselect the photo gallery. The photo gallery changes to the Slide Show layout.
6. Save the deer.htm page and save the pictures in the Web site's images folder.

To view the photo gallery, you'll view the page in a browser.

To view the photo gallery in a browser:

1. Click the **Preview** button on the Standard toolbar, and then scroll down the page so you can see the entire photo gallery.
2. Point to the first thumbnail picture on the left. The ScreenTip, "Mexican Bush Sage," is the picture's caption. The full-size picture and its caption and description appear below the thumbnail pictures.
3. Click the middle thumbnail picture (with the ScreenTip "Salvia Greggii"). The Slide Show changes to display the full-size picture, caption, and description for this Salvia Greggii picture. See Figure 4-37.

Figure 4-37 **Photo gallery with Slide Show layout**

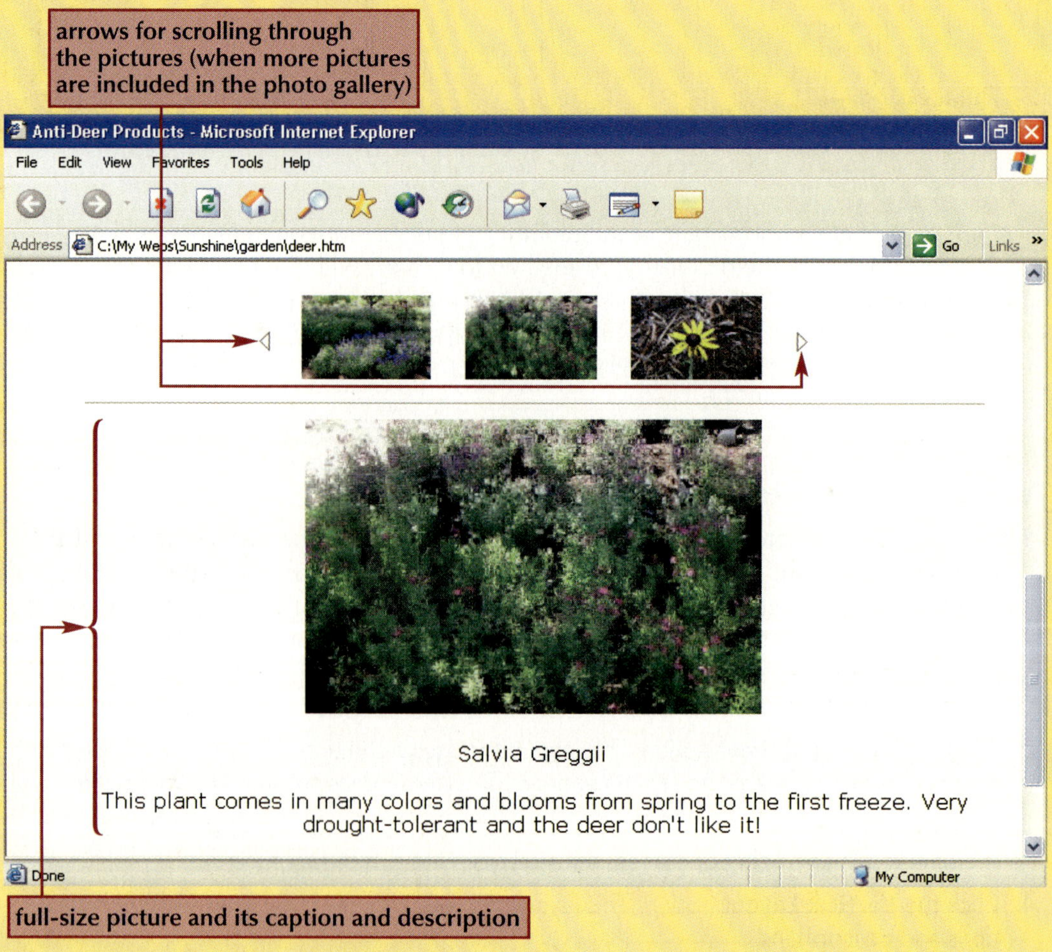

4. Click the third thumbnail picture to display it in the photo gallery.
5. Close your browser.

As you look at the completed photo gallery in the deer.htm page, Brett wonders if you can insert a heading to showcase this new feature. You suggest that instead of using a heading and plain text, you can use WordArt to create an interesting graphic from normal text.

Using Drawings, AutoShapes, and WordArt in a Page

Sometimes the content of your Web pages requires you to draw objects, such as arrows and callouts, or shapes, such as hearts or smiling faces. In other cases, you might want to format text in a special way by controlling its color, font, and appearance. In these cases, you can insert a drawing, AutoShape, or WordArt in the page.

A **drawing** is a canvas object that contains other objects, such as text boxes and arrows. For example, you might use a drawing object to create the simple diagram shown in Figure 4-38 on the home page to call attention to the nursery's sale on deer-resistant plants. If you have used the drawing tools in another program, such as Microsoft Paint, Word, or PowerPoint, you'll find that the tools in FrontPage work the same way.

Figure 4-38 Canvas object displayed by a browser

To insert a drawing into a Web page, click Insert on the menu bar, point to Picture, and then click New Drawing. A canvas object opens in the Web page, along with the Drawing and Drawing Canvas toolbars. You use the buttons on the Drawing toolbar to draw lines, change colors, and add text boxes. Clicking the Fit, Expand, or Scale Drawing buttons on the Drawing Canvas toolbar lets you control the size of the canvas object. Figure 4-39 shows the Drawing toolbar, the Drawing Canvas toolbar, and the drawing object shown in Figure 4-38 in FrontPage.

Figure 4-39 Canvas object in FrontPage

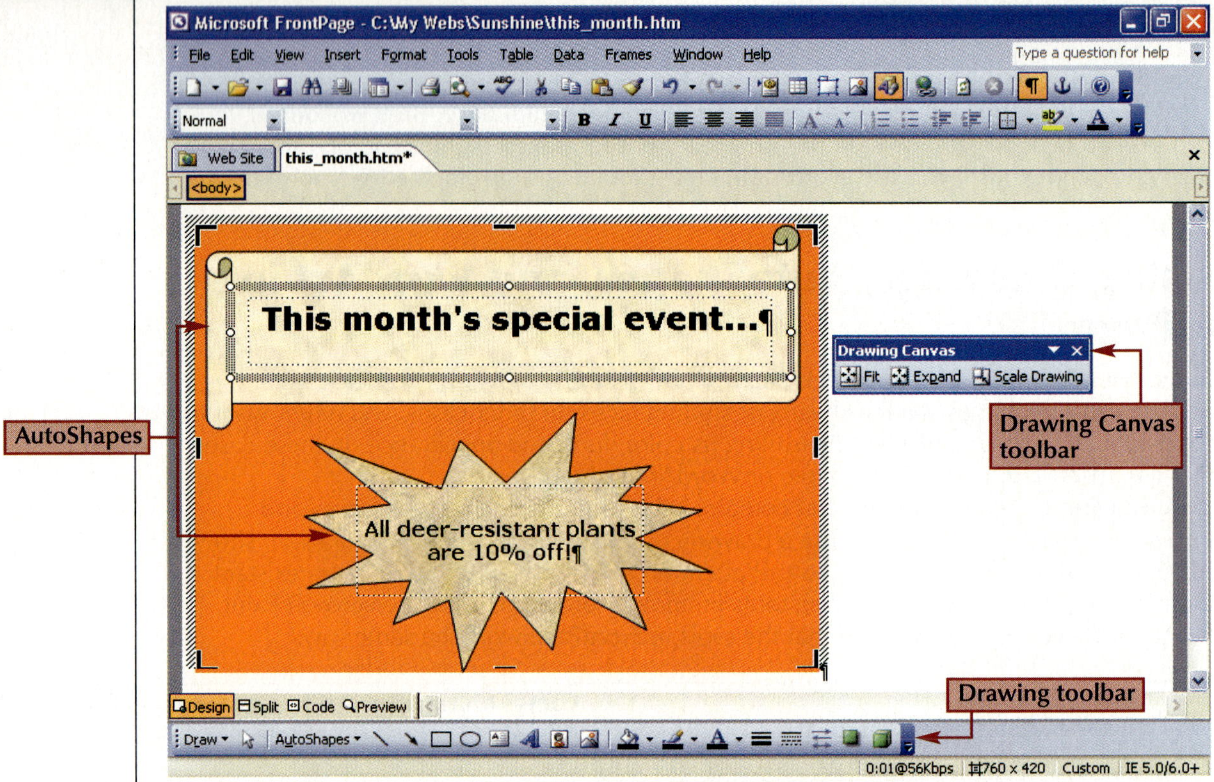

An **AutoShape** is a predesigned shape, such as an arrow, bracket, square, circle, banner, star, or callout. Figure 4-39 includes two AutoShapes—a horizontal scroll at the top of the canvas and an explosion 1 star at the bottom. You insert an AutoShape in a canvas by clicking the AutoShapes button on the Drawing toolbar to open a menu with several AutoShape categories. Pointing to the Lines AutoShape category, for example, opens a palette of line styles that you can use to draw a line. After clicking a line style, you use the pointer to draw a line in a Web page. FrontPage then automatically generates the HTML tags required to position and draw the object. You can also insert an AutoShape into a Web page (without the canvas) by clicking Insert on the menu bar, pointing to Picture, and then clicking AutoShapes. The AutoShapes toolbar then opens and provides buttons for accessing the same AutoShape styles available on the Drawing toolbar.

WordArt is a text object to which you can apply a font, font size, and special effects. When creating a WordArt object in a Web page, you can either select existing text or insert new text. In either case, when you create a WordArt object, you can select the style, font, font size, and font style for your text. After creating the WordArt object, you can use the WordArt toolbar to change its attributes or double-click the object to edit the text.

Creating a WordArt Object in a Page

Reference Window

- If necessary, select the existing text that you will format as a WordArt object.
- Click Insert on the menu bar, point to Picture, and then click WordArt. The WordArt Gallery dialog box opens.
- Click the WordArt style to use for your text, and then click the OK button. The Edit WordArt Text dialog box opens.
- Select the font, font size, and font style for your text. If necessary, type or edit the text for the WordArt object in the Text text box.
- Click the OK button.
- Use the WordArt toolbar to change the color, shape, letter height, direction, alignment, or character spacing of the WordArt object, if desired.
- Use the sizing handles on the WordArt object to resize the WordArt object, if desired.

Brett wants to use a WordArt object to add visual interest to the deer.htm page.

To create a WordArt object:

1. Scroll up the page as necessary, insert a blank paragraph above the photo gallery, and then, if necessary, position the insertion point on the new line.
2. Click **Insert** on the menu bar, point to **Picture**, and then click **WordArt**. The WordArt Gallery dialog box opens and shows the WordArt styles that you can apply to text. See Figure 4-40.

Figure 4-40 WordArt Gallery dialog box

3. Click the first style in the second row, and then click the **OK** button. The Edit WordArt Text dialog box opens. You use this dialog box to specify the font, font size, and font style for your WordArt object. Notice that default text "Your Text Here" appears in the Text text box. If you select text before creating the WordArt object, the text you selected will appear in the Text text box. In either case, you can edit or type the text to include in the WordArt object.
4. Type **This week's featured deer-resistant plants are on sale!** to replace the default text in the WordArt object.

When you create a WordArt object, the default font is Arial Black and default font size is 36 points. The WordArt text is formatted using italics because you selected a WordArt style that uses italics. The font size is large for the amount of text you entered, so you'll reduce it.

5. Click the **Size** list arrow, and then scroll up and click **14**. The text changes to use the new specifications.

6. Click the **OK** button. The WordArt object appears in the Web page and is selected, and the WordArt toolbar opens. See Figure 4-41.

Figure 4-41 **WordArt object added to the deer.htm page**

Trouble? If the WordArt toolbar blocks the WordArt object in the Web page, drag it to another location or dock it below the Formatting toolbar.

When a WordArt object is selected, the WordArt toolbar appears. The buttons on the WordArt toolbar let you change the WordArt text and the style, color, shape, letter height, direction, alignment, and character spacing of the letters in the WordArt object. There are two options for changing the alignment of a WordArt object. The first option is to align the WordArt text within the WordArt object. The second option is to align the WordArt object on the Web page. Brett likes the WordArt object but suggests that you change its color and center it on the page.

To change a WordArt object:

1. With the WordArt object selected, click the **Center** button on the Formatting toolbar. The WordArt object is centered on the page.
2. Click the **Format WordArt** button on the WordArt toolbar. The Format WordArt dialog box opens. See Figure 4-42.

Figure 4-42 **Format WordArt dialog box**

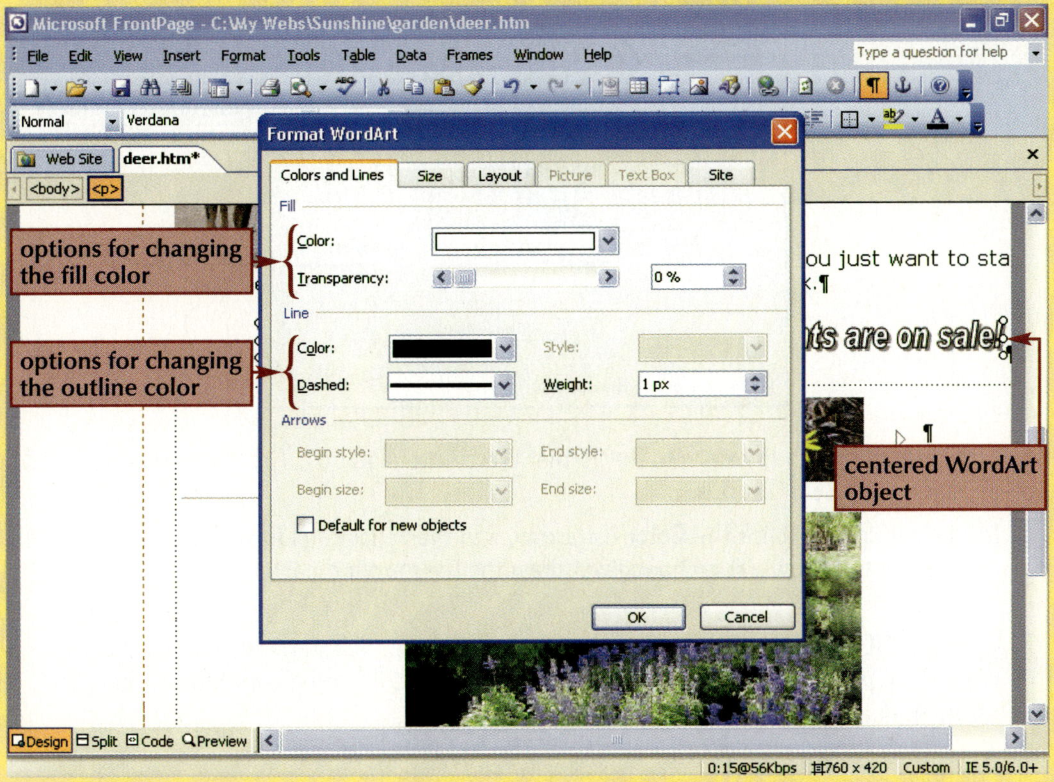

You can use the Colors and Lines tab in this dialog box to control the color, style, and weight of the lines and the fill color of the letters in the WordArt object. The Size tab lets you control the size, rotation, and scale of a WordArt object. The Layout tab lets you control the positioning style of the WordArt object. Usually, you can accept the default options on the Size and Layout tabs.

Instead of filling the WordArt object with a color, you want to show Brett how to fill the object with a pattern or a texture.

3. In the Fill section, click the **Color** list arrow, and then click **Fill Effects**. The Fill Effects dialog box opens. You can fill a WordArt object with a gradient color by applying a pattern of shading of one or more colors, a texture, a pattern, or a picture that you select. You'll apply a texture.
4. Click the **Texture** tab, and then click the last texture in the third row. After clicking the texture, its name (Bouquet) appears below the samples. See Figure 4-43.

Figure 4-43 **Fill Effects dialog box**

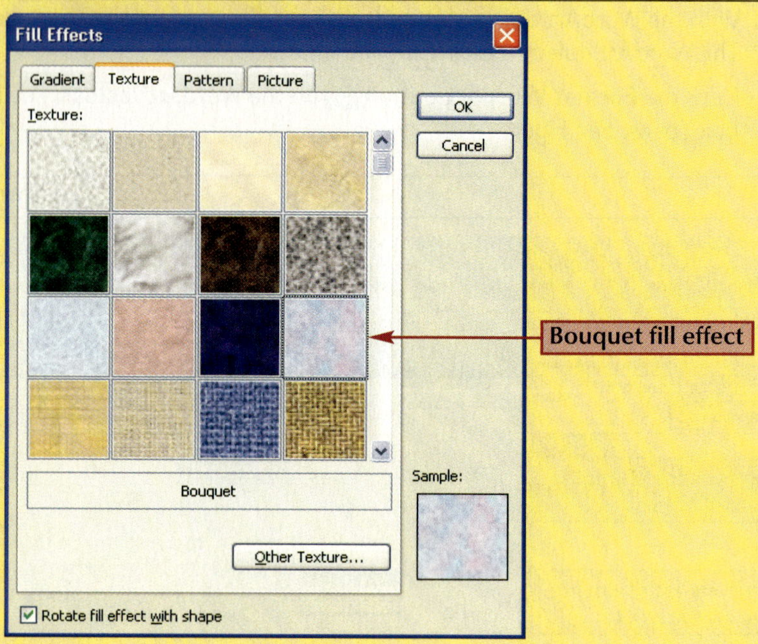

5. Click the **OK** button to return to the Format WordArt dialog box. The texture you selected appears in the Color list box.
6. In the Line section, click the **Color** list arrow, and then click the **Light Blue** color (the sixth color in the third row). This change will draw the lines around each letter using a light-blue color.
7. Click the **OK** button, and then click an empty area in the Web page to deselect the WordArt object. The WordArt object now has a textured fill and a light-blue border. See Figure 4-44.

Completed WordArt object

Figure 4-44

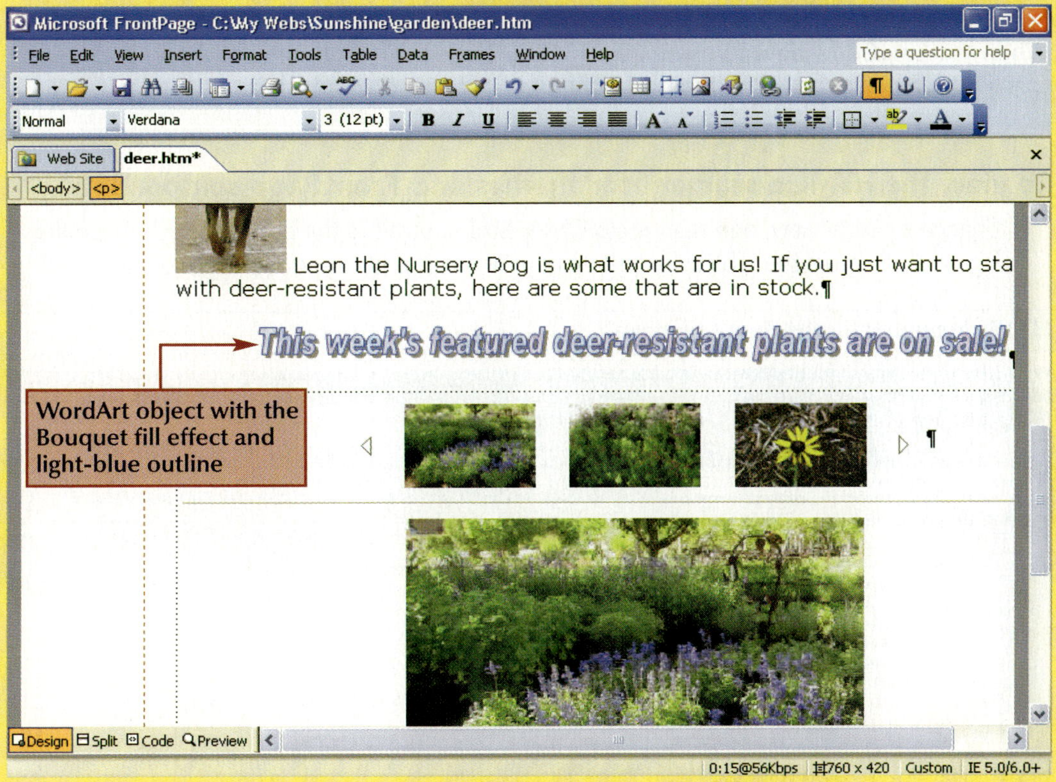

8. Save the deer.htm page, and then preview it in a browser and examine the changes you made in this page.
9. Close your browser.

You have added several new elements to the deer.htm page, and you want to show Brett the HTML tags and scripts that FrontPage created to implement them.

Examining the HTML Document for the deer.htm Page

FrontPage stores the files needed to support the photo gallery in the Web site's photogallery folder. FrontPage stores most of the files that it uses to create the interactive buttons and animations, shared borders, link bars, and themes in the Web site's hidden folders and files. The _borders and _themes folders are the primary folders in which the theme's shared border and theme files are stored. FrontPage does not display hidden folders in Folders view unless you configure it to do so by clicking Tools on the menu bar, clicking Site Settings, clicking the Advanced tab, and then selecting the Show hidden files and folders check box. After closing the Site Settings dialog box and refreshing the Web site, you can see the Web site's hidden files and folders in Folders view.

Shared borders and themes are implemented in FrontPage using meta tags (which were described in Tutorial 2). When you enable a Web site to use a theme and shared borders, FrontPage adds meta tags to the affected pages. FrontPage then uses these meta tags to display the theme and shared borders by using the files that are stored in the Web site's hidden _themes and _borders folders.

The banners and link bars were created using FrontPage Web components, which are identified in each page's HTML document with a comment tag (<!-- ... -->). If a Web browser cannot process a component, it will ignore the instructions in the comment tags. When you use Code view to examine an HTML document that contains a component, FrontPage displays the component in a different color to distinguish it.

To view the HTML document for themes and FrontPage components:

1. Change to Code view, and then press **Ctrl + End** to scroll to the bottom of the document. Figure 4-45 shows the HTML that creates the WordArt object and the photo gallery.

Figure 4-45 **HTML document for the deer.htm page**

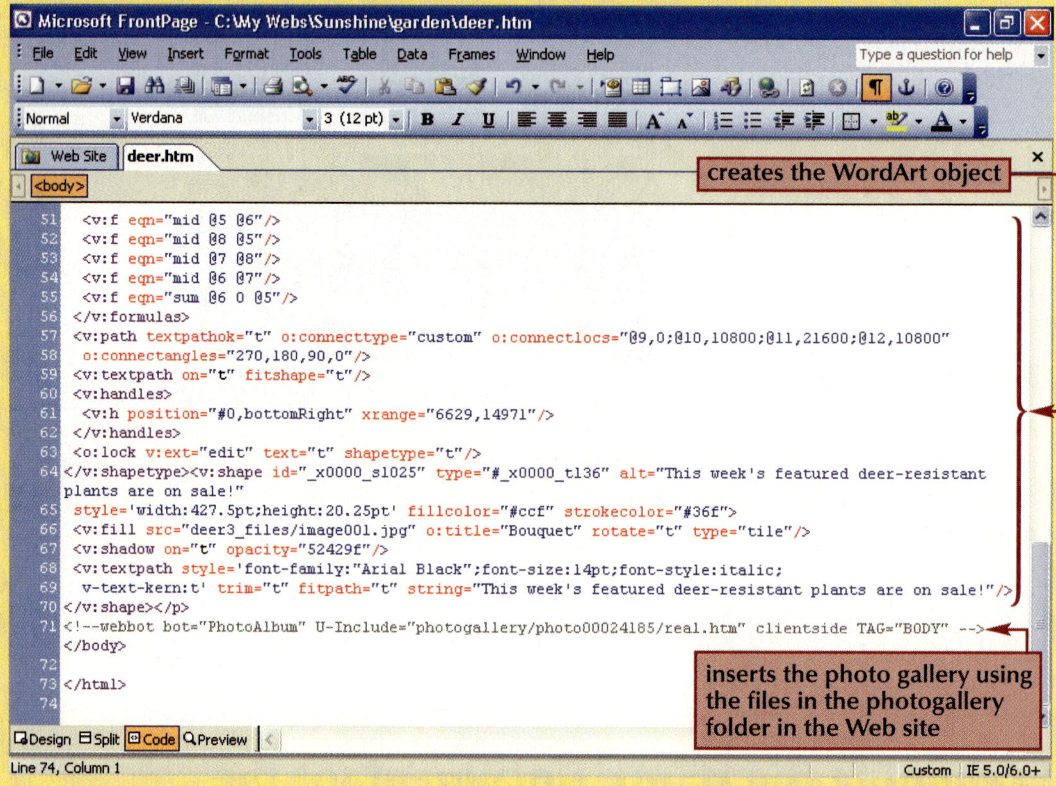

2. Scroll to the top of the page. There are two meta tags at the beginning of the document that identify the theme and the borders to include in this page.
3. Change to Design view, close the garden Web site, and then close FrontPage.

Helen and Brett like the Anti-Deer Products page and are certain that it will be a useful page in the Web site. In Tutorial 5, you will show Brett how to create tables and frames pages in a Web site.

Review

Session 4.3 Quick Check

1. True or False: When you create a caption in the photo gallery, you have the option of applying custom formatting to the text.
2. How do pictures in a photo gallery appear on the page when you apply the montage layout to the photo gallery?
3. Which photo gallery layout does not support captions?
4. The files that create a photo gallery in a Web site are stored in the site's ______________ folder.
5. What is a drawing?
6. Arrows, callouts, and special graphics such as a heart shape are examples of ______________.
7. True or False: WordArt creates a picture from text using characteristics that you specify.

Review

Tutorial Summary

In this tutorial, you learned how to use features in a Web site that are dependent upon the organization of pages in Navigation view. After positioning existing pages in the navigation structure, you learned how to create shared borders in a Web site and how to change the default presentation of links in the site's link bar components. You also learned how to turn off a shared border in a Web page and how to replace the content formerly supplied by the shared border. You also made changes in Navigation view to maintain the Web site, including removing a page from the site's link bar components, renaming a page, adding and deleting pages, and moving pages to reposition them. Finally, you learned how to create a custom link bar in a Web site to add links based on a separate navigation structure in Navigation view.

You also practiced formatting pages using preexisting, customized, and new themes. As you develop Web sites in the future, you can use existing themes and create your own themes to streamline the process of formatting your site's pages.

Finally, you inserted a photo gallery and a WordArt object in a page to organize pictures related to a single topic and to create visual interest using normal text. These features are easy to implement and enhance the appearance and utility of your Web site.

Key Terms

AutoShape	link bar component	shared border
child page	page banner	theme
color scheme	parent page	WordArt
drawing	photo gallery	

Practice

Practice the skills you learned in the tutorial using the same case scenario.

Review Assignments

Data File needed for these Review Assignments: garden99.jpg

Brett wants to make a few changes to the Web site. First, he wants to change the font used in the page banner of the Garden Web Site theme. Next, in the Anti-Deer Products page, he wants to add another plant to the photo gallery and change the WordArt object text to indicate that the featured plants are 10% off. Finally, he wants to create two child pages of the Irrigation page—one each for residential and commercial systems. Because Chad

Schomaker, supervisor of the irrigation work at Sunshine, has not yet completed these new pages, Brett wants to add them to the navigation structure but not to the site's link bars.

If necessary, start FrontPage, make sure you have your Data Files, and then do the following:

1. Open the **garden** Web site from the location where your Web sites are stored, and then open the **deer.htm** page in Design view.
2. Scroll down the **deer.htm** page, and then double-click the WordArt object. Change the text in the WordArt object to "This week's featured deer-resistant plants are 10% off!" Change the font to Verdana, the font size to 16, and the font style to bold. Close the dialog box.
3. Click the WordArt Gallery button on the WordArt toolbar, and then change the WordArt style to the first style in the first row.
4. Click the Format WordArt button on the WordArt toolbar, and then set the fill effect to a two-color, diagonal-up gradient. In the Colors section, click the Two colors option button. Click the Color 1 list arrow, and then select the Yellow color. Select Light Orange as the second color, and then click the Diagonal up option button in the Shading styles section. Click the OK button, and then set the line color to Orange.
5. Double-click the photo gallery in the **deer.htm** page, and then add the **garden99.jpg** picture from the Tutorial.04\Review folder included with your Data Files to the photo gallery. Use the caption "Mexican Butterfly Weed" and the description "This plant blooms from spring to fall. The deer don't like it, but the butterflies and hummingbirds do!"
6. Use the Move Up button to change the order of the pictures so the **garden99.jpg** picture is first in the list. Save the **deer.htm** page and save the new picture in the Web site's images folder.
7. Open the Theme task pane, and then customize the Garden Web Site theme to use a bold, 24-point, Tahoma font for the page banner. Save the revised Garden Web Site theme, and then apply it to all pages in the Web site. Save and close the **deer.htm** page.
8. Click the Garden Web Site theme in the All available themes section of the Theme task pane, click the Vivid colors check box on the Theme task pane to clear it, click the Garden Web Site theme again, and then apply the Garden Web Site theme to all pages in the Web site. (*Hint:* Do not use the Garden Web Site theme in the Web site default theme section of the Theme task pane; your changes will not be updated.) Close the Theme task pane
9. In Navigation view, create two new child pages of the Irrigation page in the navigation structure titled Residential Systems and Commercial Systems. Change to Folders view and rename these pages **res_sys.htm** and **comm_sys.htm**, respectively.
10. Return to Navigation view, and then set the pages you created in Step 9 so they will not appear in the site's link bar components.
11. Open the **irr.htm** page in Design view and confirm that links to the child pages do not appear in the left shared border, and then close the **irr.htm** page.
12. Open the home page in Design view, and then click the add link link on the custom link bar. Add the **deer.htm** page to the link bar. In the Add to Link Bar dialog box, change the Text to display to "Anti-Deer Products." Save the home page, and then preview it in a browser. Use the link bars in the site's pages to navigate the Web site. Print the Anti-Deer Products page and then close your browser.
13. In Navigation view, make sure that the Folder List is turned off, use the Zoom list arrow to change this setting to 50%, and then print Navigation view.
14. Close the **garden** Web site, and then close FrontPage.

Challenge

Expand on the skills you learned in this tutorial to customize a theme in a new way, add a picture to a shared border, and create your own WordArt object.

Case Problem 1

Data File needed for this Case Problem: bullet.gif

Buffalo Trading Post Nicole Beirne realizes that as business at Buffalo Trading Post (BTP) continues to grow, she will be adding more Web pages to the company's Web site. Nicole wants to make sure that it is easy to update the site when new pages are added. She asks you to change the existing link bars to ones generated by FrontPage, which will be updated automatically when new pages are added to the site. Also, she wants you to add a theme to the pages so they will have a consistent appearance.

If necessary, start FrontPage, make sure you have your Data Files, and then do the following:

1. Open the **buffalo** Web site from the location where your Web sites are stored. (If you did not create this Web site in Tutorial 1 and change it in Tutorials 2 and 3, ask your instructor for assistance.)
2. Change to Navigation view, and then add the existing pages as follows. The home page should be the top-level page; and the What, How, and Who pages should be child pages of the home page. If necessary, change the title of the home page to "Buffalo Trading Post."
3. Add three new pages to the navigation structure as child pages of the What page: Accessories, Women's Clothing, and Children's Clothing. After adding these pages to the navigation structure, change to Folders view and change their filenames to **acc.htm**, **women.htm**, and **child.htm**, respectively. Return to Navigation view and print it.
4. Open the home page in Design view, and then add a bottom shared border to all the pages in the Web site.
5. Select the paragraph at the bottom of the home page (it begins with the text "BTP^{TM} is"). Cut this paragraph from the page, select the comment placeholder text that appears in the bottom shared border, and then paste the paragraph into the bottom shared border. If necessary, delete any blank lines that appear in the bottom shared border.
6. Position the insertion point to the left of the "B" in "BTP" in the bottom shared border, and then insert a horizontal line.
7. **Explore** Change the background color of the bottom shared border to white. (*Hint:* Use the Border Properties dialog box to make this change.) Save the home page.
8. Apply the Poetic theme to the entire Web site. (If you do not have this theme, select another theme.) The theme should use vivid colors, active graphics, and a background picture. Save the home page, and then preview it in a browser to observe the formatting applied by the theme. When you have finished examining the home page, close your browser.
9. **Explore** Customize the Web site's default theme to make the following changes. First, change the list bullet 1 picture to the **bullet.gif** file in the Tutorial.04\Case1 folder included with your Data Files. Next, change the font of the horizontal and vertical navigation buttons to Arial Black. Save the customized theme as Buffalo Web Site, apply the Buffalo Web Site theme to all pages in the Web site, and then save the home page.
10. Delete the user-defined link bar, the **buffalo.gif** picture, and any blank paragraphs that remain at the top of the home page; open the **who.htm** page and then delete the user-defined link bar, the **who_logo.gif** picture, and any blank paragraphs that remain at the top of the page; and then open the **how.htm** page and delete the user-defined link bar and the **how_logo.gif** picture. In the **how.htm** page, move the top bookmark to the left of the "How It Works" text in the bulleted list, and then delete any blank paragraphs that appear above the bulleted list. Save all of these pages by clicking File on the menu bar, and then clicking Save All.

11. Apply top and left shared borders to the entire Web site. Include navigation buttons in both borders.

Explore

12. Open the home page, and then display the DHTML Effects toolbar. Select the animated text ("Welcome to the Buffalo Trading Post!"), and then click the Remove Effect button on the DHTML Effects toolbar. Close the DHTML Effects toolbar.
13. With the "Welcome to the Buffalo Trading Post!" heading selected, change it to a WordArt object that uses a style of your choice and a 24-point font. Center the WordArt object in the Web page and make sure that it appears on its own line. Change the WordArt object's color to plum and experiment with different formatting options to make the WordArt object easy to read and visually interesting. When you have finished, save the home page.
14. Turn off the top and left shared borders in the home page only. At the top of the page, insert a picture page banner with the text "Buffalo Trading Post." On the next line, insert a horizontal link bar based on the Web site's navigation structure with links to child-level pages formatted using the site's theme. Save the home page.

Explore

15. Click to the left of the "B" in "BTP" in the bottom shared border, and then insert the **buffalo.gif** picture from the Web site's images folder. Save the home page.
16. Open the home page in a browser and use the link bars to navigate the site's pages. Use your browser to print the home page, and then close your browser.
17. Close the **buffalo** Web site and then close FrontPage.

Create

Create a Web site's navigation structure and a new page in the Web site.

Case Problem 2

Data Files needed for this Case Problem: italy.gif, mexico.gif, and us.gif

Garden Grill Meghan Elliott and Callan Murphy want to include Garden Grill's menu in the Web site so patrons can browse it before coming to the restaurant. They anticipate including pages that feature entrees, sandwiches, appetizers, and desserts. These pages aren't ready yet, but Meghan and Callan want you to add them to the Web site now so they are part of the site's navigation structure. Meghan and Callan also want to promote the new "Today's Special" feature at Garden Grill. They also want to include the daily special on the Web site and ask you to create a new specials page. In addition to promoting the daily special, Meghan and Callan also want to include suggested dishes from Italy, Mexico, and America. After creating this content, they want you to format the Web site using a theme and link bars to ensure that the site is visually appealing and easy to navigate.

If necessary, start FrontPage, make sure you have your Data Files, and then do the following:

1. Open the **grill** Web site from the location where your Web sites are stored. (If you did not create this Web site in Tutorial 1 and change it in Tutorials 2 and 3, ask your instructor for assistance.)

Explore

2. Change to Navigation view and create the navigation structure shown in Figure 4-46. In Folders view, change the filenames for the Appetizers and Sandwiches pages to **app.htm** and **sand.htm**, respectively.

Figure 4-46

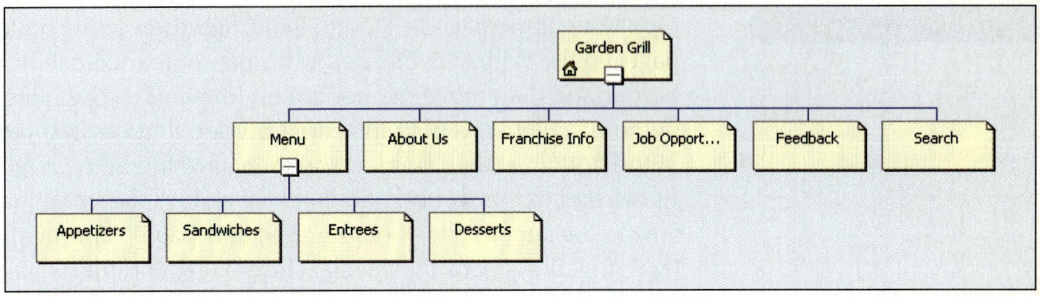

3. In Folders view, right-click any blank area in the Contents pane, point to New, and then click Blank Page. Change the filename of the new page to **specials.htm**, and then change the page title to Specials.

Explore

4. Open the Specials page in Design view, and then create the content shown in Figure 4-47. The pictures are saved in the Tutorial.04\Case2 folder included with your Data Files. When you are finished, save the page and save the pictures in the Web site's images folder.

Figure 4-47

Explore

5. Change to Navigation view, and then create a custom link bar named **Specials** that includes links to the site's home page and the Menu page. In a new centered paragraph at the top of the **specials.htm** page that is formatted with the Normal style,

insert the Specials custom link bar. Choose the options to arrange the buttons horizontally and to format them using the Web site's theme. Save the **specials.htm** page.

Explore

6. Open the home page in Design view, and then add a bottom shared border to all pages in the Web site. Delete the comment text placeholder in the bottom shared border and then move the horizontal line and the two lines at the bottom of the home page into the bottom shared border. If necessary, delete any blank paragraphs in the bottom shared border, and then save the home page.
7. At the end of the second paragraph of text on the home page, add the following sentence: "Be sure to check out our Specials page!" Format the word "Specials" as a hyperlink that opens the **specials.htm** page, and then save the home page.
8. Add the Watermark theme to the entire Web site. Be sure to select the options to use vivid colors, active graphics, and a background picture.
9. Save the home page, and then preview it in a browser. Use the links to navigate the site, use your browser to print the **specials.htm** page, and then close your browser.
10. Close the **grill** Web site and then close FrontPage.

Challenge

Create a new theme for a Web site.

Case Problem 3

Data Files needed for this Case Problem: benecr.jpg, buggy.jpg, conf.jpg, couches.jpg, manu.jpg, pic2.jpg, retail.jpg, sndcrf.jpg, sw.gif

Swenson Auctioneers Scott Swenson wants to begin working on defining the categories of auctions conducted by Swenson Auctioneers. He has some pictures that he wants you to insert into the Web site in an organized way. You suggest arranging the pictures in a photo gallery, and Scott agrees with your idea. You also want to streamline the Web site's appearance by creating a new theme that uses the existing background picture in the Web pages. By defining the background picture, fonts, and bullet characters with a theme, you can save some time by applying the theme to new pages instead of formatting these elements individually.

If necessary, start FrontPage, make sure you have your Data Files, and then do the following:

1. Open the **swenson** Web site from the location where your Web sites are stored. (If you did not create this Web site in Tutorial 1 and change it in Tutorials 2 and 3, ask your instructor for assistance.)
2. Position the site's existing pages in the navigation structure as follows. The home page is the top-level page in the Web site, and the **upcoming.htm**, **services.htm**, **team.htm**, and **mail.htm** pages are child pages of the home page.

Explore

3. Create a new theme named Swenson Web Site as follows:
   a. For the background picture, use the **back.gif** file stored in the Web site's images folder.
   b. Use the **sw.gif** file in the Tutorial.04\Case3 folder included with your Data Files as the List Bullet 1 picture.
   c. Change the body text font to Arial.
   d. Change the Heading 1, Heading 2, and Heading 3 font to Arial Black.
   e. Change the color scheme to Street Writing.
   f. Select the options for active graphics and a background picture.

Explore

4. Save the Swenson Web Site theme, and then apply it as the default theme to all pages in the Web site. (*Hint:* After creating the theme, you must apply it as the default theme from the All available themes section of the Theme task pane.)

5. Open the **services.htm** page in Design view, and then format the four paragraphs below the paragraph that begins "As skilled marketing specialists" as a bulleted list, observing the bullet characters added by the Swenson Web Site theme. Save the **services.htm** page.

Explore

6. Open the **upcoming.htm** page in Design view, and then scroll to the bottom of the page. In a new, centered paragraph, insert a WordArt object with the text "Auction Categories" and format it using a WordArt style of your choice and 24-point Arial Black font. Change the WordArt object's color fill color to red and the line color to black.

Explore

7. In a new centered paragraph below the WordArt object you created in Step 6, insert the following pictures and captions into a photo gallery as follows. Format each caption using bold text, and arrange the pictures in a Slide Show format. (*Hint:* You can add multiple pictures to the photo gallery at the same time by selecting them in the File Open dialog box, and then clicking Open. You need to set the caption to bold only once. You won't insert any descriptions.) All pictures are saved in the Tutorial.04\Case3 folder included with your Data Files.
   a. **conf.jpg**: Business Equipment & Computers
   b. **manu.jpg**: Manufacturing & Heavy Equipment
   c. **couches.jpg**: Furniture, Art, & Rugs
   d. **sndcrf.jpg**: Sound & Lighting
   e. **pic2.jpg**: Special Use
   f. **retail.jpg**: Retail FF&E
   g. **buggy.jpg**: Estates & Antiques
   h. **benecr.jpg**: Benefit Auctions
8. Save the **upcoming.htm** page and save the pictures in the Web site's images folder.
9. Preview the home page in a browser, and then print the **upcoming.htm** page with the Estates & Antiques picture displayed. (*Hint:* Click the arrow to scroll the thumbnail pictures.) Close your browser.
10. Close the **swenson** Web site and then close FrontPage.

Challenge

Customize a theme for a Web site.

Case Problem 4

There are no Data Files needed for this Case Problem.

Mortgage Services, Inc. Natalie Fuselier wants to reformat the Web site's pages to ensure that they have a consistent appearance and hyperlinks to other pages in the Web site. She asks you to make some changes to accomplish these tasks. Because she wants to distinguish the Credit Repair Services page as being separate from the rest of the site, she asks you to format this page differently.

If necessary, start FrontPage, and then do the following:

1. Open the **loan** Web site from the location where your Web sites are stored. (If you did not create this Web site in Tutorial 1 and change it in Tutorials 2 and 3, ask your instructor for assistance.)
2. Position the site's existing pages in the navigation structure as follows. The home page is the top-level page in the Web site, and the **repair.htm**, **loantype.htm**, **apply.htm**, **help.htm**, **resource.htm**, and **contact.htm** pages are child pages of the home page.

Explore

3. Set the **repair.htm** page so it is not included in the site's link bars.
4. Open the home page in Design view, and then delete the user-defined link bar, the Mortgage Services, Inc. heading, and any blank paragraphs at the top of the page. Delete these same items from the **loantype.htm**, **help.htm**, and **resource.htm** pages. Click File on the menu bar, and then click Save All to save your changes.

Explore

5. Apply the Profile theme to all pages in the Web site, and then customize the Profile theme as follows:
   a. Change the body text to Times New Roman.
   b. Change the font used in the page banner to Arial Black.
   c. Change the font and style of the horizontal navigation buttons and the vertical navigation buttons to 8-point, bold, and Arial.
   d. Save the theme using the name Loan Web Site, and then apply it to all pages in the Web site.
6. Open the **repair.htm** page in Design view, remove the theme from this page only, and then save the page.
7. Create top and left shared borders for all pages in the Web site and select the options to include navigation buttons in both shared borders.

Explore

8. In the **repair.htm** page, remove the top and left shared borders for this page only. Replace the Heading 1 paragraph at the top of the page with a picture page banner. Apply the Blends theme to the **repair.htm** page only. Select the options for vivid colors, active graphics, and a background picture. Save the **repair.htm** page and close the Theme task pane.
9. Preview the home page in a browser, and then print the home page and the **repair.htm** page. Close your browser.
10. Close the **loan** Web site and then close FrontPage.

Review

Quick Check Answers

Session 4.1

1. to identify the relationships between pages so you can create link bar components and page banners in a Web site
2. You can create shared borders at the top, bottom, left, and right. The top, left, and right shared borders can include link bar components.
3. False
4. False
5. True
6. You can delete the page from the navigation structure only (which removes the link for the page from the site's link bars), or you can delete the page from the navigation structure and the Web site.
7. Open the page in Design view, click Format on the menu bar, click Shared Borders, click the Current page option button, clear the check box for the shared border(s) to remove, and then click the OK button.
8. True

Session 4.2

1. A theme is a collection of design elements such as bullets, backgrounds, table borders, fonts, and pictures that you can apply to a Web site or one or more Web pages.
2. True
3. The theme's color scheme changes to use a brighter, more intense set of colors.
4. True
5. colors, graphics, and text
6. False

Session 4.3

1. True
2. The pictures appear as a collage.
3. All of the photo gallery layouts support captions.
4. photogallery
5. a canvas object that contains objects such as text boxes and arrows
6. AutoShapes
7. True

Objectives

Session 5.1
- Create a table in a Web page
- Align a table and its cells
- Enter data in a table
- Insert, delete, resize, merge, and split cells
- Add a caption to a table
- Apply a Table AutoFormat

Session 5.2
- Create a frames page
- Create hyperlinks in a frames page and specify their targets
- Examine and change a frame's properties
- Change a frame's target
- Add a new frame to a frames page
- Print a frames page

Creating Tables and Frames

Revising the Bulk Goods Samples and Irrigation Pages and Creating the Lawn Care Page

Case

Sunshine Landscape & Garden Center

Brett Kizer, owner of the Sunshine Landscape & Garden Center, compliments you this morning on the Web site. He really likes the theme that you applied to the site's pages and the consistency of the navigation features provided by the link bar components in the pages' shared borders. Brett is eager to finish the Web site and make it available to his customers.

As you review the site's content with Brett in your regular weekly meeting, you suggest a different arrangement of content in the existing Bulk Goods Samples page. Currently, this page includes pictures that you intend to link to child pages of the Bulk Goods Samples page. However, as you view the page with Brett, you tell him that a table might provide a better way to organize the pictures. Brett is surprised that you would suggest using a table in this manner, because he doesn't think that drawing lines around the pictures would look very good. You tell Brett that tables are used very frequently in Web pages as a way of controlling the position of objects, including pictures and text. When used as a layout tool, a table usually includes invisible borders so that the table is transparent to the user. Because most browsers interpret the HTML tags that create and format tables consistently, a table is an important Web design tool.

Student Data Files

To complete this tutorial, you will need your ending files from Tutorial 4 and the following Data Files. Additional Data Files needed to complete the end-of-tutorial exercises are listed with the Review Assignments and Case Problems.

▼**Tutorial.05**
- ▽ Tutorial folder
  - irr folder
  - lawn.htm

As you are talking with Brett, Helen Xiao, Sunshine's horticulturist, mentions that many customers have been seeking help in solving problems with their lawns. She started a Web page that will provide answers to common questions and asks if you can finish it for her. After looking at the information Helen plans to provide in this page, you tell Brett that this page is an excellent candidate for a traditional table with gridlines to identify each cell.

Earlier in the Web site development process, Chad Schomaker, Sunshine's irrigation specialist, had asked you to add two pages to the Web site—one each for residential and commercial customers. After creating the content he wants to include in the Web site, Chad decides that he doesn't have enough content to justify having different pages for different kinds of customers. He shows you the content he completed and you tell him and Brett that this content is well suited for a frames page. You'll create a frames page to display Chad's pages in the Web site.

Session 5.1

Understanding Tables

You are probably already familiar with the process of creating tables in Microsoft Word documents. In FrontPage, just as in Word, a **table** consists of one or more rows of cells that organize and arrange data. A **cell** is the smallest component of a table. You can place text or a picture in a table cell. You can also create a **nested table**, which is a table within a table cell.

If your Web site development plan includes a Web page with a table, you should sketch out the desired appearance of the table before you create it using FrontPage. Sketching a table first helps you plan how many rows and columns you will need. Although you can add or delete columns after creating the table, it is easier to create the table correctly from the start.

The steps you take to create a table using FrontPage are similar to those you would use to create a table with Word. To create a table quickly, you can use the Insert Table button; clicking that toolbar button displays the **Insert Table button grid**, a miniature table with four rows and five columns that you can use to specify the table's size. If your table is relatively small (fewer than four rows by five columns), you can click a cell in the grid to specify the desired table size. If your table is larger than four rows by five columns, you can drag the last cell in the grid to enlarge it to the desired table size; when you release the mouse button, FrontPage creates the desired table using the default settings for tables.

After creating a table, you can change its default properties, such as the size of the border, the cell padding, the cell spacing, and the table width. A **border** is a line that surrounds each cell and the entire table. **Cell padding** is the distance between the contents of a cell and the edge of the cell, measured in pixels. Increasing the cell padding adds space around the data in a cell. **Cell spacing** is the distance between table cells, also measured in pixels. Increasing the cell spacing adds space around the individual cells in a table.

You can specify the table width as a percentage of the width of the browser window or as a fixed width in pixels. Remember that a variety of computers and monitors will display your Web pages. For this reason, most developers set widths for their tables as a percentage of the screen's width (such as 85%), or as a fixed measurement (such as 620 pixels). You should specify these types of settings to ensure that all users of your Web pages will be able to view your tables correctly regardless of their particular monitors, computers, or Web browsers. A good rule of thumb for setting a table's width is to use a percentage for tables that contain mostly text and to use pixels when you need tight control over the placement of objects that have a fixed size, such as pictures.

Figure 5-1 shows a sketch of the table you will create in the Bulk Goods Samples page. The words "mulch," "soil," and "stone" are pictures that will include hyperlinks to open the mulch.htm, soil.htm, and stone.htm pages in the Web site. The pictures below each of these hyperlinks represent a sample of the medium (mulch, soil, and stone). Because the pictures have fixed sizes, you'll create the table by setting the width in pixels to ensure that the pictures appear as desired.

Figure 5-1 **Sketch of the table for the bulk2.htm page**

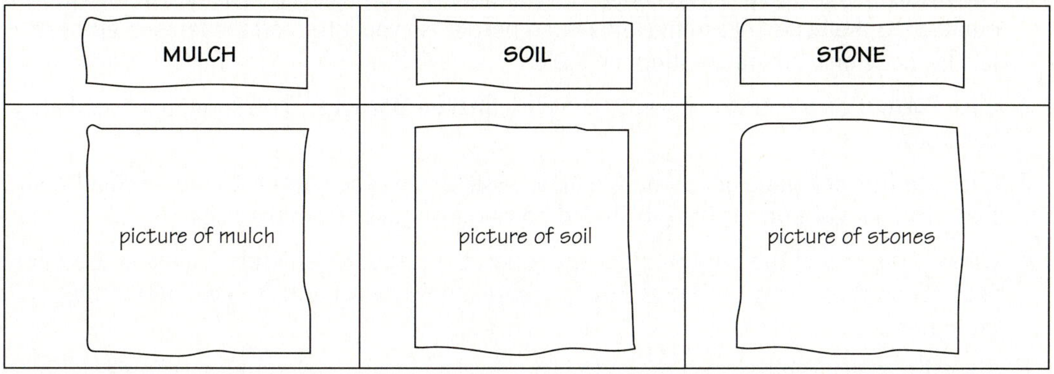

In addition to being able to create tables in a Web page, you can base the design of an entire Web page on a table. When a table is used to design a Web page, FrontPage calls it a layout table. A **layout table** is a framework that holds a page's contents. A **layout cell** is a region in a layout table that displays text, pictures, and other features in your Web page. For example, the layout table might include a cell at the top of a page to display a company's name and logo, cells that give the appearance of columns in the page, and a cell across the bottom of a page to display copyright information. FrontPage includes several templates that provide different visual appearances for a Web page. Layout table templates and options for changing them appear in the Layout Tables and Cells task pane. In this session, you'll learn about tables that appear as objects in a Web page, and not about tables that are used to design (lay out) an entire Web page's structure.

Creating a Table Using the Insert Table Button

After sketching the table, you are ready to create the new table in the desired location in the Web page.

Creating a Table in a Web Page

Reference Window

- Click the location in the Web page where you want to insert the table.
- Click the Insert Table button on the Standard toolbar to open the Insert Table button grid, click the grid cell that represents the desired table size or drag the last cell in the Insert Table button grid to expand the grid to the desired table size, and then release the mouse button.

or

- Click Table on the menu bar, point to Insert, and then click Table. In the Insert Table dialog box, specify the number of rows and columns in the Size section, and then click the OK button.

You'll show Brett how to use the Insert Table button on the Standard toolbar to make the changes to the bulk2.htm page.

To insert the table:

1. Start **FrontPage**, open the **garden** Web site from the location where your Web sites are stored, open the **bulk2.htm** page in Design view, and then if necessary click the **Show All** button ¶ on the Standard toolbar to display the nonprinting characters.

   The pictures in the page will function as hyperlinks to the Mulches, Soils, and Stones pages, duplicating the hyperlinks in the left shared border, so you'll turn off the left shared border for this page only before creating the table.

2. Click **Format** on the menu bar, and then click **Shared Borders**. The Shared Borders dialog box opens.

3. Click the **Current page** option button (if necessary), click the **Left** check box to clear it, and then click the **OK** button. The left shared border is removed from the page.

4. Click at the end of the paragraph at the top of the page (which ends "...install them for you!"), and then press the **Enter** key to create a new paragraph. You will insert the table here.

5. Click the **Insert Table** button on the Standard toolbar to open the Insert Table button grid. You might notice that it is the same Insert Table button grid that Word uses.

6. Point to the third cell in the second row, as shown in Figure 5-2. Clicking this cell will create a table with two rows and three columns.

Figure 5-2 **Insert Table button grid**

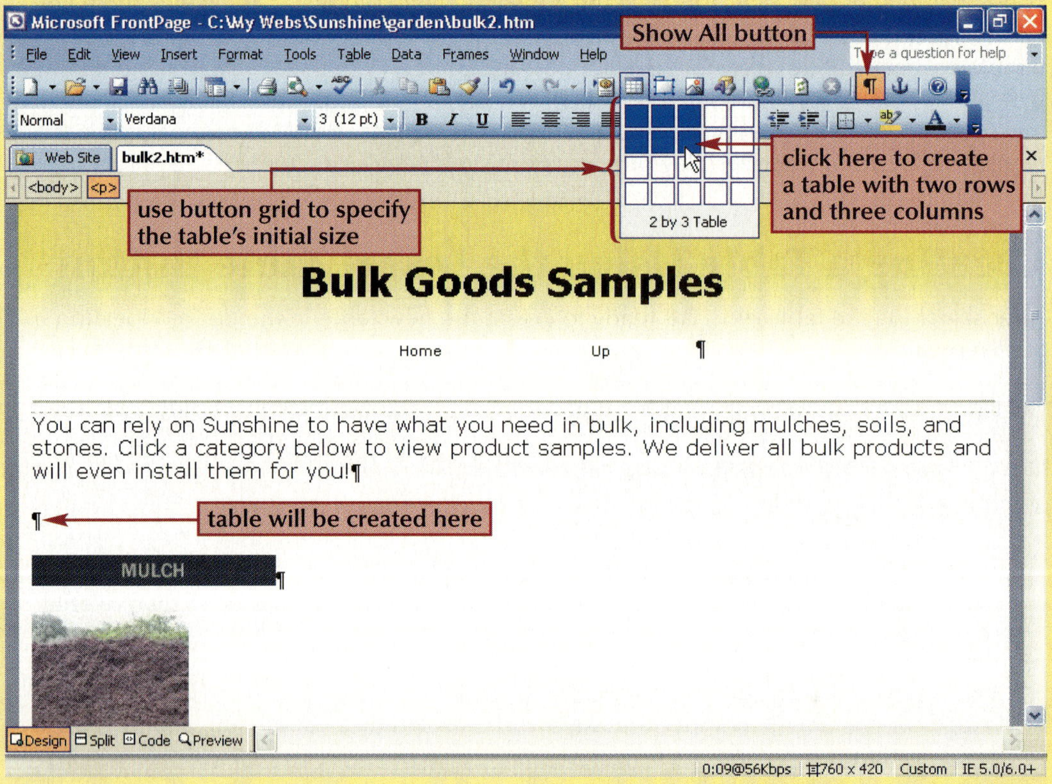

7. Click the third cell in the second row. The Insert Table button grid closes and a table with two rows and three columns is created in the Web page. The Table menu includes commands for working with tables. Displaying the Tables toolbar provides easy access to these same commands.

Trouble? If you clicked the wrong cell in the Insert Table button grid, click the Undo button on the Standard toolbar, and then repeat Steps 5 through 7.

8. Click **View** on the menu bar, point to **Toolbars**, and then click **Tables**. If necessary, drag the title bar of the Tables toolbar and dock it below the Formatting toolbar, as shown in Figure 5-3.

Figure 5-3 Table created in page

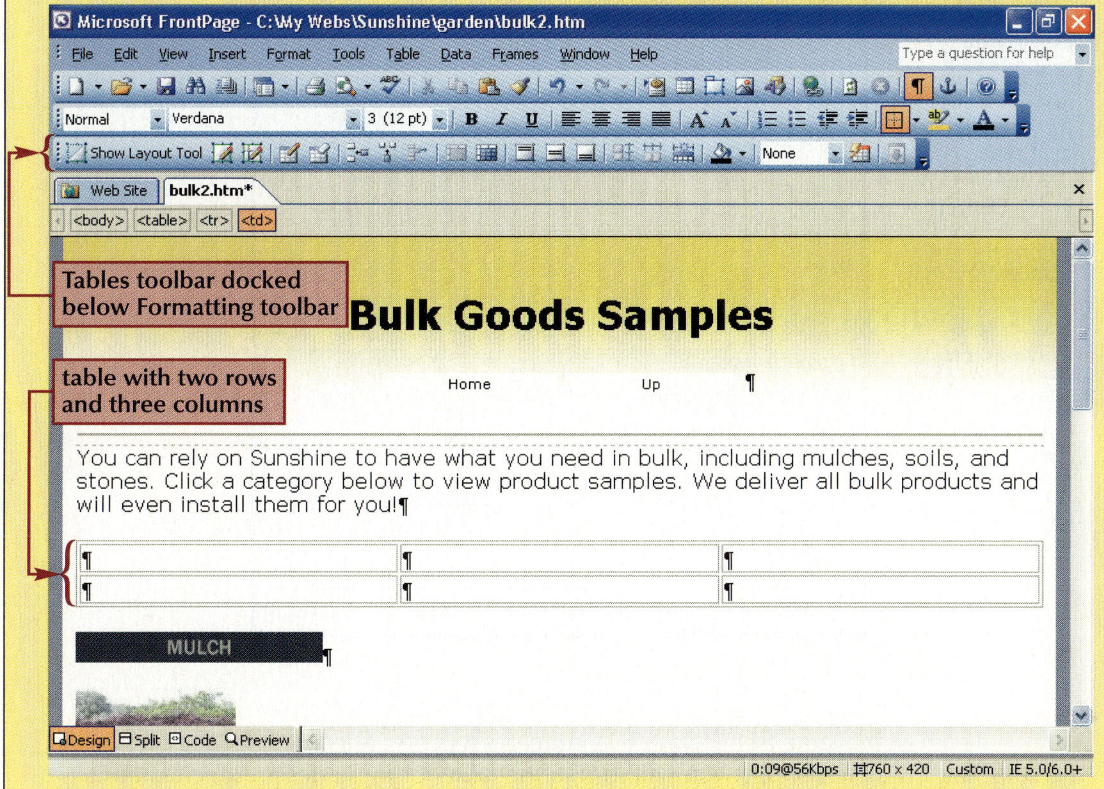

When you first create a table, FrontPage applies the default table settings to it. You can view these default settings by examining the Table Properties dialog box.

9. Right-click anywhere in the table to open the shortcut menu, and then click **Table Properties** to open the Table Properties dialog box. This dialog box lets you examine and specify the table's properties and characteristics. See Figure 5-4.

Figure 5-4 Table Properties dialog box

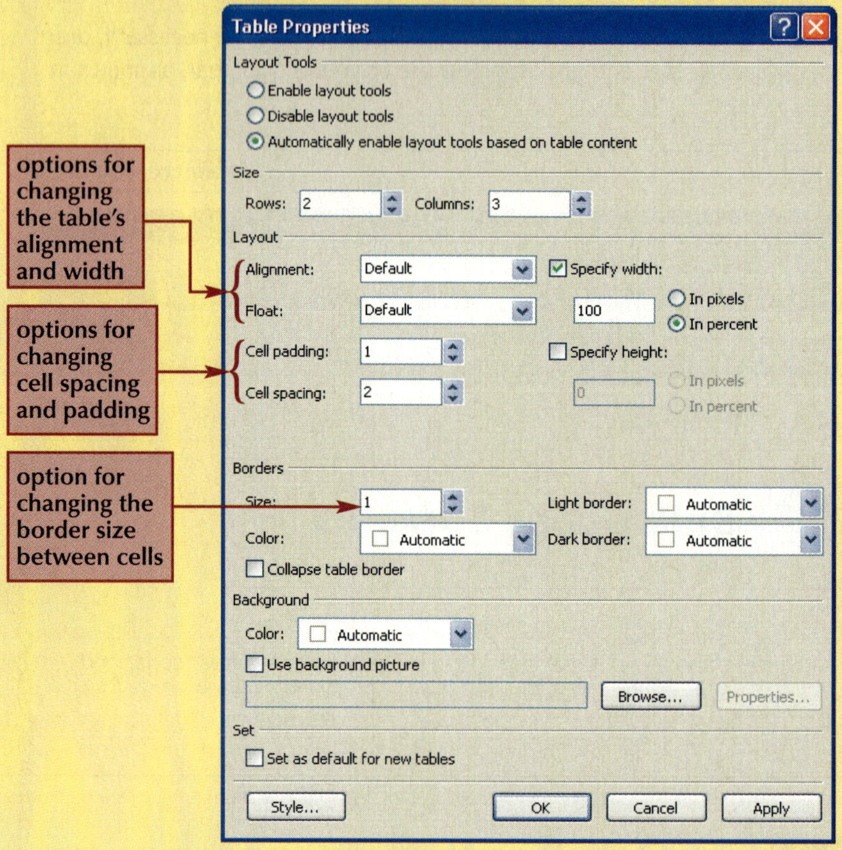

Your sketch of the table (see Figure 5-1) indicates a center alignment for the pictures in the cells and invisible borders. You will format the table for these design specifications next. In addition, because the table contains pictures with fixed sizes, you will set the table's width to 640 pixels to make sure that the pictures are always visible without scrolling the page horizontally, regardless of the user's monitor size and resolution. The minimum resolution for most monitors is 640 × 480 pixels.

To format the table:

1. Make sure that the **Specify width** check box in the Layout section contains a check mark, select the current value in the Specify width text box and type **640**, and then click the **In pixels** option button. This setting specifies that your table will be 640 pixels wide regardless of the monitor and resolution at which it is viewed. Selecting 640 pixels as the width ensures that people viewing the page with a monitor that displays 640 × 480 pixels will see the pictures without having to scroll the page horizontally. For people viewing the page using monitors with higher resolutions, the table will look narrower on the page.
2. In the Layout section, click the **Cell padding up arrow** as necessary to change the cell padding to **4**, and then click the **Cell spacing up arrow** as necessary to change the cell spacing to **3**. These settings will increase the spacing between and around cells in the table, which will make the table's contents easier to read.

3. In the Borders section, click the **Size down arrow** to change the border size to **0**. The border size is measured in pixels; a size of 0 indicates an invisible border, and a size of 1 indicates a thin border.

   There are two types of borders in a table: the border that encloses the table and the borders that enclose each cell. You can turn off the display of cell borders by adding a check mark to the Collapse table border check box. Because you have selected a border value of 0, you won't need to select the Collapse table border check box because all borders will be invisible.

4. Click the **OK** button. The Table Properties dialog box closes, and the new properties are applied to the table. Notice that a dashed outline, which identifies the position of the table and its cells, indicates the borders. The browser will not display these outlines.

When you click a cell in a table, the options on the Tables toolbar become active. Figure 5-5 describes the tools available on the Tables toolbar. You'll use some of these buttons as you create tables in the Web site.

Tables toolbar buttons and their descriptions **Figure 5-5**

Button Name	Button	Function
Show Layout Tool	Show Layout Tool	Turns on the layout tools for cells and tables
Draw Layout Table		Lets you draw a new layout table using the pointer, which changes to a shape
Draw Layout Cell		Lets you draw a new layout cell in a layout table using the pointer, which changes to a shape
Draw Table		Lets you draw a new table or modify an existing table using the pointer, which changes to a shape, to draw lines to indicate rows and columns
Eraser		Lets you use the pointer, which changes to a shape, to merge cells
Insert Rows		Inserts a new row above the selected row
Insert Columns		Inserts a new column to the left of the selected column
Delete Cells		Deletes the selected cells
Merge Cells		Merges the selected cells into one larger cell
Split Cells		Splits the selected cell into two or more cells
Align Top		Vertically aligns the data in the selected cells at the top of the cells
Center Vertically		Vertically centers the data in the selected cells
Align Bottom		Vertically aligns the data in the selected cells at the bottom of the cells
Distribute Rows Evenly		Changes the height of the selected rows to equal measurements
Distribute Columns Evenly		Changes the width of the selected columns to equal measurements
AutoFit to Contents		Increases or decreases the size of selected columns in the table to best fit the data they contain
Fill Color		Lets you change the background color of the selected cells to a standard or custom color
Table AutoFormat Combo	None	Lets you apply a Table AutoFormat to an existing table by selecting the desired Table AutoFormat from a list
Table AutoFormat		Opens the Table AutoFormat dialog box, where you can select and apply a Table AutoFormat and special formats to an existing table
Fill Down (or Fill Right)	(or)	Copies data from the topmost (or leftmost) cell in a range of selected cells and pastes it into the range of selected cells

You inserted the table in the correct location in the page, but Brett thinks that the table would look better if it were centered.

Aligning a Table

A table's alignment in a Web page differs from the alignment of data in a table's cells. A table can have only one alignment, whereas each cell in a table can have a different alignment. The alignment of a table and the alignment of a table's cells are specified using different HTML tags. To specify a different alignment for a table, you need to change the table's properties.

Reference Window

Aligning a Table in a Web Page

- Right-click anywhere in the table to open the shortcut menu, and then click Table Properties.
- In the Table Properties dialog box, click the Alignment list arrow in the Layout section, click the desired alignment, and then click the OK button.

The table that you inserted in the Bulk Goods Samples Web page is left-aligned, which is the default alignment. Brett wants this table to be centered to give it a more balanced appearance when viewed in a browser. He asks you to center the table next.

To align a table in a Web page:

1. Right-click anywhere in the table to open the shortcut menu, and then click **Table Properties** to open that dialog box.
2. In the Layout section, click the **Alignment** list arrow, and then click **Center**. Selecting this option will center the table (but not the data in the table's cells) in the page.
3. Click the **OK** button. The Table Properties dialog box closes and the table's alignment changes to centered. See Figure 5-6.

Figure 5-6 **Centered table**

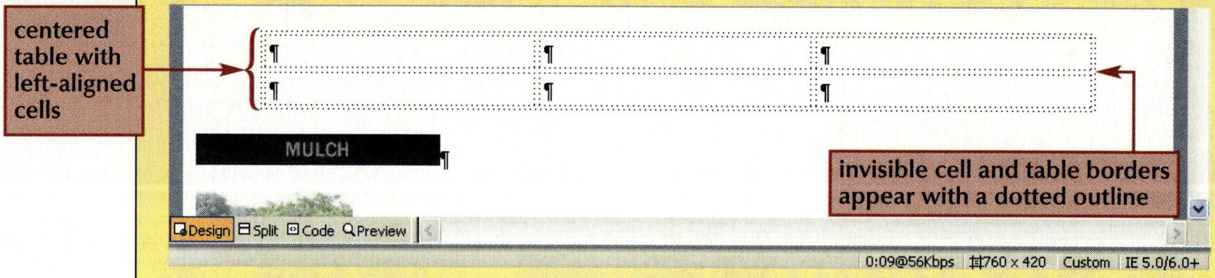

Moving Existing Data into a Table

The table that you created will contain the pictures that already exist in the Web page. You can drag the pictures into the correct cells to position them in the table. Using a table to position graphics is common on the Web because it provides good control over the positioning of objects in a Web page.

To drag existing items and position them in a table:

1. Click the picture with the word "mulch" on it to select it. Sizing handles appear around the picture.
2. Drag the picture to the first cell in the first row of the table. When the insertion point appears in the table as shown in Figure 5-7, release the mouse button. The picture now appears in the first cell of the table. The width of the first column increases after you position the first picture. This problem will correct itself after you insert all of the pictures into the table.

Moving a picture into a cell **Figure 5-7**

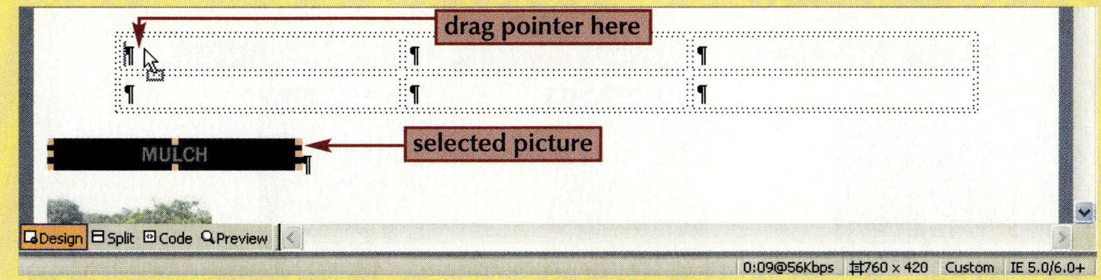

3. Drag the picture of bulk mulch from below the table and position it in the first cell in the second row.
4. Drag the picture with the word "soil" on it and its sample photo to the cells in the second column of the table.
5. Drag the picture with the word "stone" on it and its sample photo to the cells in the third column of the table.
6. Select the paragraphs below the table (but not a paragraph in the bottom shared border), and then press the **Delete** key. Figure 5-8 shows the table, which now contains six pictures. Notice that the heights of the two rows in the table were adjusted automatically to store the content they contain.

Figure 5-8 **Pictures moved into cells**

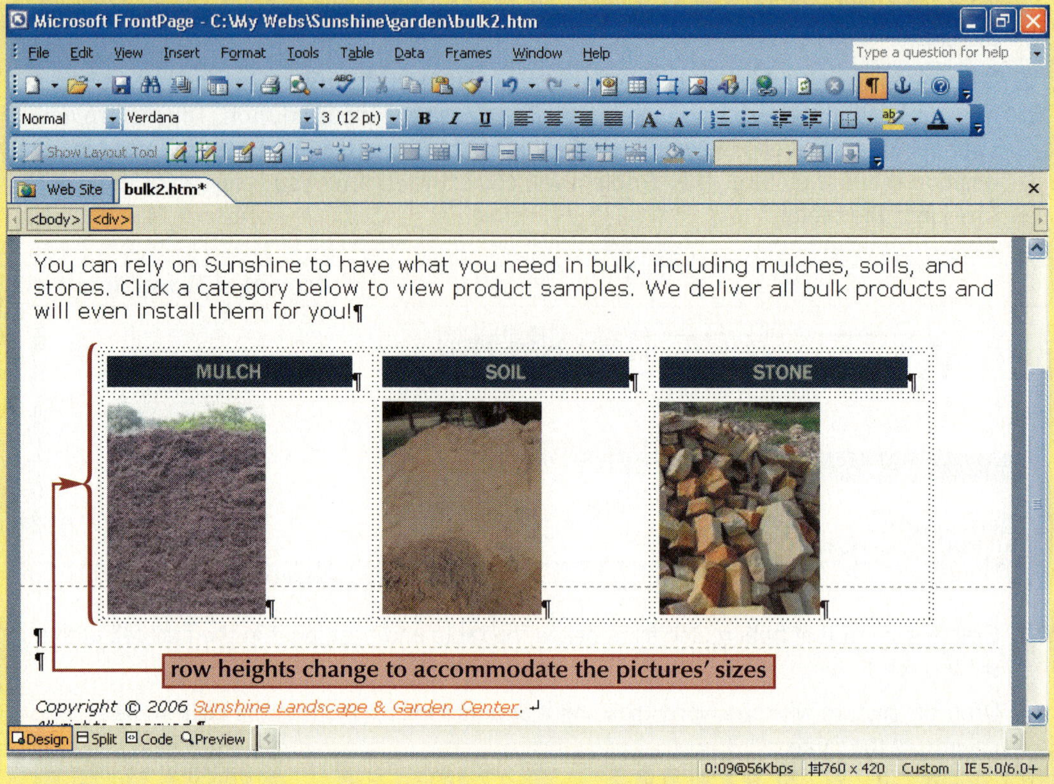

Although the table is centered in the Web page, the pictures are left-aligned within their cells. You can change the cell alignment by using the alignment buttons on the Formatting toolbar, or by opening the Cell Properties dialog box. Because the Cell Properties dialog box contains additional options for working with table cells, you want to show Brett its settings.

Aligning Cells in a Table

In addition to the horizontal alignment of left, right, center, and justified, you can select a vertical alignment of top, middle, baseline, or bottom for cells. These two alignments—horizontal and vertical—are specified using different HTML tags. Middle is the default vertical alignment, and left is the default horizontal alignment. Figure 5-9 shows the different horizontal and vertical alignments you can select for cells.

Vertical and horizontal cell alignments **Figure 5-9**

Align Top Vertical Alignment		Left Horizontal Alignment
Center Vertically (Middle) Alignment		Center Horizontal Alignment
Align Bottom Vertical Alignment		Right Horizontal Alignment
Baseline Vertical Alignment (cells in the same row are vertically aligned so the first text line in each cell has a common baseline)	This is a line of text. This is a line of text.	This cell uses the Justify horizontal alignment and the baseline vertical alignment. Notice that the lines are aligned on the right and left sides of the cell, similar to how articles appear in newspaper or magazine publications.
No baseline alignment	This is a line of text. This is a line of text.	This is a line of text. This is a line of text. Notice that the lines of text in this row are not vertically aligned in the cells.

You align cell contents by selecting the cells and specifying the desired alignment. You can align cells as a group or individually. Unlike a table, which can have only one alignment, the cells in a table can have different alignments to present data in the best manner. In some cases, cell alignment is a matter of personal preference—you might want to center data to make it look better. Numeric values, especially for currency, are usually right-aligned because this is a common practice in accounting. Vertically aligning data is also a matter of personal preference—you can select the vertical alignment that best presents your data.

Because your plan specifies that all cells in the table will have a center alignment, you could select the entire table and change the alignment once. However, you want to show Brett how to select cells, groups of cells, columns, and rows in a table first, so he can use these skills as he works with tables.

To select and align cells in a table:

1. Move the pointer to the left border of the first row in the table so that it changes to a ➡ shape, and then click the left border to select the first row of the table. See Figure 5-10.

Figure 5-10 **Selecting a row**

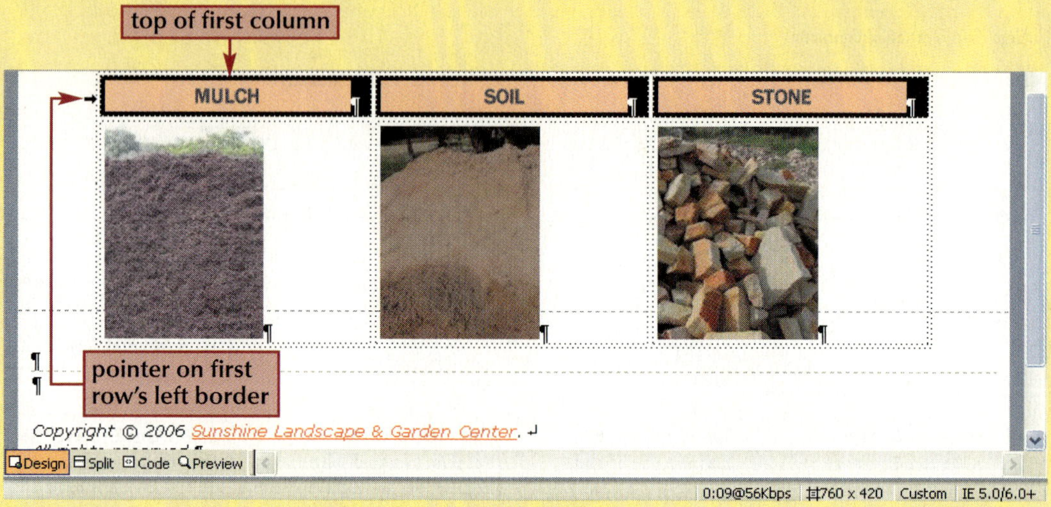

2. Hold down the **Ctrl** key, click ➡ on the border for the second row, and then release the **Ctrl** key. Now the first and second rows are selected.

   You can select sequential columns and rows in one step by dragging the pointer over the rows or columns you want to select. You'll practice this next by selecting the columns.

3. Click the first cell in the first row to deselect the rows, point to the top of the first column of the table so the pointer changes to a ⬇ shape, and then click and hold the left mouse button and drag the ⬇ pointer to the top of the third column. When all three columns are selected, release the mouse button. It doesn't matter which method you use to select all cells in a table; you can accomplish the same task by selecting all of the rows or all of the columns.

4. With all cells selected, right-click any selected cell to open the shortcut menu, and then click **Cell Properties**. The Cell Properties dialog box opens for the group of cells that you selected. See Figure 5-11.

Figure 5-11 **Cell Properties dialog box**

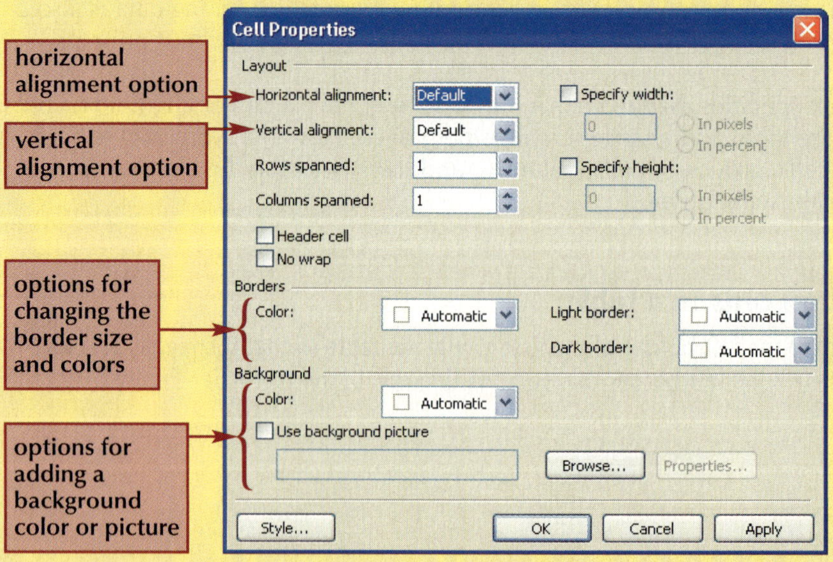

5. Click the **Horizontal alignment** list arrow in the Layout section, and then click **Center**. The data in the selected cells will be centered horizontally.
6. Click the **Vertical alignment** list arrow in the Layout section, and then click **Middle**. The data in the selected cells will use the middle alignment.

   Notice that you can change other values for selected cells, as well. For example, the Borders section includes options to change the color of individual cell borders. The Background section includes options that let you specify a background color or picture to use in individual cells.
7. Click the **OK** button, and then click any cell to deselect the cells. The data in the selected cells changes to a center horizontal alignment and a middle vertical alignment. See Figure 5-12.

Figure 5-12 Table with revised cell alignments

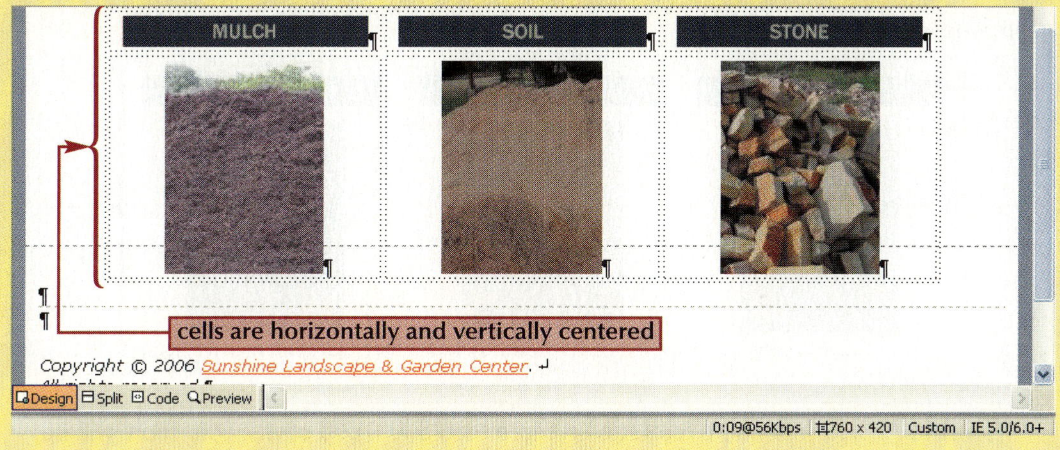

Next, Brett asks if you can format the picture with the word "mulch" on it to open the mulch.htm page.

To format a picture in a cell as a hyperlink:

1. Click the picture with the word "mulch" on it to select it.
2. Click the **Insert Hyperlink** button on the Standard toolbar. The Insert Hyperlink dialog box opens.
3. Make sure that the **Existing File or Web Page** button is selected, scroll down the list of files, click **mulch.htm**, and then click the **OK** button. Now the picture is a hyperlink that will open the mulch.htm Web page. (When you complete the Review Assignments at the end of this tutorial, you will finish creating the hyperlinks for this page.)
4. Save the bulk2.htm page, and then preview it in a browser. Figure 5-13 shows the Bulk Goods Samples page. The cells in the table are center-aligned and the borders of the table and cells are hidden. The table is centered in the Web page and its width is 640 pixels.

Figure 5-13 Completed Bulk Goods Samples page

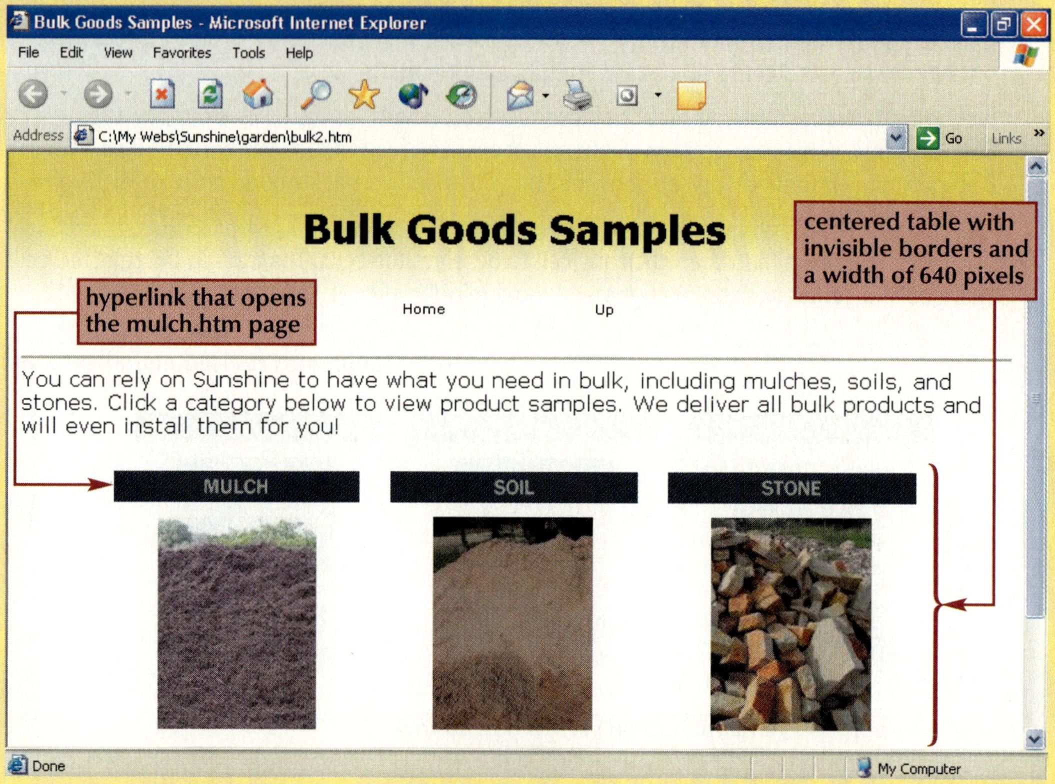

Trouble? If your monitor's resolution is more than 800 × 600 pixels, your table will be the same size but will look much narrower on the page. If your monitor's resolution is 640 × 480 pixels, your table will fill the width of the page.

5. Click the picture with the word "mulch" on it. The Mulches page opens.
6. Close your browser.

Brett likes the new appearance of the Bulk Goods Samples page and now sees how tables are used to organize Web page content. Helen Xiao stops by and mentions that she finished her draft of the new page in the Web site that will feature information about lawn care and common lawn problems. She already sent you a draft of this page via e-mail and asks you to import it into the Web site. You'll need to apply the theme and shared borders to this page, and then add the page to the Web site's navigation structure as a child page of the Garden Center page.

To import the page, apply the theme and shared borders, and add the page to the navigation structure:

1. Display the Folder List, make sure the Web site's root folder is selected, click **File** on the menu bar, click **Import**, click the **Add File** button, open the **Tutorial.05\Tutorial** folder included with your Data Files, double-click the **lawn.htm** file, and then click the **OK** button. The lawn.htm page is added to the Web site.
2. Scroll down the list of files in the Folder List, double-click the **lawn.htm** page to open it in Design view, and then close the Folder List.

3. Click **Format** on the menu bar, and then click **Theme**. The Theme task pane opens.
4. Point to the **Garden Web Site** theme in the Web site default theme section, click the **list arrow** that appears, and then click **Apply to selected page(s)**. The page is formatted by the theme.
5. Close the Theme task pane.
6. Click **Format** on the menu bar, and then click **Shared Borders**. The Shared Borders dialog box opens.
7. Make sure the **Current page** option button is selected, make sure the **Top**, **Left**, and **Bottom** check boxes contain check marks, and then click the **OK** button. Top, left, and bottom shared borders are added to the page. You need to add this page to the navigation structure, however, for these features to be displayed correctly.
8. Click the **Web Site** tab, change to Navigation view, and then display the Folder List.
9. Drag the **lawn.htm** page from the Folder List and position it in the navigation structure as a child page of the Garden Center page and to the right of the Anti-Deer Products page, as shown in Figure 5-14.

Figure 5-14 Imported lawn.htm page added to the navigation structure

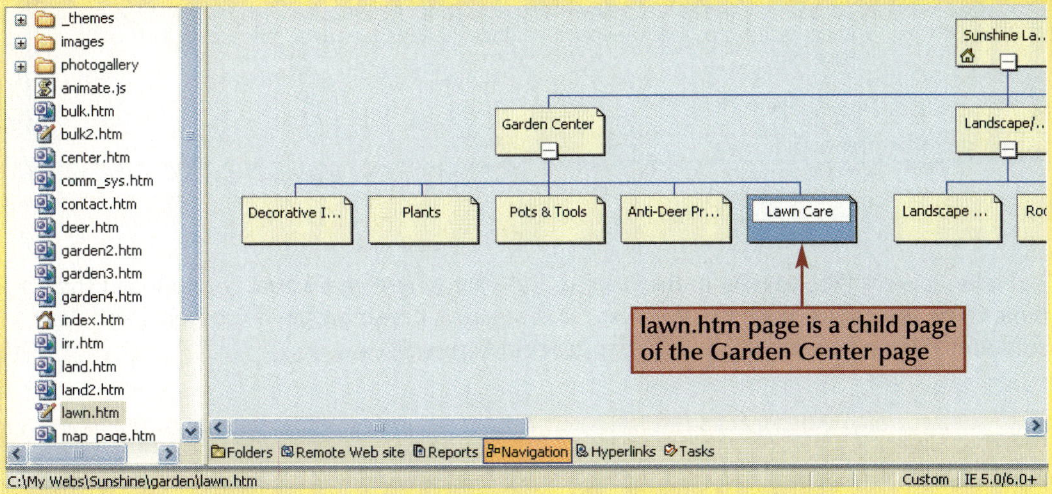

10. Close the Folder List, click the **lawn.htm** tab, and then save the lawn.htm page. The Lawn Care page now has a theme and shared borders. See Figure 5-15.

    Trouble? If a Confirm Save dialog box opens, click the Yes button.

Figure 5-15 **Lawn Care page in Design view**

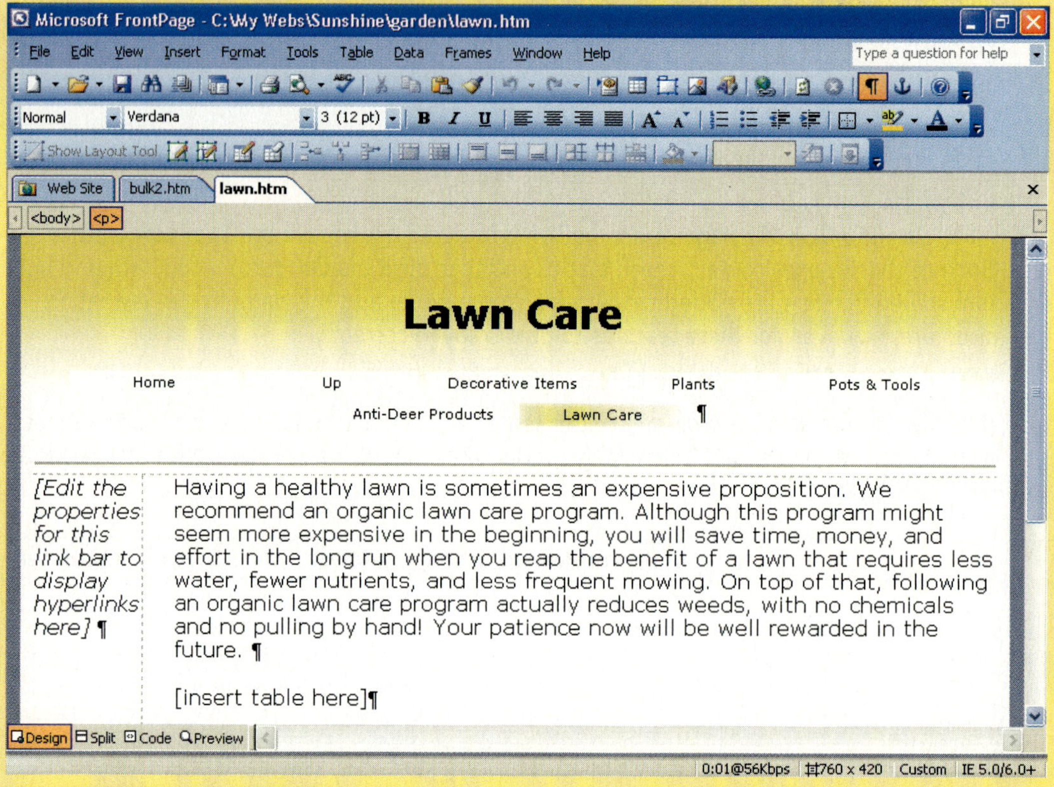

Helen typed placeholders in the page to indicate where she wants you to insert the tables. The first table you'll create is one that presents common lawn problems and their solutions. Helen's sketch of the table appears in Figure 5-16.

Figure 5-16

Sketch of the table with common lawn care problems and solutions

Problem	Occurrence	Symptoms	Treatment
Brown patch	Fall or late spring	Circular areas with brown centers and a yellow to light green outer edge.	Aerate lawn, improve drainage and soil fertility, and apply bacteria that will protect the roots from the fungus.
Take all patch	Summer	Soil disease that is similar in appearance to brown patch, but occurs in the heat of the summer.	Remove thatch buildup, and improve drainage and soil fertility.
Chinch bugs	Summer	Yellow grass that has been watered properly.	Apply insecticides such as pyrethrums or soap sprays until gone.
Grub worms	Summer	Brown grass with no roots that has been watered properly.	Apply beneficial nematodes to control infestation.
Fire ants	Anytime, especially after a rain	Dirt mounds appearing in the turf.	Treat mounds immediately with an approved pesticide.

Creating a Table Using the Insert Table Command

With Helen's sketch in hand, you can create the table. You already showed Brett how to use the Insert Table button on the Standard toolbar to create a table. When you use the Insert Table button grid, you can create a table with the default settings for new tables very quickly. After you create a table, you can use the Table Properties dialog box to make any necessary adjustments to the table's appearance. If you know that the table you want to create will require changes to the default characteristics, you can use the Table menu to create the table and change its characteristics at the same time.

Helen's table has six rows and four columns. To make the appearance of this table consistent with the one you already created in the Bulk Goods Samples page, you'll set the table's alignment to center, the cell padding to 4, and the cell spacing to 3. However, this table requires a border to look like a traditional table. You will use a border size of 2 with the default colors supplied by the Garden Web Site theme you applied to the Web site and a left cell alignment. In addition, because Helen's table contains mostly text, you'll set its width as a percentage of the browser window's width.

To create the table using the Insert Table command:

1. Scroll down the lawn.htm page, and then select the text **[insert table here]** that appears immediately above the bottom shared border. You will insert the table in this location.
2. Click **Table** on the menu bar, point to **Insert**, and then click **Table**. The Insert Table dialog box opens, as shown in Figure 5-17. This dialog box is similar to the Table Properties dialog box that you used to change the properties of the table in the Bulk Goods Samples page.

Figure 5-17 **Insert Table dialog box**

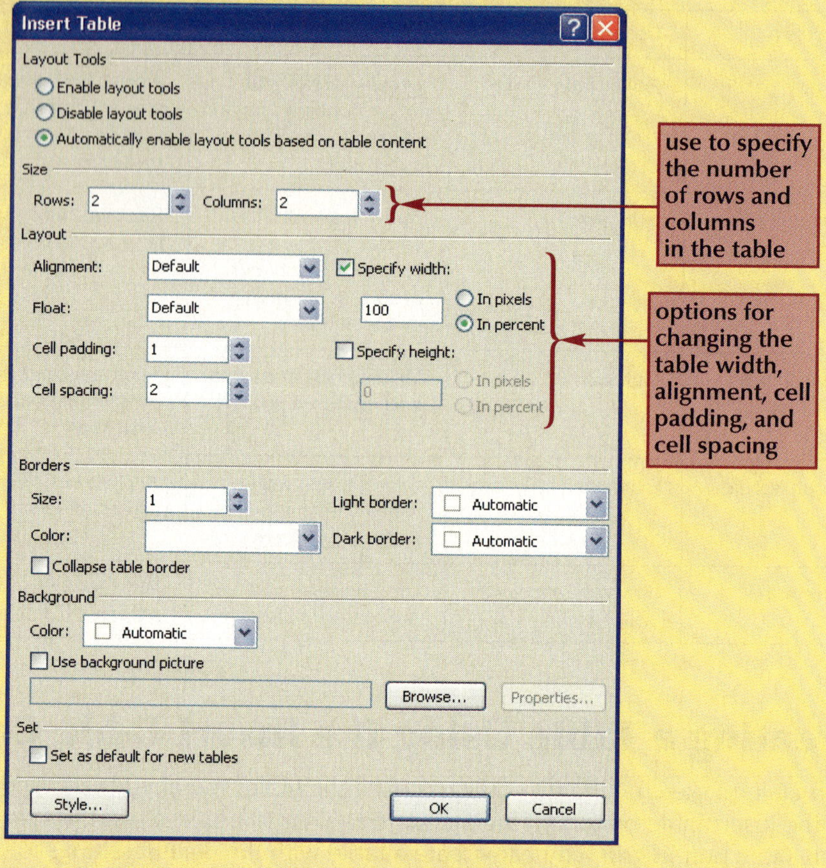

3. Select the value in the Rows list box, type **6**, press the **Tab** key to select the value in the Columns list box, and then type **4**. These settings create a table with six rows and four columns.
4. Click the **Alignment** list arrow in the Layout section, and then click **Center**. This setting will center the table in the Web page.
5. Make sure that the **Specify width** check box contains a check mark, select the value in the text box that appears below the Specify width check box, type **95**, and then make sure the **In percent** option button is selected.
6. Select the value in the Cell padding list box, type **4**, press the **Tab** key to select the value in the Cell spacing list box, and then type **3**. These settings will increase the spacing between and around cells in the table, which will make the table's contents easier to read.
7. Select the value in the Size list box in the Borders section, and then type **2**. Increasing the table's border size creates a thicker border.
8. Click the **OK** button. The Insert Table dialog box closes and a table with the characteristics you specified appears in the Web page. If necessary, scroll down the Web page so you can see the complete table, as shown in Figure 5-18.

Table created in page

Figure 5-18

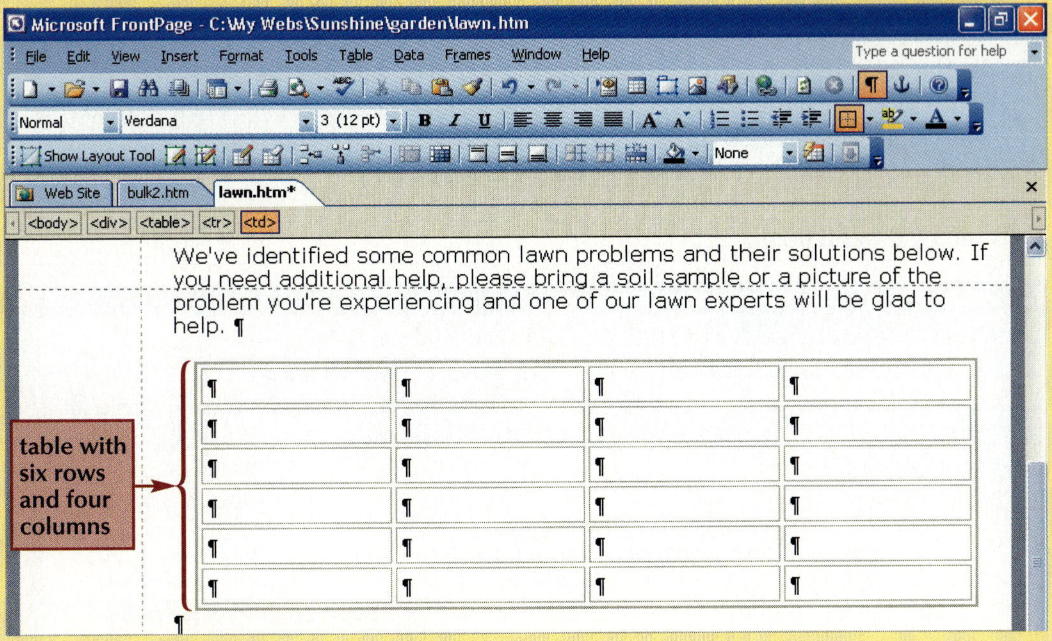

With the table created, you can use Helen's sketch to add data to its cells.

Entering Data in a Table

Entering data in a table in a Web page is similar to entering table data in a Word document or in an Excel worksheet. You position the insertion point by clicking a cell and then type the data. You move the insertion point into another cell by clicking the cell or by pressing the appropriate arrow keys or the Tab key to move to the desired cell.

When your table contains repetitive data, you can type the data once and then use the Fill Down or Fill Right buttons on the Tables toolbar to copy and paste one value into adjacent cells. You'll begin by adding the text for the column headings, which appear in the first row of the table.

To enter data in a table:

1. Click the cell in row 1, column 1, and then type **Problem**. As you type, the width of the first column increases.

   Trouble? If you aren't sure where to enter the column heading in the table, refer to the sketch shown in Figure 5-16.

2. Press the **Tab** key to move to the cell in row 1, column 2, and then type **Occurrence**.
3. Press the **Tab** key, type **Symptoms**, press the **Tab** key, type **Treatment**, and then press the **Tab** key again. The first row contains data, and the insertion point moves to the first cell in the second row.
4. Type **Brown patch**, press the **down** arrow key ↓, type **Take all patch**, press ↓, and then type the following values in the remaining cells in the first column: **Chinch bugs**, **Grub worms**, and **Fire ants**.

5. Click the cell in row 2, column 2, type **Fall or late spring**, press ↓, and then type **Summer**. Instead of typing the value "Summer" in the cells in rows 4 and 5, you can use the Fill Down button to copy the value in row 3 into rows 4 and 5.
6. Use the pointer to select the cells in rows 3, 4, and 5 of column 2, as shown in Figure 5-19. Notice that the Fill Down button on the Tables toolbar becomes active when you select cells in a column. You can also copy cells to the right of a cell; when you select cells to the right, the Fill Right button on the Tables toolbar becomes active.

Figure 5-19 **Cells selected to fill down**

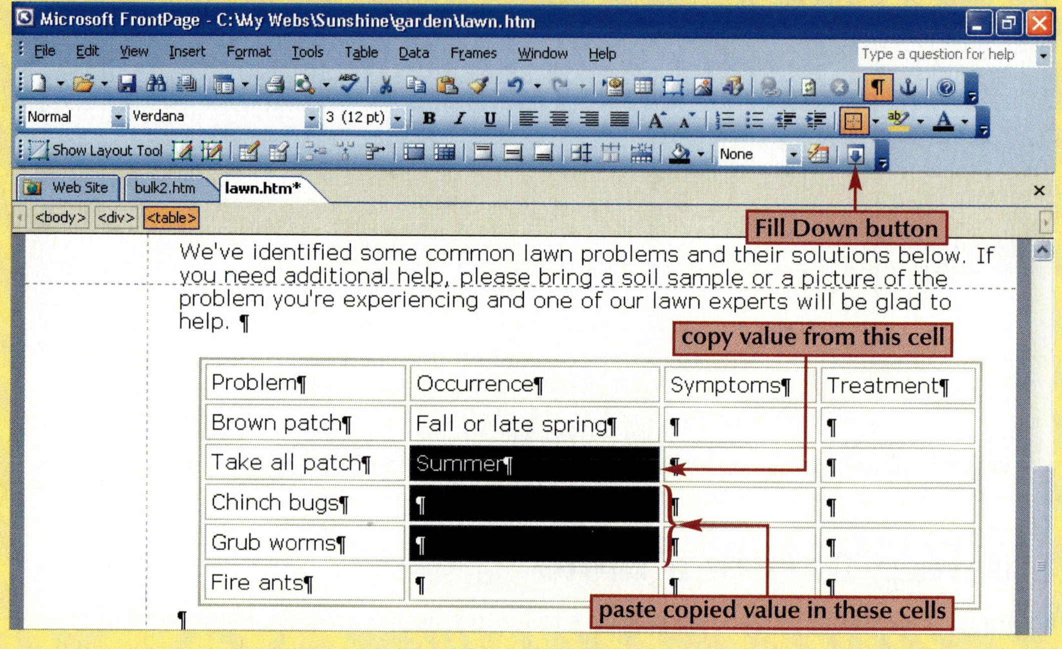

7. Click the **Fill Down** button on the Tables toolbar. The value "Summer" is entered in the selected cells.
8. Click the last cell in the second column, and then type **Anytime, especially after a rain**.
9. Use Figure 5-20 to enter the data in the rest of the table. Press the **Tab** key after typing the data in a cell to move to the next cell. Do not press the Tab key after typing the data in the last cell in the table or you will create a new row.

Table with data entered **Figure 5-20**

Problem	Occurrence	Symptoms	Treatment
Brown patch	Fall or late spring	Circular areas with brown centers and a yellow to light green outer edge.	Aerate lawn, improve drainage and soil fertility, and apply bacteria that will protect the roots from the fungus.
Take all patch	Summer	Soil disease that is similar in appearance to brown patch, but occurs in the heat of the summer.	Remove thatch buildup, and improve drainage and soil fertility.
Chinch bugs	Summer	Yellow grass that has been watered properly.	Apply insecticides such as pyrethrums or soap sprays until gone.
Grub worms	Summer	Brown grass with no roots that has been watered properly.	Apply beneficial nematodes to control infestation.
Fire ants	Anytime, especially after a rain	Dirt mounds appearing in the turf.	Treat mounds immediately with an approved pesticide.

Trouble? Don't worry if the lines in your table wrap differently than those shown in Figure 5-20. The appearance of data depends on many variables, including your monitor's resolution.

10. Save the lawn.htm page.

Helen likes the table's appearance, but wants to add a column to the table that identifies the cause of the problem. To make this change, you'll need to add a column to the table. She also wants to create a row at the top of the table that identifies the nursery's name when the table is printed. To make this change, you'll need to add a row at the top of the table.

Inserting Columns and Rows in a Table

After creating a table, you can insert additional rows and columns as needed, either before or after entering data in the table's cells.

Reference Window

Inserting a Column in a Table

- Click any cell in the column to the left of which you want to insert the new column, and then click the Insert Columns button on the Tables toolbar.

or

- Click a cell adjacent to where you want to insert the new column, click Table on the menu bar, point to Insert, and then click Rows or Columns to open the Insert Rows or Columns dialog box.
- Click the Columns option button, and then enter the number of columns to insert in the Number of columns text box.
- Click the Left of selection option button to insert the new column(s) to the left of the currently selected column, or click the Right of selection option button to insert the new column(s) to the right of the currently selected column.
- Click the OK button.

You'll start by adding a new column to the table. Helen wants the new column to appear between the Symptoms and Treatment columns.

To insert a column in the table:

1. Click the last cell in the first row, which contains the value "Treatment." When you insert the new column, it will appear to the left of the selected column.
2. Click the **Insert Columns** button on the Tables toolbar. A new column is added to the left of the Treatment column. The new column's width is very narrow. When you begin typing data in it, its width will increase automatically.
3. Use Figure 5-21 to add the content to the cells in the new column you added.

Figure 5-21 Data entered into the Causes column

Problem	Occurrence	Symptoms	Causes	Treatment
Brown patch	Fall or late spring	Circular areas with brown centers and a yellow to light green outer edge.	Poor drainage, soil compression, and overwatering.	Aerate lawn, improve drainage and soil fertility, and apply bacteria that will protect the roots from the fungus.
Take all patch	Summer	Soil disease that is similar in appearance to brown patch, but occurs in the heat of the summer.	Imbalanced soil fertility, excessive herbicide use, and overwatering.	Remove thatch buildup, and improve drainage and soil fertility.
Chinch bugs	Summer	Yellow grass that has been watered properly.	Infestation by adult chinch bugs.	Apply insecticides such as pyrethrums or soap sprays until gone.
Grub worms	Summer	Brown grass with no roots that has been watered properly.	Infestation by grub worm larvae.	Apply beneficial nematodes to control infestation.
Fire ants	Anytime, especially after a rain	Dirt mounds appearing in the turf.	Infestation by a fire ant colony.	Treat mounds immediately with an approved pesticide.

4. Save the page.

You insert a row using a similar procedure.

Inserting a Row in a Table

Reference Window

- Click any cell in the row above which you want to insert the new row, and then click the Insert Rows button on the Tables toolbar.

or

- Click a cell adjacent to where you want to insert the new row, click Table on the menu bar, point to Insert, and then click Rows or Columns to open the Insert Rows or Columns dialog box.
- Click the Rows option button, and then enter the number of rows to insert in the Number of rows text box.
- Click the Above selection option button to insert the new row(s) above the currently selected row, or click the Below selection option button to insert the new row(s) below the currently selected row.
- Click the OK button.

Helen asks you to insert the new row at the top of the table.

To insert a row in a table:

1. Click any cell in the first row. When you insert the new row, it will appear above the first row.
2. Click the **Insert Rows** button on the Tables toolbar. A new row is inserted, as shown in Figure 5-22.

Figure 5-22 **Table with new row added**

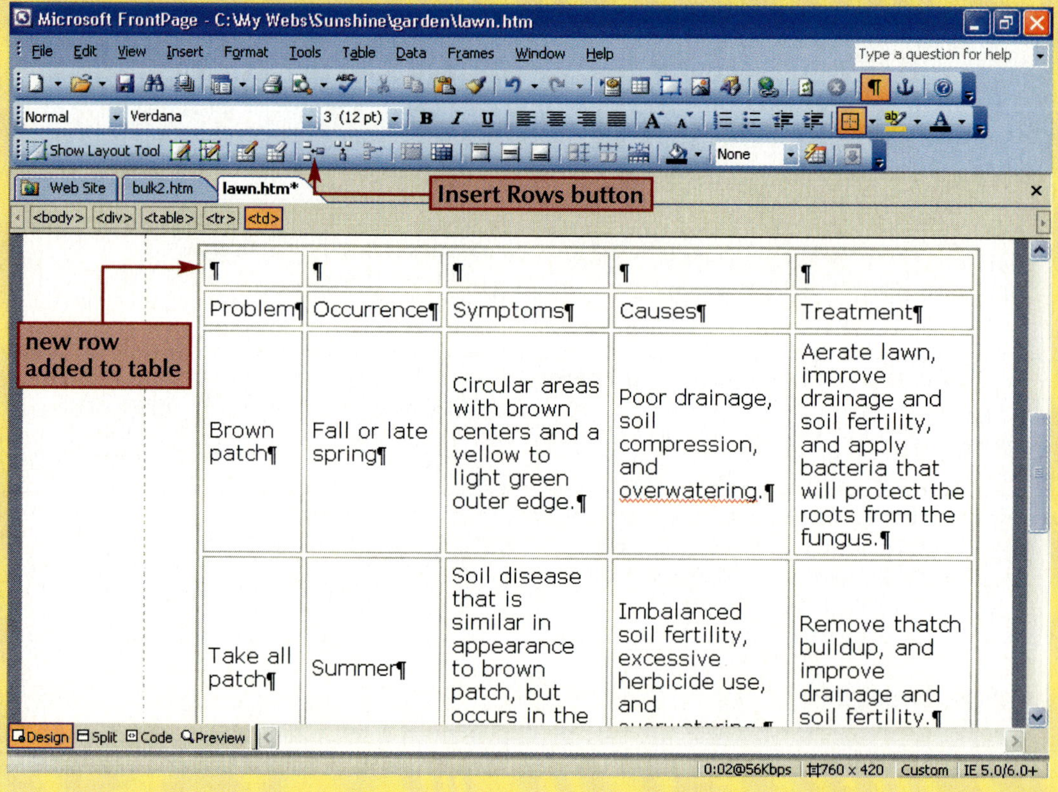

Helen asks if you can format the cells in the new row so there are no gridlines between the individual cells. You tell her that you can do this by merging the five cells in the first row to become a single cell.

Merging Table Cells

You can arrange a group of selected cells to span a row or column by merging them into a single cell. When you **merge** a group of cells, the resulting cell spans multiple columns or rows.

Merging Table Cells

Reference Window

- Select the cells to be merged, and then click the Merge Cells button on the Tables toolbar.

or

- Click the Eraser button on the Tables toolbar, and then use the pointer to erase the cell border that separates the cells to be merged.

You'll show Helen two methods for merging cells so she sees how to use each one. First, you'll merge the first two cells in the first row using a toolbar button, and then you'll use the pointer to erase the borders between the third, fourth, and fifth cells in the first row.

To merge cells:

1. Click the cell in row 1, column 1, press and hold the **Shift** key, click the cell in row 1, column 2, and then release the mouse button and the **Shift** key to select cells 1 and 2 in row 1. See Figure 5-23.

Figure 5-23 Merging cells in a table

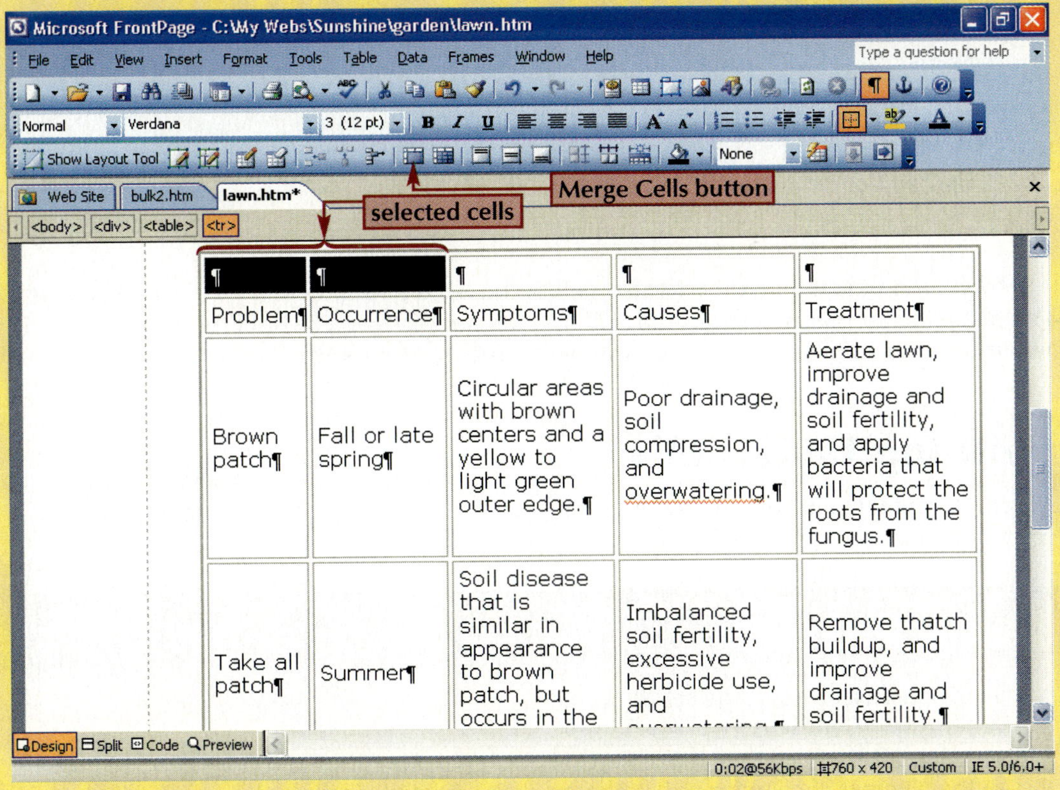

2. Click the **Merge Cells** button on the Tables toolbar, and then click the cell to the right of the selected merged cell to deselect the merged cell. The cells that were in columns 1 and 2 are joined to become a single cell.

   Now, you want to show Helen how to use the Eraser.

3. Click the **Eraser** button on the Tables toolbar to select this tool. The pointer changes to a shape when you move it over the Web page.

4. With the pointer positioned over the first cell in the first row (the merged cell), click and hold the mouse button, and then drag the pointer across the right border of the merged cell. The border turns red, as shown in Figure 5-24.

Figure 5-24 **Merging cells using the pointer**

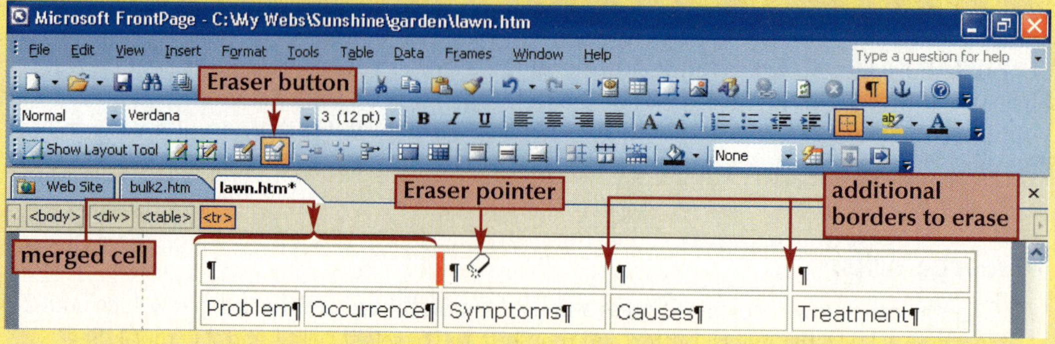

5. Release the mouse button to erase the cell border.

   Trouble? If you erase the wrong border, click the Undo button on the Standard toolbar to undo your change, and then repeat Steps 4 and 5.

6. Repeat Steps 4 and 5 to erase the borders between the remaining cells in the first row. Now the first row contains a single cell.
7. Click on the Tables toolbar to turn off the Eraser.
8. Click the **Center** button on the Formatting toolbar, and then type **Sunshine Landscape & Garden Center** in the merged cell.

Helen wants to add another merged cell to the table to display the text, "Come see us if you're having problems with your lawn!" You tell her that you can split the first row into two rows, instead of adding another row and merging its cells.

Splitting Table Cells

When you **split** a cell, you are dividing a selected cell or group of cells into two or more rows or columns.

Reference Window | **Splitting Table Cells**

- Use the pointer to select the cell(s) to split.
- Click the Split Cells button on the Tables toolbar.
- In the Split Cells dialog box, click the Split into columns or Split into rows option button.
- Use the Number of columns or Number of rows list box to indicate the number of columns or rows to split.
- Click the OK button.

You'll split the cell in row 1 into two rows.

To split a cell:

1. Make sure the insertion point is positioned in the cell in the first row (the merged cell).
2. Click the **Split Cells** button on the Tables toolbar. The Split Cells dialog box opens. See Figure 5-25.

Split Cells dialog box **Figure 5-25**

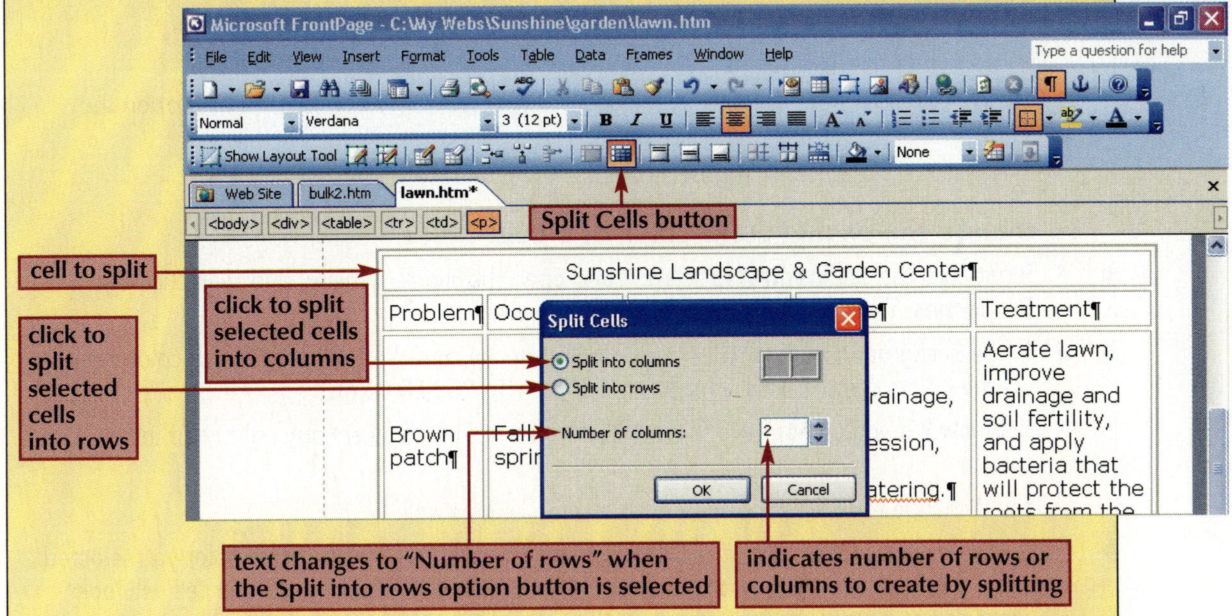

3. Click the **Split into rows** option button, make sure that **2** appears in the Number of rows list box, and then click the **OK** button. The Split Cells dialog box closes, and the table now contains a new row.
4. Click in the new row, click the **Center** button on the Formatting toolbar, and then type **Come see us if you're having problems with your lawn!** Figure 5-26 shows the revised table.

Revised table **Figure 5-26**

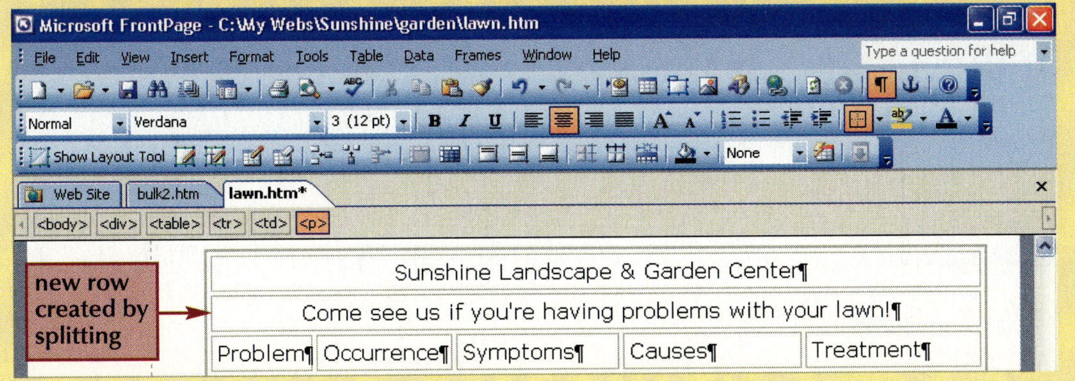

Helen likes the table's new organization. She asks if you can format the cell in the second row with a background color so its message stands out better.

Reference Window

Changing the Background Color or Picture in a Table or Cell

- Right-click anywhere in the table to open the shortcut menu, click Table Properties to change the background color of the table or click Cell Properties to change the background color of a selected cell, and then click the Color list arrow in the Background section to select a background color.

or

- Click the Use background picture check box to select it, and then click the Browse button to select a file to use as the table's background picture.

To add the message to the cell in the second row, you'll select the cell and open the Cell Properties dialog box.

To change the background color of a cell:

1. Right-click the cell in row 2 to select it and open the shortcut menu, and then click **Cell Properties**. The Cell Properties dialog box opens.
2. In the Background section, click the **Color** list arrow, and then click the fourth color in the Theme Colors section. This color has the ScreenTip RGB(EB,B6,6C).

   Trouble? If you do not have the color specified in Step 2, select any light color in the color palette.

   You'll change the border color for the selected cell, as well.
3. In the Borders section, click the **Color** list arrow, and then click the same color you selected in Step 2. By changing the border color to match the background color, the cell will look like it has no borders because they are the same color as the background.
4. Click the **OK** button. The Cell Properties dialog box closes and the cell in the second row has a background color. Because you formatted this cell's border using the same color as the background, the border seems to disappear. See Figure 5-27.

Figure 5-27 Background color added to cell

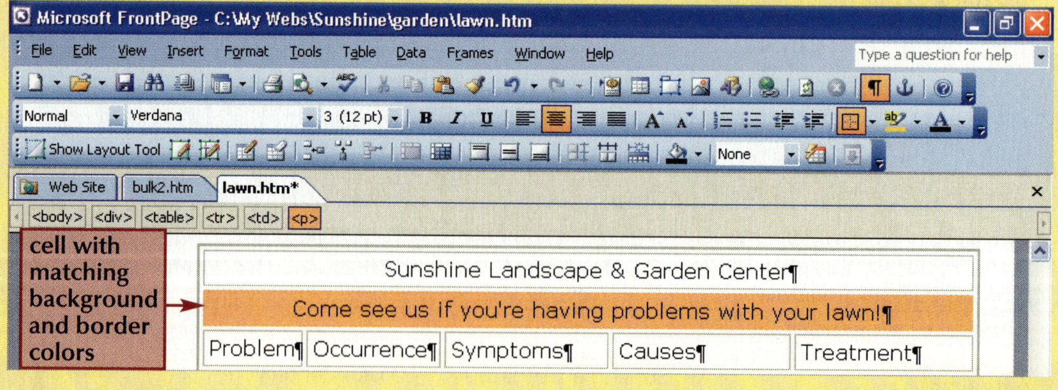

5. Save the page.

Helen likes the table's overall appearance but decides that the data in the Occurrence column isn't very usable. She asks you to delete this column from the table.

Deleting Cells from a Table

Even when you sketch a table before inserting it in a Web page, sometimes you might need to add or delete cells, including entire rows and columns, to create the right table for your data. The process of deleting cells is straightforward. First, you select the cell, row, or column that you want to delete or drag the pointer over a group of cells to select them. If you need to select additional cells, rows, or columns at the same time, press and hold the Shift key while you select them. These selection methods are similar to how you would select table cells in Word. After selecting the cells, click the Delete Cells button on the Tables toolbar.

Deleting Cells from a Table

Reference Window

- Select a single cell, group of cells, row, or column.
- Click the Delete Cells button on the Tables toolbar.

Helen's request is to delete the cells in the Occurrence column. You'll select these cells and then delete them.

To delete cells from a table:

1. Click the cell in row 3, column 2 (which contains the word "Occurrence").
2. Scroll down the table as necessary so you can see the last row, press and hold the **Shift** key, click the second cell in the last row of the table (which contains the phrase "Anytime, especially after a rain"), and then release the **Shift** key. Six cells in the second column of the table are selected.
3. Click the **Delete Cells** button on the Tables toolbar. The selected cells are deleted from the table.

After deleting the cells, Helen asks if you can resize the columns in the table. There are two methods for resizing rows and columns. The first method uses the pointer and the second method uses a toolbar button.

Resizing Rows and Columns

When you enter data in a cell, FrontPage automatically increases the size of the cell and the column in which it appears to accommodate the text that you entered. You can also manually resize a table's rows and columns to affect the overall appearance of your table.

The easiest way to resize a column is to use the pointer—you drag the column's right border to the left to decrease the column's width, or drag the column's right border to the right to increase the column's width. You can also use the pointer to drag the bottom border of a row up to decrease the row's height or down to increase its height.

Reference Window

Resizing a Row or Column in a Table Using the Mouse

- Select the row or column that you want to resize.
- For a row, drag the bottom border down to increase the row's height, or drag the bottom border up to decrease the row's height.

or

- For a column, drag the right border to the left to decrease the column's width, or drag the right border to the right to increase the column's width.

You'll start by resizing the first column to make it slightly wider.

To resize a column using the mouse:

1. Select the first column in the table by clicking the first cell in the third row, scrolling down to the first cell in the last row, pressing and holding the **Shift** key, clicking the first cell in the last row, and then releasing the **Shift** key.
2. Position the pointer on the right border of the selected column so it changes to a ↔ shape, and then click and hold down the mouse button as you drag the right border of the selected column to the right. When the dotted vertical line is positioned as shown in Figure 5-28, release the mouse button.

Figure 5-28 Changing a column's width

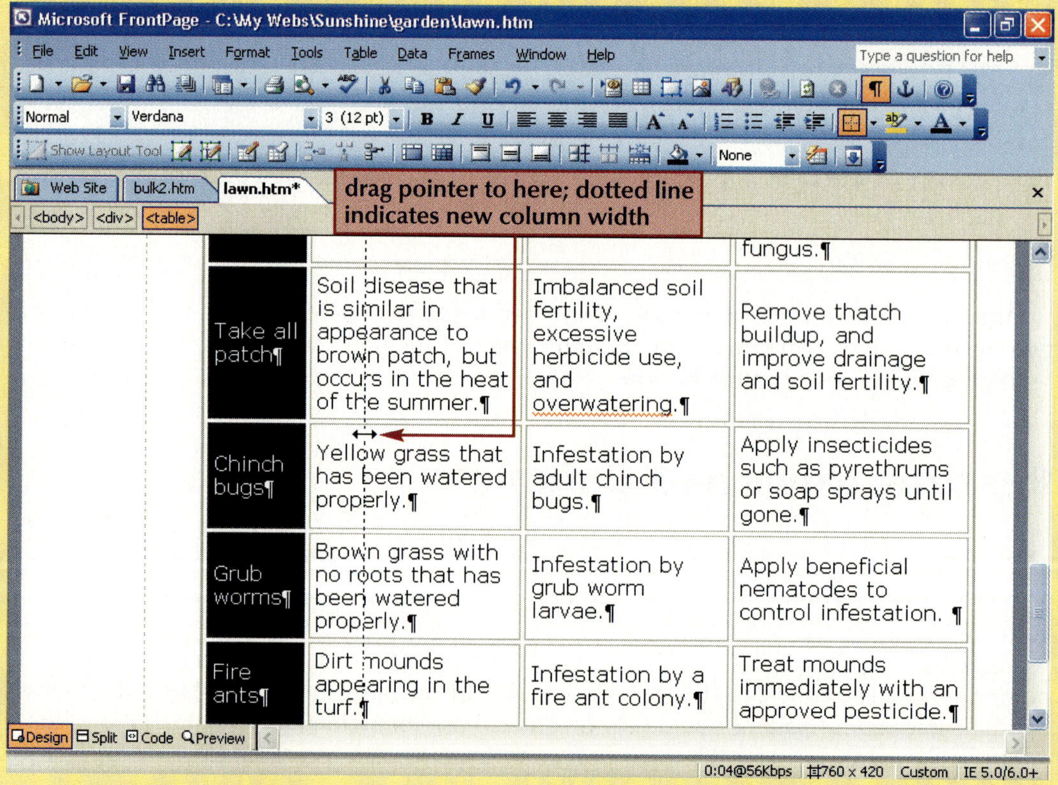

Trouble? If you do not see the dotted vertical line, drag the pointer to approximately the same location shown in Figure 5-28 and then release the mouse button.

3. Click the cell in row 3, column 1, to deselect the first column.

As you resized the first column, the width of the second column in the table decreased. You can select the second, third, and fourth columns as a group and use the Distribute Columns Evenly button on the Tables toolbar to change them to have equal widths, which is called distributing the columns evenly.

To distribute the columns evenly:

1. Click the cell in row 3, column 2, scroll down to the last row, press and hold the **Shift** key, click the cell in the last row and last column (row 8, column 4), and then release the **Shift** key. The cells are selected.
2. Click the **Distribute Columns Evenly** button on the Tables toolbar. The cells in the second, third, and fourth columns have equal widths.
3. Click the cell in row 1 to deselect the selected cells.

   When you distribute the columns evenly, FrontPage changes the width setting of the table to pixels. If you want to accept this change, you don't need to do anything. However, if you want to use a percentage as the table width, you need to reset the width property.
4. Right-click any cell in the table to open the shortcut menu, and then click **Table Properties**. The Table Properties dialog box opens. Notice that the Specify width setting changed to use pixels.
5. Select the value in the Specify width text box, type **95**, click the **In percent** option button, and then click the **OK** button. The table width is set to a percentage, but the table looks the same.

You can select rows and use the Distribute Rows Evenly button on the Tables toolbar to change the heights of a group of selected rows to the same measurement as well.

To help identify the table in the Web page, you suggest adding a table caption to it.

Adding a Table Caption

A **table caption** is a title that appears either above or below a table. It can contain one or more lines of text. Although the table caption appears to be a part of the table, it actually resides outside of the table's border and is created by a separate HTML tag. When you insert a caption, its default location is above the table. You can relocate the caption by clicking the Caption Properties command on the table's shortcut menu.

Adding a Table Caption

Reference Window

- Click anywhere in the table to select it.
- Click Table on the menu bar, point to Insert, and then click Caption.
- Type the caption at the location of the insertion point.

Because this page will contain two tables, Helen agrees that adding a caption to the tables will help clarify their functions. She asks you to add the caption above the table.

To add a table caption:

1. Click **Table** on the menu bar, point to **Insert**, and then click **Caption**. A new line appears above the table, and the insertion point moves to the new line. This new line is the table's caption. Although the caption *looks* like a paragraph in Design view, it is formatted as an HTML caption and not as a new paragraph.
2. Type **Common Lawn Problems and Solutions**.
3. Select the **Common Lawn Problems and Solutions** caption, and then click the **Bold** button **B** on the Formatting toolbar to change the caption to bold text.
4. Click anywhere in the caption to deselect it.

After adding a caption to a table, you can change its properties. For example, you might want to display the caption on two lines, or place one or more blank lines between the caption and the table. You can press Shift + Enter to create a new line in a caption. Another way to change an existing caption's properties is to use the settings in the Caption Properties dialog box.

Helen wants to see how the caption would look below the table.

To change caption properties:

1. Right-click the **Common Lawn Problems and Solutions** caption to open the shortcut menu, and then click **Caption Properties** to open that dialog box. See Figure 5-29.

Figure 5-29 **Caption Properties dialog box**

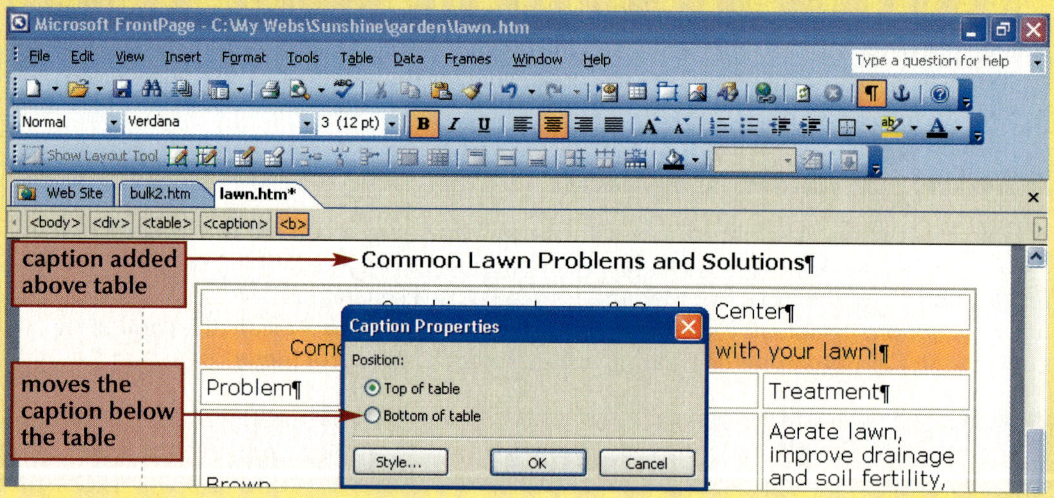

2. Click the **Bottom of table** option button, and then click the **OK** button. Now the caption appears below the table. (You might need to scroll down the table to see the caption below it.)

   Helen prefers the caption above the table, so you will undo this action.
3. Click the **Undo** button on the Standard toolbar. The caption appears above the table again.
4. Save the lawn.htm page.

Helen likes the appearance and content of the table. Before finishing it, you want to show her how to apply a Table AutoFormat to the table.

Applying a Table AutoFormat

After you create a table, you might decide to use the Table Properties and Cell Properties dialog boxes to enhance its appearance with a background color and complementary cell and table border colors. You can also format your table with a **Table AutoFormat**, which is a predefined combination of colors, colored borders, and other special effects that enhance a table's appearance. A Table AutoFormat might be simple, colorful, classic, or three-dimensional. After applying an AutoFormat, you can use the Table Properties and Cell Properties dialog boxes to change the AutoFormat to customize your table's appearance even further.

Applying a Table AutoFormat

Reference Window

- Click anywhere in the table to select it, click the list arrow for the Table AutoFormat Combo button on the Tables toolbar, and then select an AutoFormat in the list.

or

- Click anywhere in the table to select it, and then click the Table AutoFormat button on the Tables toolbar. The Table AutoFormat dialog box opens.
- Select an AutoFormat in the Formats list.
- If necessary, change the options in the Formats to apply and Apply special formats sections.
- Click the OK button.

Helen is curious to see how a Table AutoFormat might change the table's appearance. You will show her several samples to see if she likes any of them.

To apply a Table AutoFormat to the table:

1. Click any cell in the table to select the table, click the **list arrow** for the Table AutoFormat Combo button None on the Tables toolbar, and then click **Simple 3**. As shown in Figure 5-30, the table's format changes to use the styles created by the Simple 3 Table AutoFormat.

Figure 5-30 **Simple 3 Table AutoFormat applied to table**

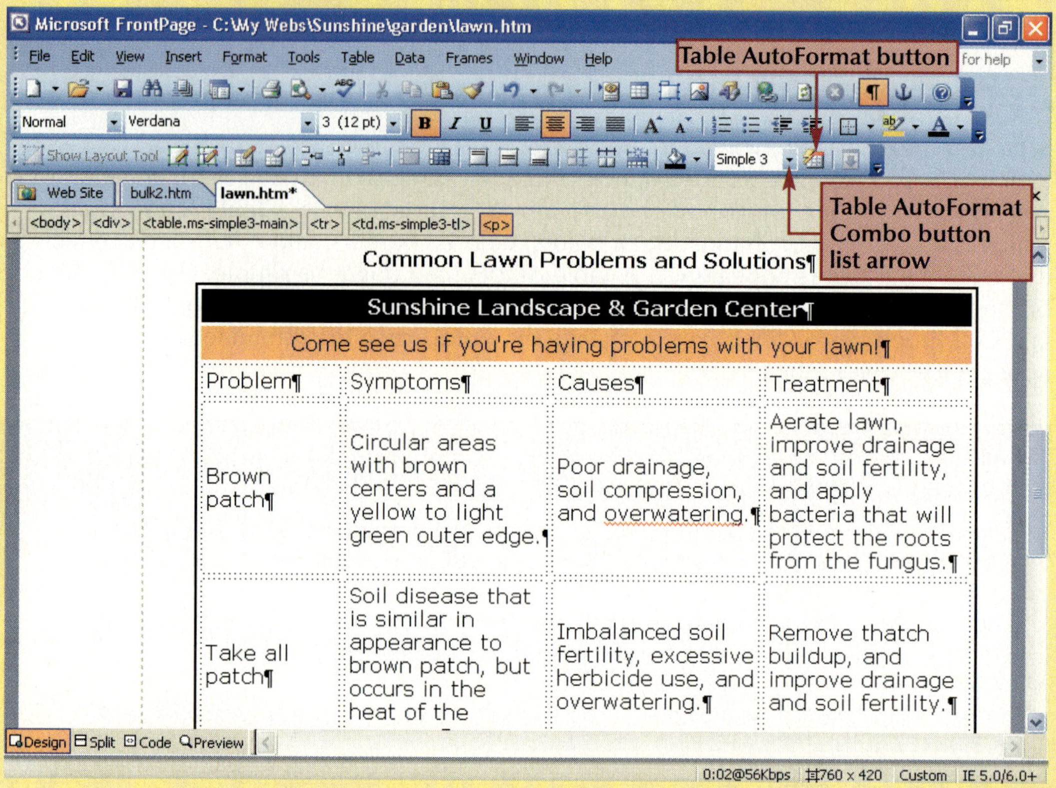

You could continue clicking the Table AutoFormat Combo button list arrow and selecting different formats. However, an easier way to find a suitable Table AutoFormat is to use the Table AutoFormat dialog box.

2. Click the **Table AutoFormat** button on the Tables toolbar. The Table AutoFormat dialog box opens. See Figure 5-31.

Figure 5-31 **Table AutoFormat dialog box**

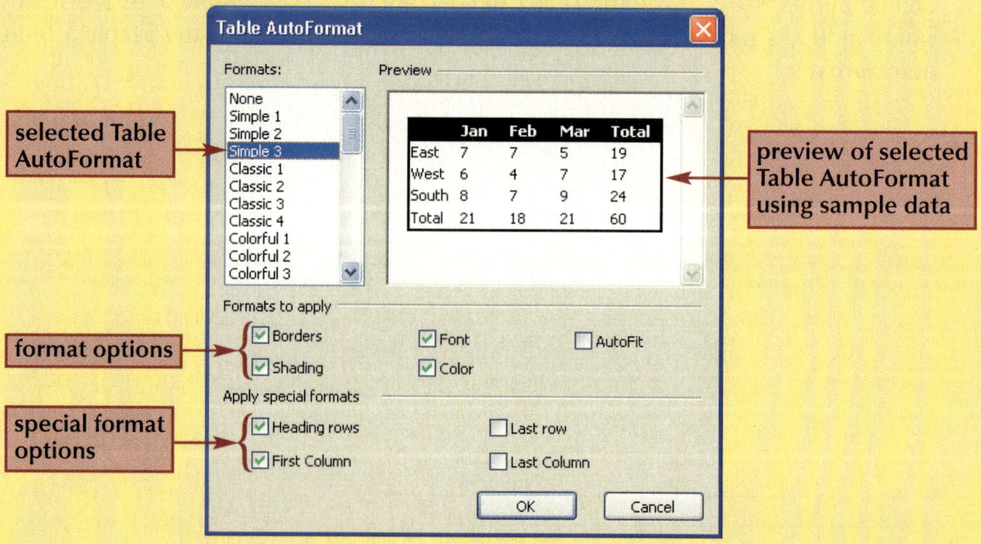

The Simple 3 format is selected, and a preview of its appearance is shown in the Preview box. Notice that you can also use this dialog box to control which formats are applied to your table. For example, deselecting a check box in the Formats to apply section omits those elements from the AutoFormat. In addition, you might want to apply or deselect special formats in your tables. A heading row is the first row in a table; it usually contains column headings. The table's first column usually contains row headings. You can also apply special formats to the last row and last column in a table when these table elements require special formatting.

Helen wants to see whether any of the AutoFormats are more appealing than the Simple 3 format that you applied.

3. Click **Classic 3** in the Formats list. The Preview box shows the appearance for the Classic 3 format. This format's dark background might make the page difficult to read. In addition, the AutoFormat's color scheme doesn't match well with the current colors in the Garden Web Site theme.
4. Scroll down the Formats list and click **3D Effects 2**. This format uses a background color with a raised effect to distinguish alternating rows in the table.
5. Scroll up the Formats list and click **Colorful 2**. This AutoFormat complements the colors in the Garden Web Site theme, so Helen asks you to apply it.
6. Click the **OK** button. The table now uses the styles from the Colorful 2 Table AutoFormat. See Figure 5-32.

Figure 5-32 **Colorful 2 Table AutoFormat applied to table**

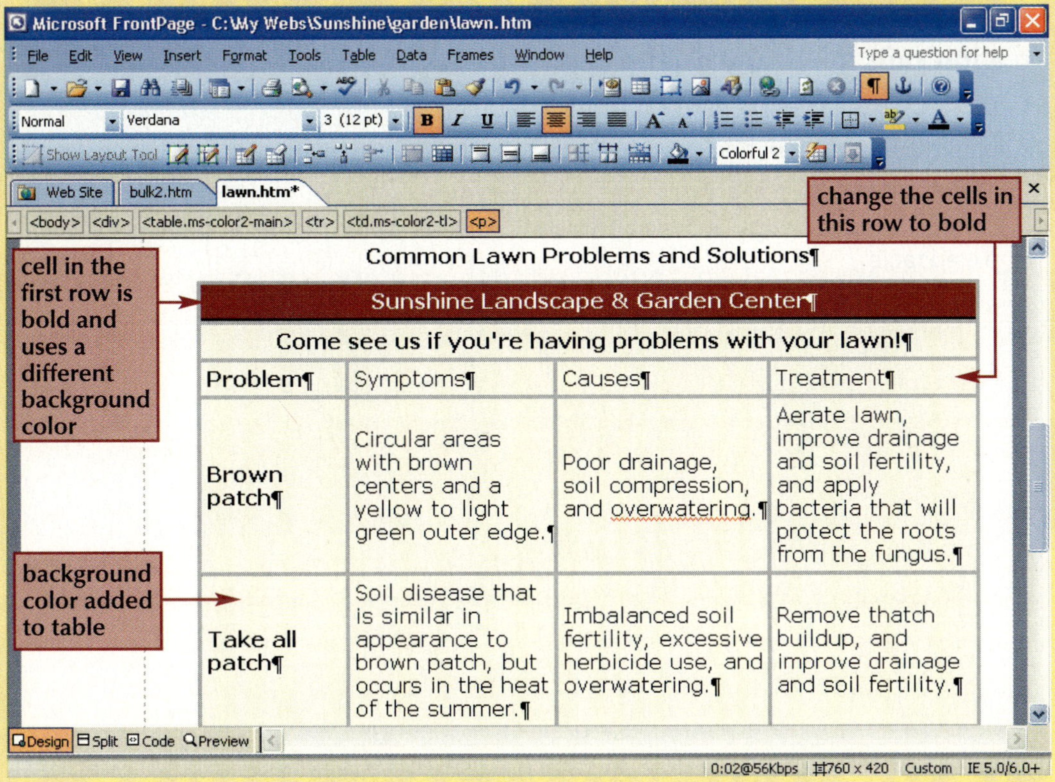

The AutoFormat changed the first cell in each row to bold. In addition, the background color from the Table AutoFormat replaced the one you created in the cell in the second row. To improve on this style, you'll manually change the column headings, which appear in the third row, to bold.

7. Select the third row in the table, and then click the **Bold** button on the Formatting toolbar. The column headings are now bold.
8. Save the page.

Now that you've completed the table, you can view it in a browser.

To view the table in a browser:

1. Click the **Preview** button on the Standard toolbar. If necessary, scroll down the page to see the table. Notice the appearance of the caption and the formatting applied by the Table AutoFormat.
2. Close your browser.

Helen wants to make one final change to the table. She asks you to change the vertical alignment of the cells in rows 4 through 8 so that the text in each cell starts at the top of the cell instead of being vertically centered in the cell.

To align cells vertically on the top:

1. Use the pointer to select rows 4 through 8.
2. Click the **Align Top** button on the Tables toolbar. The selected cells are aligned vertically at the top of the cells.
3. Save the lawn.htm page, and then preview it in your browser. Figure 5-33 shows the completed table.

Figure 5-33 Completed table

Common Lawn Problems and Solutions

Sunshine Landscape & Garden Center			
Come see us if you're having problems with your lawn!			
Problem	**Symptoms**	**Causes**	**Treatment**
Brown patch	Circular areas with brown centers and a yellow to light green outer edge.	Poor drainage, soil compression, and overwatering.	Aerate lawn, improve drainage and soil fertility, and apply bacteria that will protect the roots from the fungus.
Take all patch	Soil disease that is similar in appearance to brown patch, but occurs in the heat of the summer.	Imbalanced soil fertility, excessive herbicide use, and overwatering.	Remove thatch buildup, and improve drainage and soil fertility.
Chinch bugs	Yellow grass that has been watered properly.	Infestation by adult chinch bugs.	Apply insecticides such as pyrethrums or soap sprays until gone.
Grub worms	Brown grass with no roots that has been watered properly.	Infestation by grub worm larvae.	Apply beneficial nematodes to control infestation.
Fire ants	Dirt mounds appearing in the turf.	Infestation by a fire ant colony.	Treat mounds immediately with an approved pesticide.

bold column headings

cells aligned vertically at the top

Trouble? If you are viewing the table at 1024 × 768 resolution or higher, the spacing in your cells might differ. This difference causes no problems.

4. Close your browser.

If you are more comfortable creating a table using a spreadsheet program (such as Excel) or a word processor (such as Word), you can create a table in another program and then insert the file in the Web page. FrontPage will recognize the table and convert its content and format to HTML tags. The HTML document that FrontPage produces for a table originally created in another program is almost the same, and you can use the tools in FrontPage to edit the inserted table as if you had originally created it using FrontPage.

Viewing HTML Tags for a Table

When you create a table in a Web page, whether using FrontPage or another program, you create a complex HTML document. For example, the <table> and </table> tags specify the beginning and end of the table. The <tr> and </tr> (table row) tags indicate the beginning and end of one row in the table, whereas individual <td> and </td> (table data) tags indicate the beginning and end of each cell. FrontPage generates a separate line for each cell in a table. The <div> tag and center attribute center the table in the page.

So that you can gain a better understanding of the HTML tags that FrontPage used to create the table, you will view the HTML document for the bulk2.htm and lawn.htm pages.

To view the HTML documents that produce tables:

1. Click the **bulk2.htm** tab to display the Bulk Goods Samples page.
2. Change to Code view, and then if necessary, press **Ctrl + End** to scroll to the bottom of the HTML document. Figure 5-34 shows the HTML document that creates the bulk2.htm page. The <div align="center"> tag centers the table on the page. The <td align="center"> tag centers the data in an individual cell. The <tr> and </tr> tags indicate a single row in the table. Notice that the width for this table is set to 640 pixels.

Figure 5-34 HTML document for the bulk2.htm page

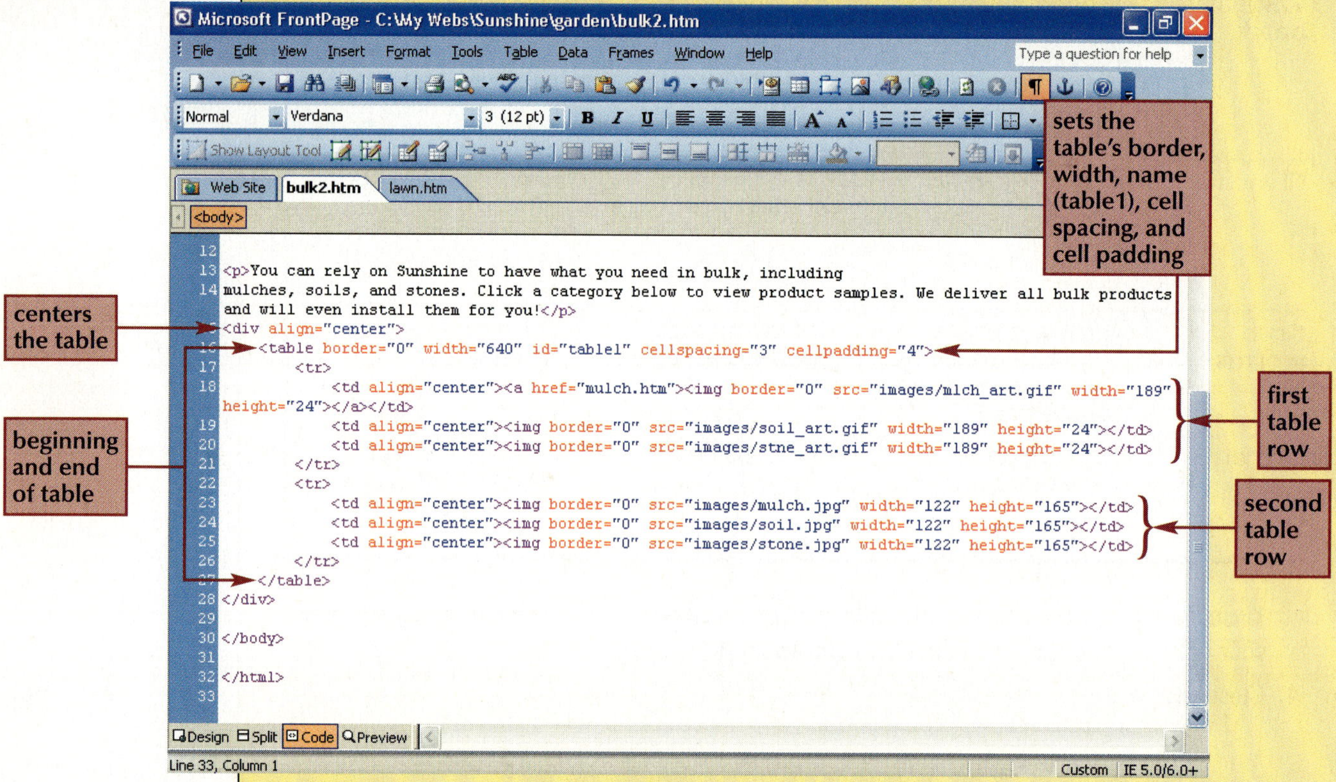

3. Change to Design view, and then close the bulk2.htm page.
4. In the lawn.htm page, click anywhere in the page to deselect the selected cells, change to Code view, and then scroll the HTML document so the <div align="center"> tag is at the top of the window, as shown in Figure 5-35. Notice the <caption> and </caption> tags, which format the table's caption. This table is also centered in the page, as indicated by the <div align="center"> tag. The opening <table> tag contains properties that format the table's border size, width in the browser window, cell spacing, cell padding, name, and the Table AutoFormat. The colspan property merges the cells in the first row. The other properties in the <td> tags were inserted by the Table AutoFormat and affect the table's appearance.

HTML document for the lawn.htm page

Figure 5-35

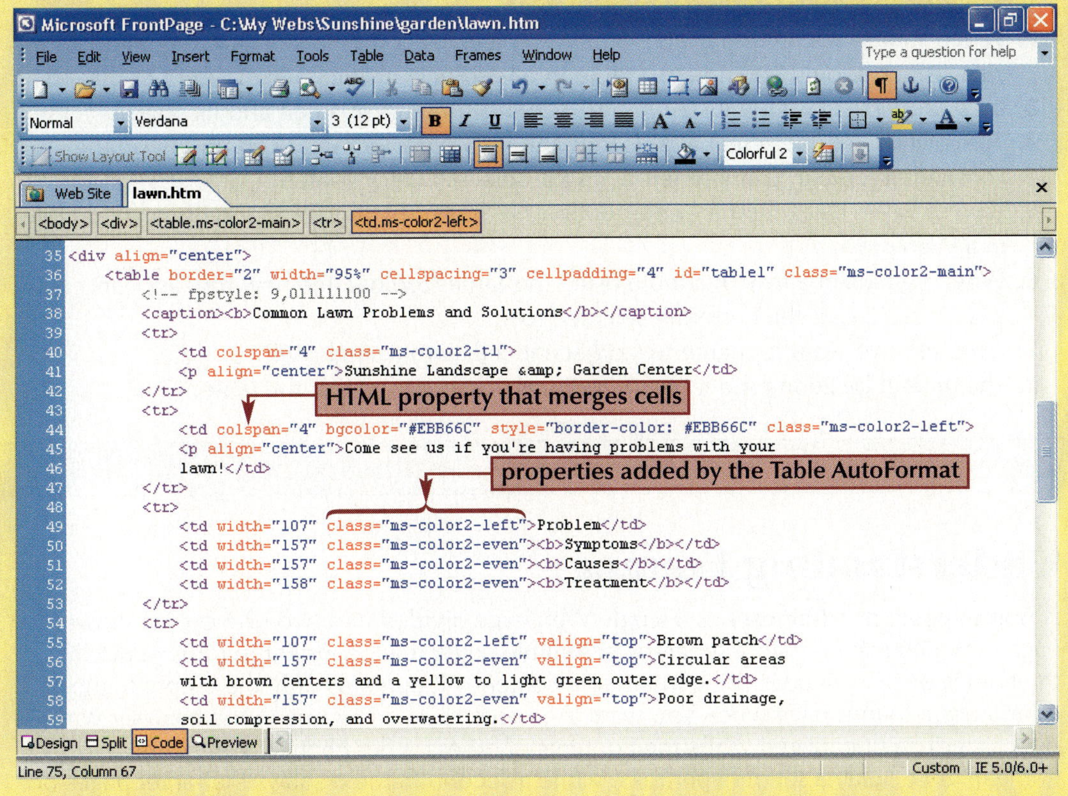

5. Press **Ctrl + End**. Notice the width property in the <td> tags, which indicates the widths of the cells in pixels. These widths represent the column widths you indicated when you resized the first column using the pointer and the remaining columns using the Distribute Columns Evenly button.

   Trouble? The widths of the second, third, and fourth columns might not be exactly equal; their measurements might vary by one or two pixels. This difference does not cause any problems.

6. Change to Design view.
7. Click **View** on the menu bar, point to **Toolbars**, and then click **Tables** to hide the Tables toolbar.
8. Close the garden Web site, and then close FrontPage.

Brett and Helen now understand how to use and create tables in a Web page. In the next session, you will create a page with frames in the Web site.

Review

Session 5.1 Quick Check

1. What is the smallest component of a table?
2. When should you create a table in a Web page using a percentage of the window size? When should you create a table in a Web page using a fixed number of pixels?
3. ______________ is the distance between the contents of a cell and its edges.
4. True or False: If you select a table cell and then click the Align Left button on the Formatting toolbar, you will left-align the selected cell's contents.
5. True or False: Clicking the Center button on the Formatting toolbar will center a table in a Web page.
6. When you insert a row in a table using the Tables toolbar, the new row appears ______________ the currently selected row.
7. Describe two ways to merge two adjacent cells into a single cell.
8. The default location for a table's caption is ______________ the table.

Session 5.2

Understanding Frames

A **frames page**, or a **frameset**, is a single Web page divided into two or more windows, each of which can contain a separate, scrollable page. It is important to understand that the frames page itself does not contain any content—it contains only the empty frames.

You use a frames page when you want the contents of one frame in the browser window to remain unchanged while the contents of other frames change. For example, one frame might display a set of hyperlinks, while a second frame displays the target pages of the hyperlinks.

Chad Schomaker wants to replace the existing Irrigation page in the Web site with a frames page. His vision of the new Irrigation page is one that lends itself very well to a frames page with three frames. He wants a page at the top of the frames page that contains navigation links to other pages in the garden Web site, and a page on the left side of the frames page that contains links to topics related to irrigation; the pages for those related irrigation topics would open in the third, or main, frame. A frames page itself is just a set of empty frames; its HTML tags specify each frame's name and size.

After planning the content of the new Irrigation page, Chad created several pages. The first page, banner.htm, is the page that will appear at the top of the frames page. The second page, contents.htm, is the page that will appear on the left side of the frames page. The pages war.htm, request.htm, faq.htm, and intro.htm will open in the main frame of the frames page. Chad saved these pages in a folder. You'll import this folder into the Web site, and then you'll create the frames page and set its pages to open in the correct frames.

When you open a frames page in a browser, the browser first opens the frames page, then it opens the pages that are specified to load into the individual frames. If the frames page contains three frames, your browser is really opening *four* separate Web pages—the frames page and one page in each of the three frames. Figure 5-36 shows the RainMaker Irrigation page that you will create and describes how it works.

RainMaker Irrigation frames page

Figure 5-36

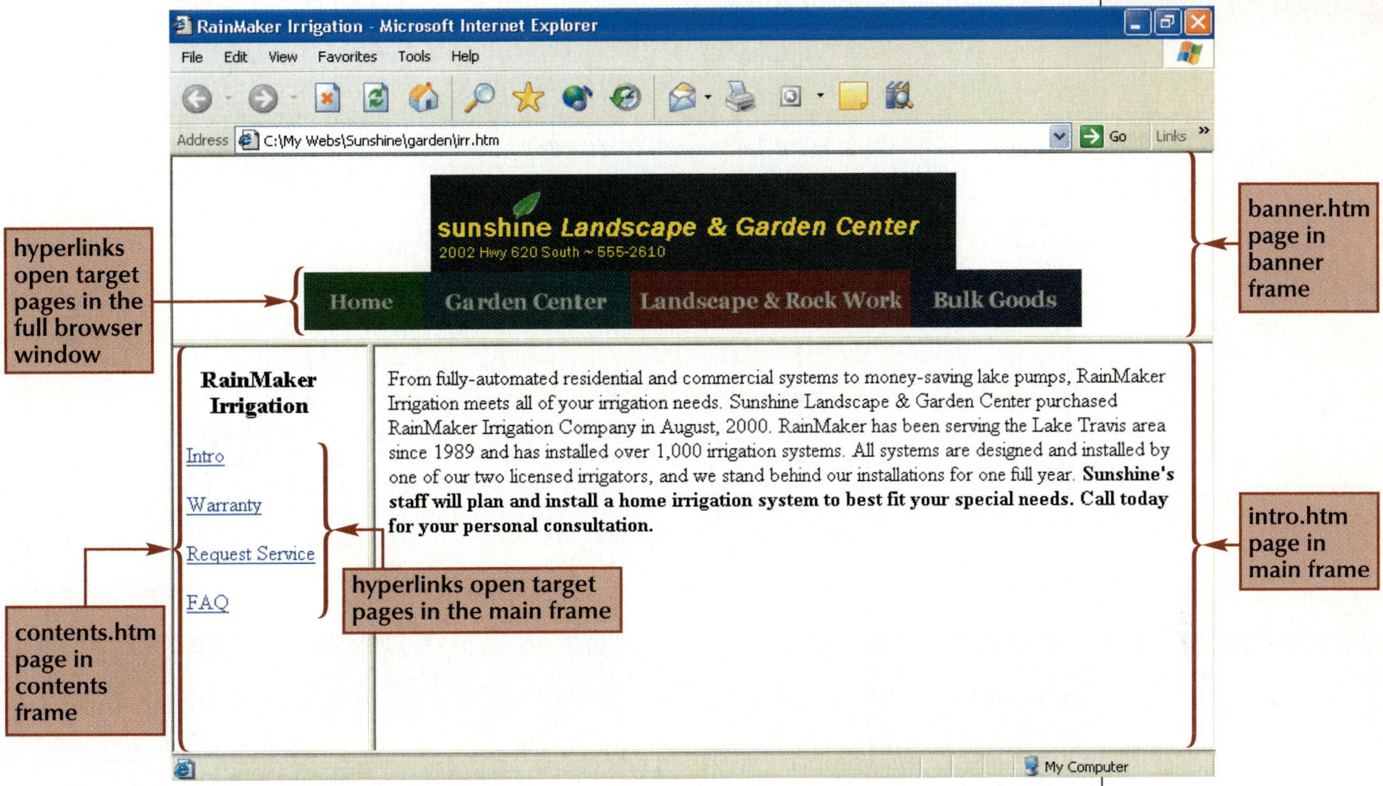

Frames provide Web site developers with a way to display two or more Web pages at once. An advantage of displaying multiple Web pages simultaneously is that the navigation links can be always visible, making it easier to navigate the site. Using a frames page has some disadvantages as well. Some browsers cannot display Web pages that contain frames, which means that some visitors to your Web site might not see the frames page with the different Web pages. Therefore, you should use frames only when you are certain that your Web site's users will be able to display them. Another concern when using a frames page is that the page displayed in the main frame appears in a smaller window than when it is displayed in the full browser window. If the page in the main frame contains a lot of text, users will need to scroll the page frequently to read its contents, which might be distracting.

Creating a Frames Page

FrontPage includes many frames page templates that you can use to create a frameset; Figure 5-36 shows just one example of a frames page that you can create. A **frames page template** is a Web page that contains the specifications for the individual locations and sizes of the frames in a frames page. When you create a frames page using a template, FrontPage assigns a default name to each frame. You can resize any of the frames in a frames page and change other frame properties after creating them.

Figure 5-37 shows the plan for the new RainMaker Irrigation page. The irr.htm page is the frames page, banner.htm contains links that open other pages in the garden Web site, contents.htm contains links that open in the main frame, and intro.htm is one of the pages that will open in the main frame.

Figure 5-37 **Sketch of the frames page**

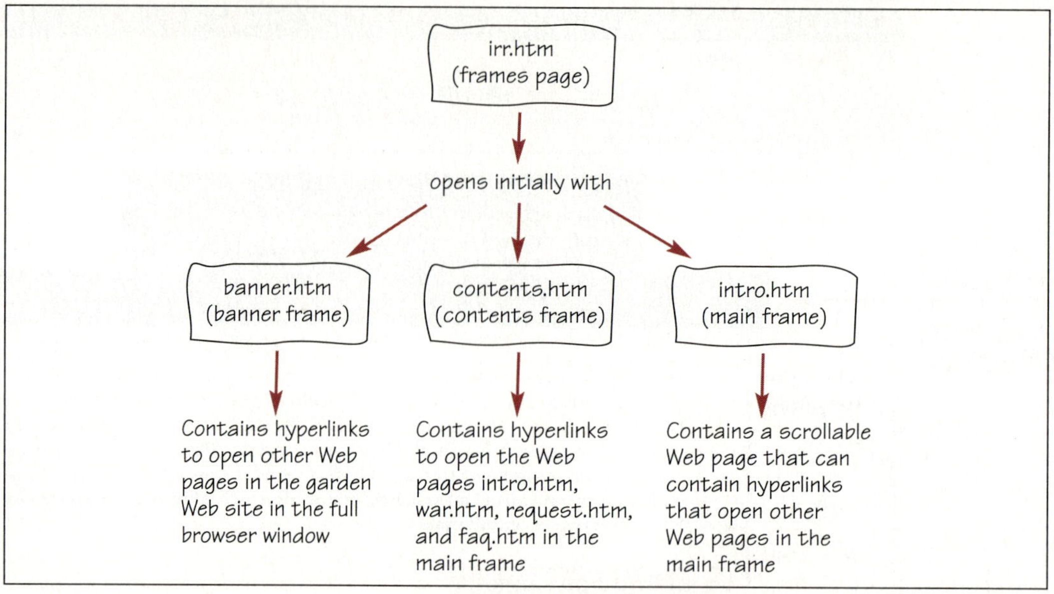

Reference Window

Creating a Frames Page

- Click File on the menu bar, and then click New.
- In the New page section of the New task pane, click More page templates.
- In the Page Templates dialog box, click the Frames Pages tab.
- Click a template to see its preview and description.
- Double-click a template icon to close the Page Templates dialog box and to create the new frames page.

You will create the new RainMaker Irrigation page using a frames page template.

To create a frames page:

1. Start **FrontPage**, and then open the **garden** Web site from the location where your Web sites are stored.
2. Click **File** on the menu bar, and then click **New**. The New task pane opens.
3. In the New page section of the New task pane, click **More page templates**. The Page Templates dialog box opens.
4. Click the **Frames Pages** tab to display a list of available frames page templates.

   You can preview a template to see its description and appearance before using it.
5. If necessary, click the **Banner and Contents** icon. A preview and description of the selected template appear on the right side of the Page Templates dialog box. See Figure 5-38.

Figure 5-38 Page Templates dialog box

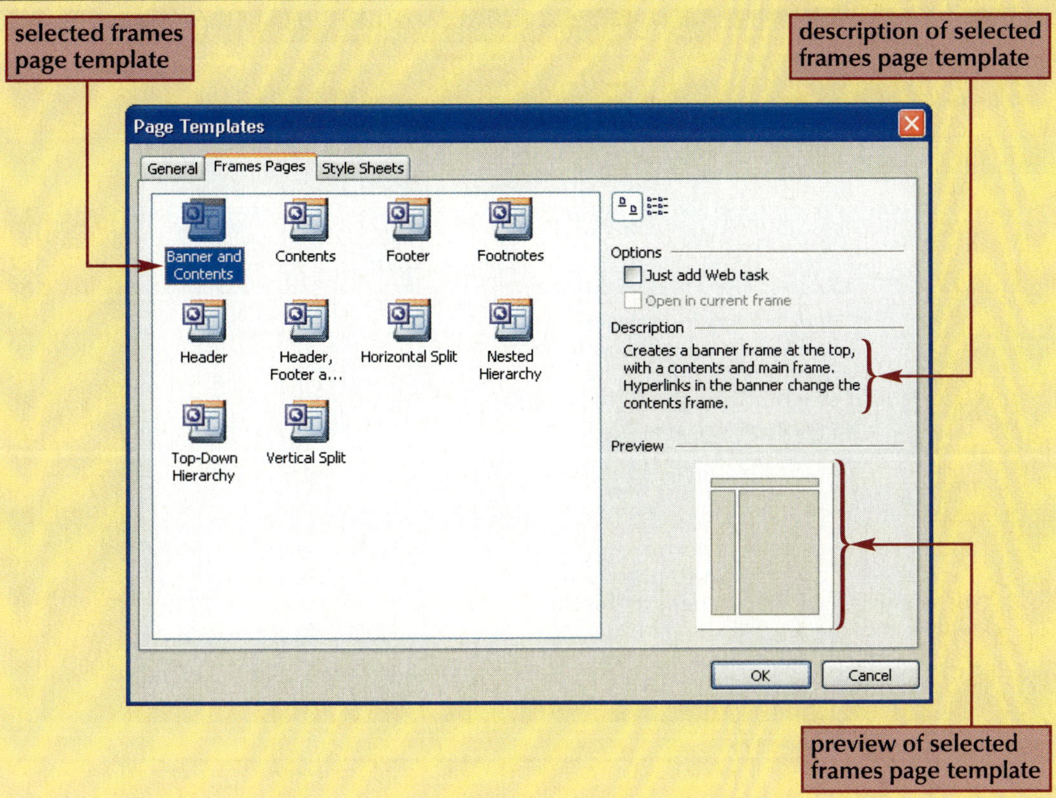

6. Select other templates and examine their previews and descriptions.

   Chad's description of the page he wants you to create most closely matches the Banner and Contents template. This template has a banner frame, a contents frame, and a main frame.

7. Double-click the **Banner and Contents** icon to close the Page Templates dialog box and the New task pane and to create the frames page, which opens in Design view with the filename new_page_1.htm. (Your page might use a different number in the filename.) See Figure 5-39.

Figure 5-39 New frames page in Design view

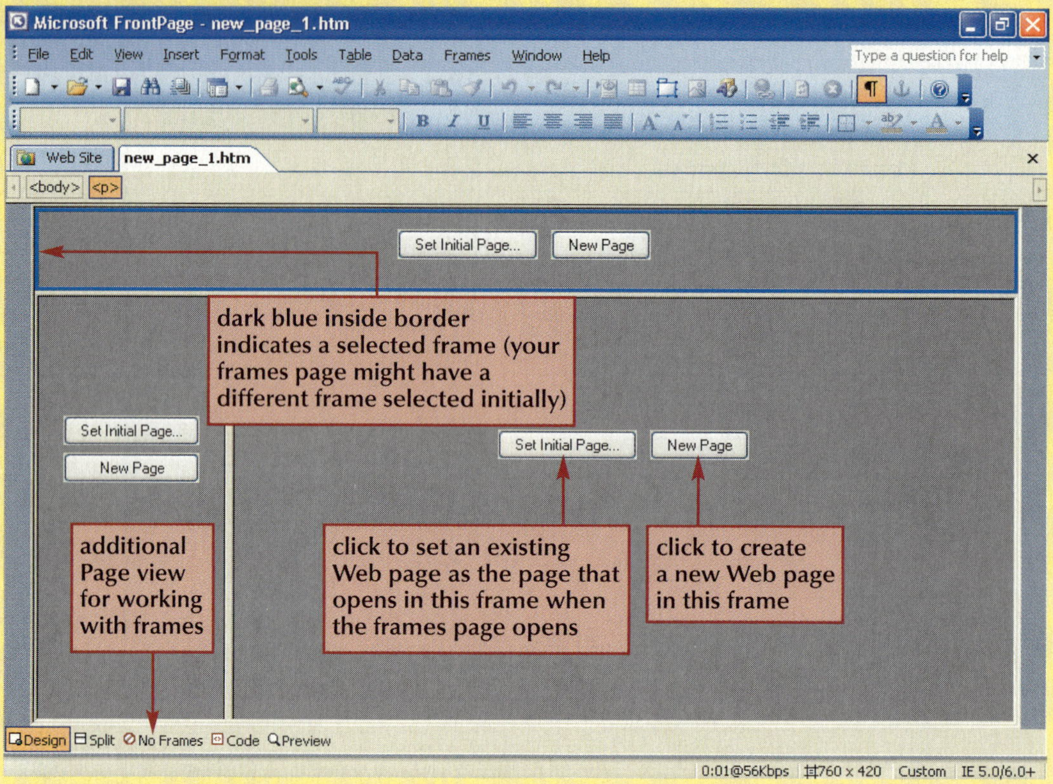

Before beginning your work, you'll save the frames page using the filename irr.htm. Because a page with this filename already exists in the Web site, you'll overwrite the existing file.

8. Click the **Save** button on the Standard toolbar. The Save As dialog box opens. See Figure 5-40.

Figure 5-40 Save As dialog box

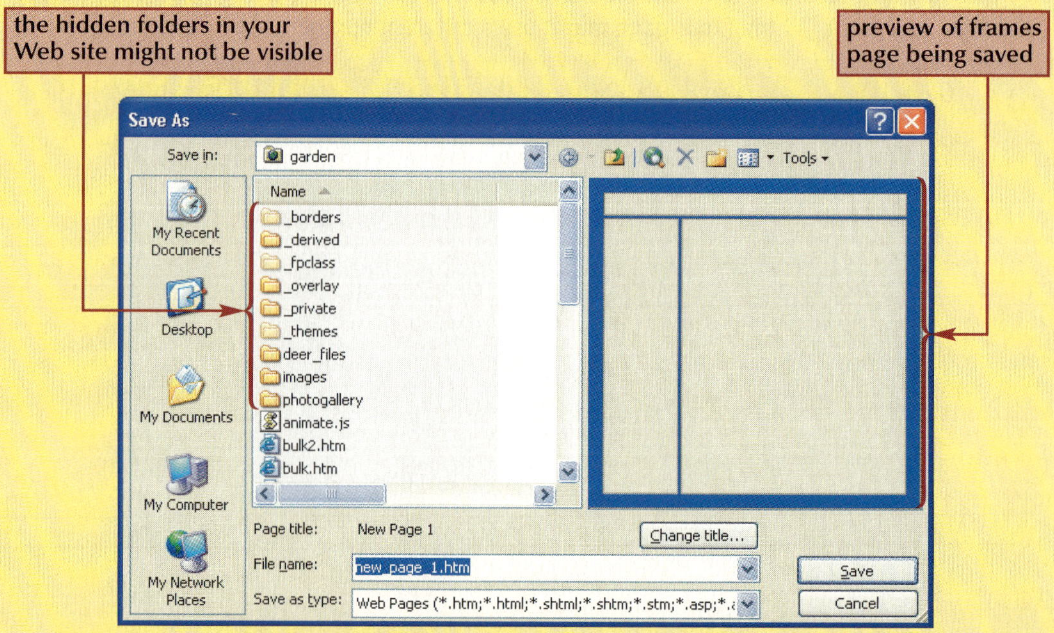

Notice that the Save As dialog box shows a preview of the frames page that you will save. The frames page contains three frames, as indicated by the thin borders. The frames page itself appears with a dark border. If you had created new pages in any of the frames, you would need to save those pages now, as well.

9. Type **irr.htm** as the filename, click the **Change title** button to open the Set Page Title dialog box, type **RainMaker Irrigation** in the Page title text box, click the **OK** button, make sure that the Save in list box displays the garden folder, and then click the **Save** button in the Save As dialog box.

   A message box opens, asking if you want to replace the existing irr.htm file in the Web site.

10. Click the **Yes** button to replace the existing page. The frames page is saved in the Web site using the filename irr.htm. When a browser displays the frames page, the title "RainMaker Irrigation" will appear in its title bar. The titles of pages displayed in the other frames will not appear anywhere in the browser. For this reason, you should create a title that is a description of all of the pages displayed by the frames page, because that title will appear the entire time the frames page is open.

Examining the HTML Document for a Frames Page

The RainMaker Irrigation page that you just created is a Web page with no content except for three empty frames named banner, contents, and main that the Banner and Contents frames page template created. Notice that one new button—No Frames—appears at the bottom of the Contents pane. This button appears when a frames page is open in Design view. A **No Frames page** provides instructions for browsers that cannot display frames.

You want to show Chad the HTML document for a frames page so he sees how the pages in the individual frames are added to the frames page.

To examine the HTML document for a No Frames page and a frames page:

1. Click the **Show No Frames View** button [No Frames] at the bottom of the Contents pane. A new page opens in Show No Frames view and completely replaces the frames page. This page contains the text, "This page uses frames, but your browser doesn't support them." FrontPage created this page automatically with your frames page. If a Web browser that cannot display frames tries to open the irr.htm page, which contains frames, this page will open in its place. You explain to Chad that he could change the content of this page to include hyperlinks to pages that would otherwise be available in the frames page. Because you expect the Web site users to have current releases of browsers that support frames, you will not modify this page.

2. Click the **Show Code View** button [Code] at the bottom of the Contents pane. The HTML document for the irr.htm frames page appears in this view. See Figure 5-41. Notice that the <frame> tags and the name properties identify the three frames created by the Banner and Contents frames page template: banner, contents, and main. Also notice that the title of the page, as specified by the <title> and </title> tags, is RainMaker Irrigation.

Figure 5-41 HTML document for the frames page

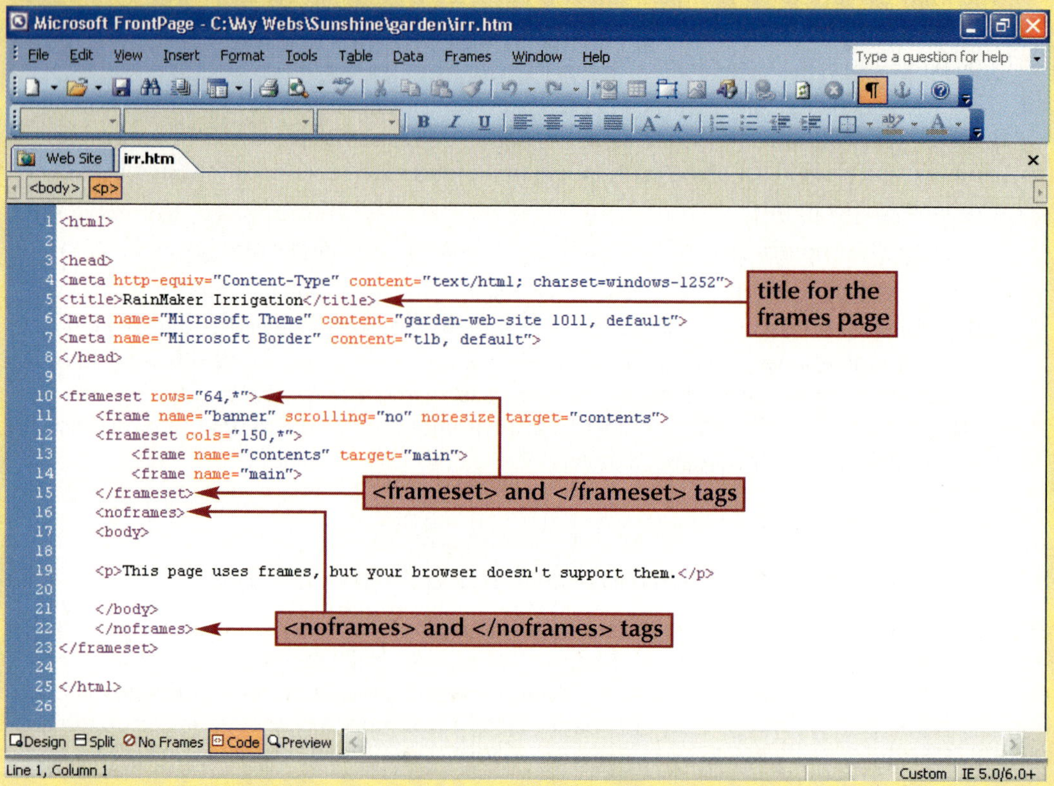

3. Click the **Show Design View** button [Design] at the bottom of the Contents pane to return to Design view for the frames page.

Your next task is to set the page that opens in each frame when a browser opens the irr.htm page. You already created these pages, so you just need to import them into the Web site.

Importing Web Pages for Use in a Frames Page

Before you can set Chad's pages to open in the RainMaker Irrigation frames page, you must import them into the Web site. Chad stored these pages in a folder, so you'll import the folder and its contents into the site to keep the pages used in the frames page organized in a single location.

To import pages for a frames page:

1. Display the Folder List, make sure the Web site's root folder is selected, click **File** on the menu bar, and then click **Import** to open the Import dialog box.
2. Click the **Add Folder** button to open the File Open dialog box. If necessary, open the **Tutorial.05\Tutorial** folder included with your Data Files, and then click the **irr** folder to select it.
3. Click the **Open** button. The Import dialog box displays six files in the irr folder.
4. Click the **OK** button to import the folder and its files into the Web site.
5. Close the Folder List.

The pages that will open in the RainMaker Irrigation page are now saved in the Web site.

Setting Initial Pages for Frames

The frames page displays three frames, each containing a Set Initial Page button and a New Page button. Clicking the Set Initial Page button lets you specify an existing Web page (from the current Web site or from another location) as the page that opens in the selected frame. Clicking the New Page button lets you create a new blank page in the Web site and open it in the frame so you can enter its content. Creating a new page for use in any of the frames in the frames page is the same as creating a new Web page in Design view—the only difference is that you are creating and editing the new page in a frame. Because you imported the Web pages that will be used with the frames page, they already exist in the Web site.

To set the initial pages for a frames page:

1. Click the **Set Initial Page** button in the banner frame. The banner frame is selected and the Insert Hyperlink dialog box opens. When you set the page, you are really creating a hyperlink to it.

   Trouble? If you accidentally click the New Page button in a frame, you will create a new page. To remove it, click Frames on the menu bar, click Frame Properties, delete the text in the Initial page text box, and then click the OK button.

2. Double-click the **irr** folder to open it, and then double-click **banner.htm**. The Insert Hyperlink dialog box closes and the banner.htm page opens in the banner frame. Notice that you cannot see all of the page's content. You will fix this problem later.

   Trouble? If you accidentally set the wrong page to open in a frame, right-click in the frame to select it and to open the shortcut menu, click Frame Properties, click the Browse button to the right of the Initial page text box to browse for and select the correct file, click the OK button, and then click the OK button again.

3. Click the **Set Initial Page** button in the contents frame, and then double-click the **contents.htm** page to set it to open in the contents frame on the left side of the frames page.

4. Click the **Set Initial Page** button in the main frame, and then double-click the **intro.htm** page to set it to open in the main frame on the right side of the frames page. You have now specified the pages to open in each frame when the browser opens the frames page. See Figure 5-42.

Figure 5-42 **Initial pages set for the frames page**

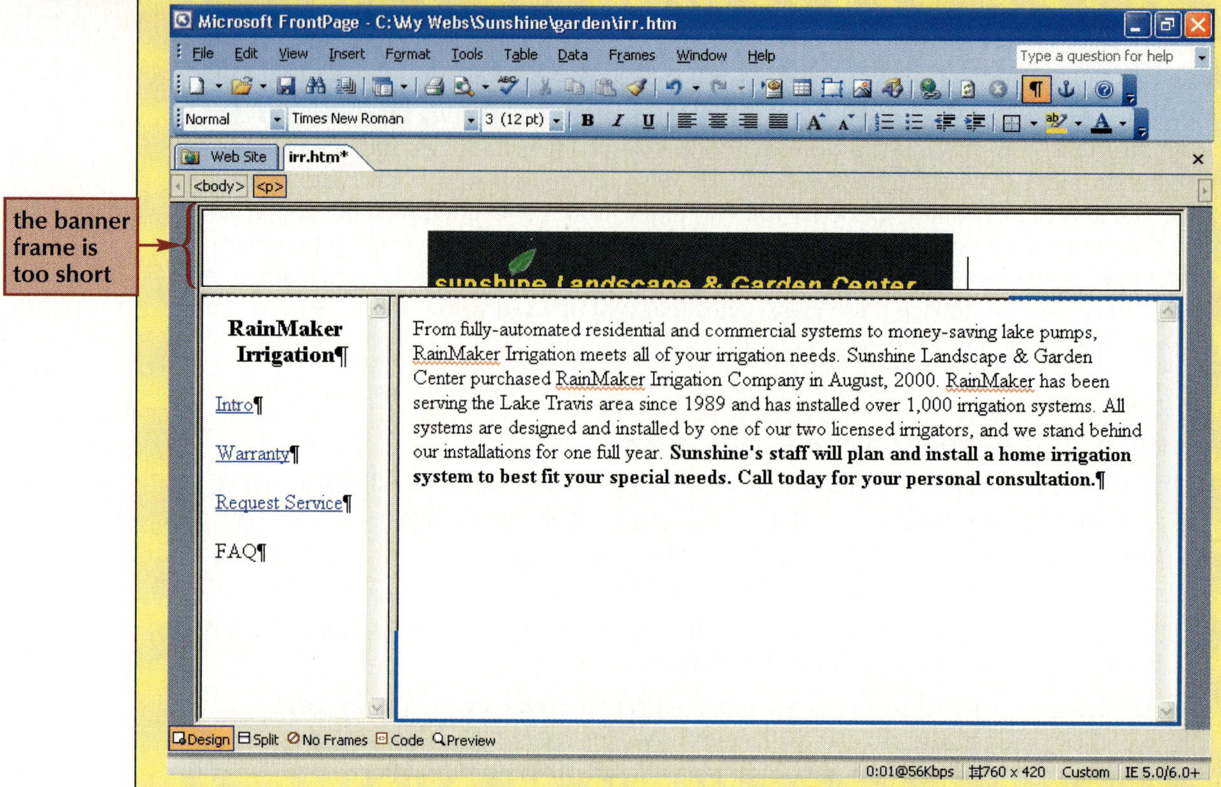

Editing the Frames in a Frames Page

The first problem you noticed is that the banner.htm page does not fit in the frame created by the Banner and Contents frames page. You could open the banner.htm page in Design view and change its contents to fit in the frame. A simpler method, however, is to increase the size of the banner frame so the existing banner.htm page will fit in it. After creating a frames page, you can use the pointer to resize any of the individual frames. Keep in mind, however, that resizing one frame resizes the other frames in the frames page, so make your adjustments carefully.

To edit the frames:

1. Click the banner frame to select it. A dark blue border appears inside the banner frame to indicate that it is selected.
2. Move the pointer to the bottom frame border of the banner frame so that the pointer changes to a ↕ shape.
3. Click and hold the mouse button on the bottom border of the banner frame, drag the frame border down about one inch, and then release the mouse button. Figure 5-43 shows the revised height of the banner frame. Notice that the size of the contents and main frames is reduced to accommodate the larger size of the banner frame.

Frames page with resized banner frame

Figure 5-43

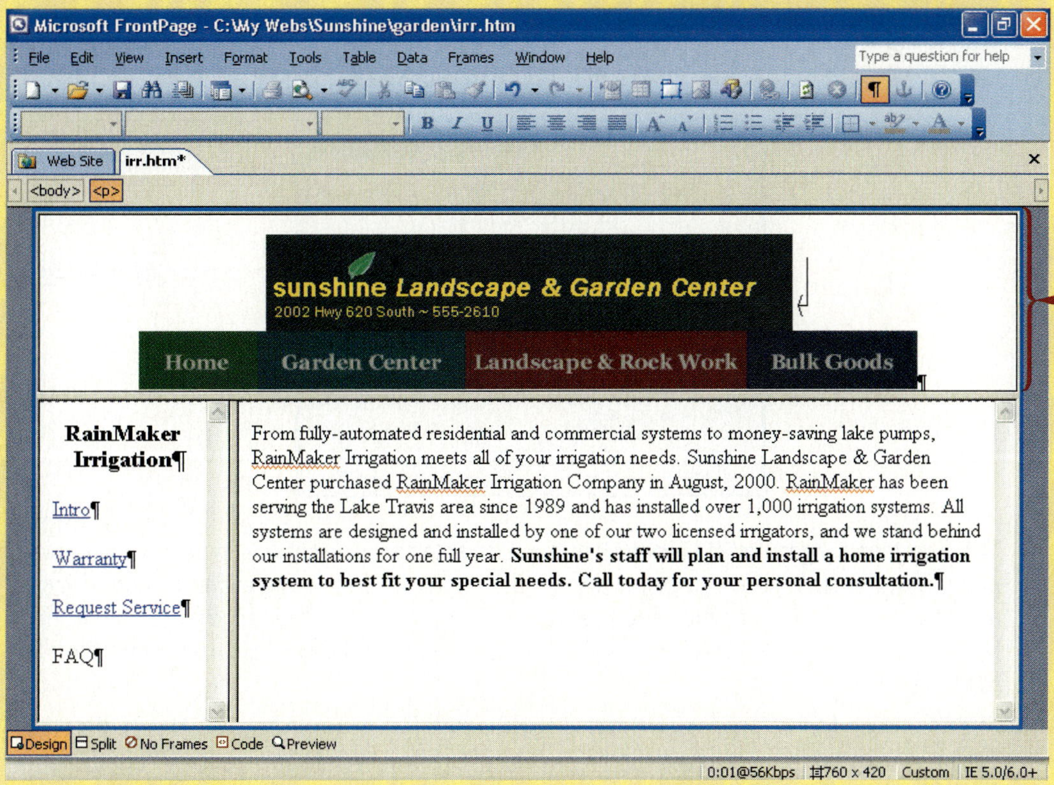

When you changed the size of the banner frame, you changed the HTML document that contains information about the frames. When you display a frames page in Design view, clicking the Save button saves the changes that you made to the pages in the frameset and to the frameset itself.

4. Click the **Save** button on the Standard toolbar to save the frames page with these initial page settings.

Now that you have updated and saved the pages that open in the frames page, you can work on specifying how pages will open in the frames page.

Creating a Hyperlink in a Frame

A **target frame** is the designated frame in a frames page in which a Web page opens. For example, the target frame for the Warranty page is the main frame of the frames page. When you imported the contents.htm page, it contained the hyperlinks, including their target frames, for the Intro, Warranty, and Request Service pages. You'll format the "FAQ" text as a hyperlink that opens the faq.htm page in the main frame of the RainMaker Irrigation page.

To specify the target frame for a page:

1. In the contents frame, select **FAQ** as the text for the hyperlink, and then click the **Insert Hyperlink** button on the Standard toolbar to open the Insert Hyperlink dialog box.
2. Click **faq.htm** to select the FAQ page.

3. Click the **Target Frame** button. The Target Frame dialog box opens. See Figure 5-44.

Figure 5-44 **Target Frame dialog box**

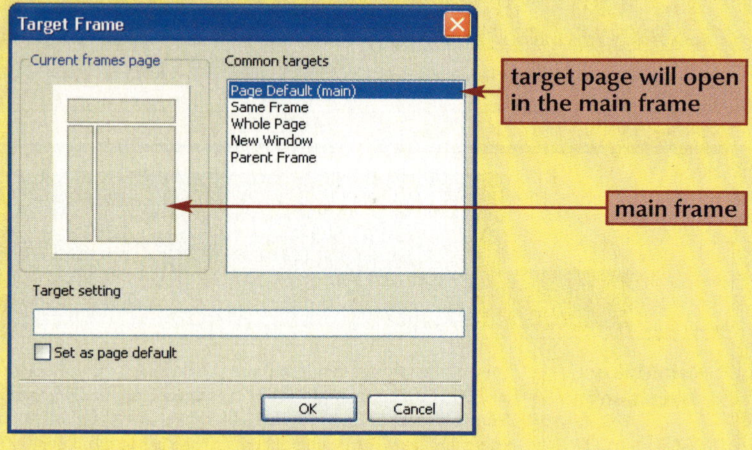

The Common targets list box identifies the available target locations in which to open a page. The Current frames page section identifies the frames in the current page. Clicking a frame in the Current frames page section sets that frame as the target location of the hyperlink. You want the faq.htm page to open in the main frame, so you'll select the main frame.

4. Click the main frame (see Figure 5-44) in the Current frames page section. Notice that the Target setting text box displays the "main" location. This is the same as the "Page Default (main)" setting in the Common targets list box. The default target for hyperlinks in the contents frame is the main frame, so this target was set correctly by the Banner and Contents frames page template.
5. Click the **OK** button to close the Target Frame dialog box, and then click the **OK** button to close the Insert Hyperlink dialog box.
6. Click **FAQ** in the contents frame to deselect it. The "FAQ" text now appears as a hyperlink.
7. Click the **Save** button on the Standard toolbar to save the changes you made to the contents.htm page.

Examining a Frame's Properties

After creating a frames page, you can verify that the pages will open in the correct frames by opening the page in a browser and testing them, or by checking the values in the Frame Properties dialog box. You want to show Chad how to verify a frame's properties.

To examine a frame's properties:

1. Right-click the main frame to select it and open the shortcut menu, and then click **Frame Properties**. The Frame Properties dialog box opens. See Figure 5-45.

Frame Properties dialog box — **Figure 5-45**

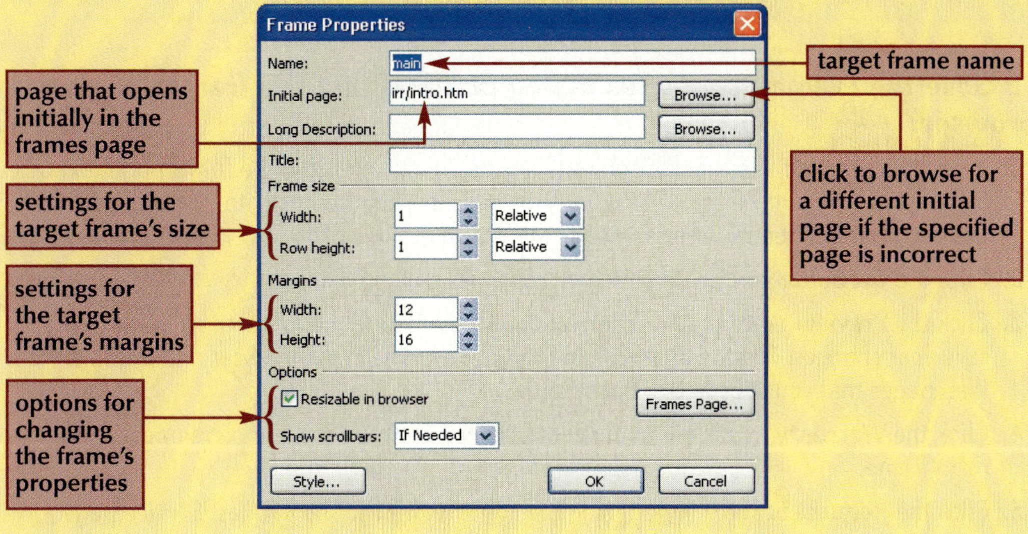

Figure 5-46 describes the changes that you can make to a selected frame using this dialog box.

Options in the Frame Properties dialog box and their descriptions — **Figure 5-46**

Option	Description
Name	The name of the selected frame in the frames page.
Initial page	The filename of the page that opens in the named frame when the frames page is opened in a browser. Click the Browse button to change or set the page that opens initially.
Long Description	The optional filename of the page that contains a description of the page used in the frame. Usually you use a long description when you need to provide a long explanation of something in the frame in a separate file.
Title	The optional short description of a page that identifies its use or function. The title is usually added for users who are visually impaired or people using text-only browsers; it appears as a ScreenTip when you move the pointer over the frame in a browser that supports the title property.
Width (Frame size section)	The frame's width. Use the list box to specify the frame's width relative to other frames, to set the width as a percentage of the browser window's size, or to set the width as a fixed number of pixels. The default width is 1 with relative sizing.
Row height (Frame size section)	The frame's height. Use the list box to specify the frame's height relative to other frames, to set the height as a percentage of the browser window's size, or to set the height as a fixed number of pixels. The default height is 1 with relative sizing.
Width (Margins section)	The frame's margin width (in pixels), which indicates the amount of left and right space to indent the content in the frame from the inside frame border.
Height (Margins section)	The frame's margin height (in pixels), which indicates the amount of top and bottom space to indent the content in the frame from the inside frame border.
Resizable in browser check box	Select this check box to let users resize the current frame using a Web browser. Clear this check box to prevent users from resizing the frame.
Frames Page button	Opens the Page Properties dialog box with the Frames tab selected so that you can change the spacing between frames or turn the display of frame borders on or off.
Show scrollbars list box	Lets you specify whether to display scroll bars as needed for longer pages or to always or never display scroll bars.
Style button	Lets you change the style of the frames in the page; this topic is beyond the scope of this tutorial.

After checking the frame properties and changing them as necessary, you can close the dialog box and test the frames in a browser.

To close the Frame Properties dialog box and test the frames page in a browser:

1. Verify that the Name text box displays the value "main" and that the Initial page text box has the value "irr/intro.htm." These settings indicate that the intro.htm page will open in the main frame when the browser loads the irr.htm frames page.
2. Click the **OK** button to close the Frame Properties dialog box.
3. Click the **Preview** button on the Standard toolbar, and then click the **Yes** button to save your changes. The RainMaker Irrigation page opens in the browser and displays the Web pages that you specified in each frame.
4. Click the **Warranty** hyperlink in the contents frame. The Warranty page opens in the main frame.
5. Click the **Request Service** hyperlink in the contents frame. The Request Service page opens in the main frame.
6. Click the **FAQ** hyperlink in the contents frame. The FAQ page opens in the main frame. If your monitor is set to 800 × 600 (or lower) resolution, a scroll bar appears on the right side of the main frame because the FAQ page exceeds the frame's size, as shown in Figure 5-47. The browser added the scroll bar so you can view the rest of this page's contents.

Figure 5-47 Frames page after clicking the FAQ hyperlink

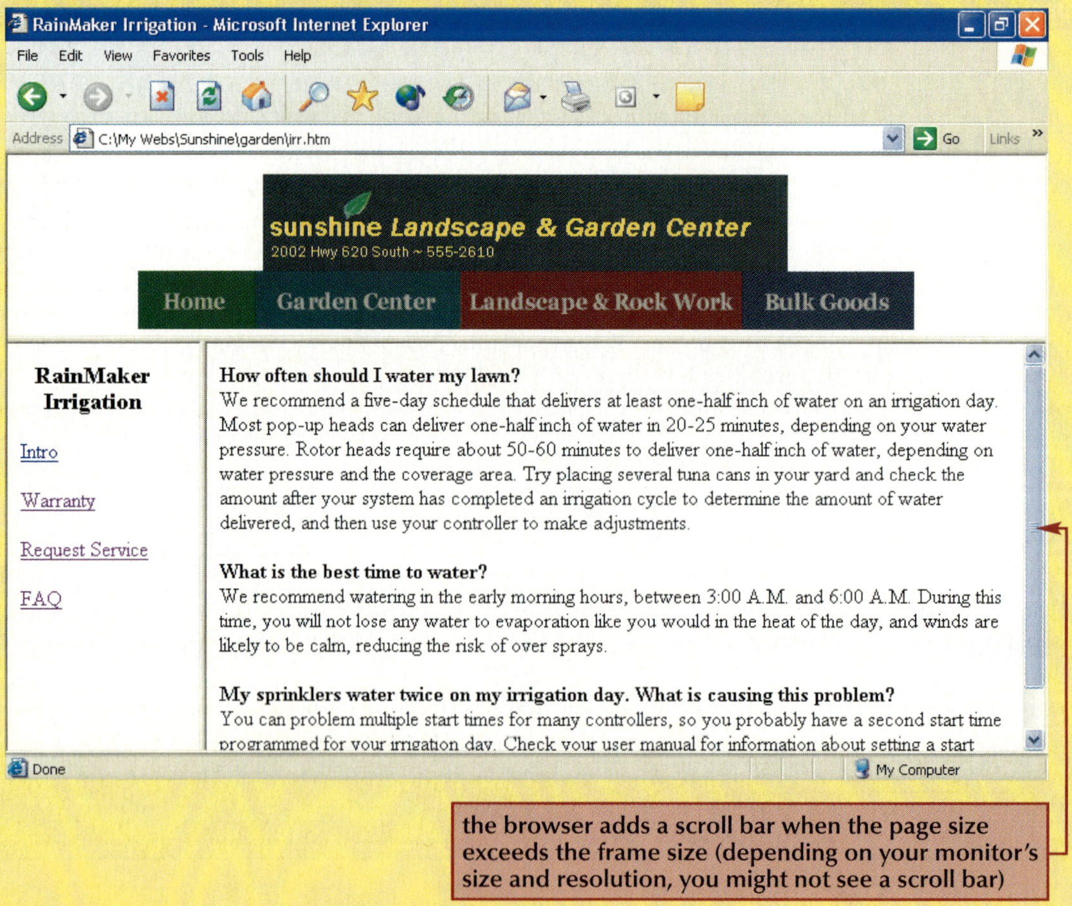

7. Click the **Garden Center** hyperlink in the link bar in the banner frame. Because this hyperlink is set to open the center.htm page in a full browser window, the frames page closes and the center.htm page opens.
8. Click the **Irrigation** link to return to the frames page, and then click the **Home** link in the banner frame.

   The home page for the garden Web site, which should open in the full browser window, opens in the contents frame. This indicates that a problem exists with the target for this hyperlink. See Figure 5-48.

Figure 5-48 Frames page after clicking the Home hyperlink

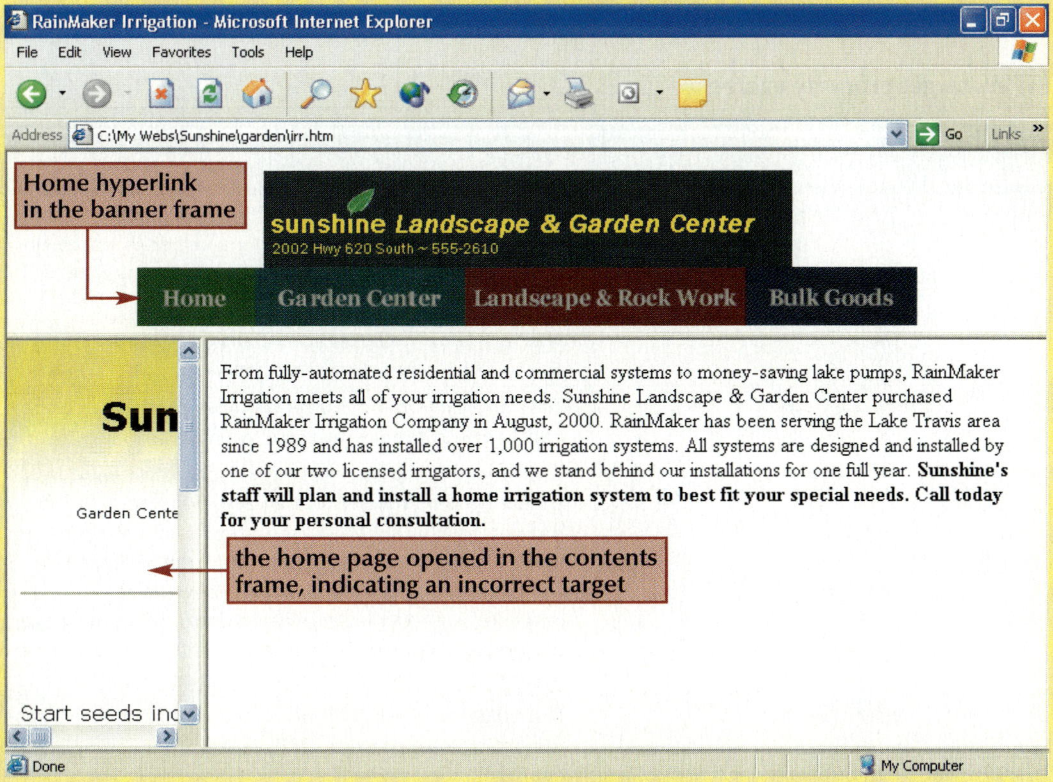

9. Click the **Landscape & Rock Work** hyperlink in the banner frame. The Landscape/Rock Work page replaces the entire RainMaker Irrigation page and opens in the full browser window. This action is the one that you want to occur when any page is opened from the link bar in the banner frame.
10. Click the **Irrigation** hyperlink in the link bar. The RainMaker Irrigation page opens and replaces the Landscape/Rock Work page in the browser window.
11. Close your browser.

When you clicked the link to the home page in the link bar in the banner frame, the page did not completely replace the frames page. Instead, the home page opened in the contents frame. You need to change the target frame for the home page by modifying its hyperlink in the link bar in the banner.htm page so that the frames page will close before the home page opens. In other words, the target of the hyperlink should open in the full browser window without any frames.

Changing a Frame's Target

When you use a FrontPage frames page template to create a frames page, the navigation between frames is already set up for you. For example, the Banner and Contents frames page template specifies that pages opened using hyperlinks in the contents frame will open in the main frame. For the irr.htm frames page, you imported the pages that open in each frame into the Web site, instead of creating them as new pages from within the frames page. Sometimes you might need to change the target frame for a hyperlink. For example, your testing in the previous section revealed that the Home hyperlink in the banner frame did not open the home page correctly.

There are five values of the HTML target property that tell a browser where to open hyperlinked pages in a frames page. Figure 5-49 describes the five values that you can use to specify target frames.

Figure 5-49 **HTML target property values**

HTML Value	Predefined Frame Name	Description
frame name	Page Default (*frame name*)	The target of the hyperlink is the *frame name* frame in the frames page. The *frame name* varies based on the frames page template you used to create the frames page.
_self	Same Frame	The target of the hyperlink opens in the same frame as the page containing the hyperlink.
_top	Whole Page	The target of the hyperlink replaces the frames page and opens in the full browser window.
_blank	New Window	The target of the hyperlink opens in a new window. A new window means that a second instance of the browser starts and opens the page. Use this option to open a page that is related to the frames page's contents, but is not part of the frames page. For example, a page that contains information about eye discomfort might include a hyperlink that opens a page related to diseases of the eye in a new browser window.
_parent	Parent Frame	The target of the hyperlink opens a page that replaces the entire frameset that defines the frame containing the hyperlink.

The default target frame for a hyperlink is Page Default (*frame name*), where *frame name* is the name of the frame in which the page will open. For example, if you create a hyperlink in a page that appears in the contents frame, the default target frame for the hyperlinked page would be Page Default (main). If you do not specify a predefined frame name when creating a hyperlink, the target of the hyperlink will open in the main frame.

When Chad created the link bar in the banner.htm page, he specified the _top target frame for every hyperlink except for the Home hyperlink. In your testing, you confirmed this problem: The home page opened in the contents frame, whereas the other hyperlinks in the banner frame correctly opened their targets in the full browser window. You need to change the target frame of a hyperlink.

To change the target frame of a hyperlink and test it in the browser:

1. Right-click the **Home** picture in the banner frame to open the shortcut menu, and then click **Hyperlink Properties** to open the Edit Hyperlink dialog box. Notice that the Target Frame section at the bottom of the dialog box identifies the target of the Home hyperlink as "contents," which is the contents frame. This target is incorrect.
2. Click the **Target Frame** button to open the Target Frame dialog box. The current target frame, Page Default (contents), appears in the Common targets list box, and the Target setting text box contains the value "contents." You need to change the target frame so that the home page opens in the full browser window, replacing the entire frames page. To do so, you must specify the Whole Page (_top) target setting.
3. Click **Whole Page** in the Common targets list box. FrontPage adds the HTML equivalent, _top, to the Target setting text box. See Figure 5-50.

Figure 5-50 Changing the frame target

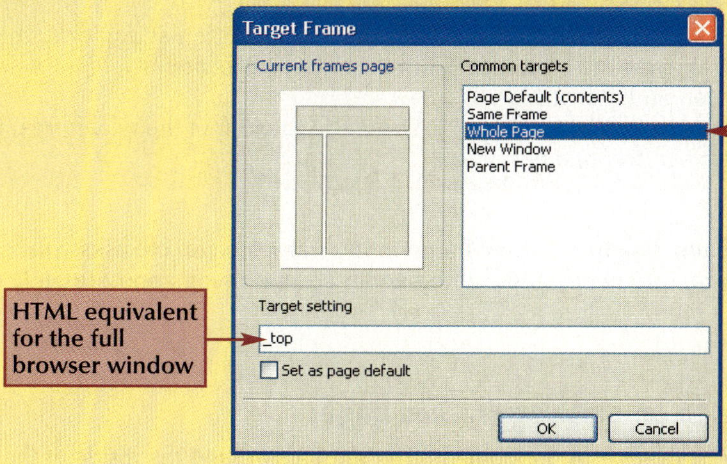

4. Click the **OK** button to close the Target Frame dialog box and return to the Edit Hyperlink dialog box. Notice that the Target Frame section now displays the correct target frame, _top.
5. Click the **OK** button to close the Edit Hyperlink dialog box, and then click the **Save** button on the Standard toolbar to save your changes.

   Trouble? If a Picture Actions button appears in the banner frame, click it, click the Resample Picture To Match Size option button, save the page, and then choose the option to overwrite the home_pic.gif file in the Web site's images folder.
6. Click the **Preview** button on the Standard toolbar to open the revised frames page in the browser.

   Now test the page again to make sure that it works correctly.
7. Click the **Home** hyperlink in the banner frame. The home page replaces the entire frames page in the browser.
8. Click the **Irrigation** link. The frames page opens. Your test is successful.
9. Close your browser.

Usually, you will need to change a target frame only when it is set incorrectly. Creating hyperlinks that open pages in frames can be a complicated chore, so it is important to test your frames pages thoroughly to ensure that all of the hyperlinked pages open correctly.

You can also use Hyperlinks view to examine all of the hyperlinks to and from a frames page, and use Reports view to search for broken links.

Adding a New Frame to an Existing Frames Page

After creating a frames page, you can add a new frame to it by dividing an existing frame into two separate frames. To divide one existing frame into two frames, press and hold the Ctrl key while dragging the border of the existing frame that you want to divide to create a new frame. After adding the new frame, you can specify a Web page to open in the new frame by using the same procedure you followed for creating other pages in the frames page.

Reference Window

Adding a New Frame to an Existing Frames Page

- Open the frames page in Design view.
- Press and hold the Ctrl key, and then click and hold the mouse button as you drag the border of an existing frame that you want to split to the desired location.
- Release the mouse button and the Ctrl key.
- Use the Set Initial Page button to specify an existing page to open in the new frame, or use the New Page button to create a new page.

Chad wants to add a sales slogan in a new frame in the frames page. He asks you to split the current main frame into two frames, with the new frame being approximately one inch high.

To add a new frame to an existing frames page:

1. Click the main frame to select it. A dark blue border appears around the inside of the main frame.
2. Press and hold the **Ctrl** key, point to the bottom border of the main frame so the pointer changes to a ↕ shape, click and hold the mouse button as you drag the border up about one inch, and then release the mouse button and the **Ctrl** key. A new frame is created, containing the Set Initial Page and New Page buttons. See Figure 5-51.

New frame created by splitting the main frame **Figure 5-51**

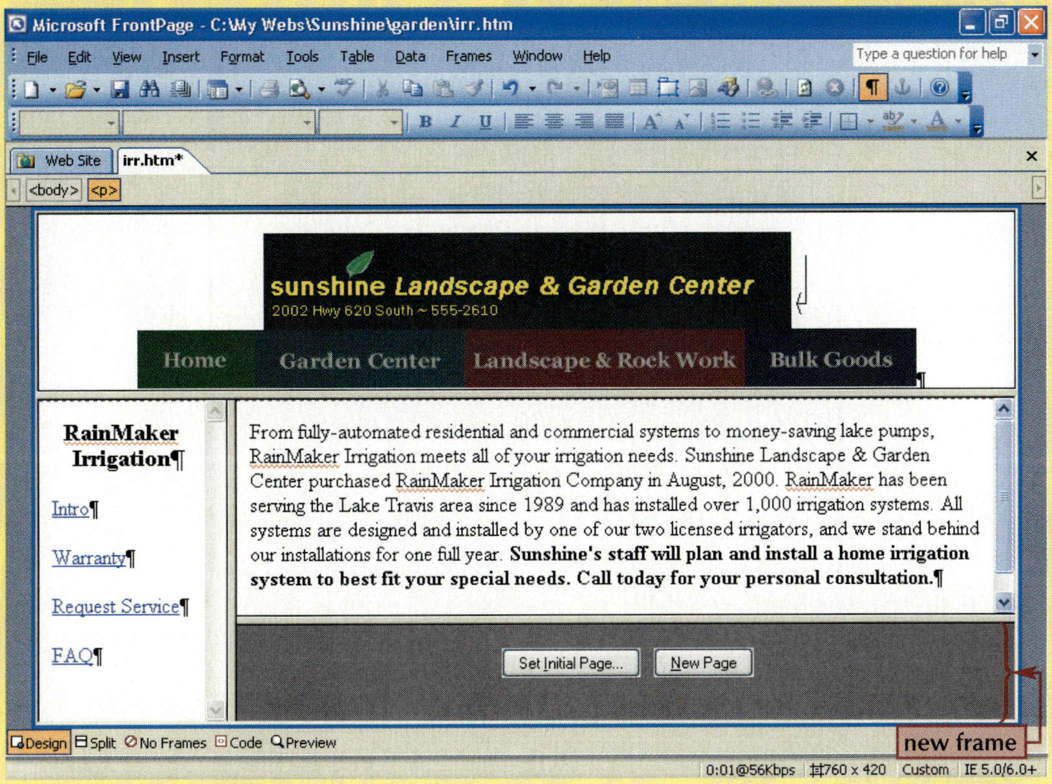

You could add the sales slogan to the new frame, but as Chad looks at the entire frames page, he realizes that the main frame is now too small to display its content effectively. He asks you to restore the main frame to its original size.

3. Click the new frame to select it, click **Frames** on the menu bar, and then click **Delete Frame**. The new frame is deleted and the main frame returns to its original size.
4. Save the page.

FrontPage lets you divide existing frames within a frames page easily and quickly to provide the best presentation for your Web pages. Nevertheless, you must exercise care to avoid making a frame too small to be useful.

Printing a Frames Page

Printing a frames page is not as straightforward as printing a Web page that does not contain frames. In FrontPage, you can print the individual Web pages that appear in each frame in a frames page, but you cannot print the frames page itself. For example, if you select the outer border for the frames page in Design view, the Print button on the Standard toolbar and the Print command on the File menu become disabled. If you select an individual frame in the frames page, you can use either of these methods to print the page that appears in that frame.

When you view a frames page in the browser, you have more options for printing a frames page. If you click File on the menu bar and then click Print, you can use the Print dialog box to select what to print. Figure 5-52 shows the Print dialog box in Internet Explorer.

Figure 5-52 **Print dialog box (Internet Explorer)**

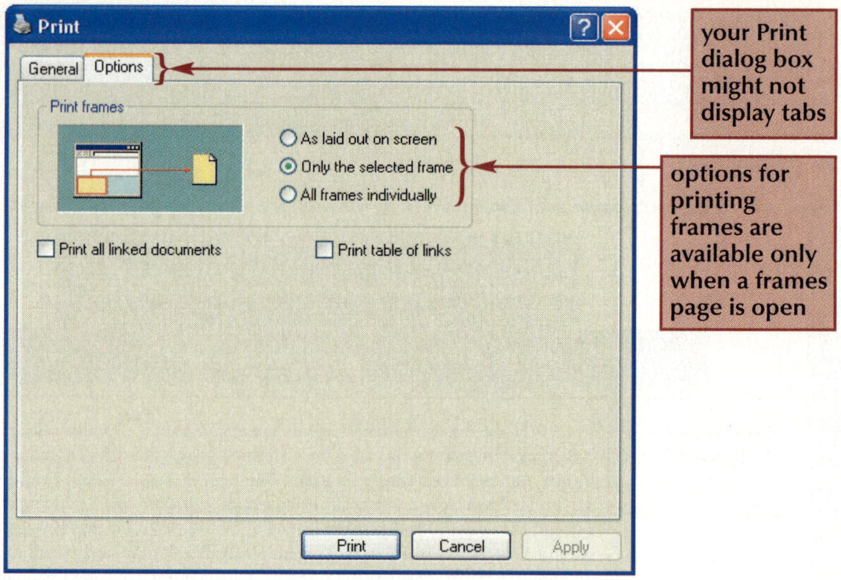

When a frames page is open in the browser, the Print frames section displays three options:

- The "As laid out on screen" option prints the frames page as it appears on the screen. In other words, this option prints the full content of the pages that you see in the browser window.
- The "Only the selected frame" option prints the active frame.
- The "All frames individually" option prints the full content of each page in the frames page on a separate sheet of paper.

Chad wants you to print the frames page, not just the individual pages contained within the frames page.

To print the frames page:

1. Click the **Preview** button on the Standard toolbar to open the RainMaker Irrigation page in the browser.
2. Click **File** on the menu bar, and then click **Print**. The Print dialog box opens. If necessary, click the **Options** tab to display those settings.

   Trouble? If you are using Netscape Navigator version 6.x or lower, you must click each frame to select it, and then click the Print button on the toolbar to print each frame's contents individually. These versions of Navigator do not have an option to print a frames page. Skip to Step 4 after printing each of the three frames.

   Trouble? If you are using Netscape Navigator version 7.x or higher, the Print Frames section of the Print dialog box contains the options for printing a frames page.
3. Click the **As laid out on screen** option button in the Print frames section, and then click the **Print** button (or the **OK** button). Internet Explorer prints the contents of the frames page as it appears on the screen.
4. Close your browser.

Viewing HTML Tags for a Frames Page

When you viewed the HTML document for the frames page earlier in this session, you saw only the HTML tags that created the frames page. Now you want to show Chad the HTML document for the frames page again, so he can see the HTML tags that FrontPage created to open the Web pages in the frames page. The <frameset> and </frameset> tags indicate the beginning and end of the frameset and specify each frame in the frames page. Within the <frame> tag, the src property indicates the filename for the target page, and the name property identifies the name of the frame in which to display the target page. The rows and columns properties of the <frameset> tag indicate the layout of the frames as a percentage of the size of the page when it is displayed in the browser. The Student Online Companion page for Tutorial 5 includes links that you can follow to learn more about HTML tags that create frames pages.

To view the HTML document for a frames page:

1. Click the **Show Code View** button [Code] at the bottom of the Contents pane to display the HTML document for the irr.htm page. See Figure 5-53. For each frame in the frames page, the HTML document specifies the frame's name (frame name), the page to open initially (src), and the size of the frame (frameset cols).

HTML document for the frames page — **Figure 5-53**

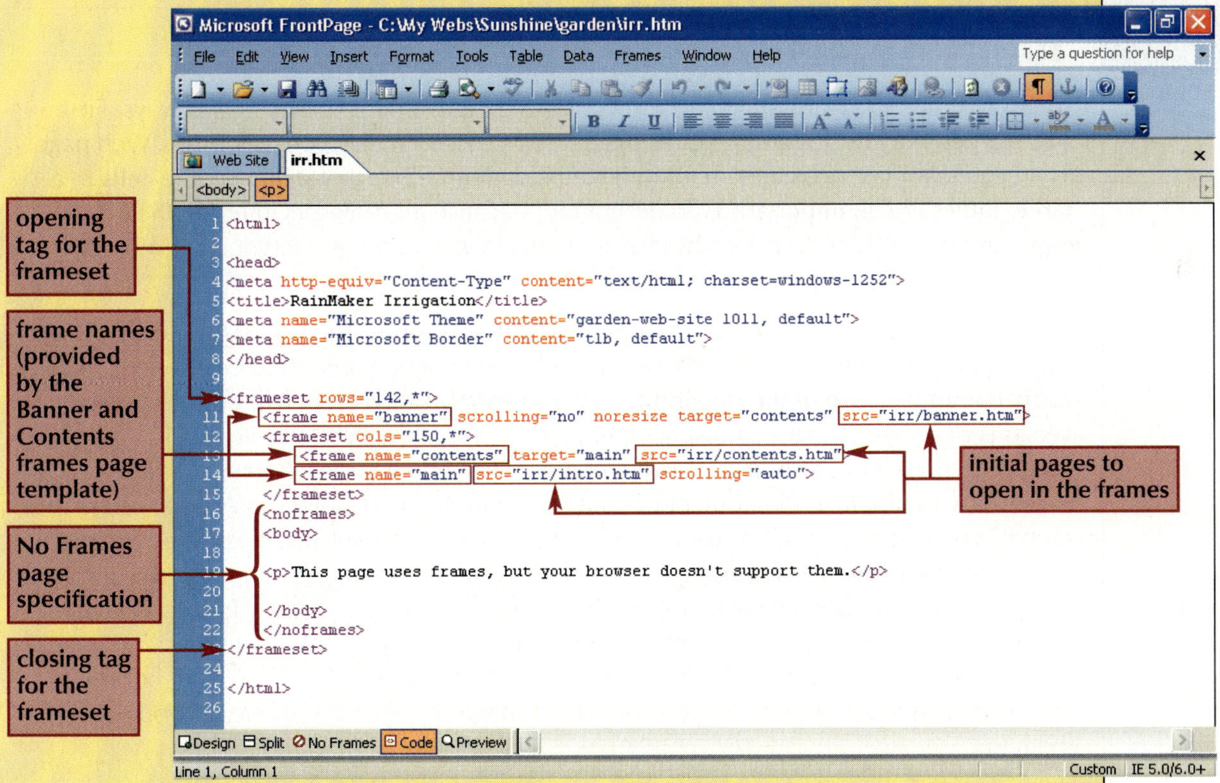

Trouble? The value you see for the rows property in the <frameset> tag might differ, depending on how you resized the banner frame in the steps. This difference causes no problems.

2. Return to Design view.
3. Close the garden Web site, and then close FrontPage.

The frames page is complete and it effectively organizes the content Chad requested. You will complete the second table for Helen's Lawn Care page in the Review Assignments. In the next tutorial, you will create forms that let visitors provide feedback and search the Web site for specific text, and then you will publish the Web site to a server.

Review

Session 5.2 Quick Check

1. True or False: A frames page does not contain any content; it contains only the specifications that define the empty frames.
2. A frames page that displays two frames will display ____________ Web pages when it is opened in a browser.
3. True or False: You can use a frames page without hesitation because all browsers can display frames.
4. Click the ____________ button in Design view to examine the HTML document that creates a frames page.
5. Click the ____________ button in an empty frame to specify an existing Web page to open when the browser loads the frames page.
6. Which predefined frame name causes the browser to remove all loaded frames pages before displaying the target of a selected hyperlink?
7. What information does the <frame> tag provide in a frameset?

Review

Tutorial Summary

In this tutorial, you learned how to use tables to organize information in two ways. First, you learned how to position pictures in a table to control their appearance in a Web page. Then you saw how to create a traditional table with gridlines that delineate the cells in a table. Tables are an important Web design tool because all browsers interpret the HTML tags that create tables consistently, thus providing a way to align content in a Web page so it always looks the way you intend it to.

You also learned how to create a frames page in this tutorial. The use of frames in a Web site is a frequent topic of debate between Web developers. Some Web developers avoid using frames because of the possibility that some Web site visitors will not have recent versions of browsers that can display them. However, many Web developers like using frames as a way of controlling Web site content. Much like tables, frames provide a consistent way to organize the content of your Web site. If you develop a Web site using frames, you can display all of your pages in frames, or just a subset of pages as you did in the garden Web site. However, be sure to check your frames pages carefully to make sure that the hyperlinks open their targets in the correct frames. If you use a frames page template to create a frames page, FrontPage will manage the hyperlink targets for you. If you add or remove a frame from the frames page created by a template, however, be sure to test your page thoroughly to make sure that the pages open in the frames as you intend them to.

Key Terms

border
cell
cell padding
cell spacing
frames page
frames page template
frameset
Insert Table button grid
layout cell
layout table
merge
nested table
No Frames page
split
table
Table AutoFormat
table caption
target frame

Practice

Practice the skills you learned in the tutorial using the same case scenario.

Review Assignments

Data Files needed for these Review Assignments: sun1.gif, tips.doc

To finish your work for today, you will need to format the remaining pictures in the table in the Bulk Goods Samples page and create the second table in the Lawn Care page. Finally, Chad wants to add a new page to the RainMaker Irrigation page, so you'll add this page to the Web site and create a hyperlink to it in the contents frame that will open the page in the main frame.

If necessary, start FrontPage, make sure you have your Data Files, and then do the following:

1. Open the **garden** Web site from the location where your Web sites are stored.
2. Open the **bulk2.htm** page in Design view. Format the pictures with the words "soil" and "stone" on them as hyperlinks that open the **soil.htm** and **stone.htm** pages, respectively.
3. Add a light yellow background color (Hex={FF,FF,CC}) to the table in the **bulk2.htm** page. Save and close the **bulk2.htm** page.
4. Open the Lawn Care page (**lawn.htm**) in Design view. Select the caption and the entire table, and then change the font size to 10 points. (*Hint:* Use the pointer to select the caption and the table.)
5. Select the text "[insert table here]" in the page, and then create the table shown in Figure 5-54. Use the same properties for the new table (alignment, size, cell padding, Table AutoFormat, font size, font style, and so on) that you used for the Common Lawn Problems and Solutions table that appears in the same page. Resize the first column in the table you are creating to match the width of the first column in the other table in the page. Change the second, third, and fourth columns to distribute them evenly, and then reset the table's width to 95%.

Figure 5-54

Sunshine Landscape & Garden Center			
The best landscape is an organic one!			
	Spring	Summer	Fall/Winter
Mowing	Mow every one to two weeks as necessary.	Mow every two weeks.	Mow every two to four weeks.
Fertilizing	Top-dress lawn with compost, and then in three to four weeks, apply an organic fertilizer (8-2-4).	Spray once a week with liquid seaweed.	Top-dress lawn with compost, and continue foliar feeding with liquid seaweed.
Watering	Water deeply when there is no rainfall.	Water deeply, in the morning or late evening, every five days.	Water deeply when there is no rainfall and before a freeze.
Other	Apply corn gluten to turf grasses to kill pre-emergent weeds.	Apply a soil activator to energize soil.	Prune oak trees and protect new plants from freezes.

6. Click the cell in column 1, row 3, of the table you created in Step 5, and then insert the **sun1.gif** picture from the Tutorial.05\Review folder included with your Data Files. Save the page and save the picture in the Web site's images folder.
7. Add the caption "Organic Lawn Care Program Recommendations" to the table you created in Step 5. After creating the caption, change its format to bold and 10 points.
8. Save the **lawn.htm** page, preview it using a browser, and then print it. Close your browser, and then close the **lawn.htm** page.
9. Open the **irr.htm** page in Design view. In the contents frame, add a new "Tips" hyperlink below the FAQ hyperlink. When you create the hyperlink, click the Create New Document button on the Link to bar in the Insert Hyperlink dialog box. Type **tips.htm** in the Name of new document text box, set the target frame so the **tips.htm** page opens in the main frame, and then click the Edit the new document now option button.
10. Remove the theme and shared borders from the **tips.htm** page only.
11. Insert the **tips.doc** file from the Tutorial.05\Review folder into the **tips.htm** page, and then save and close the page.
12. Open the RainMaker Irrigation page in a browser and test all the hyperlinks in the banner and contents frames. If necessary, return to FrontPage and correct any problems that you discover.
13. Use your browser to print the frames page with the **tips.htm** page displayed in the main frame. (If you cannot print the frames page with your browser, print each page displayed in the frames page individually.) Close your browser.
14. Close the **garden** Web site, and then close FrontPage.

Create

Create a frames page in a Web site, create a table in a Web page, and experiment with viewing a table at different screen resolutions to understand more about setting table widths.

Case Problem 1

There are no new Data Files needed for this Case Problem.

Buffalo Trading Post Retail-clothing customers usually want to know which items are the current best-sellers. Nicole Beirne, owner of Buffalo Trading Post, has decided that a list of the current top-selling items would be a great addition to the Web site. As you discuss this concept with Nicole and several sales associates, you conclude that there are three main areas of interest: women's clothing, children's clothing, and accessories. You already added these pages to the Web site, but now you want to use them in a frames page. Because the pages will not require the Web site's shared borders, you'll need to turn off the shared borders in these pages. Nicole is eager to see the new What page in the Web site.

If necessary, start FrontPage, and then do the following:

1. Open the **buffalo** Web site from the location where your Web sites are stored. (If you did not create this Web site in Tutorial 1 and change it in Tutorials 2 through 4, ask your instructor for assistance.)
2. In Folders view, select the **acc.htm**, **child.htm**, and **women.htm** pages, and then turn off the shared borders for these selected pages only. (*Hint:* To select multiple files, click the first file, press and hold the Ctrl key, select the remaining files, and then release the Ctrl key.)
3. Use the Banner and Contents frames page template to create a new frames page with the filename **what.htm** and the title What. Replace the existing **what.htm** file in the Web site that you created in Tutorial 2.

Explore

4. Create a new Web page in the banner frame with the filename **banner.htm** and the title Banner. In this new page, create a table that will contain the entries for the link bar. Your table should contain one row and five cells. Type the following text in the five cells: Home, How, Who, Where, and Contact. For the Home, How, and Who links, create hyperlinks to the appropriate pages in the Web site. Make sure to set the targets to open pages in the whole browser window.
5. Create two new Web pages in the site. The first page's filename is **where.htm** and its title is Where. The second page's filename is **contact.htm** and its title is Contact. Change to Navigation view, and then add the **where.htm** and **contact.htm** pages as child pages of the home page and to the right of the Who page.
6. In the **banner.htm** page in the frames page, format the Where and Contact text as hyperlinks that open the **where.htm** and **contact.htm** pages in the whole browser window.
7. Select the cells in the table in the banner frame, distribute the columns evenly, and then change the alignment of the data in the cells to centered. Change the table's properties so it is centered on the page.

Explore

8. Apply the Classic 1 Table AutoFormat to the table in the banner frame. Turn off the features that apply special formatting to the heading rows and the first column.
9. Change the properties of the table in the banner frame so it is 640 pixels wide, and then save the **banner.htm** page.

Explore

10. Create a new page in the contents frame with the filename **contents.htm** and the title Contents. Following your plan for the frames page, type Women's Clothing, Children's Clothing, and Accessories on separate lines in the **contents.htm** page, and then format these entries as hyperlinks that open the correct pages in the main frame.

Explore

11. Design a table that you will use to present the different top-selling items lists. The table should contain the item's category (such as "Shoes"), the item's description (such as "Sneakers and dress shoes"), and the item's price range (such as "$15 - $50").

12. Set the **women.htm** page to open initially in the main frame, add a centered heading with the Heading 2 style at the top of the page with the text "Top Women's Clothing Items," and then follow the plan you created in Step 11 to create the first table. Add the headings and five rows of data that you make up to the table, and then save it.
13. If necessary, resize the columns in your table so they best fit the data they contain. For example, the column that holds the item descriptions should be wider than the columns that hold the item names and price ranges.
14. Change the properties of the table in the **women.htm** page so it is centered in the page and 500 pixels wide, and then save it.

Explore

15. Apply the Classic 1 Table AutoFormat to the table in the **women.htm** page, and turn off the feature to apply special formatting to the first column. After applying the Table AutoFormat, change the background color of the cells in the first row to the light-yellow color in the Theme Colors section (this color is RGB(FF,FF,CC); if you do not see this color, select another light-yellow or beige color). Save your changes.
16. With the insertion point in the main frame, press Ctrl + A to select the page's content, click the Copy button on the Standard toolbar, and then use Ctrl + Click to open the **child.htm** page in the main frame. (*Hint:* Use the hyperlink in the contents frame. If you formatted this hyperlink with the correct target in Step 10, it will open in the main frame. If the page does not open in the main frame, correct the hyperlink's target, save your changes, and then resume the steps.)
17. Paste the content you copied into the **child.htm** page, and then edit the heading and table content to reflect the top-selling items in the children's clothing category.
18. Open the **acc.htm** page in the main frame, paste the table into this page, and then edit it to reflect the top-selling items in the accessories category. (Accessories are purses, jewelry, scarves, sunglasses, hats, etc.)

Explore

19. Reduce the width of the contents frame to 115 pixels. (*Hint:* Click in the contents frame, and then use the Frame Properties dialog box.)

Explore

20. Save your changes, and then open the frames page in a browser at 640 × 480 resolution and verify that clicking each hyperlink results in the appropriate action. If you encounter any problems during testing, return to FrontPage and correct them. Then use the browser to print the frames page as it appears in the browser with the Accessories page displayed in the main frame. (If you cannot print the frames page with your browser, print each page displayed in the frames page individually.) Close the browser, and then open the frames page in a browser at 800 × 600 resolution. What differences do you find between your testing at different resolutions? Why did these differences occur? Write your response and submit it to your instructor with your completed work.
21. Close your browser, the **buffalo** Web site, and FrontPage.

Apply

Apply the skills you learned in the tutorial to create a frames page in a Web site and use tables to organize pages that open in the main frame.

Case Problem 2

There are no new Data Files needed for this Case Problem.

Garden Grill Meghan Elliott and Callan Murphy just returned from a meeting with Hazel Scherer, who runs the marketing department at Garden Grill. During the meeting, Hazel asked if they could add a new page to the Web site to highlight the restaurant's weekly menu specials. As Hazel described the content she wants you to add, Meghan decided to replace the existing menu.htm page in the Web site with a frames page that will open four pages in its main frame to list specials in four menu categories: appetizers, sandwiches, entrees, and desserts. Hazel also thinks that a table would be the best way to organize the entries in each menu; she asks you to develop prototypes of these Web pages so she can approve them.

If necessary, start FrontPage, and then do the following:

1. Open the **grill** Web site from the location where your Web sites are stored. (If you did not create this Web site in Tutorial 1 and change it in Tutorials 2 through 4, ask your instructor for assistance.)

Explore

2. In Folders view, select the **app.htm**, **desserts.htm**, **entrees.htm**, and **sand.htm** pages, and then turn off the bottom shared border for these selected pages only. (*Hint:* To select multiple files, click the first file, press and hold the Ctrl key, select the remaining files, and then release the Ctrl key.)
3. Use the Contents frames page template to create a frames page. Save the page with the filename **menu.htm** and the title Menu, and overwrite the existing page in the Web site with the same name.
4. Sketch the design and contents of the table that will contain the menu items. The table should include at least three menu choices and columns for each item's name, description, and price.

Explore

5. Create a new page in the contents frame (the frame on the left) with the filename **contents.htm** and title Contents. The Contents page should include hyperlinks to the home page and to each menu page, with the main frame being the target for each of the four menu category pages. Set the target for the hyperlink to the home page so it opens in the full browser window.
6. Set the **app.htm** as the page that opens initially in the main frame.
7. Follow the plan you designed in Step 4 and create the table in the **app.htm** page. Insert a minimum of three menu items using data that you make up. Add a new first row to the table, which contains one merged cell that spans the three columns in the table. Center this merged cell, and then type "Appetizers." Set the table so it 100% of the browser's window width and uses a collapsed table border. Set the cell padding and cell spacing properties to 2. Apply a Table AutoFormat of your choice to the table. Be sure that the Table AutoFormat's colors complement the colors provided by the page's theme, and, if necessary, format the column headings and row headings in bold. With the exception of the first row, set the vertical alignment of cells to top and the horizontal alignment of cells to left. When you are finished, save the page.

Explore

8. With the insertion point in the main frame, press Ctrl + A to select the page's content, click the Copy button on the Standard toolbar, and then use Ctrl + Click to open the **sand.htm** page in the main frame. (*Hint:* Use the hyperlink in the contents frame. If you formatted this hyperlink with the correct target in Step 5, it will open in the main frame. If the page does not open in the main frame, correct the hyperlink's target, save your changes, and then resume the steps.)
9. Paste the content you copied into the **sand.htm** page, and then edit the table content to reflect menu items in the Sandwich category. Save the page.
10. Repeat Step 9 to complete the tables in the **entrees.htm** and **desserts.htm** pages. Save each page as you finish it.

Explore

11. Create a new frame in the Menu page by splitting the contents frame. Drag the bottom border of the contents frame up approximately two inches to create the new frame. Next, create a new Web page in the new frame with the filename **contact.htm** and the title Contact Us. In the new frame, type "Didn't find your favorites? Specials change each week!" If the text you typed doesn't fit in the frame, increase the size of the new frame to best fit the text. Save your changes.

12. Test the frames page in a browser. If you see a scroll bar in the frame that you added to the frames page in Step 11, return to FrontPage and increase the height of the new frame, save the page, and then refresh the frames page in the browser. Use the browser to print the frames page as it appears in the browser with the Desserts page displayed in the main frame. (If you cannot print the frames page with your browser, print each page displayed in the frames page individually.) Close your browser.
13. Use FrontPage to print the HTML document for the frames page.
14. Close the **grill** Web site, and then close FrontPage.

Apply

Use the skills you learned in the tutorial to create a frames page and expand your knowledge of working with tables by converting existing text into a table.

Case Problem 3

Data Files needed for this Case Problem: frame folder, scott.jpg, tucker.jpg

Swenson Auctioneers Scott Swenson knows that part of the reason for his company's success is the excellent word-of-mouth advertising he receives from satisfied customers when they recommend Swenson Auctioneers to their colleagues and friends. In times of economic downturns, Scott realizes that conducting an auction can be a very stressful time for a client who has lost his business. Auctions are equally stressful when they are held to sell off the estate of a loved one who has passed away. Scott has received many positive comments from former and current clients and he wants to showcase these comments on the Web site. Scott has already contacted the people who have submitted these comments and has obtained their written permission to use their remarks in the Web site. Scott asks you to add a page to the Web site that is accessible through a hyperlink on the home page. As you review the content for this page, you recommend presenting it in a frames page. Scott likes this idea and asks you to make it happen.

Scott also wants to add his picture and Tucker Griffin's picture to the Our Team page. You agree to make this change, as well, and recommend putting the pictures in a table to control their position in the page.

If necessary, start FrontPage, make sure you have your Data Files, and then do the following:

1. Open the **swenson** Web site from the location where your Web sites are stored. (If you did not create this Web site in Tutorial 1 and change it in Tutorials 2 through 4, ask your instructor for assistance.)
2. Use the New task pane to create a new Web page using the Contents frames page template. Save the frames page using the filename **clients.htm** and the title Client Comments.
3. Open the home page in Design view, select the word "clients" in the second sentence of the paragraph that begins "Established…", and then format this word as a hyperlink that opens the **clients.htm** page. Save the home page.

Explore

4. In the contents frame (the frame on the left) of the frames page, create a new page using the filename **contents.htm** and the title Contents. In the **contents.htm** page, insert the **sw_logo.gif** file from the **swenson** Web site's images folder. Format this picture as a hyperlink that opens the home page in the whole browser window. Add the alternative text "Return to Swenson Auctioneers Home Page" to the picture. Center the picture in the page, and then save the page.

Explore

5. Increase the width of the contents frame to 30%. (*Hint:* Select the contents frame, and then change the unit of measurement in the Frame size section of the Frame Properties dialog box.)

6. Import the **frame** folder and its contents from the Tutorial.05\Case3 folder included with your Data Files into the root folder of the **swenson** Web site. This folder contains eight files that you will use in the frames page. After importing this folder, open it in Folders view, select all eight files, and then apply the Swenson Web Site theme to them.
7. Set the **bus.htm** page in the **frame** folder to open initially in the main frame when the browser loads the frames page. Then add the following items to the **contents.htm** page, making sure the entries are centered and appear on separate lines: Business Equipment & Computers; Manufacturing & Heavy Equipment; Furniture, Art, & Rugs; Sound & Lighting; Special Use; Real Estate; Estates & Antiques; and Benefit Auctions. For each entry in the **contents.htm** page, create a hyperlink that opens the related page in the main frame. (The pages that these links should open are, respectively: **bus.htm**, **manu.htm**, **furn.htm**, **sound.htm**, **special.htm**, **real.htm**, **estate.htm**, and **benefit.htm**. These files are stored in the **frame** folder of the Web site.)
8. Save the **clients.htm** page, and then preview it in a browser. Test the hyperlinks that you created, including the hyperlink to open the home page and the hyperlink in the home page to open the Client Comments page. If necessary, return to FrontPage to make any corrections, resave the page, and then test it again. When you are finished, display the Sound & Lighting page in the main frame and then print the frames page. (If you cannot print the frames page with your browser, print each page displayed in the frames page individually.) Close your browser.

Explore

9. Open the **team.htm** page in Design view, and then scroll down to the bio for Scott. Scott told you that in his picture, he is facing to the left, so you will position the picture on the right side of the page so it appears that he is "looking" at the content. Select the four paragraphs below Scott's name (but not the hyperlink that scrolls to the top of the page or his name and position), and then convert this text to a table. (*Hint:* Click Table on the menu bar, point to Convert, and then click Text to Table. In the Convert Text To Table dialog box, click the None (text in single cell) option button, and then click the OK button.) The four paragraphs now appear in a table with one cell.
10. Insert a new column to the right of the single cell that you just created. In the new cell that you created, insert the **scott.jpg** file from the Tutorial.05\Case3 folder.
11. Set the table's properties so it is has a width of 100% and invisible table borders.

Explore

12. Tucker's picture shows him looking to the right, so you will insert his picture to the left of the paragraph that appears below his name and position. Select the paragraph below Tucker's name and position, convert it to a table, and then insert a column to the left of the single cell you created and insert the **tucker.jpg** picture from the Tutorial.05\Case3 folder. Set the table's properties so it has a width of 100% and invisible table borders.
13. Change the cells that contain pictures in both tables you created to the top vertical alignment.
14. Save the **team.htm** page and save the pictures in the Web site's images folder. Preview the **team.htm** page in a browser, print it, and then close your browser.
15. Close the **swenson** Web site, and then close FrontPage.

Create

Create a frames page in a Web site.

Case Problem 4

Data Files needed for this Case Problem: resource folder

Mortgage Services, Inc. As part of her Web site plan, Natalie Fuselier wants to include a page in the Web site for Mortgage Services, Inc. that provides resources for people who are moving into the area. She plans to include lists of homeowner's insurance agents, moving companies, utilities, and other helpful numbers that might assist her clients. A draft of this page appears in the current Web site, but Natalie wants you to improve it by adding the links and organizing the content so it is easy to use. She gives you the sketch shown in Figure 5-55 and asks you to make this change to the Web site. After you create the page, Natalie will begin working on compiling the links and other information to add to these new pages.

Figure 5-55

If necessary, start FrontPage, make sure you have your Data Files, and then do the following:

1. Open the **loan** Web site from the location where your Web sites are stored. (If you did not create this Web site in Tutorial 1 and change it in Tutorials 2 through 4, ask your instructor for assistance.)
2. Examine the sketch shown in Figure 5-55, and then create a new frames page in the Web site using the Contents frames page template. Save the frames page as **resource.htm** and with the title Resources, replacing the existing file in the Web site with the same name.

Explore

3. Make the following changes to the **resource.htm** frames page:
   a. Split the main frame (on the right) to create a new "top" frame. In this frame, create a new page with the filename **top.htm** and the title Top. Type and format the text shown in Figure 5-55 in the top frame. Format the word "here" as a hyperlink that opens the home page in the full browser window. If necessary, resize the height of the new frame so you can see all of the text you typed.
   b. Split the frame on the left to create a new frame at the top that is the same height as the top frame you created in the previous step. Create a new page using the filename **corner.htm** and the title Corner. Do not add any content to the page in the corner frame.
   c. Select the contents frame, and then open the Frame Properties dialog box. Click the Frames Page button and turn off the display of the frame's borders. Close the dialog boxes, save your changes, and then view the frames page in Preview view, noticing the effect created by creating the corner frame and turning off the frame's borders. (The background picture appears only in the corner and top frames because you haven't added any pages to the contents and main frames yet.)

d. Change to Code view for the frames page. Inspect the HTML document and notice the default names assigned to the two new frames you created in the frames page. Edit the HTML tag for the frame that contains the corner.htm page to change its name property to "corner." (Make sure to enclose this value in quotation marks.) Then find the HTML tag that creates the frame that contains the top.htm page and change its name property to "top." Return to Design view, and then save your changes.
e. Import the **resource** folder and its contents from the Tutorial.05\Case4 folder included with your Data Files into the **loan** Web site's root folder. After importing the folder into the Web site, open it in Folders view, select the six files it contains, and then apply the Loan Web Site theme to the selected pages.
f. In the contents frame of the frames page, create a new page using the filename **contents.htm** and the title Contents. Type the text shown in Figure 5-55 in the **contents.htm** page, and then format each item as a hyperlink that opens the related page in the main frame. The pages to open in the main frame are stored in the **resource** folder in the Web site. (*Note:* These pages contain headings, but no content.)
g. Set the **insure.htm** page to open initially in the main frame.
h. Save the frames page.

4. Preview the frames page in a browser, and then test the links that you created, including the link to the home page. Use the Resources link in the home page to return to the frames page. Display the Schools page in the main frame of the frames page, and then use the browser to print it. (If you cannot print the frames page with your browser, print each page displayed in the frames page individually.) Close your browser.
5. In FrontPage, display the HTML document for the frames page, and then print it.
6. Close the **loan** Web site, and then close FrontPage.

Review

Quick Check Answers

Session 5.1

1. a cell
2. Use a percentage for tables that contain mostly text; use pixels when you need tight control over the placement of objects that have a fixed size, such as pictures.
3. cell padding
4. True
5. False
6. above
7. Select the cells, and then click the Merge Cells button; or click the Eraser button, and then use the pointer to erase the border between the cells to merge.
8. above

Session 5.2

1. True
2. three
3. False
4. Show Code View
5. Set Initial Page
6. _top (Whole Page)
7. the frame's name, the target frame, and the initial page to load in the frame

Objectives

Session 6.1
- Create a Web page using a template
- Change the properties of a search component
- Add a form component to a Web page
- Add form fields to a form and set their properties

Session 6.2
- Validate a form field
- Use a form handler
- Open an Office document from a Web site

Session 6.3
- Publish a Web site
- Process Web pages on a server
- Create a hit counter in a Web page
- Synchronize local and remote Web sites
- Recalculate and verify hyperlinks in a Web site
- Set permissions for a Web site

Publishing a Web Site

Creating Web Pages with Components and Processing Pages on a Server

Case

Sunshine Landscape & Garden Center

In this morning's staff meeting, you spent some time presenting the Web site to the senior staff at Sunshine Landscape & Garden Center. Almost everyone has contributed content to the site and is pleased with its overall content, appearance, and organization.

As you review the pages with Sunshine's owner, Brett Kizer, you suggest adding two new pages to the site. The first page would let Web site visitors search the entire site for content based on one or more keywords that they enter in a text box. This page would let visitors find the content they need without having to navigate the entire site looking for it. Brett agrees that this page would be useful and asks you to proceed with its creation.

The second page would contain a form that a visitor can use to submit a question or a request. In talking with staff members at the nursery, you found that many customers have expressed interest in using the Web site to request a consultation about landscaping or rock work installations and to ask questions about plants and lawn care. When the new site is published, you think that this functionality will be a nice way to promote the nursery's goal of increased customer service. Brett likes this idea and sees potential for it in the future to generate lists of customers and their requests for service and installations. He asks you to create this page in the Web site, as well.

After creating these two new pages and testing the Web site, you will publish the Web site to a server where you can test the site again and make it ready for its final destination on the Web server Brett selected to host it. After publishing the Web site, it will be accessible to Internet visitors.

Student Data Files

To complete this tutorial, you will need your ending files from Tutorial 5 and the following Data Files. Additional Data Files needed to complete the end-of-tutorial exercises are listed with the Review Assignments and Case Problems.

▼**Tutorial.06**
- ▽ Tutorial
  - form.doc
  - requests.htm

Session 6.1

Creating a Page That Searches a Web Site

So far in this book, you have created pages in a Web site using a template. Some of those pages were based on the Normal Page template, which creates a blank Web page. In Tutorial 5, you used templates to create frames pages. FrontPage includes many templates that create Web pages with sample formatting and text. For example, if you need to create a Web page into which users will enter personal information, you might create your page using the Guest Book template, which includes features and sample text that are commonly found in a printed guest book. When you use a template to create a new Web page that contains sample content, you can edit it just like any other Web page. Figure 6-1 describes the general templates that you can use to create Web pages.

Figure 6-1 **General template Web pages and wizards and their descriptions**

Name	Description
Normal Page	Creates a blank Web page
Bibliography	Creates a page with references to printed or electronic works
Confirmation Form	Creates a page that confirms the receipt of information from a user of a form, discussion, or registration page
Feedback Form	Creates a page that collects data entered by a user, such as comments and personal information
Form Page Wizard	A wizard that creates a page containing a form with fields to collect information
Frequently Asked Questions	Creates a page with popular questions about a topic and their answers
Guest Book	Creates a page into which visitors to a Web site can enter comments and other information
Photo Gallery	Creates a page that contains a photo gallery with pictures, captions, and descriptions that you supply
Search Page	Creates a page that accepts keywords entered by a user and then returns a list of hyperlinks to pages with matching entries
Table of Contents	Creates a page that contains a list of hyperlinks to every page in the current Web site
User Registration	Creates a page that visitors can use to register for a restricted-access Web site

After meeting with the nursery's senior staff, your first task is to add a page to the Web site that searches the entire site using one or more keywords entered by the user. The Search Page template creates content for you and adds the necessary functionality to the page to search the site, so you'll base the new page on the Search Page template.

To create the Search page using a template:

1. Start **FrontPage**, and then open the **garden** Web site from the location where your Web sites are stored.
2. Click the **list arrow** on the Create a new normal page button on the Standard toolbar, and then click **Page**. The Page Templates dialog box opens with the General tab selected.
3. Click the **Search Page** icon to select it. See Figure 6-2. The description and preview indicate that this page will provide the capability for searching the entire Web site.

Page Templates dialog box | **Figure 6-2**

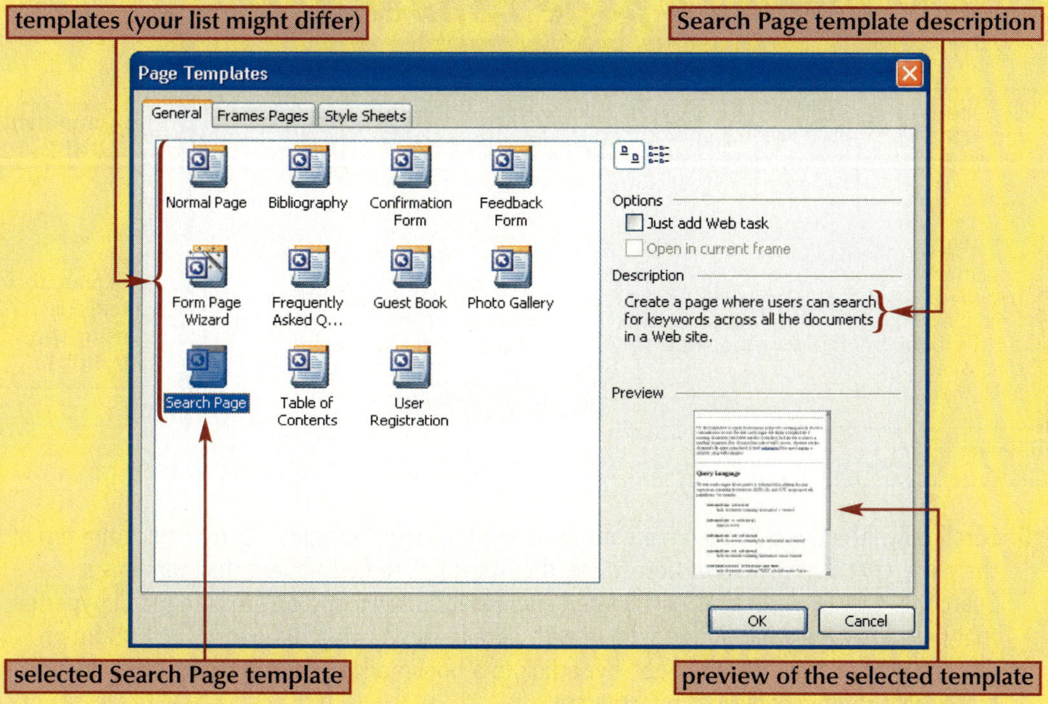

4. Click the **OK** button to create a new Web page based on the Search Page template. The new page opens in Design view, as shown in Figure 6-3. Because you have not yet added this page to the navigation structure in Navigation view, the page displays placeholder text for the page banner and link bar.

Figure 6-3 New page created using the Search Page template

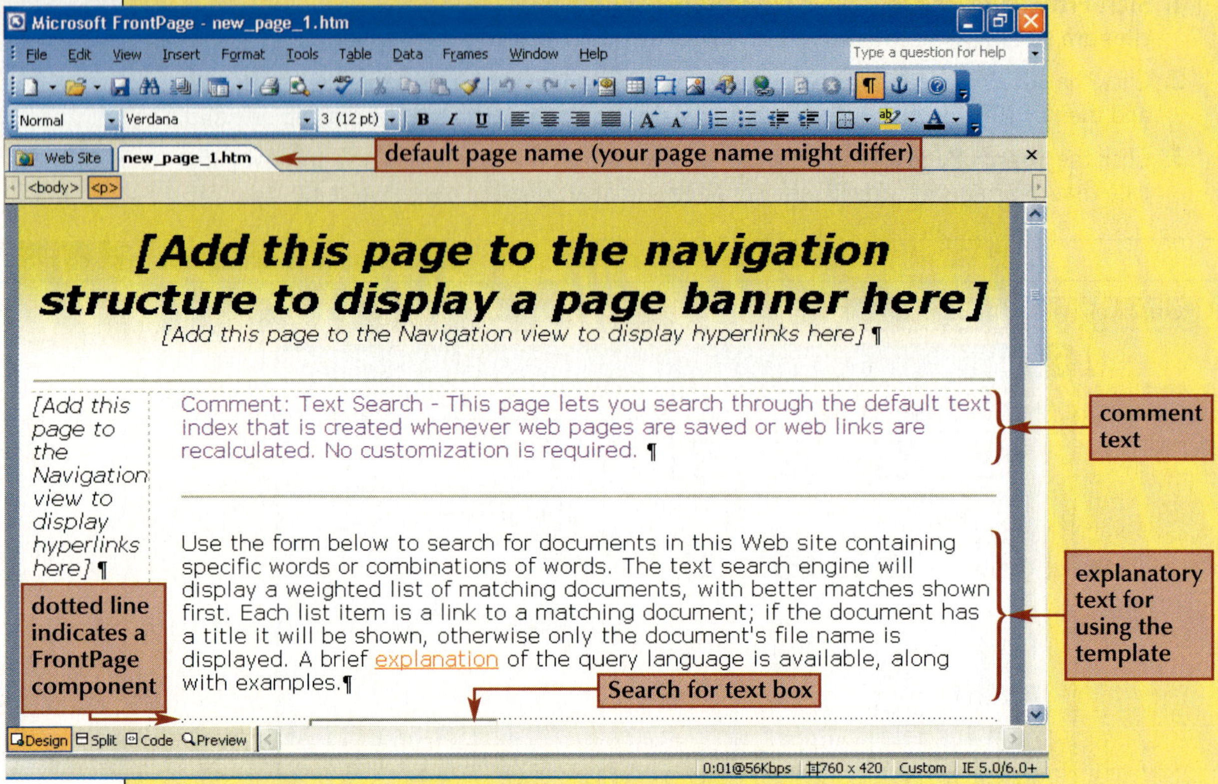

5. Scroll down the page and examine its contents. The page contains a comment at the top of the page, text that describes how to use the page, a Web component that contains a Search for text box and the Start Search and Reset buttons, and an "explanation" hyperlink that links to a Query Language section with details about using the page. The bottom of the page contains a "Back to Top" hyperlink to a bookmark at the top of the page and a footer with sample copyright information.
6. Press **Ctrl + Home** to scroll to the top of the page.

The overall design and content of the new page is similar to the page that you want to develop for the garden Web site. In reviewing the content provided by the template, you decide to make some minor changes. You will remove the comment from the top of the page, add the page to the navigation structure to display the page banner and link bar in the top shared border, and then save the page with an appropriate filename and a descriptive title.

To revise a Web page created with a template:

1. At the top of the page, point to the purple "Comment: Text Search - This page..." text at the top of the page. The pointer changes to a shape, which identifies the location of a Web component. The comment includes text you can see in Design view, but not in a Web browser.
2. Right-click the purple comment text to select it and open the shortcut menu, and then click **Cut**. The comment is deleted, and a blank line appears above the horizontal line at the top of the page.
3. Right-click the horizontal line that appears below the comment you just deleted (but not the horizontal line that appears in the top shared border), and then click **Cut** on the shortcut menu.

4. Click the **Save** button on the Standard toolbar, type **search.htm** in the File name text box, click the **Change title** button, type **Search** in the Page title text box, click the **OK** button to close the Set Page Title dialog box, and then click the **Save** button to close the Save As dialog box. The new Web page now has the filename search.htm and an appropriate title.
5. Click the **Web Site** tab at the top of the Contents pane, change to Navigation view, and, if necessary, display the Folder List.
6. If necessary, scroll the navigation structure so you can see the yellow Irrigation page in the navigation structure (but not the white Irrigation page in the custom link bar navigation structure).
7. If necessary, scroll down the Folder List so you can see the search.htm page, and then drag the **search.htm** page from the Folder List and position it as a child page of the home page and to the right of the Irrigation page. See Figure 6-4.

Figure 6-4 Search page added to the navigation structure

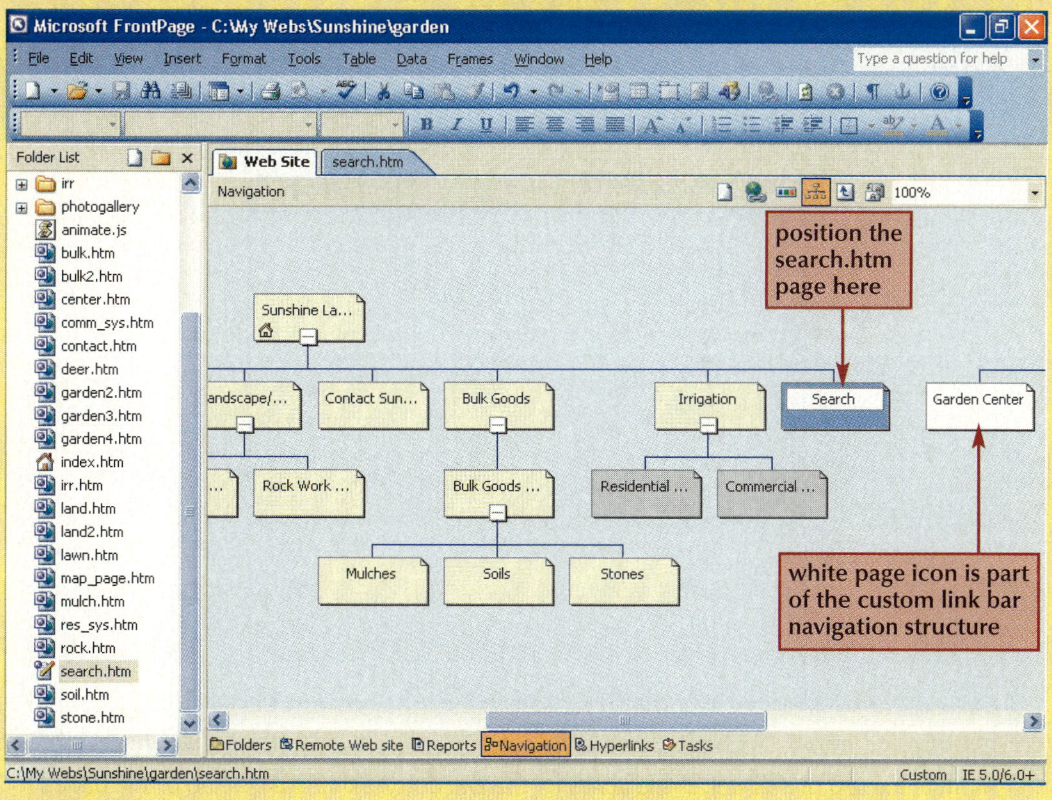

You also need to add the Search page to the custom link bar that appears in the home page.

8. Scroll the navigation structure so you can see the custom link bar navigation structure (with the white page icons), and then drag the **search.htm** page from the Folder List and position it to the right of the Anti-Deer Products page.
9. Double-click **search.htm** in the Folder List to open the page in Design view. The page now displays a page banner and a link bar in the top shared border.
10. Save the search.htm page and close the Folder List.

Changing the Search Component's Properties

When you created the Search page from the template, FrontPage automatically included a search component in it that searches the Web site using keywords entered by the user. You can also add a search component to an existing page by clicking the Web Component button on the Standard toolbar, clicking the Web Search Component type, and then following the instructions in the dialog boxes. Regardless of how you create the search component, you can change its properties as necessary. The first change you decide to make is to increase the size of the text box into which users will type keywords.

To change the properties of the search component:

1. If necessary, scroll down the Search page so you can see the Search for text box and the Start Search and Reset buttons, and then point anywhere in the dotted-line box that contains these objects so the pointer changes to a  shape.
2. Right-click anywhere in the search component to open the shortcut menu, and then click **Search Form Properties** to open the Search Form Properties dialog box. See Figure 6-5.

Figure 6-5 Search Form Properties dialog box

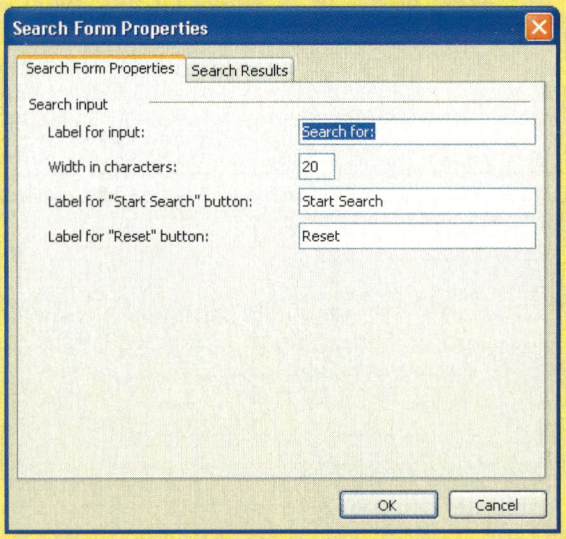

The Search Form Properties tab includes options for changing the defaults for the label and width of the text box as well as the labels for the two buttons that are created by the page's template. (A label for a button is the text that appears on the button to identify its function.) You can accept these defaults or change them, when necessary, to match your requirements. You will change the width of the Search for text box so it will display more characters.

3. Select the value in the Width in characters text box, and then type **25** to increase the size of the Search for text box. The other default settings are acceptable, so you can close the dialog box.
4. Click the **OK** button to close the dialog box and return to the Search page, and then click anywhere in the paragraph above the search component to deselect it. The size of the Search for text box has increased to 25 characters.

   The Search Page template added a horizontal line and sample copyright information at the bottom of the page. Because copyright information already appears in the bottom shared border of the Web site, you can delete the duplicate text added by the template. Because other pages in the Web site do not have a horizontal line at the bottom of the page, you'll also delete the horizontal line.

5. Press **Ctrl + End** to scroll to the bottom of the Search page, and then select the horizontal line and the three lines of text below it. (The first line of the footer you will delete is "Author information goes here.")
6. Press the **Delete** key to delete the selected items.
7. Save the search.htm page.

You can also insert a search component in a Web page that searches the Internet using keywords entered by the user. FrontPage also provides other components that you can use to create a link to a map at Expedia.com; to display stock market information; and to display business, living, travel, news, sports, and technology headlines, as well as weather forecasts from MSNBC. All of these components are available in the Insert Web Component dialog box.

Brett thinks that it would be a nice addition to the Web site to provide a component that searches the Internet, so if his customers don't find what they are looking for in the garden Web site, they can search other sites.

To insert a component that searches the Web:

1. Scroll up the Web page until the "Query Language" heading appears at the top of the Contents pane, and then click to the left of the letter "Q" in Query Language.
2. Click the **Web Component** button on the Standard toolbar. The Insert Web Component dialog box opens.
3. Scroll down the list of Component types, and then click **MSN Components**. The two MSN components—Search the Web with MSN and Stock quote—appear in the Choose a MSN component list box. See Figure 6-6.

Insert Web Component dialog box **Figure 6-6**

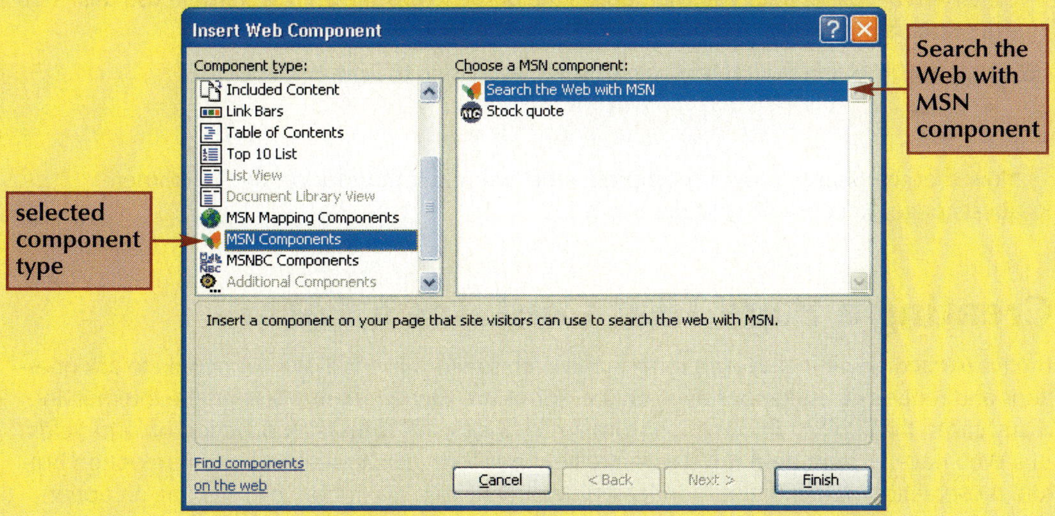

4. Make sure that the **Search the Web with MSN** component is selected, and then click the **Finish** button. A Search the Web with MSN component is inserted in the Web page. See Figure 6-7. The MSN logo appears as a broken link because this picture is not stored in the Web site.

Figure 6-7 **Search the Web with MSN component added to search.htm page**

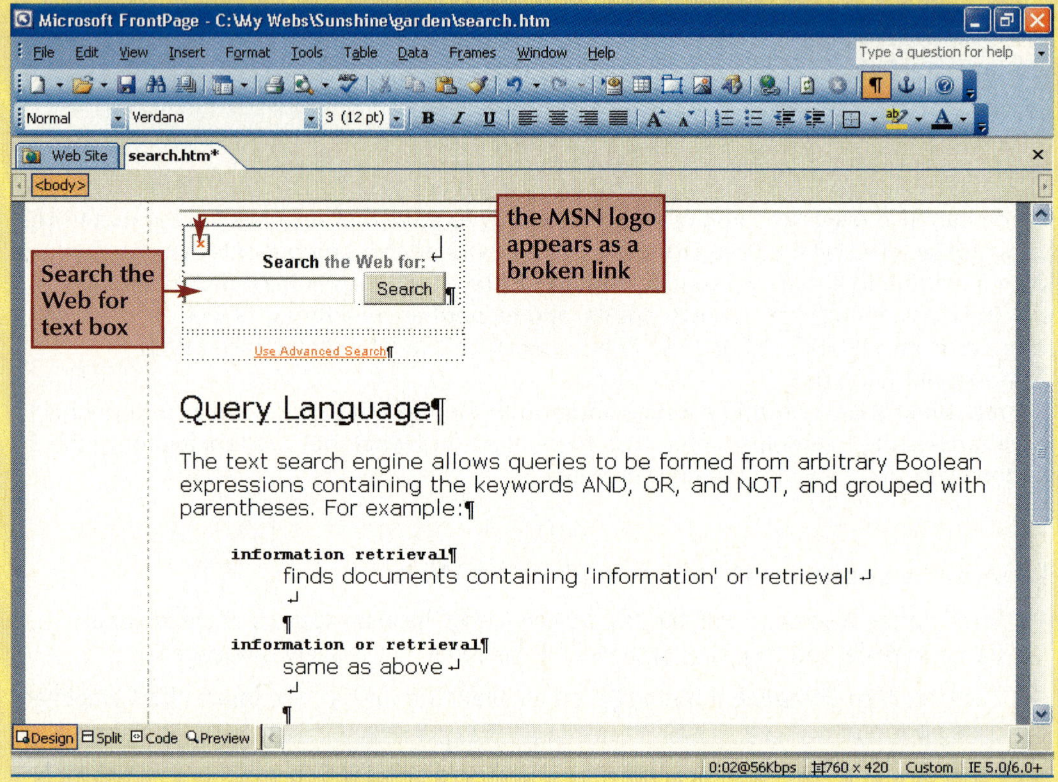

Trouble? If a Dial-up Connection dialog box opens, click the Close button to close it. You do not need an Internet connection to complete these steps.

The Search page now contains a component that will let users enter keywords to search the Internet. In Session 6.3, you will publish the garden Web site on a server and use this page to search both the site and the Internet.

5. Save and close the search.htm page, and then change to Folders view.

Now that the Search page is complete, you are ready to work on the Customer Requests page, which will contain a form.

Creating a Page That Contains a Form

Brett is excited about including a form in the Web site to make it easier for people to ask questions and request consultations and service. Forms are used in many ways on the Internet. In many cases, they collect information from a site's visitors. A **form** is a collection of form fields in a Web page. A **form field** is a data-entry field in a form, such as a text box or an option button. A user enters data into the form by typing directly into a text box, by selecting an option button or a check box, or by selecting a value from a drop-down menu. After completing the form, the user submits it to the server, where a form handler processes it. A **form handler** is a program that collects and processes the form's data in a predetermined manner. For example, you might select a form handler to save the form's data in an HTML file, or to send the form's data to an e-mail address, or both. FrontPage includes many form handlers to process common requests. If you are an experienced programmer, you can also design your own form handler and use it to process forms you create with FrontPage.

During your meeting with Sunshine's senior staff, you formulated a plan for the form that you need to create. The form will provide a text box into which customers can type a question; a section that lets the customer request a consultation or service; and a section in which the customer can enter his or her name, e-mail address, daytime phone number, and a communication preference (e-mail or phone). Brett asks if there is also a way to ask customers for the number of visits they have made to the nursery so he can determine whether new or existing customers are using the site. You tell Brett that this information is easy to collect and add it to your sketch of the form, which appears in Figure 6-8.

Figure 6-8 **Sketch of the Customer Requests page**

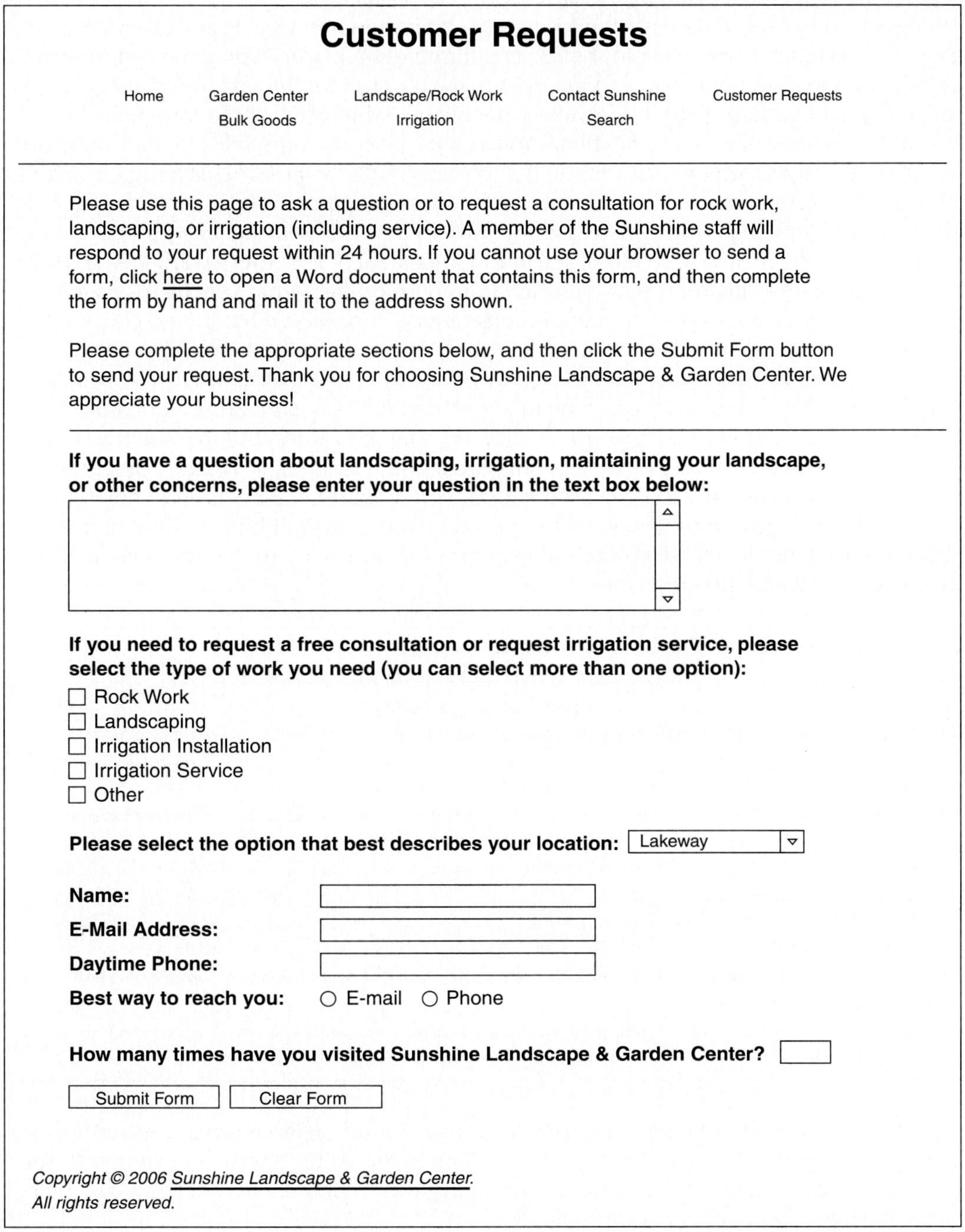

You tell Brett that there are two ways to create a form. First, you can use the **Form Page Wizard**, which asks questions about the type of form that you want to create and lets you select the form's options to create a Web page containing the form with the fields you specified. To use this option, double-click the Form Page Wizard icon in the Page Templates dialog box. You can use this method when you want to create a standard type of form, such as a form that contains billing and shipping addresses or information about products, such as quantity ordered.

The second option is to insert a form component in an existing or new Web page. The form component appears as a box with a dotted outline in Design view. You use the Form command on the Insert menu to insert the form's fields into the form. After adding a form field, you can accept its default settings or change its properties.

Regardless of how you create the form, you edit it the same way as any other Web page. For example, if you click to the left of a form field and start typing the text to serve as its label, the form field moves to the right to make room for the text. Pressing the Enter key to the left of a form field inserts a new paragraph, which causes the form field to appear at the beginning of the next line. You can cut or copy form fields to the Clipboard and paste them into another location in the form or into another form. Although a single Web page can contain more than one form, the most common approach is to create a single form in a Web page. You will create one form in the Customer Requests page.

In addition to creating a sketch of the form's appearance, it is also a good idea to determine ahead of time any rules that you want to impose on the form's use and users. For example, do you want to permit multiple selections in drop-down boxes and check box groups? Do you want to create a default selection for an option button or check box? How many characters do you want to display at one time in a text box? Do you want to limit the amount of text a user can type in a text box? Do you want any default text to appear in a text box? Do you need to validate any entered values, to force users to enter a value in a text box, or to restrict the content entered in a text box to integers or letters? To help Brett understand how to develop the form, you prepared the document shown in Figure 6-9 to list the criteria you want to impose on the form. You'll teach Brett more about the questions to ask when designing a form as you work with him to develop the form in the Customer Requests page.

Figure 6-9 **Form design criteria for the Customer Requests page**

Form Design Criteria

- The text area should be 80 characters wide and five lines high, with no initial value.
- The check box group should not contain a default selection. The results file should include the value "Yes" to indicate a selected check box.
- The drop-down box should have a height of 1 and allow only one selection. The choices are Lakeway, Dripping Springs, Austin, Lago Vista, West Lake Hills, and Other. The default selection is Lakeway. The Other selection should include a text box for the user to enter a location not in the list.
- The text boxes for the user's name, e-mail address, and daytime phone number should be 35 characters wide.
- The option button group should include two option buttons, with neither option button being selected initially.
- The text box to record the number of visits to the nursery should permit only integers from 0 to 100. This field must contain a value when the user submits the form to the server.

After meeting with Brett, you created a Web page based on the Normal Page template and entered most of the text in the page according to the sketch shown in Figure 6-8. You will import this page into the Web site, turn on the shared borders for the page, and then create the form component and form fields.

To import the page into the Web site and turn on the shared borders:

1. Display the Folder List, and then make sure the garden Web site's root folder is selected.
2. Click **File** on the menu bar, and then click **Import**. The Import dialog box opens.
3. Click the **Add File** button to open the Add File to Import List dialog box, open the **Tutorial.06\Tutorial** folder included with your Data Files, and then double-click **requests.htm**. The path to the requests.htm file included with your Data Files appears in the Import dialog box.
4. Click the **OK** button to import the requests.htm page into the garden Web site.
5. If necessary, scroll down the files in the Folder List, and then double-click **requests.htm** to open the Customer Requests page in Design view. You need to add this page to the navigation structure and to the custom link bar navigation structure, turn on the shared borders, and add the theme to the page.
6. Click the **Web Site** tab, change to Navigation view, and then position the **requests.htm** page in the navigation structure between the Contact Sunshine and Bulk Goods pages.
7. Scroll the navigation structure, and then position the **requests.htm** page in the custom link bar navigation structure between the Contact Sunshine and Bulk Goods pages.
8. Close the Folder List, and then click the **requests.htm** tab.
9. Click **Format** on the menu bar, click **Shared Borders**, make sure the **Current page** option button is selected, make sure that the **Top**, **Left**, and **Bottom** check boxes are selected, and then click the **OK** button. The top, left, and bottom shared borders appear in the requests.htm page.
10. Click **Format** on the menu bar, click **Theme**, point to the **Garden Web Site** theme in the Theme task pane, click the **list arrow** that appears, and then click **Apply to selected page(s)**. The Garden Web Site theme is applied to the requests.htm page. Now the page has the same appearance and navigation options as other pages in the Web site.
11. Close the Theme task pane, and then save the requests.htm page.

With the page imported into the Web site and the shared borders and theme added to the page, you are ready to add a form component. Then you will insert the form fields in the form component and modify their properties to match the criteria you specified in Figure 6-9.

Adding a Form Component to a Web Page

Before adding a form field to the Web page, you must add the form component that will contain the form's fields. The form component is required because it identifies the region of the page that the server will process. If you use the Form Page Wizard to create your Web page, FrontPage adds the form component to the page automatically. The Customer Requests page does not yet contain a form component. When you add a form component to a page, FrontPage creates the form component and inserts the Submit and Reset buttons automatically.

Reference Window

Creating a Form Component and Adding a Form Field

- Position the insertion point where you want to insert the form.
- Click Insert on the menu bar, point to Form, and then click Form.
- Place the insertion point inside the form component where the first form field should appear.
- Click Insert on the menu bar, point to Form, and then click the desired form field to add to the form.
- Double-click a form field object to open the form field's Properties dialog box.
- Enter the appropriate values for the form field's properties.
- Click the OK button.

Because the Customer Requests page already contains content, you will insert the form component in the page, and then cut the content from the page and paste it into the form component. The form handler on the server will process only form fields that are contained within a form component.

To insert a form component in the Customer Requests page:

1. Click to the left of the word "If" in the third paragraph to position the insertion point there. This line of text is the first one that will appear within the form.
2. Click **Insert** on the menu bar, point to **Form**, and then click **Form**. FrontPage inserts a form component above the paragraph that begins with the word "If." The insertion point moves automatically to the left of the Submit button in the form component. Notice that a dotted line identifies the form component.

   You will cut the text from the page and paste it into the form component.
3. Click to the left of the word "If," scroll to the bottom of the page, press and hold the **Shift** key, click to the right of the last line in the page (which ends "...Sunshine Landscape & Garden Center?"), and then release the **Shift** key. The text that you will cut is selected.
4. Click the **Cut** button on the Standard toolbar to cut the selected text from the page.
5. Click to the left of the Submit button, but inside the form component, to place the insertion point there. You will paste the text that you just cut here.

   Trouble? If you see selection handles around the Submit button, then you selected the button instead of the space between the form component and the Submit button. Press the left arrow key ← to deselect the Submit button and to position the insertion point to its left.
6. Click the **Paste** button on the Standard toolbar to paste the text into the form component, and then save the page. The form component now contains the text. See Figure 6-10.

Form component in the requests.htm page

Figure 6-10

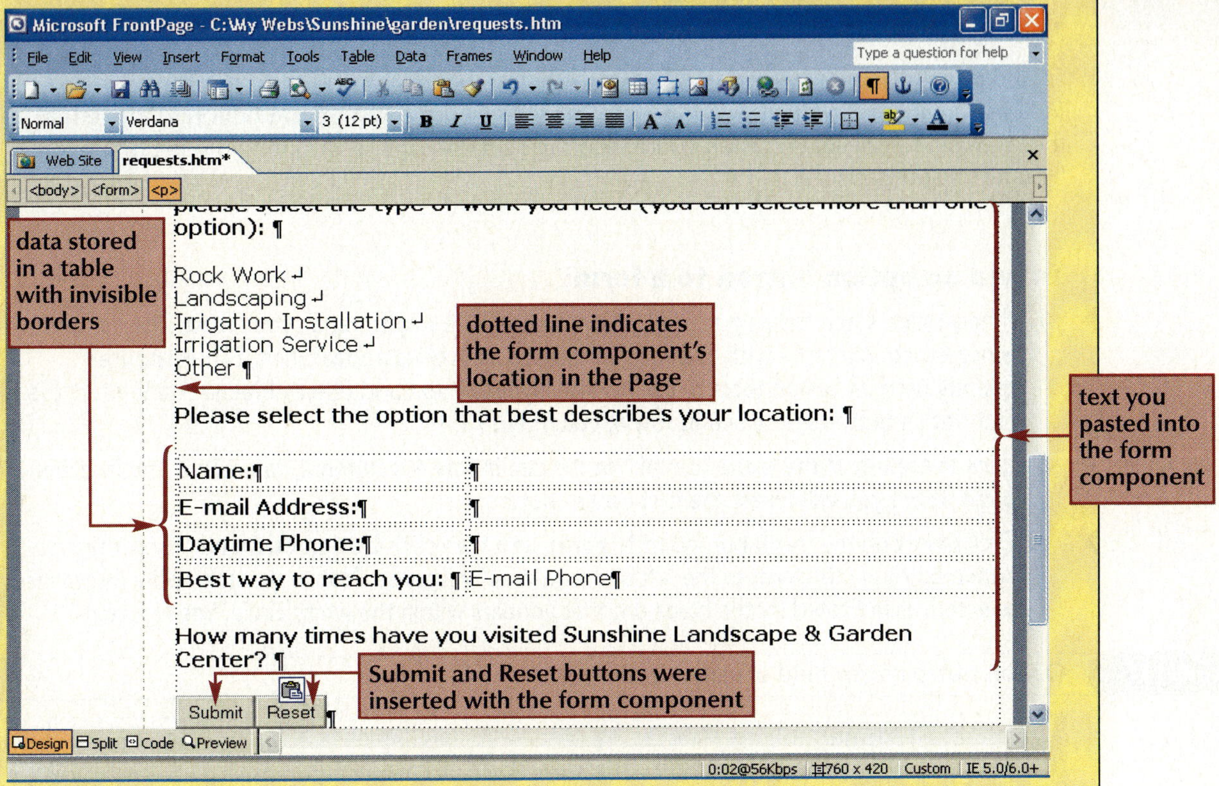

Now you can start adding fields to the form according to the sketch shown in Figure 6-8.

Adding Option Buttons to a Form

Option buttons (also called **radio buttons**) are usually arranged in groups in a form. An **option button group name** identifies a set of related option buttons. Within a group of option buttons, only one button can be selected at a time—selecting an option button automatically deselects any other selected option button. You create labels for option buttons by typing the appropriate text next to the button. For example, a form might have a section with the group name "Age" that contains corresponding option buttons with the labels "Under 25," "25-40," "41-65," and "Over 65." Option buttons are appropriate when only a few choices are available, such as when specifying age groups. A form can contain more than one option button group as long as the different option button groups use different option button group names.

The first option button you add to a form will be selected automatically when you open the form in a browser, unless you change its properties. The first option button in an option button group is usually the most common response, and selecting it automatically saves users some time so they won't need to select it if it is their choice. You can also design an option button group so that no single option button is selected, thereby forcing the form's user to make a selection.

When you create option button groups in a form, consider the following design suggestions:

- Use option buttons when you want to limit the user to selecting one of a few related and mutually exclusive choices.
- The minimum number of option buttons in a group is two, and the recommended maximum is seven.

- Clearly label each option button in a group so that users can easily determine the appropriate option button to select.
- Use a heading or text to identify the group name for the option buttons.

The sketch shown in Figure 6-8 shows an option button group for customers to use to indicate their communication preferences. You'll insert the first option button to the left of the "E-mail" response, and then you'll insert the second option button to the left of the "Phone" response.

To add an option button to a form:

1. If necessary, scroll the page so you can see the "Best way to reach you:" text. The content is organized in a table with invisible borders to control its appearance. Tables are frequently used as design tools to control the layout of text and other objects. You'll insert the first option button in the cell in row 4, column 2.
2. Click to the left of the word "E-mail" in the cell in row 4, column 2, to position the insertion point where you will insert the first option button.
3. Click **Insert** on the menu bar, point to **Form**, and then click **Option Button** to insert the first option button in the form to the left of the "E-mail" response. Notice that the option button is selected, as indicated by the black dot that appears within the white circle. See Figure 6-11.

Figure 6-11 **Option button form field inserted in the form**

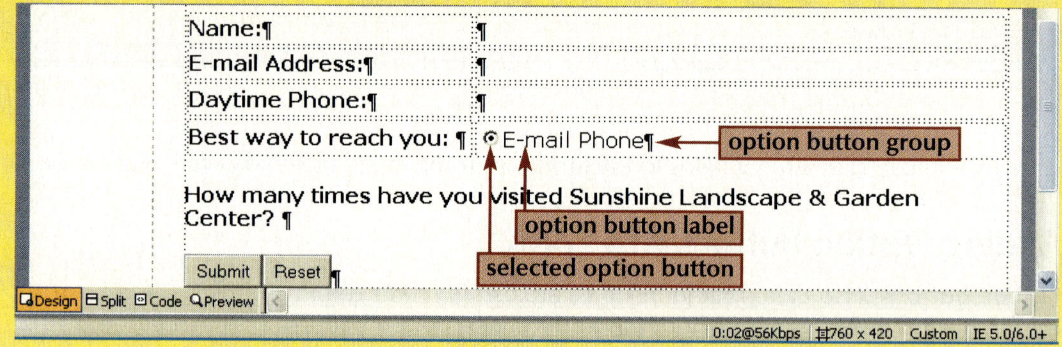

Trouble? If you insert the option button in the wrong location or insert the wrong form field, click the Undo button on the Standard toolbar to remove the form field, and then repeat the steps to insert the correct form field. You can also delete a form field by selecting it and pressing the Delete key.

You'll insert the second option button to the left of the "Phone" response.

4. Click to the left of the word "Phone" to position the insertion point, and then repeat Step 3 to insert the option button for this selection. Notice that this second option button does not appear selected, as indicated by the solid white circle.
5. Save the page.

The E-mail and Phone option buttons now belong to a group. Within this group, the user can select only one option button.

After placing a form field in the form, you can change its properties to match your needs better. For example, FrontPage assigned the group name R1 to the option button group, the value V1 to the E-mail option button, and the value V2 to the Phone option button. If you add more option buttons to this form, FrontPage will add them to the R1 group and assign sequential values to them (V3, V4, etc.). You could accept these default values for the group and button names, but you will modify the current option button properties to change the group name to CommunicationPreference and the button names to match their responses. Using more meaningful names will make the responses easier to examine and locate in the file that stores the form's results. Before changing the properties of the option buttons, you tell Brett that names for groups and form fields cannot contain spaces.

To change option button properties:

1. Double-click the **option button** to the left of the E-mail label to select it and to open the Option Button Properties dialog box. You will change the group name and the value name for the option button.
2. With the value selected in the Group name text box, type **CommunicationPreference**, press the **Tab** key to select the value in the Value text box, and then type **Email**. Now the option button group is named CommunicationPreference, and the first option button in the group is named Email. See Figure 6-12. In the Initial state section, the Selected option button is selected, indicating that the E-mail option button is the default selection.

Option Button Properties dialog box for the E-mail option button **Figure 6-12**

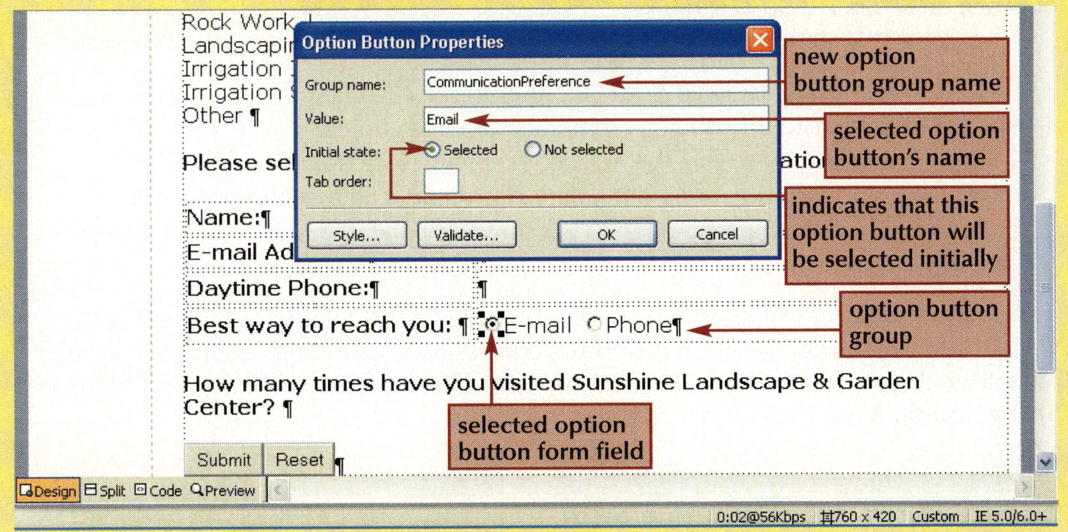

Because you want to force the user to make a choice, you'll change the initial state of the E-mail option button so it is not selected.

3. Click the **Not selected** option button to select it, and then click the **OK** button to close the dialog box. The E-mail option button changes from selected to not selected. The other changes you made appear only in the HTML document for this page.

   Trouble? If a message box opens and tells you that the name is not valid, click the OK button to continue and make sure that "CommunicationPreference" in the Group name text box does not contain a space. Click the OK button to close the dialog box.

   Next, you will change the properties of the Phone option button. When editing the properties of option buttons, make sure that the option buttons in a group have the same group name. If you change the group name for one option button, but not for another, the server will treat the option buttons as being in two groups instead of one. This problem can lead to inaccurate data because the user would be able to select an option button in each group, which might not be the action that you want.

4. Double-click the **option button** to the left of the Phone label to open the Option Button Properties dialog box for this option button.
5. With the value in the Group name text box selected, type **CommunicationPreference**, press the **Tab** key, type **Phone**, make sure the **Not selected** option button is selected, and then click the **OK** button.
6. Save the page.

Next, you will add another type of form field—a drop-down box.

Adding a Drop-Down Box to a Form

Option buttons are useful when you want a user to select a response from only a few choices. When you want to present several choices in a single form field, a **drop-down box** (also called a **drop-down menu**) is an appropriate choice because it saves space by organizing choices in an expandable list. The user displays the list by clicking a list arrow and then selects the desired choice by clicking it in the list. Although you can set a drop-down box to accept multiple selections, it is more common to limit the user to selecting only one choice in a drop-down box.

When you create drop-down boxes in a form, consider the following design suggestions:

- Use a drop-down box when you want the user to select a choice from a list.
- Drop-down boxes should contain a minimum of three choices.
- Arrange items in the list so that the most commonly selected entries appear first, or arrange items in ascending order alphabetically, numerically, or chronologically.
- The default selection in a drop-down box should be either the most used choice or the first choice in the list.

The sketch shown in Figure 6-8 includes a drop-down box located to the right of the "Please select the option that best describes your location:" text. Brett wants the customer to indicate the city or area in which he or she lives. These choices are Lakeway, Dripping Springs, Austin, Lago Vista, West Lake Hills, and Other.

To add a drop-down box to a form:

1. Scroll the form as necessary so you can see the "Please select the option that best describes your location:" text, click anywhere in the word "location," and then press the **End** key to position the insertion point in the correct location for the drop-down box. Make sure that one space appears between the colon and the insertion point.
2. Click **Insert** on the menu bar, point to **Form**, and then click **Drop-Down Box**.

FrontPage creates a drop-down box that is two characters wide. To make the drop-down box match your sketch, you will change the default settings to increase the width of the drop-down box, insert the list items, and change the default form field names.

To add choices to a drop-down box and change its properties:

1. Double-click the **drop-down box** to select it and to open the Drop-Down Box Properties dialog box. FrontPage automatically assigned the name D1 to the drop-down box. The dialog box shows that there are no choices in the list, that it has a height of one line, and that multiple selections are not permitted. You will rename the drop-down box, and then you will create the choices that will appear in the list.
2. In the Name text box, select **D1**, and then type **Location**. The drop-down box form field now has the name Location.
3. Click the **Add** button to open the Add Choice dialog box. You use this dialog box to create entries in the list. First, you will supply the item's name, or choice, which is how the item will appear in the list. Then you will supply the item's value, which is the name of the list item that will appear in the results file. Finally, you will indicate whether the item is selected or not selected in the drop-down box.
4. Type **Lakeway** in the Choice text box, and then click the **Specify Value** check box to select it. FrontPage automatically adds the value "Lakeway" to the Specify Value text box to match the choice that you entered. This value will appear in the form results file to indicate the user's choice.

   Because Brett anticipates that most of his customers live in Lakeway, where the nursery is located, he wants to program this choice as the default so it will be selected when the page opens.
5. Click the **Selected** option button in the Initial state section. See Figure 6-13. The first choice is complete.

Completed Add Choice dialog box for the Lakeway choice — **Figure 6-13**

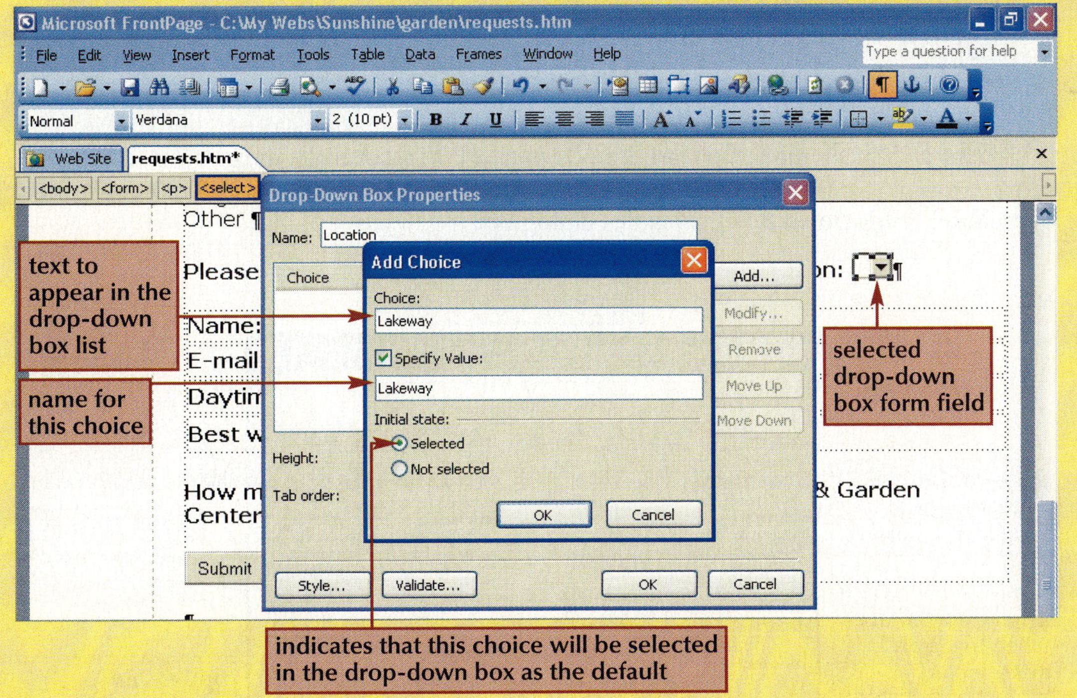

6. Click the **OK** button. The Add Choice dialog box closes and you return to the Drop-Down Box Properties dialog box, which now displays the Lakeway choice.

7. Click the **Add** button, and then type **Dripping Springs** in the Choice text box. Notice that the Specify Value text box includes a space. Because some Web servers won't process the space character, you'll need to remove it.
8. Click the **Specify Value** check box to select it. The text box below the Specify Value check box becomes active so you can edit the value. You can edit the value to make it shorter or to change it to any permissible value. In this case, you will remove the space between words.
9. Click to the left of the letter "S" in "Springs" in the Specify Value text box, press the **Backspace** key to delete the space, and then make sure the **Not selected** option button is selected. See Figure 6-14.

Figure 6-14 Add Choice dialog box for the Dripping Springs choice

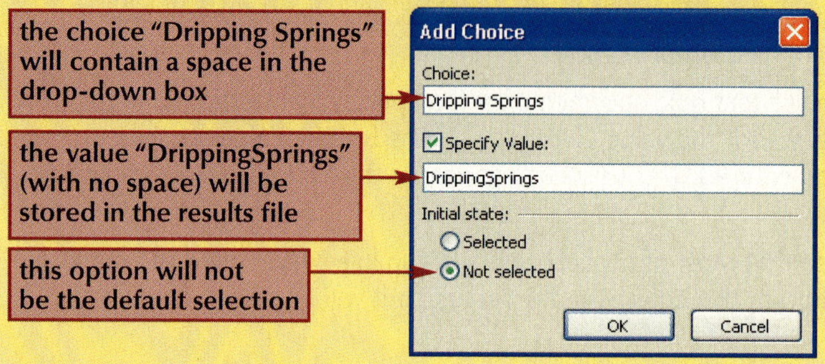

10. Click the **OK** button.
11. Add the following choices to the Location drop-down box:

Choice	Selected	Value
Austin	No	Austin
Lago Vista	No	LagoVista
West Lake Hills	No	WestLakeHills
Other	No	Other

Figure 6-15 shows the completed Drop-Down Box Properties dialog box.

Figure 6-15 Completed Drop-Down Box Properties dialog box

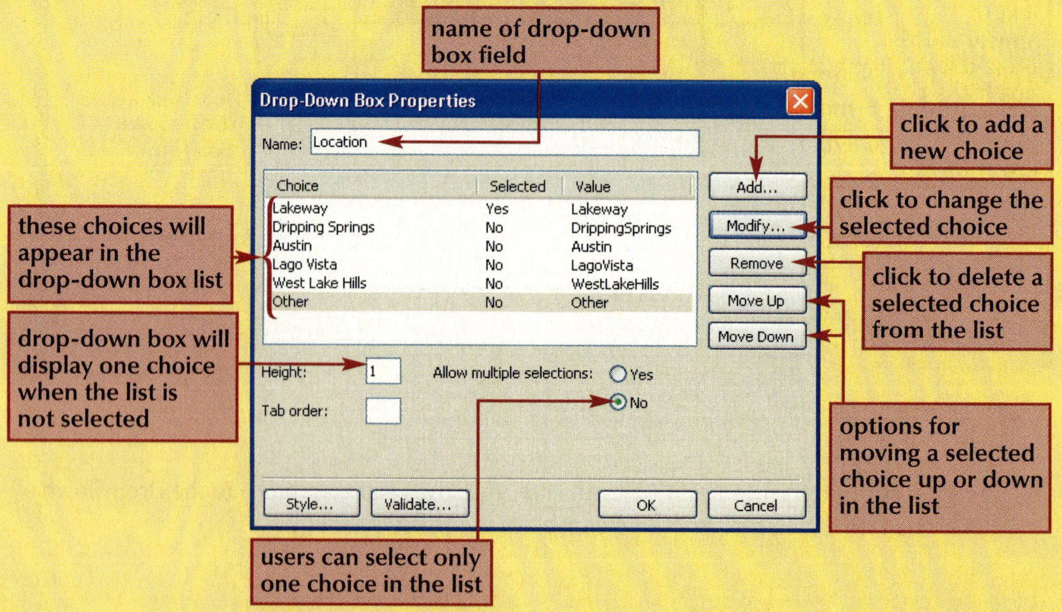

12. Click the **OK** button to close the Drop-Down Box Properties dialog box. The drop-down box appears in the form. The drop-down box is wide enough to display the longest choice in the list (Dripping Springs), and the default choice (Lakeway) appears in the list box.

    Trouble? Don't worry if the drop-down box appears on the next line. It will be displayed correctly in a browser.

If you click the list arrow on the drop-down box in Design view, you will select the form field instead of displaying the list. To see the list, you must open the page in a browser or Preview view and then click the list arrow. You will test all of the form fields in the browser after completing the form.

Your sketch includes several text boxes that collect information about the user. You'll show Brett how to add these form fields next.

Adding a Text Box to a Form

When you need a user to supply limited information in a form field that is unique or uncommon, such as a phone number or an e-mail address, you can use a text box to collect the data. A **text box** accepts typed information that you can limit to some maximum number of characters. Even though it will accept more characters than it can display, the text box itself might display a predetermined number of characters; in this case, the text scrolls to the left as the user types in the text box. You can also use a text box form field to permit users to enter a password, in which case the password appears as a series of dots or asterisks to conceal it while it is being typed.

When you create text boxes in a form, consider the following design suggestions:

- Use a text box when you want the user to enter unique or uncommon information that is limited to a single line.
- A text box can be set to limit the number of characters that a user can enter and see at one time.
- A text box can be used as a password field.

In addition to being unique, a user's name and e-mail address usually are short, making them suitable candidates for text box form fields.

To add a text box to a form:

1. Click the cell in row 1, column 2, of the table.
2. Click **Insert** on the menu bar, point to **Form**, and then click **Textbox**. FrontPage places a text box form field in the cell. By default, when you insert a text box in a form, it is 20 characters wide.
3. Press the **down** arrow key ↓ to move the insertion point to the cell in row 2, column 2, and then repeat Step 2 to insert a text box.
4. Repeat Step 3 and insert a text box in row 3, column 2.
5. Save the page.

To make it easier for visitors to enter their name and e-mail address in the appropriate text boxes, you can change the default width of the text boxes to display more characters. This change ensures that most people will be able to see their complete information in the text boxes without needing to scroll the text. Although a phone number will fit in the default text box, you'll increase its width to make the text boxes the same size.

To change the properties of a text box:

1. Double-click the **text box** in the cell in row 1, column 2, to open the Text Box Properties dialog box. FrontPage assigned the name T1 to the text box. If you want a default value to appear in the text box when the form is opened in the browser, you can set it by entering a value in the Initial value text box. You can also change the width of the text box (using a measurement indicating the maximum number of characters that will be displayed in the text box at one time), change the text box to accept a password, or change the order in which the user selects text boxes in the form when pressing the Tab key.

   You'll rename the text box to "Name" to describe its function. You will also increase the text box width from the default of 20 characters to 35 characters.

2. Type **Name** in the Name text box, press the **Tab** key twice to select the value in the Width in characters text box, and then type **35** to set the text box width to 35 characters. See Figure 6-16.

Figure 6-16 **Completed Text Box Properties dialog box**

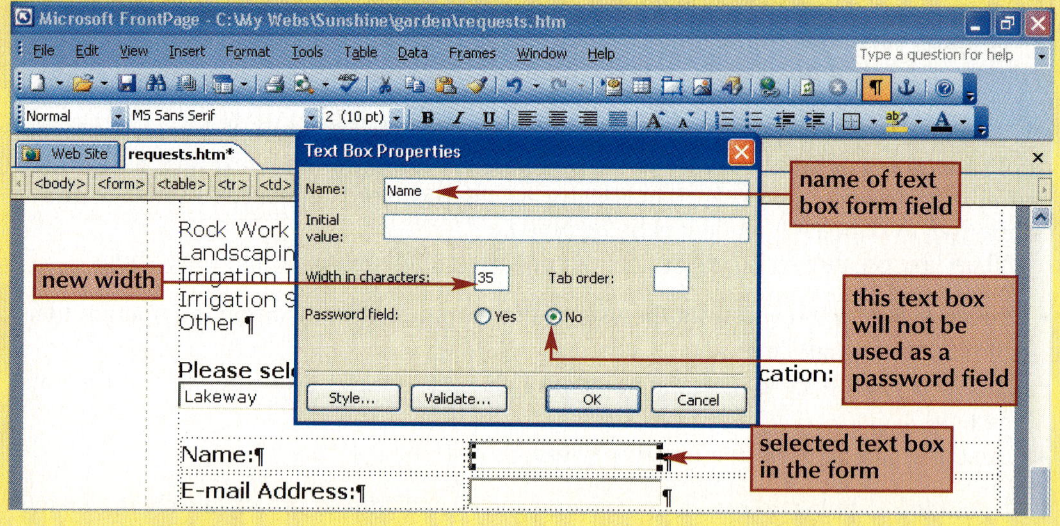

3. Click the **OK** button. The width of the Name text box increases to 35 characters.
4. Repeat Steps 1 through 3 to set the text box in the cell in row 2, column 2, to the name **Email** and a width of **35** characters.
5. Repeat Steps 1 through 3 to set the text box in the cell in row 3, column 2, to the name **Phone** and a width of **35** characters.
6. Save the page.

Text boxes are appropriate for collecting a limited amount of data, such as a name, address, or phone number. When you need to accept unique passages of longer text, such as a description of a problem or an open-ended comment, you can use a text area form field.

Adding a Text Area to a Form

A **text area** (also called a **scrolling text box**) has the same basic characteristics as a text box, except that it displays multiple lines of text and cannot be used as a password field. A text area is an effective form field when asking a user to provide comments or feedback.

When you create a text area in a form, consider the following design suggestions:

- Use a text area when you want a user to supply information that might include more than one line.
- A text area can be set to display multiple lines of text entered by the user. The size of the text area should be large enough to display several lines of text at a time.

Your sketch of the page (see Figure 6-8) includes one text area form field that allows users to enter multiple lines of text. You will add this form field next.

To add a text area to a form:

1. Scroll up the page so you can see the paragraph that begins "If you have a question," and then click the blank paragraph below it. You will insert the text area here.
2. Click **Insert** on the menu bar, point to **Form**, and then click **Text Area**. FrontPage inserts a text area in the form.

The default settings format the text area so it is 20 characters wide and two lines high. Your sketch shows a text area that nearly spans the width of the page and displays five lines. You'll need to change the properties of the text area to make these changes.

To change the properties of a text area:

1. Double-click the **text area** to open the TextArea Box Properties dialog box. FrontPage automatically assigned the name S1 to the text area. Notice that you can specify an initial value for the text area; if you leave this text box empty, then the text area will be empty when the Web page that contains it is opened in a browser. You can also set the properties for a text area to change its width and the number of lines of text displayed in the box. If the user enters more text than can be displayed in the text area, the form field will scroll the lines automatically.

   You will change the default name to be more descriptive of the text area, and then you will change the size of the text area.
2. With the value selected in the Name text box, type **Comments**, press the **Tab** key twice to move to the Width in characters text box, type **80**, press the **Tab** key twice to move to the Number of lines text box, and then type **5**. See Figure 6-17.

Figure 6-17

Completed TextArea Box Properties dialog box

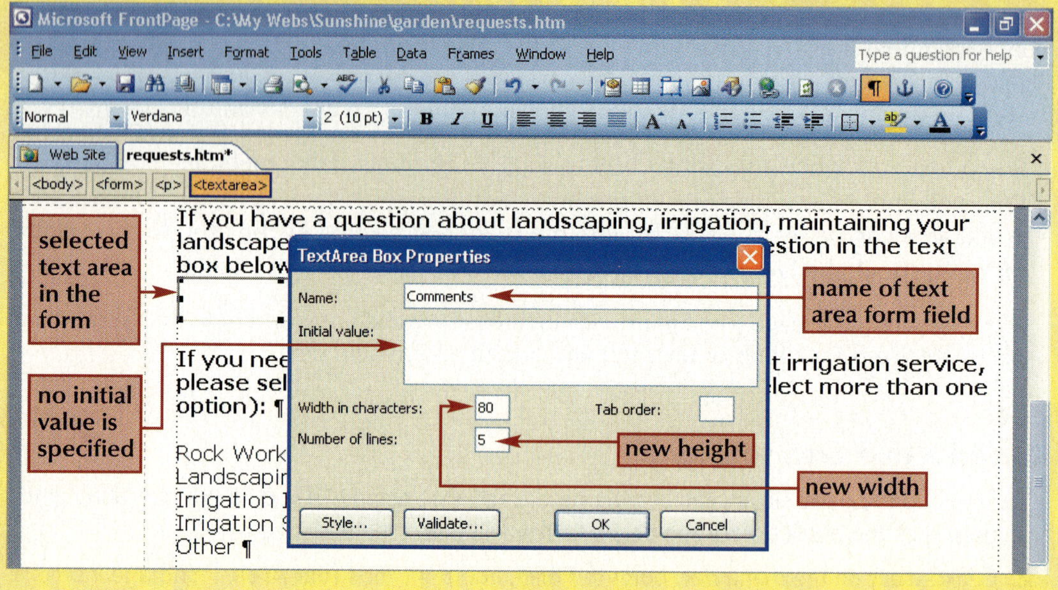

3. Click the **OK** button. The text area is displayed with the new properties—it is five lines high and 80 characters wide.
4. Save the page.
5. Close the garden Web site, and then close FrontPage.

In the next session, you will finish the Customer Requests page by adding additional form fields to it and creating rules that verify and validate the form fields so they will accept the correct data from users. You will test the Search and Customer Requests pages after you publish the Web site in Session 6.3.

Review

Session 6.1 Quick Check

1. What are the two types of search components you can insert in a Web page?
2. True or False: You can insert components in a Web page to display weather and stock market information.
3. What is a form field?
4. Before adding a form field to a Web page, you must first create a(n) ____________ in the Web page that will contain the form field.
5. What is a form handler?
6. What are two important things that you should do when planning to use a form in a Web page?
7. True or False: You can use a text box form field to enter passwords.
8. You are designing a Web page for a Canadian company that includes a list of the Canadian provinces. Which form field would you use to collect the data, which properties would you assign to the form field, and which option would be the default selection? Defend your selections.

Session 6.2

Validating a Form Field

The text boxes and text area that you added to the Customer Requests page in Session 6.1 accept unique information entered by a user. In some situations, you might want to validate the information that a user enters into these form fields. For example, if you ask a user to enter a product number into a text box and all product numbers contain four digits, you might set the properties of the text box so that it must contain four digits. By ensuring that the user enters four digits, you can reduce data-entry errors.

Validation is the process of checking the information entered by a user into one or more form fields to verify that the information is acceptable and valid. If the data entered by a user fails the validation test, then the user must change it before the browser will send the form to the server for processing. You specify data validation criteria using the form field's Properties dialog box.

The sketch of the Customer Requests page (see Figure 6-8) includes a text box that lets users enter the number of times that they have visited the Sunshine Landscape & Garden Center. Although you could retain the initial properties of this text box so that a user could enter anything or nothing in it, you tell Brett that it would be helpful to restrict entries in this text box to only positive, whole numbers (or **integers**). In other words, a user shouldn't be able to enter a negative number, a number containing a decimal, or letters in this form field. You tell Brett that it would also be helpful to restrict the value a user can enter to numbers from 0 to 100. This restriction would prevent a user from accidentally entering an unreasonable number of visits, such as 1,000, as a response. To ensure that users will not inadvertently skip this form field, you also tell Brett that you can validate this form field so that it must contain an acceptable value. In other words, users cannot submit the form if this form field is empty or contains an invalid response.

To create the text box and change its properties:

1. Start **FrontPage**, and then open the **garden** Web site from the location where your Web sites are stored.
2. Double-click **requests.htm** in the Contents pane to open the Customer Requests page in Design view.
3. Press **Ctrl + End**, click anywhere in the word "Center" in the "How many times have you visited Sunshine Landscape & Garden Center?" text, and then press the **End** key. Now the insertion point is positioned in the correct location for the text box.
4. Click **Insert** on the menu bar, point to **Form**, and then click **Textbox**. A text box is added to the form. You will change the form field's name to "Visits" and decrease its width to three characters.

   Trouble? Don't worry if the text box appears on the next line. It will be displayed correctly in a browser.
5. Double-click the **text box** that you created in Step 4 to open the Text Box Properties dialog box, type **Visits** in the Name text box, press the **Tab** key twice to move to the Width in characters text box, type **3**, and then click the **OK** button. The dialog box closes and the text box is displayed with the new width.

Next, you will set the validation criteria for the Visits text box.

To validate a text box in a form:

1. Double-click the **Visits text box** to open the Text Box Properties dialog box, and then click the **Validate** button. The Text Box Validation dialog box opens. Currently, there are no validation criteria placed on the data entered into the Visits text box, as indicated by the "No Constraints" setting in the Data type list box.
2. Click the **Data type** list arrow. You can select Text, Integer, or Number as the data type to validate. You want to make sure that this form field accepts whole numbers, so you will select Integer as the data type.
3. Click **Integer** to specify that data type. The settings in the Numeric format section become active.
4. In the Numeric format section, click the **None** option button in the Grouping category, because the data should not contain a comma or a period. You can use this option to display a number with a decimal point or a comma, such as 4.5 or 10,000.
5. In the Data length section, click the **Required** check box to select it, press the **Tab** key to move to the Min length text box, type **1**, press the **Tab** key to move to the Max length text box, and then type **3**. You specified 1 as the minimum number of digits and 3 as the maximum number of digits that a user can enter into this form field. Selecting the Required check box means that the user must enter a value—even zero—into this form field before the server will accept the form for processing.
6. In the Data value section, click the **Field must be** check box to select it, click the **Field must be** list arrow, click **Greater than or equal to** (if necessary), press the **Tab** key to move to the Value text box, and then type **0** (the number zero—not the capital letter "O"). These settings specify that an entry in the Visits text box must be greater than or equal to zero.
7. In the Data value section, click the **And must be** check box to select it, click the **And must be** list arrow, click **Less than or equal to** (if necessary), press the **Tab** key to move to the Value text box, and then type **100**. These settings specify that the integer must be less than or equal to 100. See Figure 6-18.

Completed Text Box Validation dialog box

Figure 6-18

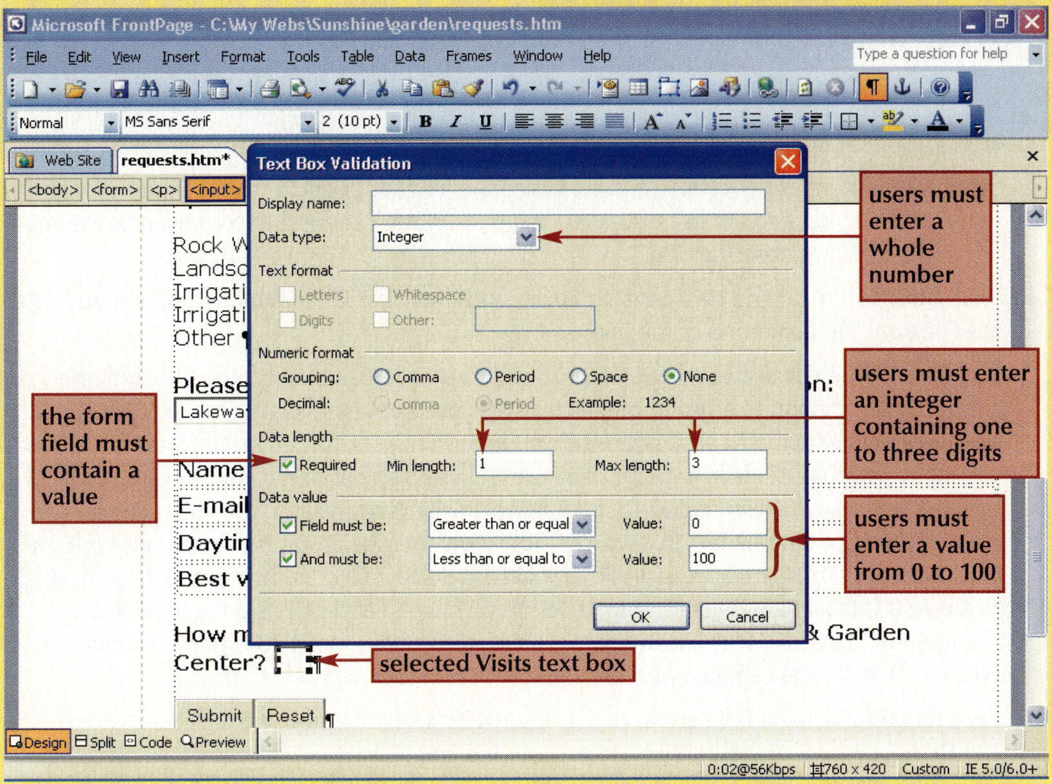

8. Click the **OK** button to close the Text Box Validation dialog box, and then click the **OK** button to close the Text Box Properties dialog box.
9. Save the page.

Now users must enter an integer from 0 to 100 in the Visits text box before the browser will send the form to the server. The final task is to add check boxes so users can request a free consultation or request irrigation service.

Adding a Check Box to a Form

You can use a **check box** by itself to collect a yes/no response to a question, or you can use check boxes in a group to let users answer yes or no for several options. Unlike option button groups, selecting one check box in a check box group does not automatically deselect another check box in the same check box group. Also, you can set the properties for each check box so that it is selected or not selected when the form opens in the browser.

When you create check boxes in a form, consider the following design suggestions:

- Use check boxes when you want a user to select from a group of one or more independent and nonexclusive choices.
- Set the default selection to the most frequently occurring selection.

- Clearly label each check box in a group.
- When necessary, use a heading or text to identify the subject of the check box group.

Based on your sketch in Figure 6-8, you will add five check boxes to the form.

To add a check box to a form and change its properties:

1. Scroll up the form as necessary so you can see the list that begins with the "Rock Work" entry, and then click to the left of the "R" in "Rock Work." You will add a check box to the left of the text that describes it.
2. Click **Insert** on the menu bar, point to **Form**, and then click **Checkbox**. FrontPage inserts a check box at the beginning of the line.
3. Double-click the **check box** to open the Check Box Properties dialog box. Although the check box will belong to a group of check boxes based on their related topics, usually you provide a unique name to each check box in the group. This strategy is different from how you name option buttons in a group. Because the user can click zero, one, several, or all of the check boxes, you need a way to identify which check box(es) the user selected. By giving this check box the name "RockWork," you know that the check box is the one with the label with the same name. In addition, the default value, "ON," indicates the value to store in the results file when the check box is selected. You can accept this default value or change it to "Yes" or "True" to indicate a positive response. Brett asks you to change the value to "Yes," so he can easily determine if the check box was selected.
4. Type **RockWork** in the Name text box, press the **Tab** key to move to the Value text box, and then type **Yes**. In the Initial state section, the Not checked option button is selected, indicating that this check box will not contain a check mark when the page is opened in a Web browser. See Figure 6-19. Because you don't want to include a default selection, this setting is correct.

Figure 6-19 **Completed Check Box Properties dialog box**

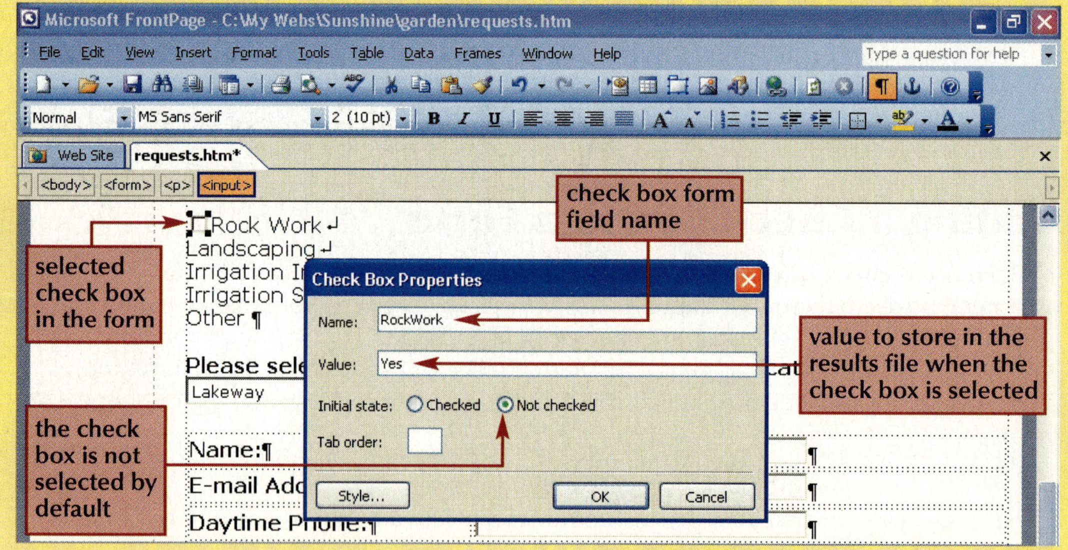

5. Click the **OK** button to close the Check Box Properties dialog box. The check box form field looks the same—changing the Name property did not affect this form field's appearance. Your changes only affected the way the server will process this form field.

You could continue inserting check boxes for the four other choices, but you want to show Brett how to copy and paste form fields to insert them into a form. After inserting the form fields, you'll need to change only the Name property for each check box to finish your work on the check boxes.

To copy and paste the check boxes:

1. If necessary, click the **RockWork** check box to select it. Sizing handles appear around the check box.
2. Click the **Copy** button on the Standard toolbar to copy the check box to the Clipboard.
3. Press the **down** arrow key ↓, press the **Home** key to move the insertion point to the beginning of the line, and then click the **Paste** button on the Standard toolbar. A check box with the name "RockWork0" and a value of "Yes" is inserted.
4. Repeat Step 3 to paste a check box at the beginning of the lines with the following text: Irrigation Installation, Irrigation Service, and Other.

   When you pasted the four copies of the check boxes, FrontPage renamed them using the name of the original check box ("RockWork") plus a digit. You will rename each check box to match its label.
5. Double-click the check box to the left of the "Landscaping" text to open its Check Box Properties dialog box, type **Landscaping** in the Name text box, and then click the **OK** button.
6. Double-click the check box to the left of the "Irrigation Installation" text to open its Check Box Properties dialog box, type **IrrigationInstallation** in the Name text box, and then click the **OK** button.
7. Double-click the check box to the left of the "Irrigation Service" text to open its Check Box Properties dialog box, type **IrrigationService** in the Name text box, and then click the **OK** button.
8. Double-click the check box to the left of the "Other" text to open its Check Box Properties dialog box, type **Other** in the Name text box, and then click the **OK** button.

   Now each check box in the page has a unique name. When the user selects a check box, the value "Yes" will appear in the results file.
9. Save the page.

You have finished adding all of the form fields that collect data from the user. To finish this form, you need to supply the user with a way of sending the Web page to the server for processing.

Working With Push Buttons

Push buttons (also called **command buttons**) are used to submit a form to the server, to clear a form's fields, or to perform specific functions programmed by the developer. You can create three types of push buttons in a form; each type implements a different processing action. You use a **Submit push button** to let a user submit a form to the server for processing. Clicking a **Reset push button** clears any previously entered data from the form. Clicking a **Normal push button** initiates a user-defined script (an advanced Web page feature that is beyond the scope of this tutorial). When you create a form, FrontPage automatically creates and programs the Submit and Reset push buttons for you. By default, the Submit push button is associated with the FrontPage form handler that processes the form results on the Web server. Because these two buttons are automatically included in the form, you can either accept their default values or edit them to suit your needs better. If you add a new push button to a form, FrontPage automatically creates a Normal push button with the value "Button." You must change the properties of the new button to change its name and function.

To match the sketch shown in Figure 6-8, you will need to change the label for the Submit push button to "Submit Form" and the label for the Reset push button to "Clear Form."

To change the properties of the Submit push button:

1. Scroll down the page as necessary, and then double-click the **Submit push button** to open the Push Button Properties dialog box.
2. Type **Submit** in the Name text box, press the **Tab** key to move to the Value/label text box, press the **End** key, press the **spacebar**, and then type **Form**. In the Button type section, the Submit option button is selected, indicating that this button submits the form's data to the Web server. See Figure 6-20.

Figure 6-20 **Completed Push Button Properties dialog box**

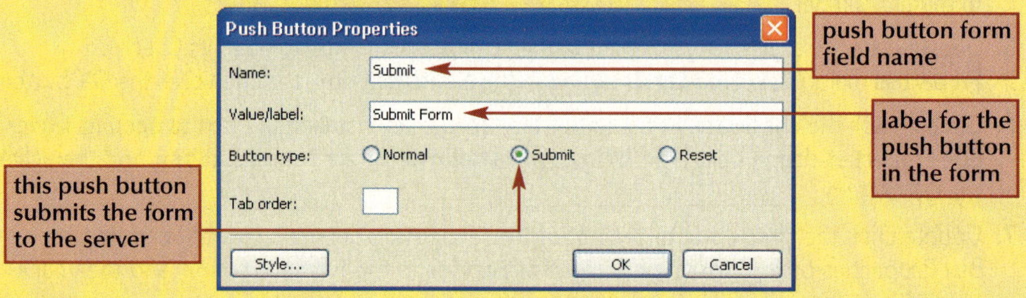

3. Click the **OK** button to close the Push Button Properties dialog box. The Submit button now displays the label "Submit Form." FrontPage automatically resizes the push button to accommodate the new label.

Next, you will change the default settings for the Reset push button to change its name to "Clear" and its label to "Clear Form."

To change the properties of the Reset push button:

1. Double-click the **Reset push button** to open the Push Button Properties dialog box.
2. Type **Clear** in the Name text box, press the **Tab** key to move to the Value/label text box, and then type **Clear Form**. The Reset option button is selected in the Button type section, indicating that this button resets the values in the form's fields to their default settings.
3. Click the **OK** button to close the Push Button Properties dialog box. The Reset push button now displays the label "Clear Form."
4. Save the page.

You have finished placing all of the form fields that collect data in the form and provided a means for the user to submit the form to the server for processing. When a form is submitted to the server, you must tell the server how to process it by specifying a form handler.

Using a Form Handler

A form handler is a program on a Web server that communicates with a browser to process form data received from the browser. You select a form handler based on how you want to process the data collected in your form. For the Customer Requests page, you will use the FrontPage Save Results form handler, which collects form data and can save that data in a variety of file formats.

The **Save Results form handler** collects data from a browser and stores it in a specified format on the server. You have the option of sending the results to a file, to an e-mail address, or to a database. The data entered by the user in the form, or the **form results**, is stored on the server in a format that you specify. The two most popular methods of storing form results are as a text file, with one line for each form that was submitted to the server, or as an HTML file, with a line for each form field name and its value (known as a **field name-data value pair**). In the text file method, the first entry, or row, contains the names of the form fields from which the data was obtained. In the HTML file method, each form field name is included as a field name-data value pair, with the name being repeated with the data from each form submission. When using either of these methods to store form results, most developers will set the results file to add the form results at the end of the file for each form submitted to the server.

In addition to storing the results in a file on the server, you can send the results to an e-mail address. To send the form results to an e-mail address, the server must be configured to send e-mail messages. Normally, the Web site's administrator, or webmaster, configures the server for this type of processing. Check with your instructor or technical support person to determine whether your FrontPage installation and server are enabled to send a form's results to an e-mail address.

Regardless of how you choose to store your form results, you can also collect optional information, such as the date on which the form was submitted and the Internet Protocol (IP) address of the user. In most cases, the results files are saved in the Web site's _private folder so they are inaccessible to the site's visitors.

You want to show Brett how to use the Save Results form handler to specify the processing method for the data collected by the Customer Requests page.

To configure the Save Results form handler:

1. Right-click anywhere in the form component to open the shortcut menu, and then click **Form Properties**. The Form Properties dialog box opens. See Figure 6-21.

Figure 6-21 Form Properties dialog box

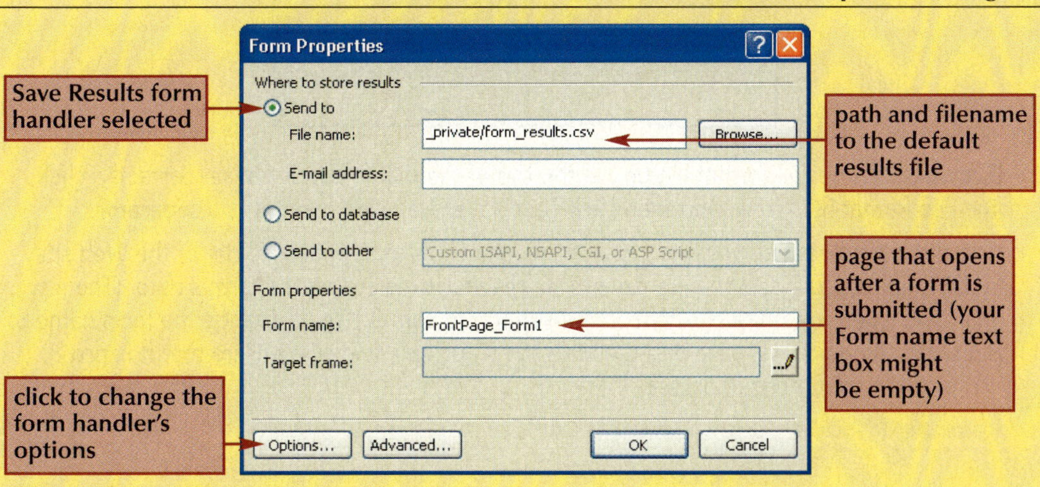

Trouble? If the Send to option button is dimmed in the Form Properties dialog box, click the Cancel button to close the dialog box. Click Tools on the menu bar, click Page Options, click the Authoring tab, and then make sure that all check boxes except Generator and ProgID tags and Downlevel image file are selected in the FrontPage and SharePoint technologies section, that Microsoft Internet Explorer only is selected in the Browsers list box, and that 5.0/6.0 browsers and later is selected in the Browser versions list box. Click the OK button, and then repeat Step 1.

The settings in this dialog box let you accept or change the default filename in which to store your results file and the optional e-mail address to which to send the results from each form submission. You can also send your form results to a database or to a location defined by a script. You use the Form properties section to supply the filename that will serve as your confirmation page. (You will learn more about confirmation pages in Session 6.3.) To change the options for any of these settings, click the Options button.

Brett wants to configure the form results to be stored in a text file and sent to an e-mail address at the nursery. You will show Brett how to configure these settings next.

2. Click the **Options** button to open the Saving Results dialog box. See Figure 6-22. The default file format listed near the top of the dialog box is "Text database using comma as a separator." This option uses a comma to separate the data entered by the user into each form field. This format, which is known as **comma-delimited text** or **comma-separated values**, is a popular choice for storing data because many different programs can read and use it.

Figure 6-22 File Results tab of the Saving Results dialog box

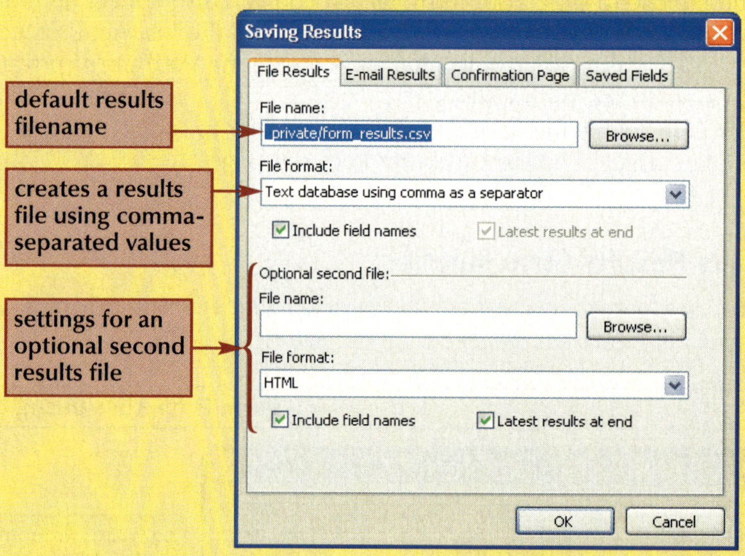

Trouble? If the File format list box at the top of the dialog box is not set correctly, click the File format list arrow, and then click Text database using comma as a separator.

The default location in which to store the results file is the _private folder of the Web site, and FrontPage suggests the filename form_results.csv to collect the form's data. (The .csv filename extension is the one for comma-separated values.) You'll change the form name to simplify it, and you will save it in the Web site's _private folder to ensure that it is protected from unauthorized access.

3. Edit the value in the File name text box at the top of the dialog box so it is **_private/results.csv**.
4. Make sure that the **Include field names** check box contains a check mark, and then click the **E-mail Results** tab.
5. Type **brett@sunshinelandscapeandgardencenter.com** in the E-mail address to receive results text box, click the **Subject line** text box, and then type **Customer Requests Web Page**. When a user submits a form to the server, the server will save the form results in the results.csv file on the server. In addition, the server will send a copy of the form results to the e-mail address you entered. By entering text in the Subject line text box, you identified the source of the message for the recipient of the e-mail message. All messages containing form results and sent to this e-mail address will have the subject "Customer Requests Web Page" so Brett can easily identify the source of the message. See Figure 6-23.

Figure 6-23 E-mail Results tab

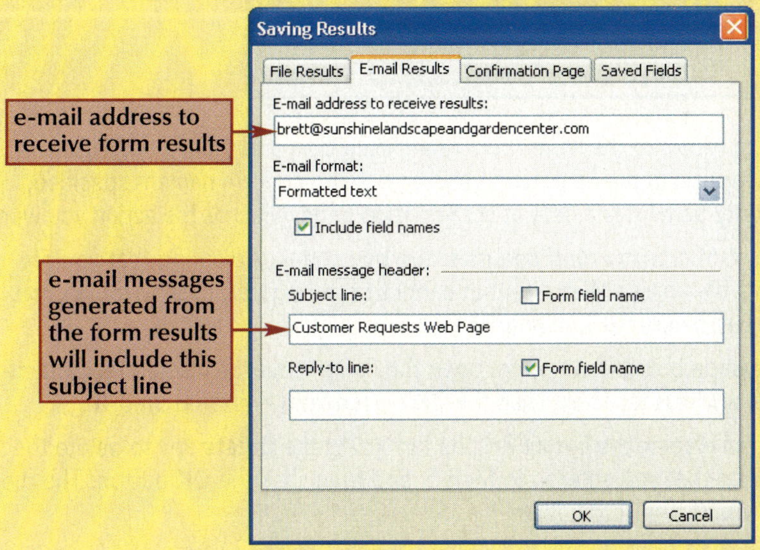

6. Click the **Saved Fields** tab to display those settings. The Form fields to save list box displays the form fields you created in the Customer Requests page. The form fields are easy to distinguish because you gave them meaningful names, instead of accepting the default names of V1, S1, and so on.
7. In the Additional information to save section, click the **Remote computer name** check box to select it. This setting will save the user's IP address in the results file with the field name "Remote Name." See Figure 6-24.

Figure 6-24 Saved Fields tab

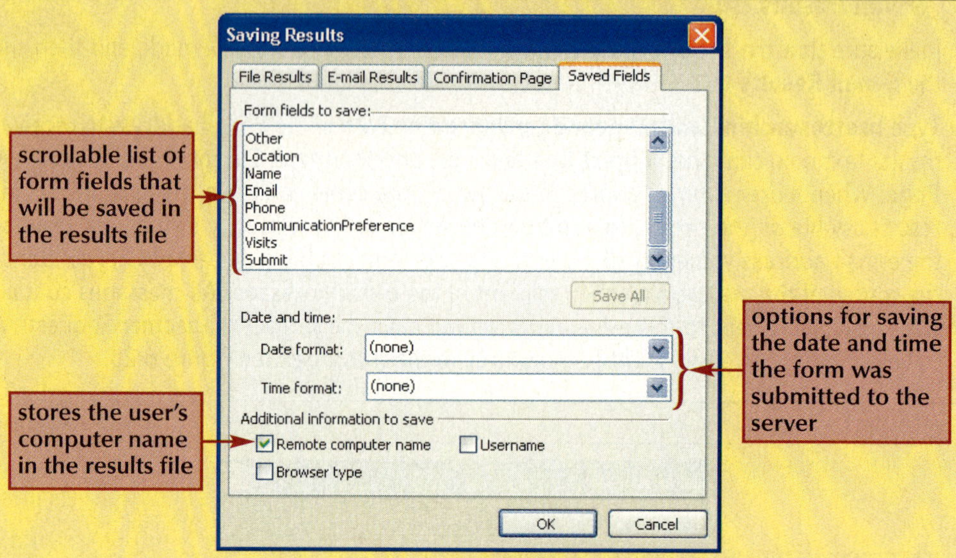

8. Click the **OK** button to return to the Form Properties dialog box, and then, if necessary, delete any text that appears in the Form name text box. When no form name is specified, FrontPage automatically generates a default confirmation page, which is the action you want.
9. Click the **OK** button. A Microsoft FrontPage message box opens, indicating that you are creating the form in a disk-based Web site that cannot be configured to send e-mail messages. For now, you will delete the e-mail address.

   Trouble? If the message box doesn't open, open the Form Properties dialog box, delete the text in the E-mail address text box, click the OK button, and then skip Step 10.
10. Click the **Yes** button to display the E-mail Results tab, press the **Delete** key to delete the selected e-mail address that you entered in Step 5, and then click the **OK** button. The dialog boxes close and you return to the form.
11. Save the page.

Now that you have identified the form handler and specified the file in which the results will be stored on the server, you need to test the form.

Testing a Form on the Client

Unlike other Web pages, you should test a page that contains a form on the client *and* on the server. When testing the form on a client, you test each form field by entering data into it. For example, you can enter text in text boxes or use drop-down boxes to ensure that they display the choices you need. Also, you can clear all data from the form and then reenter it. Any form fields that use data validation, such as the Visits text box, require a server for verification. Therefore, you cannot test form fields that are validated until you can submit the form to a server for processing.

At this point in the development of the form, you want to show Brett how to test it on the client. Your test of the form will include reviewing the layout of form fields in the form and testing their operation. You will finish testing the form in Session 6.3 after publishing the Web site on a server.

To test a form on the client:

1. Click the **Preview** button on the Standard toolbar, and then, if necessary, click the **OK** button in the message box that reminds you that some form elements won't work in a disk-based Web site. The Customer Requests page opens in the browser.
2. Scroll down the page until you see the form fields, click the text area, and then type **At what time of year do you recommend planting trees?**
3. Scroll down the page, and then click the **Rock Work** and **Irrigation Service** check boxes. Brett wants to provide a way for users to indicate the consultation or service they require, so he asks you to include a text box to the right of the Other check box. You'll add this text box when you complete the Review Assignments.
4. Click the **Please select the option that best describes your location** list arrow, and then look at the choices in the list. The blue background for the Lakeway choice indicates that this is the default selection. To select another choice, the user would need to click it.
5. Click **West Lake Hills** in the list. The menu closes and your selection appears in the drop-down box.
6. Click the **Name** text box, type your first and last names separated by a space, press the **Tab** key to move to the E-mail Address text box, type your e-mail address, press the **Tab** key, and then type your phone number.
7. Click the **E-mail** option button, and then click the **Phone** option button. Notice that you can select only one option button in the option button group.
8. Click the **Visits** text box, and then type **2000**. Because you set this form field to accept values from one to three characters, you cannot type the third zero in the number 2000.
9. Select the value **200** in the Visits text box, and then type **7**.
10. Click the **Submit Form** button. The FrontPage Run-Time Component Page opens to advise you that a server is required for the page to function correctly. You will test the page using a server later in this tutorial.
11. Click your browser's **Back** button to return to the Customer Requests page, and then click the **Clear Form** button. The data you entered is deleted from the form; this action does not require a server. Your test of the form on the client is successful.
12. Close your browser.

Although the browser performs data validation, a server is required to generate the error message that appears when the Visits text box contains an invalid entry. Even though the form appears to work correctly, you remind Brett that he needs to test this page again after publishing the Web site to a server to ensure that this page does work correctly.

Opening an Office Document from a Web Site

Brett is happy with the form and thinks that it will expedite the process of scheduling and coordinating customer requests for consultations and service. As you consider the form's use, you tell Brett that you want to make sure that people who cannot submit forms to the server—for whatever reason—will still be able to use the form to communicate with the nursery. You could ask users to use a browser to print the Customer Requests page and complete the form, but users could not indicate their location because they cannot use a drop-down box on a paper form. A better option is to save the form in another format that the user can access and print. One popular format on the Web is Portable Document Format (PDF) from Adobe Corporation. To save a document as a PDF file, the Web developer uses a program called

Adobe Acrobat to convert it to PDF. To read the PDF document, the user must install a program on his or her computer called Adobe Reader, which is a free downloadable program from Adobe. After installing the Adobe Reader program, the user's browser will start the Reader automatically when the user clicks a link to a PDF file. Because the Reader is free, easy to download, and installs automatically, PDF is a popular format on the Web for providing documents created in other programs, such as Word, Excel, and PowerPoint, because it eliminates the problem of the user not having the required program on his or her system to read the file. Brett will investigate the possibility of using PDF files in the future, but he does not have Adobe Acrobat at this time. As an alternative, you tell him that another option is to save the form as a Word document and change some of the form fields to make them easier to complete by hand. Saving documents using Word is a good second choice, because many users have Word or a compatible program (such as WordPerfect or WordPad) installed on their systems that can open Word documents.

After converting the form to a Word document, you are ready to show Brett how to create a link to the document and to open it from the Web site. First, you will import the Word document you created into the Web site.

To import the Word document into the garden Web site:

1. Display the Folder List, and then make sure the Web site's root folder is selected.
2. Click **File** on the menu bar, click **Import**, click the **Add File** button, open the **Tutorial.06\Tutorial** folder included with your Data Files, double-click **form.doc**, and then click the **OK** button in the Import dialog box to import the file.
3. Scroll down the Folder List and double-click **form.doc**. Microsoft Word starts and opens the document.

   Trouble? If a Security Warning dialog box opens and asks you to enable macros, ask your instructor or technical support person for help. If you are working on your own computer, click the Enable Macros button.

   Trouble? If Microsoft Word does not open, your installation of FrontPage might not be configured to open Office documents in the program that created them. If necessary, close the program that opened. In FrontPage, click Tools on the menu bar, click Options, and then click the Configure Editors tab. Select the Open web pages in the Office application that created them check box, and then click the OK button. Then repeat Step 3. If Word still doesn't open, it might not be installed on your computer; ask your instructor or technical support person for help.
4. Scroll down the Word document, noticing the changes to the form fields to make it easier to complete the form by hand.
5. Close Word.
6. Close the Folder List.

Next, you will create the hyperlink to the Word document.

To create a hyperlink to a Word document:

1. Scroll to the top of the Customer Requests page, and then double-click the word **here** in the third sentence of the first paragraph.
2. Click the **Insert Hyperlink** button on the Standard toolbar to open the Insert Hyperlink dialog box, scroll down the list of files in the garden Web site, and then click **form.doc**.

   As you learned in Tutorial 5, you can set hyperlinks to open in different frames in a frames page. You can also set other hyperlinks to open in different locations, even when they are not part of a frames page. For example, there are some links that you might want to open in their own browser window, such as when linking to a different Web site. This way, the user can examine the Web site that opens without closing your Web site. You can do the same thing with documents. You'll show Brett how to set a hyperlink to open in a new browser window using the New Window target.

3. Click the **Target Frame** button. The Target Frame dialog box opens, as shown in Figure 6-25. Because you are not working in a frames page, the notation "(none)" appears in the Current frames page section of the dialog box. The Common targets section lists the same targets you can set for frames.

Target Frame dialog box **Figure 6-25**

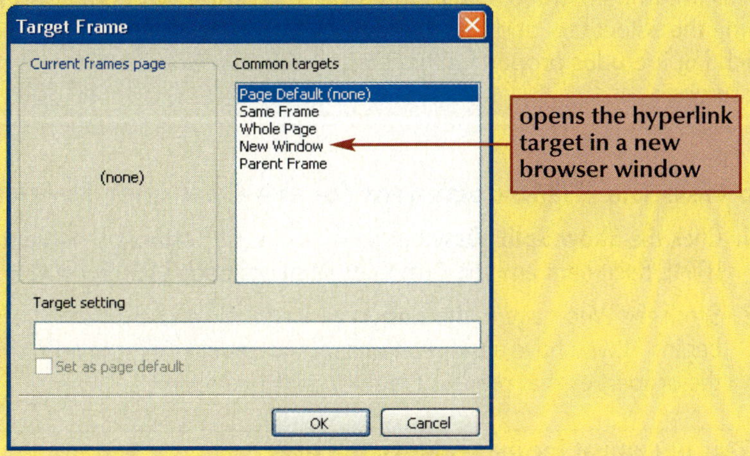

4. Click **New Window** in the Common targets list box. The HTML equivalent (_blank) appears in the Target setting text box. This setting will open the target of the hyperlink in a new browser window.
5. Click the **OK** button in the Target Frame dialog box. Notice that the Target Frame section of the Insert Hyperlink dialog box shows that this hyperlink uses the _blank target.
6. Click the **OK** button to close the Insert Hyperlink dialog box. The "here" text now contains a link to the Word document.
7. Click the **here** hyperlink to deselect it, and then save the page.

To test the here hyperlink, you need to open the Customer Requests page in a browser.

To test the hyperlink:

1. Click the **Preview** button on the Standard toolbar.
2. Click the **here** hyperlink in the first paragraph. A new browser window opens as a result of the _blank target you set. The Word document opens and the browser's menu bar changes to include commands for working with Word documents. The user would print the document, complete it using a pen or pencil, and then take or mail it to the nursery.

   Trouble? If a File Download dialog box opens, click the Open button.
3. Close the window that displays the form.doc file.
4. Close the window that displays the Customer Requests Web page.

In Session 6.3, you will publish the Web site to a server and then test the Customer Requests and Search pages again. Before finishing your work, you want to show Brett the HTML document that FrontPage created for the Customer Requests page.

Viewing the HTML Tags That Create a Form

Creating a form in a Web page results in a complex HTML document. All of the form fields are nested within the <form> and </form> tags that specify the beginning and end of the form in the Web page. The post value of the method property specifies that the data in the form will be processed by or posted to the server. The webbot property specifies the values for the Save Results form handler. The option button, text box, and check box form fields are implemented using input tags. The drop-down box form field is implemented using the select tag, and the text area form field is implemented using the textarea tag. Each tag includes properties that specify the appearance of the form field in the form and its settings.

To view the HTML document for the Customer Requests page:

1. Click the **Show Split View** button [Split] at the bottom of the Contents pane to view the HTML document and the Customer Requests page in Split view.
2. Scroll the Web page in the Design view window and click anywhere in the paragraph that begins "If you have a question about landscaping." Figure 6-26 shows the <form> tag and the properties that process the form on the server.

Figure 6-26 HTML document for the requests.htm page

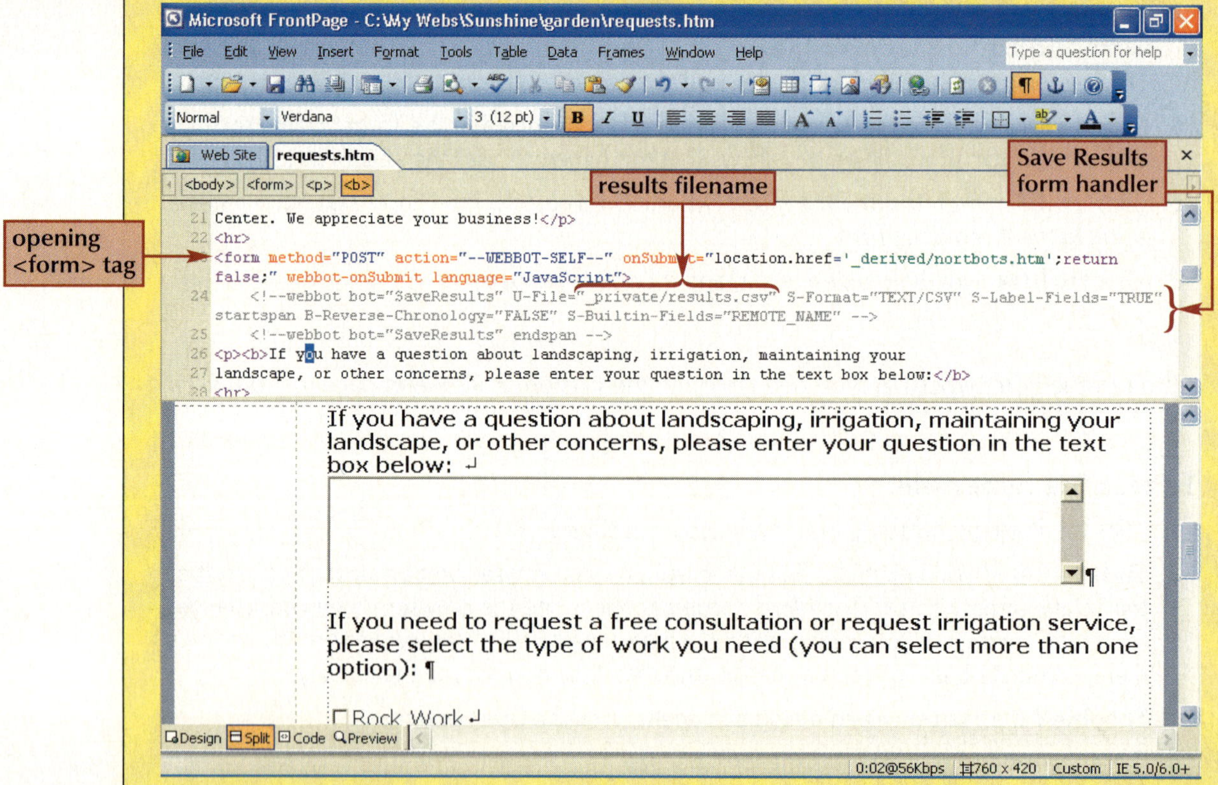

3. Scroll down the Web page in the Design view window as necessary, and then click the **text area**. The HTML textarea tag is selected in the Code view window.
4. Scroll down the Web page in the Design view window, and then click the **Other** check box. Notice that the <input> tag includes the type property "checkbox," which creates a check box in the page. The name property for each check box identifies the check box using its label in the Web page. The value property is set to "Yes," which is the value that will appear in the results file when a user selects the check box.
5. Scroll down the Web page in the Design view window, click the **drop-down box**, and then scroll down the HTML document so you can see the selected HTML <select> and </select> tags. See Figure 6-27. The <option> tags create the choices in the drop-down box. Because you specified a value to store for each choice in the list, the value property includes the name of each option.

Figure 6-27 **HTML document for the requests.htm page (continued)**

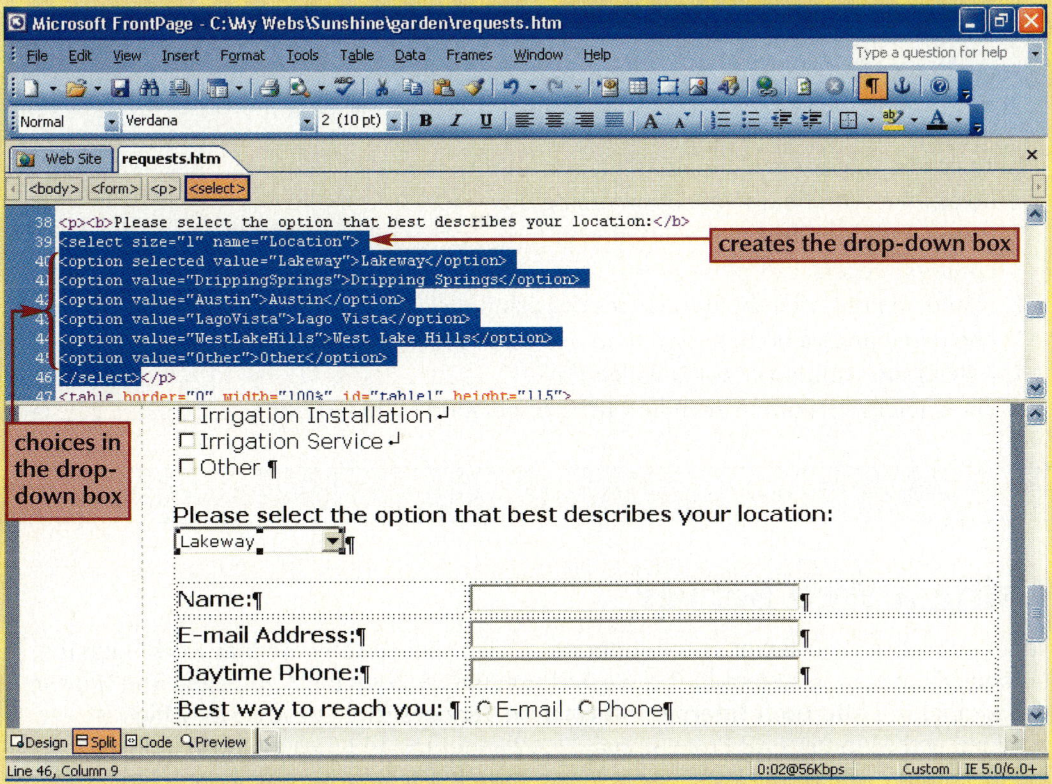

6. Scroll down the Web page in the Design view window, and then click the **Email** text box. Notice that the <input> tag includes the type, name, and size properties, which create a text box named "Email" with a width of 35 characters.
7. Scroll down the Web page in the Design view window, and then click the **E-mail** option button. An <input> tag creates the option button. Notice that its type is "radio," its value is "Email," and it belongs to an option button group named "CommunicationPreference."

8. Scroll down the Web page in the Design view window, and then click the **Visits** text box. Notice that the <input> tag includes the type, name, size, and maxlength properties. These properties create a text box with the name "Visits" that has a width of three characters. The maxlength property restricts the number of characters a user can enter into this text box to three. The HTML comment tag that appears above the <input> tag includes instructions for validating this text box so that it must contain an integer value in the range 0 to 100.
9. Click the **Submit Form** button, and then click the **Clear Form** button, noticing the HTML tags that create these form fields.
10. Return to Design view, save the requests.htm page, close the garden Web site, and then close FrontPage.

In Session 6.3, you will publish the garden Web site to a server and test the Web site. You will also enhance the Web site by adding features that require a server for processing.

Review

Session 6.2 Quick Check

1. What is validation as it relates to a form?
2. To ensure that users will enter data into a form field, click the ____________ check box in the form field's Validation dialog box.
3. Name and describe three validation criteria that you can set for a form field that will contain integers.
4. Name and describe the three types of push buttons that you can create in a form.
5. The name and value of a form field in a results file is known as a(n) ____________.
6. A Web site's administrator is called the ____________.
7. The choices in a drop-down box list are specified by the HTML ____________ tag.

Session 6.3

Using a Web Server

To function as a Web server, a computer must have special software that works with the computer's operating system to receive and execute requests for Web pages. The steps in this tutorial use **Microsoft Internet Information Services (IIS)** version 5.1, which is installed with Windows XP Professional. (You cannot install IIS using the Windows XP Home Edition, which is the operating system installed on many home computers.) The default setting starts IIS when you boot your computer. You can also start it from the Windows Control Panel.

To access a site stored on IIS, you do not need to use the "www" prefix or the server type suffix in the URL; instead, you use the computer name or the default name of **localhost**. Most Web developers use a local Web server such as IIS to develop and test a Web site before publishing it on a server and making the site available to Internet users. Because the specifications for using a local Web server vary from one computer to another, it is important to work with your instructor or technical support person to determine the correct configuration for your computer. Your instructor will note any differences that you might encounter as you complete the steps in this session.

Figure 6-28 illustrates the differences between using a disk-based Web site and using a server-based Web site to access your Web pages. In a disk-based Web site, the Web browser opens each Web page by obtaining it directly from the file stored on a disk. In a server-based Web site, also called a remote Web site, the Web browser uses the TCP/IP network protocol to send the request for a Web page to the server. The server then obtains a copy of the file stored on a disk and sends it back to the browser by way of the TCP/IP network connection, and the browser subsequently opens the file. Thus, with a local Web server, the TCP/IP network software uses the same network processing to obtain the requested files as if it were connecting to a Web server.

Figure 6-28 **File transfer comparison of a disk-based and server-based Web site**

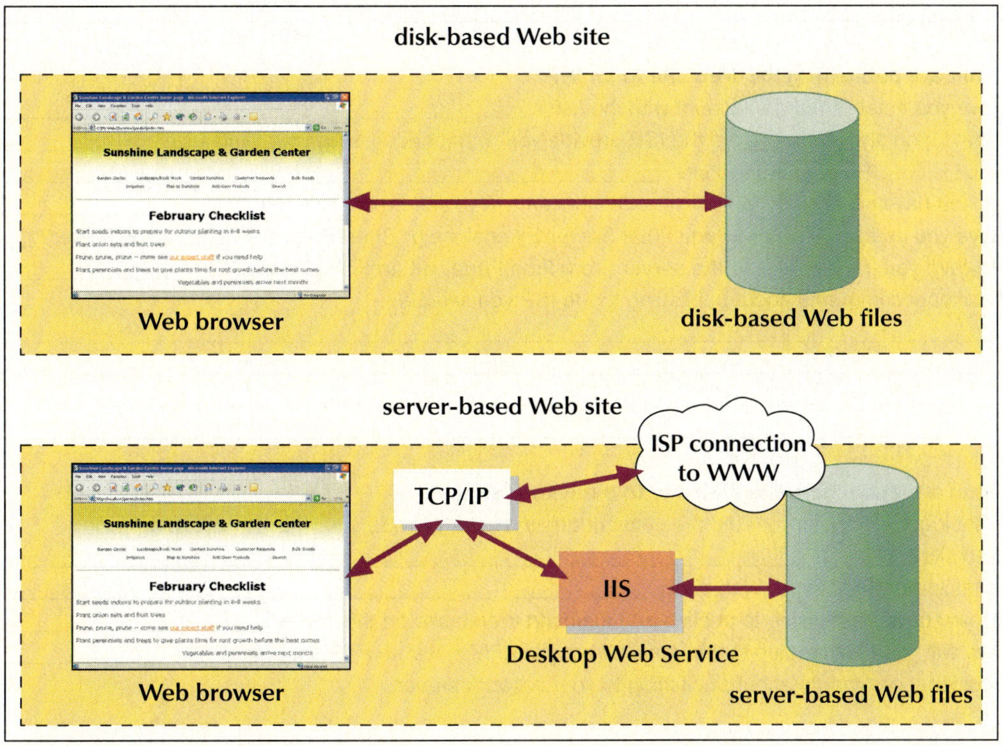

Before you can publish a Web site to a server, you need to know the proper method to transmit the files, the URL of the server, your user name and password, and any rules enforced by the server. To help you publish your Web sites, use Figure 6-29 to organize your work.

Figure 6-29 What you need to know before publishing a Web site

What You Need to Know Before Publishing a Web Site

In most cases, you should learn the answers to the following questions during the planning and development phases of the Web site. Your instructor or lab administrator can help you answer these questions. If you are working from home, you can use the resources on the Student Online Companion page for Tutorial 6 to learn more about publishing Web sites to your computer.

If you are publishing the Web site to a local Web server, such as IIS:

Is Windows 2000 or XP Professional and IIS installed and running on your computer?__________
What is your server's name?__________
Do you need to log on to the server and, if so, what is your logon and password?__________
Do you have permission to publish and maintain a Web site on the server? __________
Are the FrontPage 2002 Server Extensions or SharePoint Services installed on the server?__________
How will you transfer files to the server (from FrontPage, via an FTP site, etc.)? __________
Additional comments about publishing to IIS for your computer or lab:

____
____
____
____

If you are publishing the Web site to an ISP:

Have you established an account with the ISP?__________
What logon and password did the ISP provide you with for accessing your Web site?__________
What is the URL of your Web site?__________
Do you have permission to publish and maintain a Web site on the server?__________
Have you enabled the FrontPage 2002 Server Extensions or SharePoint Services on the server?____
How will you transfer files to the server (from FrontPage, via an FTP site, etc.)?__________
Additional comments about publishing to the ISP you selected:

____
____
____
____

If you are publishing the Web site to a network server:

What logon and password did the network administrator provide you with for accessing your Web site?__________
What is the URL of your Web site?__________
Do you have permission to publish and maintain a Web site on the server?__________
How will you transfer files to the server (from FrontPage, via an FTP site, etc.)? __________
Additional comments about publishing to your network server:

____
____
____
____

This morning, you installed and configured IIS and the FrontPage 2002 Server Extensions on Brett's computer. You used the default name for the Web server, "localhost," for Brett's computer (your computer's name might be different). You will test IIS to make sure that it is installed and operating correctly and that you can access it using your Web browser. Your instructor or technical support person will inform you of any differences that you might encounter in the lab. These steps assume a default installation of IIS or a compatible Web server and a default URL of http://localhost to access it. In addition, the FrontPage 2002 Server Extensions or SharePoint Services must be installed and configured on the Web server to which you will publish your Web sites. (*Note:* There are no FrontPage 2003 Server Extensions.)

To test IIS:

1. Start your Web browser. You do not need an Internet connection to complete these steps.
2. Select the URL in the browser's address field, type **http://localhost** (or the name or IP address provided by your instructor), and then press the **Enter** key. If IIS (or the Web server you accessed) is installed and running, the windows shown in Figure 6-30 will open. Depending on your browser's settings, the windows might open restored (as shown in Figure 6-30) or maximized, with one window on top of the other.

Figure 6-30 Checking the IIS installation

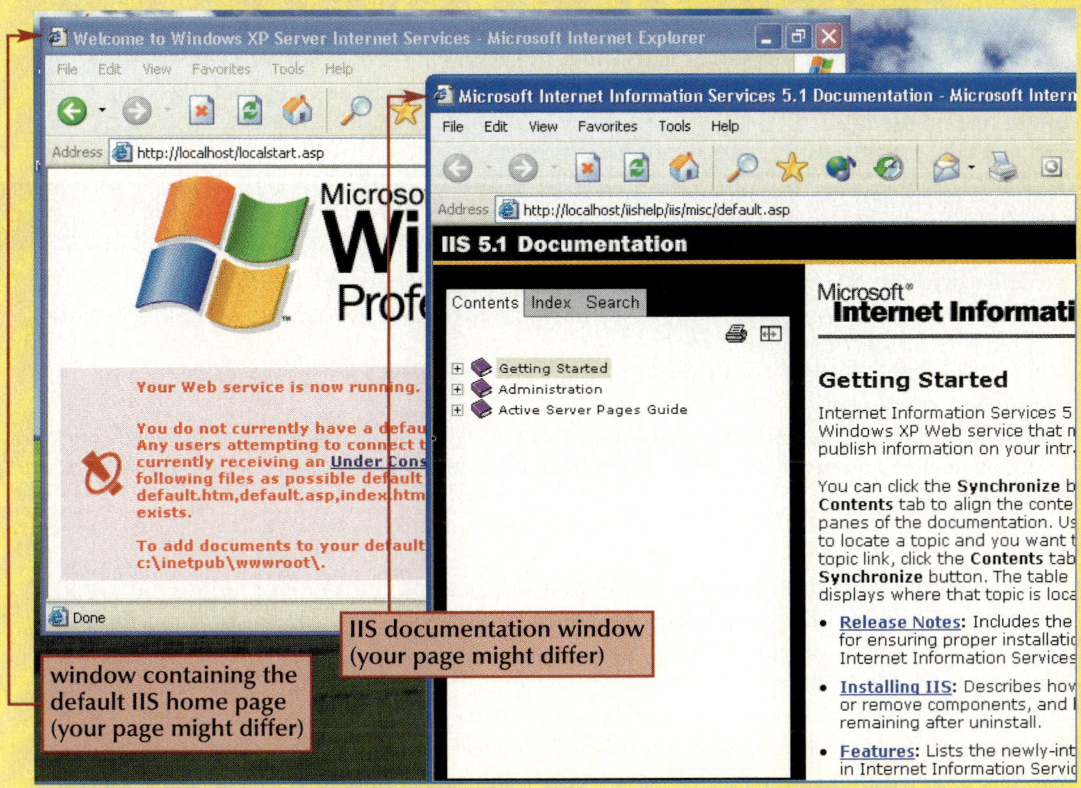

Trouble? If your browser displays a page telling you that it cannot find the page, click the Start button on the taskbar, click Control Panel, double-click the Administrative Tools icon, and then double-click the Component Services icon. (If you do not see the Component Services icon, but you do see a Personal Web Manager icon, ask your instructor or technical support person for help. If you do not see either icon, IIS might not be installed.) In the Component Services dialog box, click Services in the left pane, scroll down the services in the right pane, and then click IIS Admin in the right pane. If you see a link to Start the service, click the Start link, and then close the Component Services dialog box. If you do not see a Start link, IIS is already running and you can close the dialog box. Close the Control Panel.

Trouble? If a "Web page unavailable while offline" message box opens after you press the Enter key, click the Connect button to connect to your computer's server. You do not need to connect to your ISP, however.

Trouble? If you receive an error message or no response from the server, you might need to start, install, or configure the server. Ask your instructor or technical support person for help.

3. Close all open browser windows.

You need to move the folders and files from your disk-based Web site to the server so that you can test the garden Web site. To move the folders and files, you will publish the Web site to IIS or another server designated by your instructor.

Publishing a Web Site

You publish a Web site by copying the Web site's folders and files to your computer's server or to a Web server that is connected to the Internet. When you publish a Web site to IIS, the default server-based folder containing all server-based Web sites is C:\Inetpub\wwwroot; any Web sites that are published to IIS are stored as subfolders, or subsites, in this path.

Note: You will need to know how your computer is organized before publishing your Web site to ensure that the server is running the FrontPage 2002 Server Extensions or SharePoint Services. Your instructor will inform you of any differences that you might encounter in the lab.

Reference Window

Publishing a Web Site to Your Computer's Server

- Open the Web site in FrontPage, and then change to Remote Web Site view.
- Click the Remote Web Site Properties button on the Contents pane to open the Remote Web Site Properties dialog box.
- Click the option button in the Remote Web server type section to select the type of server you are using.
- Click the Remote Web site location list box, and then type http://localhost/ (or your server's name) and the name of the folder in which to store the Web site's files and folders.
- Click the OK button.

You can publish a disk-based Web site to a server using the same or a different Web site name. Before publishing a Web site, check with the server's administrator to find out if you need to use any special naming conventions, such as using only lowercase letters or omitting spaces in Web folder names and filenames. Even though a disk-based Web site and a server-based Web site can have the same name, you access pages in a disk-based Web site using a path to a folder or a drive. To access pages in a server-based Web site, you use the Hypertext Transfer Protocol (HTTP), the server name (in this case, localhost), and the name of the Web site, as in http://localhost/garden.

When publishing a Web site, you also need to determine the best way to transfer the files. FrontPage includes four methods for publishing files depending on the type of server to which you are publishing. If the remote Web server you selected to host your Web site supports the FrontPage 2002 Server Extensions or SharePoint Services, you choose the FrontPage or SharePoint Services option. If the remote Web server supports **Distributed Authoring and Versioning (DAV)**, which is an extension of the HTTP protocol that is used to transfer files over the Internet, select the WebDAV choice. If the remote Web server supports **File Transfer Protocol (FTP)**, an Internet protocol for transferring files between computers connected to the Internet, select the FTP option. Finally, if you are publishing the Web site to a folder on your computer or on a network, choose the File System option. This book assumes that you will publish the garden Web site to IIS or a compatible Web server running the FrontPage 2002 Server Extensions or SharePoint Services. However, you can publish the garden Web site using one of the other methods if required to do so by your instructor or your ISP.

When you publish a Web site to IIS, the site is added as a subfolder in the C:\Inetpub\wwwroot folder on your hard drive. If you are publishing changes to an existing server-based Web site, you can click the Publish Site button on the Standard toolbar and FrontPage will automatically publish the changes to the correct Web site on the server without reopening the Publish Remote Web Site Properties dialog box.

You'll show Brett how to publish the garden Web site to his computer's Web server using the FrontPage 2002 Server Extensions.

Note: You must be able to publish files to complete the steps in Session 6.3. If you cannot access IIS or a compatible Web server, read Session 6.3 without completing the steps at the computer so you will know how to publish a Web site. If your instructor asks you to publish the garden Web site to a location other than IIS, follow the instructions provided by your instructor to complete this section.

To publish a disk-based Web site to IIS:

1. Start **FrontPage**, and then open the **garden** Web site from the location where your Web sites are stored.
2. Click the **Remote Web Site View** button [Remote Web site] at the bottom of the Contents pane to change to Remote Web Site view. Because you haven't published the garden Web site to a server, this view is empty except for a message that tells you to click the Remote Web Site Properties button to set up a remote Web site.
3. Click the **Remote Web Site Properties** button on the Contents pane. The Remote Web Site Properties dialog box opens. See Figure 6-31.

Figure 6-31 Remote Web Site Properties dialog box

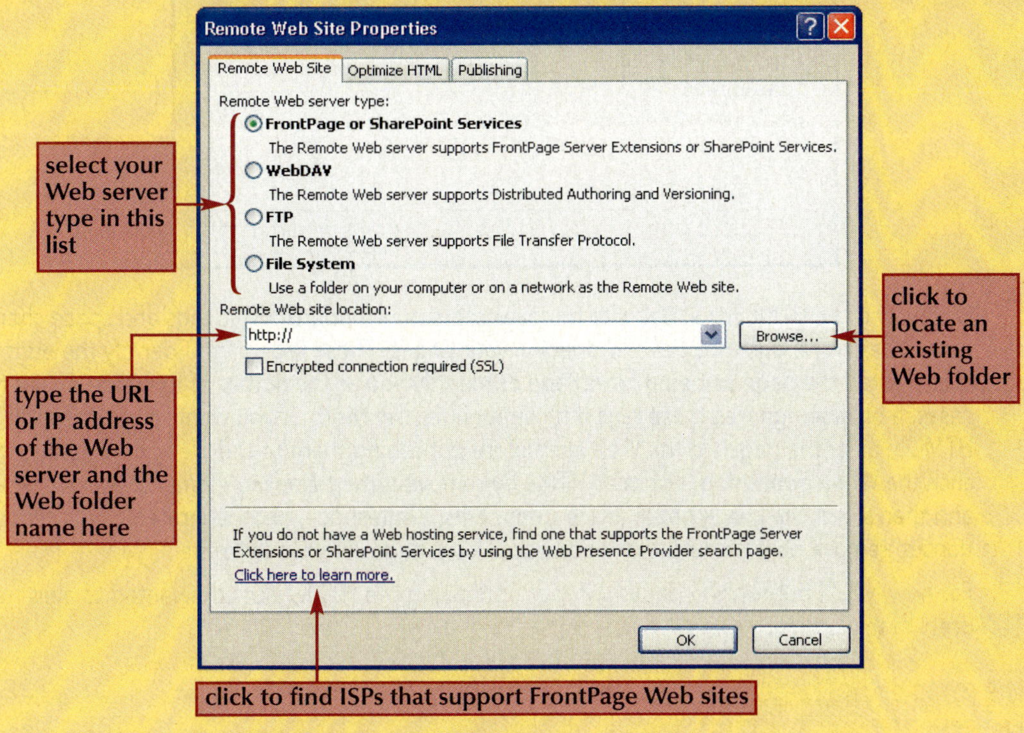

4. Make sure that the **FrontPage or SharePoint Services** option button is selected in the Remote Web server type section.

   Trouble? If your ISP or instructor asks you to select a different method for publishing the Web site, choose the appropriate option button in Step 4.

   You will enter the remote Web site location by typing the path to IIS or your server.

5. Select any text in the Remote Web site location list box (if necessary), and then type **http://localhost/garden**.

   Trouble? If your instructor provides you with a different path or computer name, or an IP address for publishing your Web site, use that path or computer name instead of the one provided in Step 5.

6. Click the **Optimize HTML** tab. See Figure 6-32.

Figure 6-32 **Optimize HTML tab**

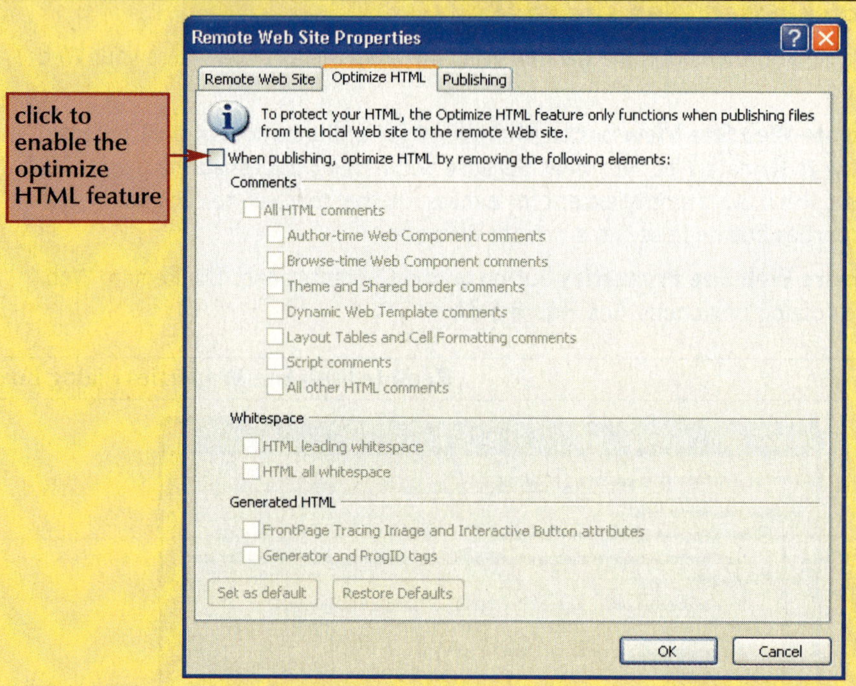

Optimizing the HTML for a Web site removes some nonstandard HTML tags and space characters that FrontPage may have inserted in your pages. These tags might identify the editor that created the page as being FrontPage or identify you as the author of the page. In most cases, a browser ignores these tags if it cannot interpret them. If you want to optimize the HTML in all of the pages in the Web site before publishing them to the Web server, you can click the When publishing, optimize HTML by removing the following elements check box, and then select the check boxes in the Comments, Whitespace, and Generated HTML sections to remove nonstandard tags and spaces from pages in your Web site.

For now, you'll publish the pages without optimizing the HTML, but you wanted to alert Brett to this option.

7. Click the **Publishing** tab. See Figure 6-33. You can change the default settings to publish either all pages or only those pages that contain changes. The advantage of publishing only changed pages is that it will speed up the publishing process. You can specify which method to use to determine a changed page: by comparing the source and destination Web sites, or by comparing the date and time that pages in the source Web site were last saved. You can publish any subsites in your Web site at the same time by selecting the Include subsites check box. Because your Web site does not include a subsite, you don't need to select this option. Finally, by selecting the Log changes during publish check box, FrontPage will create a log file when publishing the Web site. If there are errors during the publishing process, this log file can help you identify them.

Publishing tab **Figure 6-33**

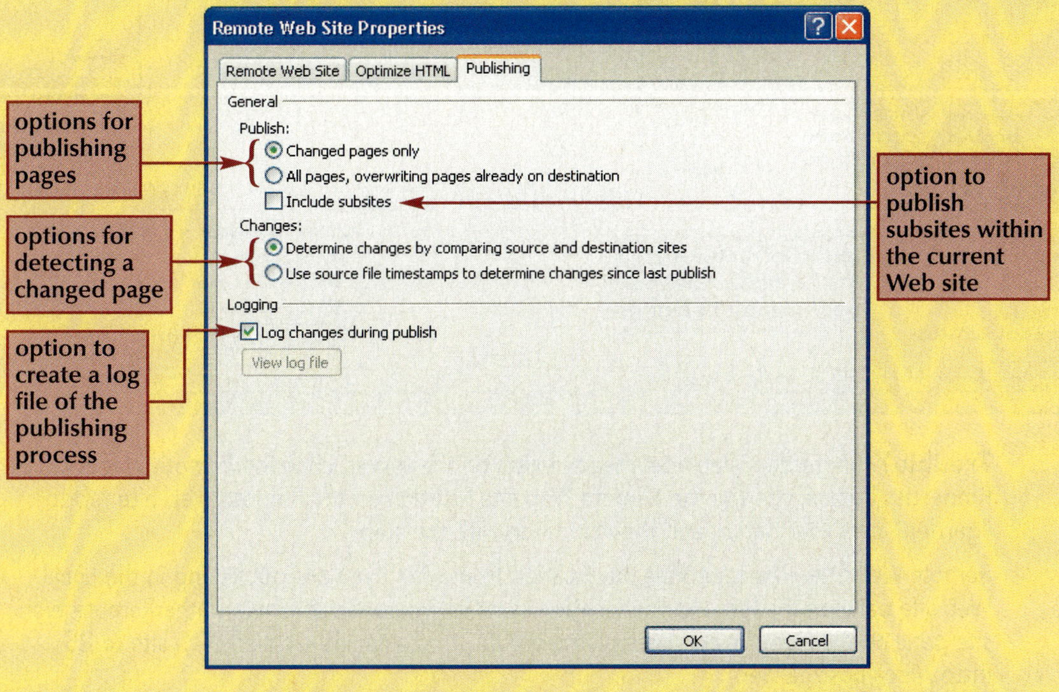

8. Make sure that the **Changed pages only** option button is selected, that the **Determine changes by comparing source and destination sites** option button is selected, and that the **Log changes during publish** check box contains a check mark, and then click the **OK** button.

   A Microsoft Office FrontPage message box opens, indicating that a Web site does not exist at the location you specified. You need to create the Web folder, so you'll click the Yes button.

9. Click the **Yes** button. Remote Web Site view now shows the folders and files in the disk-based garden Web site on the left and the remote garden Web site on the right. Because you have not yet published the garden Web site, the Remote Web site pane is empty, except for the _private and images folders that FrontPage created when you clicked the Yes button to create the Web site on the server. See Figure 6-34.

Figure 6-34 **Remote Web Site view**

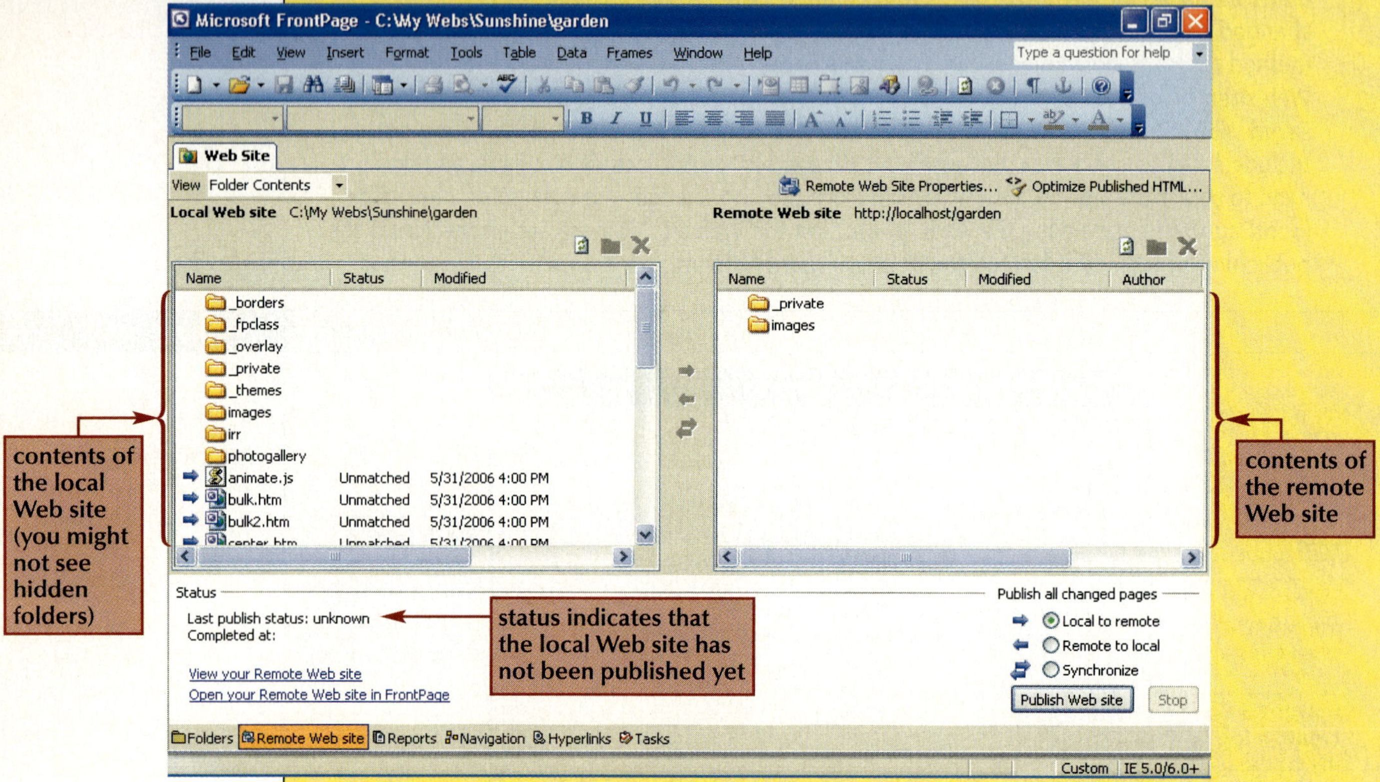

Trouble? If a garden Web site already exists on the server, click the Remote Web Site Properties button, change the Remote Web site location on the Remote Web Site tab to "garden" plus your name, and then continue with the steps.

Remote Web Site view identifies the location from which you are publishing in the Local Web site pane on the left and the location to which you are publishing in the Remote Web site pane on the right. In this case, you are publishing your disk-based Web site to IIS (http://localhost/garden).

Remote Web Site view also lists all of the folders and files in your Web site in the Local Web site pane. Each file has a status of "Unmatched" and an arrow to the left of the filename. If you had set any page so that it would not be published, the status would be "Don't publish" and a red "X" would appear instead of the arrow next to the filename. (You can set a page so that it is not published by right-clicking the filename and then clicking Don't Publish on the shortcut menu.)

The Publish all changed pages section in Remote Web Site view shows three options for publishing the Web site to the remote Web server. The first option, Local to remote, publishes the disk-based Web site to the remote Web site. This option is the one that publishes the Web site from a computer to a server. The second option, Remote to local, publishes the remote Web site to the local disk. You usually use this option to create a backup copy of the remote Web site on a local drive, such as your computer's hard drive or a removable disk. Regularly backing up your remote Web site to a hard drive or other disk is a good way to prevent data loss in the event of a problem with the Web server. The third option, Synchronize, updates the local and remote Web sites so they are identical. You can use this option when you need to update a local and remote site so they contain the same content and files. Usually you use this option when you and other users have made changes to both copies of the Web site and need to merge those changes. If there are conflicts between files on the local and remote systems during the publishing process, a Conflict dialog box opens and asks you to choose to ignore the conflict, overwrite the file with the new version (using the date), or cancel publishing the Web site.

Because you are publishing the garden Web site for the first time, you'll need to select the default option, which is to publish the local Web site to the remote Web server.

To publish the local Web site to the remote server:

1. Make sure that the **Local to remote** option button is selected, and then click the **Publish Web site** button. The Status section shows the publishing status of the Web site as FrontPage publishes the files from the local Web site to the remote Web server. When publishing is complete, the Status section displays the message "Last publish status: successful" and the date and time publishing was completed, as shown in Figure 6-35.

Figure 6-35 Successful publication of the Web site

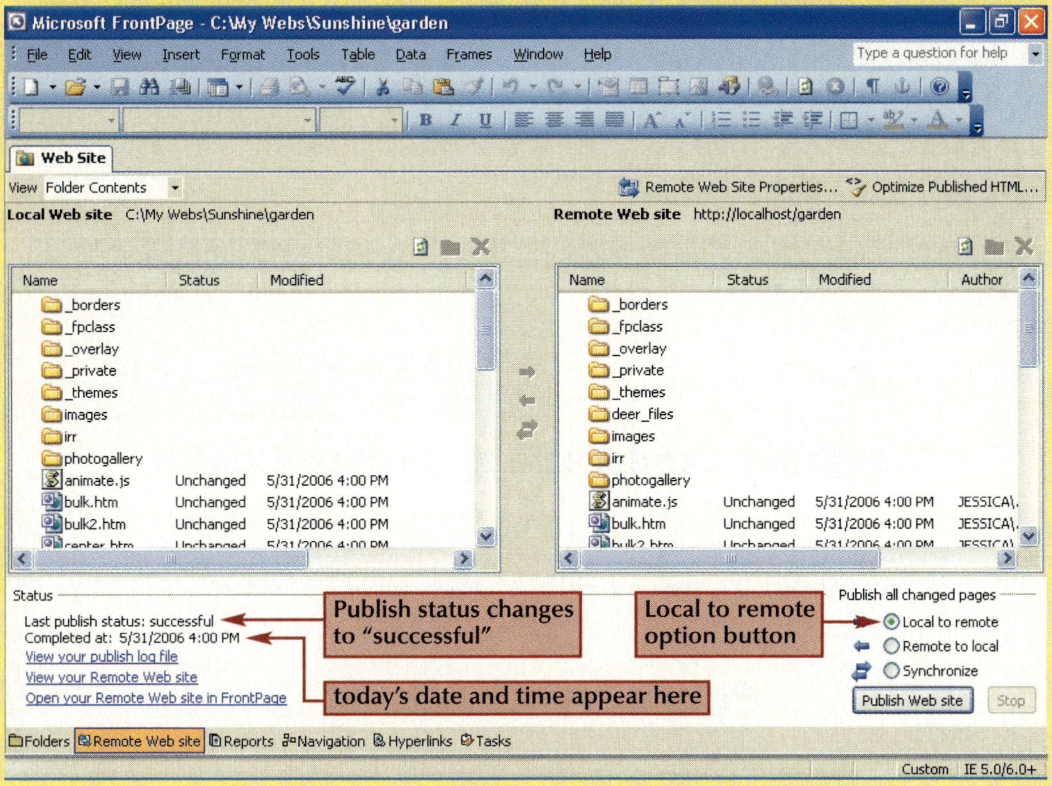

The Remote Web site pane shows the files and folders that were published to the server. If FrontPage is configured to hide the local Web site's hidden folders, you will see more folders in the Remote Web site pane than in the Local Web site pane because the Remote Web site pane shows all of the site's folders, including the hidden folders, such as _borders, which contains the files that create the Web site's shared borders, and _themes, which stores the files that create the Garden Web Site theme.

The Status section includes three hyperlinks for viewing your publish log file, viewing your remote Web site (in a browser), and opening your remote Web site in FrontPage. You'll show Brett how to work with these options next.

To view the publish log file and the remote Web site:

1. In the Status section, click **View your publish log file**. The publish log file opens in a browser and shows the actions FrontPage took to publish the Web site. As you scroll down the page, you'll see that it created each folder in and copied each file to the remote Web site. The last entries show that the navigation structure was copied and that publishing was finished. If FrontPage encountered any errors during the publishing process, these errors would appear in the publish log file.
2. Close your browser.
3. In the Status section, click the **View your Remote Web site** link. The home page for the remote Web site opens in a browser, as shown in Figure 6-36. Notice that the URL for the page is the remote Web site, http://localhost/garden (your path might differ if you published your Web site to another location). The HTTP protocol in the URL indicates that your Web browser is communicating with a server to process requests, instead of opening files directly from your computer's hard drive. The server is opening the files from the C:\Inetpub\wwwroot\garden folder on your hard drive. You can perform the same activities using this server-based Web as you did with the disk-based Web. In addition, when you open a server-based Web in FrontPage, you can edit pages, update hyperlinks, and perform other tasks, just as you did in the disk-based Web. The main difference between the two Web sites is that the server-based Web will process several key elements of the Web site, including the form that you created earlier in this tutorial.

Figure 6-36 Home page of the remote Web site

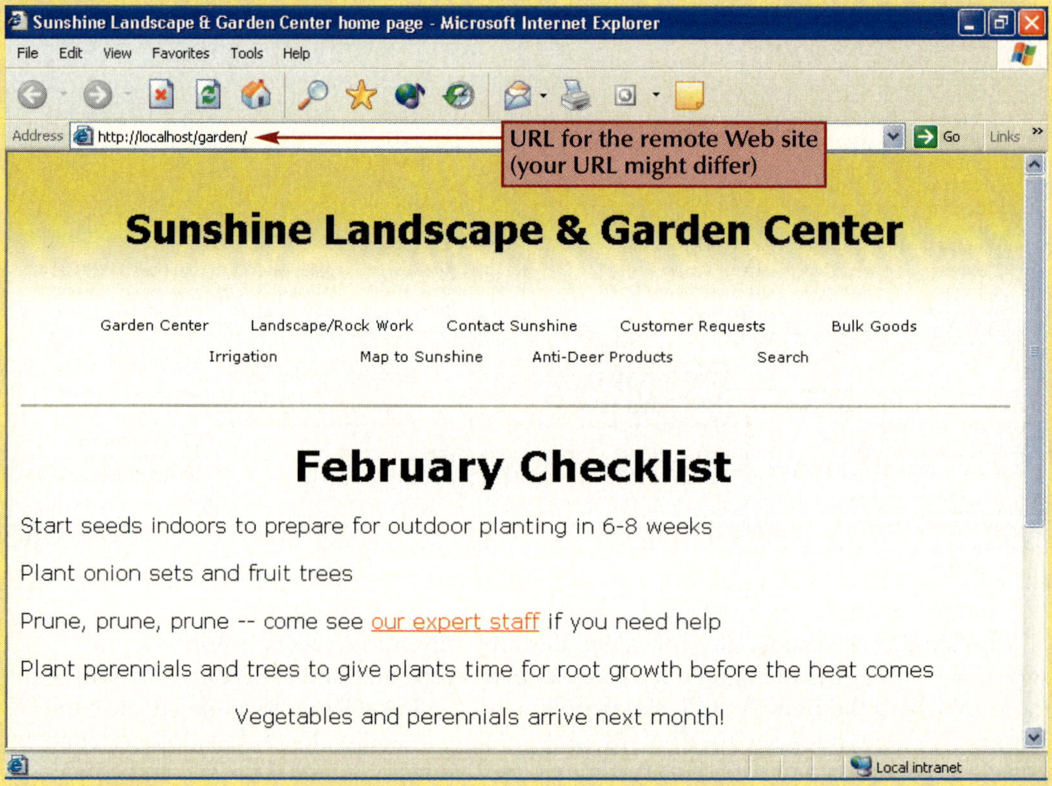

4. Follow the links on the home page to examine the pages in the remote Web site, and then close your browser.

Publishing Changes to Pages in a Web Site

As you and Brett examine the pages in the garden Web site, you notice that the marquee on the home page is set to scroll its message indefinitely. You think that this feature would be better if it scrolled twice, instead of continuously, so it doesn't become a distraction. You can make this change in the disk-based Web site and then publish the change to the remote Web server. You explain to Brett that you could also make the change in the remote Web site, but most developers make changes in the local site and then publish them. This strategy has two advantages. First, when you publish a site, you publish all of the site's changes at once, which minimizes the problems that users might encounter if they are viewing your pages as you work on them. Second, having two copies of the Web site—one on a local drive and another on the remote Web server—ensures that you can recover your files in the event of a problem.

Publishing Changes to a Server-Based Web Site

Reference Window

- In Design view, open the Web page that you need to edit, make the changes, and then save the page.
- Edit and save other Web pages, as necessary.
- Click the Publish Site button on the Standard toolbar.

You'll make the change in the home page, save the home page, and then publish the Web site.

To make a change in the home page and publish the Web site's changes:

1. Change to Folders view. The disk-based garden Web site is still open in FrontPage, as indicated by the path in the title bar.
2. Double-click **index.htm** in the Contents pane to open the home page in Design view.
3. Scroll down the page as necessary, and then double-click the marquee. (The marquee contains the text "Vegetables and perennials arrive next month!") The Marquee Properties dialog box opens.
4. In the Repeat section, click the **Continuously** check box to clear it. A "1" appears in the list box in the Repeat section. This number indicates the number of times the marquee will scroll across the page before it stops.
5. Click the **up** arrow on the list box in the Repeat section to change the value to **2**, and then click the **OK** button. This change will cause the marquee to scroll across the screen twice and then stop.
6. Save the home page, and then close it. You need to publish the Web site again to make the same change in the remote Web site.
7. Click the **Publish Site** button on the Standard toolbar. Because you have already published this Web site, you do not have to specify a location to which to publish it. You also previously set FrontPage to publish only those pages with changes, so only the index.htm page and any other pages that changed as a result of the update you made to the index.htm page will be copied to the server. The Web site appears in Remote Web Site view and the Status section shows the publishing process. When publishing is complete, the Last publish status changes to "successful."
8. Click the **View your Remote Web site** link to open the home page of the remote Web site in a browser. The marquee scrolls across the screen twice and then stops.

Processing Web Pages on a Server

In Sessions 6.1 and 6.2, you added the Search and Customer Requests pages to the Web site. You tested these pages in the disk-based Web site but your testing served primarily to confirm that the pages appeared as desired. For the Search page, you included a component to search the site using keywords entered by the user and a second component to search the Internet using keywords entered by the user. For the Customer Requests page, you inserted a form and form fields in the page to collect data, and set the form to send its results to a file in the Web site. You tested both pages, but were limited to testing individual form fields to make sure that they contained the desired choices. Now that you have published the Web site, you tell Brett that he can test these pages by entering keywords in the search components and submitting a form to the server. Even if your Web site performs perfectly when you test it on your local drive or local server, after publishing a Web site you must resume testing again to ensure that all of the site's features work correctly.

After a server processes a Web page that contains a form, it usually sends a confirmation page to the browser that sent the page. A **confirmation page** is a Web page that contains a copy of the data entered by the user and often is used for verification purposes. FrontPage can return a default confirmation page or you can create, save, and specify a custom confirmation page. When you specify a custom confirmation page, FrontPage automatically inserts the data entered by the user in the correct locations in the confirmation page and then sends it to the browser.

Next, you will test the Search and Customer Requests pages to make sure that the server processes them correctly.

To test the Search page in a browser:

1. Click the **Search** hyperlink in the link bar in the home page. The Search page opens in the browser. The page's URL references the page in the remote Web site. The link to the MSN logo picture is broken because this picture file is not stored in the Web site.

   Trouble? If a Dial-up Connection dialog box opens, click the Close button. You do not need an Internet connection to complete these steps.

   Trouble? If you published your Web site to Windows 2003 Server using Windows SharePoint Services, the search page will not return the search results because this feature is not supported with this server configuration. Read the remaining steps so you will understand how a search component works, but do not complete them at the computer.

2. Click the **Search for** text box, type **lawn**, and then click the **Start Search** button. If necessary, scroll down the page so the Search for text box is at the top of the window. The server processes your search request and returns a new Web page with two documents that match your request and contain the word "lawn." Depending on your computer's speed, the new page might appear so quickly that you won't notice it. The Search page that is displayed in the browser is the page that the server generated to contain your search results. See Figure 6-37.

Search page with search results

Figure 6-37

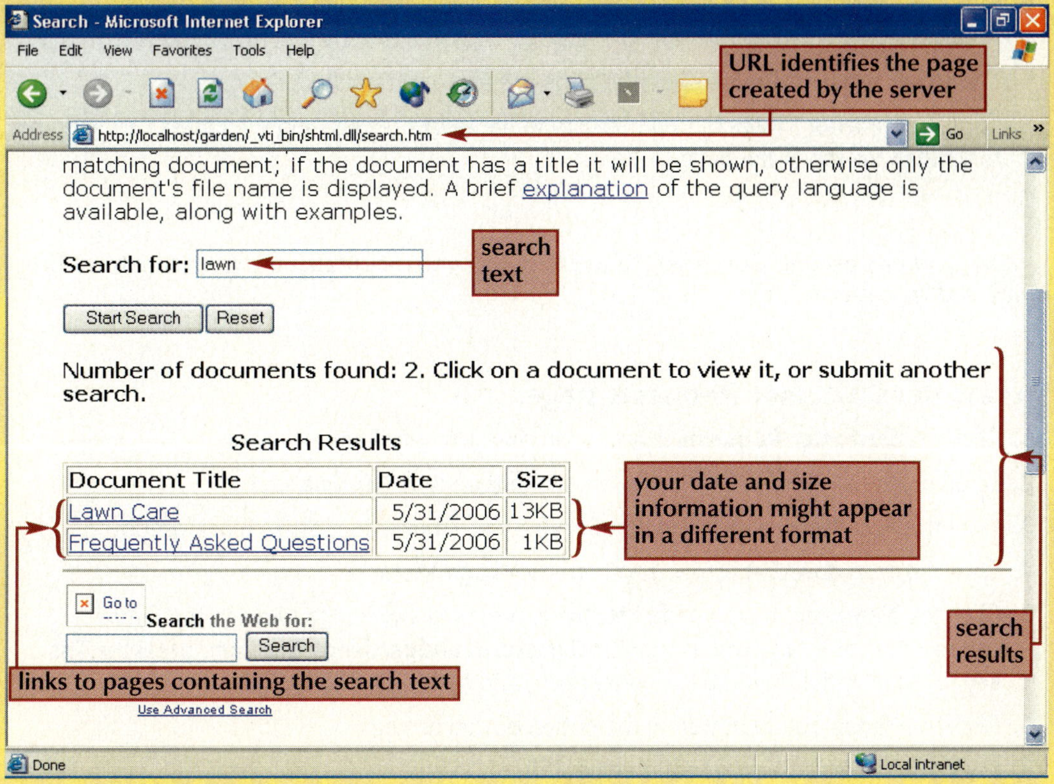

Trouble? If a page opens with the message "Service is not running" and you published the garden Web site to IIS, you will need to start the Indexing Service. Click the Start button on the taskbar, and then click Control Panel. Double-click the Administrative Tools icon, double-click the Component Services icon, and then click Services (Local) in the pane on the left. Scroll down the list of services on the right and double-click Indexing Service. Click the Startup type list arrow, and then click Automatic. Click the Start button in the Service status section. Click the OK button, close the Component Services window, close the Administrative Tools window, and then close the Control Panel. Click your browser's Back button to return to the Search page (search.htm), click the Reset button, and then repeat Step 2.

Trouble? If you published the garden Web site to IIS, it might take several minutes for the server to index the pages you just published. If you see the message "No documents found. Please try again." in the search results, click your browser's Back button to return to the Search page (search.htm), wait a few minutes for the indexing service to index the site, and then repeat Step 2.

Trouble? If an Internet Explorer dialog box opens and says that you are sending information to the local intranet, click the Yes button to continue.

3. If necessary, scroll down the Search page so you can see the search results. The server generated this revised version of the search.htm page. The Search Results table contains two entries that are formatted as hyperlinks. The Lawn Care and Frequently Asked Questions pages contain the word "lawn." Pages identified in the search results are hyperlinks that you can click to open those pages.

4. Click the **Lawn Care** hyperlink in the Search Results table. The Lawn Care Web page opens.
5. Click your browser's **Back** button to return to the search results, and then click the **Frequently Asked Questions** link. This page is part of the Irrigation frames page.

   Trouble? If a message tells you the page has expired, refresh the page.
6. Click your browser's **Back** button to return to the search results, and then press **Ctrl + Home** to scroll to the top of the page.

Now you can test the Customer Requests page, which contains the form that must be processed by a server.

To test the Customer Requests page:

1. Click the **Customer Requests** link to open the Customer Requests page.
2. Scroll down the page, click the text area, and then type **This is a test.**
3. Click the **Rock Work** and **Irrigation Service** check boxes in the check box group.
4. Click the drop-down list arrow, and then click **Lago Vista**.
5. Click the **Name** text box, type **Brett Kizer**, press the **Tab** key to move to the E-mail Address text box, type **brett@sunshinelandscapeandgardencenter.com**, press the **Tab** key to move to the Daytime Phone text box, and then type **555-2610**.
6. Click the **Phone** option button in the option button group.
7. Click the **Visits** text box, and then type **155**.
8. Click the **Submit Form** button. The Form Validation Error page opens and asks you to enter a value greater than or equal to zero and less than or equal to 100 in the Visits field. See Figure 6-38.

Figure 6-38 Form Validation Error page

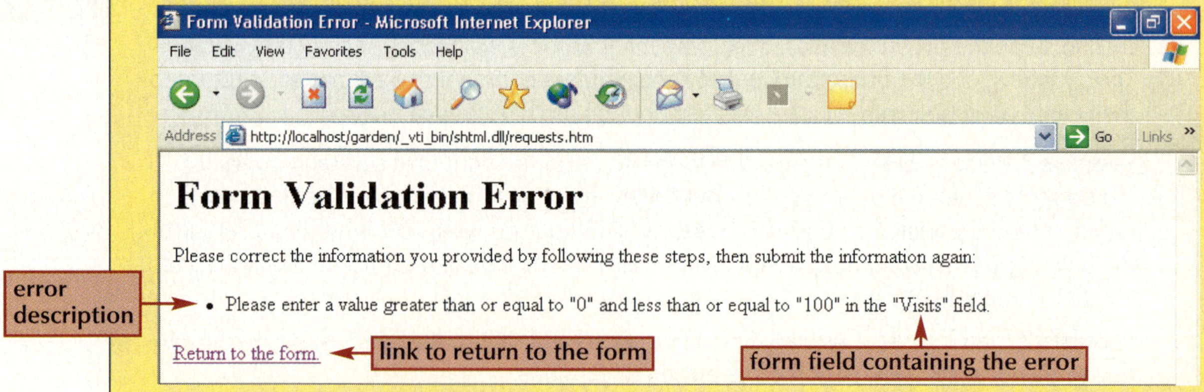

Trouble? If a dialog box opens instead of the page shown in Figure 6-38, click the OK button, and then skip clicking the Back button in Step 9.

Trouble? If an AutoComplete dialog box opens, click the No button.

9. Click your browser's **Back** button, select **155** in the Visits text box, type **15**, and then click the **Submit Form** button. The Form Confirmation page opens with a copy of the data you entered into the form. The server generated this page automatically. See Figure 6-39. Notice that the check boxes you selected contain the value "Yes." Check boxes that you did not select do not contain a value. When you clicked the Phone option button in the CommunicationPreference option button group, the value "Phone" was entered as the result.

Form Confirmation page

Figure 6-39

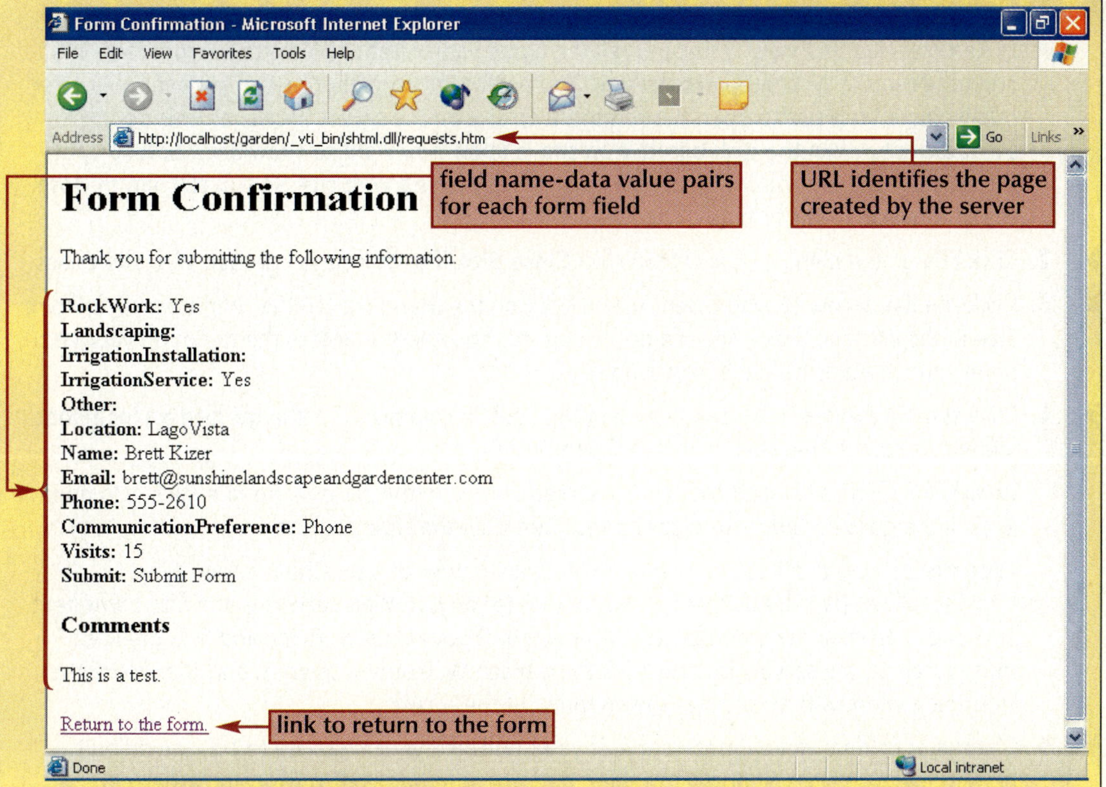

10. Click the **Return to the form** link at the bottom of the confirmation page to return to the Customer Requests Web page. Clicking the Return to the form link clears all of the form's fields and resets the form so it is ready to be completed again. Your test of the form is successful. The page correctly accepts your input, produces a confirmation page, and resets the form.

When the confirmation page was sent to your browser, the form's results were also written to the results.csv file that you specified when you created the form. You stored this file in the _private folder of the remote Web site.

Examining a Form Results File

When you set the Save Results form handler to store the form's results, you specified a comma-delimited text file format. In a comma-delimited text file, the name of each form field appears in the first line of the file. The form results from each new form submission are added as a new line at the end of the file. Unless you submitted your form more than once, the results file contains only two lines—one containing the form field names and another containing the form results from your form submission. You can examine the contents of the results file on the server at any time.

You want to show Brett how to view this file to increase his understanding of how the data submitted to the server is stored. You'll show him how to open the remote Web site in FrontPage.

To open the remote garden Web site in FrontPage:

1. Close your browser.

   In Remote Web Site view, you can click the Open your Remote Web site in FrontPage link to open the remote Web site in FrontPage. You explain to Brett that he can click this link *after* publishing a Web site to open the remote Web site on the server. However, this option is available only when the disk-based Web site is open. You want to show Brett how to open the remote Web site without first opening the disk-based Web site, so you ask him to close the disk-based Web site first.

2. Click **File** on the menu bar, and then click **Close Site**. The disk-based garden Web site closes.
3. Click the **list arrow** for the Open button on the Standard toolbar, and then click **Open Site** in the list. The Open Site dialog box opens. You need to access the folder on your computer that contains server-based Web sites.
4. Click the **My Network Places** button in the Look in column, click the **garden on localhost** folder to select it, and then click the **Open** button.

   Trouble? If you see localhost or your server's name in the list box, double-click it to open it, click the garden folder to select it, and then click the Open button.

   Trouble? If you don't see a garden on localhost folder or a localhost folder, type http://localhost (or the address for the root folder of your Web server) in the Site name text box, and then click the Open button. A new FrontPage window opens and lists the Web sites stored on the server. Double-click the garden Web site to open it, and then close the FrontPage window that displays the contents of the server.

5. Change to Folders view (if necessary). If you published your Web site to IIS, the default path to the Web site will appear in the FrontPage title bar as http://localhost/garden.

Now that the server-based Web site is open, you can examine the results file.

To examine the results file:

1. Double-click the **_private** folder, and then double-click **results.csv** in the Contents pane. The results.csv file opens and shows the field names on line 1 and the results of the form you submitted on line 2. Each value in quotation marks represents the value for one form field in the form. Notice that the last entry is Remote Name on line 1 and 127.0.0.1 on line 2. This form field collects the IP address of the user who submitted the form, which you specified when you configured the form's handler and the data to collect. The value 127.0.0.1 is the default IP address for IIS. See Figure 6-40.

Figure 6-40 Form results file

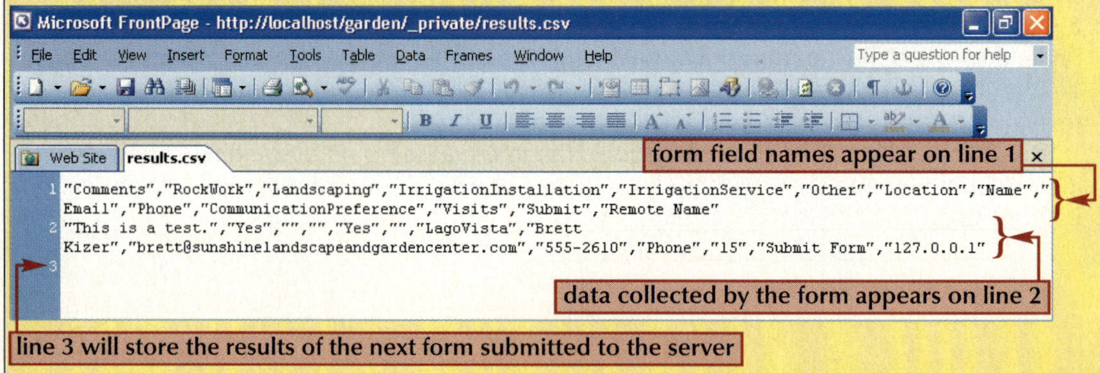

2. Click the **Close** button to close the results.csv file.
3. Click the **Up One Level** button on the Contents pane to return to the root folder of the garden Web site.

You have verified that the form's results were collected correctly and stored in the results.csv file in the _private folder of the remote garden Web site. You tell Brett that it is important to continue testing the pages in the Web site to ensure that everything is working correctly. Brett also wants to add some new features to the Web site. The first feature he wants to add is a counter that displays the number of times the home page has been accessed.

Using a Hit Counter

To fulfill Brett's request, you tell him that he will need to add a hit counter to the Web site. A **hit counter** is a component that counts the number of times a page in a Web site has been opened or refreshed using a Web browser. Usually a hit counter appears in the Web site's home page, although you can create hit counters in other pages, as well. A hit counter requires a server for processing, so you can test it only in a server-based Web site. In Web sites that do not use the FrontPage 2002 Server Extensions or SharePoint Services, you must write a program to add the functionality to a hit counter. However, if your Web site uses the FrontPage 2002 Server Extensions or SharePoint Services, you can insert a hit counter in a Web page, and FrontPage will generate the program to provide its functionality automatically. You can accept the default settings for the hit counter or change the counter style and other properties if desired. The counter style is implemented using a default or custom-designed GIF picture that contains the digits zero through nine.

Creating a Hit Counter in a Web Page

Reference Window

- Click the location in the page where you want to insert the hit counter.
- Click the Web Component button on the Standard toolbar.
- In the Component type list box, click Hit Counter.
- In the Choose a counter style list box, click the desired hit counter style, and then click the Finish button.
- In the Hit Counter Properties dialog box, set the options to reset the counter or to display a fixed number of digits as needed.
- Click the OK button.

Brett wants to insert a hit counter in the home page. Most Web developers start the counter with the number 1000 to make it look like the site is active, so you suggest doing the same. You'll also set the counter to display six digits to allow for future expansion.

To create a hit counter in the home page:

1. Double-click **index.htm** in the Contents pane to open the home page in Design view. You will insert the hit counter between the marquee and the map picture.
2. Scroll down the page, click the marquee, press the **End** key, press the **Enter** key to create a new paragraph, and then click the **Center** button on the Formatting toolbar to center the new paragraph.
3. Click the **Bold** button on the Formatting toolbar, type **You are visitor number** as the text that precedes the hit counter, and then press the **spacebar**.

4. Click the **Web Component** button on the Standard toolbar, and then in the Component type list box click **Hit Counter**. The Choose a counter style list box displays five styles of hit counters.
5. Click the fourth hit counter style in the Choose a counter style list box, and then click the **Finish** button. The Hit Counter Properties dialog box opens. See Figure 6-41.

Figure 6-41 Hit Counter Properties dialog box

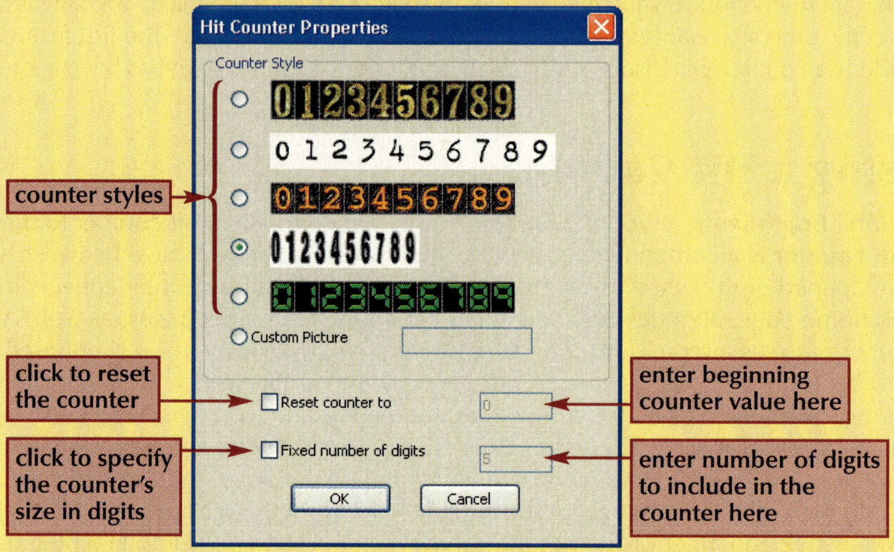

6. Click the **Reset counter to** check box to select it, press the **Tab** key to move to its text box, and then type **1000**. The hit counter will start at 1000, instead of zero. Starting the hit counter at a number other than zero or one is a common practice on the Internet.
7. Click the **Fixed number of digits** check box to select it, press the **Tab** key to move to its text box, and then type **6**. The counter will display six digits.
8. Click the **OK** button to close the Hit Counter Properties dialog box and to insert the hit counter. A picture of the hit counter appears in the page as a placeholder to indicate the hit counter's location.

   Next, complete the rest of the sentence that contains the hit counter.
9. Press the **spacebar**, and then type **to our Web site.** as the text that follows the hit counter.
10. Save the home page.

You'll need to open the home page of the remote Web site in a browser to test the hit counter.

To test the hit counter:

1. Click the **Preview** button on the Standard toolbar to open the home page in a browser.
2. If necessary, scroll down the home page to see the hit counter. You are the first visitor to the Web site. Because you set the hit counter to start with the value 1000, you are visitor number 1001.

3. Click the **Refresh** button on the toolbar to refresh the page. Now you are visitor number 1002. Each time the page is opened or refreshed, the number in the hit counter increases by one. See Figure 6-42.

Hit counter after loading and refreshing the home page **Figure 6-42**

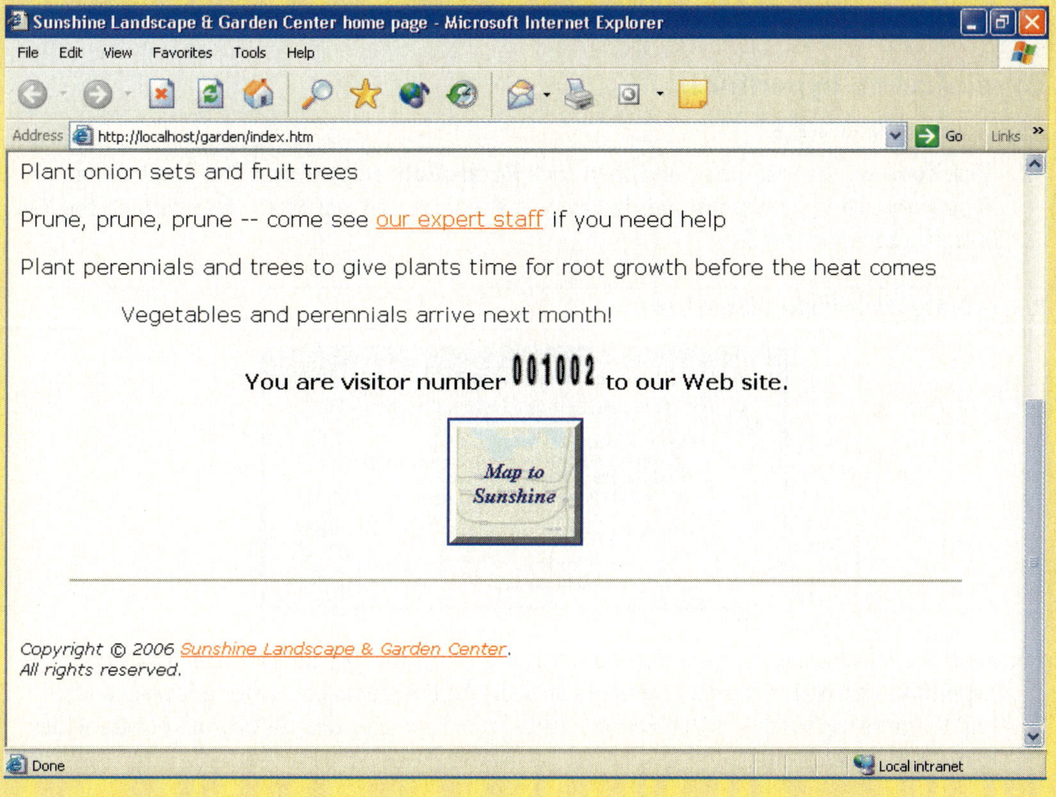

4. Close your browser.

The hit counter will count the number of times the home page has been opened. Because refreshing the page also increases the number in the counter, the counter does not indicate the exact number of visitors to a Web page, but it's a good estimate.

Recalculating and Verifying Hyperlinks

When you are working on a Web site, it is a good idea to recalculate the hyperlinks contained in it periodically. **Recalculating hyperlinks** is the process of updating the display of all views of the Web site in which you are working, including updating the text index created by a FrontPage search component (when one is used), deleting files for unused themes, and reporting any broken hyperlinks. You can recalculate the hyperlinks in a disk-based or server-based Web site. When it recalculates the hyperlinks in a server-based Web site, FrontPage updates the index that it maintains for the search component as well.

Verifying hyperlinks is the process of checking all of the hyperlinks in a Web site to identify any internal or external broken hyperlinks. An **external hyperlink** is a hyperlink to a location that is not in the current Web site, such as a hyperlink to a URL on a different Web server. Any broken hyperlinks will be listed in Reports view so you can repair them.

You can recalculate and verify hyperlinks to detect and repair broken hyperlinks. One of the primary differences between these two commands relates to how broken hyperlinks are displayed. Both commands list broken hyperlinks, but verifying hyperlinks provides a report of all broken hyperlinks (both internal and external). Both commands also provide information that is useful in locating and correcting hyperlink problems.

Recalculating Hyperlinks

First, you want to show Brett how to recalculate the hyperlinks in the remote garden Web site.

To recalculate hyperlinks:

1. Close the home page.
2. Click **Tools** on the menu bar, and then click **Recalculate Hyperlinks**. The Recalculate Hyperlinks dialog box opens and describes the actions that will occur after clicking the Yes button. See Figure 6-43.

Figure 6-43 **Recalculate Hyperlinks dialog box**

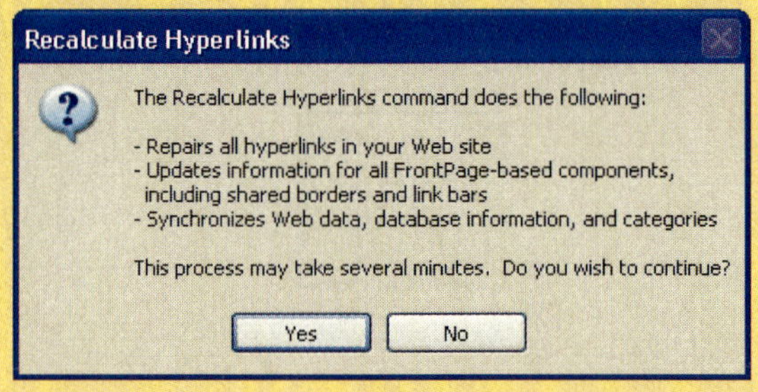

3. Read the information in the dialog box, and then click the **Yes** button. The "Updating hyperlinks and text indices..." message appears on the status bar. After a few seconds, FrontPage refreshes the files in Folders view. FrontPage also deletes any unnecessary files in the garden Web site.

The hyperlinks have been recalculated, and their display has been updated to reflect any changes. After recalculating the hyperlinks, you should verify them.

Verifying Hyperlinks

When you recalculated the hyperlinks for the garden Web site, FrontPage deleted any unnecessary files from the Web site and refreshed the Web site views. To identify broken links in a Web site, you need to switch to Reports view and verify the site's hyperlinks. When you verify hyperlinks, FrontPage checks each Web page for missing or broken hyperlinks and then displays a report of its findings.

You want to show Brett how to verify the site's hyperlinks so he can identify and correct any problems.

To verify hyperlinks:

1. Change to Reports view.
2. Click the **Verifies hyperlinks in the current web** button on the Contents pane. The Verify Hyperlinks dialog box opens.
3. Click the **Verify all hyperlinks** option button, and then click the **Start** button. The Broken Hyperlinks report lists several broken links in the current Web site. See Figure 6-44. (Your list of broken hyperlinks might differ, which is not a problem.)

Broken Hyperlinks report in Reports view

Figure 6-44

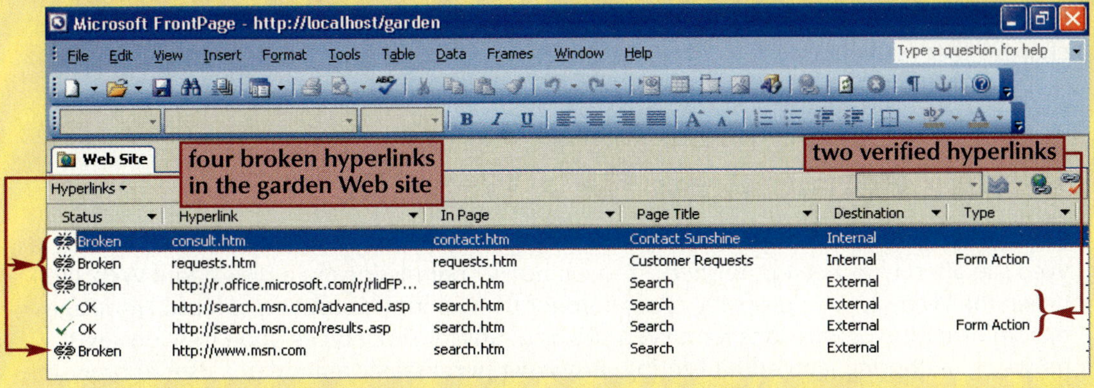

Trouble? If a Dial-up Connection dialog box opens, click the Close button.

4. Right-click the **http://www.msn.com** broken hyperlink to open the shortcut menu, and then click **Edit Page**. The search.htm page opens in Design view.
5. Scroll down the page as necessary so you can see the search components. The broken link to the picture is selected.
6. Press the **Delete** key to delete the selected broken link, and then save and close the search.htm page.
7. Click the button, and then click the **Start** button to verify the site's hyperlinks again. This time, the report shows two broken hyperlinks in the contact.htm and requests.htm pages (your broken links might differ). You'll fix these broken links when you complete the Review Assignments at the end of this tutorial.

Because you made your changes in the remote garden Web site, the local Web site is now out of date. To update the local site, you can open the local Web site in FrontPage and synchronize it with the remote Web site.

To synchronize the local and remote Web sites:

1. Close the remote Web site by clicking **File** on the menu bar, and then clicking **Close Site**.
2. Click **File** on the menu bar, point to **Recent Sites**, and then select the disk-based garden Web site to open it in FrontPage.
3. Change to Remote Web Site view.
4. Click the **Synchronize** option button in the Publish all changed pages section, and then click the **Publish Web site** button. FrontPage updates the local Web site with the changes you made in the remote Web site.
5. In the Local Web site pane, scroll down the file list as necessary and select **index.htm**, and then click the **Preview** button on the Standard toolbar. The home page of the local Web site opens in a browser. Scroll down the page and notice that the page now contains the hit counter. The synchronize action updated the local Web site with this change that you made in the remote Web site. However, because the hit counter works only in a server-based Web site, a broken link to the hit counter is displayed rather than a number.
6. Close your browser.

Recalculating and verifying hyperlinks has helped you isolate several broken hyperlinks, and possibly other problems in your Web site. After fixing any problems that you find, it is a good idea to recalculate and verify the hyperlinks again, so you can check the changes that you made.

The last thing that you want to review with Brett is how to secure a Web site.

Setting Permissions for a Web Site

Permissions allow a Web site developer to control who can browse, author, or administer a Web site after it has been published. (You cannot set permissions in a disk-based Web site.) When the Web server is properly configured for using permissions, you can use FrontPage to administer the permissions for a Web site or a subsite. Three types of permissions exist: browsing, authoring, and administering. **Browsing permissions** authorize a user to browse (open) all of the pages in a Web site, including hidden files, but the user cannot make changes to the pages. **Authoring permissions** allow a user to browse and change a site's pages by opening them in Design view. Finally, **administering permissions** allow a user to browse and change a site's pages and to set other user permissions. For example, if you do not want a user to be able to change the content of a Web site, you would set that user's permission to browsing. Permissions are hierarchical; for example, a user with administering permissions also has authoring and browsing permissions, whereas authoring permissions give a user browsing permissions but not administering permissions.

When you run IIS on a Windows NT or a Windows 2000/XP computer, users and groups are set up and maintained in Windows and cannot be created in FrontPage. In this case, the system administrator determines which users and groups can set security for Web sites that reside on that server. You will be able to set permissions for a Web site only if you have the necessary permissions to do so for the client or network on which the IIS server resides.

If the server allows permissions and the settings have not been changed, the permissions established for the root Web site are inherited by all other Web sites. The garden Web site that you published to the server is a subsite in the FrontPage root Web, which is C:\Inetput\wwwroot. Thus, any permissions that were set for the root Web also apply to the garden Web site that you published. You can change the permissions for a subsite at any time; in fact, one advantage of creating a subsite is to protect it independently of the root Web site by establishing appropriate permissions for different users.

Reference Window

Setting Permissions for a Web Site

- Open the server-based Web site in FrontPage.
- Click Tools on the menu bar, point to Server, and then click Administration Home. The Administration page opens in a browser.
- Click the Change subweb permissions link.
- Choose the Use unique permissions for this Web site option button, and then click the Submit button.
- Click the Administration link at the top of the page.
- Click the Change anonymous access settings link, use the page that opens to turn anonymous access off or on and to assign users to a role (Administrator, Advanced author, Author, Contributor, or Browser), and then click the Submit button.
- Click the Manage users link, and then click the Add a user link. Use the Configure Web User page to add a user and to select a role for the user, and then click the Add User button.
- Close the browser.

Because Brett is the administrator of the Web site, he needs to assign himself administering permissions. Brett will probably want to assign permissions to other users, such as the senior staff at the nursery, so they can make changes to pages in the Web site that represent their departments or specialties. Before setting up users, you will need to show Brett how to change the Web site to use permissions that are separate from the root Web site.

To change the garden Web site to use unique permissions:

1. Click **File** on the menu bar, and then click **Close Site**. The disk-based garden Web site closes.
2. Click **File** on the menu bar, point to **Recent Sites**, and then click the remote garden Web site.
3. Click **Tools** on the menu bar, point to **Server**, and then click **Administration Home**. The Administration page opens in a browser. Figure 6-45 shows the page in Internet Explorer. The IIS server used in these steps has the FrontPage 2002 Server Extensions installed on it. If your Web site is published on a server that uses SharePoint Services or another version of the FrontPage Server Extensions, your page will look different.

Administration page for the garden Web site **Figure 6-45**

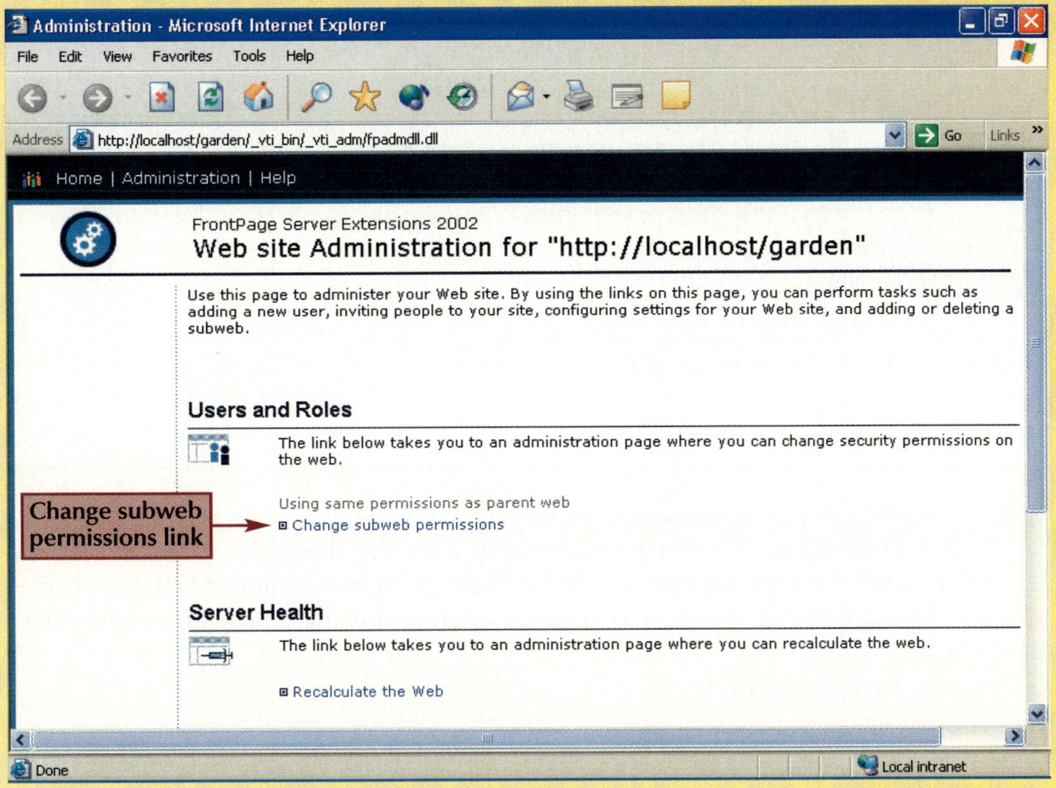

4. Click the **Change subweb permissions** link. The Edit Permissions page opens. There are two options for setting the permissions in a Web site. You can choose to use the same permissions as the parent (root) Web site, or use unique permissions for the current Web site. Brett wants to set the permissions for the current Web site.

5. Click the **Use unique permissions for this Web site** option button, and then click the **Submit** button. An Operation Results page opens while this change is being made on the server, and then the Edit Permissions page opens again.
6. Click the **Administration** link at the top of the page. The Administration page opens. As shown in Figure 6-46, the Users and Roles section has changed to reflect the fact that this Web site will have unique permissions.

Figure 6-46 **Administration page after enabling the Web site for unique permissions**

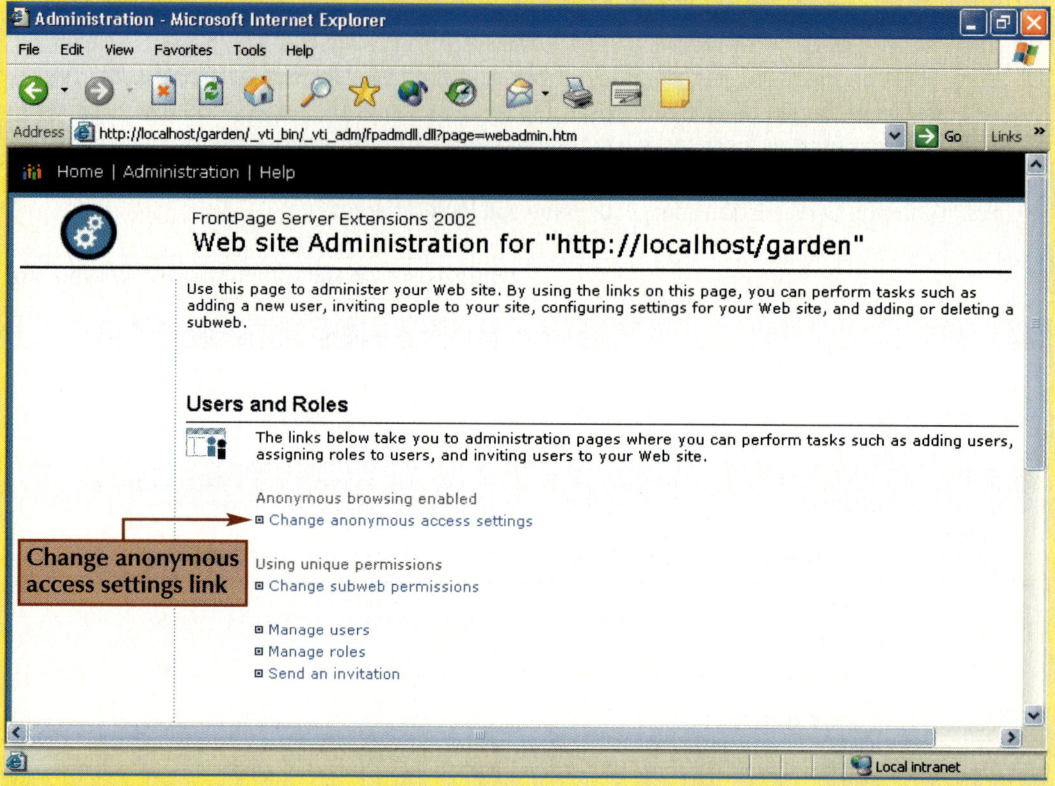

7. Click the **Change anonymous access settings** link. The Anonymous Access page opens. The default setting permits anonymous access for users with the Browser role. You tell Brett that this setting is acceptable for now. In the future, as he assigns different roles to other users, he might change the role of anonymous access to give users more authority to make changes to the Web site.
8. Click the **Cancel** button.

Brett wants to set himself as an administrator of the Web site. You'll show him how to make this change next.

To assign administering permissions to a user:

1. On the Administration page, click the **Manage users** link. The User Management page opens, as shown in Figure 6-47. You use this page to add new users, remove existing users, or assign users new permissions. The User Management page on your computer might differ if users have been assigned permissions already.

Figure 6-47 User Management page

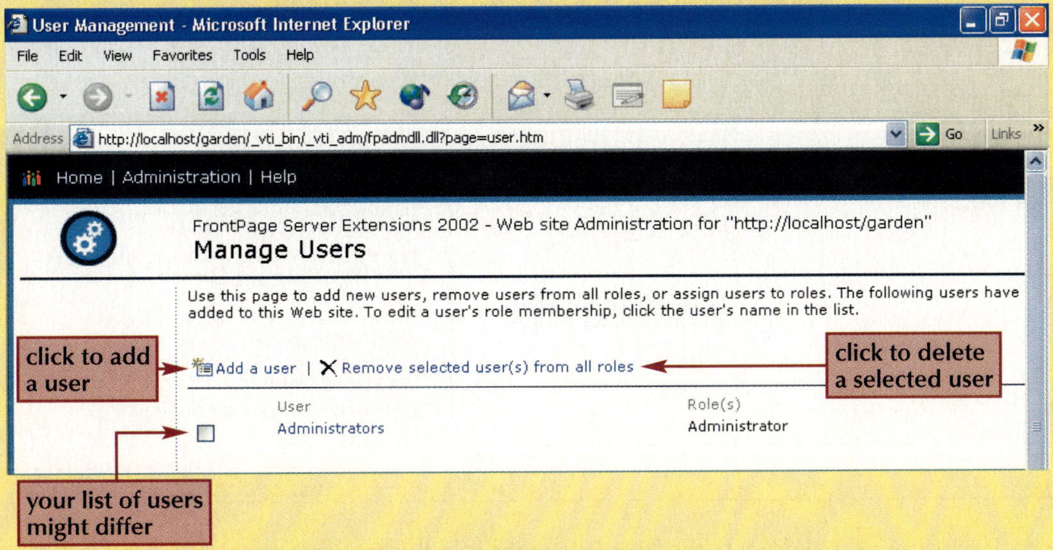

2. Click the **Add a user** link. The Configure Web User page opens. The insertion point is blinking in the User name text box.
3. Make sure that the **Add a new user with the following information** option button is selected, and then type **Brett Kizer** in the User name text box.
4. Press the **Tab** key, and then type **sunshine** as the password. As you type the password, dots or asterisks will appear instead of the letters you are typing to protect the password from being seen by others.
5. Press the **Tab** key, and then type **sunshine** to confirm the password. See Figure 6-48.

Figure 6-48 Adding a user

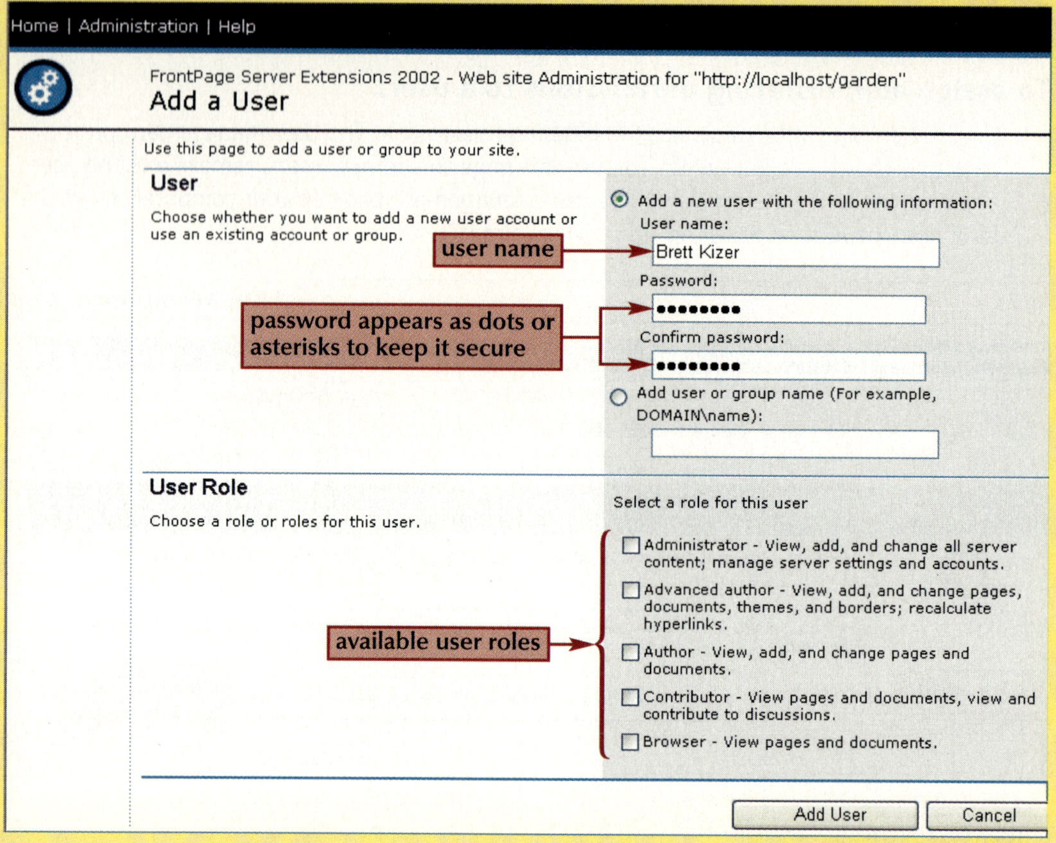

6. If necessary, scroll down to the User Role section. In this section, you select a role for the user you entered in the User section. Each role provides the user with different levels of permission for working in and changing the Web site.
7. Click the **Administrator** check box to select it, and then click the **Add User** button. On the User Management page, Brett now appears as a user with Administrator permissions.

You also want to show Brett how to change a user's permissions and how to remove a user.

To change a user's permissions and remove a user:

1. On the User Management page, click the **Brett Kizer** link but not the check box to the left of the user Brett Kizer. The Edit User Role Membership page opens. To change the role for this user, you would check the new role in the User Role section, and then click the Submit button.

   Trouble? The user Brett Kizer might be preceded by a computer name and a backslash, such as DEFAULT\Brett Kizer. Just make sure that you click the link for Brett.
2. Click the **Cancel** button. You return to the User Management page.
3. Click the **check box** to the left of the Brett Kizer user, and then click the **Remove selected user(s) from all roles** link. A message box opens to confirm your intent to delete the user.
4. Click the **OK** button. The user Brett Kizer is removed from the site's list of users.

5. Close your browser.
6. Close the garden Web site, and then close FrontPage.

Going Live

Going live is the process of publishing your Web site on a Web server to make it accessible to other users. In this tutorial, you published a disk-based Web site to a server and tested it to ensure that its features work as expected. Before publishing a Web site on a Web server, most commercial Web site developers also test the Web site using different Web browsers, screen resolutions, and connection speeds to confirm that the Web site works consistently for the many ways in which people will access it. After thoroughly testing the site, the developer or administrator publishes it on the designated Web server.

You published the garden Web site to the server on your computer. After thorough testing and analysis, you will be ready to publish the Web site to the Web server that Brett selected to host it. You would use the Remote Web Site Properties button in Remote Web Site view to enter the information for the Web server Brett selected. To publish the site to a Web server, you need the URL for the Web server and the user name and password provided by the ISP. In addition, you must have permission to publish and maintain a Web site. In most cases, when you purchase a domain name and space on a Web server, the ISP will send you an e-mail message with your user name, password, and other important information about publishing your Web site. If the ISP hosts FrontPage Web sites, you might need to read the documentation to determine how to enable the FrontPage 2002 Server Extensions for your site. In most cases, you just need to submit a request to enable the Web site to use the FrontPage 2002 Server Extensions.

Generally, an individual designated as the administrator manages a Web server. The administrator is responsible for the overall management of the server, including the management of user access to it. The administrator determines how and where a Web site will be located on the server based on the procedures that have been established for the Web server by the company or ISP that owns and operates the server. The procedures for publishing a Web site on a Web server vary; check with your site's administrator for more information about publishing a Web site.

Acceptable Use Policies

Most companies and ISPs maintain an **acceptable use policy** (**AUP**). An AUP typically consists of a published or online document that an ISP or company creates to indicate the acceptable activities permitted on the Web server. For example, an AUP for an educational institution might prohibit users from using the network to engage in commercial activities, or an AUP for an ISP might prohibit users from creating Web sites on the network that include objectionable material. It is the responsibility of the Web server's administrator to verify that the Web site will meet these standards.

FrontPage 2002 Server Extensions and SharePoint Services

In this tutorial, you learned that the FrontPage 2002 Server Extensions or SharePoint Services must be installed and properly configured before certain features of the garden Web site, such as the hit counter and form processing, will work correctly. Some ISPs do not accept Web sites with FrontPage 2002 Server Extensions because the extensions can compromise the security of the Web server on which they reside. Before creating your Web site, it is important to identify any restrictions imposed by the operator of the Web server on which your Web site will ultimately reside. You might learn that the ISP will not accept Web sites with FrontPage 2002 Server Extensions or SharePoint Services. In this case, you can either search for another ISP to host your Web site or set your installation of FrontPage to disable features that are not supported by the ISP. If you must disable features that the ISP does not support, create the Web site as usual but, before creating any of its pages, click Tools on the menu bar, click Page Options, and then click the Compatibility tab. You can use this tab to disable features that use the FrontPage 2002 Server Extensions, SharePoint Services, and other elements, as necessary.

Fortunately, most ISPs have a technical support staff available to answer questions about publishing a Web site. Your best course of action is to find and communicate with an ISP before creating your Web site to gather information about the ISP's AUP and policy for accepting FrontPage Web sites. In most cases, the ISP can provide alternative means for creating pages in the event that the server cannot accept server extensions.

Now that you and Brett have finished the Web site, you are confident that Brett will be able to add new pages to it, update the site to make changes, and assign users different roles to help maintain the site.

Review

Session 6.3 Quick Check

1. The default name of the Web server for Windows XP is ______________.
2. What is the default directory in which FrontPage publishes Web sites?
3. What are the four types of remote servers to which you can publish a FrontPage Web site?
4. What are the three options for publishing a Web site?
5. What is a confirmation page?
6. What is a comma-delimited text file?
7. What is a hit counter?
8. What happens when you recalculate the hyperlinks in a Web site?
9. What happens when you verify the hyperlinks in a Web site?

Review

Tutorial Summary

In this tutorial, you learned how to create a search component and a form in a Web page. You also learned how to use different form fields to collect different kinds of data and how to validate a form field to reduce data-entry errors and to ensure that the correct data is collected. You used a form handler to process a form on a server and viewed the form results file stored on the server. Finally, you learned how to publish a Web site from a local drive to a Web server, how to make changes in a remote Web site, and how to synchronize copies of a Web site.

As you develop Web sites in the future, you'll find other uses for forms. Forms can collect all kinds of data, from recording a visitor's name and address information to processing requests for service and collecting questions from customers. When you publish a Web site, be sure to test your forms thoroughly to ensure that they are easy to use and collect the intended data. You should also experiment with the different ways to store form data to find the one that best suits your needs. When deciding on a file format for your form results, make sure to plan ahead. For example, if you know that you will be creating a mailing list from data collected by a form, part of your testing should make sure that the data is easily imported into the program you intend to use to generate the mailing list.

When publishing a Web site, be sure to update the local site and then publish it to the remote Web server. This method ensures that you always have a local copy of the Web site that you can publish again in the case of a problem on the server.

Key Terms

acceptable use policy (AUP)
administering permission
authoring permission
browsing permission
check box
comma-delimited text
comma-separated value
command button
confirmation page
Distributed Authoring and Versioning (DAV)
drop-down box
drop-down menu
external hyperlink
field name-data value pair
File Transfer Protocol (FTP)
form
form field
form handler
Form Page Wizard
form results
going live
hit counter
integer
localhost
Microsoft Internet Information Services (IIS)
Normal push button
option button
option button group name
permission
push button
radio button
recalculating hyperlinks
Reset push button
Save Results form handler
scrolling text box
Submit push button
text area
text box
validation
verifying hyperlinks

Practice

Practice the skills you learned in the tutorial using the same case scenario.

Review Assignments

There are no new Data Files needed for these Review Assignments.

Before preparing the garden Web site for publication on a Web server and making it available to Internet visitors, Brett asks you to test the pages again and to make any necessary adjustments.

If necessary, start FrontPage, and then do the following:

1. Use My Network Places to open the **garden** Web site that you published to the server.
2. Open the Search page (**search.htm**) in Design view. Double-click the search component to open the Search Form Properties dialog box, and then make the following changes:
   a. Change the label for input to “Search the Sunshine Web Site for:”.
   b. Change the label for the Start Search button to “Search the Sunshine Web Site.”
   c. Change the information displayed in the search results to display the score (closeness of match) only.
3. Make the following changes to the Search the Web with MSN component:
   a. Change the text that identifies the text box to “Search the Internet for:”.
   b. Change the properties of the text box so its name is “InternetSearch” and its width is 25 characters.
   c. Use the pointer to increase the width of the table in which the Search the Web with MSN component is stored so it is the same width as the search component that appears above it.
   d. Change the text in the component to the default 12-point font. (*Hint:* Select the text in the component, and the click (default font) in the font list.)
   e. Change the label for the Search push button to “Search the Internet” and change its name to “Search.”
   f. Left-align the Use Advanced Search hyperlink.
   g. Delete the period that appears between the text box and the push button.
4. Save the **search.htm** page, and then close it.

5. Open the Customer Requests page (**requests.htm**) in Design view. To the right of the Other check box label, add a text box with the name "Other" and a width of 35 characters.
6. Add a new choice to the Location drop-down box. The choice name is "Round Rock," the value to store in the results file is "RoundRock," and the initial state is not selected. After adding this new choice, move it so it appears between the West Lake Hills and Other choices. Save the **requests.htm** page.
7. In Folders view, open the _private folder of the server-based Web site. Right-click the **results.csv** file to open the shortcut menu, point to Open With, and then click Microsoft Office Excel. The form results data is displayed in the worksheet using the form field names as the column headings. Resize each column to its best fit, and then print the worksheet in landscape orientation. Close Excel without saving your changes.
8. Recalculate and verify all hyperlinks in the Web site. There is a broken link in the **contact.htm** page. Right-click this broken link to open the shortcut menu, and then click Edit Page. The Contact Sunshine page opens in Design view with the broken hyperlink selected. Determine the cause of the problem and fix the broken link. (*Hint:* Read the paragraph in which the broken hyperlink appears for more information. The hyperlink's text and target both need to point to the page in the Web site that contains the form.) When you are finished, save and close the **contact.htm** page, and then recalculate and verify all hyperlinks again. Right-click any page in Reports view to open the shortcut menu, and then click Copy Report. Start Word or WordPad, and then click the Paste button on the Standard toolbar to paste the report into a new document. Click the Print button to print the report. Close Word or WordPad without saving your changes.
9. Close the server-based **garden** Web site, open the disk-based **garden** Web site, and then synchronize the remote and local Web sites. When the publishing process is complete, open the remote Web site in a browser. Thoroughly test the Web site by opening each link and examining each page. Use the Search page to conduct a search of the Web site using the keyword "deer," and then print the search results. Then use the Search the Web with MSN component to perform an Internet search using any keywords of interest. (*Note:* You must be connected to the Internet to use the Search the Web with MSN component.) Use your browser's Back button to return to the **garden** Web site.
10. Use the Customer Requests page to submit one form to the server. Print the confirmation page returned by the server.
11. Close your browser, close the **garden** Web site, and then close FrontPage.

Create

Create a page that searches a Web site and a page that contains a form. Then publish the Web site to a server and thoroughly test it.

Case Problem 1

There are no new Data Files needed for this Case Problem.

Buffalo Trading Post Many Buffalo Trading Post customers have told a sales associate that they would like to use the Web site to request more information and to add their names to a mailing list. During a recent Web site development meeting, the company's sales associates encouraged Nicole Beirne to develop a Contact Web page for customers. They agreed that the page's design should include a way for customers to add their names and addresses to the company's mailing list. Customers should also be able to send comments about items they would like to buy or sell using the categories of women's clothing, children's clothing, and accessories. The sales associates also were interested in finding out how many times a customer had visited a retail store. Nicole organized the ideas from the meeting and then met with you to review the Contact page requirements. Nicole asks you to make these enhancements to the Web site before publishing it to a server.

If necessary, start FrontPage, and then do the following:

1. Open the **buffalo** Web site from the location where your Web sites are stored. (If you did not create this Web site in Tutorial 1 and change it in Tutorials 2 through 5, ask your instructor for assistance.)

Explore

2. Open the **contact.htm** page in Design view, and then use the information supplied in the Case Problem description and Figure 6-49 to create the form. Define any necessary validation criteria to ensure that data is input correctly. Save the results collected by this form as comma-delimited text in the **contact.csv** file in the **_private** folder of the Web site. Do not save any additional fields, or the date and time the form was submitted to the server. When you are finished, save the **contact.htm** page.

Figure 6-49

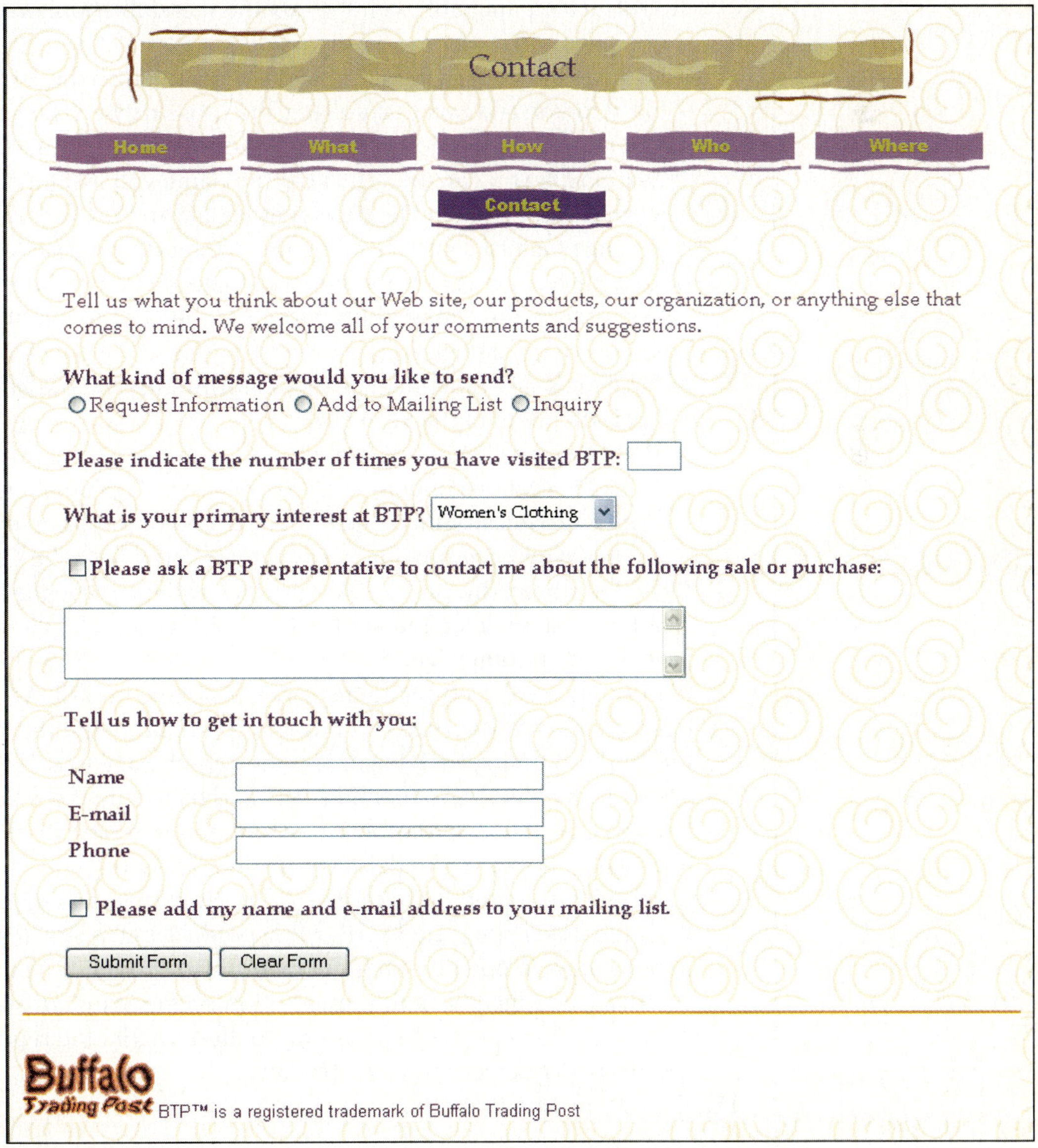

Explore

3. Use FrontPage to print the HTML document for the **contact.htm** page. On the printout, circle the tags that implement the FrontPage Save Results form handler. Close the **contact.htm** page.
4. Use a page template to create a page that searches the **buffalo** Web site. Delete the paragraph with the comment text and the horizontal line that appear at the top of the page, and then delete the copyright information and horizontal line that appear at the bottom of the page. Save the page using the filename **search.htm** and the title "Search." Add the **search.htm** page to Navigation view as a child page of the home page, positioning it to the right of the Contact page.
5. Publish the local **buffalo** Web site to the server using the same Web site name, and then use the hyperlink created by FrontPage to open the remote Web site in a browser. Test the Contact Web page that you created by completing the form, and then print the confirmation page that you receive from the server. Close your browser.

Explore

6. Use the Confirmation Form page template to create a new page in the disk-based **buffalo** Web site that confirms data submitted by the Contact page. After creating the page, do the following:
   a. Delete the paragraph with the comment and the horizontal line at the top of the page.
   b. Change the form field in the "Dear" line to match the form field name that you used for the text box that collects the user's name. (*Hint:* Double-click the field to open the Confirmation Field Properties dialog box, and then type the name of the text box. If you cannot remember the name you assigned to this field, open the **contact.htm** page in Design view to confirm it.)
   c. Change the first sentence in the first paragraph to "Thank you for your message."
   d. Change the form fields for the E-mail and Telephone lines to the form field names you used in the **contact.htm** page, and then delete the line containing the reference to a fax number.
   e. Save the page using the filename **confirm.htm** and the title "Confirmation" in the **_private** folder of the Web site.
   f. Return to the Contact Web page, and then open the Form Properties dialog box. Click the Options button, and then click the Confirmation Page tab. Type **_private/confirm.htm** in the URL of confirmation page (optional) text box to use the new Confirmation page with the form. Save the Contact page.
7. Open the **where.htm** page in Design view, and then type the following in the page: "For the location of the Buffalo Trading Post nearest you, please call 1-888-BUFFALO." Save the **where.htm** page.
8. Publish the local Web site to the server. After the publishing process is complete, open the remote Web site in a browser. Thoroughly test the Web site by opening each link and examining each page. Use the Search page to conduct a search of the Web site using the keywords "mailing list," and then print the search results.
9. Use the Contact page to submit one form to the server. Print the confirmation page returned by the server, and then close your browser.
10. Close the disk-based **buffalo** Web site in FrontPage, and then open the remote **buffalo** Web site. Recalculate and verify all hyperlinks in the site. Right-click any page in Reports view to open the shortcut menu, and then click Copy Report. Start Word or WordPad, and then click the Paste button on the Standard toolbar to paste the report into a new document. Click the Print button to print the report. Close Word or WordPad without saving your changes.
11. Change the **buffalo** Web site to use unique permissions.

12. Add yourself as a user with administrator permissions for the **buffalo** Web site by providing a user name and password of your choice. Use your browser to print the Manage Users page after adding yourself as a user.
13. Remove yourself from the Manage Users page, and then close your browser.
14. Close the **buffalo** Web site, and then close FrontPage.

Create

Create a page that searches a Web site and a page that contains a form. Then publish the Web site to a server and thoroughly test it.

Case Problem 2

There are no new Data Files needed for this Case Problem.

Garden Grill Meghan Elliott and Callan Murphy are pleased with your progress on the Garden Grill Web site. Their next priority is creating the Feedback and Search Web pages. After a meeting with the company's marketing department, Meghan wants to create a new Web page to gather customer information and feedback about diners' eating habits and their impressions about the restaurant's menu, prices, service, and Web site. Meghan asks you to make these enhancements to the Web site before publishing it to a server.

If necessary, start FrontPage, and then do the following:

1. Open the **grill** Web site from the location where your Web sites are stored. (If you did not create this Web site in Tutorial 1 and change it in Tutorials 2 through 5, ask your instructor for assistance.)
2. Use a page template to create a page that searches the **grill** Web site. Save the page using the filename **search.htm** and the title "Search," replacing the page in the Web site with the same name. Delete the paragraph with the comment text and the horizontal line that appear at the top of the page, and then delete the copyright information and horizontal line that appear at the bottom of the page. Open the **about.htm** page in Design view, copy the link bar graphic and page title ("About Us") from the top of the page, and then paste this information at the top of the **search.htm** page. Change the heading you pasted to "Search," and then save the page.

Explore

3. Open the **feedback.htm** page in Design view, and then paste the information you copied in Step 2 at the top of the page and change the heading you pasted to "Feedback." Use the information supplied in the Case Problem description and Figure 6-50 to create the form. Define any necessary validation criteria to ensure that data is input correctly. Save the results collected by this form as comma-delimited text in the **feedback.csv** file in the **_private** folder of the Web site. The choices for the drop-down box are Web Site, Food, Menu, Prices, Employees, and Other. When you are finished, save the **feedback.htm** page.

Figure 6-50

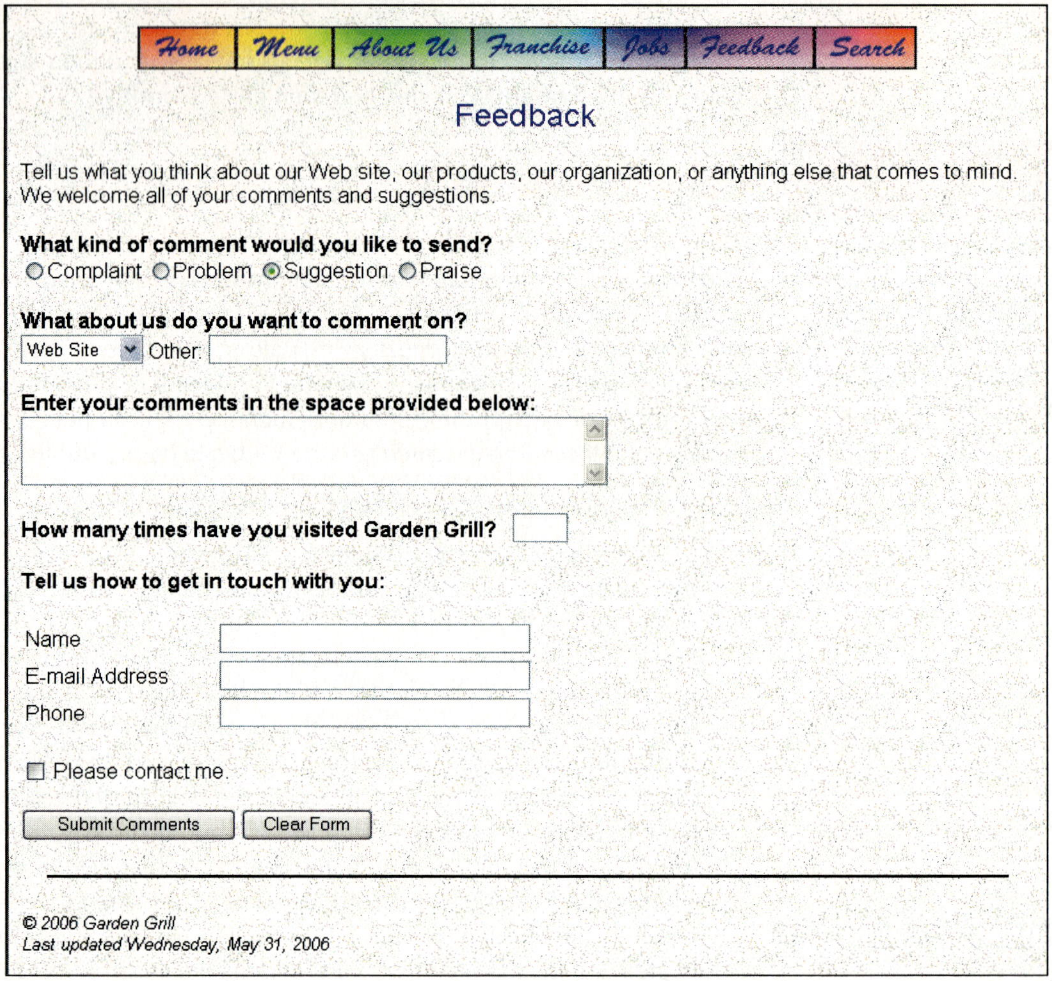

Explore

4. Use FrontPage to print the HTML document for the **feedback.htm** page. On the printout, circle the tags that implement the FrontPage Save Results form handler, the drop-down box, and the text boxes.
5. Publish the local **grill** Web site to the server using the same Web site name, and then use the hyperlink created by FrontPage to open the remote Web site in a browser. Test the Feedback Web page that you created by completing the form, and then print the confirmation page that you receive from the server. Close your browser.

Explore

6. Use the Confirmation Form page template to create a new page in the disk-based **grill** Web site that confirms data submitted by the Feedback page. After creating the page, do the following:
   a. Delete the paragraph with the comment and the horizontal line at the top of the page.
   b. Change the form field in the "Dear" line to match the form field name that you used for the text box that collects the user's name. (*Hint:* Double-click the field to open the Confirmation Field Properties dialog box and then type the name of the text box. If you cannot remember the name you assigned to this field, open the **feedback.htm** page in Design view to confirm it.)
   c. Change the first sentence in the first paragraph to "Thank you for your message."

d. Change the form fields for the E-mail and Telephone lines to the form field names you used in the **feedback.htm** page, and then delete the line containing the reference to a fax number.
e. Save the page using the filename **confirm.htm** and the title "Confirmation" in the **_private** folder of the Web site.
f. Return to the Feedback Web page, and then open the Form Properties dialog box. Click the Options button, and then click the Confirmation Page tab. Type **_private/confirm.htm** in the URL of confirmation page (optional) text box to use the new Confirmation page with the form. Save the Feedback page.

7. Open the Franchise Info page (**fran.htm**) in Design view. Paste the link bar and heading from the **about.htm** page at the top of the **fran.htm** page, and then change the heading to "Franchise Information." In a new left-aligned paragraph below the heading, type "If you are interested in opening a Garden Grill restaurant in your area, please call Katy Ricke at 1-800-555-4921 to discuss startup costs and franchise licensing." Save the **fran.htm** page.
8. Publish the local Web site to the server. (If a Conflicts dialog box opens, click the Overwrite Remote Files button.) After the publishing process is complete, open the remote Web site in a browser. Thoroughly test the Web site by opening each link and examining each page. Use the Search page to conduct a search of the Web site using the keyword "management," and then print the search results.
9. Use the Feedback page to submit one form to the server. Print the confirmation page returned by the server, and then close your browser.

Explore

10. Modify the form in the Feedback Web page in the disk-based Web site so that the Save Results form handler also stores the results in an HTML file named **feedback.htm** in the **_private** folder of the Web site. (*Hint:* Specify the second results file using the Options button in the Form Properties dialog box.) Publish your changes, and then use a browser to test the Feedback Web page using data that you create. Enter data for two different users. Close the browser, and then use FrontPage to print the **feedback.htm** page that contains the form results. (*Hint:* Open the **feedback.htm** page stored on the server.)
11. Recalculate and verify all the hyperlinks in the server-based **grill** Web site. Right-click any page in Reports view to open the shortcut menu, and then click Copy Report. Start Word or WordPad, and then click the Paste button on the Standard toolbar to paste the report into a new document. Click the Print button to print the report. Close Word or WordPad without saving your changes.

12. Change the **grill** Web site to use unique permissions.
13. Add yourself as a user with administrator permissions for the **grill** Web site by providing a user name and password of your choice. Use your browser to print the Manage Users page after adding yourself as a user.
14. Remove yourself from the Manage Users page, and then close your browser.
15. Close the **grill** Web site, and then close FrontPage.

Create

Create a form in a Web page to collect data to be used in print and electronic mailing lists. Then publish the Web site to a server and thoroughly test it.

Case Problem 3

There are no new Data Files needed for this Case Problem.

Swenson Auctioneers Scott Swenson is eager for you to finish the Swenson Auctioneers Web site so he can start giving the URL to his clients. The last task you need to complete is to finish the Mailing List page by adding a form that will collect a person's name, address, e-mail address, and phone number so the Web site can add this information to a mailing list. Scott will use this data to mail print advertisements and e-mail messages to clients who wish to receive information about upcoming auctions. Scott also wants to ask visitors to his site a few questions so he can better understand the kinds of auctions in which they are interested. After creating the form and thoroughly testing the Web site, you will publish it to a server.

If necessary, start FrontPage, and then do the following:

1. Open the **swenson** Web site from the location where your Web sites are stored. (If you did not create this Web site in Tutorial 1 and change it in Tutorials 2 through 5, ask your instructor for assistance.)
2. Open the **mail.htm** page in Design view, and then create the form shown in Figure 6-51. The choices for the drop-down box are Internet, Direct Mail, Newspaper, Trade Magazine, Word of Mouth, and Other. None of the form fields require validation. Save the results collected by this form as comma-delimited text in the **maillist.csv** file in the **_private** folder of the Web site. When you are finished, save the **mail.htm** page.

Figure 6-51

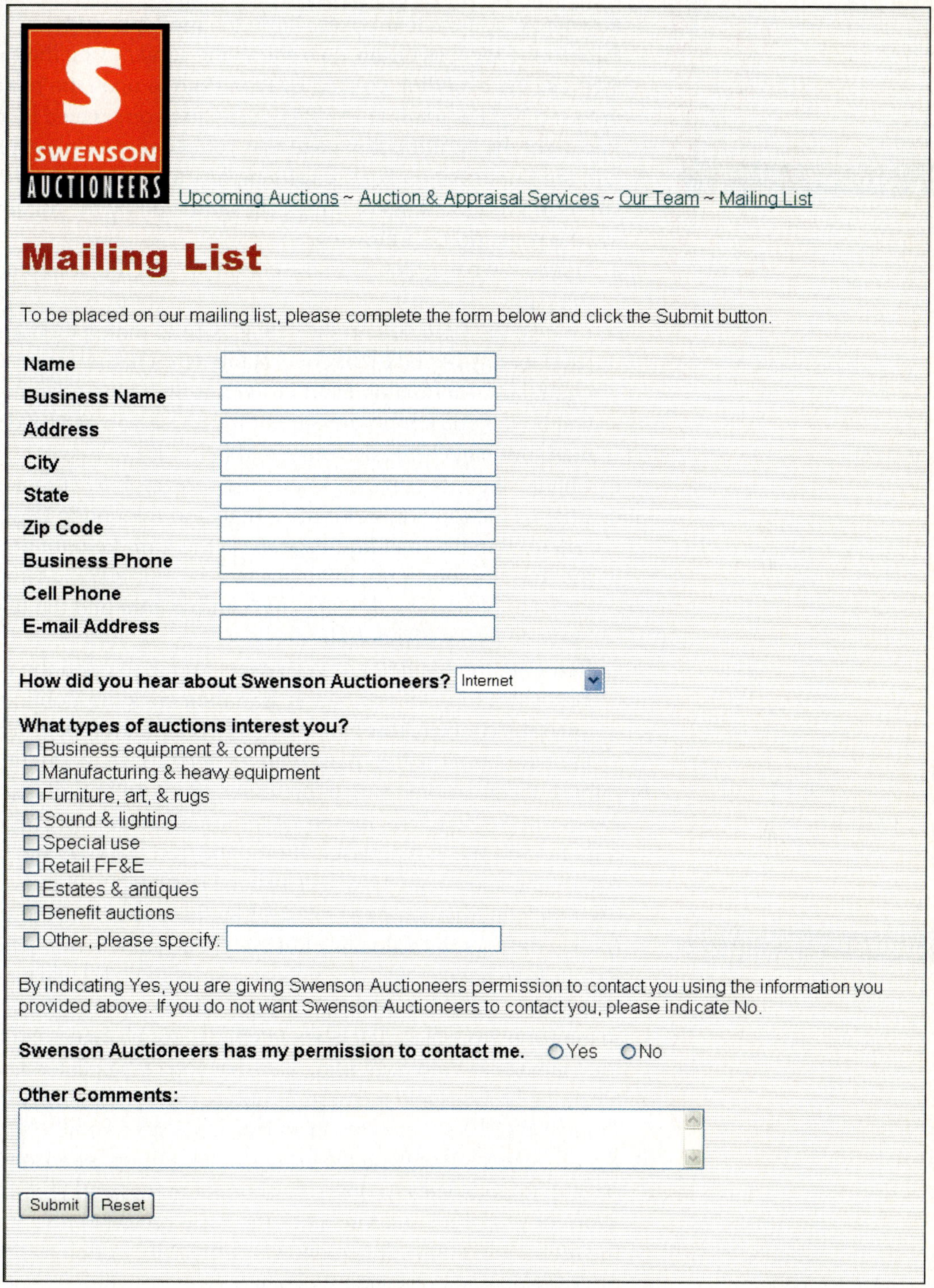
SWENSON
AUCTIONEERS
Upcoming Auctions ~ Auction & Appraisal Services ~ Our Team ~ Mailing List
Mailing List
To be placed on our mailing list, please complete the form below and click the Submit button.
Name
Business Name
Address
City
State
Zip Code
Business Phone
Cell Phone
E-mail Address
How did you hear about Swenson Auctioneers?
Internet
What types of auctions interest you?
Business equipment & computers
Manufacturing & heavy equipment
Furniture, art, & rugs
Sound & lighting
Special use
Retail FF&E
Estates & antiques
Benefit auctions
Other, please specify:
By indicating Yes, you are giving Swenson Auctioneers permission to contact you using the information you provided above. If you do not want Swenson Auctioneers to contact you, please indicate No.
Swenson Auctioneers has my permission to contact me.
Yes
No
Other Comments:
Submit
Reset

Explore

3. Use FrontPage to print the HTML document for the **mail.htm** page. On the printout, circle the tags that implement the FrontPage Save Results form handler, the drop-down box, and the text boxes. Close the **mail.htm** page.
4. Publish the local **swenson** Web site to the server using the same Web site name, and then use the hyperlink created by FrontPage to open the remote Web site in a browser. Test the Mailing List Web page that you created by completing the form, and then print the confirmation page that you receive from the server. Close your browser.

Explore

5. Use the Confirmation Form page template to create a new page in the disk-based **swenson** Web site that confirms data submitted by the Mailing List page. After creating the page, do the following:
   a. Delete the paragraph with the comment and the horizontal line at the top of the page.
   b. Change the form field in the "Dear" line to match the form field name that you used for the text box that collects the user's name. (*Hint:* Double-click the field to open the Confirmation Field Properties dialog box and then type the name of the text box. If you cannot remember the name you assigned to this field, open the **mail.htm** page in Design view to confirm it.)
   c. Change the first sentence in the first paragraph to "Thank you for your message."
   d. Change the form fields for the E-mail and Telephone lines to the form field names you used in the **mail.htm** page. (Use the form field for the business phone.) Delete the line containing the reference to a fax number.
   e. Save the page using the filename **confirm.htm** and the title "Confirmation" in the **_private** folder of the Web site.
   f. Return to the Mailing List Web page, and then open the Form Properties dialog box. Click the Options button, and then click the Confirmation Page tab. Type **_private/confirm.htm** in the URL of confirmation page (optional) text box to use the new Confirmation page with the form. Save the Mailing List page.
6. Publish the local Web site to the server. (If a Conflicts dialog box opens, click the Overwrite Remote Files button.) After the publishing process is complete, open the remote Web site in a browser. Thoroughly test the Web site by opening each link and examining each page. Use the Mailing List page to submit one form to the server. Print the confirmation page returned by the server, and then close your browser.

Explore

7. Modify the form in the Mailing List Web page in the disk-based Web site so that the Save Results form handler also stores the results in an HTML file named **form.htm** in the **_private** folder of the Web site. (*Hint:* Specify the second results file using the Options button in the Form Properties dialog box.) Publish your changes, and then use a browser to test the Mailing List Web page using data that you create. Enter data for two different users. Close the browser, and then use FrontPage to print the **form.htm** page that contains the form results. (*Hint:* Open the **form.htm** page stored on the server.)
8. Recalculate and verify all hyperlinks in the remote **swenson** Web site. Right-click any page in Reports view to open the shortcut menu, and then click Copy Report. Start Word or WordPad, and then click the Paste button on the Standard toolbar to paste the report into a new document. Click the Print button to print the report. Close Word or WordPad without saving your changes.
9. Change the **swenson** Web site to use unique permissions.
10. Add yourself as a user with administrator permissions for the **swenson** Web site by providing a user name and password of your choice. Use your browser to print the Manage Users page after adding yourself as a user.
11. Remove yourself from the Manage Users page, and then close your browser.
12. Close the **swenson** Web site, and then close FrontPage.

Create

Create a form in a Web page that serves as a loan application and a page that searches a Web site. Then publish the Web site to a server and thoroughly test it.

Case Problem 4

Data File needed for this Case Problem: apply.doc

Loan Services, Inc. Natalie Fuselier is pleased with the appearance and content of the Web site for her company, Loan Services, Inc. An important part of the Web site is the loan application form that she needs you to create in the Application page. Natalie will use this data to begin the loan process for a client. Because the range of Internet experience varies among her clients, Natalie wants to ensure that the form is easy to complete for both inexperienced and Web-savvy clients. She wants to provide a way to complete the form for those clients who are uncomfortable submitting sensitive personal information over the Internet. Natalie also wants to create a new page that searches the Web site.

If necessary, start FrontPage, make sure you have your Data Files, and then do the following:

1. Open the **loan** Web site from the location where your Web sites are stored. (If you did not create this Web site in Tutorial 1 and change it in Tutorials 2 through 5, ask your instructor for assistance.)
2. Use a page template to create a page that searches the **loan** Web site. Delete the paragraph with the comment text and the horizontal line that appear at the top of the page, and then delete the copyright information and horizontal line that appear at the bottom of the page. Save the page using the filename **search.htm** and the title "Search." Add the **search.htm** page to Navigation view as a child page of the home page, positioning it to the right of the Contact Us page.

Explore

3. Delete the **contact.htm** page from the navigation structure and from the Web site. (*Hint:* Right-click the Contact Us page icon to open the shortcut menu, and then click Delete.)

Explore

4. Open the **apply.htm** page in Design view, and then use the information supplied in the Case Problem description and Figure 6-52 to create the form.

Figure 6-52

Application
Home
Loan Types
Application
Post Application Help
Resources
Search
Important! Before you apply for a loan:
Do not quit or change jobs.
Pay your bills on time.
Do not make any purchases requiring a new line of credit, such as a car or boat.
Do not move money around to different bank accounts.
Do not apply for a new credit card or increase the balance on credit cards you currently have.
Save as much cash as you can.
Talk to your lender before you look for a house.
Click here to complete your application using a Word document that you can submit to Natalie Fuselier by regular mail.
Information About You (and Your Co-Borrower, If Applicable)
Borrower
Co-Borrower
First Name
First Name
Last Name
Last Name
Social Security Number
Social Security Number
Home Phone
Home Phone
Work Phone
Work Phone
Employer
Employer
Income
Borrower
Co-Borrower
Monthly Income
Monthly Income
Authorization
Please click Yes or No to authorize us to obtain your credit report and to verify your income.
Yes
No
Submit Form
Clear Form

Define the following validation criteria in the form:

a. The borrower's first name, last name, Social Security number, and home phone number are required fields, but there are no constraints on the data a user can enter into these fields.

b. The borrower's monthly income is a required field.

5. Save the results collected by the form using the formatted text within HTML file format and the filename **form.htm** in the **_private** folder of the Web site. Save an optional file using the formatted text file format and the filename **form.txt** in the **_private** folder of the Web site. For both results files, make sure that the option to include field names is selected.

6. Import the **apply.doc** file from the Tutorial.06\Case4 folder included with your Data Files into the root folder of the **loan** Web site. Then change the word "here" in the first paragraph of the **apply.htm** page to a link that opens the **apply.doc** file in a new browser window. When you are finished, save the **apply.htm** page.

Explore

7. Use FrontPage to print the HTML document for the **apply.htm** page. On the printout, circle the tags that implement the validation you applied in Step 4. Close the **apply.htm** page.

8. Publish the local **loan** Web site to the server using the same Web site name, and then use the hyperlink created by FrontPage to open the remote Web site in a browser. Test the Application Web page that you created by completing the form (type your first and last names in the form, but enter fictitious data for the remaining fields). Print the confirmation page that you receive from the server, and then close your browser.

Explore

9. Use the Confirmation Form page template to create a new page in the disk-based **loan** Web site that confirms data submitted by the Application page. After creating the page, do the following:

   a. Delete the paragraph with the comment and the horizontal line at the top of the page.

   b. Change the form field in the "Dear" line to match the form field name that you used for the text box that collects the borrower's first name. (*Hint:* Double-click the field to open the Confirmation Field Properties dialog box and then type the name of the text box. If you cannot remember the name you assigned to this field, open the **apply.htm** page in Design view to confirm it.)

   c. Delete the paragraphs between the salutation ("Dear") and the closing ("Sincerely"). Then type the following as a new first paragraph: "Thank you for your loan application. We will contact you in one to two business days to review your loan." Change the line below the word "Sincerely" to "Loan Services, Inc."

   d. Remove the top and left shared borders from the confirmation page.

   e. Save the page using the filename **confirm.htm** and the title "Application Received" in the **_private** folder of the Web site.

   f. Return to the Application Web page, and then open the Form Properties dialog box. Click the Options button, and then click the Confirmation Page tab. Type **_private/confirm.htm** in the URL of confirmation page (optional) text box to use the new Application Received page with the form. Save the Application page.

10. Publish the local Web site to the server. After the publishing process is complete, open the remote Web site in a browser. Thoroughly test the Web site by opening each link and examining each page. Use the Search page to conduct a search of the Web site using the keyword "FHA," and then print the search results.

11. Use the Application page to submit one form to the server (type your first and last names in the form, but enter fictitious data for the remaining fields). Print the confirmation page returned by the server, and then close your browser.

12. Close the disk-based **loan** Web site, and then open the remote **loan** Web site in FrontPage. Recalculate and verify all hyperlinks in the site. Right-click any page in Reports view to open the shortcut menu, and then click Copy Report. Start Word or WordPad, and then click the Paste button on the Standard toolbar to paste the report into a new document. Click the Print button to print the report. Close Word or WordPad without saving your changes.
13. Change the **loan** Web site to use unique permissions.
14. Add yourself as a user with administrator permissions for the **loan** Web site by providing a user name and password of your choice. Use your browser to print the Manage Users page after adding yourself as a user.
15. Remove yourself from the Manage Users page, and then close your browser.
16. Close the **loan** Web site, and then close FrontPage.

Review

Quick Check Answers

Session 6.1

1. the search component, which searches a Web site using keywords entered by the user; and the Search the Web with MSN component, which searches the Internet using keywords entered by the user
2. True
3. a data-entry field in a form, such as a text box or an option button
4. form component
5. a program that collects and processes a form's data in a predetermined manner
6. First, you should sketch the form's appearance and determine the types of form fields to use to collect the data you need. Then you should identify any rules that you want to impose on the form's users.
7. True
8. Use a drop-down box with the name "Province" and assign each value in the list a name that is equivalent to the province's name. Using a drop-down box gives the user several mutually exclusive choices. The default selection should be the most populated province or the province that is closest to the company's location.

Session 6.2

1. the process of checking the information entered by a user into one or more form fields to verify that the information is acceptable and valid in an attempt to reduce data-entry errors
2. Required
3. grouping, which edits the value to insert a comma or decimal point; data length, which specifies the minimum and maximum number of integers that the form field can contain; and data value, which lets you specify that the entered value must be greater than, equal to, less than, or in a certain range based on a predetermined value
4. Submit, which lets a user send the form to the server for processing; Reset, which clears the form's fields of any previously entered data; and Normal, which initiates a user-defined script
5. field name-data value pair
6. webmaster
7. <option>

Session 6.3

1. localhost
2. C:\Inetpub\wwwroot\
3. servers that support the following: FrontPage Server Extensions or SharePoint Services, Distributed Authoring and Versioning, File Transfer Protocol, and File System
4. publishing the local site to the remote server, publishing the remote site to the local server or drive, and synchronizing the local and remote Web sites
5. a Web page that contains a copy of the data entered by the user and often is used for verification purposes
6. a file that contains form results where the results from each form field are separated by commas
7. a component that counts the number of times a page in a Web site has been opened or refreshed using a Web browser
8. FrontPage updates the display of all views of the Web site, updates the text index created by a search component (when one is used), deletes files for unused themes, and reports broken hyperlinks.
9. FrontPage checks all of the hyperlinks in the Web site to identify any internal or external broken hyperlinks.

Glossary/Index

Note: Boldface entries include definitions.

A

B

C

I

J

L

M

Q

R

S

T

Task Reference

TASK	PAGE #	RECOMMENDED METHOD
Alternative text, add to a picture	FP 85	See Reference Window: Adding Alternative Text to a Picture
Authoring settings, change for a Web site	FP 19	Double-click the Authoring Settings pane on the status bar, select the desired technologies and browsers, click OK
Background color, change for a table or table cell	FP 292	See Reference Window: Changing the Background Color or Picture in a Table or Cell
Background color, set for a Web page	FP 70	See Reference Window: Setting the Background Color of a Web Page
Background picture, insert into a Web Page	FP 74	See Reference Window: Inserting a Background Picture into a Web Page
Bookmark, create hyperlink to	FP 157	See Reference Window: Creating a Hyperlink to a Bookmark
Bookmark, create nontext-based	FP 159	Click the location to create the bookmark, click Insert, click Bookmark, type the bookmark's name in the Bookmark name text box, click OK
Bookmark, create text-based	FP 154	See Reference Window: Creating a Text-Based Bookmark in a Web Page
Caption, add to a table	FP 295	See Reference Window: Adding a Table Caption
Cell, copy contents into adjacent cells in a column in a table	FP 284	Select cell to be copied and cells to copy into, click 
Cell, copy contents into adjacent cells in a row in a table	FP 284	Select cell to be copied and cells to copy into, click 
Cell, split in a table	FP 290	See Reference Window: Splitting Table Cells
Cells, delete from a table	FP 293	See Reference Window: Deleting Cells from a Table
Cells, merge in a table	FP 289	See Reference Window: Merging Table Cells
Check box, add to a form	FP 360	Click the desired location, click Insert, point to Form, click Checkbox
Column, insert in a table in a Web page	FP 286	See Reference Window: Inserting a Column in a Table
Column, resize in a table	FP 294	See Reference Window: Resizing a Row or Column in a Table Using the Mouse
Column, select in a table	FP 276	Click the top border of the column
Columns, distribute selected evenly in a table	FP 295	Click 
Comment, insert into a Web page	FP 165	See Reference Window: Inserting a Comment into a Web Page
Custom link bar, create in Navigation view	FP 220	See Reference Window: Creating a Custom Link Bar in Navigation View
Custom theme, delete	FP 237	See Reference Window: Deleting a Custom Theme From Your Hard Drive
Download time, estimate for a Web page	FP 84	Click the Estimated Time to Download pane on the status bar, click the desired transfer rate
Drop-down box, add to a form	FP 350	Click the desired location, click Insert, point to Form, click Drop-Down Box
Embedded file, save with a Web page	FP 75	See Reference Window: Saving a Web Page That Contains an Embedded File
File, insert into a Web page	FP 23	See Reference Window: Inserting a File into a Web Page
Folder List, open or close	FP 17	Click 
Folders view, change to	FP 179	Click 

TASK	PAGE #	RECOMMENDED METHOD
Form component, add to a Web page	FP 346	See Reference Window: Creating a Form Component and Adding a Form Field
Form field properties, change	FP 349	Double-click the form field
Form field, validate	FP 358	Double-click the form field, click Validate
Form results file, examine contents of	FP 388	Open the server-based Web site in FrontPage, click the _private folder in the Folder List, double-click the form results file
Format Painter, use to copy and paste text formatting more than once	FP 41	Select the text whose format you want to copy, double-click , select the text to which to copy the format as needed, click
Format Painter, use to copy and paste text formatting once	FP 41	Select the text whose format you want to copy, click , select the text to which to copy the format
Frame, add new to a frames page	FP 320	See Reference Window: Adding a New Frame to an Existing Frames Page
Frame, edit size of in a frames page	FP 312	In Design view, drag a border of the frame to new position
Frames page, create	FP 306	See Reference Window: Creating a Frames Page
Frames page, print in Internet Explorer	FP 322	Click File, click Print, click desired option in the Print frames section, click OK
FrontPage link bar, add to a Web page	FP 216	Click in the desired location, click Insert, Navigation, select the link bar options, click OK
FrontPage link bar, change properties of	FP 206	Double-click the link bar component, make desired changes, click OK
FrontPage, close	FP 28	Click
FrontPage, start	FP 11	Click Start, point to All Programs, point to Microsoft Office, click Microsoft Office FrontPage 2003
Heading, create in a Web page	FP 32	See Reference Window: Creating a Heading in a Web Page
Help, get in FrontPage	FP 54	Click , type a question in the Search for text box, click
Hit counter, create in a Web page	FP 389	See Reference Window: Creating a Hit Counter in a Web Page
Horizontal line, add to a Web page	FP 91	See Reference Window: Inserting a Horizontal Line and Changing Its Properties
Horizontal line, change properties of	FP 91	See Reference Window: Inserting a Horizontal Line and Changing Its Properties
Hotspot, highlight in a picture	FP 103	See Reference Window: Highlighting Hotspots in a Picture
HTML document, view for a frames page in FrontPage	FP 309	Click Code
HTML document, view for a No Frames page	FP 309	Click No Frames
HTML document, view using FrontPage	FP 47	In Page view, click Code
HTML document, view using Internet Explorer	FP 50	Click View, click Source
Hyperlink, create to another Web page	FP 96	See Reference Window: Creating a Hyperlink to an Existing Web Page in the Same Web Site
Hyperlink, create using drag and drop	FP 97	See Reference Window: Creating a Hyperlink Using Drag and Drop
Hyperlink, follow in Design view	FP 97	Press and hold the Ctrl key, click the hyperlink
Hyperlinks view, change to	FP 171	Click Hyperlinks

TASK	PAGE #	RECOMMENDED METHOD
Hyperlinks view, print	FP 176	Press the Print Screen key, click , click , click
Hyperlinks, recalculate	FP 392	Click Tools, click Recalculate Hyperlinks, click the Yes button
Hyperlinks, show or hide links to pictures	FP 172	In Hyperlinks view, right-click the Contents pane, click Hyperlinks to Pictures
Hyperlinks, verify	FP 392	In Reports view, click on the Contents pane, click the Start button
Image map, create	FP 101	See Reference Window: Creating an Image Map
Initial page, set for a frame	FP 311	Click the Set Initial Page button, double-click the desired page
Interactive button, create	FP 114	See Reference Window: Creating an Interactive Button in a Web Page
Line break, create in a Web page	FP 37	Press Shift + Enter
List, create bulleted	FP 145	See Reference Window: Creating a Bulleted List
List, create definition	FP 151	See Reference Window: Creating a Definition List
List, create nested	FP 150	See Reference Window: Creating a Nested List
List, create numbered	FP 148	See Reference Window: Creating a Numbered List
Mailto, create	FP 99	See Reference Window: Creating a Mailto
Marquee, create in a Web page	FP 78	See Reference Window: Creating a Marquee in a Web Page
Meta tag, insert into a Web page	FP 51	See Reference Window: Inserting a Meta Tag into a Web Page
Navigation structure, create	FP 195	In Navigation view, drag and drop filenames from the Folder List and position them in the navigation structure
Navigation view, change to	FP 195	Click Navigation
Nonprinting characters, hide in a Web page	FP 79	Click ¶
Nonprinting characters, show in a Web page	FP 78	Click ¶
Option button, add to a form	FP 348	Click the desired location, click Insert, point to Form, click Option Button
Page banner, create	FP 218	See Reference Window: Creating a Page Banner
Page transition, create	FP 118	See Reference Window: Applying a Page Transition
Permissions, set for a Web site	FP 394	See Reference Window: Setting Permissions for a Web Site
Photo Gallery, change properties of	FP 245	Double-click the photo gallery, change properties as necessary, click OK
Photo Gallery, create	FP 242	See Reference Window: Creating a Photo Gallery in a Page
Picture, add to a Web page	FP 81	See Reference Window: Inserting a Picture into a Web Page
Picture, animate in a Web page	FP 119	See Reference Window: Creating Animated Text or an Animated Picture in a Web Page
Picture, bevel	FP 110	Click on the Pictures toolbar
Picture, change color characteristics	FP 109	Click on the Pictures toolbar, click desired option
Picture, change color to transparent	FP 89	See Reference Window: Changing a Color in a Picture to Transparent
Picture, convert to another format	FP 88	See Reference Window: Converting a Picture to Another Format
Picture, restore all previously applied, unsaved effects	FP 108	Click on the Pictures toolbar
Picture, rotate left	FP 110	Click on the Pictures toolbar
Picture, rotate right	FP 110	Click on the Pictures toolbar
Program window, maximize	FP 55	Click

TASK	PAGE #	RECOMMENDED METHOD
Repeated hyperlinks, show or hide in Hyperlinks view	FP 175	Right-click the Contents pane, click Repeated Hyperlinks
Reports view, change to	FP 169	Click Reports
Row, insert in a table in a Web page	FP 287	See Reference Window: Inserting a Row in a Table
Row, resize in a table	FP 294	See Reference Window: Resizing a Row or Column in a Table Using the Mouse
Row, select in a table	FP 275	Click the left border of the row
Rows, distribute selected evenly in a table	FP 295	Click
Save Results component, configure	FP 363	Right-click the form component, click Form Properties
Search component properties, change	FP 340	Right-click the search component, click Search Form Properties
Search page, create in a Web site	FP 337	Click the list arrow for , click Page, double-click the Search Page icon
Shared border, disable for a Web page	FP 215	See Reference Window: Disabling Shared Borders for a Single Web Page
Shared border, edit	FP 205	In Design view, click the shared border to select it, make the desired changes
Shared borders, create for a Web site	FP 199	See Reference Window: Creating Shared Borders for a Web Site
Site settings, examine and change for a Web site	FP 166	Click Tools, click Site Settings
Special character, insert in a Web page	FP 38	Click the desired location, click Insert, click Symbol, select the desired character, click the Insert button, click the Close button
Table, align in a Web page	FP 272	See Reference Window: Aligning a Table in a Web Page
Table, apply an AutoFormat to	FP 297	See Reference Window: Applying a Table AutoFormat
Table, create in a Web page	FP 267	See Reference Window: Creating a Table in a Web Page
Target frame, specify	FP 313	Click , click the Target Frame button, select the target frame, click OK, click OK
Task history, show or hide	FP 183	Right-click any blank area in Tasks view, click Show Task History
Task pane, change	FP 163	Click the Other Task Panes list arrow, click desired task pane
Task pane, close	FP 164	Click X on the task pane
Task pane, display	FP 163	Click View, click Task Pane
Task, add in Tasks view	FP 179	See Reference Window: Adding a Task to Tasks View
Task, change in Tasks view	FP 181	Double-click the task, change the settings, click OK
Task, delete from the Tasks list	FP 183	In Tasks view, right-click the task, click Delete Task, click Yes
Task, mark as completed	FP 182	In Tasks view, right-click the task, click Mark Complete
Tasks list, sort	FP 181	In Tasks view, click the column heading on which to sort
Tasks view, change to	FP 181	Click Tasks
Text area, add to a form	FP 355	Click the desired location, click Insert, point to Form, click Text Area
Text box, add to a form	FP 353	Click the desired location, click Insert, point to Form, click Textbox
Text, add on top of a picture	FP 110	See Reference Window: Adding Text on a Picture
Text, align in a Web page	FP 34	See Reference Window: Aligning a Paragraph in a Web Page
Text, animate in a Web page	FP 119	See Reference Window: Creating Animated Text or an Animated Picture in a Web Page

TASK	PAGE #	RECOMMENDED METHOD
Text, change color of selected in a Web page	FP 40	Click the list arrow for [A], click desired color
Text, change font of selected in a Web page	FP 37	Click the Font list arrow, click new font name
Text, change selected to bold	FP 40	Click [B]
Text, change selected to italic	FP 37	Click [I]
Text, change selected to underlined	FP 31	Click [U]
Text, change size of for selected in a Web page	FP 38	Click the Font Size list arrow, click the desired font size
Text, copy and paste in a Web page	FP 26	Select the text to copy, click, click the location in which to paste the text, click
Theme, apply to a Web site	FP 226	See Reference Window: Applying a Theme to a Web Site
Theme, create new	FP 238	See Reference Window: Creating a New Theme
Theme, customize	FP 231	See Reference Window: Customizing an Existing Theme
Theme, remove	FP 241	See Reference Window: Removing a Theme From a Page or Web Site
Thumbnail picture, create	FP 108	See Reference Window: Creating a Thumbnail Picture
Title, rename in Folders view	FP 94	Click the title to select it, click it again to change to editing mode, type the new title, press Enter
Title, rename in Navigation view	FP 198	See Reference Window: Renaming a Page's title in Navigation View
Toolbar, show or hide	FP 83	Click View, point to Toolbars, click the toolbar to show or hide
Web page size, set default	FP 21	Click the Page Size pane on the status bar, click the desired page size in the list
Web page, add new to navigation structure	FP 210	See Reference Window: Creating a New Page in Navigation View
Web page, check spelling in	FP 25	See Reference Window: Spell Checking a Web Page
Web page, close in Page view	FP 28	Click [×] on the Contents pane
Web page, delete from navigation structure	FP 209	See Reference Window: Deleting a Page in Navigation View
Web page, import into a Web site	FP 93	See Reference Window: Importing an Existing Web Page into a Web Site
Web page, preview	FP 42	See Reference Window: Previewing a Web Page
Web page, print using FrontPage	FP 44	See Reference Window: Printing a Web Page
Web page, save	FP 28	See Reference Window: Saving a Web Page
Web page, scroll to bottom	FP 36	Press Ctrl + End
Web page, scroll to top	FP 40	Press Ctrl + Home
Web page, view in Design view	FP 53	Click [Design]
Web page, view in Preview view	FP 42	Click [Preview]
Web page, view in Split view	FP 48	Click [Split]
Web site, close in FrontPage	FP 28	Click File, click Close Site

TASK	PAGE #	RECOMMENDED METHOD
Web site, create new	FP 15	Click the Other Task Panes arrow, click New, click the template or Wizard to use to create the Web site, type the Web site's name in the Specify the location of the new Web site text box, click OK
Web site, open in FrontPage	FP 29	See Reference Window: Opening a Web Site
Web site, publish	FP 376	See Reference Window: Publishing a Web Site to Your Computer's Server
Web site, publish changed pages	FP 383	See Reference Window: Publishing Changes to a Server-Based Web Site
WordArt object, create	FP 249	See Reference Window: Creating a WordArt Object in a Page
WordArt object, revise selected	FP 251	Click  on the WordArt toolbar